Indian Gaming Law

Indian Gaming Law
Cases and Materials

Kathryn R.L. Rand
School of Law
University of North Dakota

Steven Andrew Light
Department of Political Science and Public Administration
University of North Dakota

Co-Directors
Institute for the Study of Tribal Gaming Law and Policy
University of North Dakota

CAROLINA ACADEMIC PRESS
Durham, North Carolina

ISBN 10: 1-59460-258-1
ISBN 13: 978-1-59460-258-0
LCCN: 2007940306

Carolina Academic Press
700 Kent Street
Durham, North Carolina 27701
Telephone (919) 489-7486
Fax (919) 493-5668
www.cap-press.com
Printed in the United States of America

for
Vaslav Bast
and
Sally Rand

Contents

Part IV
Policy Implications

Table of Cases

Preface

Although this is a legal casebook, it reflects an interdisciplinary approach to studying and understanding the law. Our collaboration on Indian gaming issues began more than a decade ago when we realized that tribal gaming gave rise to complex issues of law and public policy that crossed our respective disciplines of law and political science and public administration. At the University of North Dakota, we founded the Institute for the Study of Tribal Gaming Law and Policy in 2002 to foster research on Indian gaming and to understand its impact on intergovernmental relations and the lives of real people—Indian and non-Indian—across the U.S.

We strongly believe in the importance of informing our pedagogy with our research, and vice versa. Several years ago, one of us (Rand) taught one of the first Indian gaming law courses offered in a law school curriculum. She was amazed at how difficult it was to design the course, develop an easily understandable framework, and find appropriate readings. When the other of us (Light) sought to teach a short unit on the public administration of Indian gaming to graduate students, he was stymied by having to edit long law review articles or case law, and to guard against student reliance on inaccurate or incomplete information found on the Internet. Still today, instructors in this rapidly expanding area of interest and practice must adopt a do-it-yourself approach to assembling course materials—a difficult, time-consuming and resource-intensive task, even for an expert on federal Indian, tribal, or gambling law. Fortunately, this no longer needs to be the case.

Indian gaming is a particularly complicated and highly specialized topic for instructors, students, and practitioners alike to master. To meet the teaching and learning demands of the field, INDIAN GAMING LAW: CASES AND MATERIALS provides a clear, comprehensive, and accessible platform designed specifically for Indian gaming law and similar courses.

This casebook is one-stop resource for understanding Indian gaming law and the regulations and public policy that flow from it. This in large part is because our approach to the subject is informed by our sense that Indian gaming law and policy have evolved through political compromise as much as through litigation and law reform. Attention only to "black letter" law would be misleading as to the type and relative influence of extralegal variables that shape Indian gaming law. Similarly, discussion of the politics surrounding Indian gaming without grounding in the law would untether tribal gaming from its key legal context.

The focus of most existing casebooks that incorporate some discussion of Indian gaming is either as a form of gambling regulation or as an example of the application of federal Indian law. Our own work has emphasized that understanding Indian gaming requires explanation and exploration of both of these contexts. In this casebook, we fuse the necessary background on federal Indian law and the status of American Indian tribes in the American political system with legal approaches to regulating gambling, and provide a useful and usable overarching theoretical approach grounded in law and governance.

Students and other readers will hear from the legal, judicial, and political experts, American Indian and non-Indian alike, who shape Indian gaming today and will determine its future. We present excerpts from relevant case law, statutes, and regulations alongside excerpts from congressional testimony by noted public officials and scholarly journal articles and books written by key authorities in the fields of law, Indian studies, political science, economics, gambling studies, and more. To assist readers in working through such complex issues, we introduce teaching problems and notes and questions throughout. Accompanying the casebook is our INSTRUCTOR'S RESOURCE MANUAL FOR INDIAN GAMING LAW: CASES AND MATERIALS, in which we draw on our own experiences in the classroom to offer numerous suggestions to stimulate an engaging and exciting classroom environment.

A course in Indian gaming law has legal and political currency and thus can easily "connect" with students. But more than simply learning about current events, students should come away from such a course with a critical understanding of perhaps the most important legal and policy issues facing tribes today, and with a deeper sense of how tribal governments — the "third sovereign" — interact with the federal government as well as state and local governments in the American political system.

It is our sincere wish that students who use this casebook in a course on Indian gaming law will have the tools to enter the field as practicing attorneys, regulators, or policymakers and face with confidence the day-to-day complexities and nuances of Indian gaming law and policy. We also recognize that one of the primary functions of a law school education is to foster in students a sense of the interactions between law and society. We hope to further that important goal through this casebook's approach.

* * *

INDIAN GAMING LAW: CASES AND MATERIALS begins with Part I, Indian Gaming in Context. In this Part, we cover the necessary historical, legal, and political contexts for understanding the modern law of Indian gaming. In Chapter 1, we provide an overview of Indian gaming through multiple lenses. We discuss the growth and scope of tribal gaming and the legalized gambling industry in the U.S. before turning to an overview of how and why gambling is regulated. We then provide necessary background on the complicated area of federal Indian law and policy, and its historical and contemporary relationship to tribal sovereignty and tribal governments.

Chapter 2's focus is on the pre-statutory law that created the foundations for Indian gaming. We discuss traditional tribal games and Indian gaming's modern roots as a tool of reservation economic development, illustrated through case law arising out of state attempts to regulate tribal bingo operations in the 1970s and 1980s. The U.S. Supreme Court recognized the limits of state regulation in its landmark 1987 decision in *California v. Cabazon Band of Mission Indians*.

Part II, The Federal Regulatory Scheme, covers in detail the complex and comprehensive legal framework governing Indian gaming. In Chapter 3, we describe how *Cabazon* and the political activity it generated resulted in Congress's passage of the Indian Gaming Regulatory Act of 1988 (IGRA). IGRA's regulatory framework codified several key policy goals for Indian gaming while creating the basis for extensive civil and criminal regulation of tribal gaming at the tribal, state, and federal levels. IGRA also created a classification scheme for Indian gaming regulation.

Chapter 4 describes the statutory requirements for conducting bingo and other forms of Class II gaming. The definition of Class II gaming has generated considerable litigation and controversy, as new technology has blurred the distinction between Class II and casino-style gaming.

In Chapter 5 we focus on Class III, or casino-style, gaming. IGRA requires the negotiation in good faith of tribal-state compacts before a tribe can operate Class III games. In 1996, however, the Supreme Court in *Seminole Tribe v. Florida* held that tribes could not sue states without their consent to enforce IGRA's good-faith requirement. We examine how the post-*Seminole* environment has become increasingly politicized. IGRA limits tribal gaming to the types of games that are allowed under state public policy. The question of the scope of Class III gaming under IGRA's definitions has been extensively litigated.

Part III, Government Authority Over Indian Gaming, explores in more detail the various government officials, agencies, and institutions that exercise power over Indian gaming at the federal, tribal, and state levels. Chapter 6 discusses the scope and extent of federal authority concerning tribal gaming. IGRA delegates to the National Indian Gaming Commission extensive powers to issue opinions and approve tribal gaming ordinances, management contracts, and consulting agreements, as well as to promulgate regulations and investigate and enforce various investigation and compliance provisions. The U.S. Secretary of the Interior and other federal agencies play key roles in determinations concerning tribal-state compacts, per capita payments, and other regulations.

In Chapter 7, we consider the extent of tribal authority to formulate, implement, enforce, and interpret tribes' own gaming regulations and ordinances. Indian gaming has created many new challenges and opportunities for tribal governments to build effective and responsive governmental institutions.

Chapter 8 turns to state authority regarding tribal gaming. IGRA's tribal-state compacting requirement allowed state gaming commissions and other agencies to become involved in the implementation and enforcement of tribal gaming regulation. State courts have interpreted IGRA's provisions related to state public policy and the scope of gaming, as well as decided which state actors are authorized to negotiate compacts. In state court litigation over Indian gaming, tribes may be forced to sit on the sidelines.

In the casebook's final chapters in Part IV, Policy Implications, we bring public policy and politics to the forefront. Chapter 9 focuses on tribal gaming's socioeconomic impacts. Indian gaming has both economic and social costs and benefits that may accrue to Indian and non-Indian communities. One of the keys to developing effective Indian gaming law and public policy is using methodologically sound research to identify and weigh these effects.

Chapter 10 explores in some detail four recurring legal and political issues in Indian gaming: "off-reservation" gaming, tribal-state revenue sharing agreements, federal tribal recognition, and tribal employment issues. All four issues continue to generate legal and political controversy throughout the U.S. Overall, there is little doubt that Indian gaming is changing the calculus of intergovernmental relations as well as the meaning of tribal sovereignty.

* * *

INDIAN GAMING LAW: CASES AND MATERIALS has benefited from numerous conversations and interactions we have had with academics, practitioners, regulators, public officials, and students. All mistakes, of course, are our own. We very much would appreciate hearing from those of you who use this book. Please feel free to contact us at the Institute for the Study of Tribal Gaming Law and Policy at the University of North Dakota through our Web site, *Indian Gaming Today*, at indiangamingtoday.com or by e-mail at rand@law.und.edu or steven_light@und.nodak.edu.

As always, we are grateful for the support of our colleagues at the University of North Dakota School of Law and the Department of Political Science and Public Administration in the University of North Dakota College of Business and Public Administration. Special thanks to Kelly Jordet, Elizabeth Puthoff, and Karen Bowles for their administrative assistance, Lesley Foss and Matthew Myrick for their research assistance, and Jared Rigby for his assistance in proofreading. We are indebted to Meg Daniel, who prepared the Index and Table of Cases on short notice and with aplomb. At Carolina Academic Press, thanks to Keith Sipe for his continued enthusiasm about our work, Bob Conrow for guiding us through the publication process, Karen Clayton for her production assistance, and everyone else at the Press for their help along the way.

Kathryn R.L. Rand
Steven Andrew Light

Grand Forks, North Dakota
November 2007

Copyright Acknowledgments

We are indebted to those whose noteworthy scholarship and commentary on Indian gaming and myriad related topics inform this casebook. We gratefully acknowledge the permission granted by authors, law reviews and journals, publishers, and other organizations to reprint excerpts from the following materials.

Ansson, Richard J., & Ladine Oravetz, *Tribal Economic Development: What Challenges Lie Ahead for Tribal Nations as They Continue to Strive for Economic Diversity?*, 11 KANSAS JOURNAL OF LAW AND PUBLIC POLICY 441 (2002). Reprinted by permission.

Aronovitz, Cory, *The Regulation of Commercial Gaming*, 5 CHAPMAN LAW REVIEW 181 (2002). Reprinted by permission.

Burris, Tracy, *How Tribal Gaming Commissions Are Evolving*, 8 GAMING LAW REVIEW 243 (2004). Reprinted by permission.

Cabot, Anthony N., & Louis V. Csoka, *The Games People Play: Is It Time For a New Legal Approach to Prize Games?* 4 NEVADA LAW JOURNAL 197 (2004). Reprinted by permission.

Clinton, Robert N., *There Is No Federal Supremacy Clause for Indian Tribes*, 34 ARIZONA STATE LAW JOURNAL 113 (2002). Copyright © 2002 by Robert N. Clinton. Reprinted by permission of author.

Coffey, Wallace & Rebecca Tsosie, *Rethinking the Tribal Sovereignty Doctrine: Cultural Sovereignty and the Collective Future of Indian Nations*, 12 STANFORD LAW & POLICY REVIEW 191 (2001). Copyright © 2002 by the Board of Trustees of the Leland Stanford Junior University. Reprinted by permission.

CRAMER, RENEE ANN, CASH, COLOR, AND COLONIALISM: THE POLITICS OF TRIBAL ACKNOWLEDGMENT (2005). Copyright © 2005 by the University of Oklahoma Press, Norman, Publishing Division of the University. All rights reserved. Reprinted by permission.

DELORIA, VINE JR., & CLIFFORD M. LYTLE, AMERICAN INDIANS, AMERICAN JUSTICE (1983). Copyright © 1983. Reprinted by permission of the University of Texas Press.

FINDLAY, JOHN M., PEOPLE OF CHANCE: GAMBLING IN AMERICAN SOCIETY FROM JAMESTOWN TO LAS VEGAS 3-4 (1986). Reprinted by permission of Oxford University Press, Inc.

Fletcher, Matthew L.M., *Tribal Employment Separation: Tribal Law Enigma, Tribal Governance Paradox, and Tribal Court Conundrum*, 38 UNIVERSITY OF MICHIGAN JOURNAL OF LAW REFORM 273 (2005). Reprinted by permission.

Gerstein, Dean, et al., *Gambling Impact and Behavior Study: Report to the National Gambling Impact Study Commission* (1999). Reprinted by permission.

Gips, Robert L., *Current Trends in Tribal Economic Development*, 37 NEW ENGLAND LAW REVIEW 517 (2003). Reprinted by permission.

Reid, Harry, Commentary in INDIAN GAMING AND THE LAW 15-20 (William R. Eadington ed., 1998). Reno: Institute for the Study of Gambling & Commercial Gaming, University of Nevada, Reno. Reprinted by permission.

Santoni, Roland J., *The Indian Gaming Regulatory Act: How Did We Get Here? Where Are We Going?* 26 CREIGHTON LAW REVIEW 387 (1992-1993). Copyright © 1992-93 by Creighton University. Reprinted by permission.

SCHWARTZ, DAVID G., ROLL THE BONES: THE HISTORY OF GAMBLING (2006). Copyright © 2006 by David G. Schwartz. Used by permission of Gotham Books, an imprint of Penguin Group (USA) Inc.

Skibine, Alex Tallchief, *Gaming on Indian Reservations: Defining the Trustee's Duty in the Wake of* Seminole Tribe v. Florida, 29 ARIZONA STATE LAW JOURNAL 121 (1997). Reprinted by permission of the author.

Skibine, Alex Tallchief, *Scope of Gaming, Good Faith Negotiations and the Secretary of Interior's Class III Gaming Procedures: Is I.G.R.A. Still a Workable Framework After* Seminole?, 5 GAMING LAW REVIEW 401 (2001). Reprinted by permission.

Staudenmaier, Heidi McNeil, *Negotiating Enforceable Tribal Gaming Management Agreements*, 7 GAMING LAW REVIEW 31 (2003). Reprinted by permission.

Staudenmaier, Heidi McNeil, *Off-Reservation Native American Gaming: An Examination of the Legal and Political Hurdles*, 4 NEVADA LAW JOURNAL 301 (2004). Reprinted by permission.

Taylor, Jonathan B., Matthew B. Krepps, & Patrick Wang, *The National Evidence on the Socioeconomic Impacts of American Indian Gaming on Non-Indian Communities* (2000). Reprinted by permission.

Tsosie, Rebecca, *Negotiating Economic Survival: The Consent Principle and Tribal-State Compacts Under the Indian Gaming Regulatory Act*, 29 ARIZONA STATE LAW JOURNAL 25 (1997). Reprinted by permission of author.

Udall, Stewart L., Commentary in INDIAN GAMING AND THE LAW 22-28 (William R. Eadington ed., 1998). Reno: Institute for the Study of Gambling & Commercial Gaming, University of Nevada, Reno. Reprinted by permission.

Washburn, Kevin K., *The Mechanics of Indian Gaming Management Contract Approval*, 8 GAMING LAW REVIEW 333 (2004). Reprinted by permission.

WILKINS, DAVID E., AMERICAN INDIAN POLITICS AND THE AMERICAN POLITICAL SYSTEM (2002). Reprinted by permission.

Part I
Indian Gaming in Context

The Indian gaming industry is big and just keeps getting bigger. Gambling enterprises owned and operated by tribes are providing basic government services and fueling economic development that is fundamentally improving the quality of life for the members of many tribes across the U.S. For the first time in generations, tribal governments are in a position to exert political influence, changing the framework for intergovernmental relations among tribal, state, federal, and local governments. The rapid growth of Indian gaming mirrors or even exceeds the exploding legalized gambling industry in its many forms. Today all but two states, Utah and Hawaii, permit some form of legalized gambling, including gaming in riverboat or land-based casinos, racetrack pari-mutuel wagering, charitable gaming, and state-run lotteries. Various forms of online gambling are a mouse-click away, and the World Series of Poker is televised. Yet tribal gaming is much more controversial than most legalized gambling. Knowledge and understanding about tribal gaming are limited and myths obscure realities. The policy rationale underlying Indian gaming and a full explanation of its socioeconomic impacts remain cloudy to policymakers and the public alike.

Subject to a complex federal regulatory scheme embodied in the Indian Gaming Regulatory Act of 1988 (IGRA) as well as myriad state and tribal regulations, Indian gaming also is a growing area of legal practice. Thousands of practitioners in the public and private sectors, in tribal and non-tribal governments and enterprises alike, must develop expertise in this challenging and rapidly evolving area of law. Courses in Indian gaming law are springing up in law school curricula throughout the U.S. to meet the rising demand for attorneys, regulators, and policymakers familiar with tribal gaming law and policy. As an intersection of federal Indian law and gambling law, Indian gaming is a particularly complicated and highly specialized topic for instructors, students, and practitioners to master, giving rise to numerous complicated legal questions fraught with political and policy implications. A gaming attorney or regulatory official must know how to respond to a phenomenal array of such questions, from ones related to abstract theoretical principles or preconstitutional history to those with highly technical answers grounded in the judicial interpretation of current federal law and regulations. Here is but a sample of "need-to-knows":

- What exactly is the statutory definition of "Indian gaming," and what are its legal and political roots?

- What is "tribal sovereignty," and how has it been defined and embodied by tribes as well as by federal Indian law and policy and the U.S. Supreme Court?

1

- What key U.S. Supreme Court decision prompted Congress to enact IGRA, the federal statutory framework governing Indian gaming?

- What are the overriding federal policy goals of Indian gaming, and why are its goals different than for those of other forms of legalized gambling?

- What are IGRA's key statutory provisions?

- How does IGRA's unique classification scheme influence tribal-state intergovernmental relations, including compacting for casino-style gaming?

- How is Indian gaming regulated today by tribes, states, and the federal government?

- What has the Supreme Court had to say about tribes' ability to hold states to IGRA's requirements?

- Is there a clear legal distinction between IGRA's gaming classifications, or have the lines become blurred by advances in gaming technology?

- Who has the legal and political right to determine what type of gaming is allowed in a state?

- What is a "tribal-state compact," and what terms are negotiable under federal law?

- How much and what types of authority does the National Indian Gaming Commission, the federal agency responsible for regulating Indian gaming, have?

- What are the federal Minimum Internal Control Standards that apply to a tribal casino?

- Under what authority can tribes pursue gaming on newly acquired lands, and what are the legal and political hurdles to opening an "off-reservation" casino?

- Under what conditions may a local or state government ask a tribe to enter into a revenue-sharing agreement?

- Why is the federal recognition of tribal groups so controversial in the context of Indian gaming?

- What are the current legal and political issues that will shape the future of tribal gaming?

In this casebook, we provide the opportunity and means for students to grapple with these questions, and many, many more. Indian gaming law and policy has evolved through political compromise as much as through litigation and law reform. The full contours of Indian gaming emerge only with attention to the interactions and interdependence of law and politics. Luckily, if you're reading these words, you're probably enrolled in a course on Indian gaming law that will allow you to negotiate the fascinating terrain of the law, politics, and policy of Indian gaming now and in the future.

Chapter 1 begins with an overview of the industry, discussing the growth and scope of tribal gaming and the legalized gambling industry throughout the U.S. before turning to an overview of how and why gambling is regulated. You'll become familiar with the complicated topic of federal Indian law and policy and its historical and contemporary relation to tribal sovereignty and tribal governments. Chapter 2 discusses the sociolegal roots of Indian gaming law and policy, including the U.S. Supreme Court's landmark decision in *California v. Cabazon Band of Mission Indians*. That case set the stage for the enactment of IGRA, the primary legal framework governing Indian gaming.

Chapter 1

Introduction

A. Overview of Indian Gaming

According to the National Indian Gaming Commission (NIGC), the federal regulatory agency created by Congress through IGRA, tribal gaming has experienced steady growth, both in terms of number of operations and overall revenue, for more than a decade. Total gaming revenue quadrupled from 1995 to 2006, as Figure 1.1 illustrates.

Figure 1.1: Growth in Indian Gaming Revenue, 1995–2006 (in billions)

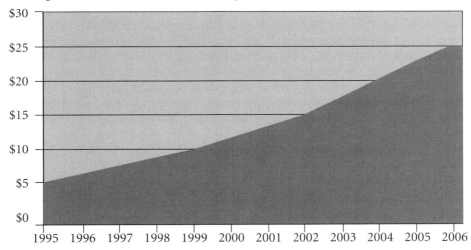

Source: Adapted from National Indian Gaming Commission

Growth and revenue are not uniform, however, across tribes, states, or gambling operations. Not surprisingly, the old adage from real estate—"location, location, location"—holds true as the most important determinative factor for gaming revenue. Tribal casinos located in or near large metropolitan areas, with ready access to literally millions of customers, earn more than those in rural locales. Though the NIGC reports tribal gaming revenue only by multi-state regions, the regions that earn the highest revenues are those that include populous states such as California (Region II), Connecticut, and New York (Region VI), as Table 1.1 indicates. A reputable independent assessment put California and Connecticut as the two highest grossing states in 2006. ALAN P. MEISTER, IN-DIAN GAMING INDUSTRY REPORT (2007–2008 ed.).

Table 1.1: Tribal Gaming Revenue by NIGC Region in 2006

Region	Number of Operations	Gaming Revenue (in millions)
I (Alaska, Idaho, Oregon, Washington)	45	2,080
II (California, northern Nevada)	56	7,675
III (Arizona, Colorado, New Mexico, southern Nevada)	45	2,928
IV (Iowa, Michigan, Minnesota, Montana, Nebraska, North Dakota, South Dakota, Wisconsin, Wyoming)	117	4,050
V (Kansas, Oklahoma, Texas)	97	2,123
VI (Alabama, Connecticut, Florida, Louisiana, Mississippi, New York, North Carolina)	27	6,219
Total	387	25,076

Source: Adapted from National Indian Gaming Commission

Tribal gaming operations in these markets earn in excess of $250 million in annual revenue—some estimates put the handful of the most lucrative tribal casinos at $1 billion in annual revenue. More typical, though, is annual revenue that amounts to a fraction of such figures. According to NIGC numbers found in Table 1.2, in 2006, under 6 percent of tribal gaming operations earned more than $250 million, accounting for nearly 45 percent of the total industry revenue, while more than half earned $25 million or less. One out of every five tribal casinos earned less than $3 million, often just enough to keep the casino doors open and to provide some modest tribal government revenue.

Table 1.2: Tribal Gaming Operations by Revenue in 2006

Gaming Revenue	Number of Operations	Revenue (in millions)	Percentage of Total Operations	Percentage of Total Revenue
$250 million or more	23	11,215	5.9	44.7
$100 million to $250 million	40	6,730	10.3	26.8
$50 million to $100 million	45	3,186	11.6	12.7
$25 million to $50 million	64	2,241	16.5	8.9
$10 million to $25 million	72	1,229	18.6	4.9
$3 million to $10 million	66	413	17.1	1.6
Under $3 million	77	62	19.9	0.2
Total	387	25,076	100.0	100.0

Source: Adapted from National Indian Gaming Commission

The size and scope of the Indian gaming industry are such that its impacts reach far beyond reservation boundaries, to local, state, regional, and national economies.

Alan P. Meister
Indian Gaming Industry Report
3–5 (2007–2008 ed.)

Indian gaming continued to exhibit strong growth in calendar year 2006. There were 228 tribes operating 423 gaming facilities in 28 states. In total, these gaming facilities generated approximately $25.5 billion in gaming revenue, an 11 percent increase over the $23.0 billion generated in 2005. Total non-gaming revenue rose approximately 12 percent, from about $2.2 billion in 2005 to $2.5 billion in 2006.

Total jobs and wages also increased substantially in the industry. Indian gaming facilities, including non-gaming operations, directly supported approximately 327,000 jobs and provided about $11.3 billion in wages in 2006. In 2005, the industry supported 301,000 jobs and provided $10.4 billion in wages.

Economically speaking, the *general nationwide* success of Indian gaming can be attributed to several factors:

- Strong demand for gaming;
- Favorable market conditions relative to commercial casinos and racinos, such as:
  ° Closer proximity to gaming patrons;
  ° Minimal local competition; and
  ° Less mature markets;
- Increased supply of gaming:
  ° Introduction of new gaming facilities;
  ° Expansion of gaming at existing gaming facilities; and
  ° Introduction/addition of new types of gaming not previously offered;
- Increased supply of non-gaming amenities at Indian gaming facilities; and
- Increased quality of Indian gaming facilities.

While Indian gaming is often talked about as if it were a single large entity, this could not be farther from the truth. It is in fact very fragmented. There were 228 *unique* tribes across 28 states operating 423 gaming facilities of varying size, scope, and quality. Thus, while the performance of Indian gaming was solid nationwide, it varied widely across facilities, tribes, and states. This reflects differences in supply and demand for gaming in different geographic areas. And the supply and demand for gaming depend on a variety of factors, including:

- The legal, regulatory, and political environments within each state;
- Market conditions (e.g., geographic location; the size of the population base; customer demographics; the degree of competition; and the maturity level of the market); and
- The scope and quality of gaming and nongaming amenities available.

When looking at Indian gaming on a state-by-state basis, variations in market performance are readily apparent. The gaming revenue growth rate for Indian gaming varied from a low of –2 percent to a high of 43 percent. Only one of the 28 states with Indian gaming had a decline in gaming revenue (Louisiana). Of the 27 states that had positive growth rates, just over one half of them experienced double-digit growth of gaming revenue. And eight of the 14 states with double-digit growth had growth of 20 percent or more.

Gaming revenue continued to be very concentrated among a small number of states. In 2006, California alone accounted for 30 percent of total gaming revenue at Indian gaming facilities. This was down slightly from 31 percent in 2005. The top two states, California and Connecticut, generated 40 percent of total gaming revenue. This was down slightly from 41 percent in 2005. Meanwhile, the top five states, which included California, Connecticut, Arizona, Oklahoma, and Florida, accounted for 62 percent of total gaming revenue in 2006. Although this level of concentration was unchanged from 2005, Florida replaced Minnesota as the fifth largest state in terms of gaming revenue at Indian gaming facilities. The level of concentration for the top 10 states, which added Minnesota, Washington, Wisconsin, New York, and Michigan to the top 5 states, was virtually unchanged from 2005. They generated 86 percent of all gaming revenue at Indian gaming facilities.

On the whole, Indian gaming continues to make significant contributions to the U.S. economy. It has stimulated economic activity, created jobs, and provided wages—all of which generated tax revenue to federal, state, and local governments. In 2006, it is estimated that Indian gaming directly and indirectly led to:

- $80.7 billion in output;
- 703,000 jobs;
- $27.8 billion in wages; and
- $11.7 billion in federal, state, and local tax revenue.

Overall, the total fiscal benefit of Indian gaming, including tax revenue and all direct payments by tribes to other governments, was $12.9 billion in 2006. Amidst some future uncertainties, the outlook for Indian gaming as a whole remains positive.

National Indian Gaming Association
An Analysis of the Economic Impact of Indian Gaming in 2005
2–4 (2006)

The benefits of Indian gaming are far reaching and extend in many directions. For example, the Mille Lacs Band of Ojibwe in Minnesota built two schools, the Oneida Nation of Wisconsin built its Turtle School to reflect Oneida culture, and the Mescalero Apache built a new K–12 school. The Salt River Pima-Maricopa Indian Community in Arizona built a dialysis clinic, the Choctaw Nation of Oklahoma built a hospital and the Shakopee Mdewakanton Sioux Community in Minnesota built a family birthing clinic. The Pueblo of Santa Ana in New Mexico recently completed a water system to provide service to its communities and the Yankton Sioux Tribe in South Dakota built a new water tower.

Tribal governments also use gaming revenues to provide essential services, such as education, health care, police and fire protection to all tribal members from toddlers in day care to grandmothers in elder care programs. The Tohono O'odham Nation in Arizona uses gaming revenue to fund police patrols of the border and 60% of its police budget is used to protect its 75 mile stretch of border with Mexico. The Pechanga Band of Luiseno Indians in California uses gaming revenue to fund its fire department which responds to frequent wildfires in nearby communities. The Rosebud Sioux Tribe in South Dakota uses gaming revenue to provide school clothes for students who need assistance at the start of each school year.

Neighboring communities see the benefits of Indian gaming as well. Indian gaming creates hundreds of thousands of jobs for non-Indians. By increasing state and local income tax revenues, Indian gaming provides funding for public schools, hospitals and roads in neighboring non-Indian communities.

Tribes also use Indian gaming revenue as a catalyst to spur economic growth. The Winnebago Tribe of Nebraska created Ho-Chunk, Inc., which provides more than 500 American jobs through economic diversification into grocery stores, housing construction, and high-tech communications. The Chickasaw Nation in Oklahoma has grown its workforce from 250 to more than 8,400 employees providing services both nationwide and worldwide, including banking, construction, property management, information technology, medical services, manufacturing and retail. The Seminole Tribe of Florida boosted its workforce to 17,000, with 7,000 people employed in gaming and 10,000 people employed in related tribal enterprises. Thus, tribal governments promote sustainable communities and create new opportunities where there were little before.

Notes and Questions

1.   *The "spectrum of success."* It remains difficult to paint an accurate portrait of Indian gaming's socioeconomic effects. The industry is large and sprawling, and there is no single agreed-upon methodological approach or plug-and-play model. Yet research on Indian gaming's social and economic impacts has proliferated in recent years as the industry has grown and changed. Some studies are the product of government agencies or academic inquiry, and may be conducted as after-the-fact assessments by independent researchers with no vested interest in the outcomes; others are impact studies commissioned to make the case for or against a proposed casino and are conducted by for-hire consulting groups; still others are the products of various advocacy groups or commercial gambling industry associations. There simply is a wide variation in origin, research design, intended audience, and other factors that a smart consumer will need to take into account.

Another major complication in the collection, assessment, and dissemination of accurate information about Indian gaming is the fact of tribal sovereignty. Tribal governments are exempted from public disclosure requirements, and many tribes choose to reveal data to the media, the public, policymakers, and even each other on a selective basis. The National Indian Gaming Association (NIGA) aggregates tribal data and produces an annual report, excerpted above. NIGA's numbers generally track those of at least two other widely cited sources: the NIGC, and the annual reports authored by economist Meister, who has gained access to otherwise confidential tribal data.

2.   *Indian gaming interest groups.* NIGA is an umbrella organization of more than 180 tribes and other associate members. It functions as a political advocacy and lobbying group and an educational resource on issues related to Indian gaming, economic development, and tribal sovereignty. NIGA maintains an online clearinghouse of external resources including studies, books, and testimonies before regulatory commissions or in legislative hearings. Throughout the U.S., regional or state tribal advocacy associations, such as the California Nations Indian Gaming Association, perform similar functions and seek to work with state and local officials as well as community organizations and the media. Through advocacy groups like NIGA, tribal governments are able to pool gaming resources and play an increasingly visible and influential role in the American political system. *See* Steven Andrew Light, *Indian Gaming and Intergovernmental Relations: State-Level Constraints on Tribal Political Influence Over Pol-*

icy Outcomes, 38 AM. REV. PUB. ADMIN. (2008). How does an organization like NIGA represent the interests of its tribal government members? What are the similarities between tribes and interest groups? What are the differences? Consider the National [State] Governors Association and the American Gaming Association, which represents commercial operators. Which organization is most analogous to NIGA? Explain your response.

    3.   Tribes' use of gaming revenue. Does the description of tribes' use of gaming revenue surprise you? As will be discussed in Chapter 3, IGRA limits how tribes may spend funds earned through Indian gaming. Tribes may use net gaming revenues for only six purposes: (1) to fund tribal government operations or programs, (2) to provide for the general welfare of the tribe and its members, (3) to promote tribal economic development, (4) to donate to charitable organizations, (5) to help fund operations of local government agencies, and, if approved by the U.S. Secretary of the Interior, (6) to make per capita payments to tribal members. Tribes do not share identical needs. Instead, the size, location, and unique history of each tribe influence its current socioeconomic circumstances and priorities. Some tribes may have little net gaming revenue to spend, others may address pressing needs related to basic government services such as housing, others may choose to invest in non-gaming economic enterprises, and still others may choose to divide a portion of the revenue among their members.

    4.   Commercial vs. charitable vs. Indian gaming. Gaming varies in its purpose and in the type of organization that conducts it. Commercial gaming is conducted by a private entity, such as a corporation, for the purpose of turning a profit. The casinos lining the Las Vegas Strip are commercial casinos, as are most race tracks and "racinos"—horse or dog race tracks that offer some casino games, such as slot machines. Charitable gambling is gaming conducted by non-profit organizations as a means of fundraising to support their missions. Charitable gaming often is limited to low-stakes bingo or card games, or limited duration raffles or "Las Vegas nights." Church bingo is a classic example of charitable gaming. Indian gaming is neither commercial nor charitable, as it is conducted by neither for-profit nor non-profit organizations. Instead, Indian gaming is conducted by governmental entities—tribal governments—for the public good. In this way, Indian gaming is more akin to state lotteries. This type of gambling is called "public gaming," referring to state or other government-run gaming whose revenues are used for purposes related to the public welfare, such as funding public schools. It sometimes is called "public sector gaming" to differentiate it from another type of so-called public gaming, that is, gambling that is publicly available through the Internet.

B. History of Gambling in the U.S.

David G. Schwartz
Roll the Bones: The History of Gambling
xviii–xix (2006)

Even before an unprecedented explosion of legal gambling in the past fifty years, the U.S. has long been a gambling nation. Poker, a game that evolved on the Mississippi River and in the American West, has become one of the world's most popular games, and with the slot machine, Americans brought gambling into the Machine Age. Bingo, an American innovation of the Depression years, has similarly crossed the oceans. The American casino hub, Las Vegas, has displaced Monte Carlo as the world's gambling capital and shows no signs of yielding the honor anytime soon.

Americans are joined by other nations in chasing fortune. Canadians have commercial and charitable casinos as well as a range of lottery and video lottery products. Australians gamble on "pokies," slots, lotteries, race and sports betting, and keno. Macao, a former Portuguese colony, has had a monopoly on casino gambling in China for nearly forty years, and it faces competition from casinos in the Philippines, South Korea, Cambodia, and Malaysia. Casinos span the African continent from Cairo to Cape Town, Latin American nations from Costa Rica to Chile have casinos and slot parlors, and Europe boasts casinos, lotteries, and bookmaking. Gambling is often as easy as buying a ticket: International lottery sales in calendar year 2001 topped $125.6 billion. In all, over two hundred and fifty jurisdictions throughout the world offer legal gambling of some kind. Casinos, pari-mutuel wagering on horses, greyhounds, and jai alai, lotteries, and other forms of betting together comprise a world betting market valued at nearly $1 trillion per year. From the tundra of Siberia to the wider shores of Tierra del Fuego, from balmy Mediterranean waters to the Nevada desert, over the oceans and across each continent, gambling unites humanity.

In the forty thousand or so years that we have thrown sticks, drawn lots, rolled dice, tossed cards, and pulled handles, humans have left ample evidence of our gambling passion in the historical record. Gambling and gamblers have left imprints throughout history in curious, sometimes surprising ways. Games of chance have evolved over many centuries, changing and maturing along with civilization. As new technologies—from block printing to the Internet—have become available, people have used them to gamble. Early mathematics and statistical sciences developed in part to explain the vagaries of chance. Gambling flourished in the neighborhood of Shakespeare's Globe Theater and in the imperial courts of China. European colonial ventures, including the Virginia Company, received financing from lotteries, and the British Stamp Tax, which included levies on playing cards, helped spur the colonies into rebellion against the Crown. The consolidation of German states into Prussia forced the closure of German casinos and led to the establishment of Monte Carlo as a gaming monopoly. Leaders from Julius Caesar to Franklin Roosevelt (who offered Americans a "New Deal") have used gambling metaphors to speak to the people.

The history of gambling has many elements of a high-stakes Texas hold 'em game: cunning calculations, audacious gambits, and reversals of fortune. Always a part of human culture, its evolution never ceases, and at every juncture of history, it seems the gambler is nearby.

John M. Findlay
People of Chance: Gambling in American Society from Jamestown to Las Vegas
3–4 (1986)

Las Vegas, Nevada, during the mid-twentieth century attested the growth of American society, its direction, and its distinctiveness. The gambling resort epitomized the restless, commercial, and middle-class orientations that made Americans a singular people. In one tourist district modeled after yesteryear and another devoted to the future, its styles evinced the borrowing as well as the innovation that had shaped American culture over the centuries, and its games typified the confident pursuit of fortune that had been the essence of so many American lives. Las Vegas gambling confirmed an insight of Alexis de Tocqueville who, one hundred years prior to the legalization of casino gaming in Nevada, had speculated on the character of the citizens of the young republic: "Those who live in the midst of democratic fluctuations have always before their eyes the image of chance; and they end by liking all undertaking in which chance plays a part."

A social history of gambling, focusing on the development of modern casino styles, indicated that the far western location of Las Vegas as index to national culture was not incidental. The qualities that identified Americans as a people of chance stood out most boldly on western frontiers, where gambling tended to flourish and where distinctly American betting games emerged for the first time. The affinity between gambling and frontiers has been forceful from the time that lotteries funded the first permanent English settlement in North America to the year when Las Vegas casinos, embodying Southern California culture, emerged as stunning new landmarks of United States civilization.

From the seventeenth century through the twentieth, both gambling and westering thrived on high expectations, risk taking, opportunism, and movement, and both activities helped to shape a distinctive culture. Like bettors, pioneers have repeatedly grasped the change to get something for nothing—to claim free land, to pick up nuggets of gold, to speculate on western real estate. Like bettors, frontiersmen have cherished risks in order to get ahead and establish identity. Like bettors, migrants to new territories have sought to begin again in a setting that made all participants equal at the start. And whenever frontier society minimized risk or engendered inequality, curtailed enterprise or submerged individuality, Westerners could still turn to gambling to recreate those vanishing ideals on a different scale, in the same fashion that Easterners regarded the frontier as an arena to test their luck anew. Both groups were just as likely to lose at gambling as they were to see their expectations fade in the gamble of life, but in a historical perspective, the dogged pursuit of success, on the frontier or at betting tables, looms larger than success or failure itself. For a people of chance, participation in migrating and gambling counted for more than winning or losing; the game mattered more than the outcome.

* * *

In 1996 Congress sought to take stock of legalized gambling's impacts on "people and places" by charging a nine-member National Gambling Impact Study Commission (NGISC) with "conduct[ing] a comprehensive legal and factual study of the social and economic impacts of gambling in the United States" on communities, social institutions, and individuals, and to assess the role of government. NGISC, FINAL REPORT 12 (1999). Although the mission and composition of the Commission were not without controversy, the NGISC's 1999 report on gambling's social and economic impacts is the most comprehensive government-sponsored attempt to capture the empirical effects of gambling. The report devotes one chapter to assessing the specific socioeconomic impacts of Indian gaming. The report's introductory chapter gives a sense of the Commission's perceived mission and hints at its general findings.

National Gambling Impact Study Commission
Final Report
1-1 to 1-7 (1999)

Today the vast majority of Americans either gamble recreationally and experience no measurable side effects related to their gambling, or they choose not to gamble at all. Regrettably, some of them gamble in ways that harm themselves, their families, and their communities. This Commission's research suggests that 86 percent of Americans report having gambled at least once during their lives. Sixty-eight percent of Americans report having gambled at least once in the past year. In 1998, people gambling in this country lost $50 billion in legal wagering, a figure that has increased every year for over two decades, and often at double-digit rates. And there is no end in sight: Every prediction that the gambling market was becoming saturated has proven to be premature.

The Expansion of Legalized Gambling

The most salient fact about gambling in America — and the impetus for the creation of the Commission — is that over the past 25 years, the United States has been transformed from a nation in which legalized gambling was a limited and a relatively rare phenomenon into one in which such activity is common and growing. Today, all but two states have some form of legalized gambling. Pari- mutuel racetracks and betting are the most widespread form and are now legal in over 40 states; lotteries have been established in 37 states and the District of Columbia, with more states poised to follow; Indian casinos operate in every region of the country. Non-Indian casino gambling has expanded from Nevada and Atlantic City to the Mississippi Gulf Coast, Midwest riverboats, and western mining towns. As gambling sites proliferate on the Internet and telephone gambling is legalized in more states, an increasingly large fraction of the public can place a bet without ever leaving home at all. Universally available, "round-the-clock" gambling may soon be a reality.

Once exotic, gambling has quickly taken its place in mainstream culture: Televised megabucks drawings; senior citizens' day-trips to nearby casinos; and the transformation of Las Vegas into family friendly theme resorts, in which gambling is but one of a menu of attractions, have become familiar backdrops to daily life.

Impact and Controversy

Not surprisingly, the spread of legalized gambling has spawned a range of public debates, infused with the drama of contests between great interests and sharpened by a visceral emotional intensity. Typically, proponents of gambling choose to stress the potential economic benefits that the gambling industry can produce, such as jobs, investment, economic development, and enhanced tax revenues; whereas opponents underline the possible social costs, such as pathological gambling, crime, and other maladies.

Many of the positive economic impacts are in fact easy to point to if not always to quantify: Sleepy backwaters have become metropolises almost overnight; skyscrapers rise on the beaches at once-fading tourist areas; legions of employees testify to the hope and opportunities that the casinos have brought them and their families; some Indian nations have leapt from prolonged neglect and deprivation to sudden abundance. Gambling has not just made the desert bloom in Las Vegas but has made it the fastest growing city in the United States. Others, however, tell a different tale — of lives and families devastated by problem gambling, of walled-off oases of prosperity surrounded by blighted communities, of a massive transfer of money from the poor to the well-off, of a Puritan work ethic giving way to a pursuit of easy money. Which of these images is true? If elements of both exist, how does one weigh them? Assuming an assessment is even possible, what should be done?

The Role of Government

Government decisions have influenced the expansion of gambling in America, and influencing those decisions is the principal objective of most of the public debates on this issue. Although some would argue that gambling is a business like any other and, consequently, should be treated as such, in fact it is almost universally regarded as something different, requiring special rules and treatment, and enhanced scrutiny by government and citizens alike. Even in the flagship state of Nevada, operation of a gambling enterprise is explicitly defined as a "privilege," an activity quite apart from running a restaurant, manufacturing furniture, or raising cotton. Unlike other businesses in which the market is the principal determinant, the shape and operation of legalized gambling has been largely a product of government decisions. This is most obvious in the state lotteries, where governments have not just sanctioned gambling but have become its enthusiastic purveyors, legislating themselves an envied monopoly; and in Native American tribal gambling, where tribal nations own, and their governments often operate, casinos and other gambling enterprises.

But the role of government is hardly less pervasive in other forms of gambling: Governments determine which kinds of gambling will be permitted and which will not; the number, location, and size of establishments allowed; the conditions under which they operate; who may utilize them and under what conditions; who may work for them; even who may own them. All of this is in addition to the normal range of governmental activity in areas such as taxes, regulations, and so forth. And, because governments determine the level and type of competition to be permitted — granting, amending, and revoking monopolies, and restricting or enhancing competition almost at will — they also are a key determinant of the various industries' potential profits and losses.

To say that gambling has grown and taken shape in obeisance to government decisions does not imply that there was a well thought-out, overall plan. All too commonly, actual results have diverged from stated intentions, at times completely surprising the decisionmakers. There are many reasons for this awkward fact.

In the U.S. federalist system, use of the term "government" can easily mislead: Far from a single actor with a clear-eyed vision and unified direction, it is in fact a mix of authorities, with functions and decisionmaking divided into many levels — federal, state, local, and others, including tribal. Each of these plays an active role in determining the shape of legalized gambling. The states have always had the primary responsibility for gambling decisions and almost certainly will continue to do so for the foreseeable future. Many states, however, have delegated considerable authority to local jurisdictions, often including such key decisions as whether or not gambling will be permitted in their communities. And the federal government plays an ever-greater role: Indian gambling sprang into being as a result of federal court decisions and congressional legislation; and even the states concede that only Washington has the potential to control gambling on the Internet.

And almost none of the actors coordinate their decisions with one another. The federal government did not poll the states when it authorized Indian gambling within their borders, nor have Mississippi and Louisiana — nor, for that matter, any other state — seen fit to adopt a common approach to gambling. In fact, rivalry and competition for investment and revenues have been far more common factors in government decisionmaking regarding gambling than have any impulses toward joint planning.

Those decisions generally have been reactive, driven more by pressures of the day than by an abstract debate about the public welfare. One of the most powerful motivations has been the pursuit of revenues. It is easy to understand the impetus: Faced with stiff public resistance to tax increases as well as incessant demands for increased or improved public services from the same citizens, tax revenues from gambling can easily be portrayed as a relatively painless method of resolving this dilemma.

Critics have asserted that this legislative pursuit of revenues has occurred at the expense of consideration of the public welfare, a serious charge indeed, albeit an unproveable one. But advocates have successfully deployed many other arguments for legalizing or expanding gambling: economic development for economically depressed areas, the general promotion of business for the investment and employment opportunities it can bring with it, undermining illegal gambling and the organized crime it supports, and so forth. There is even the eminently democratic motivation of responding to public demand: A number of election campaigns and referenda have been successfully waged on the issue of legalizing or expanding gambling.

The Lack of Information

Presumably, many of the debates could be settled if either the benefits or costs of gambling could be shown to be significantly greater than the other. But such a neat resolution has evaded would-be arbiters. Efforts to assess the various claims by proponents and opponents quickly encounter gambling's third defining characteristic—the lack of reliable information. Regarding gambling, the available information on economic and social impact is spotty at best and usually inadequate for an informed discussion let alone decision. On examination, much of what Americans think they know about gambling turns out to be exaggerated or taken out of context. And much of the information in circulation is inaccurate or even false, although often loudly voiced by adherents. Add to this the fact that many of the studies that do exist were contracted by partisans of one point of view or another and uncertainty becomes an understandable result. Nevertheless, decisions must be made and governments have shown little hesitation in making them.

The problem is not simply one of gathering information. Legalized gambling on a wide scale is a new phenomenon in modern America and much of the relevant research is in its infancy. Many phenomena are only now beginning to be recognized and defined, a prerequisite to gathering useful information. And many of the key variables are difficult to quantify: Can the dollar costs of divorce or bankruptcy adequately capture the human suffering caused by problem gambling? The more difficult the measurement; the more the weighing of competing claims retreats from science to art or, with even greater uncertainty, to politics. Nevertheless, the lack of information will not reduce the pressures on governments to make decisions.

To take but one example: What are the economic impacts of gambling? The answer in great part depends on the context selected. On an individual basis, it is obvious that some people benefit and others do not, including both gamblers and nongamblers. The larger the group examined, however, the more ambiguous the possible conclusions. Single communities boasting a positive impact can readily be found, but the radius of their concerns usually does not extend to surrounding areas where negative consequences for others may surface as a direct consequence of this good fortune, such as loss of business, increases in crime, reduced tax revenues, and problem gamblers taking their problems home.

Even when the economic benefits are clear and agreed upon, there are other equally important issues to be decided. In fact, the heart of the debate over gambling pits possible economic benefits against assumed social costs. What are the broad impacts of gambling on society, on the tenor of our communities' lives, on the weakest among us? Because they inevitably involve highly subjective, non-quantifiable factors, assessing these is a more controversial exercise than the more pleasant task of estimating economic benefits. How can one ruined life be compared with the benefits provided to another? How can the actual costs of gambling-related crime be measured? Where is the algorithm that would allow the pursuit of happiness to be measured against the blunt numbers of pathological gambling?

Notes and Questions

1.   The "lack of information." The Commission noted that publicly commissioned or otherwise independently conducted and methodologically rigorous studies that seek to assess the impacts of legalized gambling were surprisingly rare. NGISC, Final Report, at 1-6 to 1-8, 6-14. Despite the industry's continued growth and expansion into new arenas, such as television and the Internet, the Commission's conclusion continues to have currency. With gambling so prominently on the public agenda, why do you think that is the case?

C. Gambling Law

Widely regarded as the embodiment of sloth, vice, or sin, gambling in various forms has been prohibited in nearly all 50 states throughout much of U.S. history. As prohibition has given way to legalization and accompanying regulation, legalized gambling has expanded rapidly and in myriad forms, including sports books, state lotteries, bingo palaces, riverboat casinos, pari-mutuel betting, poker tournaments, Internet gaming sites, civic and charitable gaming, and, of course, Indian gaming. Market expansion has depended almost exclusively on government support through repeal or modification of anti-gambling laws and the institution of regulatory schemes. Generally, government regulation of gambling is intended to foster industry growth while limiting gambling's negative externalities and providing the state a cut of the action in the form of tax dollars or other revenue. The legalization of gambling in most jurisdictions creates different legal and regulatory regimes, which overlap in complex ways. As Professors Mason and Nelson note, "Each of the fifty states has taken a distinctive approach to gambling, ranging from the complete ban on legal gambling in Hawaii, Utah, and Tennessee [which has since authorized a state lottery] to New Jersey and Louisiana's embrace of casinos, lotteries, pari-mutuel betting, and charitable bingo." John Lyman Mason & Michael Nelson, Governing Gambling 1 (2001). Gaming attorney Cory Aronovitz identifies some common goals and mechanisms of gambling regulation.

Cory Aronovitz
The Regulation of Commercial Gaming
5 Chapman L. Rev. 181 (2002)

The gaming industry is subject to special scrutiny, beyond that given to other industries. Many people fear that gaming will produce substantial negative impacts on society, either because gaming has a colorful past filled with unsavory individuals, or because it has the potential to wreak social havoc, absent direct and continuous oversight. Therefore, all jurisdictions that allow gaming have adopted some form of regulation—a structure to govern all conduct within the gaming environment. Although certain specific policies and goals may differ among communities, all gaming regulation strives to maintain the integrity of the gaming environment and to assure the public that the games are fair.

Regulatory Models

While all gaming laws incorporate provisions designed to maintain the integrity of the games and to protect against the infiltration of organized crime, the public purpose behind these provisions differs. Two well-established, general public purposes relate to gaming, and two different regulatory models have been developed to further these distinct purposes.

The first regulatory model, commonly referred to as the "Nevada model," seeks to maximize the economic benefits of gaming, and allows the industry to meet market demands with little regulatory involvement, including determining the number, location, and size of gaming facilities. Although business decisions are vested with the industry, integrity and suitability issues are strictly regulated.

The other approach, commonly referred to as the "New Jersey model," is in stark contrast to the Nevada model. This model focuses on the potential negative impacts of gaming, and establishes a comprehensive regulatory framework that strictly governs virtually every aspect of the business. Interestingly, while Nevada has experienced tremendous growth and capital investment over the last five years, New Jersey did not have any new development for ten years, following the opening of the Taj Mahal in 1990.

In both models, the administrative investigation and enforcement functions are independent and separate from the administrative decisionmaking. In Nevada, the Gaming Control Board investigates and enforces the gaming law and submits its findings and recommendations to the Gaming Commission for its determination. In New Jersey, the Division of Gaming Enforcement investigates and enforces the gaming law, while the decision function is vested in the Casino Control Commission.

Illinois is an example of a hybrid model, midway between the Nevada and New Jersey models. This hybrid regulatory scheme is typical of the "emerging jurisdictions," including Iowa, Indiana, Missouri, and Louisiana. The hybrid model vests all regulatory functions in one agency and limits the number of casino licenses that may be issued. In addition, the same agency investigates, enforces, and decides all aspects of the gaming environment.

Components of a Comprehensive Gaming Law

There are several components to a comprehensive gaming law. These include licensing, operational controls, law enforcement, taxation, and accounting and auditing.

Licensing is governmental control that determines who will profit from gaming activities, and who may associate with the gaming industry. The level of regulatory scrutiny varies, depending on a party's level of involvement in the gaming industry. Typically, the level of regulatory scrutiny increases when there is an increased level of involvement.

Another of the main objectives of gaming regulation is to monitor the casino's day-to-day operations. To effectively monitor casinos, gaming authorities require that each casino implement and strictly follow a comprehensive system of controls. Often, the jurisdictional gaming authority will prescribe a set of minimum controls, commonly referred to as the Minimum Internal Control System Standards (MICS). The MICS typically focus on gaming activity, including the conduct of games, the handling and movement of cash, chips, tokens or other similar items of value, and the accounting and document trail for all transactions. In general, the MICS related to the conduct of games dictate a universal method of dealing, shuffling, collecting wagers, and paying winning bets. Casino operators must meet or exceed the MICS; any deviation from the MICS is a red flag to surveillance that wrongdoing, such as collusion or cheating, may have occurred.

Yet another essential element to the effective regulation of commercial gaming is the government's ability to enforce its laws and regulations. Enforcement can either take the form of detection and discipline or prevention. Detection and discipline involve discovering violations of law, regulation, or internal controls, and imposing fines or restrictions on the offending licensee. On-site agents or instruments of the gaming authority enhance the ability to detect violations. One of the most effective tools used in detection is video surveillance. A typical surveillance system incorporates sophisticated video cameras, strategically placed throughout the facility, and controlled from a remote location. The surveillance operator is highly trained in detecting deviations from the MICS, as well as in the techniques typically used in cheating. Surveillance systems allow operators to view a specific area of the facility on command, as well as to zoom in and capture detailed images. In most regulatory schemes, the on-site agents have independent surveillance command centers, separate from the operator centers. Unlike detection, prevention seeks to reduce regulatory violations through education, training, and deterrence. For instance, programs designed to identify underage and problem gamblers, as well as intoxicated patrons, are valuable to avoid a potentially dangerous situation or regulatory violation. These programs also serve to put the operator on notice of the importance of compliance and the consequences of non-compliance. However, prevention is dependent on successful detection and discipline. If regulatory violations are regularly detected and consistently disciplined, then operators and employees are deterred from both intentional and negligible regulatory violations.

Tax revenue is perhaps the primary economic benefit that a jurisdiction derives from the authorization of gaming. Gaming taxes typically focus on the patron and the casino. Taxes on patrons include admission, sales, and income taxes. Casino taxes include state and local taxes on gross, adjusted gross, or net revenues; the quantity of games or gaming devices; the size of the casino floor; or the license privilege. When determining how much tax should be assessed, jurisdictions must consider competing markets and other leisure activities. If gaming taxes are too high, then casinos may pass the expense on to the customer in the form of higher costs, making the gaming product less attractive in comparison to other activities and gaming markets.

Accounting and audit procedures, whether pursuant to law or regulation, are necessary to control and protect the revenues generated from gaming activities. Accounting procedures provide a detailed picture of cash flow and can assist in detecting internal theft, commonly referred to as "skimming." Furthermore, accounting procedures can determine whether unlicensed, and possibly unsuitable, persons are profiting from gaming activities. The audit function of accounting is a companion tool that can identify non-compliance with internal controls.

All jurisdictions that allow gaming adopt some form of regulation. Regardless of the regulatory scheme, the ultimate goal of regulation should be maintaining the integrity of the gaming environment and assuring the public that the games are fair. The successful regulation of commercial gaming combines well-drafted legislation with administrative implementation.

Well-drafted legislation stems from a clear understanding of the reason for authorizing gaming. Lawmakers that take the time to develop a public policy for gaming will be able to incorporate provisions that have meaning and purpose. Issues of specific concern or importance to a community are properly addressed in legislation, along with the key elements addressed herein. The essential elements will preserve the integrity of the gaming environment and allow the regulatory body to implement the law.

Gaming has evolved into a corporate format that focuses on customer satisfaction, brand name recognition, and social concerns. The transformation from an industry that many thought was controlled by unsavory individuals, to today's ownership and management structure, is largely attributable to advancements in government regulation.

* * *

Now that we understand what gambling law is and what regulatory models fall under such schemes, we might ask whether, in the eyes of the law, there are any distinctions among types of gambling. As explained in the following excerpt, gaming attorneys Anthony Cabot and Louis Csoka are certain that such differentiation exists, but are more quizzical about the legitimacy of the policy rationales that underpin these distinctions. In this article, they offered a framework for considering the type of regulation that best meets a jurisdiction's goals.

Anthony N. Cabot & Louis V. Csoka
The Games People Play:
Is It Time For a New Legal Approach to Prize Games?
4 Nev. L.J. 197 (2004)

Almost all countries of the world afford their citizens some form of legal prize gaming. It could be, for example, betting on a hot stock rumor, buying a ticket in a state-run lottery, wagering on a horse, or checking the bottom of a soda can to see if you won a trip to the World Cup. There is an old saying that "[i]f you bet on a horse, that's gambling. If you bet you can make three spades, that's entertainment. If you bet cotton will go up three points, that's business. See the difference?" Of course, given the analytical similarity between the foregoing activities, it is difficult to justify why some activities are spurned, while others are legal.

Prize gaming is any activity where the participant is attempting to win a prize. There are three basic forms of prize gaming: gambling, sweepstakes, and contests. In general, court decisions typically analyze gambling offenses as financial schemes where (1) individuals pay consideration (usually money) (2) to participate in a game of chance (3) for the opportunity to win a prize (usually even more money). A sweepstake is similar, but involves activities where the participant does not pay consideration. Likewise, a contest differs from gambling only because the winner is determined primarily by skill as opposed to chance.

Increasingly, prize gaming scenarios appear to defy classification under such simple analytical models. For example, why is it legal to risk your money (consideration) on the chance that cotton stock will go up three points (a chance event) in hopes of making a profit (prize), while risking your money on the finish of a horse at the track may be prohibited?

In many instances, historic reasons, based on politics rather than analytical reasoning, exist for such distinctions. One argument is that those forms of prize gaming activities that were popular with the upper class tended to be legal (i.e., stock trading, horse racing, and golf contests for a prize), while those that were popular with the "lower classes" tended to remain illegal (i.e., numbers [lotteries], general sports wagering, and card games for a prize). Legislation and case law dealing with prize gaming often appears to be intellectually incongruous.

"Gambling" itself does not have a single definition; it is made up of three separate categories. In the first category of gambling games are "lotteries" or chance games involving schemes where a person pays valuable consideration for the chance to win a prize based on a game of chance. "Casino-style gaming" is generally a subset of lotteries or chance gaming. This subset encompasses such well-known chance games as slot machines, roulette tables, craps, and the like. In these games, participants risk something for the chance to win something of greater value than that which was risked.

The second category of gambling games is "bookmaking." Bookmaking occurs when a person risks something of value on the outcome of an uncertain event, in which the bettor does not exercise any control, but has the opportunity to win something of greater value than that which was risked. Whether sports wagering is an activity predominately determined by chance or skill can be the subject of much debate. Most states avoid this debate by enacting separate laws defining bookmaking as a criminal offense. The key difference between bookmaking and lottery laws is that a predominant element of chance, a prerequisite in many states to illegal gambling, is not a specific prerequisite to a bookmaking violation. Bookmaking is typically associated with wagering on sporting events.

"Pari-mutuel wagering" is a unique form of sports wagering. Unlike other forms of sports wagering, pari-mutuel horse wagering is legal in most states. Pari-mutuel wagering is important to the success of wagering on horse races. The popularity of pari-mutuel wagering assures that horse track operators have the gross profits necessary to maintain horse track facilities and compensate the horse owners and others involved in the industry. Gross profit is assured because the track or off-track betting ("OTB") operator takes a commission from each wager and places the remaining amounts into pools to be divided among winning bettors. The commission retained by the operator is called the "takeout." Takeouts vary between states and tracks and are often set by law or regulation. Typically the takeout on win, place, and show bets is about fifteen percent and is slightly higher on "exotic" bets, such as exactas and trifectas. Pari-mutuel wagering is most commonly used for events such as horseracing, dog racing, and motor sports.

The final category of "gambling" involves activities that are predominantly skill-based "contests," but because state legislatures want to eradicate these types of activities, they have grouped them with illegal gambling. The best example of this type of activity is poker.

The prize gaming universe—containing sweepstakes, skill-games, lotteries, pari-mutuel wagering, casino gaming, bookmaking, equity trading, and many other forms of gaming—is very complex. It is full of anomalies and inherent contradictions.

State governments have never taken a comprehensive approach to creating prize gaming policy. More often, the underlying public policy has taken an inferior position to historical, political, or economic realities that drove a particular piece of legislation. For example, economics normally dictate when a deficit in school funding drives support for creating a state lottery. As a result, the general subcategories of horse racing, lotteries, sports wagering, and casino-style gambling each have their unique anomalies, without any overarching, carefully reasoned policy rationale. Moreover, laws regarding gambling, contests, and sweepstakes have evolved from different historical bases, which appear to have led to another layer of contradictions.

To avoid anomalies and to better achieve the state's public policy goals, the state must utilize consistent criteria to determine whether to permit the different forms of gambling, sweepstakes, and contests in their community. In other words, those that enact laws should have rational answers as to why one activity is allowed and another activity is prohibited; or why one activity is heavily regulated, while another is left unregulated.

Any reasoned debate on prize gaming policy must start with a clear articulation of the government's underlying prize gaming public policy goals. There are three distinct approaches to this issue: (1) prize gaming should be prohibited because it is immoral, (2) prize gaming should be permitted as a fundamental aspect of individual freedom, or (3) prize gaming should be permitted only to the extent that government can achieve a positive economic benefit, while minimizing negative economic or social consequences.

Moralists maintain their positions based on subjective, personal feelings dictated either by theology or personal notions of social order. Moralists claim that gambling influences the values and priorities of the general public. In essence, people may interact differently in a community with gambling as opposed to in a community where it is banned. The argument is that the emphasis on hedonism, luck, and wealth created by gambling may affect the nature of these societal interactions. Undesirable attributes in the community at large may emerge, including that persons are better off trying their luck gambling than working hard. This line of reasoning extends even further; wealth is the most important social attribute in this culture, therefore everyone must have a price.

Where state policy is based on morals, a re-examination of the application of those morals to the various forms of prize gaming is appropriate. For example, does logic dictate that casino gambling should be morally prohibited while allowing minors access to prize arcades and trading cards with chase cards? Likewise, if the prohibition on gambling is based on promoting the notion that persons are better off working hard than taking their chance at luck, a million dollar sweepstakes is difficult to justify. Here, again, consistency alone in the application of a public policy will begin to eliminate the anomalies found in prize gaming.

States that go beyond moralism and attempt to assess prize gaming based on pragmatic considerations face a more daunting task. Regarding legalized casinos, some state governments have undertaken, at least on the surface, a pragmatic consideration of the economic and social costs and benefits associated with legalized gambling. Under this approach, state officials must consider the benefits, negative externalities, and feasibility of implementation before deciding on a policy approach. If the benefits exceed the externalities, the activity should be permitted, but regulated, to further maximize the benefits.

Even if negative externalities exceed the benefits, the state may decide not to end legalized prize gaming in the state. Instead, policy makers may look toward alternatives to reduce or avoid those externalities. Only if the reduced negative externalities exceed the benefits would a government normally prohibit the activity, unless the activity is inevitable. Specifically, where the externalities caused by illegal gambling are worse than the externalities caused by regulated gambling, regulating the activity with the goal of minimizing the externalities is the preferred approach.

Governments often distinguish their gaming public policy choices based on the beneficiary of the offered activity. Prize gaming can benefit four principal groups: government, charities, disadvantaged groups, and private interests. Where the gambling activity was designed to help charities or, generally, a socially important cause, then it has often been deemed acceptable because of its targeted nature. Lotteries, for instance, are probably one of the best and earliest examples of a gambling activity that became sanctioned or legalized to help support socially important causes. With respect to certain forms of casino-style gaming, similar observations can again be made. As the United States Congress explained, the purpose of the Indian Gaming Regulatory Act of 1988 was to establish a "statutory basis for the operation of gaming by Indian tribes as a means of promoting tribal economic development, tribal self-sufficiency, and strong tribal governments."

Once a society formulates a public policy toward gambling, it must implement that policy. Implementation concerns the way in which the government carries out its policy goals. While policy goals are the desired ends, implementation is the means of arriving at those desired ends. Implementation usually involves both adopting and enforcing laws. While the government can achieve policy goals through the adoption of laws that restrict, mediate, or promote the activities of private parties, regulation is the most common method of implementation. Specifically, regulation is the process by which the government achieves policy goals by restricting the choices of private parties. Nevertheless, no perfect regulatory system exists or can exist. The best that a jurisdiction can hope for is that it tailors a regulatory system that meets its goals efficiently. In some limited cases, effective regulation in one jurisdiction may prove to be unworkable in another.

Between the extreme approaches of eradication and non-enforcement lies the middle road of legalization and control through regulation. Three approaches to gaming regulation predominate in societies that allow legal gaming: (1) the Player Protection Model; (2) the Government Neutral Model; and (3) the Government Protection Model.

Player Protection Model

The Player Protection Model is a system that protects the player. Under this approach, the government allows the gaming activity, but attempts to regulate the operators to minimize undesirable social consequences. This model is often based on the underlying premise that the activity is not subject to prohibition, therefore legalizing it with the goal toward minimizing externalities is the preferred public policy. Under the Player Protection Model—applicable to all forms of prize gaming—are three basic principles. First, the game should be fair. Second, the game should be honest. The third basic principal is that players who win should be paid.

Another aspect of the Player Protection Model is the philosophy that the operator should not engage in exploitation by encouraging gaming activity, encouraging players to wager more than they can afford to lose, or encouraging players to wager more than they would if not encouraged to do so. These societies often achieve this goal through the adoption of laws that prevent operators from advertising or conducting any other activities that might stimulate interest in gaming.

Government Neutral Model

The second way that government may approach legal gambling is by adopting a Government Neutral Model. In places where gaming is legal, this is the least common approach. The Government Neutral Model involves little or no regulation of a legal casino industry. Under this model, the casino industry would not be subject to any more licensing or regulatory scrutiny than other businesses, such as automobile dealers. In the rare instances where this approach is taken, government usually requires that proceeds from legal gambling be given to charities. Charitable gaming is common in many American states and in foreign countries where commercial casino gaming is prohibited.

While the government may approach licensing of charitable gaming with no more intensity than the licensing of other businesses, the revenues generated by charitable gaming are often significant. This model does not reflect a moral or social/economic bias against gambling; nor does it recognize that the government has any special obligation to protect the industry.

The government may also decide that small-stakes gambling is harmless, but that patrons need protection from high-stakes gambling. These governments may apply a Government Neutral Model to some forms of low-stakes gambling and a Government Protection Model to high-stakes gambling, or even ban high-stakes gambling altogether. In Mississippi, for example, licenses to conduct low-stakes bingo games are routinely granted with little regulatory scrutiny, while applicants wishing to operate high-stakes games must undergo more rigorous licensing and follow more stringent regulations.

Government Protection Model

Like the Player Protection Model, the Government Protection Model involves strict regulation of a legal industry. While the Player Protection Model provides regulation to protect the patron, the Government Protection Model provides regulation that protects the economic interests of the state. Not surprisingly, the Government Protection Model is often found where the government relies heavily on the industry to meet tax expectations.

The government has four roles in this model. The first and most important role is to act as a vehicle for the industry to gain and maintain credibility. Its existence in many places is tenuous. Public perception of the benefits and burdens of legal gaming may change and influence the legality of the activity.

The second role of the government in the Government Protection Model is to promote and defend the industry. This requires the government to take an active interest in convincing the outside world that the regulatory system has successfully excluded organized crime, and is protecting the honesty of the games. When attacked, the government must defend the industry against its critics.

A third role that the government plays in the Government Protection Model is to provide a vehicle for solving the industry's problems. For example, no single casino may be capable of testing equipment or games sold by distributors to assure that they cannot be manipulated or cheated to the operator's detriment. Equipping and maintaining a lab and employing trained personnel would be too costly for a single casino.

Another governmental role in this model is to assure that it accounts for all government benefits. Because the primary benefit is often tax revenues, the government provides such accounting controls and audit functions as it deems reasonable to assure it receives its fixed share. In other instances, where the benefits are ancillary services, employment, or the like, government checks to assure that the operators comply with all legislative mandates.

Hybrid models also exist, borrowing elements of the Government Protection, Government Neutral, and Player Protection models. Often, underlying these hybrids are the public policy that seeks to tap the economic benefits from gambling and minimize costs. Here, government believes the financial reward from gambling is greater than the potential harm. These hybrid systems often attempt to realize the revenues from gambling while eliminating the harm, particularly to its citizens.

Notes and Questions

1. ***Illegal gambling.*** As noted above, while legalized gambling in the U.S. has varied over time, illegal gambling has been something of a constant. From backroom poker and "numbers" games banked by organized crime to office "March Madness" sports pools, illegal gambling continues to flourish despite government prohibition. Some illegal gambling may be tacitly sanctioned by the fact of nonenforcement. The illegal gambling market arguably has grown exponentially with the advent of Internet gaming. Professors Barker and Britz believe that the illegal gambling market is "huge":

> The estimates for illegal sports betting along vary from $30 to $100 billion annually. Illegal gambling may be larger in terms of people involved and money gambled if we take into account full-time bookies, numbers runners, illegal slot machines, and part-time operators who run sports, cards, poker, and craps games. Illegal gambling also takes place in sports pools, poker games, and "gray"

machines (designated for amusement only but [which actually] pay off) in fraternal, veterans, and social clubs. We simply don't know the extent and monies bet. No one does.... Furthermore, this illegal gambling is unlicensed, unregulated, and untaxed....

Thomas Barker & Marjorie Britz, Jokers Wild: Legalized Gambling in the Twenty-First Century 5 (2000). How does illegal gambling figure in the models of government regulation?

  2.   *Indian gaming and regulatory models.* As analytical frameworks, can one square the various models of government regulation offered by Aronovitz with those explicated by Cabot and Csoka? Where does Indian gaming fit into these models? Does tribal gaming share the policy goals for state intervention identified by the authors of the above articles? If so, which ones, and if not, why not?

  3.   *Economic vs. moral regulation generally.* For a discussion of other "vices" where government regulation is influenced by both economic interests and morality, such as alcohol and tobacco sales, see Jerome H. Skolnick, *The Social Transformation of Vice*, 51 Law & Contemp. Probs. 9 (1988).

D. Tribal Governments and Federal Indian Law and Policy

Appropriate and effective regulation of gambling is a complex endeavor, made more difficult by lack of a clear and consistent public policy to guide government action. Indian gaming adds a further complicating dimension: the legal and political status of tribal governments. In this section, we examine the foundations of tribes' unique status in the American political system.

David E. Wilkins
American Indian Politics and the American Political System
41–49 (2002)

The situation of the 561 indigenous polities in North America is and has always been distinctive in comparison to the status and place of African Americans, Asian Americans, Latino Americans, women, and other racial or ethnic groups in the country. This is so far a number of important reasons, some obvious, some little known. First, tribal people are the *original—the indigenous—inhabitants* of North America and they are *nations* in the most fundamental sense of the word. That is, they are separate peoples inhabiting specific territories that they wield some governmental control or jurisdiction over.

Second, the preexistence of over six hundred independent tribal nations, bands, pueblos, etc., well in advance of the formation of the United States, each having a number of integral attributes, including a bounded land base, and appropriate economic system, a governmental system, and sociocultural distinctiveness, necessitated the practice of aboriginal sovereigns negotiating political compacts, treaties, and alliances with European nations and later the United States. The fact of *treaty making*, which no other resident American group (states are also precluded from negotiating treaties) participated in, and the products of that process—the actual treaties, agreements, and negotiated settlements—

confirmed a nation-to-nation relationship between the negotiating tribe and nontribal parties. A large number, over five hundred, of these important contractual arrangements form the baseline parameters of the political relationship between tribes and the United States and are still legally valid, though their enforceability has always been problematic. A majority of these treaties involved land cessions by tribes and reservations of lands not ceded or sold to the federal government.

As tribes are treaty-recognized sovereigns, tribal rights are not based on or subject to U.S. constitutional law and are therefore not protected by the Constitution. This is because as preexisting sovereigns tribes do not derive their inherent governmental powers from the federal or state government. Thus, tribal nations have an extraconstitutional relationship to the United States that no other group has.

A third feature differentiating indigenous peoples from other racial/ethnic groups is the *trust doctrine*. While the federal government and tribes have rarely been in agreement on what the trust principle entails, President Clinton, in an executive order on May 14, 1998, put forth a clear description of what the trust relationship entails from the federal government's perspective: "The United States has a unique legal relationship with Indian tribal governments as set forth in the Constitution of the United States, treaties, statutes, executive orders, and court decisions. Since the formation of the Union, the United States has recognized Indian tribes as domestic dependent nations under its protections." In this statement the president sought to assure Indians that the United States recognized that tribes have a sovereign status which the federal government, as a separate though connected sovereign, is bound to respect under its own law. The hundreds of treaties and agreements that were negotiated in which the tribes were guaranteed all the rights and resources (e.g., rights to water and lands; to hunt, fish, and gather; to exercise criminal and civil jurisdiction; to tax) they had not ceded to the federal government when they sold or exchanged the majority of their lands—most of North America—were contractual rights that were also protected by the trust doctrine, which is the federal government's legal and moral pledge to respect those reserved Indian rights.

More important was the president's use of the phrase "under its [the government's] protection." This is a declaration that the federal government has a protectorate obligation to support indigenous people legally, culturally, economically, and politically.

Tribal nations tend to think of "trust" as entailing four interrelated components: that the federal government—or its agents—was pledged to protect tribal property and sovereignty and would not move for or against tribes without first securing tribal consent; that the United States would act with the utmost integrity in its legal and political commitments to Indian peoples as outlined in treaties or governmental policies (e.g., provide health care, educational support, housing assistance); that the United States would act in a moral manner regarding tribal rights, as the Judeo-Christian nation is historically professed to be in its dealing with tribes; and that the United States would continue to support any additional duties and responsibilities in its self-assumed role as the Indians' "protectors."

A fourth concept, congressional plenary power, is yet another distinctive feature of the tribal-federal relationship that separates tribal nations from all other racial/ethnic groups in the United States. Basically put, "plenary" means complete in all aspects or meanings in federal Indian policy and law. First, it means *exclusive*. The federal Constitution, in the commerce clause (article 1, section 8, clause 3), vests in Congress the sole authority to "regulate Commerce with foreign Nations, and among the several States, *and with the Indian tribes*." In other words, the founders of the American republic believed that the power to engage in treaty making with tribes should rest with the legislative branch of the federal government, not with the states.

Second, and related to the first definition, plenary also means *preemptive*. That is, Congress may enact legislation which effectively precludes—preempts—state governments from acting in Indian-related matters. Finally, and most controversially, since this definition lacks a constitutional basis, plenary means *unlimited* or *absolute*. This judicially constructed definition (*United States v. Kagama*, 1886) means that the Congress has vested in itself, without a constitutional mooring, virtually boundless governmental authority and jurisdiction over tribal nations, their lands, and their resources. As recently as 1978 the Supreme Court, in *United States v. Wheeler*, held that "Congress has plenary authority to legislate for the Indian tribes in all matters, including their form of government."

Federal plenary power when defined as unlimited and absolute should give one reason to pause from a democratic theory perspective. The idea that a democracy has exercised and continues to assert that it has the power to wield absolute authority over tribal people—and without tribal consent—whose members are today citizens of the United States, is deeply disturbing, yet that reality persists for indigenous peoples and their citizens, notwithstanding their treaty and trust rights as citizens of sovereign governments and, since 1924, with citizenship status in the states and federal government as well.

Plenary power, like the trust doctrine, has proven to be a mixed blessing for Indian peoples. On the positive side, Congress, under its plenary power, has been able to pass legislation that accords Indians unique treatment that other groups and individuals are ineligible for—medical care, Indian preference hiring practices in the BIA, educational benefits, housing aid, tax exemptions, etc. Such legislation and policy action is possible, again, because of the extraconstitutional status of tribes, which places them outside the protections of the Constitution. Tribal members are entitled to these distinctive considerations, and Congress is empowered to exercise a great deal of authority in Indian affairs because it must be "immune from ordinary challenges which might otherwise hamper the wise administration of Indian affairs."

On the negative side, plenary power has been interpreted by the Supreme Court to allow the federal government to pass laws and enact regulations which prohibit Indians in some situations from selling their own land to whomever they wish. Congress may also confiscate Indian lands held under aboriginal title and is not required to pay just compensation under the Fifth Amendment to the Constitution. Congress may punish Indians under federal law for certain crimes, even if this means the individuals will be punished more severely than non-Indians who commit the same crime under state law. And Congress may literally terminate the legal existence of tribal nations.

How are Congress and Supreme Court able to justify such discriminatory action if the Constitution prohibits discrimination on the basis of race? It is because while tribal nations certainly constitute separate racial groups, more important is that fact that they constitute separate political groups, recognized in the treaty relationship, the trust doctrine, and the placement of tribes in the commerce clause. In other words, Europeans nations and the United States did not enter into treaties with tribes because of their racial differences, but because they were separate sovereigns—oftentimes with impressive military and economic clout—that the United States wanted and needed to establish diplomatic ties with. Hence, the relationship the United States has with tribes as political entities, and as governments, is at its heart a political, not racial, alliance. Congressional action, therefore, that is based on plenary power does not violate the equal protection and due process clauses of the Constitution that prohibit discrimination on the basis of race.

What all the preceding concepts confirm is that tribal peoples, unlike any other groups in the United States, are *sovereign nations*, not minority groups. A sovereign nation is a distinct political entity which exercises a measure of jurisdictional power over a specific territory. It is not an absolute or fully independent power in a pure sense because no nation or tribe in the world today, regardless of its geographic girth, population base, or gross national product, is completely or fully sovereign.

The sovereignty of tribes, it is important to note, was not delegated to them by the federal or state governments—it is original and inherent power. Tribal sovereignty has to do, on one hand, with a tribe's right to retain a measure of independence from outside entities and the power of regulating one's internal affairs, including the ability to make and execute laws, to impose and collect taxes, and to make alliances with other governments. On the other hand, tribal sovereignty has a unique cultural and spiritual dimension which differentiates it from the sovereign power of a state or the federal government.

Because of the doctrines discussed above, the sovereign interactions of the tribes, the states and the United States entail an ongoing and awkward minuet whose choreography has too often been unilaterally prepared by the federal government, with little regard for the inherent rights of the tribes, the original minuet partners.

Consequently, tribal nations find that their collective rights, lands, and even inherent sovereignty lack substantive protection from the very government, the federal government, which is charged by treaties, by the trust doctrine, and by constitutional acknowledgement in the commerce clause with protecting Indian tribes. The internal political affairs of tribal nations and the relationship between tribal nations and the United States is, thus, full of perplexity.

Robert B. Porter
A Proposal to the Hanodaganyas to Decolonize Federal Indian Control Law
31 U. Mich. J.L. Reform 899 (1998)

Greetings Hanodaganyas:

For over 200 years, the Seneca Nation has maintained a peaceful relationship with the United States in accordance with the Treaty of Canandaigua. While it is true that both of our nations have benefited from this Treaty, mine has sacrificed greatly: because of the American people's colonization, we have lost almost all of our aboriginal lands and much of our traditional way of life. These losses resulted from federal and state governmental actions over the generations that violated the letter and spirit of our Treaty and that interfered with our sovereign right of self-determination.

The effect of these violations on our ability to survive as distinct peoples has been dramatic. Indeed, because of what America and its colonizing predecessors have done to deny us the opportunity to choose our own future, it is my belief that Indigenous people are in grave danger of becoming extinct.

Despite this history and the effect that it has had on us, I remain committed to the belief that we can revitalize our sovereignty and thus ensure the survival of our future generations. In order to do so, we must find ways to generate economic opportunity for all of our people, to preserve our unique languages and cultures, and to develop vibrant tribal governments. Perhaps as never before, some of us currently have resources that might allow us to accomplish these goals and to cast off the hardship associated with the last few hundred years. While we know that much of the blame for our condition can be placed at the feet of your Nation, we fully accept that the burden of safeguarding our future rests on our own shoulders.

Nevertheless, no matter how much responsibility we assume for the redevelopment of our sovereignty, the United States remains a barrier to our forward progress. America, because of its geography, its people, its culture, and its media, is an overwhelming influence on the Indigenous nations located within its borders. As a result, tremendous forces inhibit the preservation and strengthening of the unique fabric of our nations and thus form considerable obstacles to our redevelopment.

One of the most significant barriers to our redevelopment lies in the body of American law. Since its founding, the United States has developed an extensive body of law — so-called "federal Indian law" — to define and regulate its relationship with the Indian nations remaining within its borders. While this law may seem to have a neutral purpose, it would be more accurate to say that "federal Indian law" is really "federal Indian control law" because it has the twofold mission of establishing the legal bases for American colonization of the continent and perpetuating American power and control over the Indian nations. Unfortunately, in addition to this foundational problem, the law itself is not simple or uniform. Federal Indian control law is a hodgepodge of statutes, cases, executive orders, and administrative regulations that embody a wide variety of divergent policies towards the Indian nations since the time the United States was established. Because old laws reflecting these old policies have rarely been repealed when new ones reflecting new policies have been adopted, any efforts that might be taken by the Indian nations and the federal government to strengthen Indian self-determination must first cut through the legal muck created by over 200 years of prior federal efforts to accomplish precisely the opposite result.

As I see it, this legal minefield profoundly affects tribal sovereignty. For example, conflicting federal laws — such as those that provide for the federal government's protective trust responsibility over Indian affairs and those that allow federal, state, and private interests to interfere with tribal self-government — make it impossible for the Indian nations to exercise fully their sovereign right of self-determination. As past efforts to destroy our sovereign existence continue to have their corrosive effect, so too, in my view, does the natural result of those efforts: the destruction of Indigenous culture and the eventual assimilation of Indian people into American society. Inevitably, in the absence of any affirmative efforts to decolonize both the Indian nations and federal Indian control law, I believe that our distinct native identity will continue to erode, and with it, the existence of our nations.

I realize that the challenge of revitalizing tribal sovereignty is a difficult one and that this problem is unlikely to be resolved quickly. Even if desired, several hundred years' worth of colonizing influence will never be totally undone; to the extent that it can be undone, it will not be undone easily. The most reasonable and prudent course for our Indigenous nations to pursue is to attempt to harmonize the good things that have been forced upon us by others with the good things that are unique to and traditional within our own societies.

The Colonial Foundation of Federal Indian Control Law

The primary reason why federal Indian control law is a significant barrier to the greater assertion of tribal sovereignty is because the United States originally approached relations with the Indian nations from a singular, self-interested perspective — how to achieve the complete colonization of the American continent and the "civilization" of the Indigenous peoples. The colonization of the "New World" raised the possibility that at some point the colonists would have to generate a legal basis for taking lands that were already occupied. The failure of disease to exterminate the Indigenous population by the time of the American Revolution ensured that the United States would be required to develop a body of law to rationalize its continued expansion and assertion of hegemony over those lands and peoples.

The architect of modern federal Indian control law was U.S. Supreme Court Chief Justice John Marshall. In a series of opinions that he wrote during the early nineteenth century, *Johnson v. M'Intosh, Cherokee Nation v. Georgia*, and *Worcester v. Georgia*, Marshall laid out the analytical framework for how American law would address the quandary of the Indian nations.

In *Johnson v. M'Intosh*, the Supreme Court was called upon to decide whether the Piankeshaw Indians could pass land title to private individual colonists, and thus to address the fundamental question of how the United States originally gained legal title to the land upon which it rested. Writing for the court, Marshall concluded that America, as a colonizing nation, had the superior right over other nations to extinguish Indian titles "either by purchase or by conquest." This principle — which is called the "doctrine of discovery" — meant that under federal Indian control law, the Indian nations "had no theoretical, independent right to sovereignty that a European discoverer might be required to recognize under Europe's Law of Nations." Marshall further reasoned that because the Indian nations did not possess the full panoply of inherent sovereign powers vis-à-vis the colonizing nation, they were thus only vested with a permanent "right of occupancy" to their aboriginal lands. Therefore, the Indians could not pass good title to non-Indians because they had no title to pass in the first place.

Since he was writing without the benefit of much domestic precedent on this issue, one might wonder where Marshall got the idea that the Indians should be divested of legal title to their lands solely by virtue of being "discovered" by the Anglo-European colonists. Marshall's opinion in *Johnson v. M'Intosh* represents the American incorporation of the medievally-derived "heathen subjugation" theory [or the idea that Christian Europeans possessed a moral and religious right to subjugate non-Christian "pagans"]. This was a view shared commonly by the Founding Fathers. Thus, in accordance with his perspective, Marshall had little choice but to vanquish the Indian nations under American law — either they owned the land or the United States did. This was truly a monumental problem; ruling that the Indians actually owned their own land would have up-ended the entire American land tenure system and might have bankrupted the new nation's already weakened federal treasury if compensation had to be paid for the illegal takings accomplished to date. Viewed this way, the *Johnson* decision might simply be understood as nothing more than the perfect political compromise. Affording the Indians a permanent "right of occupancy" under federal law eliminated the difficult problem associated with actually having to remove them.

But Marshall, in concluding that the Indian nations had been "conquered" and thus divested of title to the land, went beyond mere political compromise and incorporated fully the "heathen subjugation" theory that had been used for centuries to justify the domination of non-Christian peoples and their lands. In describing the manner in which American colonization had occurred, Marshall observed:

> On the discovery of this immense continent, the great nations of Europe were eager to appropriate to themselves so much of it as they could respectively acquire. Its vast extent offered an ample field to the ambition and enterprise of all;

and the character and religion of its inhabitants afforded an apology for considering them as a people over whom the superior genius of Europe might claim an ascendancy. The potentates of the old world found no difficulty in convincing themselves that they made ample compensation to the inhabitants of the new, by bestowing on them civilization and Christianity, in exchange for unlimited independence. As a result, Great Britain's successor, the United States, as a nation of "civilized inhabitants," acceded to its land title pursuant to the rule that "discovery gave an exclusive right to extinguish the Indian title of occupancy."

In some respects, Marshall suggested that he might not agree with the conclusion that he "must" draw: that "[c]onquest gives a title which the Courts of the conqueror cannot deny." Nonetheless, while he professed not "to engage in the defence of those principles which Europeans have applied to Indian title," he did find justification "in the character and habits of the people whose rights have been wrested from them." In so doing, Marshall accepted the basic tenets of Western colonization theory, and thus incorporated them into the foundation of federal law dealing with the Indian nations by describing how colonization is "supposed" to work. He explained:

> The title by conquest is acquired and maintained by force. The conqueror prescribes its limits. Humanity, however, acting on public opinion, has established, as a general rule, that the conquered shall not be wantonly oppressed, and that their condition shall remain as eligible as is compatible with the objects of the conquest. Most usually, they are incorporated with the victorious nation, and become subjects or citizens of the government with which they are connected. The new and old members of the society mingle with each other; the distinction between them is gradually lost, and they make one people.

But Marshall did acknowledge a problem, perhaps unique, associated with dealing with America's Indigenous people:

> [T]he tribes of Indians inhabiting this country were fierce savages, whose occupation was war, and whose subsistence was drawn chiefly from the forest. To leave them in possession of their country, was to leave the country a wilderness; to govern them as a distinct people, was impossible, because they were as brave and as high spirited as they were fierce, and were ready to repel by arms every attempt on their independence.

As a result, Marshall concluded that this "law which regulates, and ought to regulate in general," the relationship with the Indians could not be applied. Thus, Marshall acknowledged that no "conquest" had actually occurred, but concluded that the United States had no recourse but to leave the Indians in possession of the land and to preserve the possibility that the United States' legal claim to the land could be perfected in the future. While this appears to be an honest conclusion, it nonetheless rests on the weak assumption that the United States has no legitimate right to its land other than by virtue of its self-proclaimed status over the Indians.

Marshall continued to expand upon his overall theory of colonization in *Cherokee Nation v. Georgia*, in which the Supreme Court was called upon to decide whether the Cherokee Nation could invoke the original jurisdiction of the Supreme Court on the ground that it was a foreign nation. Marshall concluded that the Court could not exercise original jurisdiction in the case because the Cherokee Nation was not a foreign nation or state, but only a "domestic dependent nation." Simply by declaring this proposition, Marshall eliminated under American law the independent sovereign status not only of the Cherokees, but also of all Indian nations.

While this conclusion was based significantly upon a textual reading of the Constitution, Marshall expanded his analysis in dicta to address the precise nature of the federal-tribal relationship. In so doing, he developed the most important and longstanding mechanism utilized by the United States for exercising control over the lives and lands of Indian people: the federal government's trust responsibility.

In denying the Cherokee Nation the status of a foreign nation with the right to invoke the Supreme Court's original jurisdiction, Marshall memorialized in federal law the self-interested determination that the Indians were a subservient people dependent upon the United States. It is not a far stretch to conclude from this opinion that Marshall continued to perceive the aboriginal inhabitants of the continent as uncivilized heathens. Indians "in a state of pupilage" could never be thought to appeal to "an American court of justice for an assertion of right or a redress of wrong" — "[t]heir appeal was to the tomahawk, or to the government." Marshall's opinion in *Cherokee Nation* furthered the rationalization of American colonization by concluding that the Indian nations are merely "domestic dependent nations" and thus are barred from exercising the rights of self-determination inherent in all free peoples.

The last of the foundational federal Indian control law decisions written by Marshall was *Worcester v. Georgia. Worcester* addressed whether a state could extend its legislative authority to regulate the conduct of non-Indians within Indian territory. Marshall concluded that the State of Georgia had no authority to enforce its laws within Cherokee territory because relations with Indian nations were an exclusively federal matter.

In obvious respects, Marshall's reasoning in *Worcester* diverged significantly from the reasoning contained in *Johnson* and *Cherokee Nation.* He analyzed in great detail the sovereign existence of the Cherokee Nation, mainly utilizing the Treaty of Hopewell between the Cherokees and the United States as his vehicle. He concluded that while the Treaty provides that the Cherokees shall be under the protection of the United States, such a provision should not be construed as a relinquishment of Cherokee sovereignty: "Protection does not imply the destruction of the protected." Indeed, his reasoning in this regard seems almost totally at odds with his reasoning in *Cherokee Nation.*

Despite this apparent departure from his prior practice of suppressing the Indian nations within American law, Marshall's *Worcester* opinion can easily be read as consistent with *Johnson* and *Cherokee Nation* if it is viewed as another instance in which federal power is deemed paramount in the face of a competing interest — in this case, the interest of a State. Thus despite his hearty acknowledgment of Cherokee sovereignty in *Worcester*, much of Marshall's reasoning defending and rationalizing colonization from his earlier opinions remained in the decision.

In many ways, *Worcester*, through its majority and concurring opinions, revealed the tension between competing theories — accommodation versus colonization — of how America should deal with the Indian nations. Nonetheless, in deciding *Johnson* and *Cherokee Nation*, the Supreme Court was called upon to address fundamental questions associated with Indian relations that were tied critically to the future development of the United States. Viewed from this simple perspective, it can perhaps be rationalized that the actions taken by the United States to deal with the Indians in the early years of the Republic — such as warfare, forced removal, and outright stealing of Indian lands — were simply a matter of perceived necessity. But the reality is that Indian peoples and lands were colonized in order to remove a barrier to the pursuit of wealth, territory, and freedom for the colonizing people. In the course of Western colonization of "heathen" peoples, demonizing, devaluing, and degrading those who are to be colonized all have been tools to facilitate total subjugation.

While Marshall revealed in *Worcester* that he may have thought his prior conclusions about federal authority over Indian affairs overreached, and therefore sought to distance himself from them, it is significant that only after he had established the legal justification for American colonial policies designed to secure wealth, resources, and opportunity for the emerging nation, did he find it comfortable to defend the sovereignty of the Indian nations. Marshall, like all leaders, had choices to make when he wrote these important cases. Ultimately, he chose to follow the "underlying medievally-derived ideology—that normatively divergent 'savage' peoples could be denied equal rights and status accorded to the civilized nations of Europe." In so doing, he embedded this ideology firmly within the fabric of the American law dealing with the Indian nations.

The Evolution of Federal Indian Policy: The Different Faces of Colonization

Most scholars of federal Indian control law and policy hold the view that the United States has never successfully developed and carried out an effective policy for dealing with the Indian nations located within its borders. This view holds that throughout the 222 years of United States history, every conceivable policy objective has been attempted, ranging from the pursuit of peaceful coexistence—through the Treaty, Reorganization, and Self-Determination policies—to outright genocide—through the Warfare, Removal, Reservation, Allotment, and Termination policies. On its face, the historical record makes it easy to conclude that the United States has had a cyclical and inconsistent policy in Indian affairs.

I hold a contrary view. Looking at the same evidence and apparent policy fluctuations as others, it is clear to me that American policy toward the Indians has always revolved around the same central theme: to wit; how can "we," the superior, enlightened, Christian people, help/destroy "them," the inferior, uncivilized, pagan people; in such a way as to eliminate our/their problem with them/us. It is obvious that policies such as Warfare, Allotment, and Termination had the clear intent of simply eliminating Indian people as members of distinct societies. But even the so-called "benevolent" policies, like Reorganization, ended up achieving the same objective as the most destructive policies. In their efforts to help Indian people, the reformers, usually motivated by Christian and Western values, have supported policies that have had the direct and indirect effect of assimilating Indian people into the American way of life.

Treaty Policy. In the early years of the American Republic, Indian affairs management focused on securing the neutrality of the Indian nations to allow for stability and growth in the new nation. American officials relied upon negotiation and treaty-making in dealing with the Indians. The primary reason for relying on these methods was the fact that the Indian nations were militarily powerful and still a threat to the young United States. Moreover, the Articles of Confederation supported a state role in managing Indian affairs and left the federal government with little power other than the ability to enter into treaties. Given the weakness associated with the federal government of the new United States, diplomacy and treaty making were the only viable options for addressing Indian affairs.

Upon the Constitution's adoption and ratification, all questions concerning the states' role in managing Indian affairs were resolved in favor of the federal government. The Commerce Clause vested full and exclusive authority in the United States to regulate "Commerce ... with the Indian tribes." Accordingly, the first Congress asserted this new authority by enacting the Indian Trade and Intercourse Act of 1790, which prohibited any purchase of Indian land by individuals or states without federal approval. Until the early part of the nineteenth century, federal Indian policy and legislation was mostly limited to managing Indian trade relations.

Removal Policy. After the turn of the nineteenth century, as the United States established its military superiority over the Indian nations, it developed an alternative to diplomacy for dealing with Indian affairs—physical removal of the Indians to western lands. American colonization through settlement and economic development generated tremendous conflict between the Indian nations and the states: the most famous of these disputes involved the State of Georgia's efforts to eradicate Cherokee sovereignty through its own legislation, precipitating a constitutional crisis in 1832 due to President Jackson's refusal to enforce the Supreme Court's decision in *Worcester v. Georgia.*

The conflict between the Indian nations and the nascent United States presented a policy quandary that allowed for several possibilities. Other policy options available to Jackson at the time included simply killing the Indians off, assimilating them rapidly, or "protecting" them on their "ancestral lands in the East." All were rejected. Outright killing of the Indians was not seriously considered (although it was the policy of "aggressive frontiersmen"), most likely because it was thought too inhumane and not politically salable. Rapid assimilation was rejected as unworkable, despite the Jeffersonian-inspired belief that the Indians could be absorbed into American society within a generation. The retention of aboriginal reservations—the preferred policy of Jackson's critics—was rejected because the United States simply did not have the political or military ability to defend Indian territory from encroaching white society. Given those options, Jackson chose Removal.

Having made his choice, Jackson initiated a Removal policy that confiscated Indian land without adequate compensation and cost the lives of scores of Indian people. Jackson forcibly removed the Cherokees, among others, (such as in the infamous "Trail of Tears" in which many Cherokee died) to the so-called "Indian Territory" located west of the Mississippi. While Jackson initiated, in his view, a liberal policy and entered into treaties with the Cherokees and other Indian nations to secure them new lands in the west, the forced nature of the removal process was physically and emotionally destructive and weakened the Indian nations dramatically. Nonetheless, throughout this period, the federal Indian control law reflected in the opinions of Jackson's ideological opponent, John Marshall, continued to recognize that the Indian nations had a measure of inherent sovereignty over their members and their remaining territory.

Reservation Policy. Inevitably, the pace of American colonization and expansion made the Removal Policy unworkable by itself. By the mid-nineteenth century, an alternative plan to establish formal reservations for the Indians within the various states and territories had evolved. Using treaties, statutes, and executive orders supported by force, starvation, and disease, the United States secured peace with and obtained land title from the Indian nations, reserving significantly reduced tracts for Indian occupation and use. Accordingly, states were required to relinquish all claims to authority over Indian territories located within their borders.

The policies formulated during the middle and late nineteenth century were heavily influenced by the Christian nationalism that had rationalized American colonization in the first place. Although federal Indian policy during most of this period was still affected by the sentiment that the Indian nations were the "enemy," the social reformers and "friends of the Indian" were singularly focused on resolving the "Indian problem" by converting the Indians to Christianity and assimilating them into the American way of life.

Peace Policy. With the end of the Civil War, President Ulysses S. Grant initiated what became known as the "Peace Policy," which funded missionary expeditions among the Indians and used religious groups to nominate government agents to deal with federal Indian affairs. Although Congress had appropriated funds to establish missions among the Indians as early as 1776, the Peace Policy represented a formal adoption of government funding and support for religious groups to deal with the "problem" of the Indian nations.

Ironically, the Peace Policy was implemented concurrently with the United States' heavy involvement in warfare with the Plains Indians. Indeed, the violent conflicts between the military, the settlers, and the Indians, especially after Custer's defeat at Little Big Horn, precipitated the demise of the Peace Policy in favor of a more aggressive military approach. Eventually, however, the United States succeeded in eliminating any Indian military threat to further American colonization, and Congress formally ended Indian treaty-making in 1871.

Allotment Policy. Federal Indian policy between 1871 and 1934 reflected America's continuing belief that it had an "Indian problem" and that efforts should be focused on assimilating the Indians into American life by destroying their tribal identity. Reflecting the still-dominant American view that American society and culture were superior to Indian society and culture, the social reformers acted in concert with the speculators, who were eager to appropriate the remaining Indian land base by urging Congress to privatize Indian lands and eradicate the traditional tribal lifestyle. Indeed, the "Americanization" of the Indians "became the all-embracing goal of the reformers in the last two decades of the century."

These reformers, led by groups like the Indian Rights Association and the Women's National Indian Association, drew upon the common refrain that the Indians should be converted to Christianity, but added a twist by focusing on the destruction of tribal Indian life:

> [I]f civilization, education and Christianity are to do their work, they must get at the individual. They must lay hold of men and women and children, one by one. The deadening sway of tribal custom must be interfered with. The sad uniformity of savage tribal life must be broken up! Individuality must be cultivated.... At last, as a nation, we are coming to recognize the great truth that if we would do justice to the Indians, we must get at them, one by one, with American ideals, American schools, American laws, the privileges and the pressure of American rights and duties.

The means for facilitating this transformation was the allotment of the remaining tribal land base to individual Indian ownership. With support from the speculators and settlers eager for new lands to colonize, the government focused on "educating" the Indians. In 1887, Congress passed the Indian General Allotment Act, which established a mechanism for converting tribal land to private Indian ownership. The reformers were no doubt elated because they believed that:

> [land allotment] is a mighty pulverizing engine for breaking up the tribal mass. It has nothing to say to the tribe, nothing to do with the tribe. It breaks up that vast "bulk of things" which the tribal life sought to keep unchanged. It finds its way straight to the family and to the individual.

Over the next fifty years, the Allotment Act had just such an effect on many reservation Indians. The fee patent program and the surplus lands program served as the vehicles for transferring eighty-seven million acres — approximately 65% of all Indian land — to white owners.

At the same time that the Allotment Act was being implemented, Congress and the Supreme Court were involved in other efforts to further solidify legal and political hegemony over the Indian nations. Much of this development came after 1883, when the Court held in *Ex parte Crow Dog* that federal criminal jurisdiction did not extend to the murder of one Indian by another in Indian territory. This decision was reluctantly given effect by officials in the Bureau of Indian Affairs (BIA), who thought that this recognition of tribal sovereignty only frustrated their assimilation policies. As a result, they initiated a campaign to have Congress grant such jurisdiction to the federal courts. In 1885, Congress acceded to this request and enacted the Indian Major Crimes Act, one of the most important federal laws granting federal authority to interfere with internal Indian affairs. In addition, Congress granted the Secretary of the Interior sweeping administrative authority to establish a wide variety of assimilating institutions within Indian reservation communities, such as Western judicial and law enforcement systems, boarding schools, and mission schools.

As Congress was asserting federal law and power over the internal affairs of the Indian nations, the Supreme Court was providing the legal rationale for doing so. In *U.S. v. Kagama*, the Court upheld the constitutionality of the Indian Major Crimes Act merely upon the grounds that the United States had a "duty of protection" of the Indians and that the "Indian tribes are the wards of the nation." And in *Lone Wolf v. Hitchcock*, the Court upheld the abrogation of Indian treaties on the grounds that the courts did not have any power to interfere with Congress' "plenary authority" over Indian affairs. Thus, by the early twentieth century, John Marshall's early understanding of federal-tribal relations—that the United States had "conquered" the Indian nations—had become a reality under American law.

Efforts to appropriate Indian land and otherwise destroy Indian tribal life were extremely successful. The Indian nations had been stripped of most of their aboriginal lands and deprived of their traditional governmental, social, and cultural institutions. As a result, Indian economies were destroyed and many Indian people were thrown into poverty, which, in some cases, made them heavily dependent upon the federal government and its distributions for survival. The failure of the Allotment Policy was documented in the tremendously influential Meriam Report, which was issued in 1928. Given their obvious effects, it was generally accepted that the Allotment and Assimilation Policies had failed and that a new approach toward Indian affairs should be taken.

Reorganization Policy. In 1933, a new Commissioner of Indian Affairs, John Collier, was appointed, and the United States initiated changes in its Indian policy. At Collier's urging, Congress passed the Indian Reorganization Act (IRA) in 1934. The IRA ended allotment and provided a mechanism for tribes to revitalize themselves by adopting written tribal constitutions and business charters. In doing so, Congress had apparently reversed its Indian policy from one intent on destroying tribal sovereignty and self-government to one in favor of supporting both of these ideals.

While some have heralded the IRA as a good thing for the Indian nations, it is easy to see that even this "beneficial" initiative could not be totally divorced from the colonial foundations common to all of the previous federal Indian policies. While the IRA did acknowledge that the Indian nations were separate sovereigns, it nonetheless provided that their governmental reorganization could only occur pursuant to federal law and only in accordance with a written constitution and/or a business corporation. As a result, the IRA heavily "embodied elements of the very colonialism it sought to end," and thus has only received qualified praise from historians.

Despite these flaws, which ensured that the federal government would perpetuate its colonial authority, some measure of the IRA's detrimental effect was offset by the fact that it was the first federal Indian policy in over 100 years that did not have the explicit purpose of undermining the status of the Indian nations.

Termination Policy. The Reorganization Policy, however, was short-lived. In the 1940s, likely as a result of the nationalism associated with America's successful participation in World War II, Congress responded to the deficiency in Indian "Americanization" by abandoning its effort to protect and strengthen tribal self-government. In a dramatic and direct assault on the Indian nations, Congress began to implement a policy of relinquishing federal "supervision" over certain aspects of Indian relations to the states. Thus, in the 1940s, Congress acted initially to vest certain states with criminal and civil jurisdiction over the Indian territories located within their boundaries. Eventually, it authorized a standing mechanism for any state to do so when it enacted Public Law 280.

The Termination Policy was formally conceived in 1953 when Congress adopted House Concurrent Resolution 108. Eventually, 109 tribes and bands were terminated, that is, denied recognition as separate political entities, in furtherance of this policy. Tribal lands were allotted, tribal funds were distributed, and tribal governments were effectively disbanded. Consistent with its radical assimilationist purposes, the BIA even set up a relocation program to move Indians to the cities, which significantly increased the urban Indian population.

Fortunately, like all previous federal Indian policies, the Termination Policy failed, because separating Indian people from their tribal lands and tribal way of life did not dramatically improve their condition, as had been predicted. Many Indian nations, like the Menominee of Wisconsin, never gave up the fight for recognition of their sovereignty and eventually were "restored" to federal recognition. Moreover, many states began to feel the brunt of assuming social service responsibility for former reservation communities. These factors, combined with criticism of the federal government's haste and a lack of Indian input in implementing the policy, led to the abandonment in practice of the Termination Policy in the early 1960s.

In 1968, Congress again focused on the Indian nations and, as was the national tenor at the time, on the treatment of minorities by the federal government. Acting on the basis of information alleging rights abuses by tribal governments, Congress passed the Indian Civil Rights Act (ICRA), which was designed to apply most of the provisions of the Bill of Rights to the actions of tribal government. Here again, Congress professed to support tribal government. But the ICRA, by imposing on tribal governments external standards of appropriate governmental conduct, was clearly more federal intrusion into tribal government affairs. In its effort to "help" the situation, Congress again undermined tribal sovereignty because it could only see a solution to the problem of individual Indian rights abuses in terms that it could understand and with which it was familiar—a declaration of individual rights through law.

Self-Determination Policy. It is generally believed that the Termination Era formally ended and the Self-Determination Era began when President Nixon notified Congress that he intended to help the Indian nations achieve self-sufficiency. Nixon's policy statement marked the formal end of the Termination Policy and was the most significant improvement in the revitalization of tribal self-government in American history. Nixon's message to Congress showed that the change in policy was unmistakable:

> For years we have talked about encouraging Indians to exercise greater self-determination, but our progress has never been commensurate with our promises. Part of the reason for this situation has been the threat of termination. But another reason is the fact that when a decision is made as to whether a Federal pro-

gram will be turned over to Indian administration, it is the Federal authorities and not the Indian people who finally make that decision.

This situation should be reversed. In my judgment, it should be up to the Indian tribe to determine whether it is willing to assume administrative responsibility for a service program which is presently administered by a Federal agency.

In 1975, Congress passed the Indian Self-Determination and Education Assistance Act, which provided a mechanism to assist the Indian nations financially in their revitalization efforts. In 1976, the American Indian Policy Review Commission issued its report supporting greater federal support for tribal sovereignty and self-government. And in 1978, Congress passed the Indian Child Welfare Act, which protected Indian children against removal from Indian homes by state and county social services for culturally-biased reasons. Various acts were also passed to restore the federally-recognized status of Indian nations that had earlier been terminated.

Throughout this period, the Supreme Court began to address Indian issues in earnest. The "modern" era in federal Indian control law generally is thought to have begun in 1959 when the Court decided the case of *Williams v. Lee*. *Williams* reaffirmed the residual doctrinal foundations of *Worcester*, holding that the state courts did not have jurisdiction over a case arising out of an on-reservation transaction involving an Indian and a non-Indian. Since 1959, the Supreme Court has continued to address Indian law cases in disproportionate significance. It has not, however, retreated from the fundamental covenants that affirm federal power and control over the Indian nations.

Because of its deep foundation, colonization remains firmly embedded in the body of modern federal Indian control law and policy. This observation should be of little surprise, because all federal policies for dealing with the Indian nations—the Removal Policy, the Reservation Policy, the Peace Policy, the Allotment Policy, the Reorganization Policy, the Termination Policy—and the "archaic, European-derived law" supporting them have been "ultimately genocidal in both practice and intent." Only since the ushering in of the Self-Determination Policy in the early 1970s, has the United States avoided using the language of subjugation and assimilation in creating and carrying out its policy toward the Indian nations. So long as the United States preserves the colonial foundation of its Indian law, it will be unable to formulate an effective and mutually beneficial policy for dealing with the Indian nations.

Notes and Questions

1. *Federal Indian policy.* For a more detailed treatment of the historical eras of federal Indian law and federal Indian policy, see Rennard Strickland et al., Felix S. Cohen's Handbook of Federal Indian Law (1982); Francis Paul Prucha, American Indian Policy in the Formative Years: The Indian Trade and Intercourse Acts, 1790–1834 (1962); Angie Debo, A History of the Indians of the United States (1970).

2. *The Marshall Trilogy.* The Marshall Trilogy deservedly has been the object of extensive critique. Yet despite—and in part because of—subsequent legal and political developments, the Trilogy informs much of federal Indian law and policy. Legal scholars have generated a large body of critical literature on the cases as well as the nature and scope of federal authority "over" tribal nations. For a lengthy critical analysis of the Marshall Trilogy and similar subjects, including the "doctrine of discovery," see David E. Wilkins & K. Tsianina Lomawaima, Uneven Ground: American Indian Sovereignty

AND FEDERAL LAW (2001); DAVID E. WILKINS, AMERICAN INDIAN SOVEREIGNTY AND THE U.S. SUPREME COURT: THE MASKING OF JUSTICE (1997); see also Eric Kades, *History and Interpretation of the Great Case of* Johnson v. M'Intosh, 19 LAW & HIST. REV. 70 (2001); Philip P. Frickey, *Marshalling Past and Present: Colonialism, Constitutionalism, and Interpretation in Federal Indian Law*, 107 HARV. L. REV. 381 (1993); Robert A. Williams, Jr., *The Algebra of Federal Indian Law: The Hard Trial of Decolonization and Americanizing the White Man's Indian Jurisprudence*, 1986 WIS. L. REV. 219; Nell Jessup Newton, *Federal Power Over Indians: Its Sources, Scope and Limitations*, 132 U. PA. L. REV. 195 (1984).

3.   *The federal legal doctrine of tribal sovereignty.* The contemporary legal doctrine of tribal sovereignty essentially means that the U.S. recognizes tribes as independent sovereign nations whose location within the boundaries of a state does not subject them to the application of state law. Tribes nevertheless are bound by the trust relationship with the federal government and retain only the political and legal authority that Congress has not expressly abrogated under its asserted plenary power pursuant to the U.S. Constitution's Indian Commerce Clause. *See* U.S. CONST., art. I, § 8, cl. 3 ("The Congress shall have Power ... to regulate commerce ... with the Indian tribes...."). The federal legal doctrine of tribal sovereignty effectively means that tribes, in fact, are "semi-sovereign." In the following article, Professor Clinton challenged the foundation for tribes' "semi-sovereign" status under federal law.

Robert N. Clinton
There Is No Federal Supremacy Clause for Indian Tribes
34 ARIZ. ST. L.J. 113 (2002)

During the American Revolution, the Continental Congress sought to out-position British military contingents. The British presence in Canada and the Crown's forts and other outposts on the St. Lawrence and on the Great Lakes constituted one of the major threats to the Continental Army led by George Washington. American troops could only reach these outposts by crossing through the territory of the Haudenosaunee (the Iroquois Confederation) in upstate New York and through the territory of Lenni Lenape (the Delaware) in the western Pennsylvania and Ohio valleys. The Continental Congress and the Army undertook major efforts to secure the alliance, or at least neutrality, of these tribes. These efforts produced an alliance with the Oneida. Ultimately, that alliance militarily split the Iroquois Confederation and violated the central norm of the Great Law of Peace of the Iroquois, the long revered constitutional tradition and law of the confederation. The Great Law of Peace that created a confederation of the constituent original five tribes of the Haudenosaunee (Onondaga, Cayuga, Mohawk, Seneca and Oneida) contained a central organizing principle that stipulated that they not make war on one another, a norm violated by the alliances created during the American Revolution.

These federal diplomatic initiatives by the United States also resulted in the nation's first ratified treaty with an Indian tribe, the Treaty of Fort Pitt of 1778, signed with the Delaware Nation. The lands of the Lenni Lenape (Delaware) were located within the newly independent states (established by imprecise colonial charters). Consequently, Delaware tribal lands were within the exterior boundaries of the United States. Since Indian title to the land had not been extinguished by cession, the Continental Congress assumed that neither the national government nor the states had any authority to enter or otherwise govern the territory. Thus, in Article III of the Treaty of Fort Pitt, the fledgling government of the United States clearly negotiated for permission from the Delaware Nation authorizing General Washington's army to reach the British outposts "by passing through the country of the Delaware nation" and by "permitting free passage through their country to the troops aforesaid." Both parties to the treaty clearly assumed that continuing Indian ownership and possession of aboriginal lands included the Indians' right to govern, control, and exclude anyone on their lands, including Washington's army. Tribal permission, therefore, was legally required to enter the Delaware Nation's territory and the United States formally sought that permission so that Washington's military forces could strike at the menacing British outposts to the north and northwest.

Article III of the Treaty of Fort Pitt expressly contemplated joint establishment of a system for handling offenders who might disturb the chain of friendship that bound the two treaty parties together. This system can only be described as a process of international agreement. It contemplated that neither signatory to the treaty would attempt to inflict punishment on the offenders of the other party until "[t]he mode of such trials [could] be hereafter fixed by the wise men of the United States in Congress assembled, with the assistance of such deputies of the Delaware nation, as may be appointed to act in concert with them in adjusting this matter to their mutual liking." The article implicitly recognized that either sovereign party to the treaty might have the right to punish or otherwise seek restitution or retribution from the others' citizens who committed crimes outside the borders of their own country, but it exhorted the parties to stay their hands in the interest of the "chain of friendship" until a workable middle ground procedure was established agreeable to both.

In short, the general thrust of the nation's first ratified treaty with an Indian tribe appears to contain all of the hallmarks of international diplomacy. It embodied a paradigm for tribal federal relations that can only be described as one of international self-determination. The Lenni Lenape (Delaware) people constituted a nation with which the United States negotiated treaties. All presumed the Delaware Nation controlled its territory so pervasively that the United States required its formal permission for Washington's army to enter into and pass through its lands, both to recognize the sovereign control of the Delaware Nation over their territories located within United States boundaries and to avoid causes for disruption in the relationship. The internal sovereignty of the Lenni Lenape, therefore, was considered identical to the internal sovereignty of any nation—encompassing complete territorial control of all persons and property located within their territory.

While premised on a model of international diplomacy, the Treaty of Fort Pitt nevertheless contained two provisions, the broad contours of which haunt tribal federal relations to the present day. The issues on which they touch serve as the focus of a never-ending debate about the place of Indian nations within the federal structure. First, under Article VI, the United States assumed a federal treaty obligation of protecting the territorial integrity of the Delaware Nation. The terms of the agreement are instructive since they illuminate the purpose of the duty of protection, that later ripened into the so-called federal trust doctrine:

> Whereas the enemies of the United States have endeavored, by every artifice in their power, to possess the Indians in general with an opinion, that it is the design of the States aforesaid, to extirpate the Indians and take possession of their country: to obviate such false suggestion, the United States do engage to guarantee to the aforesaid nation of Delawares, and their heirs, all their territorial rights in the fullest and most ample manner, as it has been bounded by former treaties, as long as they the said Delaware nation shall abide by, and hold fast the chain of friendship now entered into.

This provision imposed an obligation of protection on the United States for one and only one purpose—"to guarantee to the aforesaid nation of Delawares, and their heirs, all of their territorial rights in the fullest and the most ample manner." It contemplated the continued permanent occupation of islands of Indian sovereignty and control within the territorial borders of the United States. The federal trust supervision over Indian land therefore had only one purpose—the full protection of the territorial integrity and sovereignty of the Indian tribe. Since the Indian trust doctrine would later be used to subvert the sovereign rights of Indian tribes, the importance of this language in reflecting the original understanding of the federal protective trusteeship cannot be understated. The United States' apparent concern that the Delaware Nation might not "hold fast the chain of friendship now entered into" is ironic since today the Lenni Lanape hold none of the aboriginal lands guaranteed them in the Treaty of Fort Pitt. As a result of the Tribe's sad history of dispossession and removal at the hands of the federal government, many of the Delaware descendants were incorporated into the Cherokee Nation of Oklahoma, and their separate national identity submerged for long periods, until the Department of the Interior granted separate federal recognition in 1996. Other Delaware descendants wound up living on Indian lands with the Wichitas and Caddos.

The second provision of significant interest and, perhaps, prescience, is also found in Article VI of the Treaty of Fort Pitt. The provision involves the promise by the United States of statehood "should it for the future be found conducive for the mutual interest of both parties to invite any other tribes who have been friends to the interest of the United States, to join the present confederation, and to form a state whereof the Delaware nation shall be the head, and to have representation in Congress." The striking provision requires some explanation. At the time of the Treaty of Fort Pitt ratification, the Indian Nations were composed of native peoples who were not citizens of the United States. As Chief Justice Marshall later put the matter in *Cherokee Nation v. Georgia*, Indians were "aliens, not owing allegiance to the United States." The United States Constitution clearly recognized and ratified the status of Indian tribes as nations originally outside the federal union. The provisions in the Article I, section 2 census clause expressly exclude "Indians not taxed" from the count in the census. This exclusion had no roots in the abhorrent history of race relations and slavery that originally resulted in slaves being counted as three-fifths of a person. Rather, it constituted a recognition that Indians, while geographically located within territory claimed by the United States, were not in any political sense part of the nation and should not be counted for representational purposes.

Nevertheless, by holding out the promise of statehood and representation in Congress, the Treaty of Fort Pitt confronts a problem that has perplexed federal Indian law ever since. Should the Indian tribes be incorporated as separate sovereign peoples and nations into the federal union and, if so, by what procedure and on whose terms? The Continental Congress, the Constitutional Convention of 1787 and subsequent state ratification conventions clearly answered such questions for the states. While the Treaty of Fort Pitt contained promises of a like resolution for the tribes, no such bilateral agreement between the people of the United States and the various peoples of the Indian tribes ever emerged that ultimately produced Indian statehood. Obviously, Article VI contemplated a consensual change in tribal federal relations. It envisioned moving from a model of international self-determination and sovereignty toward a new federalism paradigm, by tribal consent.

The parties contemplated ultimate inclusion of the tribes within the federal union as one or more separate Indian states. This idea was later echoed in treaty promises made to the Cherokee Nation that contemplated Cherokee representation in Congress and in later proposals repeatedly heard throughout the second half of the nineteenth century with respect to incorporating all or parts of the Indian Territory as an Indian state. Of course, these late-nineteenth century proposals were rejected when the Indian Territory was later incorporated (in violation of express treaty promises) into the multiracial, pluralistic state of Oklahoma. Nevertheless, from the start, statehood for Indian tribes and inclusion of them within the federal union contemplated (1) the consent of the tribes through treaty and (2) representation in Congress as separate constituent Indian states within the union. It did not assume the exercise of direct federal legislative power over Indian nations without their consent or representation.

This baseline original understanding of the tribal federal relationship was also evident in the nation's constitutional documents and early history. While the Articles of Confederation contained no antecedents of the Foreign and Interstate Commerce Clauses of the United States Constitution, the Articles did contain the seeds of the Indian Commerce Clause. Article IX of the Articles of Confederation delegated to the Continental Congress "the sole and exclusive right and power of ... regulating the trade and managing all affairs with the Indian tribes, not members of any of the States, provided that the legislative right of any State within its own limits be not infringed or violated." This power was the culmination of a movement commencing with Benjamin Franklin's draft of a plan of union at the Albany Congress in 1754, a Congress that actually was part of a larger treaty conference with the Haudenosaunee (the Iroquois Confederation). Franklin's idea of a unified government for the states derived from his desire to coordinate Indian policy in negotiating with and confronting the unified Five Nations Confederation of the Haudenosaunee. Indeed, in the Franklin draft, the power to handle trade and affairs with the Indian tribes was the first, and perhaps, most important power delegated to the national government.

When understood against this backdrop, the adoption of the Indian Commerce Clause and the reference to "Indians not taxed" in the census clause clearly reflect the original baseline understanding of the tribal federal relationship established by review of the Fort Pitt Treaty provisions. Indians tribes constituted separate nations. The United States Constitution recognized tribal sovereignty in two ways. First, since the tribes constituted separate peoples owing no political allegiance to the United States beyond their existing treaty obligations, they were not citizens and formed no part of the "We the people of the United States" who created the United States Constitution and their members, consequently, were excluded from the census and from political participation by the "Indians not taxed" clause. Second, and too often overlooked in discussions of tribal sovereignty, the Indian Tribes are expressly included in the Commerce Clause, together with two other sovereigns — foreign nations and the states. The text of the United States Constitution, therefore, unquestionably recognizes the sovereignty of the Indian tribes. More importantly, the Indian Commerce Clause eliminated the two provisos in the Articles reserving state authority that so plagued management of Indian affairs by the Continental Congress under the Articles of Confederation.

Understanding the proper original meaning of the Indian Commerce Clause within the larger framework of the Commerce Clause further reinforces the notion that the United States Constitution not only recognized, but constitutionalized, this original baseline understanding. Since the Commerce Clause governs commerce with foreign nations, with which the United States maintained diplomatic contact, the covered commerce, at least in that context, must be the United States' side of various bilateral exchanges with foreign nations, including not only trade with those nations but the maintenance of embassies, consulates and other forms of diplomatic contacts and exchanges, i.e., "intercourse." Interpreting "commerce with foreign nations" to subsume regulatory power over the internal commerce of foreign nations would, of course, self-evidently invade the sovereignty of such foreign nations and, therefore, never has been contemplated as a legitimate exercise of federal authority under the Foreign Commerce Clause. Similarly, the renewed debate currently raging over the limitations of Congressional power under the Interstate Commerce Clause should be seen, but to date has not been waged, as a debate over the precise boundary of "Commerce among the Several States." Finally, the Indian Commerce Clause employs precisely the same phrase used in the Foreign Commerce Clause, i.e., "Commerce ... with the Indian Tribes." Presumably, by employing the same language within the same clause, the Framers meant the Indian commerce power to have precisely the same meaning and scope as the foreign commerce power, i.e., the regulation of the United States' side of the various bilateral exchanges, economic, political and diplomatic, with the Indian tribes.

The most basic tenet of American constitutional law has long sought to analyze the legitimacy of the exercise of federal governing power by grounding and confining such authority to the scope of the popular delegation contained in the Constitution. The touchstone of constitutional exercises of federal power involves confining the exercises of federal power to express and implied grants of authority delegated by the people in the document and not running afoul of any prohibition on the exercise of power contained in the Bill of Rights and elsewhere. American constitutional theory, therefore, is fundamentally grounded upon and enforces the idea of popular delegation of authority.

This constitutional understanding has been, both expressly and impliedly, at the center of recent debates over the Supreme Court's increased judicial activism on federalism questions in favor of state sovereignty and autonomy. Indeed, it has been the theoretical cornerstone for much of the judicial activism witnessed in recent years in the name of enforcing federalism [such as the Court's decisions in *United States v. Lopez* and *New York v. United States*].

This reminder that the historical and contemporary theory of popular delegation provides the basis for determining the constitutional legitimacy of the exercise of governmental power fully explains the foundation in American constitutional law for the baseline understanding of the limited nature of federal power in Indian affairs. The Indian tribes and their members, unlike the states and their citizens, were not part of the "We the People of the United States" who drafted the United States Constitution. They constituted separate sovereign peoples which federal Indian law would later label domestic dependent nations. They were outside the federal union and owed no allegiance to it other than bi-national alliances created by treaty. The very exclusion of tribal Indians from the census by the "Indians not taxed" clause contained in Article I clearly recognizes that status in the text of the Constitution itself. As such, unlike the states, the citizens of the tribes never delegated any power to the federal government!

Any review of the cases cited by the Court amply demonstrates the questionable lineage of these precedents in the American history of race relations and colonialism. Its proof of the plenary power of Congress to "limit, modify or eliminate" the sovereignty of Indian tribes, therefore, rests entirely on cases derived from late-nineteenth century "white man's burden" racial-superiority arguments. Yet, the Supreme Court continues to cite them as controlling precedent. The closest analogy might be the Court unabashedly citing *Dred Scott v. Sanford* or *Plessy v. Ferguson* to make a controlling point in a modern affirmative action case. If such an event occurred, the uproar from the public and the academic and legal community undoubtedly would be deafening. Yet, unfortunately, no one notices, cares or comments when the federal courts cite and rely upon precedents of like ilk in modern Indian law decisions.

Because Indian tribes constituted no part of the federal union at the time the Constitution was drafted, no structural protections exist to protect their sovereignty within the framework of the federal government. While the Treaty of Fort Pitt and later similar proposals expressly contemplated that Indian tribal statehood might accomplish that objective by tribal consent, such tribal statehood, with appropriate votes in the Senate and the Electoral College to structurally protect their interests, never emerged. Furthermore, today Indians constitute a very small minority of the United States population with no great likelihood to significantly affect the political process through the ballot box. Thus, most traditional theories of the need for judicial intervention suggest that federal judicial protection for tribal sovereignty against federal initiatives should be required. Yet, as a result of the federal Indian plenary power doctrine derived from late-nineteenth century notions of supposed racial-superiority and the "white man's burden," the Supreme Court perpetuates and reinforces a colonial authority in Indian country that cannot be justified under traditional American constitutional analysis and values.

Today, Indian tribes face a problem they have not previously confronted—whether to honor federally developed Indian law. At first glance, the problem may appear simple, but it involves a far more complex set of choices than may be apparent. Most tribes made no agreement expressly giving up their sovereignty and some even negotiated for and received express treaty promises of complete territorial jurisdiction over their reservations. While such guarantees were explicit in some treaties, implicit in all creation of Indian country, at least until recently, was the assumption created by the baseline understanding of the tribal federal relationship—that Indian reservations or other areas of Indian country were set aside for exclusive governance by the Indian tribes governing the areas. The Indian tribes still recognize those promises and the original understanding of the tribal federal relationship. Since there is no easy way for the tribes to seek rescission and get their ceded lands back as a result of federal breaches of treaty promises, the tribes insist that Congress and the federal courts honor the original bargain.

Notes and Questions

1.   *Federal Indian law and the "New Federalism."* Professor Clinton referred to the U.S. Supreme Court's "new federalism" decisions in *United States v. Lopez*, 514 U.S. 549 (1995), and *New York v. United States*, 505 U.S. 144 (1992), to support his argument that the constitutional principle of the "popular delegation" of political authority to the federal government is inapplicable when it comes to American Indian tribal nations. Both of these cases stand for the proposition that Congress's ability to abrogate state sovereignty is limited, and that those limitations may be judicially enforced. Thus, as Clinton's argument went, there is an even stronger basis to limit Congress's ability to abrogate tribal sovereignty, as tribes have not delegated any power to the federal government. For more on constitutional law and tribal governments, see Symposium, *Native Americans and the Constitution*, 5 U. Pa. J. Const. L. 219 (2003).

2.   *Practical application of critiques of federal Indian law.* How would Porter's and Clinton's theoretical arguments play out in practical application? What would be the result of "decolonizing" federal Indian law?

3.   *Tribal sovereignty.* As the preceding readings demonstrate, federal Indian law and its conception of tribes' inherent powers and political status, though entrenched, are not unassailable. The federal legal doctrine of tribal sovereignty is not the only definition of tribal sovereignty. Some have argued that sovereignty in fact has much broader connotations rooted in self-determination; that is, the inherent right of a nation to chart its own future. Tribal self-determination would encompass or embrace tribal sovereignty in its legal, political, cultural, and spiritual dimensions. Comanche Nation Tribal Chair Coffey and Professor Tsosie discussed the significance of a cultural conception of tribal sovereignty in the excerpt below.

Wallace Coffey & Rebecca Tsosie
Rethinking the Tribal Sovereignty Doctrine:
Cultural Sovereignty and the Collective Future of Indian Nations
12 Stan. L. & Pol'y Rev. 191 (2001)

This article is the result of a dialogue between colleagues who live and work within a particular universe which Indian people know very well and non-Indians know very little: the cultural existence of an Indian nation with its own territory, identity, and history, that has been enveloped by another nation in a contemporary "pluralistic" and "multicultural" society. This universe is governed by "Federal Indian Law," the most byzantine series of statutes, regulations, treaties, and court opinions that any nation has ever possessed. However, it is not defined by Federal Indian Law, but by the moral vision that has always guided Indian nations in their collective existence as distinctive peoples. It is a universe that is beset with jurisdictional, social, and economic problems. But it is also the universe that encompasses our lives as Indian people, and it is what unites us, inspires us, gives us hope that there is a future, and gives us hope that our collective future as Indian nations will define the terms of our existence in the twenty-first century.

Contemporary legal battles center around the concept of political sovereignty as Indian nations attempt to define and defend the boundaries of their jurisdictional authority. However, these legal struggles for political sovereignty coincide with a larger battle: the battle to protect and defend tribal cultures from the multitude of forces that threaten the cultural survival of Indian nations. After enduring nearly two centuries of government policies directed at the forcible assimilation of Indian people, we stand at a moment in time in which our languages, ceremonies, and ways of life are increasingly jeopardized by the forces of mass media, the educational system, and a host of court decisions failing to protect the religious or cultural rights of Native peoples.

The concept of cultural sovereignty is valuable because it allows us, as Native people, to chart a course for the future. In that sense, cultural sovereignty may well become a tool to protect our rights to language, religion, art, tradition, and the distinctive norms and customs that guide our societies. Indeed, cultural sovereignty may ultimately prove to be our most valuable legal tool. However, it is important to construct this tool from within our Native societies, rather than looking to external definitions of "sovereignty" to determine what the concept means. Too often, we as Indian people are forced to litigate our rights within the dominant society's appraisal of tribal sovereignty. We cite the Marshall Trilogy as if the concept of "domestic dependent nation" really means something in terms of our legal rights. To the extent that we litigate our right to sovereignty within this legal framework, we have lost the true essence of our sovereignty.

The central challenge of cultural sovereignty is to reach an understanding of sovereignty that is generated from within tribal societies and carries a cultural meaning consistent with those traditions. The idea of sovereignty is one that has historically been defined by Western political thought. In particular, Western tradition has posited a dichotomy between individuals and the "state" or "nation." Individuals organize collectively as "states" in a political association designed to secure the advantage of its members through positive assertions of sovereignty: exclusive jurisdiction, territorial integrity, and nonintervention in domestic affairs. Within this moral universe, the primacy of the individual is

unquestioned. Under Western thought, group sovereignty may also be considered a social compact intended to maximize the well-being of the individual members of the civil
society. Consequently, government power (the authority of the group) is necessarily limited by individual rights.

The disjunction between Western and indigenous understandings of the relationship
between individuals and their encompassing cultural and political structures is vividly
represented by the idea within domestic jurisprudence that Indian nations are "domestic dependent nations"—in other words, that they are subordinate societies within the
dominant civil society of the United States. The effort to construct a concept of cultural
sovereignty rejects that premise in favor of defining our relationships to each other and
to the United States from within an indigenous understanding of what those relationships entail.

For Indian nations, the process of building community is an essential part of the exercise of sovereignty. The concept of community has always been central to Indian nations,
and thus, to some extent, this process comprises a return to tradition. However, it is not
a static notion of "tradition" based upon some past era and adherence to an "unchang-
ing and unchangeable set of activities," but rather a dynamic process that becomes "part
of the life of a community as it struggles to exercise its sovereignty." This process, of
course, requires some level of change and innovation to meet new conditions.

As Iroquois leader Oren Lyons describes the traditional governments of the Iroquois
Confederacy, they are bound to ensure that each of their actions is "for the benefit of the
seventh generation." That is, the collective welfare of the group is paramount, including
the future generations of the group. Both individual and collective actions are limited by
the spiritual instructions which demand respect for the other living beings which share
this earth, and for the future generations who will inherit this earth. Thus, unlike the
Western notion of sovereignty, which is devoid of spiritual content (and at least in the United
States, demands a complete separation between church and state) the indigenous notion
of sovereignty may be founded upon a spiritual core that defines the overriding values and
content of governance.

As Lyons' account demonstrates, an indigenous concept of sovereignty which is founded
upon notions of relationship, respect, and continuity between generations is quite distinct
from the Western view of the sovereign as an entity set up to maximize the happiness and
preferences of the constituent citizens that comprise the nation.

Cultural sovereignty is a means by which Native peoples can constitute their own histories and identities in a manner which, among other things, will counterbalance the false
images that have been presented as truth by non-Natives. The history of America has typically been portrayed as the story of European migration to and settlement of the "New
World." Under this story, the United States originates as a heroic response to Old World
oppression—both political and religious. The history of America is a white history:
African, Hispanic and Native peoples play supporting roles in the mythology of America's "creation."

Not surprisingly, the histories that have been constructed about Native people are often
inaccurate and have been used to justify the dispossession of Native peoples from their
lands, resources, and even their cultural identity. Supreme Court cases routinely adopt
the script that emerges from historical accounts, depicting Indians as nomadic savages
without property rights and white settlers as the bearers of civilization in a brave new
land. Federal policy relied on the myth of "cultural inferiority" to justify the federal government's authority to forcibly assimilate and acculturate Indian people for their own

good. Thus, until rescinded by the 1934 Indian Reorganization Act, multiple federal policies such as allotment, criminalization of Native religion, forcible removal of Native children to remote boarding schools (where they were forbidden to speak their languages
and, in many cases, to see their relatives), were constructed to obliterate Indian cultures
and, in the process, destroy the separate political identity of Indian people.

Cultural sovereignty seeks to provide a different context for political sovereignty, one
rooted in autonomy of Native people as distinct cultural groups. So what does a return
to tradition suggest for Indian people? Must tribes give up the accoutrements of Western
society and culture? Must they be purists in their return to a past existence untainted by
the presence of Anglo-Americans? To accept these propositions is to accept the same type
of linear thinking that makes sovereignty so problematic for Indian people. We would
suggest a different type of thinking, one that sees past and future generations as related
to the present generation by core elements of cultural existence which may not be destroyed or removed. This is the essence of cultural sovereignty, which posits that culture
is the living basis for the survival of Indian nations as distinct political and cultural groups.

Admittedly, achieving cultural sovereignty poses a significant challenge for Indian nations. It requires a change in our thinking and perhaps also a change in our priorities. Our
focus in the future must be on nation-building, on institutional development that starts
within tribal communities, builds upon our traditional forms of governance, and responds to the contemporary needs of our communities. This process can be assisted by
federal law to some extent, but the real work remains to be done by tribal communities
themselves.

The concept of cultural sovereignty encompasses the spiritual, emotional, mental, and
physical aspects of our lives. Because of this, only Native people can decide what the ultimate contours of Native sovereignty will be.

Notes and Questions

1. *Practical application of cultural sovereignty.* Coffey and Tsosie put forth the case
for cultural sovereignty as the key determinant of tribal self-determination. How would
you define "culture" or "tradition," and how might those definitions inform a tribe-specific model of cultural sovereignty? Can cultural sovereignty be reconciled with the legal
and political doctrine of tribal sovereignty? How does the concept of cultural sovereignty
fit into Professors Porter's and Clinton's critiques of federal Indian law? What would a
legal doctrine of cultural sovereignty look like? For a synopsis of cultural sovereignty and
other alternatives to the federal legal doctrine, see Steven Andrew Light & Kathryn R.L.
Rand, Indian Gaming and Tribal Sovereignty: The Casino Compromise 18–25
(2005) (summarizing and describing tribes' "inherent right of self-determination" as a
broader and more accurate definition of indigenous conceptions of tribal sovereignty).

2. *Tribal sovereignty and "nation building."* Coffey and Tsosie connected tribal sovereignty to the necessity for strong tribal governments to address the needs of tribal communities. As noted above, the federal government maintains a trust relationship with
federally recognized tribes. Undergirding federal responsibilities to protect tribal interests
is an elaborate administrative structure comprised of independent executive agencies with
multiple and sometimes overlapping jurisdictions. The federal bureaucracy embodies yet
another dimension of the peculiar and paradoxical tenets of federal Indian law and policy. Federal agencies are obliged by federal law and constitutional duty to secure or further tribal interests, while at the same time those obligations may run squarely against the

wishes of tribal nations or undercut tribal sovereignty. At the same time, like all executive agencies, the federal bureaucracy that is supposed to work for tribes is subject to Congress's power of the purse as well as legislative oversight; that is, to both budgetary and political constraints. The U.S. Commission on Civil Rights recently assessed a number of the socioeconomic deficits facing Indian country as well as the status of key federal agencies and programs designed to address those disparities. The Commission's conclusions are framed by its sense of the federal government's trust obligations to tribes.

U.S. Commission on Civil Rights
A Quiet Crisis: Federal Funding and Unmet Needs in Indian Country
ix–xii, 1–9 (2003)

Executive Summary

The federal government has a long-established special relationship with Native Americans characterized by their status as governmentally independent entities, dependent on the United States for support and protection. In exchange for land and in compensation for forced removal from their original homelands, the government promised through laws, treaties, and pledges to support and protect Native Americans. However, funding for programs associated with those promises has fallen short, and Native peoples continue to suffer the consequences of a discriminatory history. Federal efforts to raise Native American living conditions to the standards of others have long been in motion, but Native Americans still suffer higher rates of poverty, poor educational achievement, substandard housing, and higher rates of disease and illness. Native Americans continue to rank at or near the bottom of nearly every social, health, and economic indicator.

Small in numbers and relatively poor, Native Americans often have had a difficult time ensuring fair and equal treatment on their own. Unfortunately, relying on the goodwill of the nation to honor its obligation to Native Americans clearly has not resulted in desired outcomes. Its small size and geographic apartness from the rest of American society induces some to designate the Native American population the "invisible minority." To many, the government's promises to Native Americans go largely unfulfilled. Thus, the U.S. Commission on Civil Rights, through this report, gives voice to a quiet crisis.

Over the last 10 years, federal funding for Native American programs has increased significantly. However, this has not been nearly enough to compensate for a decline in spending power, which had been evident for decades before that, nor to overcome a long and sad history of neglect and discrimination. Thus, there persists a large deficit in funding Native American programs that needs to be paid to eliminate the backlog of unmet Native American needs, an essential predicate to raising their standards of living to that of other Americans. Native Americans living on tribal lands do not have access to the same services and programs available to other Americans, even though the government has a binding trust obligation to provide them.

The Bureau of Indian Affairs (BIA), within [the U.S. Department of the Interior], bears the primary responsibility for providing the 562 federally recognized Native American tribes with federal services. BIA's mismanagement of Individual Indian Money trust accounts has denied Native Americans financial resources that could be applied toward basic needs that BIA programs fail to provide. Insufficient program funding resulted in $7.4 billion in unmet needs among Native Americans in 2000. BIA and its programs play a pivotal role in the lives of Native Americans, but mismanagement and lack of funding have undercut the agency's ability to improve living conditions in Native communities.

Native Americans have a lower life expectancy than any other racial/ethnic group and higher rates of many diseases, including diabetes, tuberculosis, and alcoholism. Yet, health facilities are frequently inaccessible and medically obsolete, and preventive care and specialty services are not readily available. Most Native Americans do not have private health insurance and thus rely exclusively on the Indian Health Service (IHS) for health care. The federal government spends less per capita on Native American health care than on any other group for which it has this responsibility, including Medicaid recipients, prisoners, veterans, and military personnel. Annually, IHS spends 60 percent less on its beneficiaries than the average per person health care expenditure nationwide. By most accounts, IHS has done well to work within its resource limitations. However, the agency currently operates with an estimated 59 percent of the amount necessary to stem the crisis. If funded sufficiently, IHS could provide more money to needs such as contract care, urban health programs, health facility construction and renovation, and sanitation services.

The availability of safe, sanitary housing in Indian Country is significantly less than the need. Overcrowding and its effects are a persistent problem. Furthermore, existing housing structures are substandard: approximately 40 percent of on-reservation housing is considered inadequate, and one in five reservation homes lacks complete plumbing. Native Americans also have less access to home-ownership resources, due to limited access to credit, land ownership restrictions, geographic isolation, and harsh environmental conditions that make construction difficult and expensive. Housing needs on reservations and tribal lands cannot be met with the same interventions that [the U.S. Department of Housing and Urban Development] uses to meet rental housing or homeownership goals in the suburbs or inner cities. Innovation and a more comprehensive approach are needed, and the government's trust responsibility to provide housing to Native Americans must be fully factored into these efforts.

All three components of law enforcement—policing, justice, and corrections—are substandard in Indian Country compared with the rest of the nation. Native Americans are twice as likely as any other racial/ethnic group to be the victims of crime. Yet, per capita spending on law enforcement in Native American communities is roughly 60 percent of the national average. Correctional facilities in Indian Country are also more overcrowded than even the most crowded state and federal prisons. In addition, Native Americans have long held that tribal court systems have not been funded sufficiently or consistently, and hence, are not equal to other court systems. Law enforcement professionals concede that the dire situation in Indian Country is understated. While [the U.S. Department of Justice] should be commended for its stated intention to meet its obligations to Native Americans, promising projects have suffered from inconsistent or discontinued funding. Native American law enforcement funding increased almost 85 percent between 1998 and 2003, but the amount allocated was so small to begin with that its proportion to the department's total budget hardly changed. Native American programs make up roughly 1 percent of the agency's total budget. A downward trend in funding has begun that, if continued, will severely compromise public safety in Native communities. Additionally, many Native Americans have lost faith in the justice system, in part due to perceived bias. Many attribute disproportionately high incarceration rates to unfair treatment by the criminal justice system, including racial profiling, disparities in prosecution, and lack of access to legal representation. Solving these problems is vital to restoring public safety and justice in Indian Country.

As a group, Native American students are not afforded educational opportunities equal to other American students. They routinely face deteriorating school facilities, underpaid teachers, weak curricula, discriminatory treatment, outdated learning tools, and cultural isolation. As a result, achievement gaps persist with Native American students scoring lower than any other racial/ethnic group in basic levels of reading, math, and history. Native American students are also more likely to drop out. The lack of educational opportunities in Native communities extends to postsecondary and vocational programs. Special Programs for Indian Adults has not been funded since 1995, and vocational rehabilitation programs are too poorly funded to meet the abundant need. Tribal colleges and universities receive 60 percent less federal funding per student than other public community colleges. The federal government has sole responsibility for providing education to these students—an obligation it is failing to meet.

The [U.S. Department of Agriculture] is largely responsible for rural development and farm and business supplements in rural communities. Native Americans rely on such programs to foster conditions that encourage and sustain economic investments. However, insufficient funding has limited the success of development programs and perpetuated unstable economies. Poor economic conditions have resulted in food shortages and hunger. Native Americans are more than twice as likely as the general population to face hunger and food insecurity at any given time. The inaccessibility of food and economic development programs compromises their usefulness. By its failure to make programs accessible to Native Americans, the federal government has denied them the opportunity to receive benefits routinely available to other citizens. The continuously high rates of hunger and poverty in Native communities are the strongest evidence that existing funds are not enough.

In short, the Commission finds evidence of a crisis in the persistence and growth of unmet needs. The conditions in Indian Country could be greatly relieved if the federal government honored its commitment to funding, paid greater attention to building basic infrastructure in Indian Country, and promoted self-determination among tribes. Failure to act will signify that this country's agreements with Native people, and other legal rights to which they are entitled, are little more than empty promises. Focused federal attention and resolve to remedy the quiet crises occurring in Indian Country, embodied in these recommendations and the results that flow from them, would signal a decisive moment in this nation's history. That moment would constitute America's rededication to live up to its trust responsibility for its Native people. Only through sustained systemic commitment and action will this federal responsibility be realized.

The Trust Relationship

The federal government has obligations to tribes on the basis of agreements and treaties that were established when tribes relinquished their lands in exchange for services and other protections. The federal government, as trustee, thus has a responsibility to protect tribal lands, and holds title to ensure against their divestiture from tribal governments. Three components define the trust relationship: land, self-governance, and social services.

Although the federal trust responsibility is rooted in the U.S. government's obligation to compensate Native Americans, the unique government-to-government relationship that resulted has proven beneficial and detrimental. One benefit to tribes is the power to transact directly with the federal government and to receive federal funds without state involvement. However, some states have encroached on tribal sovereignty, primarily through attempts to limit tribal government jurisdiction and to tax and regulate tribal enterprise. A common misconception is that Native Americans do not pay taxes and thus should not benefit from state programs. While Native American lands are not taxed, Native Americans themselves pay considerable business, sales, and federal income taxes. Denial of services based on this premise ignores the true character of tribes' economic contributions to states. A study by the Arizona Commission of Indian Affairs found that for every dollar the state spent on a tribe, nearly $42 was returned to the state through taxes assessed on businesses that operated on reservations and sales taxes that Native Americans paid on goods purchased off the reservation. Another study found that, in 1999, tribes contributed more than $1 billion to Washington State's economy, much more than the state paid to provide services to Native Americans.

Another misconception is that Native Americans do not need state assistance because they benefit from tax-free wealth generated by casino gaming. In reality, very few tribes have generated significant wealth from casino revenues; and casino income is taxed. Taxation and gaming are complex and outside the scope of this report, but it is important to note that the perception of casino-generated wealth is creating a new anti-Indian backlash and resistance to support funding for much-needed social services.

Trust Fulfillment as a Civil Right

Before the passage of federal civil rights laws, Native Americans faced (as did African Americans and other groups) other, less subtle forms of legally sanctioned discrimination based on religion, culture, and race. In several states, for instance, not only did water fountains exist for "Whites" and "Coloreds," but also for "Indians." Separation of the three groups, and the segregation of African Americans and Native Americans from whites, also occurred in public places such as movie theaters, which designated separate areas for "Colored" and "Indian." Until 1954, one of the most common offenses in Arizona courts was "selling liquor to an Indian," a practice that was prohibited by Arizona's constitution.

Efforts to raise Native American living conditions to the standards enjoyed by other groups have only been in full motion since the 1960s, largely inspired by the drive of other disadvantaged groups. But the goals of Native Americans were, and are, somewhat distinct. While integration was a governmental objective for many antidiscrimination programs affecting blacks and Hispanics, this was not always the objective of government policy toward Native Americans. As noted above, in early years the federal government engaged in a policy of removal and segregation. In the era of termination (1946–1965), however, federal policy shifted toward one of forced acculturation, pushing thousands of Native Americans into urban areas, away from cultural and familial ties, and creating another form of isolation with brutal consequences.

At the height of the civil rights movement, Native Americans resisted policies of forced integration and fought to preserve their unique cultural identities. Many Native Americans came to view civil rights as collective entitlements for which their ancestors bargained. It was around this time that the federal government recognized the need to establish a comprehensive Indian policy, which would acknowledge the hundreds of historical treaties, through legislation supporting Native American self-determination. The goal of self-determination maintains the federal protective role while increasing tribal participation in government. This goal has been eagerly embraced by Native Americans further asserting their rights and demanding redress for centuries of failed policies. Through their struggle, Indian tribes have retained most powers of government, such as public school administration, health care provision, and the administration of justice.

Today, Native Americans are subject to the same protections as other racial/ethnic and religious groups and are entitled to opportunities because of their unique status as (1) original inhabitants of U.S. land and (2) self-governing peoples. However, although current federal policies support self-determination, the lingering effects of past injustices remain. Attempts to self-govern and undo damages are undermined by the lack of resources and infrastructure necessary to adequately serve tribal members. At least in policy, the nation has clearly stated its promise to Native Americans. But laws and policies are meaningless without resources to enforce them. Resources are an important demonstration of the U.S. government's commitment to its responsibilities, including the obligation to preserve civil and other rights.

For more than 40 years, the U.S. Commission on Civil Rights has documented the dismal conditions in Native communities. Sadly, conditions in Indian Country are current-day reflections of some of the Commission's earliest works, despite continued funding and promises to improve. To what degree the federal government has failed to live up to its obligations and the implications of that failure are questions to which the Commission now addresses itself. In every area reviewed—health, housing, law enforcement, education, food distribution—funding and services are inadequate, as they have been historically. Some observers have labeled the economic condition in Indian Country "termination by funding cuts," as funding has so severely limited the ability of tribal governments to provide the services needed to sustain life on reservations.

The Native American Population

Compared with other racial and ethnic groups in the United States, Native Americans make up a relatively small proportion of the population. Often considered the "invisible minority," their numbers are relatively small and percentages too minute to register on established government-reported tracking scales. In addition, their geographic location leaves those who reside, attend school, or work on reservations isolated from the rest of society. The tendency of American society to respond foremost to visible problems results in Native Americans being overlooked and, in the minds of many, forgotten. However, there are nearly 2.5 million individuals in the United States who identify themselves as American Indian or Alaska Native (0.9 percent of the population); another 1.6 million identify as part American Indian or Alaska Native. According to the 2000 census, nearly 60 percent of Native Americans live in urban areas, compared with roughly 38 percent in 1990. The remaining 40 percent live on reservations, trust lands, or bordering rural areas.

The socioeconomic condition of the Native American population in the United States reveals a dire need for increased national attention. Native Americans rank at or near the bottom of nearly every social, health, and economic indicator. For example, the national poverty rate in the Unites States for the period between 1999 and 2001 was 11.6 percent. For Native Americans nationally, the average annual poverty rate was 24.5 percent. That is, nearly a quarter of Native Americans—more than twice the national average—live in poverty. Nearly one in three (31.2 percent) of those residing on reservations live in poverty. The unemployment rate in the Native American population nationwide is 12.4 percent, more than twice the general unemployment rate. On reservations, unemployment averages 13.6 percent, but varies widely across the nation. Unemployment among the Navajo, for example, is 25 percent; on the Pine Ridge and Rosebud reservations in South Dakota, unemployment exceeds 33 percent; and on the Kickapoo reservation in Texas, unemployment is nearly 70 percent. Of Native Americans aged 18 to 24, only 63.2 percent have graduated from high school (compared with 76.5 percent of the United States population) and of those 25 years and older, only 9.4 percent have completed four or more years of college (compared with 20.3 percent nationally).

The poor socioeconomic status of Native Americans resonates through myriad aspects of social and fiduciary policy from education to health care to housing. Stunted economic development in Native communities calls for increased national commitment that preserves the right to self-governance and self-determination. History has shown that self-governance and self-determination, in spite of promises, have come at the cost of constant struggle.

Notes and Questions

1.   Federal spending and the "quiet crisis." In its evaluation of the budgets and expenditures of six key federal agencies that administer more than 90 percent of all federal spending on American Indians, the Commission concluded,

> While some agencies are more proficient at managing funds and addressing the needs of Native Americans than others, the government's failure is systemic. The Commission identified several areas of jurisdictional overlap, inadequate collaboration, and a lack of articulation among agencies. The result is inefficiency, service delay, and wasted resources. Fragmented funding and lack of coordination not only complicate the application and distribution processes, but also dilute the benefit potential of the funds.

U.S. Commission on Civil Rights, at xii.

2.   American Indian demographics. For a useful compendium of the federal government's most current demographic reports and other information concerning American Indian tribes and people, see U.S. Bureau of the Census, *American Indian and Alaska Native (AIAN) Data and Links*, at http://factfinder.census.gov/home/aian/index.html; see also generally Harvard Project on American Indian Economic Development et al., The State of the Native Nations: Conditions Under U.S. Policies of Self-Determination (2007).

3.   Indian gaming and the "quiet crisis." What are the implications of the readings in this section with regard to Indian gaming law? How does Indian gaming reflect federal Indian law? What is — or should be — the role of tribal sovereignty? Recall that the U.S. Commission on Civil Rights commented,

> Another misconception is that Native Americans do not need state assistance because they benefit from tax-free wealth generated by casino gaming. In reality, very few tribes have generated significant wealth from casino revenues; and casino income is taxed. Taxation and gaming are complex and outside the scope of this report, but it is important to note that the perception of casino-generated wealth is creating a new anti-Indian backlash and resistance to support funding for much-needed social services.

U.S. Commission on Civil Rights, at 4.

How does the stereotype of the gaming-rich tribe affect Indian gaming law and policy? To what extent should Indian gaming law and policy be influenced by continuing poverty, unemployment, and other socioeconomic ills on reservations?

Problem 1: A Regulatory Model for Indian Gaming

After reading the above section on tribal governments and federal Indian law and policy, reconsider the various models of government regulation offered by Aronovitz and by Cabot and Csoka. Which regulatory model do you think best fits Indian gaming? What public policy goals should guide the selection and application of the model? What modifications, if any, would you make to the model to provide a better fit for regulating Indian gaming, and why?

Chapter 2

Pre-Statutory Law

A. Overview

In addition to its connections to over 200 years of federal Indian policy and the relatively modern U.S. history of legalized gambling discussed in the prior Chapter, what today is known as "Indian gaming" has foundations in longstanding North American tribal practice. Like many cultures, American Indian tribes have engaged in traditional games of chance that may look familiar to students of gambling.

Indian gaming's modern roots, however, stem from the imperatives of reservation economic development. As late-twentieth century goals of federal Indian policy shifted toward a focus on encouraging tribal self-sufficiency, tribes explored various means to capitalize on the limited resources available to them. As a few tribal bingo operations saw some financial success, they drew the interest of states, which sought to regulate them. Several legal challenges ensued that illustrate how various courts struggled with the extent to which state law and public policy would control the fledgling tribal gaming industry. The U.S. Supreme Court ultimately recognized the limits of state regulation in its landmark 1987 decision in *California v. Cabazon Band of Mission Indians*.

B. Traditional Tribal Games

Paul Pasquaretta
Gambling and Survival in Native North America
118–23 (2003)

Not surprisingly, public comment on the Indian gaming industry has tended to emphasize vicious gambling over virtuous speculation. This attitude is the product of envy, legitimate concerns about the social and economic effects of for-profit gaming, and the habit of applying the stigmas European-Americans attach to their own practices and behaviors to Native cultural institutions. This is most clearly illustrated in the historical commentary on traditional Indian gaming. When viewed through the vicious gambling/virtuous speculation paradigm, such practices are associated with wastefulness and the lack of thrift and industry, and never with productive risk and speculation. By the early seventeenth century, Indian gaming was already the focus of censure for incoming settlement communities. The gambling, lazy, and wasteful Indian male that William Wood described eventually became a stock character in European-American representations of Indians. Among the most notable scholars to proliferate this stereotype were Thomas Jefferson, Francis Parkman, and Lewis Henry Morgan. Commenting on the subject of Indian gambling, Jefferson declared the Natives' "vivacity and activity of mind" to be equal to that of whites; "hence, his eagerness for hunting, and for games of chance." While Jefferson intends to prove that Indians are endowed with the same talents as whites, an important consideration for him as he sought to defend aboriginal man from the degeneracy theory of European naturalists, he can find few better examples of the Indians' intellectual and physical capacities than their penchant for gambling.

Writing about his travels through Lakota/Sioux territories in the 1840s, New England historian Francis Parkman recalls one night when "a monotonous thumping of Indian drum, mixed with occasional sharp yells, and a chorus chanted by twenty voices," kept him anxiously awake. These ceremonies, which Parkman uses to illustrate a savage frenzy, were actually part of a ritual Lakota game, most likely *hanpa-pe-cunpi*, the "moccasin" or "hand game" described by Luther Standing Bear in *My People the Sioux*. For Standing Bear, hanpa-pe-cunpi was a communal celebration and wholesome entertainment. He relates how the entire camp would attend the matches, with everyone watching intently as the adults played on into the night. "No drinks were served," he stresses, "which took away the senses of our men and women, so no one grew boisterous. We had no bad words in our language, so none were used." Writing in the twentieth century, Standing Bear clearly is aware of the negative associations his white readers may have about Indian ceremonies. Typical of this biased viewpoint, Parkman compares the proceeding at the Lakota camp to the "desperate gambling" that occurs in the "hells of Paris." Although based on an eyewitness account of the Lakota gambling contest, Parkman's analysis reflects a pre-existing discourse on Indianness that designated Native gaming practices a sign of cultural pathology.

Lewis Henry Morgan, a contemporary of Parkman, sounded a similar note in his 1851 work, *League of the Ho-De-No-Sau-Nee or Iroquois*. A founding father of American ethnography, Morgan wrote his book with the intention of encouraging a "kinder feeling towards the Indian, founded upon a truer knowledge of his civil and domestic institutions." Nonetheless, Morgan saw nothing praiseworthy in Indian gaming practices. Betting, as he writes, was never "reprobated" by Native religious teachers; instead, they encouraged it. According to Morgan, this led a dangerous overindulgence: "It often happened that the Indian gambled away every valuable article which he possessed; his tomahawk, his medal, his ornaments, and even his blanket. The excitement and eagerness with which he watched the shifting tide of the game, was more uncontrollable than the delirious agitation of the pale-face at the race-course, or even the gambling table." Like most commentators of their day, Parkman and Morgan see Native gambling only in European-American terms and never attempt to understand the practice from a Native perspective.

A radical shift in the way whites perceived Indian gaming practices occurred near the turn of the nineteenth century. As Kathryn Gabriel reports, a chance meeting at the 1893 Columbian Exposition in Chicago between two American ethnologists, Stewart Culin and Frank Hamilton Cushing, led to a dramatic reappraisal. What resulted was Culin's tome-like work, *Games of the North American Indians*. Published in 1903 by the Smithsonian's Bureau of American Ethnology, this book included material on 229 different Native groups in North American and Mexico. It identified thirty-six different types of games, which Culin divided into two categories: games of skill and dexterity, and games of chance.

Although Culin devoted most of his text to describing individual games, he did offer an interpretation of the cultural aspects of indigenous gaming practices. Culin correctly perceived them to be "rites pleasing to the gods to secure their favor, or as processes of sympathetic magic, to drive away sickness, avert other evil, or produce rain and the fertilization and reproduction of plants and animals, or other beneficial results." Unlike the earlier commentaries, Culin's ethnographical discourse offers no hint of condemnation. Writing at a time when Indians were no longer a threat to expansion, his views reflect a developing interest in Native American culture as an object of study.

As Culin pointed out to his non-Indian readers, gaming has ancient roots in native North America. Associated with rituals of play and storytelling, games of chance connect the people to their communal origins and destiny. This tradition is most profoundly evident among Haudenosaunee who consider Gus-ka-eh, the Sacred Bowl Game, a divine amusement made by the Creator for the happiness of the people. Taught to humans when the world was young, it is an important rite of the *Midiwis*, or Mid-winter Ceremony. According to Trudie Lamb, a Schaghticoke Indian writer, "the Midiwis concludes the end of one cycle and marks the beginning of another. The Sacred Bowl Game is one of the Four Scared Rituals of Mid-winter and symbolizes the struggle of the Twin Boys to win control over the earth. The Mid-winter is a time of praying and awaiting the rebirth, a renewal of life. It is a time of giving thanks to the spirit forces and to the Creator." Also known as the Peach Stone Game, Gus-ka-eh is played with a wooden or cane bowl and flat stones, fruit pits, nut shells, or some other flat, two-sided object. Players take turns shaking the bowl and betting on the probability of different showing of the pieces. Each bowl shaker has a set number of bean or corn seeds, a portion of which is staked on each round of the game. The winning player is the one who collects all the beans or kernels. When played during the four-day Mid-winter, the game is said to amuse the life-giving forces, please the plant and animal kingdoms, and make the Creator laugh.

The twin boys referred to by Lamb are known in Iroquoian as Teharonhiawako (Sky-holder) and Sawiskera (Troublemaker). The grandchildren of Sky-Woman, the earth mother who remakes the world in the image of the Sky-World, the twins are born with opposite personalities; continual conflict is the result. Their ongoing rivalry, symbolizing the dualism of nature, is creative and destructive by turns. The bowl game is played to end their feuding. In a version of the story, Skyholder gains a winning edge when he substitutes the regular playing pieces for the severed heads of some small birds he had created. Killing the birds is a great sacrifice for Skyholder, but a necessary one if he is to defeat his powerful twin. Troublemaker, having been defeated in this sacred game, is relegated to the darkness, where he continues to exercise considerable power. When played in its ceremonial contexts, Gus-ka-eh commemorates this divine struggle.

As the ceremonial nature of Gus-ka-eh demonstrates, traditional Indian gaming practices are associated with communal rituals and celebrations. Generally speaking, gambling ceremonials are team competitions to be participated in by whole communities. This social aspect of traditional Indian gaming is evident in Mourning Dove's description of the Salishan stick game:

> In the evening, people made large bonfires in the open air and challenged other tribes to play stick games. Lively songs were sung by both sides, and each team tries to distract the other while it was trying to hide the two bones. The object of the game was for the other side to guess which hand had a particular bone. Each side had a long pole stretched across in front and pounded on it with a short stick, keeping time with the songs. Bets of robes, blankets, coins and so forth were piled in the middle. Anyone could bet on a team, even women. Women also had their betting games, which could last for a few hours or several days. All bets had to be absolutely matched. Anyone who wanted to make a bet had to match it against one for the other side. After the game, a winner got back double of the bet.... All gambling required good sportsmanship. It was shameful for a poor loser to grieve. They would get no sympathy.

The Haudenosaunee bowl game is likewise practiced as a team competition. In the mid-nineteenth century, Morgan reported that it was routinely played between neighboring communities and different clans within a particular town. The victory belonged to both the gambler and his clan, town, or nation. Thus, based on their skill at betting or throwing dice, gamblers were chosen by the whole group.

Notes and Questions

1.   *Traditional tribal games.* As Pasquaretta notes, Culin divided tribal games into two categories: games of dexterity and games of chance. Dexterity games, such as foot races, lacrosse, archery, and "hoop and pole" (a games that requires a player to throw a dart or shoot an arrow through a target), require physical skill. Community members often wagered on the athletes competing in games of dexterity. Games of chance also involve betting, and include dice games and guessing games such as stick games and the moccasin game. Traditional dice games are little different from the casino game of "craps": players throw dice, made of stones, buttons, seeds, or similar objects, against a blanket or hide. In stick games, players guess at the number of sticks in a group, or which group contains a specially marked stick. The moccasin game is a version of the familiar shell game in which the player guesses which moccasin hides an object.

2.   *Gambling as a vice.* As discussed in Chapter 1, the history of legalized gambling in the U.S. reflects the view of gambling as a vice. Pasquaretta, a contemporary cultural anthropologist, uncovers a historical thread of unease about Indian gaming that stems back to European-American observers' association of gambling with sin, vice, and laziness. Subsequent early-twentieth century documentation of the varied manifestations of tribal games exemplified fascination with the practices of more "primitive" cultures. This documentation, too, represents the anthropological method as it existed at the time. Pasquaretta's point was that the biases of observers colored early accounts, calling into question not only the value judgments attached to such accounts but the accuracy of the accounts themselves. Could a similar argument be made about accounts of contemporary Indian gaming?

3.   *Gambling and moral lessons.* Although many tribes engaged in the practice of gambling, they did not necessarily recognize it as a universal good. The social and societal tensions inherent to gambling are found in the teachings of many tribes. Traditional games of chance often were connected to broad myths and legends that teach moral lessons about good and bad. Gambling was portrayed as leading to the loss of possessions, family, or worse. The protagonist of such stories recognized the evils of gambling and rescued those caught in its grasp. Kathryn Gabriel captured elements of this ambivalence in GAMBLER WAY: INDIAN GAMING IN MYTHOLOGY, HISTORY AND ARCHEOLOGY IN NORTH AMERICA 17–18 (1996):

> The core plot of most gambler myths plays on the often real consequences of ordinary people who gamble too much, and then takes the plot to the extreme. Typically, the people live near an ominous gambler whose gaming challenges are irresistible to the people. They systematically lose their possessions, a piece at a time, until they are naked and destitute. They lose their families, village/tribal members, and finally themselves. In the worst case, losers go into slavery or forfeit their body parts during one play after another, working up to decapitation, and then they may be burned or eaten. The losers' heads, eyes, hands, and ears are strung up as trophies or made into a soup and fed to the hero(s) in order to thwart the rescue mission.

Through gambling contests of all kinds, the divinely sanctioned hero usually overcomes the dangerous opponent with superior skill, cunning, or magic. Equipped with covert schemes and special gaming implements (which often serve the dual purpose of hunting and warring) the divine representative, be it human, animal, or natural medium, helps the hero beat the bad gambler. The bad gambler tries to renege on his wager, but the hero calls him on it, and the same misery the gambler dispensed to others is visited upon himself. The people are then restored to life and freedom.

C. Modern Roots

Modern Indian gaming is shaped by federal Indian law and its repeated attempts to balance tribal and state sovereignty to implement federal Indian policy. As discussed in Chapter 1, jurisdictional contestation between states and tribes is nothing new. In the context of Indian gaming, states' efforts to exert regulatory authority on tribal lands resulted in the legal foundation for modern tribal gaming. We begin by examining Public Law 280, a Termination Era federal statute that delegated criminal and civil jurisdiction over reservation lands to several states. Pub. L. 280 provided the basis for states' arguments that tribal gaming was subject to state law.

Carole E. Goldberg
Public Law 280:
The Limits of State Jurisdiction Over Reservation Indians
22 UCLA L. Rev. 535 (1975)

Passed in 1953, [Public Law 280] (PL-280) was an attempt at compromise between wholly abandoning the Indians to the states and maintaining them as federally protected wards, subject only to federal or tribal jurisdiction. The statute originally transferred to five willing states* and offered all others civil and criminal jurisdiction over reservation

---

* The five were California, Minnesota, Nebraska, Oregon, and Wisconsin. Alaska was added in 1958. With respect to civil jurisdiction the Act provides:

Each of the States or Territories [sic] listed shall have jurisdiction over civil causes of action between Indians or to which Indians are parties which arise in the areas of Indian country listed opposite the name of the State or Territory to the same extent that such State or Territory has jurisdiction over other civil causes of action, and those civil laws of such State or Territory that are of general application to private persons or private property shall have the same force and effect within such Indian country as they have elsewhere within the State or Territory:
Alaska: All Indian country within the Territory.
California: All Indian country within the State.
Minnesota: All Indian country within the State, except the Red Lake Reservation.
Nebraska: All Indian country within the State.
Oregon: All Indian country within the State, except the Warm Springs Reservation.
Wisconsin: All Indian country within the State.
In regard to criminal jurisdiction in the mandatory states the Act provides:
Each of the States or Territories [sic] shall have jurisdiction over offenses committed by or against Indians in the areas of Indian country listed opposite the name of the State or Territory to the same extent that such State or Territory has jurisdiction over offenses committed elsewhere within the State or Territory, and the criminal laws of such State or Territory

Indians regardless of the Indians' preference for continued autonomy. PL-280 did not, however, terminate the trust status of reservation lands.

From the outset, PL-280 left both the Indians and the states dissatisfied, the Indians because they did not want state jurisdiction thrust upon them against their will, the states because they resented the remaining federal protection which seemed to deprive them of the ability to finance their newly acquired powers.

The expansion of metropolitan areas near Indian reservations has increased the states' interest in regulating and exploiting residential and recreational development on trust land. The discovery of substantial energy resources on reservations, and consequent industrial development, have spurred similar state interest in regulating and taxing those activities. At the same time, tribal governments have been receiving encouragement from the federal government to develop tribal enterprises and strengthen their administrative apparatus, increasing their interest in freedom from state power. Finally, growing demands on the part of Indians that they receive their share of state services and their share of representation in state legislatures have produced concomitant demands on the part of the states that Indians submit to state jurisdiction.

The jurisdictional stakes are considerably higher today than they were when PL-280 was enacted; at the same time federal Indian policy is more devoted to fulfilling federal responsibility for Indians and building effective tribal governments. Broadly speaking, the model for federal Indian policy seems to be changing from one favoring state power with minimum protection for Indian interests to one favoring tribal autonomy with minimum protection for state interests. Nevertheless, since PL-280 is the most direct evidence of congressional intent with respect to state jurisdiction, the debate over the scope of state power on Indian reservations must contend with policy choices Congress made when PL-280 was enacted. Amendments to the act adopted in 1969 did, however, bring PL-280 more in conformity with current policy by rendering all *future* assertions of state jurisdiction under the Act subject to the affected Indians' consent, and authorizing states to return jurisdiction to the federal government.

PL-280 differed from earlier relinquishments of federal Indian jurisdiction in that it authorized every state to assume jurisdiction at any time in the future. Although PL-280 itself had begun as an attempt to confer jurisdiction on California only, by the time it was reported out of the Senate, the prevailing view was that "any legislation in [the] area should be on a general basis, making provision for all affected States to come within its terms." The Senate Report indicates the foremost concern of Congress at the time of enacting of PL-280 was the lawlessness on the reservations and the accompanying threat to Anglos living nearby. In 1953, responsibility for law enforcement on the reservations was irrationally fractionated. If a non-Indian committed a crime against another non-Indian or a crime without an apparent victim, such as gambling or drunk driving, only state au-

---

shall have the same force and effect within such Indian country as they have elsewhere within the State or Territory:

Alaska: All Indian country within the State, except that on Annette Islands, the Metlakatla Indian community may exercise jurisdiction over offenses committed by Indians in the same manner in which such jurisdiction may be exercised by Indian tribes in Indian country over which State jurisdiction has not been extended.

California: All Indian country within the State.

Minnesota: All Indian country within the State, except the Red Lake Reservation.

Nebraska: All Indian country within the State.

Oregon: All Indian country within the State, except the Warm Springs Reservation.

Wisconsin: All Indian country within the State.

thorities could prosecute him under state law. But if either the offender or victim was Indian, the federal government had exclusive jurisdiction to prosecute, applying state law in federal court under the Assimilative Crimes Act. Finally, if offender and victim were both Indians, the federal government had exclusive jurisdiction if the offense was one of the "Ten Major Crimes"; otherwise, tribal courts had exclusive jurisdiction. Since federal law enforcement was typically neither well-financed nor vigorous, and tribal courts often lacked the resources and skills to be effective, the result was "[t]he complete breakdown of law and order on many of the Indian reservations." The primary law enforcement thrust of PL-280 is further evidenced by the fact that several predecessor bills offered the states criminal jurisdiction only, and PL-280 itself exempted several reservations completely from state jurisdiction solely because they had legal systems and organizations "functioning in a reasonably satisfactory manner."

There is much less evidence of the congressional rationale for conferring civil jurisdiction on the states, and much less factual support for that decision. State civil jurisdiction over reservation Indians was believed to have been somewhat more extensive than state criminal jurisdiction, though typically, state courts were powerless to resolve claims against reservation Indians arising on the reservation. Since federal law governed many important civil relations involving Indians, the B.I.A. was charged with administering these laws, and played a considerable governing role on the reservations. In this context, the Senate Report on PL-280 declared that the Indians "have reached a stage of acculturation and development that makes desirables extension of State civil jurisdiction." The implications of this and similar statements was that Indians were just as socially advanced as other state citizens, and should therefore be released from second-class citizenship as well as the paternalistic supervision of the B.I.A.

Considering the absence of any significant investigation of the Indians' stage of social development prior to the broad delegation of jurisdiction to every state by PL-280, it seems unlikely that Congress knew or cared about the Indians' readiness for state jurisdiction. Furthermore, it is difficult to reconcile this theme of advanced acculturation with the prevailing notion that state criminal jurisdiction was necessary because the Indians were disorderly and incapable of self-government. Most likely, civil jurisdiction was an afterthought in a measure aimed primarily at bringing law and order to the reservations, added because it comported with the pro-assimilationist drift of federal policy, and because it was convenient and cheap.

In 1968, Congress eliminated the need for self-imposed limits on state jurisdiction in the future by establishing a tribal consent provision in PL-280 itself. Congress provided in the Civil Rights Act of 1968 that henceforth no state could acquire PL-280 jurisdiction over the objections of the affected Indians. This change in PL-280 is significant evidence of a shift in federal Indian policy from the pro-assimilationist orientation of the 1950's to a greater concern for strengthening tribal institutions and encouraging economic development on reservations. Interestingly, the opposition to tribal consent was not couched in law and order language this time. Rather, the opponents stressed the need for state control of economic development on the reservations, a need which has precipitated much conflict over PL-280 in recent years, especially in the Southwest.

The significance of the addition of a tribal consent provision to PL-280 lies not only in its recognition of the principle of Indian self-determination, but also in its new conception of the role of state jurisdiction on reservations. The tribal consent provision transformed PL-280 from a law which justified state jurisdiction on law enforcement, budgetary, and assimilationist grounds to one which justified state jurisdiction as a means of providing services to Indian communities. Among the strongest arguments in favor of the 1968

Act's amendment was that the institution of state jurisdiction under PL-280, far from improving reservation law and order and elevating Indians from second-class citizenship, had subjected them to discriminatory treatment in the courts, as well as discrimination in the provision of state services. Once tribal consent became a prerequisite to state jurisdiction, and jurisdiction could be acquired one subject matter at a time, the way was opened for tribes and states to negotiate for the extension of state jurisdiction in those situations where it was to their mutual advantage.

The beneficial impact of the 1968 amendments to PL-280 should not be overemphasized, however. The Indian consent provision was not made retroactive, and thus earlier assumptions of state jurisdiction over Indian objections were not affected. Moreover, it did not enable Indians who had consented to state jurisdiction under a state-initiated consent provision to reconsider their decisions.

Notes and Questions

1. *Public Law 280 and the Termination Era.* In 1953, Congress adopted a resolution that stated: "It is the policy of Congress, as rapidly as possible, to make the Indians within the territorial limits of the United States subject to the same laws and entitled to the same privileges and responsibilities as are applicable to other citizens of the United States, [and] to end their status as wards of the United States." H.R. Con. Res. 108, 83d Cong., 1st Sess., 67 Stat. B132 (1953). Pub. L. 280 was a keystone in the federal Indian policy known as "termination," which was intended to cut tribes loose from federal support and dismantle the federal programs that supported tribal communities. *See, e.g.,* Charles F. Wilkinson & Eric R. Biggs, *The Evolution of the Termination Policy*, 5 Am. Indian L. Rev. 151 (1977).

2. *Termination to Self-Determination.* Professor Goldberg wrote the article excerpted above in the mid-1970s, in the early years of the Self-Determination Era of federal Indian policy. Her sense of a shift in federal Indian policy "from one favoring state power with minimum protection for Indian interests to one favoring tribal autonomy with minimum protection for state interests" accurately reflected this era's move toward encouraging tribal self-determination and, later, self-governance. During this period Congress passed various laws allowing tribes to assume control of federally funded programs and intended to promote reservation economic development and self-governance, including the Indian Self-Determination and Education Assistance Act of 1975 and the Indian Child Welfare Act of 1978. This federal encouragement of tribal self-sufficiency and self-determination was furthered in the 1980s by the Reagan administration, in part reflecting President Reagan's general approach of decreasing federal spending, downsizing the federal bureaucracy, and devolving political power to the states. As Reagan said during his Indian Policy Statement of January 24, 1983, "It is important to the concept of self-government that tribes reduce their dependence on Federal funds by providing a greater percentage of the cost of their self-government." Some observers, however, saw this rationale as cloaking the administration's general lack of "respect [for] the historical implications of the sovereign political status of tribes." Samuel R. Cook, *Ronald Reagan's Indian Policy in Retrospect: Economic Crisis and Political Irony*, 24 Pol'y Stud. J. 11 (1996).

3. *Criminal jurisdiction in Indian country.* Under the federal Major Crimes Act of 1885, serious violent felonies, including murder, kidnapping, assault, and arson, committed by Indians in Indian country fall within exclusive federal jurisdiction. *See* 18 U.S.C. § 1153. The Major Crimes Act defines "Indian country" as reservation lands, dependent Indian communities, and Indian allotments. *Id.* § 1151. This definition is used throughout fed-

eral law, so that "Indian country" has become a legal term of art. Through Pub. L. 280, Congress transferred its exclusive jurisdiction over serious felonies in Indian country to the handful of states identified in the statute. Professor Kevin Washburn has criticized federal criminal jurisdiction in Indian country as undermining the fundamental purpose of criminal law as reflecting the morality of the local community. *See* Kevin K. Washburn, *Federal Criminal Law and Tribal Self-Determination*, 84 N.C. L. Rev. 779 (2006); Kevin K. Washburn, *American Indians, Crime, and the Law*, Mich. L. Rev. 709 (2006).

4. ***State control and Indian gaming.*** Referring to Pub. L. 280, Professor Goldberg commented, "Interestingly, the opposition to tribal consent was not couched in law and order language this time. Rather, the opponents stressed the need for state control of economic development on the reservations, a need which has precipitated much conflict over PL-280 in recent years...." Goldberg, at 550. Her observation seems prescient, since states relied on Pub. L. 280 to regulate early tribal gaming enterprises, as seen in the cases that follow.

Seminole Tribe of Florida v. Butterworth
658 F.2d 310 (5th Cir. 1981)

MORGAN, Circuit Judge.

[The Seminole Tribe planned to build a bingo hall on its reservation in Broward County, Florida. The county sheriff informed the informed the tribe that he would make arrests for any violations of Fla. Stat. §849.093, the state law authorizing limited charitable bingo. The Tribe then brought this action seeking a declaration that the state lacked jurisdiction to enforce its bingo regulations on the Tribe's reservation. The state argued that because Florida opted to assume criminal jurisdiction over tribes in the state under Public Law 280, it had power to enforce the criminal provisions of its bingo statute.]

In *Bryan v. Itasca County*, [426 U.S. 373 (1976)], the Supreme Court interpreted Public Law 280 as granting civil jurisdiction to the states only to the extent necessary to resolve private disputes between Indians and Indians and private citizens. In *Bryan* the petitioner Indian sought relief from a personal property tax that the state had levied against his mobile home. The Court interpreted [Public Law 280's grant of civil jurisdiction as limited, as it read the law as] "seem[ing] to have been primarily intended to redress the lack of Indian forums for resolving private legal disputes between reservation Indians, and between Indians and other private citizens, by permitting the courts of the States to decide such disputes.... [The statute] authorizes application by the state courts of their rules of decision to decide such disputes." After further discussion the Court concluded that "if Congress in enacting Pub. L. 280 had intended to confer upon the States general civil regulatory powers, including taxation over reservation Indians, it would have expressly said so." Although the Supreme Court was interpreting the language of Public Law 280 as directed at the six mandatory states, it is clear that these same limitations on civil jurisdiction would apply to a state that assumed jurisdiction pursuant to [the section allowing states to unilaterally assume jurisdiction prior to the 1968 tribal consent requirement]. Thus, the mandate from the Supreme Court is that states do not have general regulatory power over the Indian tribes.

The difficult question remaining in a case such as the present one is whether the statute in question represents an exercise of the state's regulatory or prohibitory authority. Thus, under a civil/regulatory versus criminal/prohibitory analysis, we consider the Florida statute in question to determine whether the operation of bingo games is prohibited as against the public policy of the state or merely regulated by the state.

Fla. Stat. § 849.093 provides that the general prohibition against lotteries does not apply to prevent "nonprofit or veterans' organizations engaged in charitable, civic, community, benevolent, religious or scholastic works or other similar activities ... from conducting bingo games, provided that the entire proceeds derived from the conduct of such games shall be donated by such organizations to the endeavors mentioned above." The remaining sections of the statute state restrictions for the operation of bingo games and penal sanctions for violation of those provisions. Although the inclusion of penal sanctions makes it tempting at first glance to classify the statute as prohibitory, the statute cannot be automatically classified as such. A simplistic rule depending on whether the statute includes penal sanctions could result in the conversion of every regulatory statute into a prohibitory one. The classification of the statute is more complex, and requires a consideration of the public policy of the state on the issue of bingo and the intent of the legislature in enacting the bingo statute.

Bingo appears to fall in a category of gambling that the state has chosen to regulate by imposing certain limitations to avoid abuses. Where the state regulates the operation of bingo halls to prevent the game of bingo from becoming a money-making business, the Seminole Indian tribe is not subject to that regulation and cannot be prosecuted for violating the limitations imposed.

Although the Florida Constitution, the Florida Supreme Court, and the Florida legislature have in various forms denounced the "evils of gambling," it is clear from the provisions of the bingo statute in question and the statutory scheme of the Florida gambling provisions considered as a whole that the playing of bingo and operation of bingo halls is not contrary to the public policy of the state. This case presents a close and difficult question. The [*Bryan*] Court stated that "statutes passed for the benefit of dependent Indian tribes ... are to be liberally construed, doubtful expressions being resolved in favor of the Indians." Although the regulatory bingo statute may arguably be interpreted as prohibitory, the resolution must be in favor of the Indian tribe.

RONEY, Circuit Judge, dissenting.

I respectfully dissent on the ground that the State of Florida has prohibited, not regulated, the precise kind of bingo operation which the plaintiff seeks to conduct. As a matter of fact, it is because such activity is prohibited in Florida that this business was started and is successful. The reasons that Florida laws prohibit such a bingo business, focusing on the indirect consequences of it, whether right or wrong, are as applicable to a bingo casino on the Indian reservation as they are to such a business off a reservation. If only Indians were involved, or if the effects of the bingo casino were shown to be confined to the reservation, the decisions relied upon by the Court might be applicable. Without such a showing, in my opinion, they are not. I would reverse.

Barona Group of the Capitan Grande Band of Mission Indians v. Duffy
694 F.2d 1185 (9th Cir. 1982)

BOOCHEVER, Circuit Judge.

Barona is an independent Indian Nation recognized by federal statute with its reservation in the County of San Diego. On April 20, 1981, the Tribal Council of the Barona Tribe, the Tribe's governing body, enacted a Tribal Ordinance authorizing, with certain restrictions, the playing of bingo within the reservation. The Tribe subsequently entered into a management agreement with American Amusement Management, Inc., to commence a bingo operation within the reservation.

On June 25, 1981 the undersheriff of the County informed representatives of Barona that the bingo ordinance of the County of San Diego prohibited the Tribe's bingo operation. The undersheriff also said that the ordinance would be enforced to the extent of entry on Indian territory to cite or arrest the participants in the bingo operation. The Tribe then sought injunctive and declaratory relief against the Sheriff on the ground that the Sheriff is without lawful authority to enforce the state or county laws regarding bingo on the Barona Reservation.

The California legislature, in accordance with state constitutional limitations [which generally prohibit lotteries but allow charitable bingo], adopted Cal. Penal Code § 326.5 which controls the conduct of bingo games. This statute removes from the general prohibition of various forms of gambling the conduct of bingo games pursuant to city or county ordinance as provided in the California Constitution. The County passed such an ordinance allowing bingo games conducted by certain charitable organizations. Barona contends that these provisions do not apply to them because the state and county lacked a grant of power from the federal government to impose or enforce these laws within the confines of the reservation. The County contends that such power is granted under [Public Law 280].

Public Law 280 does provide some applicability of state law over on-reservation activities, [by granting] states civil jurisdiction over Indian reservations in words that on the surface seem to make all state laws of general application effective. The Supreme Court, however, has construed this section to mean that states have jurisdiction only over private civil litigation involving reservation Indians in state court. *Bryan v. Itasca County*. Thus, a state may not impose general civil/regulatory laws on the reservation. [Public Law 280] however, confers on certain states, including California, full criminal jurisdiction over offenses committed by Indians on the reservation. Thus, whether the state and county laws apply to the Tribe's bingo enterprise depends on whether the laws are classified as civil/regulatory or criminal/prohibitory.

We find *Seminole Tribe of Florida v. Butterworth*, 658 F.2d 310 (5th Cir. 1981), *cert. denied*, 455 U.S. 1020 (1982), persuasive. In *Butterworth*, like the present case, pursuant to a state constitutional grant of power, the state statute excepted bingo operations by certain charitable organizations and under certain conditions from a general prohibition of gambling. The Fifth Circuit determined that whether a statute may be classified as regulatory or prohibitory depended on whether the legislature deemed the activity to be against the public policy of the state. Evaluating the statute, the court determined that the legislature meant only to regulate bingo. The court based this determination on the fact that bingo is allowed in Florida as a form of recreation, that certain worthy organizations are allowed to benefit from bingo and that the state regulates bingo halls only to prevent the game of bingo from becoming a money-making venture.

The scope of Public Law 280 as applied to bingo games is also addressed in *Oneida Tribe of Indians v. Wisconsin*, 518 F. Supp. 712 (W.D.Wis. 1981). In *Oneida* the district court was confronted with a factual situation and state statutory scheme virtually identical to those found in *Butterworth*. The *Oneida* court also determined that the bingo laws were regulatory and not prohibitory. The court rested its decision primarily on the fact that the Wisconsin statute only provided penalties for operation of bingo games not in accordance with the statute. The general populace was allowed to *play* at will. Thus, the court reasoned that bingo was not contrary to public policy.

Although the test for determining when a state statutory scheme such as the present one should apply to tribal members on their reservation is not susceptible of easy application, we conclude for a number of reasons that the County's bingo laws are regulatory and of a civil nature.

First, the state statute authorizes bingo operations by tax exempt organizations including, for example, fraternal societies, recreational clubs, senior citizen organizations, real estate boards and labor and agricultural groups. There is no general prohibition against playing bingo. As in *Butterworth*, the California statute regulates bingo as a money making venture by limiting size of prizes, requiring that all proceeds be applied to charitable purposes, and requiring that the game be operated by volunteers from the authorized organization. The fact that so many diverse organizations are allowed to conduct bingo operations, albeit under strict regulation, is contrary to a finding that such operations violate California public policy.

Second, as was pointed out in the *Oneida* case, the general public is allowed to play bingo at will in an authorized game. This cuts against a public policy prohibition.

Third, the Supreme Court has laid down several rules of construction applicable to statutes affecting Indian affairs which undercut application of the bingo laws in this case. Ambiguities in statutes concerning dependent tribes are to be resolved in favor of the Indians. *Oliphant v. Suquamish Indian Tribe,* 435 U.S. 191, 208 n. 17 (1978). State jurisdiction over reservations, historically, is strongly disfavored. *McClanahan v. Arizona State Tax Commission,* 411 U.S. 164, 168 (1973). Moreover, enforcement of the bingo laws is contrary to the present federal policy of encouraging tribal self-government. The decisions addressing similar bingo statutes have acknowledged the closeness of the question, but have found in favor of the reservation Indians on the basis of these strong policies.

Finally, the stated purpose of the tribal bingo ordinance is to collect money "for the support of programs to promote the health, education and general welfare" of the Barona Tribe. This intent to better the Indian community is as worthy as the other charitable purposes to which bingo proceeds are lawfully authorized under the California statute. Although the Barona bingo operation does not fully comply with the letter of the statutory scheme, it does at least fall within the general tenor of its permissive intent.

Notes and Questions

1.   Early Indian gaming. In the late 1970s and early 1980s, several tribes in Florida, California, and elsewhere saw high-stakes bingo halls as attractive vehicles for reservation economic development. With low start-up and operational costs and a relatively high rate of return on tribes' minimal investments, gaming presented a sensible option on often isolated and resource-poor reservation lands. *See, e.g.,* Eduardo E. Cordeiro, *The Economics of Bingo: Factors Influencing the Success of Bingo Operations on American Indian Reservations,* in WHAT CAN TRIBES DO? STRATEGIES AND INSTITUTIONS IN AMERICAN INDIAN ECONOMIC DEVELOPMENT (Stephen Cornell & Joseph P. Kalt eds., 1992).

2.   The civil/regulatory-criminal/prohibitory dichotomy. Both the *Butterworth* and *Barona* courts assessed Congress's authorization of state jurisdiction in Pub. L. 280 and found that Florida and California, respectively, only had authority to enforce criminal prohibitions on tribal lands. How did the courts reach the conclusion that state authority did not extend to civil regulatory laws? Why weren't Florida's bingo laws, which provided for criminal penalties, an extension of allowable state jurisdiction over tribes? Why weren't California's? How would you articulate the "test" applied by the courts? In *Butterworth*, the court notes that the question is a "close and difficult" one, a sentiment echoed by the *Barona* court. What exactly makes the question a close one for the courts?

3.   *The Indian canon of construction.* As the *Butterworth* and *Barona* courts noted, the U.S. Supreme Court has directed that special interpretational rules apply to treaties and laws concerning tribes, including the canon that "statutes passed for the benefit of dependent Indian tribes are to be liberally construed, doubtful expressions being resolved in favor of the Indians." Put another way, "statutes are to be construed liberally in favor of the Indians, with ambiguous provisions interpreted to their benefit." *Montana v. Blackfeet Tribe of Indians*, 471 U.S. 759, 766 (1985); *see also McClanahan v. Arizona State Tax Comm'n*, 411 U.S. 164 (1973); *Choate v. Trapp*, 224 U.S. 665 (1912). The Supreme Court has tied the so-called Indian canon of construction to the federal government's trust obligations. *See Montana v. Blackfeet Tribe of Indians*, 471 U.S. at 766; *Oneida County v. Oneida Indian Nation*, 470 U.S. 226, 247 (1985) ("The canons of construction applicable in Indian law are rooted in the unique trust relationship between the United States and the Indians."). Would the *Butterworth* and *Barona* courts have reached the same conclusion without applying the canon of construction in the tribes' favor? Why or why not?

4.   **Oneida Tribe of Indians v. Wisconsin.** In *Oneida Tribe*, 518 F. Supp. 712 (W.D. Wis. 1981), the district court reached the same conclusion as did *Butterworth* and *Barona* regarding the state's ability to apply its bingo regulations on tribal lands. The court reasoned, "[B]ecause it appears that Wisconsin's bingo laws are not designed to prohibit the general populace from playing bingo, it seems that those laws are regulatory rather than prohibitory." The court continued, "[I]t also appears that the Wisconsin legislature and the general populace, as evidenced by the constitutional amendment of 1973 [authorizing charitable bingo], have determined that bingo playing is generally beneficial and have 'chosen to regulate rather than prohibit.' Thus, it appears that Wisconsin's bingo laws are civil-regulatory and, [under *Bryan v. Itasca County*], not enforceable by the state in Indian country." Nevertheless, the court expressed "a certain uneasiness in reaching that conclusion," criticizing the civil/regulatory-criminal/prohibitory analysis as "a rather mechanical approach to the issue presented." Like the *Butterworth* and *Barona* courts, the *Oneida* court used the Indian canon of construction to bolster its conclusion.

California v. Cabazon Band of Mission Indians
480 U.S. 202 (1987)

Justice WHITE delivered the opinion of the Court.

The Cabazon and Morongo Bands of Mission Indians, federally recognized Indian Tribes, occupy reservations in Riverside County, California. Each Band conducts bingo games on its reservation. The Cabazon Band has also opened a card club at which draw poker and other card games are played. The games are open to the public and are played predominantly by non-Indians coming onto the reservations. The games are a major source of employment for tribal members, and the profits are the Tribes' sole source of income. The State of California seeks to apply to the two Tribes Cal. Penal Code § 326.5. That statute does not entirely prohibit the playing of bingo but permits it when the games are operated and staffed by members of designated charitable organizations who may not be paid for their services. Profits must be kept in special accounts and used only for charitable purposes; prizes may not exceed $250 per game. Asserting that the bingo games on the two reservations violated each of these restrictions, California insisted that the Tribes comply with state law. Riverside County also sought to apply its local Ordinance No. 558, regulating bingo, as well as its Ordinance No. 331, prohibiting the playing of draw poker and the other card games.

I

The Court has consistently recognized that Indian tribes retain "attributes of sovereignty over both their members and their territory," *United States v. Mazurie,* 419 U.S. 544 (1975), and that "tribal sovereignty is dependent on, and subordinate to, only the Federal Government, not the States," *Washington v. Confederated Tribes of Colville Indian Reservation,* 447 U.S. 134 (1980). It is clear, however, that state laws may be applied to tribal Indians on their reservations if Congress has expressly so provided. Here, the State insists that Congress has twice given its express consent: first in Pub. L. 280 in 1953 and second in the Organized Crime Control Act in 1970 [18 U.S.C. § 1955]. We disagree in both respects.

In Pub. L. 280, Congress expressly granted six States, including California, jurisdiction over specified areas of Indian country within the States and provided for the assumption of jurisdiction by other States. California was granted broad criminal jurisdiction over offenses committed by or against Indians within all Indian country within the State. [Pub. L. 280's] grant of civil jurisdiction was more limited. In *Bryan v. Itasca County,* 426 U.S. 373 (1976), we interpreted [Pub. L. 280] to grant States jurisdiction over private civil litigation involving reservation Indians in state court, but not to grant general civil regulatory authority. We held, therefore, that Minnesota could not apply its personal property tax within the reservation. Congress' primary concern in enacting Pub. L. 280 was combating lawlessness on reservations. The Act plainly was not intended to effect total assimilation of Indian tribes into mainstream American society. We recognized that a grant to States of general civil regulatory power over Indian reservations would result in the destruction of tribal institutions and values. Accordingly, when a State seeks to enforce a law within an Indian reservation under the authority of Pub. L. 280, it must be determined whether the law is criminal in nature, and thus fully applicable to the reservation, or civil in nature, and applicable only as it may be relevant to private civil litigation in state court.

The Minnesota personal property tax at issue in *Bryan* was unquestionably civil in nature. The California bingo statute is not so easily categorized. California law permits bingo games to be conducted only by charitable and other specified organizations, and then only by their members who may not receive any wage or profit for doing so; prizes are limited and receipts are to be segregated and used only for charitable purposes. Violation of any of these provisions is a misdemeanor. California insists that these are criminal laws which Pub. L. 280 permits it to enforce on the reservations.

Following its earlier decision in *Barona Group of Capitan Grande Band of Mission Indians* which also involved the applicability of § 326.5 of the California Penal Code to Indian reservations, the Court of Appeals rejected this submission. In *Barona,* applying what it thought to be the civil/criminal dichotomy drawn in *Bryan v. Itasca County,* the Court of Appeals drew a distinction between state "criminal/prohibitory" laws and state "civil/regulatory" laws: if the intent of a state law is generally to prohibit certain conduct, it falls within Pub. L. 280's grant of criminal jurisdiction, but if the state law generally permits the conduct at issue, subject to regulation, it must be classified as civil/regulatory and Pub. L. 280 does not authorize its enforcement on an Indian reservation. The shorthand test is whether the conduct at issue violates the State's public policy. Inquiring into the nature of § 326.5, the Court of Appeals held that it was regulatory rather than prohibitory. This was the analysis employed, with similar results, by the Court of Appeals for the Fifth Circuit in *Seminole Tribe of Florida v. Butterworth,* which the Ninth Circuit found persuasive.

We are persuaded that the prohibitory/regulatory distinction is consistent with *Bryan*'s construction of Pub. L. 280. It is not a bright-line rule, however; and as the Ninth Circuit itself observed, an argument of some weight may be made that the bingo statute is prohibitory rather than regulatory. But in the present case, the court reexamined the state law and reaffirmed its holding in *Barona,* and we are reluctant to disagree with that court's view of the nature and intent of the state law at issue here.

There is surely a fair basis for its conclusion. California does not prohibit all forms of gambling. California itself operates a state lottery, and daily encourages its citizens to participate in this state-run gambling. California also permits parimutuel horse-race betting. Although certain enumerated gambling games are prohibited under the state's penal code, games not enumerated, including the card games played in the Cabazon card club, are permissible. The Tribes assert that more than 400 card rooms similar to the Cabazon card club flourish in California, and the State does not dispute this fact. Also, as the Court of Appeals noted, bingo is legally sponsored by many different organizations and is widely played in California. There is no effort to forbid the playing of bingo by any member of the public over the age of 18. Indeed, the permitted bingo games *must* be open to the general public. Nor is there any limit on the number of games which eligible organizations may operate, the receipts which they may obtain from the games, the number of games which a participant may play, or the amount of money which a participant may spend, either per game or in total. In light of the fact that California permits a substantial amount of gambling activity, including bingo, and actually promotes gambling through its state lottery, we must conclude that California regulates rather than prohibits gambling in general and bingo in particular.

California argues, however, that high stakes, *unregulated* bingo, the conduct which attracts organized crime, is a misdemeanor in California and may be prohibited on Indian reservations. But that an otherwise regulatory law is enforceable by criminal as well as civil means does not necessarily convert it into a criminal law within the meaning of Pub. L. 280. Otherwise, the distinction between [the grant of criminal jurisdiction] and [the grant of civil jurisdiction] of that law could easily be avoided and total assimilation permitted. This view, adopted here and by the Fifth Circuit in the *Butterworth* case, we find persuasive. Accordingly, we conclude that Pub. L. 280 does not authorize California to enforce Cal. Penal Code § 326.5 within the Cabazon and Morongo Reservations.

California and Riverside County also argue that the Organized Crime Control Act (OCCA) authorizes the application of their gambling laws to the tribal bingo enterprises. The OCCA makes certain violations of state and local gambling laws violations of federal law. [Specifically, 18 U.S.C. § 1955 provides that "[w]hoever conducts, finances, manages, supervises, directs, or owns all or part of an illegal gambling business shall be fined not more that $20,000 or imprisoned not more than five years, or both," and defines "illegal gambling business" as one that violates the law of the state in which it is conducted.]

Since the OCCA standard is simply whether the gambling business is being operated in "violation of the law of a State," there is no basis for the regulatory/prohibitory distinction that it agreed is suitable in construing and applying Pub. L. 280. And because enforcement of OCCA is an exercise of federal rather than state authority, there is no danger of state encroachment on Indian tribal sovereignty. This latter observation exposes the flaw in appellants' reliance on OCCA. That enactment is indeed a federal law that, among other things, defines certain federal crimes over which the district courts have exclusive jurisdiction [under 18 U.S.C. § 3231, which provides: "The district courts of the United States shall have original jurisdiction, exclusive of the courts of the States, of all offenses against the laws of the United States."] There is nothing in OCCA indicating that the States are to have any part in enforcing federal criminal laws or are authorized to make arrests on Indian reservations that in the absence of OCCA they could not effect. We are not informed of any federal efforts to employ OCCA to prosecute the playing of bingo on Indian reservations, although there are more than 100 such enterprises currently in operation, many of which have been in existence for several years, for the most part with the encouragement of the Federal Government. There is no warrant for California to make arrests on reservations and thus, through OCCA, enforce its gambling laws against Indian tribes.

II

Because the state and county laws at issue here are imposed directly on the Tribes that operate the games, and are not expressly permitted by Congress, the Tribes argue that the judgment below should be affirmed without more. They rely on the statement in *McClanahan v. Arizona State Tax Comm'n*, 411 U.S. 164 (1973), that "[s]tate laws generally are not applicable to tribal Indians on an Indian reservation except where Congress has expressly provided that State laws shall apply." Our cases, however, have not established an inflexible *per se* rule precluding state jurisdiction over tribes and tribal members in the absence of express congressional consent. "[U]nder certain circumstances a State may validly assert authority over the activities of nonmembers on a reservation, and ... in exceptional circumstances a State may assert jurisdiction over the on-reservation activities of tribal members." *New Mexico v. Mescalero Apache Tribe*, 462 U.S. 324 (1983). Both *Moe v. Confederated Salish and Kootenai Tribes*, 425 U.S. 463 (1976), and *Washington v. Confederated Tribes of Colville Indian Reservation*, 447 U.S. 134 (1980), are illustrative. In those decisions we held that, in the absence of express congressional permission, a State could require tribal smokeshops on Indian reservations to collect state sales tax from their non-Indian customers. Both cases involved nonmembers entering and purchasing tobacco products on the reservations involved. The State's interest in assuring the collection of sales taxes from non-Indians enjoying the off-reservation services of the State was sufficient to warrant the minimal burden imposed on the tribal smokeshop operators.

This case also involves a state burden on tribal Indians in the context of their dealings with non-Indians since the question is whether the State may prevent the Tribes from making available high stakes bingo games to non-Indians coming from outside the reservations. Decision in this case turns on whether state authority is pre-empted by the operation of federal law; and "[s]tate jurisdiction is pre-empted ... if it interferes or is incompatible with federal and tribal interests reflected in federal law, unless the state interests at stake are sufficient to justify the assertion of state authority." *Mescalero*. The inquiry is to proceed in light of traditional notions of Indian sovereignty and the congressional goal of Indian self-government, including its "overriding goal" of encouraging tribal self-sufficiency and economic development.

These are important federal interests. They were reaffirmed by the President's 1983 Statement on Indian Policy: ["It is important to the concept of self-government that tribes reduce their dependence on Federal funds by providing a greater percentage of the cost of their self-government."] More specifically, the Department of the Interior, which has the primary responsibility for carrying out the Federal Government's trust obligations to Indian tribes, has sought to implement these policies by promoting tribal bingo enterprises. Under the Indian Financing Act of 1974, the Secretary of the Interior has made grants and has guaranteed loans for the purpose of constructing bingo facilities. The Department of Housing and Urban Development and the Department of Health and Human Services have also provided financial assistance to develop tribal gaming enterprises. Here, the Secretary of the Interior has approved tribal ordinances establishing and regulating the gaming activities involved. The Secretary has also exercised his authority to review tribal bingo management contracts under 25 U.S.C. § 81, and has issued detailed guidelines governing that review.

These policies and actions, which demonstrate the Government's approval and active promotion of tribal bingo enterprises, are of particular relevance in this case. The Cabazon and Morongo Reservations contain no natural resources which can be exploited. The tribal games at present provide the sole source of revenues for the operation of the tribal governments and the provision of tribal services. They are also the major sources of employment on the reservations. Self-determination and economic development are not within reach if the Tribes cannot raise revenues and provide employment for their members. The Tribes' interests obviously parallel the federal interests.

California seeks to diminish the weight of these seemingly important tribal interests by asserting that the Tribes are merely marketing an exemption from state gambling laws. In *Washington v. Confederated Tribes of Colville Indian Reservation,* we held that the State could tax cigarettes sold by tribal smokeshops to non-Indians, even though it would eliminate their competitive advantage and substantially reduce revenues used to provide tribal services, because the Tribes had no right "to market an exemption from state taxation to persons who would normally do their business elsewhere." We stated that "[i]t is painfully apparent that the value marketed by the smokeshops to persons coming from outside is not generated on the reservations by activities in which the Tribes have a significant interest." Here, however, the Tribes are not merely importing a product onto the reservations for immediate resale to non-Indians. They have built modern facilities which provide recreational opportunities and ancillary services to their patrons, who do not simply drive onto the reservations, make purchases and depart, but spend extended periods of time there enjoying the services the Tribes provide. The Tribes have a strong incentive to provide comfortable, clean, and attractive facilities and well-run games in order to increase attendance at the games. The tribal bingo enterprises are similar to the resort complex, featuring hunting and fishing, that the Mescalero Apache Tribe operates on its reservation through the "concerted and sustained" management of reservation land and wildlife resources. *Mescalero.* The Mescalero project generates funds for essential tribal services and provides employment for tribal members. We there rejected the notion that the Tribe is merely marketing an exemption from state hunting and fishing regulations and concluded that New Mexico could not regulate on-reservation fishing and hunting by non-Indians. Similarly, the Cabazon and Morongo Bands are generating value on the reservations through activities in which they have a substantial interest.

The State also relies on *Rice v. Rehner,* 463 U.S. 713 (1983), in which we held that California could require a tribal member and a federally licensed Indian trader operating a general store on a reservation to obtain a state license in order to sell liquor for off-premises consumption. But our decision there rested on the grounds that Congress had never recognized any sovereign tribal interest in regulating liquor traffic and that Congress, historically, had plainly anticipated that the States would exercise concurrent authority to regulate the use and distribution of liquor on Indian reservations. There is no such traditional federal view governing the outcome of this case, since, as we have explained, the current federal policy is to promote precisely what California seeks to prevent.

The sole interest asserted by the State to justify the imposition of its bingo laws on the Tribes is in preventing the infiltration of the tribal games by organized crime. To the extent that the State seeks to prevent any and all bingo games from being played on tribal lands while permitting regulated, off-reservation games, this asserted interest is irrelevant and the state and county laws are pre-empted. Even to the extent that the State and county seek to regulate short of prohibition, the laws are pre-empted. The State insists that the high stakes offered at tribal games are attractive to organized crime, whereas the controlled games authorized under California law are not. This is surely a legitimate concern, but we are unconvinced that it is sufficient to escape the pre-emptive force of federal and tribal interests apparent in this case. California does not allege any present criminal involvement in the Cabazon and Morongo enterprises, and the Ninth Circuit discerned none. An official of the Department of Justice has expressed some concern about tribal bingo operations, but far from any action being taken evidencing this concern—and surely the Federal Government has the authority to forbid Indian gambling enterprises— the prevailing federal policy continues to support these tribal enterprises, including those of the Tribes involved in this case.

We conclude that the State's interest in preventing the infiltration of the tribal bingo enterprises by organized crime does not justify state regulation of the tribal bingo enterprises in light of the compelling federal and tribal interests supporting them. State regulation would impermissibly infringe on tribal government, and this conclusion applies equally to the county's attempted regulation of the Cabazon card club. We therefore affirm the judgment of the Court of Appeals and remand the case for further proceedings consistent with this opinion.

Justice STEVENS, with whom Justice O'CONNOR and Justice SCALIA join, dissenting.

Unless and until Congress exempts Indian-managed gambling from state law and subjects it to federal supervision, I believe that a State may enforce its laws prohibiting high-stakes gambling on Indian reservations within its borders. Congress has not pre-empted California's prohibition against high-stakes bingo games and the Secretary of the Interior plainly has no authority to do so. While gambling provides needed employment and income for Indian tribes, these benefits do not, in my opinion, justify tribal operation of currently unlawful commercial activities. Accepting the majority's reasoning would require exemptions for cockfighting, tattoo parlors, nude dancing, houses of prostitution, and other illegal but profitable enterprises. As the law now stands, I believe tribal entrepreneurs, like others who might derive profits from catering to non-Indian customers, must obey applicable state laws.

In my opinion the plain language of Pub. L. 280 authorizes California to enforce its prohibition against commercial gambling on Indian reservations. The State prohibits bingo games that are not operated by members of designated charitable organizations or which offer prizes in excess of $250 per game. In Pub. L. 280, Congress expressly provided that the criminal laws of the State of California "shall have the same force and effect within such Indian country as they have elsewhere within the State." Moreover, it provided that the civil laws of California "that are of general application to private persons or private property shall have the same force and effect within such Indian country as they have elsewhere within the State."

It is true that in *Bryan v. Itasca County,* we held that Pub. L. 280 did not confer civil jurisdiction on a State to impose a personal property tax on a mobile home that was owned by a reservation Indian and located within the reservation. Moreover, the reasoning of that decision recognizes the importance of preserving the traditional aspects of tribal sovereignty over the relationships among reservation Indians. Our more recent cases have made it clear, however, that commercial transactions between Indians and non-Indians—even when conducted on a reservation—do not enjoy any blanket immunity from state regulation. In *Rice v. Rehner,* respondent, a federally licensed Indian trader, was a tribal member operating a general store on an Indian reservation. We held that the State could require Rehner to obtain a state license to sell liquor for off-premises consumption. The Court attempts to distinguish *Rice v. Rehner* as resting on the absence of a sovereign tribal interest in the regulation of liquor traffic to the exclusion of the

States. But as a necessary step on our way to deciding that the State could regulate all tribal liquor sales in Indian country, we recognized the State's authority over transactions, whether they be liquor sales or gambling, between Indians and non-Indians: "If there is any interest in tribal sovereignty implicated by imposition of California's alcoholic beverage regulation, it exists only insofar as the State attempts to regulate Rehner's sale of liquor to other members of the Pala Tribe on the Pala Reservation." Similarly, in *Washington v. Confederated Tribes of Colville Indian Reservation,* we held that a State could impose its sales and cigarette taxes on non-Indian customers of smokeshops on Indian reservations.

Today the Court seems prepared to acknowledge that an Indian tribe's commercial transactions with non-Indians may violate "the State's public policy." The Court reasons, however, that the operation of high-stakes bingo games does not run afoul of California's public policy because the State permits some forms of gambling and, specifically, some forms of bingo. I find this approach to "public policy" curious, to say the least. The State's policy concerning gambling is to authorize certain specific gambling activities that comply with carefully defined regulation and that provide revenues either for the State itself or for certain charitable purposes, and to prohibit all unregulated commercial lotteries that are operated for private profit. To argue that the tribal bingo games comply with the public policy of California because the State permits some other gambling is tantamount to arguing that driving over 60 miles an hour is consistent with public policy because the State allows driving at speeds of up to 55 miles an hour.

In my view, Congress has permitted the State to apply its prohibitions against commercial gambling to Indian tribes. Even if Congress had not done so, however, the State has the authority to assert jurisdiction over appellees' gambling activities. In *Washington v. Confederated Tribes,* the tribal smokeshops offered their customers the same products, services, and facilities that other tobacconists offered to their customers. Although the smokeshops were more modest than the bingo palaces involved in this case, presumably they were equally the product of tribal labor and tribal capital. What made them successful, however, was the value of the exemption that was offered to non-Indians "who would normally do their business elsewhere." [As we concluded,] "What the smokeshops offer these customers, and what is not available elsewhere, is solely an exemption from state taxation."

Similarly, it is painfully obvious that the value of the Tribe's asserted exemption from California's gambling laws is the primary attraction to customers who would normally do their gambling elsewhere. The Cabazon Band of Mission Indians has no tradition or special expertise in the operation of large bingo parlors. Indeed, the entire membership of the Cabazon Tribe—it has only 25 enrolled members—is barely adequate to operate a bingo game that is patronized by hundreds of non-Indians nightly. How this small and formerly impoverished Band of Indians could have attracted the investment capital for its enterprise without benefit of the claimed exemption is certainly a mystery to me.

I am entirely unpersuaded by the Court's view that the State of California has no legitimate interest in requiring appellees' gambling business to comply with the same standards that the operators of other bingo games must observe. The State's interest is both economic and protective. Presumably the State has determined that its interest in generating revenues for the public fisc and for certain charities outweighs the benefits from a total prohibition against publicly sponsored games of chance. Whatever revenues the Tribes receive from their unregulated bingo games drain funds from the state-approved recipients of lottery revenues—just as the tax-free cigarette sales in the *Confederated Tribes* case diminished the receipts that the tax collector would otherwise have received.

Moreover, I am unwilling to dismiss as readily as the Court does the State's concern that these unregulated high-stakes bingo games may attract organized criminal infiltration. Comprehensive regulation of the commercial gambling ventures that a State elects to license is obviously justified as a prophylactic measure even if there is presently no criminal activity associated with casino gambling in the State. Indeed, California regulates charitable bingo, horseracing, and its own lottery. The State of California requires that charitable bingo games may only be operated and staffed by members of designated charitable organizations, and that proceeds from the games may only be used for charitable purposes. These requirements for staffing and for dispersal of profits provide bulwarks against criminal activity; neither safeguard exists for bingo games on Indian reservations. In my judgment, unless Congress authorizes and regulates these commercial gambling ventures catering to non-Indians, the State has a legitimate law enforcement interest in proscribing them.

Appellants and the Secretary of the Interior may well be correct, in the abstract, that gambling facilities are a sensible way to generate revenues that are badly needed by reservation Indians. But the decision to adopt, to reject, or to define the precise contours of such a course of action, and thereby to set aside the substantial public policy concerns of a sovereign State, should be made by the Congress of the United States. It should not be made by this Court, by the temporary occupant of the Office of the Secretary of the Interior, or by non-Indian entrepreneurs who are experts in gambling management but not necessarily dedicated to serving the future well-being of Indian tribes.

Notes and Questions

1. *State authority.* Of particular importance to the holding in *Cabazon* was the Court's analysis of state jurisdiction under Pub. L. 280. As a "mandatory" Pub. L. 280 state, California had a relatively strong argument for state regulation of tribal gaming enterprises—at least a stronger argument than had "voluntary" states, such as Florida, and non-Pub. L. 280 states.

2. *Revisiting the civil/regulatory-criminal/prohibitory dichotomy.* As it did in *Barona Group*, California argued that Pub. L. 280 authorized the application of state and local law on the tribes' reservations. In *Bryan v. Itasca County*, the Supreme Court ruled that Pub. L. 280's grant of civil jurisdiction was not a broad authority for the states to regulate the tribes generally; instead, Pub. L. 280's grant of civil jurisdiction related only to private civil litigation in state court. The Court's interpretation of Pub. L. 280 was based on its reading of congressional intent not to grant states broad regulatory authority over tribes, as that "would result in the destruction of tribal institutions and values." Thus, if California's laws were criminal prohibitions against gambling, then the state would have authority to enforce them against the tribe under Pub. L. 280. But if California's gambling laws were civil regulatory laws, then the state would *not* have authority to enforce them against the tribe under Pub. L. 280.

In determining whether state law was civil/regulatory or criminal/prohibitory, the Supreme Court adopted the approach of the Ninth Circuit in *Barona v. Duffy*:

> [A court should draw] a distinction between state "criminal/prohibitory" laws and state "civil/regulatory" laws: if the intent of a state law is generally to prohibit certain conduct, it falls within Pub. L. 280's grant of criminal jurisdiction, but if the state law generally permits the conduct at issue, subject to regulation, it must be classified as civil/regulatory and Pub. L. 280 does not authorize its

enforcement on an Indian reservation. The shorthand test is whether the conduct at issue violates the State's public policy.

Cabazon, at 209.

The question is more involved than whether the state law provides for criminal penalties. Under California law, violation of its gambling regulations is a criminal misdemeanor. The Court explained, "But that an otherwise regulatory law is enforceable by criminal as well as civil means does not necessarily convert it into a criminal law within the meaning of Pub. L. 280." *Cabazon*, at 211. California operated a state lottery and permitted pari-mutuel horse-race betting, bingo, and card games. As the Court concluded, "In light of the fact that California permits a substantial amount of gambling activity, including bingo, and actually promotes gambling through its state lottery, we must conclude that California regulates rather than prohibits gambling in general and bingo in particular." *Id.* at 210–11. In a footnote, the Court further elaborated, "Nothing in this opinion suggests that cockfighting, tattoo parlors, nude dancing, and prostitution are permissible on Indian reservations within California. The applicable state laws governing an activity must be examined in detail before they can be characterized as regulatory or prohibitory. The lower courts have not demonstrated an inability to identify prohibitory laws." *Id.* at 211 n.10.

In light of *Cabazon*, how would you articulate the civil/regulatory-criminal/prohibitory test? What facts are relevant to the distinction? Should the court examine the entire body of state law governing gambling, or just the state law applicable to the particular game at issue?

    3.   Local government authority. Recall that Riverside County argued that its local ordinances applied on the tribes' reservations as well. The Court found even less basis for the application of local laws under Pub. L. 280:

> Nor does Pub. L. 280 authorize the county to apply its gambling ordinances to the reservations. We note initially that it is doubtful that Pub. L. 280 authorizes the application of any local laws to Indian reservations. Pub. L. 280 provides that the criminal laws of the "State" shall have the same force and effect within Indian country as they have elsewhere. This language seems clearly to exclude local laws. We need not decide this issue, however, because even if Pub. L. 280 does make local criminal/prohibitory laws applicable on Indian reservations, the ordinances in question here do not apply. Consistent with our analysis of Cal. Penal Code § 326.5 above, we conclude that Ordinance No. 558, the bingo ordinance, is regulatory in nature. Although Ordinance No. 331 prohibits gambling on all card games, including the games played in the Cabazon card club, the county does not prohibit municipalities within the county from enacting municipal ordinances permitting these card games, and two municipalities have in fact done so. It is clear, therefore, that Ordinance No. 331 does not prohibit these card games for purposes of Pub. L. 280.

Cabazon, at 212 n.11.

Consider the Court's conclusion that Ordinance No. 331 fell within the civil/regulatory category. Why didn't the County's prohibition on gambling on card games evidence a public policy against gambling on card games? Does the Court's reasoning on this point add anything to your understanding of the civil/regulatory-criminal/prohibitory dichotomy?

    4.   Tribal sovereignty. Although the Court relied heavily on Pub. L. 280's civil/regulatory-criminal/prohibitory distinction, the legal doctrine of tribal sovereignty also came into play. How and why? In which portions of the Court's opinion did tribal sovereignty and the authority of tribal governments seem most relevant? Recall the readings in Chapter 1. How does the Court's opinion reflect the tenets of federal Indian law?

5.   *Federal preemption.* Review the Court's analysis of "exceptional circumstances" which may warrant state jurisdiction. In *Washington v. Confederated Tribes of Colville Indian Reservation*, 447 U.S. 134, 155 (1980), the Supreme Court held that the state's interest in collecting taxes from cigarette sales to non-Indians was sufficient to warrant application of state law in the absence of express congressional authorization because there was not a "significant" tribal interest at stake. The tribes were simply marketing "an exemption from state taxation to persons who would normally do their business elsewhere." As both are economic enterprises, what distinguishes the Cabazon and Morongo Bands' bingo enterprises from tribal smokeshops? Is an "exemption from state taxation" different than an "exemption" from other state regulation, such as limits on high-stakes gaming?

6.   *Pub. L. 280 and assimilation.* The Court stated that Pub. L. 280 "plainly was not intended to effect total assimilation of Indian tribes into mainstream American society." Termination policy, however, was assimilationist in intent, and Pub. L. 280 was a product of the Termination Era, as discussed in the Goldberg excerpt at the start of this Chapter. Is the Court's interpretation of Pub. L. 280 true to Congress's intent, or was the Court's interpretation driven by the shift in federal Indian policy to self-determination?

7.   *State law and the OCCA.* As the Court explained, the federal Organized Crime Control Act (OCCA) incorporated state law by defining an illegal gambling operation as one that violates state law. Why did the state's argument that OCCA authorized the application of their gambling laws to the tribal bingo enterprises fail?

8.   ***Indian gaming and tribal economic development.*** The Court characterized federal Indian policy as encouraging tribal self-sufficiency and economic development. It noted congressional statements of policy in two statutes. In the Indian Financing Act of 1974, Congress declared its policy to be to "help develop and utilize Indian resources, both physical and human, to a point where the Indians will fully exercise responsibility for the utilization and management of their own resources and ... enjoy a standard of living from their own productive efforts comparable to that enjoyed by non-Indians in neighboring communities." 25 U.S.C. § 1451. In the Indian Self-Determination and Education Assistance Act of 1975, Congress declared

> its commitment to the maintenance of the Federal Government's unique and continuing relationship with and responsibility to the Indian people through the establishment of a meaningful Indian self-determination policy which will permit an orderly transition from Federal domination of programs for and services to Indians to effective and meaningful participation by the Indian people in the planning, conduct, and administration of those programs and services.

25 U.S.C. § 450a(b).

The Court also noted the U.S. Department of Interior's position on tribal gaming enterprises as supported by current federal Indian policy:

> A policy directive issued by the Assistant Secretary of the Interior on March 2, 1983, stated that the Department would "strongly oppose" any proposed legislation that would subject tribes or tribal members to state gambling regulation. "Such a proposal is inconsistent with the President's Indian Policy Statement of January 24, 1983 [quoted in the Court's opinion].... A number of tribes have begun

to engage in bingo and similar gambling operations on their reservations for the very purpose enunciated in the President's Message. Given the often limited resources which tribes have for revenue-producing activities, it is believed that this kind of revenue-producing possibility should be protected and enhanced." According to an affidavit submitted by the Director of Indian Services, Bureau of Indian Affairs, on behalf of the Tribes' position: "It is the department's position that tribal bingo enterprises are an appropriate means by which tribes can further their economic self-sufficiency, the economic development of reservations and tribal self-determination. All of these are federal goals for the tribes. Furthermore, it is the Department's position that the development of tribal bingo enterprises is consistent with and in furtherance of President Reagan's Indian Policy Statement of January 24, 1983."

Cabazon, at 218 n.21.

The federal government's "overriding goal" of encouraging tribal self-sufficiency and economic development mirrored the goals of the Cabazon and Morongo Bands in conducting gaming. As the Court stated, "Self-determination and economic development are not within reach if the Tribes cannot raise revenues and provide employment for their members. The Tribes' interests obviously parallel the federal interests." How important was federal Indian policy to the Court's analysis? Tribal policy?

9.   *State interests.* In weighing the state's interest in regulating the tribes' gaming enterprises, the Court stated, "The sole interest asserted by the State to justify the imposition of its bingo laws on the Tribes is in preventing the infiltration of the tribal games by organized crime." What other state interests existed in this case? Would a stronger state interest have produced a different outcome?

10.   *State public policy.* In his dissent, Justice Stevens argued that a state may have a public policy against gambling generally, even while allowing some types or forms of games: "To argue that the tribal bingo games comply with the public policy of California because the State permits some other gambling is tantamount to arguing that driving over 60 miles an hour is consistent with public policy because the State allows driving at speeds of up to 55 miles an hour." Does this analogy hold water? How is public policy different than the detailed specifications of state law? In other words, what level of specificity is appropriate in identifying a state's public policy? Did California's public policy permit bingo? Permit charitable bingo? Permit charitable bingo with pot limits? What about the specific game at issue? If California law permitted bingo, card games, pari-mutuel betting, and a state lottery, does that reflect a different public policy than a state that permits commercial casinos? Than a state that permits only charitable bingo? Than a state that permits charitable bingo, pari-mutuel betting, and a state lottery, but not card games? How and why?

11.   *From bingo to prostitution?* Justice Stevens also argued that accepting the majority's rationale in this case would lead down the slippery slope to allowing other, presumably even less palatable, illegal commercial transactions, such as "cockfighting, tattoo parlors, nude dancing, [and] houses of prostitution" to take place without criminal penalty on Indian reservations. Is this conclusion mere legal rhetoric, or a real possibility?

12.   *Tribes' use of gaming revenue.* The Court stated that the tribes' gaming operations were their "sole source of income." At the time, the Cabazon Band had 25 enrolled members and the Morongo Band had approximately 730 enrolled members. To what degree did the tribes' specific economic circumstances and needs influence the Court's reasoning? The Court also noted that each tribe limited its use of gaming revenues.

The Cabazon ordinance authorizes the Band to sponsor bingo games within the reservation "[i]n order to promote economic development of the Cabazon Indian Reservation and to generate tribal revenues" and provides that net revenues from the games shall be kept in a separate fund to be used "for the purpose of promoting the health, education, welfare and well being of the Cabazon Indian Reservation and for other tribal purposes."…. The Morongo ordinance similarly authorizes the establishment of a tribal bingo enterprise and dedicates revenues to programs to promote the health, education, and general welfare of tribal members.

Cabazon, at 206 n.2. Were the tribes' uses of gaming revenue important to the Court's decision? Why or why not?

Problem 2: Applying *Cabazon*

Suppose that following the Court's decision in *Cabazon*, the Cabazon Band added a room of slot machines to its bingo hall. At the time, California's constitution prohibited the state legislature from authorizing "casinos of the type operating in Las Vegas." Could California close down the Band's slot room? Explain your answer, referencing the *Cabazon* Court's reasoning.

Part II

The Federal Regulatory Scheme

IGRA provides that tribes have the right to regulate gaming activity if that activity is not prohibited by federal law or against state public policy. This latter requirement is a codification of *Cabazon*'s recognition of tribal sovereignty as giving rise to tribes' right to conduct gaming, so that state law generally does not apply, and its "shorthand test" of state public policy as determining whether state law is criminal/prohibitory and thus enforceable on tribal lands. Note, though, that IGRA extends the state public policy limitation of *Cabazon* to *all* tribes, regardless of whether they are located in a Pub. L. 280 state.

Stated simply, IGRA allocates jurisdictional responsibility for regulating Indian gaming according to the type of gaming involved. In so doing, IGRA establishes three classes of gaming:

Class I gaming. Class I gaming includes social games associated with traditional Native American ceremonies. Class I gaming is subject to exclusive tribal jurisdiction on tribal lands. IGRA's provisions do not apply to Class I gaming.

Class II gaming. Class II gaming includes bingo and its variants, as well as non-house-banked card games, such as poker, that meet certain state provisions. Class II gaming specifically excludes house-banked card games, slot machines, and other electronic facsimiles of games of chance. Class II gaming is allowed on tribal lands in states that permit such gaming for any purpose by any person, *Cabazon*'s "shorthand test" of state public policy. Tribes may regulate Class II gaming with oversight by the National Indian Gaming Commission (NIGC), an independent federal regulatory agency in the Department of Interior created by Congress through IGRA. Other than the initial question of state public policy, there is no role for state regulation of Class II gaming.

Class III gaming. Class III gaming is a residual category, including all other types of gaming not included in Class I or Class II. The "catch-all" nature of Class III gaming heightens the stakes of the definition of Class II gaming, as any game that does not qualify as Class II will fall within Class III. Class III games, typically high-stakes, include slot machines, house-banked card games, pari-mutuel betting, roulette, jai alai, and other casino games. Unlike Class I or Class II, Class III gaming creates a regulatory role for the states through the tribal-state compact requirement, the centerpiece of Class III regulation.

Chapter 3

The Indian Gaming Regulatory Act of 1988

A. Overview

In the U.S. political system, the Supreme Court plays an important role not only in interpreting the law, but in mobilizing various interests and organizations and catalyzing direct legal and policy responses to its decisions in the coordinate political branches. This clearly was the case in the aftermath of *California v. Cabazon Band of Mission Indians*. The Court's opinion circumscribed state authority over tribal gaming and opened the field to industry expansion, generating concerns among federal and state actors as well as commercial casino interests.

Congress, which had been closely monitoring the progress of the *Cabazon* case, promptly took up the question of how best to craft a statutory framework to govern Indian gaming that would satisfy widely disparate interests. Although taking state and commercial interests into account, Congress also sought to comport with the tenets of tribal sovereignty and further the goals of contemporary federal Indian policy.

In this Chapter, we focus on IGRA's legislative history, and also provide an overview of the regulatory framework that will be examined in detail in Chapters 4 and 5. As you consider IGRA's legislative history and regulatory framework, pay special attention to the various legal, political, and policy compromises undergirding this landmark legislation.

B. Legislative History

Steven Andrew Light & Kathryn R.L. Rand
Indian Gaming and Tribal Sovereignty: The Casino Compromise
42–44 (2005)

As the Supreme Court considered *Cabazon*, states and tribes lobbied Congress to pass legislation governing Indian gaming. The growth in Indian gaming during the 1980s and the accompanying tensions between state power and tribal sovereignty attracted Congress' attention as early as 1985, when it held hearings on tribal gaming. At that time, the Department of the Interior estimated that about 80 tribes were conducting gaming on their reservations. Some of the tribal high-stakes bingo halls grossed nearly $1 million each month. Many tribes owned and operated their gaming establishments, while others had contracted with outside management companies and a few were owned and operated by individual tribal members.

The states wanted Congress to exercise its power to limit tribal sovereignty by authorizing state regulation of tribal gaming operations, citing the state interest in preventing the infiltration of organized crime into Indian gaming. Nevada was particularly concerned that any incidence of organized crime at a tribal casino would trigger a federal crackdown on state-licensed gaming as well. The states also asserted economic interests, asking Congress to abolish the tribal "exemption" from state regulation to place tribes on a level playing field with private and charitable gaming operations. The states further argued for federal law allowing states to tax Indian gaming operations.

The tribes opposed state regulation, and lobbied for exclusive tribal regulation. The tribes' position was grounded in preservation of tribal sovereignty generally, as well as protection of Indian gaming as an economic development strategy for tribal governments. The success of some tribal bingo operations cast gaming as one of the very few viable avenues for reservation economic development and job creation. In Florida, for example, the Seminole Tribe's bingo hall had slashed reservation unemployment from 60 percent to less than 20 percent, and improvements in the quality of life on the reservation were apparent in upgraded housing and increased high school graduation rates. Anticipating that Congress would insist on some form of regulation of Indian gaming, however, tribes supported federal regulation over state regulation.

Initially, federal legislative efforts concerning Indian gaming focused on preserving it in the face of an anticipated decision against the tribes in *Cabazon*. Early versions of a tribal gaming bill sought to maintain Indian gaming as a means of tribal economic development by preempting state regulation. The tribes' unexpected victory in *Cabazon*, however, "threw the ball into Congress's lap to do something, fast." The Court's holding catalyzed Indian gaming opponents, who vociferously lobbied for state regulation. According to U.S. Senator Harry Reid (D-Nev.), after the Court decided *Cabazon*, "there was little choice except for Congress to enact laws regulating gaming on Indian lands. The alternative would have been for the rapid and uncontrolled expansion of unregulated casino-type gambling on Indian lands." As Reid saw it, a political compromise was necessary to bridge the gap between the state and tribal positions, as well as to ensure that gaming was available to tribal governments as a means of generating revenue in accord with federal interests in tribal self-sufficiency and economic development.

Reid, along with Senator Daniel Inoyue (D-Haw.) and Representative Morris Udall (D-Ariz.), then-chairs of the Senate Indian Affairs Committee and the House Interior Committee respectively, began work on a bill to regulate Indian gaming. One of the key innovations of the bill was to categorize types of gambling and to assign regulatory authority accordingly. Traditional tribal games of chance were left to exclusive tribal jurisdiction. With almost a decade of tribal experience and relatively few problems, bingo would continue to be regulated by the tribes, with some federal oversight.

Casino-style gambling, however, was seen as potentially a greater regulatory problem than bingo. As a "cash business," many believed that casino gaming necessarily attracted crime, whether organized or unorganized. As one commentator noted, "The problem was not that it was Indian gambling, but that it was gambling, period." The states' interests in preventing the infiltration of organized crime and controlling gambling generally appeared most persuasive in the context of casino-style gaming. As Reid told it, "[t]here was no intention of diminishing the significance of the *Cabazon* decision," but the Supreme

Court's reasoning, in the eyes of the bill's drafters, was tied to the bingo and poker games at issue in the case, rather than to casino gambling.

To balance competing state and tribal interests in casino gambling, Congress conceived of "tribal-state compacts," in which a state and tribe would negotiate the regulatory structure for casino-style gaming on the tribe's reservation. Reid credits the compact provision amendment in the Senate with breaking the "logjam" of competing interests holding up the federal legislation: "[the bill] provided protection to the states without violating either the *Cabazon* decision or the concept of Indian sovereignty." Yet the tribal-state compact provision was not limited to states with greater authority over tribes under Public Law 280, but applied in all states—thus expanding state power over tribes and diminishing tribal sovereignty.

The Indian Gaming Regulatory Act (IGRA) was enacted on October 17, 1988. It first passed the Senate, and then was moved through the House without referral to committee or amendment in hopes of a quick passage. In the end, IGRA significantly changed the law of Indian gaming after *Cabazon* through Congress' attempt to balance the competing interests of the federal government, the tribes, the states, and non-Native gaming operators.

Roland J. Santoni
The Indian Gaming Regulatory Act:
How Did We Get Here? Where Are We Going?
26 Creighton L. Rev. 387 (1993)

During the period from 1983–1988, numerous bills were introduced in Congress to address the issues presented by increased gaming in Indian country. Tracing the fate of these bills and the emergence of the IGRA provides valuable insight into the alternatives discussed and the ultimate compromise that was reached.

On November 18, 1983, Representative Morris Udall, D-Ariz., introduced H.R. 4566. This bill provided that if gambling activity was not specifically prohibited within Indian country by federal law, or within a state by state public policy as a matter of criminal law, gambling activity within Indian country would be regulated only by the Secretary of the Interior ("Secretary"). The bill authorized the Secretary to approve or disapprove tribal gaming ordinances. Tribal licensing requirements and other tribal gambling regulations were to be at least as restrictive as the state laws governing similar gambling. H.R. 4566 was not intended to change existing law with respect to the rights of tribes to engage in gambling activities; it merely was to establish minimum federal standards. In H.R. 4566, Congress appeared to codify the decisions in *Oneida* and *Butterworth*, while imposing limited federal regulation.

Hearings on H.R. 4566 were held in June, 1984, and significant dissatisfaction was expressed. The United States Department of Justice did not think that the Secretary of the Interior could provide the supervision necessary to prevent organized crime from infiltrating Indian gaming, nor did it think that Indian tribes would be effective regulators. The National Tribal Chairmen's Association opposed H.R. 4566, arguing that tribes already possessed the powers that H.R. 4566 granted, and that federal regulation of tribal gambling was unnecessary. As a result of this dissatisfaction, no vote was taken on H.R. 4566.

On April 2, 1985, Representative Udall introduced H.R. 1920 ("Indian Gambling Control Act"), which was similar to H.R. 4566. On May 7, 1985, Representative Norman Shumway, R-Cal., introduced H.R. 2404 ("Indian Country Gambling Regulation Act").

Both bills were submitted to the House Committee on Interior and Insular Affairs, and hearings were held in November of 1985. H.R. 2404, like H.R. 1920, authorized the Secretary of the Interior to approve tribal ordinances with respect to gaming on Indian lands. However, under H.R. 2404, before the Secretary could approve a tribal ordinance, he had to determine that the specific *form* of gambling and the *manner* and *extent* of the gambling authorized by the ordinance did not violate the public policy of a state. Before making his determination, the Secretary had to consult with the governor of the state and request comments on the state's public policy with respect to gambling. The bill also provided that if a state, a political subdivision, or a nonprofit charitable organization operated a gambling activity, such activity would not be against the public policy of the state and could be conducted by a tribe. Both H.R. 1920 and H.R. 2404 relied on tribal and federal regulation of gambling on Indian lands, rather that state regulation and enforcement.

On April 4, 1985, Senator Dennis DeConcini, D-Ariz., introduced S. 902 (the "Indian Gambling Control Act"), which was similar to H.R. 1920. Unlike prior legislative bills, S. 902 proposed the creation of regional Indian gaming commissions for each Bureau of Indian Affairs ("BIA") district. The Indian tribes located within the administrative jurisdiction of each BIA district were to organize and establish each regional commission. The regional commissions would perform the functions that the Secretary of the Interior was to perform under H.R. 1920 and H.R. 4566—approve or disapprove tribal ordinances and management contracts. A number of Indian tribes opposed the concept of regional commissions. They were concerned that tribes with gaming operations would control the commissions and would oppose additional gaming.

S. 902, like H.R. 1920 and H.R. 2404, failed to satisfy the groups interested in the implications of gambling in Indian country. The Arizona Attorney General, Robert Corbin, expressed a view shared by many state gaming regulators. He stated: "I believe very strongly that the prime responsibility for establishing and enforcing public policy on matter with such a particularly localized impact as those relating to gambling are uniquely within the province of the States and not the Federal Government."   Corbin thought that the civil/regulatory, criminal/prohibitory distinctions articulated in the cases were artificial and should not be followed in the future. Rather, he reasoned that all state laws with respect to gaming should apply in Indian country and be enforced by the states. In his opinion, the states must have the regulatory and enforcement responsibility because neither the Secretary of the Interior not the tribes could provide the monitoring necessary to prevent infiltration of organized crime.

On the other hand, Donald Antone, Sr., Governor of the Gila River Indian Community in Arizona, stated:

> We believe there is a need for legislation which clearly establishes Federal standards for and control of gaming activities within Indian country. Such Federal legislation will indicate the limited roles that State government has in regulating Indian gaming activities on Indian reservations. Any proposed legislation must be consistent with the general rule that State laws ordinarily do not extend to an Indian reservation.

Other groups that opposed S. 902 included the Nevada gaming interests and the American Horse Council. Both the Nevada gaming interests and the American Horse Council thought that the federal government did not want to allocate resources to promulgate or enforce regulations with respect to Indian gaming; therefore, the practical result of the bills would be rapid, unregulated expansion of gaming in Indian country.

Further objections to S. 902 came from certain tribes opposed to any federal legislation that would prohibit gaming on Indian lands because state public policy opposed
such gaming. In addition to general resistance to any diminishment of tribal sovereignty,
the tribes had two concerns: (1) who would determine a state's public policy with respect
to gaming, and (2) how would that determination be made. The result of the continuing controversy was that neither H.R. 1920, H.R. 2404, nor S. 902 was voted on in 1985.

The original H.R. 1920, which had been introduced on April 2, 1985, was amended
and reported to the Committee of the Whole House on March 10, 1986. This amendment changed the name of the Act to the "Indian Gaming Regulatory Act," modified the
wording of the congressional findings, established the National Indian Gaming Commission (composed of eight members), and defined three different classes of gaming.
Class I gaming (primarily traditional tribal games) was within the exclusive jurisdiction
of the Indian tribes and not subject to the Act. The National Indian Gaming Commission
("Commission") was given the power to approve tribal ordinances with respect to Class
II gaming (primarily bingo) and Class III gaming (everything other than Class I or II) in
Indian country, unless such gaming activity was prohibited by the state within which
such tribe was located as a matter of state public policy and criminal law. The Act also prohibited Indian tribes from engaging in Class II or Class III gaming activities on Indian lands
within the State of Nevada. The Commission was to adopt comprehensive gaming regulations for Class II gaming that would be identical to those provided by the State for the
same or similar gaming activity.

Thus, as amended, H.R. 1920 placed substantial power in the hands of the Commission. The Commission had authority to approve or disapprove tribal ordinances and
adopt Class III gaming regulations. In addition, it was to perform an oversight role. Representative Udall viewed the amended H.R. 1920 as compromise legislation and was unwilling to grant any additional jurisdiction or power to the states. In his opinion,
"[c]onferring State jurisdiction over tribal governments and their gaming activities would
not insure a 'level playing field,' but would guarantee that Indian tribes could not gamble at all."

The pari-mutuel gaming industry and gaming interests, other than those in Nevada,
opposed H.R. 1920, as amended. One of their supporters, Representative Tony Coelho,
D-Cal., was able to obtain a modification of Representative Udall's bill, and on April 22,
1986, an amended version of H.R. 1920 was referred to the Senate Select Committee on
Indian Affairs. The bill provided for a four-year moratorium on any new Class III gaming on Indian lands. In addition, the Comptroller General was required under the bill to
conduct a study of Class III gaming, and report to Congress an assessment of whether regulation of Class III gaming by the tribes, the states, or the United States would be most
suitable.

Throughout the summer of 1986, the gaming interests worked with the Senate Select
Committee on Indian Affairs ("Senate Select Committee"), and another version of H.R.
1920 was reported on September 26, 1986. The Senate Select Committee version of H.R.
1920 provided for state regulation of Class III gaming. Class III gaming was unlawful on
Indian lands, unless a tribe requested that the Secretary of the Interior transfer specific
jurisdiction over the gaming enterprise to the state, and the state and the Secretary agreed
to the transfer. Under this version of H.R. 1920, the National Indian Gaming Commission was given the power to approve tribal ordinances concerning Class II gaming, but
Class II gaming was within the jurisdiction of the tribe "where such Indian gaming is located within a State that permits such gaming for any purposes by any person, organization or entity (and such gaming is not otherwise prohibited by Federal law)." The Senate

Select Committee report described the new federal Indian gaming regulatory policy with respect to Class II and Class III gaming as follows:

> H.R. 1920, as reported out by the Select Committee on Indian Affairs, does not rest on the criminal/prohibitory, civil/regulatory distinction in the law as developed in court decisions discussed in this report. The bill recognizes the need to provide a regulatory scheme for the conduct of games by Indian tribes and does this by stating that tribes may conduct certain defined games (bingo, lotto and cards) under the Federal regulatory framework, provided the laws of the state allow such games to be played at all. All other games are prohibited as a matter of Federal law unless a tribe agrees with a state for the application of the state regulatory and criminal laws respecting such gaming operations, including the licensing of such games.

While this new version of H.R. 1920 was being drafted, the United States Supreme Court granted certiorari in *Cabazon*, in which the Ninth Circuit, applying the civil/regulatory, criminal/prohibitory analysis, had held that a tribe could conduct bingo and certain card games without being subject to state regulation. This caused the parties interested in gaming legislation to reassess their positions. Tribes supporting federal legislation ensuring the continued viability of their bingo operations realized that a favorable decision by the Supreme Court in *Cabazon* would provide more tribal autonomy than legislation which granted regulatory and oversight authority to the National Indian Gaming Commission. On the other hand, those opposed to gaming on Indian lands realized that a reversal of the Ninth Circuit's decision in *Cabazon* might result in all Indian gaming, including bingo, being subject to state civil and criminal regulation. Moreover, the states and gaming interests concerned primarily with Class III gaming—although pleased with what they had accomplished in Congress during the summer of 1986—had to assess the wisdom of lobbying for passage of revised H.R. 1920, which might be unnecessary if the Supreme Court decided *Cabazon* in a manner favorable to their interests. These reassessments reduced the overall lobbying pressure, and the Senate failed to pass H.R. 1920 before the adjournment of the Ninety-ninth Congress.

In early 1987, just six days before the Supreme Court's decision in *Cabazon*, S. 555 was introduced by Senators Daniel Inouye, D-Haw.; Daniel Evans, R-Wash.; and Thomas Daschle, D-S.D. S. 555 was based on the amended version of H.R. 1920 pending at the end of the Ninety-ninth Congress. At about the same time, the Supreme Court affirmed the Ninth Circuit's decision in *Cabazon*. In affirming the Ninth Circuit's decision, the Supreme Court stated:

> In light of the fact that California permits a substantial amount of gambling activity, including bingo, and actually promotes gambling through its state lottery, we must conclude that California regulates rather than prohibits gambling in general and bingo in particular.

Subsequent to the Supreme Court's decision in *Cabazon*, Representative Udall introduced H.R. 2507. Unlike H.R. 1920, H.R. 2507 stated that both Class II and Class III gaming were within the jurisdiction of the Indian tribes, provided that such gaming was located within a state that permitted such gaming "for any purpose by any person, organization or entity." Under H.R. 2507, the tribes would not have to consent to state jurisdiction. Tribal ordinances concerning Class II and Class III gaming were to be approved by the Chairman of the National Indian Gaming Commission.

In addition, with respect to Class III gaming, the Commission had to make a determination that the tribe could operate the gaming activity in accordance with the gaming codes established by the Commission. These Commission gaming codes were to be adopted by the Commission after consultation with the tribes and officials of the state in which such activity was to be conducted. The gaming codes were to be identical to state regulation of the same activity, except that the Chairman could modify regulations clearly inappropriate for Indian tribes.

Senators John McCain, R-Ariz., Inouye, and Evans introduced S. 1303, which was the same as H.R. 2507. The Senate Select Committee on Indian Affairs was given the opportunity to resolve the differences between S. 1303 and S. 555. The main difference between the two bills was the treatment of Class III gaming. Under S. 555, no Class III gaming would be permitted on Indian land unless a tribe consented to state jurisdiction over the gaming activity. Tribes would be compelled to observe state licensing and regulatory requirements, and would be subject to state enforcement of state civil and criminal gaming regulations. In contrast, under S. 1303, the Chairman of the National Indian Gaming Commission would construct the regulatory scheme that the tribes would have to follow. The Chairman was to draft regulations identical to state regulations relating to the same activity. If the Chairman adopted state criminal penalties, a state, at least Public Law 280 states, would have jurisdiction to enforce these penalties.

On June 18, 1987, the Select Committee on Indian Affairs held a hearing on S. 555 and S. 1303. Senator Inouye, the Chairman of the Committee, stated that S. 1303 was favored by the tribes. Senator Inouye stated that under S. 1303, "[c]lass III would be regulated much like class II, with a role for both tribes and the Federal Government, but with the addition that State laws governing class III games would be incorporated into tribal and Federal law." However, for some reason, certain senators thought that S. 1303 put "substantially all regulatory control in the hands of the Indian tribes themselves." Moreover, some parties continued to argue that the states should regulate all gaming on Indian lands. For example, Ross Swimmer, the Assistant Secretary for Indian Affairs, objected to S. 1303 because it "effectively [put] hard-core gaming under self-regulation by Indian tribes." Senator McCain criticized Secretary Swimmer's position and argued that the states, if given jurisdiction over gaming on Indian lands, would not give the "Indians a fair shake."

After the hearings in the summer of 1987, the congressional staffs continued to work toward a compromise between S. 555 and S. 1303. In August, 1988, the Senate Select Committee on Indian Affairs reported favorably on a new version of S. 555. This because the Indian Gaming Regulatory Act, enacted on October 17, 1988. The IGRA was a compromise bill. The provisions with respect to Class III gaming were materially changed. In an attempt to solve the dilemma concerning appropriate jurisdiction over Class III gaming, the Act introduced the Tribal-State compact concept.

Notes and Questions

1.   *Alternative realities.* Professor Santoni traced the trajectories of the various bills introduced both prior to and after the Supreme Court's *Cabazon* decision. How would the landscape for Indian gaming differ if these proposals had been adopted? Based on what you know so far, which of the bills would you have recommended Congress enact, and why?

2.   *Competing interests.* Throughout the process of drafting what became IGRA, which governmental or organizational interests do you think were most influential in obtaining their desired outcomes, and why?

3.   *Continuing issues.* IGRA's legislative history previews a number of issues that become subjects of litigation after the statute's enactment. Santoni mentioned one in connection to objections to S. 902: "[T]he tribes had two concerns: (1) who would deter-

mine a state's public policy with respect to gaming, and (2) how would that determination be made." Why do these questions concern the tribes? What are the answers to those questions under *Cabazon*? Keep this issue in mind, as under IGRA, this morphs into the "scope of gaming" problem discussed in detail in Chapter 5.

Harry Reid
U.S. Senator (D-Nev.)
Commentary in Indian Gaming and the Law
15–20 (William R. Eadington ed., 1990)

Enactment of the Act to Regulate Indian Gaming is certainly the most significant expansion of gaming activity since New Jersey voters chose to legalize casino gambling in Atlantic City in 1976. In the long run, though, it may prove even more significant than the actions in New Jersey. It's no secret that I was opposed to expanding gaming on Indian Lands. I think that it is still a poor tool for economic development in Indian Country and the social ills that it is likely to bring with it may completely overshadow any economic benefits.

In Nevada, we understand the social costs associated with large-scale commercial gaming, and we've learned over the more than fifty years of its legal existence to deal with it and compensate for it.

I think it goes without saying that when the commodity is cash, as it is with casino gaming, that it is difficult to control. But I don't think it is necessary to take my words, someone who was born and raised in the state of Nevada, on the negative effect of gaming on Indians. I think one only has to look at the final report of the President's Commission on Gambling which was commissioned by President Nixon, received and approved by President Ford in 1976 [Commission on the Review of the National Policy Towards Gambling, Gambling in America (1976)]. Even though this study was done in the 1970's, its findings are relevant today.

The Commission found that there were hidden costs associated with the proliferation of gambling. For example, it found that lower income groups spent a greater percentage of their income on gambling than did upper income groups. In fact, that report clearly showed that the poorer you were, the greater the tendency there was to gamble. Also, the more availability there was of gambling, the more people would gamble. Furthermore, the proliferation of legalized gambling led to increased illegal gambling and other general illegal activities. Thus the Commission concluded that legalization of casino gaming should be restricted principally to Nevada.

Nevada is separated by the Mojave Desert from the population centers of southern California and by the Sierra Nevada mountains to the population centers in northern California. The study found that to be extremely important, that it was difficult for people to get to Nevada. Clearly, the Commission did not believe that the expansion of high stakes gambling was in society's best interest.

I have to say that those studies undertaken about Atlantic City indicate that that is the case. There is some disagreement about the social and economic impacts of casinos in Atlantic City, but not a great deal. I think Atlantic City has proven what the Commission stated. At this stage the only people who have made money with the Atlantic City venture have been the casinos and their owners.

Following the Supreme Court's ruling in the *Cabazon* case though, there was little choice except for Congress to enact laws regulating gaming on Indian lands. The alternative would have been for the rapid and uncontrolled expansion of unregulated casino-type gambling on Indian lands.

Therefore in the spring of 1987, there were two basic positions in regard to Indian gaming. On the other hand many tribes believed that the *Cabazon* decision and the concept of Indian sovereignty meant that gaming on Indian lands should be controlled exclusively by the tribes, with little or no oversight by the federal government. On the other hand, many law makers and state and local government officials believed that the states should have the right to directly regulate gaming on Indian lands. So it was clear to me at the time that neither one of these two positions was likely to garner enough support in Congress to pass, and therefore a stalemate was likely. We were going to have to find some realistic middle ground or face the consequences of continued inaction in this area.

I began discussions with Chairman Daniel Inouye (D-Haw.) and Chairman Morris Udall (D-Ariz.), the Senate Indian Affairs Committee and the House Interior Committee chairs respectively. There were two basic questions: how should different types of gaming operations be categorized or classified, and what is the appropriate level of regulation for each class of gaming? Some discussions were relatively simple. Traditional Indian games of chance were to be left to the sole control of the respective Indian governments. Also, bingo, with which Indian gaming operators have had years of experience, was to be left primarily in Indian hands as well with some federal oversight.

Other decisions were certainly more complicated. There was no intention of diminishing the significance of the *Cabazon* decision. It was understood that the *Cabazon* decision dealt directly with poker games on Indian lands, so percentage card games were included in Class II activities along with bingo. On the other hand it was generally agreed that casino-style card games such as blackjack and baccarat, along with pari-mutuel betting and other casino style gambling including video and slot machines, should be subject to the tighter regulation required under Class III gaming operations.

The remaining difficulty, a major one, was to find an appropriate regulatory scheme for Class III gaming. It was clear that the Indian community would not accept direct state control. It was equally clear that the states demanded a role in regulating Class III gaming. The reason was very simple. If we had been dealing with gaming on Indian lands, operated by Indians for the participation of Indians, then such gaming would have been left solely to Indian control. However, there is no question that the majority of participants in Indian gaming and certainly a large percentage of the operators were and were going to be non-Indian.

State and local government officials and law officers felt that they had to have some role in saying that Indian gaming did not have detrimental effects on their citizens. To deal with this problem I suggested to Chairman Inouye that we use the concept of Tribal-State compacts to determine the regulatory structure of Class III gaming.

Under such compacts, states and tribes, as if they were foreign entities, would negotiate the regulatory structure for Class III gaming. We also built in safeguards for the tribes and states against bad-faith bargaining on either side. This legislative process took a lot of time, but the compact approach to Class III gaming broke the logjam and allowed us to eventually pass the Indian Gaming Bill in both houses without even having a recorded vote, something that is very rare for an issue this controversial.

I believe it passed for two main reasons. First, the bill was as fair as we could make it, and it provided protection to states without violating either the *Cabazon* decision or the concept of Indian sovereignty. Second, although nobody agreed with every provision of the legislation, it was the only bill that could pass, and there were no alternatives that could become law.

The reason I've taken the time to discuss the way the law came into being is to emphasize the very careful compromise that was drafted. It was a fragile compromise, at that time, and it is still a fragile compromise. If such a compromise, though, is to work, everyone involved in Indian gaming, the Indian communities who wish to have gaming, the operators of the gaming, state and local governments, and federal regulators must understand the intent of the law and agree to abide by it.

Unless everyone works together to make this fragile compromise work, this compromise could collapse, and very quickly and we could find ourselves back where we started two years ago. Only this time the fight could become very negative, and the result could undermine the very future of Indian gaming itself.

The Indian gaming laws are like any other law, they are living documents, and therefore undoubtedly have to be modified on occasion; thus, they are subject to change. Over the years, for the Indian gaming laws to work properly, I am sure there will have to be modifications and changes. But we must stay within the confines of the intent of the basic compromise that underlies this very critical legislation, or risk destroying what is the fairest, and the only workable approach, in my opinion, to legalized Indian gambling.

Notes and Questions

1. Expansion of gambling. With further hindsight, Senator Reid's assessment in 1990 that IGRA embodied the most significant expansion of legalized gambling since casino-style gaming was authorized in Atlantic City seems accurate. At the same time, as is discussed in Chapter 1, the growth of Indian gaming has coincided with a massive expansion of gambling in numerous forms: lotteries, pull-tabs, riverboat casinos, Internet sites, poker tournaments (live, televised, and online), sports wagering, and mega-resorts on the Las Vegas Strip. All of these manifestations require the express sanction of public policy. Reid suggested that IGRA itself was the cause of this expansion, as opposed to state public policies that permitted or even encouraged gambling, such as the California policy examined in *Cabazon*.

2. Geographic isolation as a constraint on legalized gambling. Senator Reid also stated that Nevada's relative geographic isolation lends itself to the containment of gambling's negative socioeconomic impacts. Does the same argument apply to the location of most tribal casinos? Has the expansion of legalized gambling generally undermined the asserted necessity of geographic isolation, or proved Reid's point?

3. Tribal-state compacts. Senator Reid referenced IGRA's requirement that before a tribe may operate Class III, or casino-style, gaming, it must enter into an agreement or "compact" with the state. The compact requirement is the centerpiece of IGRA in many ways, and is discussed in detail in Chapter 5. As you continue to read about Congress's intent in enacting IGRA, pay attention to the compacting requirement.

Stewart L. Udall
Former Secretary of the Interior
Commentary in Indian Gaming and the Law
22–28 (William R. Eadington ed., 1990)

In 1961, when I became Secretary of the Interior under Kennedy, I wanted two things to make a fresh start on Indian issues. I wanted an *Indian* Indian Commissioner, and I wanted an *Indian* solicitor, a lawyer who was an Indian to be the top person in the solicitor's office. However, I couldn't find any.

Today we have a cadre of highly qualified Indian lawyers. This has given Indians a strength that they didn't have before. More importantly, there is a competence in terms of Indian leadership today that is almost amazing compared to what existed when I became Secretary of Interior in 1961. This has been largely a process of education. There are more college trained Indians, although many of the Indian leaders never got much education, though they have demonstrated a lot of native ability. What has developed is just plain, pure competence of Indians to lead, to deal with their affairs, to deal with the state, and to deal with federal entities. I consider this one of the major beneficial historical developments of the last three decades.

Indians, as indicated by the Indian Gaming Act, may not be as strong in the Senate or the House as they would like to be. One of the stupidest things that happens and has happened over the years is that people in state government in states where there are Indians—and particularly State tax commissions and sometimes even Attorneys General—either do not want to understand Indian sovereignty or just do not give a damn.

The reason for this is that there has been hostility and there still is hostility, by some state government officials toward Indian tribes. Some of these people do not want to understand Indian sovereignty, and others do not like it. Their idea of a level playing field is that Indian sovereignty be abolished and Indians be placed under the jurisdiction of state law.

We all know that Congress has plenary [power], and ultimately if the Indians lose their sovereignty, it will happen, in my opinion, not through another termination. Instead, it will occur by a Congressional salami process of cutting off little pieces here and there, until some day it will all be gone.

This is why we have to look carefully at the Indian Gaming Act. Harry Reid and my brother, Morris Udall, were involved in this legislation, and I know it was a compromise. It is important to understand this, because four or five years ago when I first saw the first Indian gaming bills, I asked myself two questions. Where is the abuse with Indian bingo? And where is the evidence that there is an invasion of organized crime or criminal activity in Indian gaming? There was no evidence of criminal infiltration. So there was not a very strong case law to justify the legislation. Furthermore, the initial bills put the Secretary of Interior in charge of Indian bingo. That, to me, was a crazy idea.

I have ambivalence about Indian gaming, and from comments made by tribal leaders, I am apparently not alone in my feelings. Actually, by having their budgets squeezed by the Federal government, Indian tribes in the 1980s deliberately have been forced to become more and more independent, to generate their own economic future, to do things themselves, to develop their own businesses. Some tribes have turned to Indian gaming because it was an available niche; opportunities were provided by bingo and gaming. This has become very important with some Indian tribes, although others have chosen not to experiment with gaming at all. But the success of limited Indian gaming has encouraged some tribes to consider other gaming ventures.

When I first explored the motivations behind the legislation, I thought that probably Nevada interests were behind this. Now I think I was wrong on that first assessment. I don't think that was the main thrust; rather, I think it was the states. States and state governments simply said, let's stop Indians, let's make them conform to our law and let's not let them have the freedom to introduce other forms of gaming. Let's stop Indian gaming in its tracks before it gains momentum and enlarges the status quo.

The idea that Indians might go beyond bingo to racing to casinos or to sports betting or slots machines made a lot of people antagonistic. Some of them simply did not want the competition. Some of them wanted to stop the normal evolution economically and culturally that Indians would go through. And yet, Indians, because of where they are located and because of other factors, have enormous economic disadvantages. However, for those who are located near interstate highways, or near large cities, or in other places where they can enter into business and prosper, the prospect of additional revenue from gaming has been one of the few advantages some Indian groups had.

We have a situation now where Indians are confronted with limited economic opportunities based on unusual circumstances. Gaming is one, and cigarette sale are another. States are taxing cigarettes to the point where the tax is greater than the value of the commodity; because they are exempt from state taxes, that is a niche where the Indians have established themselves. That is an area where they have been able to be competitive.

But my advice to Indian tribes as they develop these opportunities is not to make the differences between themselves and their competitors all that dramatic. They should have taxes of their own, to narrow the gap somewhat. By lessening their competitive advantage they can take some of the wind out of the sails of their critics.

I also suggest to those tribes who want to enter into Class III gaming compacts with states, don't rush in without careful thought. If it is going to be logical for Indians to have other kinds of gaming opportunities, both economically and geographically, this law is going to test the good will of the states.

So the opportunities are there and I believe the Indians have the leadership now to seize these opportunities and deal with them in a sensitive way. If the states are going to smash Indian tribes in the face, the tribes are going to have to go to court. Let us see if the states will deal fairly with these compacts. The Act is a law, so test it out, try it. If it doesn't work, go back to Congress and get it changed.

Notes and Questions

1.   *Perceptions of IGRA.* Former Secretary Udall presented a less pragmatic and less optimistic view of the legal and political compromises in IGRA than did Reid. Do their differing perceptions stem from different views of tribal sovereignty? If so, how?

2.   *Alternative realities from a different perspective.* Recall the different bills introduced prior to IGRA's passage, as described by Santoni. Which do you think Udall would have supported, and why?

Senate Report No. 100-446
100th Cong., 2d Sess.
1988 U.S.C.C.A.N. 3071

The Select Committee on Indian Affairs, to which was referred the bill (S. 555) to regulate gaming on Indian lands, having considered the same, reports favorably thereon with an amendment in the nature of a substitute and recommends that the bill as amended do pass.

Purpose

S. 555 provides for a system for joint regulation by tribes and the Federal Government of class II gaming on Indian lands and a system for compacts between tribes and States for regulation of class III gaming. The bill establishes a National Indian Gaming Commission as an independent agency within the Department of the Interior. The Commission will have a regulatory role for class II gaming and an oversight role with respect to class III.

Background

S. 555 is the outgrowth of several years of discussions and negotiations between gaming tribes, States, the gaming industry, the administration, and the Congress, in an attempt to formulate a system for regulating gaming on Indian lands. In developing the legislation, the issue has been how best to preserve the right of tribes to self-government while, at the same time, to protect both the tribes and the gaming public from unscrupulous persons. An additional objective inherent in any government regulatory scheme is to achieve a fair balancing of competitive economic interests.

The need for Federal and/or State regulation of gaming, in addition to, or instead of, tribal regulation, has been expressed by various State and Federal law enforcement officials out of fear that Indian bingo and other gambling enterprises may become targets for infiltration by criminal elements. While some States have attempted to assert jurisdiction over tribal bingo games, tribes have very strenuously resisted these attempts. It was this conflict which gave rise to the California v. Cabazon Band of Mission Indians case (*Cabazon*), decided by the Supreme Court on February 25, 1987. The Court, using a balancing test between Federal, State, and tribal interests, found that tribes, in States that otherwise allow gaming, have a right to conduct gaming activities on Indian lands unhindered by State regulation. This decision followed a long line of cases that began with the case of Seminole v. Butterworth.

Since the Seminole Tribe opened its game and succeeded in court, over 100 bingo games have been started on Indian lands in states where bingo is otherwise legal. As established in testimony presented to the Committee, it was determined that collectively, these games generate more than $100 million in annual revenues to tribes. Indian tribal elected officials demonstrated to the Committee that bingo revenues have enabled tribes, like lotteries and other games have done for State and local governments, to provide a wider range of government services to tribal citizens and reservation residents than would otherwise have been possible. For various reasons, not all tribes can engage in profitable gaming operations. However, for those tribes that have entered into the business of business, the income often means the difference between an adequate governmental program and a skeletal program that is totally dependent on Federal funding.

In deciding the *Cabazon* case, the Supreme Court used a balancing test, weighing the interests of States, tribes and the Federal Government. The Court relied heavily on the fact that the Department of the Interior, as trustee for Indian tribes, reviews tribal gaming ordinances and approves or disapproves them, as well as all joint venture and management contracts with outside firms. The court also emphasized the Federal Government's interest in Indian self-government, including the goal of encouraging tribal self-sufficiency and economic development.

However, in the final analysis, it is the responsibility of the Congress, consistent with its plenary power over Indian affairs, to balance competing policy interests and to adjust, where appropriate, the jurisdictional framework for regulation of gaming on Indian lands. S. 555 recognizes primary tribal jurisdiction over bingo and card parlor operations although oversight and certain other powers are vested in a federally established National Indian Gaming Commission. For class III casino, parimutuel and slot machine gaming, the bill authorizes tribal governments and State governments to enter into tribal-State compacts to address regulatory and jurisdictional issues.

Over the course of the development of the legislation, the definition of class I has remained constant but class II and class III definitions have been subject to much debate. Class I is the term consistently used to describe traditional gaming conducted at Indian pow-wows and ceremonies, gaming activities which are entirely free of outside regulation or oversight. Under S. 555, class II is the term used for bingo, lotto, some types of card games, as well as other forms of bingo-type gaming such as pull-tabs, punch cards, tip jars, and the like. Class III is all other forms of gaming—slot machines, casino games including banking card games, horse and dog racing, pari-mutuel, jai-alai, and so forth.

> . . . .

Statement of Policy

The regulation of gaming activities on Indian lands has been the subject of much controversy. Representatives of States with experience in regulating some forms of gaming activities, such as Nevada and California, have expressed concern over the potential for the infiltration of organized crime or criminal elements in Indian gaming activities. The criminal division of the U.S. Department of Justice has expressed similar concerns, although as stated in the additional views of Senator John McCain, in 15 years of gaming activity on Indian reservations, there has never been one clearly proven case of organized criminal activity.

Recognizing that the extension of State jurisdiction on Indian lands has traditionally been inimical to Indian interests, some have suggested the creation of a Federal regulatory agency to regulate class II and class III gaming activities on Indian lands. Justice Department officials were opposed to this approach, arguing that the expertise to regulate gaming activities and to enforce laws related to gaming could be found in state agencies, and thus that there was no need to duplicate those mechanisms on a Federal level.

It is a long- and well-established principle of Federal Indian law as expressed in the United States Constitution, reflected in Federal statutes, and articulated in decisions of the Supreme Court, that unless authorized by an act of Congress, the jurisdiction of State governments and the application of state laws do not extend to Indian lands. In modern times, even when Congress has enacted laws to allow a limited application of State law on Indian lands, the Congress has required the consent of tribal governments before State jurisdiction can be extended to tribal lands.

In determining what patterns of jurisdiction and regulation should govern the conduct of gaming activities on Indian lands, the Committee has sought to preserve the principles which have guided the evolution of Federal Indian law for over 150 years. In so doing, the Committee has attempted to balance the need for sound enforcement of gaming laws and regulations, with the strong Federal interest in preserving the sovereign rights of tribal governments to regulate activities and enforce laws on Indian land. The Committee recognizes and affirms the principle that by virtue of their original tribal sovereignty, tribes reserved certain rights when entering into treaties with the United States, and that today, tribal governments retain all rights that were not expressly relinquished.

Consistent with these principles, the Committee has developed a framework for the regulation of gaming activities on Indian lands which provides that in the exercise of its sovereign rights, unless a tribe affirmatively elects to have State laws and State jurisdiction extend to tribal lands, the Congress will not unilaterally impose or allow State jurisdiction on Indian lands for the regulation of Indian gaming activities.

The mechanism for facilitating the unusual relationship in which a tribe might affirmatively seek the extension of State jurisdiction and the application of state laws to activities conducted on Indian land is a tribal-State compact. In no instance, does S. 555 contemplate the extension of State jurisdiction or the application of State laws for any other purpose. Further, it is the Committee's intention that to the extent tribal governments elect to relinquish rights in a tribal-State compact that they might have otherwise reserved, the relinquishment of such rights shall be specific to the tribe so making the election, and shall not be construed to extend to other tribes, or as a general abrogation of other reserved rights or of tribal sovereignty.

It is also true that S. 555 does not contemplate and does not provide for the conduct of class III gaming activities on Indian lands in the absence of a tribal-State compact. In adopting this position, the Committee has carefully considered the law enforcement concerns of tribal and State governments, as well as those of the Federal Government, and the need to fashion a means by which differing public policies of these respective governmental entities can be accommodated and reconciled. This legislation is intended to provide a means by which tribal and State governments can realize their unique and individual governmental objectives, while at the same time, work together to develop a regulatory and jurisdictional pattern that will foster a consistency and uniformity in the manner in which laws regulating the conduct of gaming activities are applied.

S. 555 is intended to expressly preempt the field in the governance of gaming activities on Indian lands. Consequently, Federal courts should not balance competing Federal, State, and tribal interests to determine the extent to which various gaming activities are allowed.

Finally, the Committee anticipates that Federal courts will rely on the distinction between State criminal laws which prohibit certain activities and the civil laws of a State which impose a regulatory scheme upon those activities to determine whether class II games are allowed in certain States. This distinction has been discussed by the Federal courts many times, most recently and notably by the Supreme Court in *Cabazon*. Under Public Law 83-280, the prohibitory/regulatory distinction is used to determine the extent to which State laws apply through the assertion of State court jurisdiction on Indian lands in Public Law 280 States. The Committee wishes to make clear that, under S. 555, application of the prohibitory/regulatory distinction is markedly different from the application of the distinction in the context of Public Law 83-280. Here, the courts will consider the distinction between a State's civil and criminal laws to determine whether a body of law is applicable, as a matter of Federal law, to either allow or prohibit certain activities. The Committee does not intend for S. 555 to be used in any way to subject Indian tribes or their members who engage in class II games to the criminal jurisdiction of States in which criminal laws prohibit class II games.

Explanation of Major Provisions

Definitions. Class I gaming is defined in section [2703](7). The Committee was hesitant to attempt to define traditional or ceremonial gaming as it is clearly an area of tribal self-government. However, the necessity of classifying all types of gaming requires the mention of this form of gaming and the Committee's intent is to make certain that such gaming is never considered either as class II or class III.

Class II gaming is defined in section [2703](8)(A)(B)(C) and (D). Consistent with tribal rights that were recognized and affirmed in the Cabazon decision, the Committee intends in section [2703](8)(A)(i) that tribes have maximum flexibility to utilize games such as bingo and lotto for tribal economic development. The Committee specifically rejects any inference that tribes should restrict class II games to existing games sizes, levels of participation, or current technology. The Committee intends that tribes be given the opportunity to take advantage of modern methods of conducting class II games and the language regarding technology is designed to provide maximum flexibility. In this regard, the Committee recognizes that tribes may wish to join with other tribes to coordinate their class II operations and thereby enhance the potential of increasing revenues. For example, linking participant players at various reservations whether in the same or different States, by means of telephone, cable, television or satellite may be a reasonable approach for tribes to take. Simultaneous games participation between and among reservations can be made practical by use of computers and telecommunications technology as long as the use of such technology does not change the fundamental characteristics of the bingo or lotto games and as long as such games are otherwise operated in accordance with applicable Federal communications law. In other words, such technology would merely broaden the potential participation levels and is readily distinguishable from the use of electronic facsimiles in which a single participant plays a game with or against a machine rather than with or against other players.

Section [2703](8)(A) also makes clear the Committee's intent that pull-tabs, punch boards, tip jars, instant bingo and similar sub-games may be played as integral parts of bingo enterprises regulated by the act and, as opposed to free standing enterprises of these sub-games, state regulatory laws are not applicable to such sub-games, just as they are not applicable to Indian bingo.

Section [2703](8)(A)(ii) provides that certain card games are regulated as class II games, with the rest being set apart and defined as class III games under section [2703](9) and regulated pursuant to section [2710](d). The distinction is between those games where players play against each other rather than the house and those games where players play against the house and the house acts as banker. The former games, such as those conducted by the Cabazon Band of Mission Indians, are also referred to as non-banking games, and are subject to the class II regulatory provisions pursuant to section [2710](a)(2). Subparagraphs (I) and (II) are to be read in conjunction with sections [2710](a)(2) and (b)(1)(A) to determine which particular card games are within the scope of class II. No additional restrictions are intended by these subparagraphs. The Committee notes that, while existing law does not require that Indian card games conform with State law, it agreed to adoption of bill language to provide that these card games be operated in conformity with laws of statewide application with respect to hours or periods of operation, or limitations on wagers or pot sizes for such card games.

Subparagraph [2703](8)(B) specifically excludes from class II, and thus from regulation by a tribe and the National Indian Gaming Commission, so-called banking card games and slot machines. The Committee's intent in this instance is to acknowledge the important difference in regulation that such games and machines require and to acknowledge that a tribal-State compact for regulation of such games is preferable to Commission regulation.

. . . .

Class III gaming is defined in section [2703](9) as all gaming that is not included as class I or class II. All class III gaming will be subject to the terms and conditions of Tribal-State compacts agreed to under section [2710](d).

. . . .

Jurisdiction.... Class II. Section [2710](a)(2) stipulates that class II gaming remains within tribal jurisdiction but is subject to the provisions of the act where two conditions are met: The State within which the tribe is located must permit such gaming for any purpose by any entity; and such gaming is not otherwise prohibited by Federal law. The Committee recognizes that tribal jurisdiction over class II gaming has not been previously addressed by Federal statute and thus there has heretofore been no divestment or transfer of such inherent tribal governmental powers by the Congress.

There are five States (Arkansas, Hawaii, Indiana, Mississippi, and Utah) that criminally prohibit any type of gaming, including bingo. S. 555 bars any tribe within those States, as a matter of Federal law, from operating bingo or any other type of gaming. In the other 45 States, some forms of bingo are permitted and tribes with Indian lands in those States are free to operate bingo on Indian lands, subject to the regulatory scheme set forth in the bill. The card games regulated as class II gaming are permitted by far fewer States and are subject to requirements set forth in section [2703](8). The phrase "for any purpose by any person, organization or entity" makes no distinction between State laws that allow class II gaming for charitable, commercial, or governmental purposes, or the nature of the entity conducting the gaming. If such gaming is not criminally prohibited by the State in which tribes are located, then tribes, as governments, are free to engage in such gaming.

The phrase "not otherwise prohibited by Federal Law" refers to gaming that utilizes mechanical devices as defined in 15 U.S.C. § 1175. That section prohibits gambling devices on Indian lands but does not apply to devices used in connection with bingo and lotto. It is the Committee's intent that with the passage of this act, no other Federal statute, such as those listed below, will preclude the use of otherwise legal devices used solely in aid of or in conjunction with bingo or lotto or other such gaming on or off Indian lands. The Committee specifically notes the following sections in connection with this paragraph: 18 U.S.C. sections 13, 371, 1084, 1303–1307, 1952–1955 and 1961–1968; 39 U.S.C. § 3005; and except as noted above, 15 U.S.C. §§ 1171–1178. However, it is the intention of the Committee that nothing in the provision of this section or in this act will supersede any specific restriction or specific grant of Federal authority or jurisdiction to a State which may be encompassed in another Federal statute, including the Rhode Island Claims Settlement Act (Act of September 30, 1978, 92 Stat. 813; P.L. 95-395) and the Marine Indian Claim Settlement Act (Act of October 10, 1980; 94 Stat. 1785; P.L. 96-420).

      ....

Class III — tribal-State compacts. Section [2710](d) encompasses provisions relating to tribal-State compacts that will govern the operation of class III gaming on Indian lands. After lengthy hearings, negotiations and discussions, the Committee concluded that the use of compacts between tribes and states is the best mechanism to assure that the interests of both sovereign entities are met with respect to the regulation of complex gaming enterprises such as parimutuel horse and dog racing, casino gaming, jai alai and so forth. The Committee notes the strong concerns of states that state laws and regulations relating to sophisticated forms of class III gaming be respected on Indian lands where, with few exceptions, such laws and regulations do not now apply. The Committee balanced these concerns against the strong tribal opposition to any imposition of State jurisdiction over activities on Indian lands. The Committee concluded that the compact process is a viable mechanism for setting various matters between two equal sovereigns. The State of Nevada and the Fort Mojave Indian tribe negotiated a compact to govern future casino gaming on the Nevada portion of the tribe's reservation. While that compact itself may not be an appropriate model for other compacts, the issues addressed by the compact are the same issues that the Committee considers may be the subject of negotiations between other States and tribes.

In the Committee's view, both State and tribal governments have significant governmental interests in the conduct of class III gaming. States and tribes are encouraged to conduct negotiations within the context of the mutual benefits that can flow to and from tribes and States. This is a strong and serious presumption that must provide the framework for negotiations. A tribe's governmental interests include raising revenues to provide governmental services for the benefit of the tribal community and reservation residents, promoting public safety as well as law and order on tribal lands, realizing the objectives of economic self-sufficiency and Indian self-determination, and regulating activities of persons within its jurisdictional borders. A State's governmental interests with respect to class III gaming on Indian lands include the interplay of such gaming with the State's public policy, safety, law and other interests, as well as impacts on the State's regulatory system, including its economic interest in raising revenue for its citizens. It is the Committee's intent that the compact requirement for class III not be used as a justification by a State for excluding Indian tribes from such gaming or for the protection of other State-licensed gaming enterprises from free market competition with Indian tribes.

The practical problem in formulating statutory language to accomplish the desired result is the need to provide some incentive for States to negotiate with tribes in good faith because tribes will be unable to enter into such gaming unless a compact is in place. That incentive for the States had proved elusive. Nevertheless, the Committee notes that there is no adequate Federal regulatory system in place for class III gaming, nor do tribes have such systems for the regulation of class III gaming currently in place. Thus a logical choice is to make use of existing State regulatory systems, although the adoption of State law is not tantamount to an accession to State jurisdiction. The use of State regulatory systems can be accomplished through negotiated compacts but this is not to say that tribal governments can have no role to play in regulation of class III gaming—many can and will.

The terms of each compact may vary extensively depending on the type of gaming, the location, the previous relationship of the tribe and State, etc. Section [2710](d)(3)(C) describes the issues that may be the subject of negotiations between a tribe and a State in reaching a compact. The Committee recognizes that subparts of each of the broad areas may be more inclusive. For example, licensing issues under clause vi may include agreements on days and hours of operation, wage and pot limits, types of wagers, and size and capacity of the proposed facility. A compact may allocate most or all of the jurisdictional responsibility to the tribe, to the State or to any variation in between. The Committee does not intend that compacts be used as a subterfuge for imposing State jurisdiction on tribal lands.

The Committee does view the concession to any implicit tribal agreement to the application of State law for class III gaming as unique and does not consider such agreement to be precedent for any other incursion of State law onto Indian lands. Gaming by its very nature is a unique form of economic enterprise and the Committee is strongly opposed to the application of the jurisdictional elections authorized by this bill to any other economic or regulatory issue that may arise between tribes and States in the future.

Finally, the bill allows States to consider negative impacts on existing gaming activities. That is not to say that the bill would allow States to reject Indian gaming on the mere showing that Indian gaming will compete with non-Indian games. Rather, States must show that economic consequences will be severe and that they will clearly outweigh positive economic consequences.

Burden of proof. Section [2710](d)(7) grants a tribe the right to sue a State if compact negotiations are not concluded. This section is the result of the Committee balancing the interests and rights of tribes to engage in gaming against the interests of States in regulating such gaming. Under this act, Indian tribes will be required to give up any legal right they may now have to engage in class III gaming if: (1) they choose to forgo gaming rather than to opt for a compact that may involve State jurisdiction; or (2) they opt for a compact and, for whatever reason, a compact is not successfully negotiated. In contrast, States are not required to forgo any State governmental rights to engage in or regulate class III gaming except whatever they may voluntarily cede to a tribe under a compact. Thus, given this unequal balance, the issue before the Committee was how best to encourage States to deal fairly with tribes as sovereign governments. The Committee elected, as the least offensive option, to grant tribes the right to sue a State if a compact is not negotiated and chose to apply the good faith standard as the legal barometer for the State's dealings with tribes in class III gaming negotiations. While a tribe must show a prima facie case, after doing so the burden will shift to the State to prove that it did act in good faith. The Committee notes that it is States, not tribes, that have crucial information in their possession that will prove or disprove tribal allegations of failure to act in good faith. Furthermore, the bill provides that the court, in making its determination, may consider any of the number of issues listed in this section, including the State's public interest and other claims. The Committee recognizes that this may include issues of a very general nature and, and course, trusts that courts will interpret any ambiguities on these issues in a manner that will be most favorable to tribal interests consistent with the legal standard used by courts for over 150 years in deciding cases involving Indian tribes.

Management contracts. As used in section [2711] and throughout the bill, the term "management contract" refers to agreements governing the overall management and operation of an Indian gaming facility by an entity other than the tribe or its employees. The term "management contract" does not include contracts or agreements for the procurement of particular services, materials or supplies. These service or supply agreements, including the supply of gaming aids such as pulltabs, computers, punch boards, and communications or other equipment, are subject to regulation under section [2710](b)(2)(D). Charges associated with such services, materials, supplies or equipment are to be included as part of the total operating expenses in determining the net revenues under section [2703](10).

. . . .

Additional Views of Mr. McCain

This is the fourth consecutive year that I have been involved in the debate regarding the issue of Federal standards and regulations for the conduct of gaming on Indian reservations and lands. It is with great reluctance that I am supporting S. 555 as reported by the Committee.

I characterize my support as reluctant because I believe a different and more favorable result for Tribes could have been achieved. Unfortunately, Tribes never banded together and offered their own gaming proposal. They also never found a consensus for supporting any particular legislative solution. Some would say that Tribes were united in calling for no gaming legislation, but such a position ignores the whole debate, and, more importantly, it provides no support to those Members of Congress who have attempted to craft legislation which would be sensitive to tribal concerns. The issue has never been: should there be federal regulation of Indian gaming? Four years of continuous debate on Indian gaming should lead even the most casual observer of the legislative process to realize that legislation was inevitable. The focus of debate has always been on what standards and regulations should govern the conduct of gaming on Indian reservations and lands.

As a participant in the debate, I offered S. 1303, the companion to H.R. 2507 as introduced by Congressman Udall. This bill would have allowed Tribes to continue gaming activities that are consistent with current law under Federal regulations and standards, without State intrusion, while ensuring that adequate safeguards and careful monitoring are maintained to prevent criminal activity as called for by States. Unfortunately, I received no more than a handful of letters supporting this measure; only more calls for "no legislation". I believe Tribes and tribal organizations share part of the burden for the direction that Indian gaming legislation has taken.

As the debate unfolded, it became clear that the interests of the states and of the gaming industry extended far beyond their expressed concern about organized crime. Their true interest was protection of their own games from a new source of economic competition. Never mind the fact that tribes have used gaming revenues, and S. 1303 would have restricted their use, to support tribal governmental functions as well as addressing the health, education, social and economic needs of their members. Never mind the fact that in 15 years of gaming activity on Indian reservations there has never been one clearly proven case of organized criminal activity. In spite of these and other reasons, the State and gaming industry have always come to the table with the position that what is theirs is theirs and what the Tribe[s] have is negotiable.

The debate now focuses on S. 555, as amended. The Committee Report is clear as to the purpose of Tribal/State compacts as called for in Section [2710](d). I understand Senator Evans' concerns regarding the potential overextension of the intended scope of the Tribal/State compact approach. Toward this end, I believe it is important to again underscore the statement of the Report: "The Committee does not intend to authorize any wholesale transfer of jurisdiction from a tribe to a state." From time immemorial, Tribes have been and will continue to be permanent governmental bodies exercising those basic powers of government, as do Federal and State governments, to fulfill the needs of their members. Under our constitutional system of government, the right of Tribes to be self-governing and to share in our federal system must not be diminished.

Finally, some Members of Congress, including myself, have stated that they would rather see Tribes involved in other revenue raising activities. We must ask ourselves, however, if we have provided Tribes with sufficient opportunities to generate non-gaming revenues and thereby allow Tribes to increase their economic self-sufficiency. The answer is a resounding no. We have not done enough. Once this gaming debate is over, I challenge those involved in this debate to devote their energies toward increasing long-term economic development opportunities for Indian Tribes.

JOHN McCAIN.

Additional Views of Mr. Evans

I voted in Committee to report this bill to the full Senate, but I did so with great reluctance. I am troubled by the potential implications S. 555 may have for the fundamental legal relationship between the United States and the several Indian tribes and on the established principles of Federal Indian Law which guide that relationship. S. 555, the Indian Gaming Regulatory Act, should not be construed as a departure from established principles of the legal relationship between the tribes and the United States. Instead, the bill should be considered within the line of developed case law extending over a century and a half by the United States Supreme Court, including the basic principles set forth in California v. Cabazon Band of Mission Indians.

The bill's statement of purpose is generally a sound analysis of the law as it applies to jurisdiction in Indian Country pursuant to Public Law 83-280, specifically as established by the Court in Seminole Tribe v. Butterworth and *Cabazon*. In light of the Committee statement I am confident that the Federal courts will interpret S. 555 in the proper jurisdictional context. Nevertheless, I believe it is necessary to underscore an important distinction between this bill and Public Law 83-280. Under Public 83-280, the courts distinguish between a State's criminal laws which are prohibitory in nature and its civil laws which are regulatory in nature. This distinction is used to determine the extent to which State laws apply through the assertion of State court jurisdiction on Indian lands in Public Law 280 states. Under S. 555, application of the prohibitory/regulatory distinction is markedly different from the application of the distinction in the context of Public Law 83-280. Here, the courts will consider the distinction between a State's civil and criminal laws to determine whether a body of law is applicable, as a matter of federal law, to prohibit Class II games. S. 555 should not be interpreted in any way to subject Indian tribes or their members who engage in Class II games to the criminal jurisdiction of States in which criminal laws prohibit Class II games.

S. 555 should not be interpreted as going beyond Public Law 83-280 in another respect. Public Law 83-280 transferred to the States jurisdiction over criminal and civil causes of action in Indian Country. In other words Public Law 280 only subjected the actions of individual Indians to State enforcement. Public Law 83-280 did not subject the governing processes of the tribes to State law and public policy constraints, which would be a fundamental derogation of tribal self-government. Likewise, S. 555 should be construed not to subject tribal governance to State court jurisdiction.

Section [2709] purports to delegate the Secretary's trust responsibility to the Gaming Commission. I am troubled to think that this section of the Act and the accompanying report language may be read to suggest that the Secretary's charge to carry out the United States' trust responsibility ends where that of the Commission begins. The entire Federal Government owes a trust obligation to the tribes and the Secretary is still charged with carrying out that overall responsibility, especially in areas only incidentally affected by gaming and S. 555 in Indian Country. The Act should not be construed to relieve the Secretary, or any other Federal officer, of trust obligations to the tribes.

Finally, this bill should be construed as an explicit preemption of the field of gaming in Indian Country. Thus, in accordance with the fundamental legal principles upon which the Supreme Court relied in deciding *Cabazon*, where the Federal Government has preempted a field affecting Indians or Indian tribes, there should be no balancing of State public policy and interests when they conflict with tribal rights except where expressly provided in this bill. It is my understanding that S. 555 acknowledges that inherent rights are expressly reserved to the tribes. This bill allows tribes to relinquish some of those rights by way of compacts with the States, in accordance with the Federal Government's trust obligation to the tribes. This bill should not be construed, however, to require tribes to unilaterally relinquish any other rights, powers, or authority.

We should be candid about gambling. This issue is not one of crime control, morality, or economic fairness. Lotteries and other forms of gambling abound in many States, charities, and church organizations nationwide. It would be hypocritical indeed to impose on Indian people more stringent moral standards than those by which the rest of our citizenry chooses to live. Moreover, Indian tribes may have a competitive economic advantage because, rightly or wrongly, many states have chosen not to allow the same types of gaming in which tribes are empowered to engage. Ironically, the strongest opponents of tribal authority over gaming on Indian lands are from States whose liberal gaming policies would allow them to compete on an equal basis with the tribes.

I am no more fond of gambling than any other member of this Committee and no less aware of the potential dangers of organized criminal infiltration of Indian gaming. In 15 years of commercial gaming on Indian reservations, however, tribes have proven more capable of controlling this potential problem than have States in which high stakes gambling is played. Given this fact, the bill should not be construed, either inside or outside the field of gaming, as a derogation of the tribes' right to govern themselves and to attain economic self-sufficiency.

DANIEL J. EVANS.

Notes and Questions

1.   Cabazon as a catalyst. How and why did the Supreme Court's decision in *Cabazon* prompt Congress to act to create an overarching regulatory framework for Indian gaming? To what extent is IGRA a codification of *Cabazon*? To what extent did Congress legislatively "overrule" *Cabazon* by enacting IGRA?

2.   Balancing tribal, state, and federal interests. Through IGRA, Congress balanced the interests of tribes, states, and the federal government, as well as commercial casino operators. Several commentators refer to the compromises Congress made. Whose interests came out on top? Did Congress sufficiently account for tribal sovereignty?

3.   Indian gaming and devolution. In establishing the groundwork for states to play a role in the regulation of Indian gaming, was IGRA a byproduct of the Reagan administration's general policy of devolving federal authority to the states? Or did it simply coincide with that sense of the appropriate roles for state and federal governments?

4.   Continuing spread of legalized gambling. The Senate Report noted, "There are five States (Arkansas, Hawaii, Indiana, Mississippi, and Utah) that criminally prohibit any type of gaming, including bingo." By 1994, only Hawaii and Utah continued to completely prohibit gambling as a matter of state public policy.

5.   Federal preemption. Recall *Cabazon's* discussion of federal preemption and the strength of state interests. If Congress intended IGRA to preempt the field of Indian gaming, how should the Court's analysis of the preemption issue have changed after IGRA's enactment? How would the Indian gaming industry look today if Congress had exercised its power to preclude state regulation of tribal gaming? *See* Alexander Tallchief Skibine, Cabazon *and Its Implications for Indian Gaming*, in INDIAN GAMING: WHO WINS? 68 (Angela Mullis & David Kamper eds., 2000).

6.   IGRA and the Johnson Act. As the Senate Report referenced, 15 U.S.C. § 1175(a), a provision of the Johnson Act sometimes referred to as the "Indian Gambling Act," prohibits the possession or use of "gambling devices" in Indian country. Note the Senate Report's characterization of the Johnson Act: "The phrase 'not otherwise prohibited by Federal Law' refers to gaming that utilizes mechanical devices as defined in 15 U.S.C. § 1175. That section prohibits gambling devices on Indian lands but does not apply to devices used in connection with bingo and lotto." In recent years, the U.S. Department of Justice and the NIGC have taken different views of whether the Johnson Act prohibits Class II gambling devices that are otherwise legal under IGRA. This issue is described in more detail in Chapter 4.

The Senate Report referenced other federal criminal statutes: 18 U.S.C. §§ 13 (incorporating state law for violations not specifically prohibited by other federal statutes in areas of federal jurisdiction), 371 (conspiracy to defraud the United States), 1084 (the "Wire

Act," which prohibits using wire communications in connection with betting), 1303–1307 (the "Lottery Act," which prohibits interstate transport of lottery tickets), 1952–1955 (prohibiting racketeering, including illegal gambling businesses and interstate transportation of wagering paraphernalia, as well as the "Travel Act," which prohibits interstate transportation in aid of racketeering), and 1961–1968 (the Racketeer Influenced and Corrupt Organizations Act (RICO)); 39 U.S.C. §3005 (restrictions on mailing lottery materials).

   7.   ***Additional comments of Senator McCain.*** Senator McCain suggested that federal legislation was inevitable. On what basis—legally, politically, or practically?

   8.   ***Additional comments of Senator Evans.*** Why did Senator Evans write separately to clarify what S. 555, the proposed Indian Gaming Regulatory Act, did *not* do regarding the transfer of state criminal jurisdiction, state court jurisdiction over tribal governments, and federal trust responsibility?

C. IGRA's Regulatory Framework

The Senate Report provided a general overview of IGRA's regulation of Class II and Class III gaming, discussed in detail in Chapters 4 and 5, respectively. IGRA's provisions related to the NIGC and its powers are discussed in Chapter 6. Here, we set forth a number of IGRA's other key provisions, including its policy goals, the "Indian tribe" and "Indian lands" requirements, and criminal provisions.

1. Policy Goals

In IGRA, Congress adopted specific findings and policy goals to explain the regulatory framework and guide its application. Its findings include:

> (1) numerous Indian tribes have become engaged in or have licensed gaming activities on Indian lands as a means of generating tribal governmental revenue;

> (2) Federal courts have held that section 81 of this title requires Secretarial review of management contracts dealing with Indian gaming, but does not provide standards for approval of such contracts;

> (3) existing Federal law does not provide clear standards or regulations for the conduct of gaming on Indian lands;

> (4) a principal goal of Federal Indian policy is to promote tribal economic development, tribal self-sufficiency, and strong tribal governments; and

> (5) Indian tribes have the exclusive right to regulate gaming activity on Indian lands if the gaming activity is not specifically prohibited by Federal law and is conducted within a State which does not, as a matter of criminal law and public policy, prohibit such gaming activity.

25 U.S.C. §2701.

Congress's declaration of policy covers two broad areas: connecting Indian gaming to the general federal policy of tribal self-determination, and providing effective regulation for Indian gaming. Specifically, IGRA's purpose is:

(1) to provide a statutory basis for the operation of gaming by Indian tribes as a means of promoting tribal economic development, self-sufficiency, and strong tribal governments;

(2) to provide a statutory basis for the regulation of gaming by an Indian tribe adequate to shield it from organized crime and other corrupting influences, to ensure that the Indian tribe is the primary beneficiary of the gaming operation, and to assure that gaming is conducted fairly and honestly by both the operator and players; and

(3) to declare that the establishment of independent Federal regulatory authority for gaming on Indian lands, the establishment of Federal standards for gaming on Indian lands, and the establishment of a National Indian Gaming Commission are necessary to meet congressional concerns regarding gaming and to protect such gaming as a means of generating tribal revenue.

Id. § 2702.

2. Definition of "Indian Gaming"

IGRA authorizes "Indian gaming," or gaming conducted by an "Indian tribe" on "Indian lands." As with other comprehensive federal statutes, IGRA's definitions section provides key information. An Indian tribe is defined as a tribe or other organized group that is eligible for federal Indian programs and services and has been recognized as possessing powers of self-government. Indian lands are defined as reservation lands as well as trust and restricted lands over which a tribe exercises governmental authority:

(4) The term "Indian lands" means—

(A) all lands within the limits of any Indian reservation; and

(B) any lands title to which is either held in trust by the United States for the benefit of any Indian tribe or individual or held by any Indian tribe or individual subject to restriction by the United States against alienation and over which an Indian tribe exercises governmental power.

(5) The term "Indian tribe" means any Indian tribe, band, nation, or other organized group or community of Indians which—

(A) is recognized as eligible by the Secretary for the special programs and services provided by the United States to Indians because of their status as Indians, and

(B) is recognized as possessing powers of self-government.

25 U.S.C. § 2703. The NIGC promulgated federal regulations that rephrase the statutory definitions of these two key terms:

Indian lands means:

(a) Land within the limits of an Indian reservation; or

(b) Land over which an Indian tribe exercises governmental power and that is either—

(1) Held in trust by the United States for the benefit of any Indian tribe or individual; or

(2) Held by an Indian tribe or individual subject to restriction by the United States against alienation.

Indian tribe means any Indian tribe, band, nation, or other organized group or community of Indians that the Secretary recognizes as—

(a) Eligible for the special programs and services provided by the United States to Indians because of their status as Indians; and

(b) Having powers of self-government.

25 C.F.R. §§ 502.12, 502.13.

Thus, two fundamental prerequisites for both Class II and Class III gaming are that the games must be conducted by a federally recognized tribe on lands that satisfy the statutory definition. As the "Indian tribe" and "Indian lands" requirements are significant but often overlooked or misunderstood constraints on tribal gaming, each is worth closer examination.

a. *Indian Tribes*

To be eligible for federal Indian programs and services, as required by IGRA's definition of "Indian tribe," a tribe ordinarily must be acknowledged or "recognized" by the federal government. A tribe may be federally recognized through treaty, statute, executive or administrative order, or long-standing practice of the federal government treating the tribe as a political entity.

In 1978, the U.S. Department of the Interior adopted mandatory recognition criteria to assess the eligibility of Native American groups that had not been federally recognized. *See* 25 C.F.R. pt. 83 (excerpted in Chapter 10). In essence, the group must show that it has maintained a "substantially continuous" tribal existence and has functioned as an autonomous government entity "from historical times until the present." This status includes continuous identification as an "American Indian entity" since 1900 through interactions, as a tribe, with federal, state, local, or tribal governments, historical records, and anthropological scholarly opinion; existence as a "distinct community" from the first sustained contact with colonizers to the present, including evidence of political leadership and authority over members and appropriate governing documents; and a membership consisting of descendants of a tribe that existed in historical times and who are not members of other tribes and have not been subject to termination of tribal status by Congress.

Many federally acknowledged tribes have long histories of federal recognition, marked by legal and political interactions with the U.S. in the eighteenth and nineteenth centuries. Others have sought recognition in recent years, often through federal statute or the Interior Department's acknowledgment process. The Federally Recognized Indian Tribe List Act of 1994, Pub. L. 103-454, 108 Stat. 4791, requires the annual publication in the Federal Register of a list of all federally recognized tribes. Indian gaming's influence on the federal recognition process is discussed in Chapter 10.

Mark D. Myers

Federal Recognition of Indian Tribes in the United States

12 Stan. L. & Pol'y Rev. 271 (2001)

The [Bureau of Indian Affairs (BIA)] uses the term "tribe" to refer to a group of people indigenous to North America ("Indians") presently constituting a distinct social or political unit. Federal recognition of a tribe is often interpreted as a stamp of approval indicating that a certain group is indeed a bona fide tribe of Indians. However, the most precise definition of federal recognition describes it as the federal government's decision to establish a government-to-government relationship by recognizing a group of Indians as a dependent tribe under its guardianship.

In the mid 1970s, a dramatic increase in the number of Indian groups requesting federal recognition led to increased formalization of the recognition process. Pro-Indian Senator James Abourezk (S.D.) persuaded Congress to fund the American Indian Policy Review Commission (AIPRC), which delivered a final report in 1977. This report identified 133 unrecognized tribes and urged that they be recognized. However, the BIA had developed its own acknowledgement program through the Federal Acknowledgment Project (FAP). Critics of the BIA charged that the Bureau, fearing that recognizing multiple new tribes would overstrain its budget, "raced to draft [these] administrative guidelines that would quell Congress' appetite for legislation," and that "[a]fter endless negotiations, and several revisions, it succeeded." According to the BIA's Branch of Acknowledgment Research (BAR), however, the regulations were simply an attempt to deal with the increasing number of groups pursuing federal recognition and to formalize what had been until then an ad hoc process. In any event, Congress never enacted legislation proposed by the AIPRC in its report. Since 1978, with the promulgation of 25 C.F.R. pt. 83, the BIA has had the authority to recognize a tribe, or deny it recognition, through the federal acknowledgement process. In addition, 25 C.F.R. pt. 83 made it possible for the first time for Indian groups to seek administrative, and potentially judicial, appeals from adverse findings.

The institution of the federal acknowledgement process was also a radical departure from previous practice in that it allowed smaller, less visible groups to be heard. Previously, the executive and legislative branches dealt out of necessity and convenience with select tribes in ways constituting federal recognition. Groups of Indians with whom the federal government did not have contact — due, e.g., to the tribe's small size, relative inculturation, or remote location — were not recognized. Federal recognition was thus entirely plenary. Under the current federal acknowledgement process, however, all qualifying groups of Indians may, in theory, be recognized. Federal recognition under the federal acknowledgement process has effectively become an entitlement.

There are many reasons a tribe might remain unrecognized. In some cases, entire tribal groups were never recognized due to their small size or the fact that that they never had significant dealings with the U.S. government. Many of these tribes never made war on the U.S., or they reached agreements only with the British crown or colonial governments. The AIPRC's final report to Congress identified a variety of "historical accidents" that seem to explain why some tribes have not been federally recognized. Examples of tribes that were overlooked in this way are the Lumbees of North Carolina, the Shinnecock Tribe of New York, the Mashpee of Massachusetts, and the Hattadare of Virginia.

Other unrecognized tribes represent branches of tribes whose principal bands or nations had already been federally recognized, but who sought their own separate tribal status. The AIPRC's final report to Congress includes many examples of these tribes as well. This is by far the largest category of petitioners. Examples include the Kansas Wyandots, Indiana Miamis, Northern Cherokees, Georgia Cherokees, Mowa Choctaws, Mississippi Chickasaws, Ohio Shawnees, and Caddo Adais. These tribes are typically groups with ties to the main band who, for various reasons, settled elsewhere. For example, some groups independently emigrated from the traditional settlement area, such as the Texas Cherokees and Old Settler ancestors of Northern Cherokees in Missouri and

Arkansas. Some stayed in one place while the main body of the tribe emigrated else-where, such as the Georgia Cherokees, Mowa Choctaws, Mississippi Chickasaws, Caddo Adais, and Ohio Shawnees. Some were removed but stopped before reaching their final destination, such as the Kansas Wyandots and some Northern Cherokees. And some continued to move after arriving at their federally designated resettlement area, such as the Delawares of Idaho, Comanche Penateka of Texas, and Calusa-Seminole Nation of California. A number of federally recognized tribes also fall into this category. For instance, bands of Sioux and Shoshone in different locations are recognized as separate tribes by the federal government.

Other unrecognized tribes represent amalgamations of members of two or more tribes that were not historically a single tribe. The possibility of acknowledgement for this kind of tribe is specifically mentioned in § 83.7(e), which allows recognition of a group whose members "descend from a historical Indian tribe or from historical Indian tribes which combined and functioned as a single autonomous entity." Examples of unrecognized tribes in this category include the United Houma Nation of Louisiana, the Lumbees, and the Delaware-Muncie. This description would have applied historically to other federally recognized groups that amalgamated of their own accord, such as the Catawbas, the Creek confederation, the Sac and Fox, the Cheyenne-Arapaho, and the Ojibwes. In addition, many petitioners are identified as Indian or inter-tribal associations, such as the Coharie Intra-Tribal Council and the Santee Indian Organization. These associations parallel the arrangements of some federally recognized tribes, such as the Fort Belknap Indian Community in Montana, which includes members of two ethnic tribes, the Gros Ventre and Assiniboine.

A shrinking category of federally unrecognized tribes consists of those formerly recognized tribes whose status was terminated or who had their recognition withdrawn in some other fashion. This category formerly included the Ottawa, Modoc, Quapaw, and Seneca tribes of Oklahoma, the Catawbas, the Menominee, and many California tribes and rancherias. Many of these have now been re-recognized, although some still remain unrecognized, including ten tribes in California. In some cases it is not clear whether the tribe will ever be restored or whether termination destroyed the tribal relationship so completely that there remains no tribe to be restored. This category also includes tribes which formerly had dealings with the federal government but which were never fully recognized, those which were dissolved, or those which the Department of the Interior determined not to treat as eligible for BIA services. Some of these are the Lumbees of North Carolina, the Miamis of Indiana, and the Muwekma Ohlone Tribe of California. The Chinook Indian Tribe of Washington was recently removed from this list when the BAR discovered that its recognition had mistakenly been withheld in what Kevin Gover, former Assistant Secretary for Indian Affairs, called an "egregious oversight."

Some tribal organizations do not seek federal recognition. One example is the Cherokees of California, who have not petitioned for federal recognition. Such groups may choose not to seek federal recognition for a variety of reasons. For instance, some may already be state recognized, some do not wish to undergo the recognition process, and some recognize that they cannot satisfy one of the requirements of § 83.7. Others simply want to be left alone by the federal government.

Some Indian and non-Indian critics believe that a number of Indian groups petitioning for recognition are not composed of genuine Indians, but are merely seeking the benefits of being Indian. Observers have noted that these "wannabes" may be motivated by New Age religious beliefs or the desire to associate themselves with an idealized image of Indian as a social or ethnic category.

Another strong motivation for groups seeking federal recognition may be the significant financial benefits of recognized tribal status. Many of their opponents clearly suspect that non-Indians are attempting to tap into already meager Indian resources by achieving unmerited recognition. This has been one of the strongest arguments for maintaining the stringent requirements of the recognition process. Another criticism lodged at unrecognized groups, sometimes by those who currently enjoy federally recognized tribal status, is that such groups are acculturated to the point of losing their Indian character and identity.

Although these criticisms raise legitimate concerns, the authentic Indian identity of a group's membership is usually not the basis for denial of recognition. An examination of BIA findings regarding the qualifications of unsuccessful petitioners demonstrates that most have been denied federal acknowledgement, not because their members are not Indians as required by §83.7(e), but on other grounds, such as failure to show that "[t]he petitioner has been identified as an American Indian entity on a substantially continuous basis since 1900" or because the group has been "the subject of congressional legislation that has expressly terminated or forbidden the federal relationship." In other words, a group's failure to prove that it meets the more technical requirements of §83.7 is a much more common basis for denial of acknowledgment by the BIA than the tribe's failure to demonstrate Indian ancestry.

Even in cases where a group's Indian origin is questioned, the analysis and findings of the Branch of Acknowledgement and Research (BAR)—the entity within the BIA that carries out the technical research associated with the acknowledgement process—could reasonably be criticized as being poorly conceived, organized, and presented. Although the reports of the BAR are subject to peer review and are reviewed by several other officers, they can be difficult to follow. The BAR has also been criticized for failing to allow petitioners an adequate opportunity to cross-examine the authors of BAR final determinations. It is also important to recognize that the burden is on the petitioning tribe to show that it meets all requirements. Despite objections by political opponents of non-federally recognized tribes, a group's failure to be recognized is properly understood as a failure to provide sufficient evidence to overcome the BAR's presumption that it is not an Indian tribe under the meaning of pt. 83; it is not determinative of whether the group is actually an Indian tribe.

The BIA acknowledgement program, which is administered by the BAR, was promulgated within the Department of the Interior through the Federal Acknowledgment Project (FAP) and the first set of regulations became effective October 2, 1978. The acknowledgement process begins when a petitioning Indian group files a letter of intent signed by its governing body with the Assistant Secretary of Indian Affairs, as described in §83.4. The BAR then publishes a notice in the Federal Register, publishes a legal notice in a local newspaper, notifies the governor and attorney general of the tribe's state, sends a letter of response to the tribe, and establishes an administrative file. The tribe then has an unlimited time to submit a petition with supporting documentation. Once the petition is complete, the BAR evaluates it and conducts field interviews with tribal members, and issues a Technical Assistance Letter, usually within three months, as provided for under §83.10(b)(2). The tribe may send in additional material in response to the Technical Assistance Letter and may request another Technical Assistance Review. At this point, the tribe's petition is placed on the "ready" list for active consideration and the petitioner and other interested parties are notified. After reviewing the completed petition, the BAR publishes a preliminary decision, called a Proposed Finding, in the Federal Register. Following publication, petitioner as well as third parties may submit arguments or evidence to support or rebut the proposed finding.

BIA regulations enacted are more stringent in many significant respects than the recommendations made by the congressional commission. It is fair to say that the goal of the commission, to recognize all legitimate Indian tribes, is apparently not the goal of pt. 83. Although the AIPRC recommended that an Indian group be acknowledged as a tribe if the group could meet any of seven definitional factors, regulations generated internally by the BIA through the FAP set seven mandatory criteria that all petitioners must satisfy. Although the BIA maintains that no considerations determine acknowledgement other than whether the group meets the seven mandatory criteria outlined in § 83.7, critics have alleged that other, unwritten policy considerations are at work. For example, the BIA has been criticized for failing to acknowledge larger groups because of the strain it would place on the Bureau's budget. In some cases, such as where a tribe's claim to urban territory provokes opposition from local and state government, it has been speculated that political opposition may play a part, although the BAR denies this.

As of October 29, 1999, fourteen petitioners had been acknowledged through the BIA's process. Where this has happened, the tribe's fortunes have typically taken a dramatic upturn. For instance, Alabama's Poarch Band of Creeks, whose acknowledgement became effective August 10, 1984, rose from poverty to relative prosperity and prominence within a decade.

If, on the other hand, the BIA declines to recognize a tribe, which is more likely, the group may appeal to the Interior Board of Indian Appeals, and after exhausting its remedies within the Department of the Interior, it may appeal to a federal court. Much of the BAR's time and resources is spent dealing with appeals from unsuccessful petitioners, and the courts have only overturned the Branch's decision in a single case, that of the Samish Tribe of Washington. If a tribe's petition to the BAR fails to satisfy mandatory requirements outlined in § 83.7(e), (f), or (g), the Branch may decline to acknowledge the group without a full review of the petition, pursuant to § 83.10(e). The BAR calls this an "expedited negative finding."

Under § 83.10(e) a tribe can also be determined to be ineligible to petition because it cannot satisfy the requirement of § 83.7(g) that "[n]either the petitioner nor its members are the subject of congressional legislation that has expressly terminated or forbidden the Federal relationship." Six North Carolina tribes fall within this category, all effectively barred from being recognized by the 1956 legislation extending limited recognition to the Lumbees. Denial on these minor grounds has a great impact on the survival of tribes.

By far the largest group, representing a total of 158 petitioners, consists of those who have not yet completed applications. Of these, 44 have incomplete petitions on file, 103 have submitted letters of intent only, and eleven have submitted a letter of intent to petition but are no longer in contact with the BIA. Of the petitioners with some documentation submitted, a full thirteen have been actively seeking acknowledgement since the 1970s. The earliest application is from the Little Shell Band of North Dakota, which initiated the acknowledgement process on November 11, 1975, well before the present BIA program was in place.

This brings to the forefront an often-criticized aspect of the recognition process: the burden it places on petitioners. Although many Indian groups would like to be federally acknowledged, it is evident from the numbers above that non-federally recognized Indian groups are finding the acknowledgement process to be too burdensome. This is certainly true financially; tribes with few resources are forced to pay an estimated average of $250,000–300,000 over the course of the recognition process. It is estimated that some tribes have spent as much as $750,000 only to be denied acknowledgement. Grants available for this purpose from the Administration of Native American Programs amount to only $100,000 per petitioner. The BAR recommends that petitioners obtain additional funds from private donors, such as foundations and church groups, or hold fund-raising events to make up the difference. It is possible that many of these petitioners will never complete the process.

Whether a tribe is ultimately recognized, denied acknowledgement, or simply left to languish for years without its status resolved, the acknowledgement process as it is presently conducted places a substantial burden on tribes.

Critics have charged that part of the reason tribes spend so much money and take such a long time to complete their petitions is that "the branch's evidentiary standards are impossibly high." Moreover, the BIA's findings, while not flatly determinative of whether a group is a tribe within the meaning of federal law, are res judicata for purposes of the BIA acknowledgement process; § 83.3(f) prohibits unsuccessful petitioners from re-petitioning.

The sacrifices of money and time required to complete the BIA acknowledgement process may also affect the quality of evidence. The BAR is aware of these costs and recommends that petitioners save money by having genealogical and historical work done by volunteers. The Branch also warns petitioners of the cost of employing a large staff including "professional researchers, consultants, lawyers, and a staff that more or less parallels the BAR: a genealogist, a historian, and an anthropologist," noting that "[a] staff of this size is clearly beyond the resources of many small groups." However, in view of the difficult standards by which petitions will be evaluated and possibly reviewed on appeal, and the dire consequences of failing to be acknowledged, it is clear that petitioners have some legitimate reasons for hiring professional researchers, consultants, and attorneys rather than relying on volunteers and the BAR staff.

Lengthy delays in the review process even after submission of complete petitions appear to bear heavily on petitioning groups. To review all petitions, the BAR has no more than ten full-time employees, and sometimes fewer. Currently eleven petitions are listed as "Ready, Waiting for Active Consideration," six of which have been waiting since 1996, three since 1997, and two since 1998. The petition review rate, according to outside observers, is slightly more than one petition per year. While BIA officials have been optimistic in the past about the length of time review of petitions would take, critics reasonably charge that the entire process is moving at a "snail's pace," or, as characterized by one federal court, in a "leisurely manner."

At its present rate of petition review, assuming that most of the present petitioners eventually submit complete documentation, the BAR will not have worked through its backlog until well into the twenty-second century. There are at least 170 tribes whose status has yet to be resolved, and the BAR handles roughly 1.3 per year.

In spite of the burden it places on petitioners, however, even those observers who are most critical do not find the process entirely without its merits. Both supporters and critics of the process agree that there are a number of groups fraudulently claiming to be Indian tribes and that the acknowledgement process successfully weeds them out. In addition, the process has been identified as helping prepare some groups for the responsibility that federal recognition brings.

Notes and Questions

   1.   *Tribal recognition and tribal sovereignty.* Myers asserted that recognition represents the "federal government's decision to establish a government-to-government rela-

tionship by recognizing a group of Indians as a dependent tribe under its guardianship." In other words, under federal law, only federally recognized tribes are entitled to exercise tribal sovereignty (though some non-recognized groups may be entitled to some federal benefits). It is important to understand that tribal recognition reflects a political status, rather than a racial or ethnic category, though race and ethnicity certainly are tied up in federal recognition (and in the history of federal-tribal relations generally). As Myers mentioned, many tribes are state-recognized, but not federally recognized. Such tribes exist in a number of states, including Alabama, Connecticut, Louisiana, Massachusetts, Michigan, New Jersey, New York, North Carolina, Ohio, Oklahoma, and Virginia. Tribes whose governmental authority is recognized only by the state are not "Indian tribes" under IGRA.

2.   *Agency expertise.* When brought under the auspices of the BIA, the federal recognition process was seen as institutionalizing objective and depoliticized standards, appropriately housed within an agency that would make complicated determinations on the basis of evidence and expertise. Yet today the administrative process has been criticized as subjective and politicized. What has changed, if anything? Myers asserted that Indian "authenticity" is not the usual reason why the BIA fails to recognize a tribal group; rather, such denials usually are on technical grounds. Authenticity, however, is at the core of most criticism of the federal recognition process. Is the administrative process an effective gatekeeper for those who might wish to obtain federal recognition to capitalize on the various benefits or entitlement programs available to American Indians or tribal entities? If so, why is the perception so prevalent that gaming is the inevitable result of a petition for recognition?

3.   *The "Indian tribe" requirement.* There has not been much litigation under IGRA concerning a tribe's status as an Indian tribe, so long as the tribe has federal recognition. (The status of land as satisfying the "Indian lands" requirement is a different story, as we'll see in the next section.) That is not to say that federal recognition is not controversial, as Myers discussed. In addition to the issues he raised, Indian gaming has influenced political and policy discourse surrounding the recognition process, if not swayed the process itself. Since the advent of tribal gaming, the process has come under political fire, and the Interior Department's decisions have been vigorously challenged on a number of fronts. Federal acknowledgment is portrayed as an avenue to gaming, and groups seeking recognition are criticized as opportunist, especially if their efforts are bankrolled by outside investors. This can also cause intertribal tensions, as there sometimes are political divides among newly recognized tribes and "treaty" tribes. We provide a specific example of the scrutiny Indian gaming has brought to the recognition process through our discussion of the Schaghticoke Tribal Nation in northwestern Connecticut, just one example of what critics see as "would-be tribes," in Light & Rand, Indian Gaming and Tribal Sovereignty, at 59–63.

4.   *Legislative recognition.* Although infrequent, Congress continues to exercise its power to bestow federal recognition on tribal groups through legislation, often to settle disputed tribal claims to land. A highly controversial example related to Indian gaming is Congress's recognition of the Mashantucket Pequots through the Connecticut Indian Land Claims Settlement Act of 1983, 25 U.S.C. §§ 1751–1760. More recently, state-recognized tribes in Virginia have sought legislation that would grant them federal recognition.

b. *Indian Lands*

Until the introduction of the term "Indian lands" in IGRA, most federal laws used the term "Indian country," with a similar, but not identical, definition. *See* 18 U.S.C. § 1151 (defining "Indian country"). Because Congress chose to use a different term with a different definition in IGRA, it is plain that "Indian lands" and "Indian country" are not necessarily the same; that is, lands that qualify as "Indian country" may not qualify as "Indian lands" under IGRA. The lands within the bounds of current reservations qualify as "Indian lands," as do what typically are called "trust" lands, or lands held in trust by the U.S. for the benefit of a tribe, and "restricted" lands, or lands protected from alienation (absolute conveyance of real property) but not held in trust by the federal government. Indian lands do not include fee land allotments. For non-reservation land, IGRA requires that the tribe "exercise governmental power" over the lands in order to qualify as "Indian lands" under § 2703(4).

For most tribes with reservations, the question of whether a location qualifies as Indian lands is straightforward. For some tribes with less clearly defined reservations, and for other tribes pursuing casinos nearer non-tribal metropolitan areas, the question may depend on a complex history of tribal-federal interactions, as the following case illustrates.

Kansas v. United States
249 F.3d 1213 (10th Cir. 2001)

BALDOCK, Circuit Judge.

In 1995, the Miami Tribe of Oklahoma, pursuant to IGRA, unsuccessfully requested the NIGC approve a proposed gaming management contract between the Tribe and Defendant Butler National Service Corporation. If approved, the contract would have authorized the Tribe to establish Class II gaming facilities on the Maria Christiana Reserve No. 35, an undeveloped thirty-five acre tract of non-reservation land within the State of Kansas located 180 miles from the Tribe's reservation in Oklahoma.

One condition for Class II Indian gaming is that such gaming occur only on "Indian lands within such tribe's jurisdiction." § 2710(b). In addition to reservation lands and lands held in trust by the United States, IGRA defines "Indian lands" as "any lands title to which is ... held by any Indian tribe or individual subject to restriction by the United States against alienation and over which an Indian tribe exercises governmental power." § 2703(4). The NIGC refused to approve the gaming management contract because, in the NIGC's opinion, the Tribe did not exercise governmental power over the undeveloped tract. Therefore, the NIGC concluded the tract encompassed under the proposed contract did not constitute "Indian lands" within the meaning of § 2703(4).

On review, the district court upheld the NIGC's decision that the tract did not constitute "Indian lands" within the meaning of IGRA. *Miami Tribe of Okla. v. United States*, 927 F. Supp. 1419 (D. Kan. 1996) (*Miami Tribe I*). Carefully analyzing the detailed and complicated history of the tract, including applicable legislation and treaties, the district court had "no difficulty concluding from [a] series of events that [the Tribe] unmistakably relinquished its jurisdiction over Reserve No. 35."

To summarize, the court reasoned that under an 1867 treaty with the Tribe and an 1873 federal enactment affecting the Tribe, Congress "unambiguously intended to abrogate the Tribe's authority over its lands in Kansas and move the Tribe to new lands in Oklahoma." The court further noted that in 1891, the United States, at the direction of the Court of Claims, compensated the Miami Tribe in the amount of $61,971 for the Kansas lands. This compensation included payment to the Tribe for the subject tract, which the Government acknowledged had been *erroneously* allotted by restricted fee patent around 1858 to the infant Marie Christiana DeRome, a non-member of the Miami Tribe. In 1960, the Miami Tribe sought interest on the 1891 compensation and secured a judgment for an additional $100,072. Based on this historical analysis, the district court concluded the Tribe had no jurisdiction over the tract, and thus necessarily exercised no governmental power over the tract (recognizing that under 25 U.S.C. §2703(4) "a necessary prelude to the exercise of governmental power is the existence of jurisdiction").

The Tribe did not appeal the district court's conclusion in *Miami Tribe I* that, based on historical events, the tract did not constitute "Indian lands" under IGRA. Rather, in 1996, the Miami Tribe amended its constitution to remove the blood quantum requirement for membership in the Tribe. Subsequently, the Tribe passed an ordinance adopting the twenty-plus non-Indian owners of the tract, numerous heirs of Marie Christiana DeRome, into the Tribe. The owners in turn leased the tract to the Tribe and consented to the Tribe's exercise of jurisdiction over the tract. To provide access to the tract from the nearest public road, the tribe obtained a right-of-way road easement from an adjoining land owner. At the entrance to the tract, the Tribe placed a sign reading "Welcome to the Miami Indian Reserve in Kansas Territory established 1840." [Under an 1840 treaty with the United States, the Miami Tribe of Indiana agreed to cede its lands in Indiana and move to lands in the federal territory of Kansas. Subsequently, in 1873, the Tribe agreed to cede its lands in Kansas and move to lands in the federal territory of Oklahoma.] The Tribe raised its flag over the tract, extended "periodic" law enforcement protection to the tract, and established a smoke shop and outreach center on the tract. With this change in circumstances, the Tribe requested the NIGC reconsider its refusal to approve the proposed gaming management contract.

The NIGC again determined that the tract did not constitute "Indian lands" under IGRA, and again refused to approve the contract. Like the district court in *Miami Tribe I*, the NIGC focused largely on the history of the tract, noting that the Tribe had agreed years ago to move to Oklahoma and cede its interest in the entirety of its Kansas lands. The NIGC did not address in detail the effect, if any, of the Tribe's leasehold over the tract or recent tribal activities on the tract. The NIGC, however, concluded that "the admission of the owners of the land into the Tribe is alone not sufficient evidence of tribal authority to bring the land within the definition of 'Indian lands' under IGRA." Once again, the Tribe sought review of the NIGC's decision in the district court.

This time the Tribe argued before the district court, "without reference to and despite the history of the Reserve," that the Tribe's activities with regard to the tract subsequent to Miami Tribe I established the Tribe's jurisdiction over the tract. The court in *Miami Tribe II*, however, declined to resolve the Tribe's argument. Rather, the court concluded that the NIGC's decision not to approve the proposed gaming management contract should be set aside as an abuse of discretion because the NIGC failed to provide a "reasoned explanation" why the Tribe, in view of its recent activities, had not established jurisdiction over the tract, and did not now exercise governmental power over the tract. The court further noted that limitations in the administrative record prevented it from concluding the NIGC's decision was the product of "reasoned decisionmaking." The court cited as troublesome the NIGC's lack of reference to tribal ordinances and other activities that the Tribe asserted were examples of its exercise of jurisdiction and governmental power over the tract. The district court therefore remanded the matter to the NIGC for further proceedings related to the proposed gaming management contract.

After twice previously opining that the tract did not constitute "Indian lands" under IGRA, the NIGC, on remand from *Miami Tribe II*, decided based on events subsequent to *Miami Tribe I*, that the Tribe now exercised governmental power over the tract, and that the tract did in fact constitute "Indian lands" within the meaning of IGRA. The NIGC, however, failed to specifically address the jurisdictional concerns which the district court raised in *Miami Tribe II*. Nevertheless, the NIGC approved the proposed Class II gaming management contract between the Tribe and Butler National, and issued a gaming permit to the Tribe.

At last armed with a favorable NIGC decision, the Tribe next formally requested that the State of Kansas negotiate with the Tribe a gaming compact for Class III casino gaming on the Tribe's "Indian lands" in Kansas. Like Class II gaming, a condition for Class III casino gaming under IGRA is that such gaming occur only on a tribe's "Indian lands." The State of Kansas [then] instituted this suit under the Administrative Procedure Act (APA), [5 U.S.C. §§ 701–706,] seeking declaratory and injunctive relief from the NIGC's decision that the thirty-five acre tract of land in Kansas constituted "Indian lands" within the meaning of IGRA.

The penultimate issue pervading this litigation is whether the NIGC properly determined that the Kansas tract constitutes "Indian lands" within the meaning of IGRA for Indian gaming purposes. The NIGC's binding decision (absent judicial review) is crucial to the Miami Tribe's efforts to establish gaming facilities within the State of Kansas.

For the Kansas tract to qualify as "Indian lands" of the Miami Tribe within the meaning of IGRA, (1) the Tribe must have jurisdiction over the tract, (2) fee title to the tract must be restricted or not freely alienable, and (3) the Tribe must exercise governmental power over the tract. *See* 25 U.S.C. §§ 2703(4)(B), 2710(b)(1), (d)(1)(A)(i). Unfortunately, IGRA sheds little light on the question of whether under the present circumstances the tract constitutes "Indian lands" of the Miami Tribe. Where, as here, Congress has not "directly spoken to the precise question at issue," a court is required to uphold the agency's interpretation "if it is based on a permissible construction of the statute." Notwithstanding this deferential review standard, the agency "must ... articulate a satisfactory explanation for its action including a rational connection between the facts found and the choice made.... Normally, an agency ... [decision] would be arbitrary and capricious if the agency ... entirely failed to consider an important aspect of the problem."

In remanding the "Indian lands" question to the NIGC, the *Miami Tribe II* court was particularly concerned with the threshold question of whether the Tribe had jurisdiction over the tract. After the court in *Miami Tribe II* reversed the NIGC's decision that the tract was not "Indian lands" for purposes of IGRA, federal officials conducted a site visit to the tract. Subsequently, after twice ruling the tract was not "Indian lands," the NIGC concluded that the tract was "Indian lands" of the Miami Tribe subject to IGRA. Rather than focusing on the Tribe's jurisdiction over the tract, however, the NIGC's decision focused solely on whether the Tribe presently exercised governmental power over the tract.

The NIGC's failure to thoroughly analyze the jurisdictional question in its most recent decision likely renders its conclusion that the tract constitutes "Indian lands" within the meaning of IGRA arbitrary and capricious. In concluding that the Tribe exercised governmental power over the tract without first establishing the Tribe's jurisdiction over the tract, the NIGC, in effect, put the cart before the horse. We agree with the *Miami Tribe I* court that before a sovereign may exercise governmental power over land, the sovereign, in its sovereign capacity, must have jurisdiction over that land. A proper analysis of whether the tract is "Indian lands" under IGRA begins with the threshold question of the Tribe's jurisdiction. That inquiry, in turn, focuses principally on congressional intent and purpose, rather than recent unilateral actions of the Miami Tribe.

An Indian tribe may not unilaterally create sovereign rights in itself that do not otherwise exist. An Indian tribe retains only those aspects of sovereignty not withdrawn by treaty or statute. The most probative evidence of congressional intent and purpose in this case is the language of the legislation and treaties which the State of Kansas suggests (and *Miami Tribe I* held) eliminate the Miami Tribe's sovereign rights over the tract. To a lesser extent, we may also consider events occurring within a reasonable time after passage of these laws and treaties to discern congressional intent.

The difficulty with the Government's position is that the district court in Miami Tribe I thoroughly analyzed the question of the Tribe's jurisdiction over the tract based upon the United States' treatment of the tract. The court concluded that no lawful basis existed to suggest the Tribe presently had jurisdiction over the tract. Rather, Congress years ago "*unambiguously* intended to abrogate the Tribe's authority of its lands in Kansas and move the Tribe to new lands in Oklahoma."

Because the Tribe did not appeal *Miami Tribe I*, the district court's findings and conclusions regarding the status of the tract, including its construction of the relevant legislation and treaties, are now res judicata and we need not revisit them here. Notably, none of the Defendants have ever challenged *Miami Tribe I*'s findings and conclusions regarding the status of the tract. Rather, they rely solely on the Tribe's activities subsequent to *Miami Tribe I* to claim tribal jurisdiction over the tract—namely (1) the Tribe's adoption of the tract's twenty-plus owners into the Tribe, (2) those owners' consent to tribal jurisdiction pursuant to a lease with the Tribe, and (3) the Tribe's recent development of the tract. None of these recent events, however, alters the conclusion that Congress abrogated the Tribe's jurisdiction over the tract long ago, and has done nothing since to change the status of the tract. An Indian tribe's jurisdiction derives from the will of Congress, not from the consent of fee owners pursuant to a lease under which the lessee acts.

Notes and Questions

1. ***Indian lands and Indian country.*** Recall that the Major Crimes Act defines "Indian country," a legal term of art widely used to refer to tribal lands. Indian country is defined as "(a) all land within the limits of any Indian reservation under the jurisdiction of the United States Government…, (b) all dependent Indian communities within the borders of the United States…, and (c) all Indian allotments the Indian title to which have not been extinguished…." 18 U.S.C. § 1151. Was the land at issue in *Kansas* "Indian country"? How exactly does IGRA's definition of "Indian lands" differ from the definition of Indian country? Why do you think Congress adopted a different term in IGRA? What does requiring gaming to occur on Indian lands accomplish that mandating only that gaming occur in Indian country would not?

2. ***Jurisdiction vs. exercise of governmental authority.*** *Rhode Island v. Narragansett Indian Tribe*, 19 F.3d 685 (1st Cir. 1994), illustrates that judicial inquiries into the status of the land as held in trust or restricted, and whether the tribe exercises governmental power over the land, can be extremely complicated and require careful examination of legal sources. As seems to be the usual approach, the *Rhode Island* court treated the questions of tribal jurisdiction and tribal governmental power as two separate issues. In that case, the question of jurisdiction was complicated by the terms of a land claim settlement, codified by Congress, between the tribe and the state. The court concluded that the tribe retained concurrent jurisdiction over the settlement lands, even though the federal statute granted the state jurisdiction. Because the statute did not expressly deprive the tribe of jurisdiction, the court applied the Indian canon of construction and held that the tribe had jurisdiction over the land. The court then turned to the question of whether the tribe exercised governmental power over the land, as evidenced by "concrete manifestations"

of such authority. The court was persuaded that the tribe's establishment of a housing authority, participation in HUD programs, and "state" status granted by the EPA for purposes of the Clean Water Act adequately demonstrated tribe's exercise of governmental power over settlement lands.

Similarly, in *Cheyenne River Sioux Tribe v. South Dakota*, 830 F. Supp. 523 (D.S.D. 1993), the district court cited the NIGC regulatory definition of Indian lands, *see* 25 C.F.R. § 502.12, summarizing the requirements: "In order to qualify as Indian lands under IGRA, non-reservation land must meet three requirements: the tribe must exercise jurisdiction over the land, fee title to the land must be restricted or not freely alienable, and the tribe must exercise governmental power over the land." As in *Kansas* and *Rhode Island*, the court treated jurisdiction and exercise of governmental authority as separate questions. In the case, the court found there was insufficient evidence on the issue of governmental authority: "There is nothing in the record to determine: (1) whether the areas are developed; (2) whether tribal members reside in those areas; (3) whether any governmental services are provided and by whom; (4) whether law enforcement on the lands in question is provided by the Tribe or the State; and (5) other indicia as to who exercises governmental power over those areas."

In *City of Sherrill v. Oneida Indian Nation*, 544 U.S. 197 (2005), the Supreme Court added a new wrinkle. In that case, the Oneida Indian Nation of New York purchased property within Sherrill's city limits. The property had been part of the Oneida's reservation until 1805, when the state reacquired the land. In an earlier case, *County of Oneida v. Oneida Indian Nation*, 470 U.S. 226 (1985), the Court had held that the tribe had a claim that the state's 1805 transaction was in violation of federal law. After the tribe bought the land in 1997 and 1998, it resisted paying city tax on the property, arguing that the tribe, rather than the city, had governmental authority over the land. The Court held that despite the fact that the land formerly had been part of the tribe's reservation, "the Tribe cannot unilaterally revive its ancient sovereignty, in whole or in part, over the parcels at issue. The Oneidas long ago relinquished the reins of government and cannot regain them through open-market purchases from current titleholders." Although the status of the property as "Indian lands" under IGRA was not at issue in the case, the Court's holding would seem to preclude the property from qualifying as "Indian lands." It remains to be seen whether courts will rely on *City of Sherrill* to find that tribes may not exercise governmental authority over non-reservation lands.

3.   *Indian lands as a prerequisite to compact negotiations.* In *Match-E-Be-Nash-She-Wish Band of Pottawatomi Indians v. Engler*, 304 F.3d 616 (6th Cir. 2002), the Court of Appeals for the Sixth Circuit held that a state was not obliged to enter into tribal-state compact negotiations for Class III gaming unless and until the tribe possessed "Indian lands" under IGRA.

4.   *NIGC land determinations.* As is evident from *Kansas*, the NIGC's Office of General Counsel makes initial determinations as to whether land qualifies as Indian lands. The NIGC makes its land determinations available through its Web site. *See* NIGC, *Indian Land Opinions*, http://www.nigc.gov/ReadingRoom/IndianLandOpinions/tabid/120/Default.aspx.

As also discussed in Chapter 6, the NIGC's final agency decisions are reviewable in federal district court. The Administrative Procedure Act (APA), 5 U.S.C. §§ 501 *et seq.*, governs the actions of federal agencies and is a cornerstone of administrative law. As the *Kansas* court articulated above, where Congress has not "directly spoken to the precise question at issue," a court must uphold an agency's interpretation "if it is based on a permissible construction of the statute." The agency also "must ... articulate a satisfactory explanation for its action including a rational connection between the facts found and the choice made." A reviewing court ordinarily would find an agency decision to be "arbitrary and capricious" and thus unlawful under the APA "if the agency ... entirely failed to consider an important aspect of the problem."

As is indicated by 25 C.F.R. § 502.12, the NIGC treats reservation lands differently than non-reservation lands. If the NIGC finds that the land at issue is part of a tribe's reservation, then the NIGC will conclude that the tribe may conduct gaming on the land without further inquiry, as the tribe "preemptively" is assumed to have jurisdiction and to exercise governmental authority over reservation lands. This "preemptive" effect of reservation lands is reflected in IGRA's definition of Indian lands (and more clearly expressed in the NIGC's regulatory definition of Indian lands). Only for non-reservation lands does the NIGC inquire as to the tribe's jurisdiction and exercise of governmental authority over the lands. The NIGC explained its approach in a recent opinion:

> The NIGC Office of General Counsel (OGC) has revised its analytic approach to Indian lands within reservation boundaries. The analysis used through the past few years included a two-part determination whenever an Indian lands question was raised—OGC looked first to determine whether the lands constituted Indian lands; OGC then looked to whether the tribe exercised jurisdiction over those lands.... Despite [the holding in *Kansas v. United States*, excerpted above], the NIGC has concluded that, in some instances IGRA's preemptive effect negates the need for a complete jurisdictional analysis. IGRA specifically defines Indian lands as any "[l]ands within the limits of an Indian Reservation." This finding is a prerequisite for a tribe to be able to conduct gaming under IGRA. IGRA gives tribes the exclusive right to regulate gaming on Indian lands if the Indian lands in question are within "such tribe's jurisdiction." A tribe is presumed to have jurisdiction over its own reservation. Therefore, if the gaming is to occur within a tribe's reservation, under IGRA, we can presume that jurisdiction exists.

> It is still appropriate under the second 2703(B) definition of Indian lands [i.e., for lands that do not satisfy section 2703(A)'s definition as "all lands within the limits of any Indian reservation"] to conduct a separate jurisdictional analysis when determining whether a tribe exercises governmental powers. This is because a necessary prerequisite to the exercise of governmental powers is the theoretical and inherent authority to exercise such power. However, with respect to the first definition of Indian lands—that the lands are within the reservation boundaries, we conclude that the preemptive effect of IGRA eliminates the need for a separate jurisdictional analysis.

NIGC Office of General Counsel, Indian Land Opinion, Buena Vista Rancheria of Me-Wuk Indians (June 30, 2005).

5.   *Tribes as indispensable parties.* Note that *Kansas* nominally was a dispute between the state and the federal government, and that because the case could proceed without the tribe, it was not a party to the suit. Although the court construed the fundamental issue as one of agency authority in view of the APA, tribal interests very much were at stake. The case highlights how federal and state court decisions that do not directly implicate IGRA or Indian gaming may determine gaming-related legal outcomes. Federal and state courts are more likely sources of authority on Indian gaming than are tribal courts. Tribes,

of course, may have different reasons to intervene or choose not to intervene in such disputes; regardless, a court may decide tribal intervention is not allowed or that other nontribal interests represented in the dispute are functionally identical. One might consider the implications for tribal sovereignty if a state or federal court makes decisions that obviously impact tribal interests—especially a state court which otherwise usually lacks jurisdiction over tribes. This issue is explored in greater depth in Chapter 8.

3. Criminal Regulation

In addition to the civil regulatory framework for Indian gaming, IGRA also contains criminal provisions related to tribal gaming, found in Title 18. The first, titled "Gambling in Indian country," incorporates state law to define the federal violation of unauthorized Indian gaming (note the exceptions for gaming conducted in compliance with IGRA in subsection (c)):

> (a) Subject to subsection (c), for purposes of Federal law, all State laws pertaining to the licensing, regulation, or prohibition of gambling, including but not limited to criminal sanctions applicable thereto, shall apply in Indian country in the same manner and to the same extent as such laws apply elsewhere in the State.

> (b) Whoever in Indian country is guilty of any act or omission involving gambling, whether or not conducted or sanctioned by an Indian tribe, which, although not made punishable by any enactment of Congress, would be punishable if committed or omitted within the jurisdiction of the State in which the act or omission occurred, under the laws governing the licensing, regulation, or prohibition of gambling in force at the time of such act or omission, shall be guilty of a like offense and subject to a like punishment.

> (c) For the purpose of this section, the term "gambling" does not include—

>> (1) class I gaming or class II gaming regulated by the Indian Gaming Regulatory Act, or

>> (2) class III gaming conducted under a Tribal-State compact approved by the Secretary of the Interior under section [2710](d)(8) of the Indian Gaming Regulatory Act that is in effect.

> (d) The United States shall have exclusive jurisdiction over criminal prosecutions of violations of State gambling laws that are made applicable under this section to Indian country, unless an Indian tribe pursuant to a Tribal-State compact approved by the Secretary of the Interior under section [2710](d)(8) of the Indian Gaming Regulatory Act, or under any other provision of Federal law, has consented to the transfer to the State of criminal jurisdiction with respect to gambling on the lands of the Indian tribe.

18 U.S.C. § 1166.

IGRA also adopted criminal provisions, 18 U.S.C. §§ 1167 ("Theft from gaming establishments on Indian lands") and 1168 ("Theft by officers or employees of gaming establishments on Indian lands"), to protect tribe's gaming revenue. Section 1167 makes it illegal to steal from a tribal gaming establishment (thefts of more than $1,000 are punishable as felonies); the similarly worded § 1168 provides steeper penalties for thefts by employees, officers, and licensees.

Sycuan Band of Mission Indians v. Roache

54 F.3d 535 (9th Cir. 1995)

CANBY, Circuit Judge.

[After obtaining search warrants in state court, San Diego County sheriff's deputies raided casinos operated by the Barona, Sycuan, and Viejas Bands of Mission Indians on their reservations. The deputies seized video pull-tab machines, cash, and records from the casinos, and the local district attorney commenced prosecutions against four casino employees for operating games in contravention of state law. The state characterized the video pull-tab machines as Class III "slot machines" and argued that because the machines were not operated in accordance with a tribal-state compact, they were illegal under both IGRA and state law.]

IGRA extends state laws punishing certain types of gambling into Indian country, but it also contains a highly explicit limitation on jurisdiction to enforce those laws: "The United States shall have exclusive jurisdiction over criminal prosecutions of violations of State gambling laws that are made applicable under this section to Indian country, unless an Indian tribe pursuant to a Tribal-State compact ... has consented to the transfer to the State of criminal jurisdiction with respect to the gambling on the lands of the Indian tribe." 18 U.S.C. § 1166(d). The Bands have not consented to the transfer of criminal jurisdiction to the State. As far as IGRA is concerned, therefore, the State had no authority to prosecute the Bands' employees for conducting the Bands' gaming.

The State points out that section 1166(d) provides for exclusive federal enforcement of state criminal laws "made applicable *under this section* to Indian country." It argues that California had preexisting authority to enforce its criminal laws in Indian country under Public Law 280, 18 U.S.C. § 1162. Accordingly, the State contends that the prosecutions were lawfully maintained under the State's Public Law 280 jurisdiction.

We reject the State's arguments for two reasons. First, we do not agree that the State had jurisdiction over the Bands' gaming activities under Public Law 280. That statute granted California and certain other states jurisdiction over criminal violations and civil causes of action on Indian reservations. It left civil regulatory jurisdiction in the hands of the Tribes. In *California v. Cabazon Band of Mission Indians,* the Supreme Court made it clear that state law in a Public Law 280 state may be excluded from Indian country as "regulatory" even though the regulatory aspects of the law are enforced by criminal penalties.

[Second,] IGRA provides that "[t]he United States shall have exclusive jurisdiction over criminal prosecutions of violations of State gambling laws that are made applicable under this section to Indian country" in the absence of a compact providing for state jurisdiction. The State emphasizes "made applicable under this section" and draws an implication that, if it can find another source (i.e., Public Law 280) making its laws applicable in Indian country, then it can prosecute violations. But that conclusion does not follow, nor is it a sensible application of section 1166(d). If the Bands' electronic pull-tab machines are Class III gaming devices, then section 1166(d) makes the State's law against such machines applicable in Indian country. Section 1166(d) also grants the federal government exclusive power to enforce *that law.* Even if there were some other route making that same state law applicable in Indian country, the Federal government's right to enforce *that law* is still exclusive. If that exclusivity is incompatible with any provision of Public Law 280, then the Public Law 280 provision has been impliedly repealed by section 1166(d). Whether IGRA has made broader inroads on Public Law 280 we need not decide; it has clearly made criminal enforcement of the State's laws prohibiting "slot machines" the exclusive province of the federal government.

Notes and Questions

1.   Section 1166, Pub. L. 280, and the OCCA. Recall the *Cabazon* Court's analysis of the applicability of the Organized Crime Control Act. There, California argued that the OCCA's incorporation of state law meant that the state could enforce its laws against the tribal gaming operations. The Supreme Court rejected this argument based on the exclusive federal jurisdiction to enforce federal criminal statutes, even those that incorporate state law. And, of course, the *Cabazon* Court held that Pub. L. 280 did not allow California to enforce its gambling laws on the tribes' reservations. Are the state's arguments in *Sycuan Band* regarding section 1166 and Pub. L. 280 specious? Why or why not?

The *Sycuan Band* case is revisited in Chapter 5 in the context of scope of gaming.

2.   Other criminal statutes. As discussed in the Senate Report, other federal criminal statutes may apply to illegal gambling in Indian country. The most notable is the Johnson Act, particularly the so-called Indian Gambling Act provision, found in 15 U.S.C. § 1175(a):

> It shall be unlawful to manufacture, recondition, repair, sell, transport, possess, or use any gambling device in the District of Columbia, in any possession of the United States, within Indian country as defined in section 1151 of Title 18 [the Major Crimes Act] or within the special maritime and territorial jurisdiction of the United States. . . .

The Johnson Act defines "gambling device" broadly:

> The term "gambling device" means—
>
> (1) any so-called "slot machine" or any other machine or mechanical device an essential part of which is a drum or reel with insignia thereon, and (A) which when operated may deliver, as the result of the application of an element of chance, any money or property, or (B) by the operation of which a person may become entitled to receive, as the result of the application of an element of chance, any money or property; or
>
> (2) any other machine or mechanical device (including, but not limited to, roulette wheels and similar devices) designed and manufactured primarily for use in connection with gambling, and (A) which when operated may deliver, as the result of the application of an element of chance, any money or property, or (B) by the operation of which a person may become entitled to receive, as the result of the application of an element of chance, any money or property; or
>
> (3) any subassembly or essential part intended to be used in connection with any such machine or mechanical device, but which is not attached to any such machine or mechanical device as a constituent part.

15 U.S.C. 1171(a).

IGRA specifically excludes from the Johnson Act Class III gaming conducted under a tribal-state compact:

> The provisions of section 1175 of title 15 shall not apply to any gaming conducted under a Tribal-State compact that—
>
> (A) is entered into under paragraph (3) by a State in which gambling devices are legal, and
>
> (B) is in effect.

25 U.S.C. § 2710(d)(6).

One issue is the import of the phrase "by a State in which gambling devices are legal." In *Citizen Band Potawatomi Indian Tribe v. Green*, 995 F.2d 179 (10th Cir. 1993), the court held that whether gaming devices were legal in a particular state should be determined by state law, not the terms of the compact in effect. "Congress must have meant," reasoned the court, "that gambling devices be legal absent the Tribal-State compact; otherwise it would not have been necessary to require both that gambling devices be legal and that the compact be 'in effect.'" The implications of state law and the legality of games authorized by a compact are discussed in Chapters 5 and 8. Another issue arises with regard to Class II gambling devices, which, because they are not conducted under a compact, are not expressly excluded from the Johnson Act under § 2710(d)(6). The Johnson Act's applicability to Class II devices is discussed in Chapter 4.

Problem 3: "Something for Everyone to Hate"

According to one commentator, "Like most compromises, IGRA has something for everyone to hate." Which aspects of IGRA do you think would be most "hated" by the following groups and interests, and why?

- Tribes generally
- Tribes with Class II operations
- Tribes with Class III operations
- Tribes without any gaming operations
- States with charitable gaming only
- States with commercial gaming
- States with lotteries
- Charities engaged in gaming
- Commercial gambling interests
- Local law enforcement
- State gaming commissions
- Federal courts
- U.S. Department of Interior

Chapter 4

Bingo and Other Forms of Class II Gaming

A. Overview

IGRA regulates two classes of gaming, Class II and Class III (recall from Chapter 3 that Class I or traditional tribal gaming is not subject to IGRA), under two separate regulatory schemes that are similar in some respects, and very different in others. Most significant, regulation of Class II gaming, generally referred to as "bingo," falls under tribal and federal jurisdiction; the state has no formal regulatory role.

Although seemingly eclipsed by the more lucrative and expanding Class III market, Class II gaming remains important—and controversial—for at least two reasons. First, tribes may operate Class II games in states that do not allow or refuse to negotiate casino-style gaming. Nearly every state permits bingo, opening the door to Class II tribal gaming in those states. Even in states that allow Class III gaming, a tribe may use Class II gaming to increase, for example, the number of gaming machines allowed under the compact. Second, the Class II market created by IGRA has inspired new technology—in short, this is not your grandmother's bingo—that greatly enhances the profitability of Class II gaming. In Florida, where the state has refused to negotiate a Class III compact, Class II tribal gaming revenue topped $1 billion in 2006. Alan P. Meister, Indian Gaming Industry Report (2007–2008 ed.).

In this Chapter, we lay out the statutory requirements for Class II gaming and discuss some of the complicated issues arising out of IGRA's treatment of Class II gaming.

B. Conducting Class II Gaming

1. Statutory Requirements

Class II games include bingo and other non-house-banked games similar to bingo, such as pull-tabs, lotto, and punch boards, if played in the same location as bingo. 25 U.S.C. § 2703(7); 25 C.F.R. §§ 502.3, 502.9. The general statutory requirements for Class II gaming are set out in § 2710(b) in IGRA. In addition to the prerequisites that gaming may be conducted only by an Indian tribe and only on Indian lands within the tribe's jurisdiction, discussed in Chapter 3, subsection (b)(1) contains two further requirements:

> (1) An Indian tribe may engage in, or license and regulate, class II gaming on Indian lands within such tribe's jurisdiction, if—

(A) such Indian gaming is located within a State that permits such gaming for any purpose by any person, organization or entity (and such gaming is not otherwise specifically prohibited on Indian lands by Federal law), and

(B) the governing body of the Indian tribe adopts an ordinance or resolution which is approved by the Chairman.

The "permits such gaming" requirement in §2710(b)(1)(A) for the most part easily is met in the context of Class II, as nearly all states allow charitable bingo. We discuss this requirement further in Chapter 5, in the more controversial context of Class III gaming.

Section 2710(b)(1)(A) requires a tribal government to exercise its political authority to enact legislation authorizing Class II gaming yet subjects that ordinance or resolution to NIGC scrutiny and approval. Subsection (b)(2) further describes the content of the required tribal ordinance:

(2) The Chairman shall approve any tribal ordinance or resolution concerning the conduct, or regulation of class II gaming on the Indian lands within the tribe's jurisdiction if such ordinance or resolution provides that—

(A) except as provided in paragraph (4) [which allows a tribe to license non-tribal Class II gaming operations on tribal lands in general conformance with state regulation of similar activities], the Indian tribe will have the sole proprietary interest and responsibility for the conduct of any gaming activity;

(B) net revenues from any tribal gaming are not to be used for purposes other than—

(i) to fund tribal government operations or programs;

(ii) to provide for the general welfare of the Indian tribe and its members;

(iii) to promote tribal economic development;

(iv) to donate to charitable organizations; or

(v) to help fund operations of local government agencies;

(C) annual outside audits of the gaming, which may be encompassed within existing independent tribal audit systems, will be provided by the Indian tribe to the Commission;

(D) all contracts for supplies, services, or concessions for a contract amount in excess of $25,000 annually (except contracts for professional legal or accounting services) relating to such gaming shall be subject to such independent audits;

(E) the construction and maintenance of the gaming facility, and the operation of that gaming is conducted in a manner which adequately protects the environment and the public health and safety; and

(F) there is an adequate system which—

(i) ensures that background investigations are conducted on the primary management officials and key employees of the gaming enterprise and that oversight of such officials and their management is conducted on an ongoing basis; and

(ii) includes—

(I) tribal licenses for primary management officials and key employees of the gaming enterprise with prompt notification to the Commission of the issuance of such licenses;

(II) a standard whereby any person whose prior activities, criminal record, if any, or reputation, habits and associations pose a threat to the public interest or to the effective regulation of gaming, or create or enhance the dangers of unsuitable, unfair, or illegal practices and methods and activities in the conduct of gaming shall not be eligible for employment; and

(III) notification by the Indian tribe to the Commission of the results of such background check before the issuance of any of such licenses.

In addition to the five basic permitted government uses of gaming revenue in (b)(2), which in turn are key elements of the development and implementation of tribal public policy, subsection (b)(3) authorizes per capita payments to individual tribal members:

(3) Net revenues from any class II gaming activities conducted or licensed by any Indian tribe may be used to make per capita payments to members of the Indian tribe only if—

(A) the Indian tribe has prepared a plan to allocate revenues to uses authorized by paragraph (2)(B);

(B) the plan is approved by the Secretary as adequate, particularly with respect to uses described in clause (i) or (iii) of paragraph (2)(B);

(C) the interests of minors and other legally incompetent persons who are entitled to receive any of the per capita payments are protected and preserved and the per capita payments are disbursed to the parents or legal guardian of such minors or legal incompetents in such amounts as may be necessary for the health, education, or welfare, of the minor or other legally incompetent person under a plan approved by the Secretary and the governing body of the Indian tribe; and

(D) the per capita payments are subject to Federal taxation and tribes notify members of such tax liability when payments are made.

Before a tribe may operate Class II gaming, then, it must enact an authorizing ordinance and submit it to the NIGC chair for approval. *See* 25 C.F.R. pt. 522. The Commission has developed a model tribal ordinance that meets the requirements of subsection (b)(2) as well as federal regulations; the model ordinance is excerpted and discussed in Chapter 7. The NIGC also will determine whether Class II gaming is permitted "for any purpose by any person, organization or entity" under state law. The NIGC's regulatory authority, including its power to enforce IGRA and federal regulations, is discussed in more detail in Chapter 6.

Notes and Questions

1.   Federal regulation of Class II gaming. Recall from Chapters 2 and 3 that beginning in 1979 with the Seminole Tribe's bingo hall, tribes successfully operated bingo and other games prior to IGRA's passage. As the Senate Report noted,

Since the Seminole Tribe opened its game and succeeded in court, over 100 bingo games have been started on Indian lands in states where bingo is otherwise legal.... [T]hese games generate more than $100 million in annual revenues to the tribes, ... [enabling them], like lotteries and other games have done for State and local governments, to provide a wider range of government services to tribal citizens and reservation residents than would otherwise have been possible.

With regard to the Cabazon and Morongo Bands' operations, the *Cabazon* Court noted that "California does not allege any present criminal involvement in the [tribes'] enterprises, and the Ninth Circuit discerned none." Senator McCain, in his separate statement in the Senate Report, stated that "in 15 years of gaming activity on Indian reservations there has never been one clearly proven case of organized criminal activity." If all of that was true—that tribes were profitably operating bingo and card games, using the revenue to improve the general welfare of the tribes and their members, and successfully shielding the games from organized crime—then why was additional federal oversight necessary or appropriate? What purpose do the statutory requirements serve?

2.   *Tribes' use of net revenues.* A significant constraint on tribal sovereignty is IGRA's limited authorized uses of net gaming revenue. At the same time, as governments, tribes generally were held to IGRA's broad categories of appropriate uses even before the statute was passed. As the industry has grown, the issue of how tribes use gaming revenue has become more controversial, with increasing calls for tribal accountability. During a recent Senate oversight hearing, however, NIGC Chair Philip N. Hogen stated that "[t]he overwhelming majority of tribes ... do an excellent job of ensuring that the gaming revenues from their operations are used for the purposes authorized under IGRA." Oversight Hearing Before the S. Comm. on Indian Affairs on the Regulation of Indian Gaming, 109th Cong., 1st Sess. 12 (Apr. 27, 2005) (statement of NIGC Chair Philip N. Hogen). Consider this perspective on the issue:

> A frequently expressed concern is that despite IGRA's mandate, tribes make questionable or unauthorized use of their gaming revenue. Tribal accounts, including testimony by tribal leaders before the National Gambling Impact Study Commission and the Senate Committee on Indian Affairs, consistently describe appropriate use of tribal gaming revenue within IGRA's constraints. Although some tribes make per capita payments to members as allowed under IGRA, the overwhelming majority of gaming tribes focus on strengthening tribal government institutions and enhancing public services to tribal members. A number of studies support these accounts, as does the 2000 U.S. Census findings of socioeconomic improvements on many reservations.
>
> Due respect for tribes as governments requires that tribal accounts of revenue use not be inappropriately discounted.... [W]e urge Congress to exercise caution in adopting a blanket solution that appears, based on current evidence, to be more of a possibility than a widespread reality. The "vast, vast majority" of tribes do a good job of regulating their enterprises and act to ensure that gaming revenue is used to benefit tribes and tribal members in accordance with IGRA.

Kathryn R.L. Rand & Steven Andrew Light, *How Congress Can and Should "Fix" the Indian Gaming Regulatory Act: Recommendations for Law and Policy Reform*, 13 Va. J. Soc. Pol'y & L. 396, 456–58 (2006). Are you persuaded? What is the strongest argument in favor of strengthened accountability measures for tribes' use of gaming revenue?

3.   *Per capita payments.* IGRA permits a tribe to make per capita distributions of net gaming revenue to its members if the uses in § 2710(b)(2)(B) are adequately met and the tribe's distribution plan is approved by the Interior Secretary. Whether gaming revenue is sufficient to meet other basic needs of the tribe, including funding of tribal government operations and programs and promoting tribal economic development, plainly depends on a number of factors. The size and socioeconomic baseline of the tribe, the profitability of its gaming operation, and the level of existing government services and programs affect a tribe's decision—and ability—to make per capita payments. About

three-quarters of tribes with gaming operations do not make per capita payments, choosing instead to use net revenues to fund tribal government services and provide for the general welfare of tribal members. Among tribes with per capita distribution plans, individual payments to members range from a few hundred dollars a year to tens of thousands of dollars each month. Typically, the largest per capita payments are made by a handful of small tribes with casinos in extremely lucrative markets. Per capita payments fuel the perception of "casino-rich Indians," a theme that permeates criticism of Indian gaming. *See, e.g.*, Light & Rand, Indian Gaming and Tribal Sovereignty, at 121–34.

Because per capita payments are limited to tribal members, the membership determinations of some tribes are coming under scrutiny as well. Generally speaking, tribal sovereignty encompasses the exclusive right to make membership determinations. *See Santa Clara Pueblo v. Martinez*, 436 U.S. 49 (1978). Accordingly, federal courts have been reluctant to review a tribe's distribution of such payments. Two federal district courts, in *Maxam v. Lower Sioux Indian Community*, 829 F. Supp. 277 (D. Minn. 1993), and *Ross v. Flandreau Santee Sioux Tribe*, 809 F. Supp. 738 (D.S.D. 1992), have ruled that the court may prevent a tribe from distributing per capita payments in violation of IGRA. In both cases, the tribe's per capita payment plan had not yet been approved by the Interior Secretary, and the courts enjoined the tribes from making per capita payments. In *Smith v. Babbitt*, 875 F. Supp. 1353 (D. Minn. 1995), *aff'd*, 100 F. 3d 556 (8th Cir. 1996), the district court held that federal jurisdiction under *Maxam* and *Ross* was limited to determining compliance with IGRA's per capita payment requirements and did not extend to examining the legitimacy of a tribe's membership determinations. *See also Lincoln v. Saginaw Chippewa Indian Tribe*, 967 F. Supp. 966 (E.D. Mich. 1997) (declining to review the tribe's membership determinations in the context of a duly approved per capita payment plan). In *Hein v. Capitan Grande Band of Diegueno Mission Indians*, 201 F.3d 1256 (9th Cir. 2000), the Court of Appeals for the Ninth Circuit held that because there is no general private right of action to enforce IGRA's provisions, a tribal "splinter group" could not sue in federal court under IGRA to recover their purported share of the tribe's gaming revenue.

Controversy over tribes' banishment or disenrollment of members also has been fueled by per capita payments. For a discussion of *Ross* and *Maxam* in the context of a call for reform to address "disenfranchisement and other abuses under the IGRA," see Eric Reitman, Note, *An Argument for the Partial Abrogation of Federally Recognized Indian Tribes' Sovereign Power Over Membership*, 92 Va. L. Rev. 793 (2006). For more on Indian gaming and tribal membership generally, see Kathryn R.L. Rand & Steven A. Light, *Virtue or Vice? How IGRA Shapes the Politics of Native American Gaming, Sovereignty, and Identity*, 4 Va. J. Soc. Pol'y & L. 381 (1997). For more on tribal banishment, see Patrice H. Kunesh, *Banishment as Cultural Justice in Contemporary Tribal Legal Systems*, 37 N.M. L. Rev. 85 (2007); see also Angela R. Riley, *Good (Native) Governance*, 107 Colum. L. Rev. 1049 (2007).

2. Tribal "Self-Regulation"

After a tribe has operated a Class II gaming establishment for three years, it may apply for a "certificate of self-regulation" under § 2710(c):

> (3) Any Indian tribe which operates a class II gaming activity and which—
>
>> (A) has continuously conducted such activity for a period of not less than three years, including at least one year after October 17, 1988; and

(B) has otherwise complied with the provisions of this section may petition the Commission for a certificate of self-regulation.

(4) The Commission shall issue a certificate of self-regulation if it determines from available information, and after a hearing if requested by the tribe, that the tribe has—

(A) conducted its gaming activity in a manner which—

(i) has resulted in an effective and honest accounting of all revenues;

(ii) has resulted in a reputation for safe, fair, and honest operation of the activity; and

(iii) has been generally free of evidence of criminal or dishonest activity;

(B) adopted and is implementing adequate systems for—

(i) accounting for all revenues from the activity;

(ii) investigation, licensing, and monitoring of all employees of the gaming activity; and

(iii) investigation, enforcement and prosecution of violations of its gaming ordinance and regulations; and

(C) conducted the operation on a fiscally and economically sound basis.

(5) During any year in which a tribe has a certificate for self-regulation—

(A) the tribe shall not be subject to the provisions of paragraphs (1), (2), (3), and (4) of section 2706(b) of this title;

(B) the tribe shall continue to submit an annual independent audit as required by subsection (b)(2)(C) of this section and shall submit to the Commission a complete resume on all employees hired and licensed by the tribe subsequent to the issuance of a certificate of self-regulation; and

(C) the Commission may not assess a fee on such activity pursuant to § 2717 of this title in excess of one quarter of 1 per centum of the gross revenue.

(6) The Commission may, for just cause and after an opportunity for a hearing, remove a certificate of self-regulation by majority vote of its members.

The NIGC's Office of Self-Regulation issues certificates in accordance with § 2710(c) and Commission regulations (25 C.F.R. pt. 518). A self-regulation certificate reduces but does not remove the NIGC's oversight authority over the tribe's Class II gaming operations. The NIGC continues to exercise its power to enforce the tribe's compliance with IGRA, federal regulations, and the tribal gaming ordinance.

A tribe must notify the NIGC of any circumstances that might cause the Commission to reassess the tribe's self-regulation status, such as the casino's financial instability or a new management contract. Like the other final agency decisions of the NIGC, the decision to remove a certificate of self-regulation is reviewable in federal district court.

Notes and Questions

1.   *Self-regulation limited to Class II gaming.* Why did Congress include the possibility of tribal self-regulation of Class II gaming? Congress did not include a similar provision for Class III gaming. Why not?

2.   *Eligibility for self-regulation status.* Under NIGC regulations, relevant evidence for determining whether a tribe has met the criteria for self-regulation under § 2710(c)(4) includes:

- Tribe's adoption of adequate minimum internal control standards (MICS) (and a reporting system for the casino's compliance with the same)
- Stringent suitability standards for tribal gaming regulators
- Policies concerning conflicts of interest
- An adequate system for prosecuting violations of tribal ordinances
- Tribe's establishment of an adequately funded independent regulatory agency with specified powers and responsibilities
- Records indicating the casino's financial stability
- Compliance with applicable health and safety codes, the availability of emergency services, and other indicators that the casino is operated safely

See 25 C.F.R § 518.4. NIGC regulations place the burden on the tribe to establish that it has met the statutory criteria.

C. Defining Class II Gaming

As explained above, IGRA lays out a comprehensive regulatory scheme for Class II gaming. Unlike the regulatory framework for Class III gaming, the scheme for Class II gaming involves only the federal government and tribal governments. Class II gaming does not require negotiation of a tribal-state compact, a requirement for Class III gaming that has proven to be quite onerous in some circumstances. Though some tribes may be precluded from conducting Class III gaming as a matter of state public policy and thus have no choice but to pursue Class II gaming, other tribes may choose to pursue Class II gaming even in states that permit Class III gaming. One advantage of Class II gaming is that there is no direct involvement of the state. Accordingly, whether a game falls within Class II or Class III is crucial. If it falls within Class II, it may be operated in the absence of a tribal-state compact; if it falls outside Class II, it will be classified as Class III and its operation will be illegal without a valid tribal-state compact.

On its face, IGRA's definition of Class II gaming in § 2703(7) appears straightforward:

(A) The term "class II gaming" means —

(i) the game of chance commonly known as bingo (whether or not electronic, computer, or other technologic aids are used in connection therewith) —

(I) which is played for prizes, including monetary prizes, with cards bearing numbers or other designations,

(II) in which the holder of the card covers such numbers or designations when objects, similarly numbered or designated, are drawn or electronically determined, and

(III) in which the game is won by the first person covering a previously designated arrangement of numbers or designations on such cards, including (if played in the same location) pull-tabs, lotto, punch boards, tip jars, instant bingo, and other games similar to bingo, and

(ii) card games that —

(I) are explicitly authorized by the laws of the State, or

(II) are not explicitly prohibited by the laws of the State and are played at any location in the State, but only if such card games are played in conformity with those laws and regulations (if any) of the State regarding hours or periods of operation of such card games or limitations on wagers or pot sizes in such card games.

(B) The term "class II gaming" does not include—

(i) any banking card games, including baccarat, chemin de fer, or blackjack (21), or

(ii) electronic or electromechanical facsimiles of any game of chance or slot machines of any kind.

A few games and operations, specified in subsections (7)(C)–(F), also are "grandfathered" in Class II. For the most part, though, Class II gaming consists of bingo, pull-tabs and similar games, and non-house-banked card games. Significantly, Congress noted that Class II games could be played in connection with "electronic, computer, or other technologic aids," though the statutory definition expressly excludes from Class II "electronic or electromechanical facsimiles of any game of chance or slot machines of any kind." This distinction is discussed in detail in the next section. The NIGC has promulgated regulatory definitions for Class II gaming that, for the most part, restate the statutory definitions. *See* 25 C.F.R. § 502.3.

As the next cases illustrate, Congress's definition of Class II gaming may not be as simple as it appears.

Shakopee Mdewakanton Sioux Community v. Hope
16 F.3d 261 (8th Cir. 1994)

BEAM, Circuit Judge.

Under IGRA, gaming on Indian land is divided into three categories. Class II gaming consists of bingo, "games similar to bingo," and certain card games. In April 1992, the [National Indian Gaming Commission] issued regulations classifying keno as class III gaming. [The regulation, 25 C.F.R. § 502.4, provides that Class III gaming includes "[a]ny house banking game, including but not limited to ... [c]asino games such as roulette, craps, and keno."] On appeal, the Tribe contends that the Commission's decision to classify keno as a class III game is arbitrary and capricious.

In [*Chevron v. Natural Resources Defense Council*, 467 U.S. 837 (1984)], the Supreme Court detailed the test that a court must employ when reviewing agency decisions which apply or interpret the statute that the agency administers. The *Chevron* test has two parts. A reviewing court must first determine whether congressional intent is clear from the plain language of the statute. If analysis of the statutory language does not yield an unambiguous congressional intent, the court must then look to the legislative history. When this expanded analysis reveals a clear congressional intent, an agency interpretation of the statute contrary to that intent is not entitled to deference. However, if the language of the statute is ambiguous, and the legislative history reveals no clear congressional intent, a reviewing court must defer to a reasonable agency interpretation of the statutory provision.

We find the term game "similar to bingo" in section 2703(7)(A)(i) of IGRA to be ambiguous. Our review of the legislative history does not reveal any clear congressional intent to include keno as a game "similar to bingo." On the contrary, keno was rarely mentioned during congressional deliberations, and nothing in the legislative history evinces a clear congressional intent with regard to the classification of keno under the statute. Having concluded that Congress expressed no clear intent for the classification of keno, we turn to the second part of our *Chevron* analysis: consideration of whether the Commission acted arbitrarily by classifying keno as class III gaming.

The Tribe's briefs elaborate the common history of keno and bingo in an attempt to demonstrate the close relationship between the two games. If this court were empowered to weigh evidence or to review the Commission's determination de novo, we might well be persuaded. However, review of the Commission's decision under *Chevron* is narrow. Unless we find the Commission's classification of keno to be impermissible, we must uphold the Commission's interpretation of the ambiguous statutory provision.

The Commission classified keno as class III gaming because keno is a house banking game. The Tribe contends that in light of the avowed purpose of the statute to increase Tribal economic development and Tribal self-sufficiency, this classification is arbitrary and capricious. The Tribe points out that it is a tenet of statutory construction that "statutes are to be construed liberally in favor of the Indians, with ambiguous provisions interpreted to their benefit."* *South Dakota v. Bourland,* 508 U.S. 679 (1993). [But] the dual purpose behind IGRA [includes providing] "a statutory basis for the regulation of gaming by an Indian tribe adequate to shield it from organized crime and other corrupting influences, to ensure that the Indian tribe is the primary beneficiary of the gaming operation, and to assure that gaming is conducted fairly and honestly by both the operator and players." 25 U.S.C. §2702.

In an attempt to effectuate the second purpose of the statute, and to shield Indian gaming from corruption, the Commission drew a bright line between house banking games and other types of gaming. We cannot find this decision to be counter to the requirement that statutes be interpreted in favor of the Indian Tribes. The balance to be struck between competing statutory purposes is exactly the sort of determination that is best left to agency discretion.

The Tribe does not suggest that the Commission refused to hear evidence concerning the common history of keno and bingo. Nor is there any evidence that the Commission otherwise abused the rulemaking process. To the contrary, the Commission conducted public hearings and solicited comments before promulgating rules under its statutory authority. Therefore, the Tribe's contentions boil down to an argument that the Commission made an incorrect decision. In light of the Commission's thorough consideration of the issues raised by the Tribes, we cannot conclude that the Commission acted arbitrarily simply because it reached a disfavored result. We need not be persuaded that an agency reached the best possible decision in order to uphold reasonable agency action.

---

* We note that the notion of interpreting a statute "in favor of the Indian Tribes" is problematic in a case like this. The Commission concluded that classifying keno as class III gaming protected Indian gaming from corrupting influences. The Tribe, however, vigorously rejects the contention that such an interpretation is "in favor of the Indian Tribes." The reviewing court is left with the dilemma of what exactly "in favor of the Indian Tribes" means. In this case, the Commission has considered the welfare of Indian Tribes in applying the statute, and has effectuated a clear statutory purpose drafted with the interests of the Indian Tribes in mind. Therefore, on the facts of this case, the Commission has satisfied the requirement that statutes be interpreted "in favor of the Indian Tribes" even though the Tribe contests the agency determination.

Notes and Questions

1.   *Judicial review of agency actions.* Note that the issue before the court was not whether keno should fall within Class II or Class III, but whether the NIGC's classification of keno as a Class III game was a reasonable agency action. Section 2714 specifies that the NIGC's final decisions are "final agency decisions for purposes of appeal to the appropriate Federal district court pursuant to" the APA. Section 706 of the APA requires the reviewing court to "hold unlawful and set aside" agency actions that are found to be, *inter alia,* "arbitrary, capricious, an abuse of discretion, or otherwise not in accordance with law."

2.   *"In favor of the Indian tribes."* Note the court's uncertainty about the proper application of the Indian canon of construction to construe statutes in favor of the tribe. If the NIGC's ruling is intended to fulfill IGRA's purpose of shielding Indian gaming from organized crime and other corrupting influences, is its interpretation of the Class II definition in favor of the tribe? Or is making keno more accessible to tribal operation by placing it in Class II in favor of the tribe? What's the difference between interpreting a statute "in favor of" tribes, and interpreting a statute in tribes' "best interests"? Does one articulation better serve the purpose of the Indian canon of construction?

United States v. 103 Electronic Gambling Devices

223 F.3d 1091 (9th Cir. 2000)

BERZON, Circuit Judge.

This case poses the question, what is bingo? In particular, we determine whether an electronic game called MegaMania, manufactured and sold by Multimedia Games, Inc. ("Multimedia"), is "bingo" as that term is defined in the Indian Gaming Regulatory Act.

In MegaMania, players compete against each other in a single, interlinked electronic game via a network of individual computer terminals located at tribal gaming facilities throughout the country. At their respective terminals, players may make an initial purchase at 25 cents per card of up to four electronic game "cards," displayed on the video screens of each terminal. A participant may play up to four cards at a time.

MegaMania does not commence until at least twelve people begin playing a minimum of 48 cards collectively. Once the game begins the players start receiving a series of three-number draws displayed on-screen and announced through audio channels. The numbers in each draw are generated by a machine which, until the Government seized it, was located at the Choctaw gaming facility in Arrowhead, Oklahoma. The machine "blows" approximately forty numbered ping pong balls (out of a pool of seventy-five balls) into a tube. A human operator keys into a computer the number of each ball in the forty-number sequence. The computer then feeds those numbers into the "game host," which in turn transmits the numbers three at a time to remote host computers at participating gaming facilities. Finally, the remote hosts transmit each three-number sequence to the terminals in their respective facilities. For each three number draw a player must pay 25 cents per card that he or she is playing (e.g., if a player has three cards on her screen, she must pay 75 cents per draw). This pay-per-draw style of play is called "ante up" bingo. After a set of numbers is drawn players must press a "Daub Cards" button to "cover" the called numbers on the cards. When a player presses the daub button, the computer automatically covers corresponding numbers on the player's cards. After each three-number draw is displayed a player has eight seconds to decide whether to continue playing the card(s) for another draw.

When a player covers a straight line either horizontally, vertically or diagonally and declares "bingo" (by pressing the daub button) on one or more cards, every player in every facility nationwide is notified of the bingo. Once a player gets bingo, this straight-line game ends. Each player with bingo wins a monetary prize, the amount of which is based on the total number of cards being played in the game, the number of balls drawn since the game began, and the number of players reaching bingo simultaneously. The top jackpot on the straight-line game is $5000, awarded for a bingo achieved after the first four numbers are drawn, the earliest point at which a player can get bingo.

In addition to the traditional straight-line game, there is a "corners game" ("Corner-Mania"). In the corners game, each player who covers two, three, or four corners of a card gets a prize. The corners game is played continuously until the straight-line game ends, so there can be one or more CornerMania winners on each draw after the first. If no corners game prize has been awarded before the straight-line game ends, additional numbers are drawn three at a time until at least one corner prize is given out.

Before considering whether MegaMania satisfies the three criteria for a class II bingo game set forth in 25 U.S.C. § 2703(7)(A)(i)(I)–(III), we turn to the Government's argument that these three factors are not the only criteria a game must meet to be an IGRA class II bingo game: The Government maintains that because IGRA uses the phrase "the game of chance commonly known as bingo" before spelling out the three criteria, *other* features that have traditionally characterized bingo games are also pertinent in determining whether or not a game is a class II bingo game. The Government contends, specifically, that (i) traditional bingo games lack the ante-up feature MegaMania possesses, (ii) in a traditional bingo game, unlike CornerMania, earnings depend on those of other players, and (iii) Mega-Mania's "manic pace" and potentially high stakes are markedly different than the placid tranquility and token rewards and losses associated with a traditional bingo game, *see* Alice Andrews, *Hooked on Bingo* 11 (1988) ("There is a calm and peacefulness in playing Bingo. There is a get-away-from-it-all feeling, kind of like bamboo fishing.").

The Government's efforts to capture more completely the Platonic "essence" of tradi-tional bingo are not helpful. Whatever a nostalgic inquiry into the vital characteristics of the game as it was played in our childhoods or hometowns might discover, IGRA's three explicit criteria, we hold, constitute the sole *legal* requirements for a game to count as class II bingo.

There would have been no point to Congress's putting the three very specific factors in the statute if there were also other, implicit criteria. The three included in the statute are in no way arcane if one knows anything about bingo, so why would Congress have in-cluded them if they were not meant to be exclusive?

Moreover, IGRA's definition of class II bingo includes "other games similar to bingo," explicitly precluding any reliance on the exact attributes of the children's pastime.

Finally, and critically, the NIGC's interpretation of both IGRA and the NIGC's pri-mary IGRA implementing regulation, 25 C.F.R. pt. 502, rests on the proposition that nei-ther Congress nor the Commission intended to "limit bingo to its classic form." *See* Action for Final Rule 25 C.F.R. pt. 502 ("502 Action"), 57 Fed.Reg. 12382, 12382 ("The Com-mission does not believe Congress intended to limit bingo to its classic form. If it had, it could have spelled out further requirements such as cards having the letters BINGO across the top, with numbers 1–15 in the first column, etc. In defining class II to include games similar to bingo, Congress intended to include more than 'bingo in its classic form' in that class."). The NIGC's conception of what counts as bingo under IGRA is entitled to substantial deference.

All told, IGRA's definition of "the game of chance commonly known as bingo" is broader than the Government would have us read it. We decline the invitation to impose restrictions on its meaning besides those Congress explicitly set forth in the statute. Class II bingo under IGRA is not limited to the game we played as children.

[We now turn to the statutory requirements. The Government concedes that Mega-Mania satisfies the first two requirements in section 2703(7)(A)(i).] As stated, IGRA defines bingo as, *inter alia*, a game "(III) in which the game is won by the first person covering a previously designated arrangement of numbers ... on such cards." 25 U.S.C. § 2703(7)(A)(i); *see also* 25 C.F.R. § 502.3. The Government contends the "continuous-win" feature of CornerMania does not comply with this requirement, because CornerMania can result in multiple payouts before the straight-line game ends, and each CornerMania payout does not depend on the number of other players receiving CornerMania prize money but rather on the number of corners covered on each draw and on the number of balls drawn since the game began. For these two reasons, maintains the Government, MegaMania is not "won by the first person covering a previously designated arrangement of numbers or designations on such cards." The question before us, though, is whether MegaMania, not one of its constituent components, satisfies IGRA's statutory criteria for class II gaming. Thus, MegaMania *as a whole* is "the game" to which [the statutory definition] pertains.

Turning to the question of whether MegaMania satisfies § 2703(7)(A)(i)(III), as an initial matter, there is no reason that the "previously designated arrangement" to which the statute refers must be a straight line. Indeed, the statutory description just quoted quite clearly permits *any* pattern to yield a prize, as long as the pattern is "previously designated." Moreover, even if we were to resort for this purpose to the inquiry into "essential" bingo we have already rejected, we would not rule otherwise, [as examples of common pre-designated winning patterns include the traditional straight line, four corners, letters X or L, or covering the full card].

As for the ultimate question of whether MegaMania is "won" by the first person covering a previously designated arrangement, assuming that in a given game of MegaMania players win several rounds of CornerMania before the straight-line game ends, it would appear that each such player has "won" by "covering a previously designated arrangement." The first focus of this issue is nothing less than the meaning of the word "win": Can someone "win" a game even though the other players may also "win"? That is, does "win" necessarily mean "beat"?

The answer, according to Webster's Dictionary, is that "win" can mean "beat" but need not: That dictionary's first definition of "win" is "'[t]o achieve victory over others in a competition or contest,'" while the second is "'[t]o receive [money] as a prize or a reward for performance.'" So, for example, in an instant lottery game, everyone whose scratch card entitles them to ten dollars "wins" a prize, with no effect on how many others may win or in what amount. Because "winning" does not *necessarily* entail vanquishing one's opponents, the meaning of "win" in the statute is at worst ambiguous. In light of that ambiguity, we look for indications that Congress intended to preclude the award of multiple prizes in a single game of bingo.

The record in this case establishes that, in addition to the usual straight-line prize, some traditional live bingo games also make interim payouts to players who cover the corners of their cards; we presume those players believe that they have "won" prizes, even though the game has not ended and others may "win" as much or more. Additionally, as already stated, IGRA explicitly designates instant bingo as a class II game if it is played "in the same location" as a bingo game. That Congress would permit this variant of bingo, yielding interim prizes while the main game is ongoing, indicates it did not intend to forbid interim prizes like those CornerMania awards during a game of MegaMania.

In light of the foregoing considerations, it is telling that IGRA does not state the game has to *end* when the first person wins anything. Had Congress intended to proscribe interim prizes, the statute could have been drafted to say that "the game ends" instead of "the game is won," or could have included an express restriction that only one prize be given during the game. The sum of the matter is that the IGRA requirement that a "bingo" game be "won" by the "first player" covering a pre-designated pattern does not mean the game must *end* when one player does so, so that everyone else wins nothing. We conclude, therefore, that MegaMania *is* "won by the first person covering a previously designated arrangement of numbers … on [his or her] cards," within the meaning of IGRA.

IGRA's implementing regulations designate any house banking game as class III gaming. 25 C.F.R. § 502.4(a). A house banking game is "any game of chance that is played with the house as a participant in the game, where the house takes on all players, collects from all losers, and pays all winners, and the house can win." 25 C.F.R. § 502.11. The Government reasons that MegaMania fits within this definition because CornerMania's payouts do not hinge on the success of other players but are instead based on a mathematical formula that ensures that over time the house will net fifteen percent of players' antes.

In MegaMania, however, the house is not a participant in the game the way it is in blackjack, for example, where the house plays a hand, and the success of the players depends on the success of the house. And the mere fact that the house nets a percentage of the players' fees for playing certainly cannot define a "house banking" game. In any church-hall bingo game, the "house" regularly nets some portion of the money it takes in, or there would be no point in sponsoring the game. Thus, while the house does indeed earn a fixed percentage of players' antes over time, that fact cannot shoehorn MegaMania into the definition of a house banking game. Just because the house turns a profit on players' deposits doesn't make the house "a participant in the game" that "takes on all players" and that "can win."

Notes and Questions

1.   *House-banked games.* IGRA excludes "banking card games" from its definition of Class II games. As the court noted, the NIGC's regulations define "house banking game" as "any game of chance that is played with the house as a participant in the game, where the house takes on all players, collects from all losers, and pays all winners, and the house can win." 25 C.F.R. § 502.11. Any "house banking game" falls within Class III under NIGC regulations. *Id.* § 502.4. The more widely used term is "house-banked game." A poker game in which players play only against each other is not house-banked; the typical blackjack game, in which players play against the dealer who hands out payment for winning hands, is house-banked. The *103 Electronic Gambling Devices* court concluded that the fact that the house profits from games played on the "MegaMania" machines did not make the games house-banked, and therefore within Class III, under IGRA's and the NIGC's definitions. In *United States v. 162 MegaMania Gambling Devices*, 231 F.3d 713 (10th Cir. 2000), the Tenth Circuit reached the same conclusion. "House-banked," then, is different than whether the house profits from the game. Thus, a poker game for which the house charges each player an entry fee is not house-banked. As the Ninth Circuit reasoned, "In any church-hall bingo game, the 'house' regularly nets some portion of the money it takes in, or there would be no point in sponsoring the game."

*2.	**What is bingo?*** As the Ninth Circuit said at the start of its opinion, "This case poses the question, what is bingo?" What's the answer?

D. Class II Technologic Aids and Class III Facsimiles

IGRA's definition of Class II gaming allows games to be played in connection with "electronic, computer, or other technologic aids," but specifically excludes "electronic or electromechanical facsimiles of any game of chance or slot machines of any kind." 25 U.S.C. § 2703(7). Electronic facsimiles of Class II games and slot machines fall within the residual category of Class III. Perhaps the most vexing question relative to Class II gaming is the line between a Class II electronic aid and a Class III electronic facsimile. The issue is an important one. A tribe may operate Class II "aids" in states that allow bingo, but not casino-style games, and without the necessity of negotiating a tribal-state compact. Class II machines may also supplement slot machines, where the number of slots a tribe may operate is limited by the compact. Class III "facsimiles" and slot machines, on the other hand, are legal (and exempt from the Johnson Act's criminal prohibitions) only if operated in conformance with a valid compact.

The Senate Report casts some light on Congress's intent in this regard:

> Consistent with tribal rights that were recognized and affirmed in the *Cabazon* decision, the Committee intends … that tribes have maximum flexibility to utilize games such as bingo and lotto for tribal economic development. The Committee specifically rejects any inference that tribes should restrict class II games to existing games sizes, levels of participation, or current technology. The Committee intends that tribes be given the opportunity to take advantage of modern methods of conducting class II games and the language regarding technology is designed to provide maximum flexibility. In this regard, the Committee recognizes that tribes may wish to join with other tribes to coordinate their class II operations and thereby enhance the potential of increasing revenues. For example, linking participant players at various reservations whether in the same or different States, by means of telephone, cable, television or satellite may be a reasonable approach for tribes to take. Simultaneous games participation between and among reservations can be made practical by use of computers and telecommunications technology as long as the use of such technology does not change the fundamental characteristics of the bingo or lotto games and as long as such games are otherwise operated in accordance with applicable Federal communications law. In other words, such technology would merely broaden the potential participation levels and is readily distinguishable from the use of electronic facsimiles in which a single participant plays a game with or against a machine rather than with or against other players.

S. Rep. 100-446, 100th Cong., 2d Sess., 1988 U.S.C.C.A.N. 3071.

IGRA's Class II category essentially created a niche market for gaming manufacturers to develop exciting and entertaining electronic bingo machines while staying within the statutory definition of an electronic aid. The machines have rapidly evolved from the handheld "electronic bingo cards" often used on cruise ships to consoles with spinning video reels that resemble, at least superficially, slot machines. While the "box"—the console—may look like a slot machine, the game played on the machine is a live, external bingo game rather than the individual, internal random number generator contained in a slot machine.

As happens when technological innovation intersects with law, the federal courts (and the NIGC) have struggled to give substance to IGRA's vague definitions.

Cabazon Band of Mission Indians v. NIGC
14 F.3d 633 (D.C. Cir. 1994)

RANDOLPH, Circuit Judge.

Seven federally recognized Indian Tribes claim that new regulations of the National Indian Gaming Commission improperly consider certain computerized games to be in a different regulatory category than their non-computerized counterparts.

The game at issue in this case is "pull-tabs," one of the games included in the definition of class II gaming. The most common form of pull-tabs is the paper version. Gamblers purchase a card from a deck. The set of cards ("the deal") contains a predetermined number of winners. Upon purchasing the card, the gambler pulls the paper tab open to find out if he is a winner. In the paper version each gambler competes against all other gamblers in the hall playing the game. There is now a computerized version of pull-tabs. The computer randomly selects a card for the gambler, pulls the tab at the gambler's direction, and displays the result on the screen. The computer version, like the paper version, has a fixed number of winning cards in each deal. The computers may be interconnected so that each gambler simultaneously plays against other gamblers in "pods" or "banks" of as many as forty machines.

The Tribes concede that the video version of pull-tabs is the same game as the paper version. Because class II gaming does not include "electronic or electromechanical facsimiles of any game of chance," this concession alone demonstrates that the video game is not in the class II category. As commonly understood, facsimiles are exact copies, or duplicates. Although there may be room for a broader interpretation of "facsimile," the video version of pull-tabs falls within the core meaning of electronic facsimile. It exactly replicates the paper version of the game, and if that is not sufficient to make it a facsimile, we doubt that anything could qualify.

The Tribes' contrary position is this: The *only* point at which the use of electronics or other technology could fall into the class III category is where a different game — a copy, or imitation, something other than the genuine article; in plain English, a "facsimile" — is created by such technology. All other uses of technology, according to the Tribes, should be considered "aids." We view it as something other than "plain English" to say that only electronic versions of games different from the originals are exact duplicates. The meanings of words in a statute do not necessarily correspond with dictionary definitions. Context matters. So often does history. Yet there are limits to how far language, written in the formal style of a statute, may be wrenched. We would no sooner take "yes" to signify "no" than we would take "same" to denote only "different." One might stretch "facsimiles" to cover inexact copies, but the possibility of such a construction does not assist the Tribes. In short, at the least, IGRA's exclusion of electronic facsimiles removes games from the class II category when those games are wholly incorporated into an electronic or electromechanical version.

The sentences in the Senate Committee report to which the Tribes refer do not alter our judgment. Near the end of a lengthy paragraph discussing how separate Tribes might coordinate their gaming businesses, the following appears: "Simultaneous games participation between and among reservations can be made practical by use of computers and telecommunications technology as long as the use of such technology does not change the fundamental characteristics of the bingo or lotto games." Pointing to the Report's caution about not using technology to change the "fundamental characteristics" of the games, the Tribes argue that an electronic version of a game cannot be a "facsimile" unless it fundamentally changes the game. While the Report is less than clear about the distinction between electronic aids and electronic facsimiles, this portion of the Report focuses not on how using technology might create an electronic facsimile, but on "*communications* technology that might be used to link bingo players in several remote locations." That sort of technology is, as the Report itself recognizes, distinguishable from electronic facsimiles of the game itself. To be sure, the only supposed electronic "facsimiles" mentioned in this paragraph of the Report are those in which "a single participant plays a game with or against a machine rather than with or against other players." Although in video pull-tabs the gambler is playing the game "with ... a machine," the Tribes are right that, as in paper pull-tabs, the gambler also is playing against other gamblers. But the Tribes are wrong to suppose that the example mentioned in this passage must be the only type of electronic copies Congress meant to include under section 2703(7)(B)(ii). An illustration given in one sentence of a committee report scarcely excludes the possibility of other examples. Still less does it, rather than the language of the statute, express the will of Congress.

Ambiguous statutes, the Tribes tell us, should be construed in favor of the Indians. *See Montana v. Blackfeet Tribe of Indians*, 471 U.S. 759 (1985). Congress believed the Indian Gaming Regulatory Act would benefit Indians in several ways. The Tribes focus on the Act's objective of advancing tribal economic interests. The Act has another objective, however: protecting tribes and their members from the dangers associated with large-scale gaming operations. Which construction of the Act favors the Indians, the one including electronic pull-tab games under class II gaming or the one placing this version of the game under the more restrictive category of class III? In this case there is no need to choose. When the statutory language is clear, as it is here, the canon may not be employed.

Notes and Questions

1.   *The meaning of "facsimile."* The court concluded that the video pull-tab machine at issue "exactly replicates the paper version of the game, and if that is not sufficient to make it a facsimile, we doubt that anything could qualify." What is the line between an electronic facsimile of a game, and an electronic aid that, in the words of the Senate Report, "does not change the fundamental characteristics" of the game? The Ninth Circuit considered a similar machine in *Sycuan Band of Mission Indians v. Roache*, 54 F.3d 535 (9th Cir. 1994). In that case, the court relied on the common definition of "facsimile" and *Cabazon Band v. NIGC* to hold that the electronic pull-tab machine was an electronic copy of the paper version. The court stated,

> We conclude that the machines present the player with "electronic facsimiles" of the pull-tab game. We do so in part because it is extremely difficult for us to conceive what Congress meant by the term "facsimile" if it does not include the games played by use of these machines.... The pull-tab machines present self-contained computer games copying the pull-tab principle, and they are played electronically.

Sycuan Band, 54 F.3d at 542. In *Cabazon Band v. NIGC*, the tribe argued that Congress's statement that electronic aids should not alter the fundamental characteristics of the game undermined the court's "plain language" approach to the meaning of "facsimile." In response to the same argument, the *Sycuan Band* court explained,

This passage, it seems to us, cuts both ways. It supports the Band's argument that electronic devices are permissible "aids" if they do not alter the "fundamental characteristics" of the game. The Band emphasizes that the computer in electronic pull-tab games duplicates the characteristics of the original game: there are a certain pre-established number of winning tickets and the prizes are known and fixed in advance. Thus, the Band argues, the player plays not against the machine using random odds, but against other players in a closed board.

The Band's argument is not without force, but the passage from the Committee report also reinforces the notion that electronic aids are essentially aimed at communications to enable broader participation in a common game. The pull-tab machines have that effect over time, perhaps, but any given player is faced with a self-contained machine into which he or she places money and loses it or receives winning tickets after the electronic operations are conducted. In that sense, the gambler plays "with the machine" even though not against it. The machine is not being used to facilitate "[s]imultaneous games participation between and among Reservations" or even among players on the same reservation. In any event, whatever the implications of the Senate Committee report, we are still left with the statute's plain term "electronic facsimile" (to say nothing of "slot machines of any kind") that is excluded from Class II gaming. That language compels our result.

Sycuan Band, 54 F.3d at 543.

Do you agree that Congress meant to limit electronic aids to those utilizing communications technology to "enable broader participation"? Consider the reasoning of the Ninth Circuit in *United States v. 103 Electronic Gambling Devices*. After determining that the game played on the MegaMania terminals constituted bingo under IGRA (as excerpted above), the court then turned to the question of whether the terminals were Class II electronic aids or Class III electronic facsimiles.

The distinction under IGRA between an electronic "aid" and an electronic "facsimile" is one that has been litigated and decided before. Relying on the Senate Report, [the court in *Spokane Indian Tribe v. United States*, 972 F.2d 1090 (9th Cir. 1992),] noted that an "electronic aid" "enhance[s] the participation of more than one person in ... Class II gaming activities." *See also Sycuan Band of Mission Indians v. Roache*, 54 F.3d 535, 542 (9th Cir. 1994) ("[A]n 'electronic aid' to a class II game can be viewed as a device that offers some sort of *communications* technology to permit broader participation in the basic game being played, as when a bingo game is televised to several rooms or locations.") (citing *Cabazon Band of Mission Indians v. National Indian Gaming Comm'n*, 14 F.3d 633, 637 (D.C. Cir. 1994)). Because the Pick 6 game at issue in the [*Spokane*] case involved only "a single participant play[ing] against the machine," the court held that it was an electronic facsimile rather than an electronic aid. *See also Sycuan Band*, 54 F.3d at 542–43 (concluding that electronic pull-tab game in which one player played against machine was exact, self-contained, copy of paper version of game and was thus a class III electronic facsimile thereof).

The MegaMania terminal, in contrast, does "link[ ] participant players at various reservations whether in the same or different States [thereby] broaden[ing] the potential participation levels." As such, the MegaMania terminal is not a "facsimile of any game of chance," or, indeed, a facsimile of anything. Rather, the terminal is merely an electronic aid to human players of bingo, something like electronic mail with a graphic user interface. And, while the government has argued that MegaMania resembles a slot machine in certain limited respects, there has been no argument that the terminal *is* a "slot machine," which it plainly is not. Unlike a slot machine, MegaMania is in truth being played outside the terminal; the terminal merely permits a person to connect to a network of players comprising each MegaMania game, and without a network of at least 12 other players playing at other terminals, an individual terminal is useless.

> In short, the MegaMania terminal is just an electronic aid to bingo, because it "merely broaden[s] the potential participation levels." As such, the MegaMania terminal is class II gaming under IGRA.

103 Electronic Gambling Devices, 223 F.3d at 1100–01. In *United States v. 162 MegaMania Gambling Devices*, 231 F.3d 713 (10th Cir. 2000), the Tenth Circuit reached the same conclusion, relying on similar considerations:

> First, the MegaMania machines link up many different players, thus broadening the participation level of the traditional game of bingo. Second, because each player competes against other players to achieve a "bingo" rather than with or against a machine or the "house," the machines are an aid to bingo, rather than a facsimile.... Finally, although MegaMania satisfies the statutory criteria for a Class II game, it cannot fairly be described as an exact copy or replica of the traditional game of bingo, as required to satisfy the plain-meaning definition of "facsimile."

Id. at 724–25.

Is there another way to read the Senate Report and statutory language? Could a machine be an "aid" without broadening the potential participation levels? What would a technologic aid for the game of pull-tabs look like under *Cabazon Band v. NIGC* and *Sycuan Band v. Roache*? In other words, how would a machine broaden the potential participation levels in a pull-tabs game? Would making the play of the game more exciting broaden potential participation levels or "take advantage of modern methods of conducting Class II games" in a way consistent with Congress's intent?

    2.   Applying the Indian canon of construction. Recall the *Shakopee* court's uncertainty about the proper application of the Indian canon of construction to construe statutes in favor of the tribe in the context of Indian gaming and IGRA's purpose of shielding tribal gaming from organized crime and other corrupting influences. In the case below, the D.C. Circuit identified an additional tension: the fact that IGRA also has the purpose of promoting tribal economic development. There appears to be little argument with the assertion that the machines in question are more entertaining, and therefore more profitable, than the traditional paper game of pull-tabs.

Diamond Game Enterprises, Inc. v. Reno
230 F.3d 365 (D.C. Cir. 2000)

TATEL, Circuit Judge.

This case requires us to determine whether a gambling machine known as the Lucky Tab II, an electromechanical device that dispenses paper pull-tabs and then displays their contents on a video monitor, should be classified under the Indian Gaming Regulatory Act as a Class II "aid" or a Class III "facsimile."

[NIGC] regulations define Class II aids and Class III facsimiles. An aid is "a device ... that when used ... [i]s not a game of chance but merely assists a player or the playing of a game [and] is readily distinguishable from the playing of a game of chance on an electronic or electromechanical facsimile." A facsimile is "any gambling device as defined in [the Johnson Act]." Predating IGRA by more than 30 years, the Johnson Act prohibits the use of gambling devices on federal land, in interstate commerce, and in "Indian country." *See* 15 U.S.C. §§ 1171–78 (1953). Both the Commission's regulations and this court have interpreted IGRA as limiting the Johnson Act prohibition to devices that are neither Class II games approved by the Commission nor Class III games covered by tribal-state compacts.

This case concerns a game known as pull-tabs. A small, two-ply paper card, a pull-tab bears symbols and patterns similar to tic-tac-toe that appear when players peel off the pull-tab's top layer. The pattern of the symbols determines whether the player wins a prize. In the traditional pull-tabs game, bingo hall clerks sell pull-tabs from counters or mobile carts, and winners present the tabs to either clerks or cashiers to collect prizes. Pull-tabs are sold from large pools known as "deals." Containing anywhere from 1200 to 100,000 pull-tabs, deals have a fixed number of winners and losers.

At issue in this case is the proper classification of a gambling device known as the Lucky Tab II, an electromechanical dispenser of paper pull-tabs. The machine dispenses pull-tabs from a roll containing approximately 7500 tabs. About 100 rolls comprise a deal, within which winning pull-tabs are randomly distributed. The machine cuts the pull-tab from the roll and drops it into a tray. A bar code scanner inside the machine automatically reads the tab and then displays its contents on a video screen. A placard on the machine informs players that "[v]ideo images may vary from actual images on pull tabs. Each tab must be opened to verify." To collect prizes, players must present the actual winning tab to a clerk. In many bingo halls, players purchase pull-tabs either from a Lucky Tab II or from clerks; in such cases, machines and clerks cut pull-tabs from rolls that are part of the same deal.

In 1994, the Kickapoo Traditional Tribe of Texas and Diamond Game Enterprises, the manufacturer of the Lucky Tab II, asked the Commission to classify the machine as a Class II aid. Two years passed without Commission action. In August 1996, the Kickapoo Tribe began operating approximately 100 Lucky Tab II machines. At this point, the record becomes complicated and, to say the least, confusing. As far as we can tell, the following events of significance to this case transpired: The Commission's Director of Enforcement advised the Tribe that the machines were Class III gambling devices that could only be operated pursuant to a tribal-state compact. Notwithstanding the Director's action, the members of the Commission were apparently divided over the proper classification of the Lucky Tab II, some thinking it an aid and others a facsimile. Because of this disagreement, the Commission sought advice from the Department of Justice, but DOJ lawyers were themselves divided over the proper classification of the machine. The Commission never formally responded to the request to classify the Lucky Tab II.

According to the Tribe and Diamond Game, certain members of the Commission recommended that the Tribe and the company file a declaratory judgment action in federal court to resolve the issue. Acting on that advice, they filed this action in the U.S. District Court for the District of Columbia seeking, among other things, a declaratory judgment that the machine qualifies as a Class II aid. The Cheyenne and Arapaho Tribes of Oklahoma intervened as plaintiffs. Alabama, California, and Florida intervened as defendants. Finding that the Lucky Tab II "performs all the functions that a player of the traditional pull-tab game would have performed," the district court found the machine to be a Class III facsimile.

Unlike the legal issues presented in this case, the policy questions are both interesting and challenging. In determining the proper classification of the Lucky Tab II, how do we further Congress' objective of allowing Indian tribes to use gaming as a means of "promoting tribal economic development, self-sufficiency, and strong tribal governments," while at the same time "shield[ing] [Indian tribes] from organized crime and other corrupting influences?" Will the Lucky Tab II enable tribes to "take advantage of modern methods of conducting class II games"? Or does the machine increase the risk of corruption or excessive gambling losses, concerns that the government argues require its classification as a Class III device? To resolve such issues, Congress created the NIGC; yet whether because of bureaucratic gridlock or, as the tribes allege, because of congressional interference, we have no idea what the Commission thinks about the policy questions presented by the Lucky Tab II. Not only does this leave us with no agency position to which we might defer, but the Commission's IGRA regulations provide no assistance in interpreting the statute. Boiled down to their essence, the regulations tell us little more than that a Class II aid is something that is not a Class III facsimile. We mention this not to escape our duty to decide this case but to highlight the fact that we have no choice but to proceed without the benefit of a Commission position, a situation we expect Congress neither anticipated nor would appreciate.

Diamond Game and the Tribes contend that the Lucky Tab II acts as a permitted "electronic aid" to the Class II game of pull-tabs. They emphasize that the machine's operation depends entirely on pre-printed paper pull-tabs that can be (and in fact are) played without the mechanical dispenser. The Lucky Tab II, in other words, cannot function without rolls of paper pull-tabs. The Tribes also emphasize that despite the fact that the Lucky Tab II presents a video image of the contents of the pull-tabs it dispenses, the machine does not give the player the final word on the game; players must still peel off the top layer to verify its contents and present it to a clerk to receive their winnings. For all of these reasons, they argue, the Lucky Tab II cannot be considered a facsimile of the paper game of pull-tabs. According to the government, because the machine mirrors the traditional game played by purchasing cards from clerks, it is a Class III facsimile, not a Class II aid, as for all practical purposes the Lucky Tab II is a duplicate of the paper version.

Both sides claim support from *Cabazon Band Mission Indians v. NIGC*, 14 F.3d 633 (D.C. Cir. 1994). There, we held that a video pull-tabs game was a "computerized version" of pull-tabs and therefore a Class III facsimile. The machine randomly selects a card for the gambler, pulls the tab at the gambler's direction, and displays the result on the screen. Finding that video pull-tabs "exactly replicate[s]" the game of pull-tabs in computer form, we concluded that it amounted to a facsimile of the game.

The Lucky Tab II is quite different from the video pull-tabs game. To begin with, the Lucky Tab II is not a computerized version of pull-tabs. Although the Lucky Tab II has a video screen, the screen merely displays the contents of a paper pull-tab. Instead of using a computer to select patterns, the Lucky Tab II actually cuts tabs from paper rolls and dispenses them to players. In other words, the game is in the paper rolls, not in a computer. The machine functions as an aid—it assists the paper game of pull-tabs. Without the paper rolls, the machine has no gaming function at all. It is, in essence, little more than a high-tech dealer. Viewed this way, the game played with the Lucky Tab II is not a facsimile of paper pull-tabs, it *is* paper pull-tabs.

Another difference between the Lucky Tab II and the video pull-tabs machine reinforces our belief that the Lucky Tab II should be classified as a Class II aid. The video pull-tabs machine plays the game of pull-tabs in its entirety, dispensing receipts for players to redeem winnings. By contrast, the Lucky Tab II dispenses actual paper pull-tabs that players must peel and display to a clerk before they can obtain prizes. Although the Lucky Tab II's scanner apparently commits few errors when reading paper pull-tabs, the fact remains that unlike the video pull-tabs machine, the Lucky Tab II is technically not final. It is, in other words, an aid to the game of pull-tabs.

The government insists that the Lucky Tab II is a Class III device. At oral argument, the government even asserted that removing the video screen would not convert the Lucky Tab II into a Class II aid. Asked what in the government's view would be an aid, counsel pointed us to an electronic scanner called the "Tab Force Validation System." As we understand this device, after a clerk dispenses a paper pull-tab, instead of peeling off the top layer, the player inserts the pull-tab into the machine, which scans the bar code and displays the results on a video screen. We see no principled difference between the Tab Force and the Lucky Tab II. Both devices electronically "read" paper pull-tabs and display their contents on a screen, and neither contains an internal computer that generates the game. Rather, both machines facilitate the playing of paper pull-tabs. They are thus Class II aids.

The government makes two additional arguments in support of its position that the Lucky Tab II is a Class III facsimile. First, it relies on language from a Senate Indian Affairs Committee report describing a Class II aid as a device that enables tribes to "take advantage of modern methods of conducting class II games" by, for example, "join[ing] with other tribes to coordinate their class II operations and thereby enhance the potential of increasing revenues." Unlike computers, cables, or telephone lines that connect bingo games on different reservations — examples the Senate Report gives of aids that expand participation — the Lucky Tab II, the government argues, neither increases participation levels nor enhances competition among players. Second, the government claims that the Lucky Tab II makes it easier for players to play pull-tabs, thus increasing the potential for players to "lose the rent money." These statutory interpretations, resting as they do on the policy underlying IGRA, are interesting and might even be worthy of *Chevron* deference had they been offered by the Commission. But they come only from appellate counsel — indeed the "lose-the-rent" argument surfaced for the first time at oral argument. Moreover, nothing in the Senate Report suggests that an electronic device *must* link players on different reservations to qualify as a Class II aid. Accordingly, because of the similarities between the Lucky Tab II and the Tab Force Validation System, which the Commission has found to be a Class II aid, and because of the differences between the Lucky Tab II and the Class III video pull-tabs device at issue in *Cabazon,* we reverse.

Notes and Questions

1.   Differences between the machines. In its conclusion, the court made note of the "differences between the Lucky Tab II and the Class III video pull-tabs device at issue in *Cabazon.*" What exactly were the relevant differences between the machines, and why? Was it the difference between a computerized pull-tab "deal," and a paper roll (that no doubt was printed from a computerized "deal" by the manufacturer)? Was it the player's physical "pulling" of the tab in the Lucky Tab II? What support is there in IGRA or its legislative history for the determinative nature of these distinctions?

2.   Need for "lodestar" policy. Echoing the tension identified by prior decisions in the context of application of the Indian canon of construction, the court noted the absence of a clear policy to guide effective application of the statutory definitions. The court stated,

> Unlike the legal issue presented in this case, the policy questions are both interesting and challenging. In determining the proper classification of the Lucky Tab II, how do we further Congress' objective of allowing Indian tribes to use gaming as a means of "promoting tribal economic development, self-sufficiency, and

strong tribal governments," while at the same time "shield[ing] [Indian tribes] from organized crime and other corrupting influences?" Will the Lucky Tab II enable tribes to "take advantage of modern methods of conducting class II games"? Or does the machine increase the risk of corruption or excessive gambling losses, concerns that the government argues require its classification as a Class III device? To resolve such issues, Congress created the NIGC; yet whether because of bureaucratic gridlock or, as the tribes allege, because of congressional interference, we have no idea what the Commission thinks about the policy questions presented by the Lucky Tab II.

The government took the position that the Lucky Tab II increased at least the risk of gambling losses, arguing that the machine made it easier to play pull-tabs, and thus easier to lose money. The court dismissed the federal government's "lose-the-rent" argument, but not necessarily on its merits. Is the essence of Class II games that players don't lose as much money as quickly when compared to Class III games? If the game's rate of speed was at a "manic pace," *United States v. 103 Electronic Gambling Devices* (excerpted above), would that change the court's view that "Lucky Tab II is not a facsimile of paper pull-tabs, it *is* paper pull-tabs"? Is there support in IGRA or its legislative history for the idea that "speed of play" is an important distinction between Class II and Class III machines? Or, put another way, what makes a slot machine a slot machine? Is it the game played — betting against the random number generator — or is it the speed of play?

3. Effectiveness of the NIGC and its regulations. The D.C. Circuit criticized the NIGC on a number of fronts. First was the court's implicit critique of the NIGC's failure to issue a classification opinion on the Lucky Tab II. The tribe, the court noted, waited two years for the NIGC to issue its opinion on the machine before installing it on the casino floor. The tribe was faced with the decision either to risk a federal enforcement action under IGRA and criminal prosecution under the Johnson Act or to continue to forgo the revenue the machines would produce. At what point, if any, does the NIGC's failure to act create a defense against legal action to remove the machines and fine the tribe?

The court also criticized the NIGC's regulations as "provid[ing] no assistance in interpreting the statute. Boiled down to their essence, the regulations tell us little more than that a Class II aid is something that is not a Class III facsimile." The federal government, it seemed, was not itself clear on the distinction. As the Tenth Circuit noted in *United States v. 162 MegaMania Gambling Devices*, 231 F.3d 713 (10th Cir. 2000):

> The Tribes and Multimedia contend the government should be judicially estopped from claiming MegaMania is anything other than a Class II game. In another case, *Diamond Game Enter., Inc. v. Reno*, 9 F. Supp.2d 13 (D.D.C. 1998), the government used MegaMania as an example of a valid Class II game to support its argument another game, Lucky Tab II, utilized an illegal gambling device under the Johnson Act. The Tribes and Multimedia point to the apparent irony of the government's reliance on *Diamond* in contesting MegaMania's Class II classification in this case.

Id. at 725.

In 2002, drawing on the federal courts' interpretation of IGRA and its legislative history, the NIGC issued amended regulations defining Class II electronic aids and Class III electronic facsimiles.

§ 502.7 Electronic, computer or other technologic aid.

(a) *Electronic, computer or other technologic aid* means any machine or device that:

(1) Assists a player or the playing of a game;

(2) Is not an electronic or electromechanical facsimile; and

(3) Is operated in accordance with applicable Federal communications law.

(b) Electronic, computer or other technologic aids include, but are not limited to, machines or devices that:

(1) Broaden the participation levels in a common game;

(2) Facilitate communication between and among gaming sites; or

(3) Allow a player to play a game with or against other players rather than with or against a machine.

(c) Examples of electronic, computer or other technologic aids include pull tab dispensers and/or readers, telephones, cables, televisions, screens, satellites, bingo blowers, electronic player stations, or electronic cards for participants in bingo games.

§ 502.8 Electronic or electromechanical facsimile. Electronic or electromechanical facsimile means a game played in an electronic or electromechanical format that replicates a game of chance by incorporating all of the characteristics of the game, except when, for bingo, lotto, and other games similar to bingo, the electronic or electromechanical format broadens participation by allowing multiple players to play with or against each other rather than with or against a machine.

In the next set of cases, the courts considered the amended regulations in distinguishing between Class II aids and Class III facsimiles. In the first case, the Court of Appeals for the Eighth Circuit interpreted the amended regulations to support its holding that the Lucky Tab II pull-tab dispenser (the same machine at issue in *Diamond Game*, excerpted above) was a Class II aid. The case arose in the context of Nebraska's refusal to enter into a Class III compact with the Santee Sioux Tribe, and the protracted litigation resulting from the Tribe's continued operation of Class III games in the absence of a compact. The NIGC suggested that the Tribe replace its Class III gaming devices with the Lucky Tab II machines, as the NIGC considered the Lucky Tab II to be a Class II electronic aid. The Tribe did so, hoping to avoid continued fines. The U.S. Department of Justice, however, took the position that the Lucky Tab II was a Class III electronic facsimile.

United States v. Santee Sioux Tribe of Nebraska
324 F.3d 607 (8th Cir. 2003)

BEAM, Circuit Judge.

At trial, the following evidence was adduced regarding the Lucky Tab II machines. First, the instruments look and sound very much like traditional slot machines. Internally, the device is essentially a computer. It also has a manual feed for money, a roll of paper pull-tabs, a bar code reader to read the back of each pull-tab, a rubber roller to dispense the pull-tabs, a cutter which cuts the pull-tabs from the roll, and a cash drawer. The bar code reader reads the pull-tab as it passes through the machine to the player, and based on this reading, a video screen displays the contents of the pull-tab—whether it is a winner or loser. The machine also emits different sounds, depending on whether it has read a winning or losing ticket.

A player begins playing by feeding money into the machine. The player presses a start button and after approximately two and a half seconds an animated display appears, announcing winner or loser status. The machine then dispenses the paper pull-tab to the player. At this point, the player can either pull back the paper tab to verify the contents, or continue playing by feeding more money into the machine and pressing the start button again. If the pull-tab is a winner, the machine cannot pay the player or give credits for accumulated wins; instead, the machine tells the player to go to the cashier and present the pull-tab to redeem winnings.

The pull-tabs themselves are small, preprinted, two-ply paper cards. The player peels off the top layer to reveal symbols and patterns which indicate a winning or losing card. The pull-tabs also indicate the number manufactured, game type, and unique sequence number. The back of the pull-tab shows an encrypted bar code with fifteen characters. The bar code must be scanned with a laser light to determine if the card is a winner or a loser. Because the information is encrypted, the data on the bar code is unknowable without the proprietary software from the manufacturer, World Gaming Technologies. Also, anti-tampering devices ensure that a pull-tab that has already been scanned will be rejected and that the tabs will be dispensed in the correct sequence. Without a roll of paper pull-tabs in place, the machine cannot function—it will not accept money or display any symbols.

The evidence suggested that, as a practical matter, players often take the winning tickets, unopened, to the cashier for redemption. Furthermore, players frequently leave the losing tickets, unopened, in the dispenser drawer of the Lucky Tab II machines.

The district court, following the reasoning in *Diamond Game Enters., Inc. v. Reno*, 230 F.3d 365 (D.C. Cir. 2000), found that the machines at issue were class II devices because: the machines do not determine the winner or loser, pull-tabs can be played without these machines, the player does not play against the machine, and no winnings are paid or accumulated by the machines.

The government argues that Lucky Tab II machines are electromechanical facsimiles of the game of pull-tabs, making their use prohibited class III gaming. The Tribe argues that these machines are technological "aids," and therefore fall within the parameters of permitted class II gaming. We do not fully agree with either of these positions, and in that regard, we pause to clarify a terminology issue.

Other courts have construed this statute and concluded that the phrase "whether or not electronic, computer, or other technologic aids are used in connection therewith" modifies both the game of bingo and also other games mentioned later in the section, specifically "pull-tabs, lotto, punch boards, tip jars, instant bingo, and other games similar to bingo." These courts thus have found that games other than bingo could be technologically aided. *E.g., Diamond Game*, 230 F.3d at 367 (noting that pull-tabs is a class II game by statute, and that the IGRA specifically allows use of technologic aids "in connection with class II games"). We disagree with this reading of the statute. Instead, we believe that the phrase "whether or not electronic, computer, or other technologic aids are used in connection therewith" applies only to bingo. However, we also note that nothing in the statute *proscribes* the use of technological aids for any games, so long as the resulting exercise falls short of being a facsimile. Therefore, while we quarrel somewhat with the posture in which the parties, and other cases, have placed the issues, we agree with the ultimate conclusion that if the devices are not facsimiles within the meaning of the statute, they are not prohibited, regardless of whether or not they are labeled technological "aids." With that caveat, we apply the "aids" and "facsimiles" terminology.

[In addition to the D.C. Circuit's reasoning in *Diamond Game*,] the prior law of this case is also instructive on this question. In *Santee I*, the Tribe argued that the State of Nebraska, through its SLOTS keno reading system, was already conducting class III gaming. [The SLOTS keno reading system allows players to view game results by pressing one or more buttons on a video display terminal. The game results are displayed in slot-machine like fashion with the use of symbols (cherries, bars, etc.) rather than the typical number display.] We rejected that argument and held that the SLOTS keno reading system was a class II gaming device because it was only a means of allowing keno players to *view keno results,* and, unlike a slot machine, was not a means of conducting the game itself. [T]he device merely displays the results of the game in a novel way and does not directly affect the outcome of the game.

The Lucky Tab II machines, much like the SLOTS system described in *Santee I,* "display[ ] the results of the game in a novel way and do[ ] not directly affect the outcome of the game." While the Lucky Tab II machines read the pull-tab card for the player and display the results on screen in a novel way, the paper pull-tab card itself is the player's only path to winning. The machines have nothing to do with the outcome of the game.

While this case presents a close call, we think the better view is that operation of the Lucky Tab II machines does not change the fundamental fact that the player receives a traditional paper pull-tab from a machine, and whether he or she decides to pull the tab or not, must present that card to the cashier to redeem winnings. We agree with the reasoning of the *Diamond Game* court that the machines do not replicate pull-tabs; rather, the player using the machines *is playing* pull-tabs.

The most recent amendments to the NIGC-enacted regulations also support this conclusion. Prior to July 2002, the regulations defined facsimile with direct reference to the Johnson Act. The regulation in effect as of July 17, 2002, defines "facsimile" as "a game played in an electronic or electromechanical format that replicates a game of chance by incorporating all of the characteristics of the game, except when, for bingo, lotto, and other games similar to bingo, the electronic or electromechanical format broadens participation by allowing multiple players to play with or against each other rather than with or against a machine." 25 C.F.R. § 502.8.

Furthermore, the regulations effective July 17, 2002, define an "aid" as an electronic, computer, or other technologic device that assists the playing of a game. Significantly, the regulation gives the following examples of gaming aids, "*pull tab dispensers and/or readers,* telephones, cables, televisions, screens, satellites, bingo blowers, electronic player stations, or electronic cards for participants in bingo games." *Id.* § 502.7 (emphasis added).

The current regulations seem to expressly contemplate the use of Lucky Tab II pull-tab dispensers/readers, suggesting that the NIGC has now given its imprimatur to these types of machines. *Cf. Diamond Game* (noting at that time that the NIGC took no official position on the Lucky Tab II's class of gaming). Based on our review of the record and of the case law, the NIGC's conclusion that Lucky Tab II is a permissible class II gaming device seems to be a reasonable interpretation of the IGRA.

Notes and Questions

1.   *Aids for bingo only?* The Eighth Circuit noted that it believed that IGRA permits "electronic, computer, or other technologic aids" only in connection to the game of bingo, rather than in connection with any Class II game. The court went on to state that

> nothing in the statute *proscribes* the use of technological aids for any games, so long as the resulting exercise falls short of being a facsimile. Therefore, while we quarrel somewhat with the posture in which the parties, and other cases, have placed the issues, we agree with the ultimate conclusion that if the devices are not

facsimiles within the meaning of the statute, they are not prohibited, regardless of whether or not they are labeled technological "aids."

What, then, is the point of the court's interpretation? Considering a pull-tab machine, does it clarify the issue to say that the machine must not be a facsimile, rather than to say that it must be an aid? Do the 2002 regulations moot this point?

2. *Relevant aspects of the machine.* In prior cases, the courts seemed to take into account whether the machine contained a "computerized" version of the game as opposed to a paper deal, whether the player was required to physically "pull" the tab, and whether the machine served to broaden participation in the game. What did the *Santee Sioux* court deem relevant about the Lucky Tab II machine, and why? What, under the 2002 regulations, are the relevant aspects of a machine? Consider the video pull-tab machine at issue in *Cabazon v. NIGC* (excerpted above). How would the machine be classified under the 2002 regulations, and why?

Seneca-Cayuga Tribe of Oklahoma v. NIGC
327 F.3d 1019 (10th Cir. 2003)

HENRY, Circuit Judge.

[The Seneca-Cayuga Tribe of Oklahoma operated the Magical Irish Instant Bingo Dispenser System (the "Machine"). At the time, the Tribe had not entered into a Class III compact with Oklahoma, as state law allowed only Class II games. The NIGC classified the Magical Irish machine as a Class III device, and the federal government threatened prosecution for the continued use of the machines. In the district court, the court sided with the Tribe, holding that the machines were Class II aids.]

The Machine is an electro-magnetic dispenser manufactured by Diamond Game Enterprises. Three physically separate components constitute the Machine—the dispenser, the base, and the verifier. The Machine dispenses paper pull-tabs from a roll of a maximum of 7,500 tabs that are part of a larger pull-tab deal. Other rolls within the same deal may be dispensed by another dispenser or a gaming hall clerk. When a player inserts money into the Machine and presses the button marked "DISPENSE," the Machine cuts the next pull-tab card from the pre-printed roll within its dispenser compartment and drops the tab into a tray for the player to receive. The Machine has a "verify" feature that allows players to see the results for a given pull-tab posted on a video display. When this feature is enabled, the Machine's display screen scans a bar code that has been previously printed on the back of a paper tab. After the tab is dispensed, the screen displays the contents of the paper tab on a video screen approximately six seconds later. The video screen depicts a grid that is similar in appearance to that of a slot machine. Whether or not the "verify" function is enabled, any winning tabs dispensed by the Machine must be presented for in-person inspection by a gaming hall clerk before the player receives payment. The clerk must confirm that the paper pull-tab contains a winning prize, and only then may the clerk award the appropriate (pecuniary) prize.

The game played with the Machine can be a high-stakes, high-speed affair. A winning ticket pays up to $1,199 per one-dollar play. When working properly, the Machine completes one play every seven seconds.

The government's argument that IGRA does not authorize technologic aids for pull-tabs is directly contrary to the NIGC's most recent amendments to the Code of Federal Regulations. On July 17, 2002, the NIGC issued revised regulations stating that "pull tab dispensers and/or readers" are among the games included as IGRA Class II "electronic, computer, or other technologic aids." 25 C.F.R. §502.7(a), (c). These revised regulations are applicable because rather than being newly promulgated regulations, they are merely amendments, and do not operate retroactively since they do not "attach new legal consequences to events completed before enactment." The government has conceded that the Machine is "an electromechanical dispenser and reader of paper pull-tabs." Thus, if we adopt the NIGC's construction of IGRA, we need only decide whether the Machine constitutes an "electronic, computer, or other technologic aid[ ]" to pull-tabs.

Contrary to the government's assertion, the game played with the Machine falls within the definition of pull-tabs. IGRA does not define pull-tabs. Nor do the NIGC's regulations. This court, though, has provided a definition. In *Chickasaw Nation v. United States,* 208 F.3d 871 (10th Cir. 2000), *aff'd,* 534 U.S. 84 (2001), we stated that pull-tabs is a "scheme by which prizes are randomly distributed to the winners among the persons who have paid for a chance to win them, i.e. by purchasing one or more pull-tab tickets in a series." We noted that in pull-tabs, after players purchase a tab from a clerk or from the given dispensing machine, they must peel back the top layer to determine whether the tab contains a winning combination of symbols, and that if players purchase a winning tab, they must present it to the cashier.

The Machine meets this definition. It dispenses paper pull-tabs from a roll that is part of a larger deal, and the deal contains a predetermined number of randomly distributed winning tabs. Although a pull-tabs player may opt to view the video display regarding the contents of the paper pull-tabs, players of the Machine must still manually peel back the top layer of the pull-tab to confirm victory, and it is that tab presented for visual inspection to a gaming hall clerk that entitles players to winnings. We thus reject the government's argument that the game played with the Machine is [the equivalent of a slot machine]: although we acknowledge some superficial similarities between the two, pull-tabs, even when sped up, placed under lights, and depicted with a spinning machine on the side, is still pull-tabs. We hold that the Machine is used in connection with the playing of pull-tabs.

IGRA does not define "technologic aids." The NIGC, however, recently issued regulations, which state:

(a) Electronic, computer or other technologic aid means any machine or device that:

(1) Assists a player or the playing of a game;

(2) Is not an electronic or electromechanical facsimile; and

(3) Is operated in accordance with applicable Federal communications law.

(b) Electronic, computer or other technologic aids include, but are not limited to, machines, or devices that:

(1) Broaden the participation levels in a common game;

(2) Facilitate communication between and among gaming sites;

(3) Allow a player to play with or against other players rather than with or against a machine.

(c) Examples of electronic, computer or other technologic aids include pull-tab dispensers and/or readers, telephones, cables, televisions, screens, satellites, bingo blowers, electronic player stations, or electronic cards for participants in bingo games.

25 C.F.R. §502.7. The government does not dispute that the three requirements identified in 25 C.F.R. §502.7(a) must be met for a device to qualify as a Class II technologic aid; rather, the government argues that we should impose an additional requirement. Ac-

cording to the government, the Machine is not a Class II technologic aid because Class II aids must "broaden participation" in the games. *See* [Senate Report], 1988 U.S.C.C.A.N. at 3079 (stating that use of an aid that "would merely broaden the participation levels is readily distinguishable from the use of electronic facsimiles in which a single participant plays a game with or against a machine rather than with or against other players"). The government argues that in *MegaMania*, we endorsed the "broaden participation" requirement, and also points to the Ninth Circuit's statement [in *Sycuan Band of Mission Indians v. Roache*, 54 F.3d 535, 543–44 (9th Cir. 1995)] that "the passage from the Committee report also reinforces the notion that electronic aids are essentially aimed at communications to enable broader participation in a common game."

For several reasons, we are unpersuaded that the "broaden participation" requirement suggested by the government should be grafted onto IGRA. First, we reject the government's characterization of our holding in *MegaMania*. In *MegaMania*, we held that the device at issue was a technologic aid *in part* because it broadened participation in the underlying game of bingo. We did not hold that broadening participation was a requirement, nor did we endorse any such categorical rule. Rather, like the subsequently published NIGC regulations, we identified the broadening of participation as a factor favoring a finding that a device is a Class II aid. Second, we conclude that the NIGC's definition of "aid," which does not include the "broaden participation" requirement, is entitled to deference. Moreover, adopting the government's strict proposed definition of "aid" would run counter to the Committee Report's exhortation that "tribes be given the opportunity to take advantage of modern methods of conducting Class II games and the language regarding technology is designed to provide maximum flexibility."

In *Diamond Game*, [the D.C. Circuit] concluded that the Lucky Tab II functions as an aid to the game of pull-tabs because the Lucky Tab II literally "helps or supports" or "assists" the playing of pull-tabs. The opinion emphasized that Lucky Tab II physically cuts tabs from paper rolls and dispenses them to players, and merely displays the contents of the paper tab on its video screen for view by players, who must still peel and display any winning tabs to a clerk to obtain a prize. Concluding that the Lucky Tab is "little more than a high-tech dealer," and that the pull-tabs game with the Lucky Tab II is in the paper rolls, not the device, the D.C. Circuit held that the Lucky Tab II is a Class II technologic aid. We are persuaded that the D.C. Circuit's interpretation of "aid" as the term is used in IGRA is correct.

Because the NIGC's definition controls, the Machine is a Class II aid if it "(1) [a]ssists a player or the playing of a game; (2) [i]s not an electronic or electromechanical facsimile; and (3) [i]s operated in accordance with applicable Federal communications law." With its last gasp, the government contends that the Machine fails the second and third of these requirements.

We disagree. Like the Lucky Tab II, the Machine (1) cuts tabs from paper rolls and dispenses them to players, and when its "verify" feature is enabled, displays the contents of the paper pull-tab on the video screen; (2) does not use a computer to select the patterns of the pull-tabs it dispenses; and (3) requires players to peel each pull-tab to confirm the result and provide the pull-tab to a clerk for inspection prior to receiving any prize. As with the Lucky Tab II, with the Machine, the Machine is not the game of pull-tabs; rather, the Machine facilitates the playing of pull-tabs, "the game is in the paper rolls." As such, the Machine is not a "computerized version" of pull-tabs. Nor, put in terms of the NIGC's regulations implementing IGRA, is the Machine an "electronic or electromechanical facsimile." Thus, contrary to the government's suggestion, the Machine does not change the fundamental characteristics of pull-tabs as played by the user.

Notes and Questions

1.   *"Broaden participation" as a requirement?* The 2002 regulations expressly did not limit Class II aids to those that serve to broaden participation levels in a common game (though such devices are likely to qualify as Class II aids). In *Seneca-Cayuga*, the Tenth Circuit reinforced that in order to be classified as a Class II aid, a machine is not required to broaden player participation in the game, reading its prior decision in *United States v. 162 MegaMania Gambling Devices* to hold only that whether the machine broadens participation is a consideration in favor of classification as a Class II aid. The court referred to the statements in the Senate Report that IGRA's inclusion of technologic aids in Class II was intended to give tribes "maximum flexibility" in taking advantage of "modern methods of conducting Class II games."

2.   *IGRA and the Johnson Act.* As mentioned above, the Johnson Act prohibits "gambling devices" in Indian country (as defined by 18 U.S.C. § 1151). Gambling devices include any

> slot machine ... [or] other machine or mechanical device (including but not limited to, roulette wheels and similar devices) designed and manufactured primarily for use in connection with gambling, and (A) which when operated may deliver, as the result of the application of an element of chance, any money or property, or (B) by the operation of which a person may become entitled to receive, as the result of the application of an element of chance, any money or property.

15 U.S.C. § 1171(a)(1), (2). Courts have construed this definition broadly, reasoning that Congress, through the Johnson Act, intended to "anticipate the ingeniousness of gambling machine designers" in "separating the public from its money on a large scale." *Lion Mfg. Corp. v. Kennedy*, 330 F.2d 833 (D.C. Cir. 1964).

IGRA specifically excludes from the Johnson Act gaming devices operated by a tribe in accordance with a tribal-state compact "entered into ... by a State in which gambling devices are legal." 25 U.S.C. § 2710(d)(6). In arguable contrast, IGRA's criminal prohibition against gambling in Indian country in violation of state law excludes both Class III gaming (conducted under a tribal-state compact) and Class II gaming. 18 U.S.C. § 1166(c).

As noted above, a tribe's operation of a Class III device in the absence of a valid compact not only violates IGRA, but subjects the tribe to criminal liability under the Johnson Act as well. Where the NIGC concludes that a machine is a Class III facsimile rather than a Class II aid, it is predictable that the U.S. Department of Justice would initiate criminal prosecution under the Johnson Act for continued use of the machine in the absence of a compact. Interestingly, though, the Justice Department took the position that Class II aids were nevertheless prohibited gaming devices under the Johnson Act as well. The logical conclusion of the Justice Department's position appeared to be that a statutory amendment to IGRA or the Johnson Act was necessary in order for tribes to legally operate Class II aids approved by the NIGC.

In *United States v. 103 Electronic Gambling Devices*, 223 F.3d 1091 (9th Cir. 2000), the Ninth Circuit addressed the government's contention that the MegaMania bingo terminal, despite constituting a Class II aid under IGRA, nonetheless violated the Johnson Act:

> IGRA explicitly repealed the application of the Johnson Act to class III gaming devices used pursuant to tribal-state compacts, but did not explicitly address the relationship between IGRA and the Johnson Act as applied to class II gaming. We are not aware of any authority pre-dating IGRA that addresses how the

Johnson Act applied to bingo aids. In any event, there is little point at this juncture in engaging in time travel to determine how the Johnson Act would have applied to bingo in Indian country in the absence of IGRA. What matters *now* is how the two are to be read together—that is, how two enactments by Congress over thirty-five years apart most comfortably coexist, giving each enacting Congress's legislation the greatest continuing effect.

The text of IGRA quite explicitly indicates that Congress did not intend to allow the Johnson Act to reach bingo aids. The statute provides that bingo using "electronic, computer, or other technologic aids" is class II gaming, and therefore permitted in Indian country. Reading the Johnson Act to forbid such aids would render the quoted language a nullity. Why would Congress carefully protect such technologic aids through the text of [IGRA], yet leave them to the wolves of a Johnson Act forfeiture action? We cannot presume that in enacting IGRA, Congress performed such "a useless act." By deeming aids to bingo class II gaming in the text of IGRA, Congress specifically authorized the use of such aids as long as the class II provisions of IGRA are complied with. In short, while complete, self-contained electronic or mechanical facsimiles of a game of chance, including bingo, may indeed be forbidden by the Johnson Act after the enactment of IGRA, we hold that mere technologic aids to bingo, such as the MegaMania terminal, are not.

Id. at 1101–02.

In *Seneca-Cayuga Tribe v. NIGC*, the Tenth Circuit reached the same conclusion:

Absent clear evidence to the contrary, we will not ascribe to Congress the intent both to carefully craft through IGRA the protection afforded to users of Class II technologic aids and to simultaneously eviscerate those protections by exposing users of Class II technologic aids to Johnson Act liability for the very conduct authorized by IGRA. A better reading of the statutory scheme is that through IGRA, Congress specifically and affirmatively authorized the use of Class II technologic aids, subject to compliance with the other IGRA provisions that govern Class II gaming.

Moreover, by shielding Indian country users of IGRA Class II technologic aids from Johnson Act liability, this construction gives meaning to both statutes, rather than neutering one of legal import. This understanding of the two statutes recognizes that the Johnson Act may remain a tool for criminal prosecution of conduct outside Indian country or conduct within Indian country not authorized by federal law, but that through IGRA, Congress spoke *specifically* to the federal government's regulatory scheme over certain forms of authorized gambling within Indian country.

This common-sense reading of the two statutes is directly supported by legislative history. The sole congressional committee report accompanying the passage of IGRA stated that "[it] is the Committee's intent that with the passage of this act, no other Federal statute, such as those listed below [including the Johnson Act] will preclude the use of otherwise legal devices used solely in aid of or in conjunction with bingo or lotto or other such gaming on or off Indian lands." Read in conjunction with Congress's inclusion of "pull-tabs" in a list of games "similar to bingo," this statement in the Committee Report is direct evidence that Congress did not intend the Johnson Act to apply to the use of Class II technologic aids in Indian country.

Against these authorities, the government draws on the maxim of statutory construction *expressio unius est exclusio alterius,* which means "inclusion of one thing indicates exclusion of the other." In this context, "the notion is one of negative implication: the enumeration of certain things in a statute suggests that the legislature had no intent of including things not listed or embraced." The government points to the statement in IGRA that the Johnson Act "shall not apply to any gaming conducted under a Tribal-State compact" that is entered into between "any Indian Tribe having jurisdiction over the Indian country upon which a *Class III* gaming activity is being conducted" and "a state in which gambling devices are illegal," 25 U.S.C. §2710(d)(3), (6) (emphasis supplied). Because the quoted language is the only express exception provided for in IGRA to the general applicability of the Johnson Act, contends the government, the necessary corollary to that express exception is that, where there is no such compact, gambling devices may not be used in Indian country.

We disagree. The persuasive evidence from IGRA's legislative history seriously undermines the government's rather bald *expressio unius* argument. Because the canon's purpose is to resolve a question not answered by the statute, the canon is not particularly useful where legislative history clearly evinces congressional intent, especially in this context of construing statutes governing Native American affairs.

Accordingly, consistent with our holding in *MegaMania,* we hold that *if* a piece of equipment is a technologic aid to an IGRA Class II game, its use, sale, possession or transportation within Indian country is then necessarily not proscribed as a gambling device under the Johnson Act. If a piece of equipment is an IGRA Class II technologic aid, a court need not assess whether, independently of IGRA, that piece of equipment is a "gambling device" proscribed by the Johnson Act.

Id. at 1032–35.

In *United States v. Santee Sioux Tribe,* the Eighth Circuit reached a similar conclusion. It rejected the government's contention that the Lucky Tab II (which had been classified as a Class II aid by the NIGC) was an illegal gambling device, but its reasoning differed significantly from that of the Ninth and Tenth Circuits:

The government argues that if Lucky Tab II is construed to be a class II gaming device, it is still a "gambling device" within the parameters of the Johnson Act and therefore prohibited. If that is the case, the Tribe cannot be granted relief from the contempt order. Because class II gaming is permitted under one federal law (the IGRA), but the machines which facilitate class II gaming are arguably prohibited under another (the Johnson Act), the Tribe argues that the IGRA has repealed the Johnson Act by implication.

The IGRA, in section 2710(b)(1)(A), states that an Indian tribe may engage in class II gaming where the state in which it is located permits similar games "and such gaming is not otherwise specifically prohibited on Indian lands by Federal law." This section clearly states that class II devices may be regulated by another federal statute—obviously the Johnson Act. Thus, the argument that the IGRA implicitly repeals the Johnson Act with respect to class II devices is not well taken, even though some version of this view has been expressed by several courts. *See, e.g., 162 MegaMania Gambling Devices,* 231 F.3d at 725 (noting that the IGRA indicates Congress did not intend to allow the Johnson Act to reach class II devices); *Diamond Game,* 230 F.3d at 367 (finding that the IGRA limits "the Johnson Act prohibition to devices that are neither Class II games approved by the commission nor Class III games covered by tribal-state compacts"). We find that the IGRA and the Johnson Act can be read together, are not irreconcilable, and the Tribe must not violate either act if it is to gain relief from the prior order of contempt.

The government argues that if the Johnson Act applies, the Lucky Tab II machines are prohibited "gambling devices" under that act, and the Tribe is still operating gambling equipment in contravention of federal law. We disagree because we do not believe the Lucky Tab II machines are "gambling devices" within the meaning of the Johnson Act. Lucky Tab II machines are not slot machines, because they do not randomly generate patterns displayed on a screen, pay out money or otherwise determine the outcome of a game of chance. Nor do these machines fall within the strictures of sections 1171(a)(2)(A) and (B), which state, as earlier indicated, that a gambling device includes any machine:

> designed and manufactured primarily for use in connection with gambling, and (A) which when operated may deliver, as the result of the application of an element of chance, any money or property, or (B) by the operation of which a person may become entitled to receive, as the result of the application of an element of chance, any money or property.

Lucky Tab II machines clearly do not fall within subsection A because the machines do not deliver any money or property. Subsection B seems a more likely candidate to ensnare these machines, but upon close examination, we find it does not. This section states that the operation of a machine designed and manufactured primarily for gambling use is a gambling device if *as the result of the application of an element of chance* a person can be entitled to receive money or property. The key words are highlighted, and demonstrate why the Lucky Tab II devices do not fit within this definition. These machines do not generate random patterns with an element of chance. They simply distribute the pull-tab tickets and display the contents of the tickets on a screen for the user. The user of the machine does not become entitled to receive money or property as a result of the *machine's* application of an element of chance, which is what the statute clearly contemplates.

The Johnson Act does not bar this type of machine, because it is merely a high-tech dispenser of pull-tabs. If, however, the Lucky Tab II machines were computer-generated versions of the game of pull-tabs itself, or perhaps, even if it randomly chose which pull-tab from the roll it would dispense, it could fall within this subsection. However, it is clear the machines do neither of these things. Instead, they dispense, in identical order from the roll as physically placed in the machine, pull-tabs from that roll. Therefore, although we find that the IGRA does not repeal the Johnson Act, either explicitly or implicitly, we also find that the Tribe does not violate the Johnson Act by operating the Lucky Tab II machines.

Id. at 611–13.

3. ***Pending NIGC regulations.*** As the court noted in *Seneca-Cayuga Tribe v. NIGC,* because the Johnson Act is a federal criminal statute separate from IGRA and enforced by the U.S. Department of Justice, the NIGC's interpretation of the Johnson Act is not entitled to the same deference as its interpretation of IGRA. Though agency officials were not uniform in their reading of the statutes, generally speaking the NIGC and the Justice Department disagreed over the Johnson Act's applicability to Class II aids. In 2005, the Justice Department sought legislation that would include Class II gambling devices within the scope of the Johnson Act. The Justice Department's proposal was met with tribal opposition, and failed to find a sponsor in Congress.

In the meantime, though, the NIGC was in the protracted process of issuing new, highly technical regulations governing Class II electronic aids. The proposed regulations stemmed from the NIGC's concern

> that the industry is dangerously close to obscuring the line between Class II and Class III.... The future success of Indian gaming under IGRA depends upon tribes, states, and manufacturers being able to recognize when games fall within the ambit of tribal-state compacts and when they do not.

National Indian Gaming Commission, Proposed Rule (Preamble), *Definition for Electronic or Electromechanical Facsimile* and *Classification Standards for Bingo, Lotto, Other Games Similar to Bingo, Pull-tabs and Instant Bingo as Class II Gaming When Played Through an Electronic Medium Using "Electronic, Computer, or Other Technological Aids,"* 71 Fed. Reg. 30231, 30239 (May 25, 2006).

The 2006 proposed classification and technical regulations were criticized on two grounds. First, in requiring slower play, the rules would undermine the Class II market. An economic impact study concerning the proposed regulations commissioned by the NIGC found the rules would have "a significant negative impact" on Class II gaming revenue, and therefore on the tribes that operate such games. The study concluded that the proposed changes would reduce gaming revenue by $142.7 million, with an accompanying loss of $9.6 million in non-gaming revenue and a $17.4 million reduction in tribal government revenue. Alan Meister, *The Potential Economic Impact of Proposed Changes to Class II Gaming Regulations*, Report Submitted to the National Indian Gaming Commission (Nov. 3, 2006). Second, the regulations would trigger IGRA's tribal-state compacting requirement. In drawing a bright line between Class II and Class III games, the proposed regulations would shift some Class II games into the Class III category. To cotinue to operate the games, tribes in states that allow Class III gaming would need to convince the state to negotiate a new compact, opening up the process to the whims and vagaries of state politics and the possibility of state-mandated revenue sharing.

Originally slated for formal issuance in 2005, interagency contestation with the Department of Justice and continued criticism from tribes and game manufacturers considerably slowed the process. Following the initial announcement of the proposed standards, a group of prominent manufacturers formed the Technical Standards Work Group (TSWG) to draft an alternative regulatory scheme to submit to the NIGC. Together with the Technical Standards Tribal Advisory Committee, a group of tribal operators and experts that had been advising the NIGC, the TSWG submitted alternative Technical Standards to the Commission in early 2007. The Working Group lauded the NIGC for its willingness to listen to tribal and manufacturer concerns. *See* Frank Legato, *Class II Manufacturers & Operators United Front*, GLOBAL GAMING BUSINESS (March 2007). The NIGC announced in 2007 that it would issue the new rules in summer 2007. (As of this writing, rules had not yet been adopted.) For more on the pending NIGC regulations, see Heidi McNeil Staudenmaier, *Proposed NIGC Class II Game Classification Standards: End of Class II Gaming Debate ... or Just Further Fuel for Fire?*, 10 GAMING L. REV. 527 (2006); Heidi McNeil Staudenmaier & Andrew D. Lynch, *The Class II Gaming Debate: The Johnson Act vs. the Indian Gaming Regulatory Act*, 74 MISS. L.J. 843 (2005).

Computer technology does not stand still, and regulation is the mother of invention. Regardless of the outcome concerning the NIGC's proposed regulations, technological innovation will continue to push the bounds of the legal distinction between Class II and Class III games.

According to economist Alan Meister, in 2006, fewer states continued to allow only Class II gaming, while tribes in those states worked to expand the types and number of games permitted:

> In terms of performance by type of gaming, Class III continues to generate the vast majority (93 percent) of gaming revenue at Indian gaming facilities nationwide. In 2006, the five states [down from eight states in 2005, and nine in 2004] with *only* Class II gaming (Alabama, Alaska, Florida, Nebraska, and Texas) generated just over $1.7 billion in gaming revenue. Of this amount, approximately 91 percent, or $1.6 billion, was generated in Florida alone. The remaining 23 states with at least some Class III Indian gaming generated approximately $23.7 billion.
>
> Despite its smaller size, Class II gaming generally grew at a faster rate than Class III gaming. In 2006, gaming revenue grew a total of 20 percent for Class II only states and 10 percent for Class III states. The growth of the Class II only state was largely driven by strong growth in Florida (22 percent). However, a number of Class II only states experienced sizable growth. In fact, of all states with Indian gaming, the three fastest growing states in terms of gaming revenue were Class II only states (Nebraska, Alaska, and Texas). Interestingly enough though, Class II only states included the two lowest and four of the eight lowest in terms of gaming revenue generation.

ALAN P. MEISTER, INDIAN GAMING INDUSTRY REPORT 4 (2007–2008 ed.).

Problem 4: Class II Technologic Aid or Class III Electronic Facsimile?

1. First consider IGRA and applicable legislative history. Imagine that it is 1989, and IGRA's provisions are the only guidance you have (that is, there are not yet any federal regulations or case law on point). You are an NIGC attorney. You've been charged with writing a memorandum outlining the difference between a Class II technologic aid and a Class III electronic facsimile. What are the defining characteristics of a technologic aid? Of a facsimile? How would you articulate a legal standard that distinguishes between the two?

2. Now consider the case law prior to 2002. Reading those cases together, what is the best synthesis of the legal standard? What, according to the cases, are the defining characteristics of a technologic aid? Of a facsimile? How would you accurately and concisely state the courts' legal standard that distinguishes between the two?

3. With the statute and early case law in mind from the first two questions, now consider the NIGC's 2002 regulations and the courts' decisions in *United States v. Santee Sioux Tribe* and *Seneca-Cayuga Tribe v. NIGC*. What is the best synthesis of the legal standard? What, according to the cases, are the defining characteristics of a technologic aid? Of a facsimile? How would you accurately and concisely state the courts' legal standard that distinguishes between the two?

4. Finally, consider whether you think the 2002 regulations and subsequent cases set forth a workable legal standard. Are there questions left unanswered? Will the stan-

dard survive changes in technology? Does it serve the purposes Congress intended? Does the legal standard provide a viable public policy framework? What changes, if any, would you recommend to the NIGC regulations?

Chapter 5

Casino-Style or Class III Gaming

A. Overview

Though widely popular at casinos in Reno, Las Vegas, and Atlantic City, as well as on riverboat casinos scattered throughout the U.S., casino-style gambling remains controversial and is the most highly regulated form of commercial gaming. The same is true for the Indian gaming industry.

Recall that IGRA defines Class III or casino-style gaming as all other games not included in Class I or Class II. 25 U.S.C. § 2703(8). These games, typically high-stakes, include slot machines, roulette, craps, keno, house-banked card games such as baccarat, chemin de fer, blackjack, and pai gow poker, and such diverse activities as lotteries, parimutuel betting, and jai alai. 25 C.F.R. § 502.4. Class III gaming requires a negotiated agreement between a tribe and a state called a "tribal-state compact." In this Chapter, we cover the requirements and complexities of the compacting process, including IGRA's mandate that states negotiate in good faith with tribes. Or must they? The U.S. Supreme Court upset IGRA's carefully crafted legal and political compromise between tribal and state authority over Class III gaming when it handed down its landmark decision in *Seminole Tribe v. Florida*, 517 U.S. 44 (1996). We explore the ramifications of that decision before turning to three categorical approaches to IGRA's provisions concerning Class III gaming in relation to the scope of state public policy.

B. Statutory Requirements for Conducting Class III Gaming

Set forth in 25 U.S.C. § 2710(d), IGRA's requirements for Class III gaming largely mimic those for Class II gaming, which are discussed in Chapter 4. In addition to the prerequisites that also apply to Class II gaming (note the references to "subsection (b) of this section," meaning § 2710(b)), IGRA also requires that a tribe enter into an agreement with the state, called a "tribal-state compact," before it may conduct Class III gaming.

(1) Class III gaming activities shall be lawful on Indian lands only if such activities are—

    (A) authorized by an ordinance or resolution that—

        (i) is adopted by the governing body of the Indian tribe having jurisdiction over such lands,

        (ii) meets the requirements of subsection (b) of this section, and

(iii) is approved by the Chairman,

(B) located in a State that permits such gaming for any purpose by any person, organization, or entity, and

(C) conducted in conformance with a Tribal-State compact entered into by the Indian tribe and the State under paragraph (3) that is in effect.

(2)(A) If any Indian tribe proposes to engage in, or to authorize any person or entity to engage in, a class III gaming activity on Indian lands of the Indian tribe, the governing body of the Indian tribe shall adopt and submit to the Chairman an ordinance or resolution that meets the requirements of subsection (b) of this section....

(3)(A) Any Indian tribe having jurisdiction over the Indian lands upon which a class III gaming activity is being conducted, or is to be conducted, shall request the State in which such lands are located to enter into negotiations for the purpose of entering into a Tribal-State compact governing the conduct of gaming activities. Upon receiving such a request, the State shall negotiate with the Indian tribe in good faith to enter into such a compact.

(B) Any State and any Indian tribe may enter into a Tribal-State compact governing gaming activities on the Indian lands of the Indian tribe, but such compact shall take effect only when notice of approval by the Secretary of such compact has been published by the Secretary in the Federal Register.

(C) Any Tribal-State compact negotiated under subparagraph (A) may include provisions relating to—

(i) the application of the criminal and civil laws and regulations of the Indian tribe or the State that are directly related to, and necessary for, the licensing and regulation of such activity;

(ii) the allocation of criminal and civil jurisdiction between the State and the Indian tribe necessary for the enforcement of such laws and regulations;

(iii) the assessment by the State of such activities in such amounts as are necessary to defray the costs of regulating such activity;

(iv) taxation by the Indian tribe of such activity in amounts comparable to amounts assessed by the State for comparable activities;

(v) remedies for breach of contract;

(vi) standards for the operation of such activity and maintenance of the gaming facility, including licensing; and

(vii) any other subjects that are directly related to the operation of gaming activities.

(4) Except for any assessments that may be agreed to under paragraph (3)(C)(iii) of this subsection, nothing in this section shall be interpreted as conferring upon a State or any of its political subdivisions authority to impose any tax, fee, charge, or other assessment upon an Indian tribe or upon any other person or entity authorized by an Indian tribe to engage in a class III activity. No State may refuse to enter into the negotiations described in paragraph (3)(A) based upon the lack of authority in such State, or its political subdivisions, to impose such a tax, fee, charge, or other assessment.

(5) Nothing in this subsection shall impair the right of an Indian tribe to regulate class III gaming on its Indian lands concurrently with the State, except to the extent that such regulation is inconsistent with, or less stringent than, the State laws and

regulations made applicable by any Tribal-State compact entered into by the Indian tribe under paragraph (3) that is in effect.

(6) The provisions of section 1175 of title 15 [the Johnson Act, discussed in Chapter 4] shall not apply to any gaming conducted under a Tribal-State compact that—

> (A) is entered into under paragraph (3) by a State in which gambling devices are legal, and

> (B) is in effect.

As with Class II gaming, an "Indian tribe" may operate Class III gaming on "Indian lands" only in states that permit such gaming for any purpose by any person. 25 U.S.C. § 2710(d)(1)(B). Class III gaming encompasses only "such gaming [that] is not otherwise specifically prohibited on Indian lands by Federal law." *Id.* § 2710(d)(1)(A)(ii). Although many casino games ordinarily are illegal under the Johnson Act, games offered in compliance with IGRA's provisions are exempt from federal proscription. *Id.* § 2710(d)(6); *see also* 18 U.S.C. § 1166.

Before opening a Class III casino, a tribe must adopt a regulatory ordinance subject to approval by the NIGC Chair. 25 U.S.C. § 2710(d)(1)(A). The tribal ordinance must incorporate the same specific provisions required for Class II gaming outlined in Chapter 4, including:

- Tribe's sole proprietary interest
- Use of net gaming revenue
- Annual outside of audits of gaming
- Contracts subject to independent audit
- Maintenance of facility to protect environment and public health and safety
- Adequate system of oversight and background checks for management officials and key employees

Id. § 2710(d)(2)(A). (The NIGC encourages tribes to adopt, with appropriate modifications, its Revised Model Tribal Gaming Ordinance, discussed in Chapter 7.) A tribe has "sole discretion" to revoke an ordinance authorizing Class III gaming on its reservation. *Id.* § 2710(d)(2)(D). As with Class II gaming, the tribe may enter into an approved management contract for the operation of a Class III casino. *Id.* § 2710(d)(9). In addition to the Class II requirements, however, the tribe must enter into a compact with the state. *Id.* § 2710(d)(3)(A).

C. Tribal-State Compacts

If a tribe wants to conduct Class III gaming, it first must formally request that the state enter into compact negotiations. Once the state receives the tribe's request, "the State shall negotiate with the Indian tribe in good faith to enter into such a compact." 25 U.S.C. § 2710(d)(3)(A). Which state official or branch of state government has authority to negotiate and enter into a compact on behalf of the state is not addressed by IGRA; it therefore is a question of state law and separation of powers principles. *See, e.g., Panzer v. Doyle*, 680 N.W.2d 666 (Wis. 2004) (detailing state law concerning governor's authority to negotiate compacts and to agree to certain provisions); *Saratoga County Cham-*

ber of Commerce v. Pataki, 798 N.E.2d 1047 (N.Y. 2003) (holding that compact negoti-ations involve policymaking and thus fall within the state legislature's authority). The issue of who may negotiate and enter into a compact on behalf of the state is discussed further in Chapter 8.

As enforcement mechanisms for the compact requirement, IGRA authorizes three fed-eral causes of action. First, a tribe may sue a state in federal court for failing to negotiate in good faith a tribal-state compact. Second, the Secretary of the Interior may sue to en-force the compact procedures promulgated through a tribe's suit against the state. Third, either a tribe or a state may sue to stop a Class III gaming activity that violates the gov-erning tribal-state compact. 25 U.S.C. § 2710(d)(7)(A).

In § 2710(7)(B), IGRA sets forth highly detailed procedures governing a tribe's cause of action against the state for its failure to negotiate in good faith:

> (i) An Indian tribe may initiate a cause of action described in subparagraph (A)(i) only after the close of the 180-day period beginning on the date on which the Indian tribe requested the State to enter into negotiations under paragraph (3)(A).

> (ii) In any action described in subparagraph (A)(i), upon the introduction of evi-dence by an Indian tribe that—

>> (I) a Tribal-State compact has not been entered into under paragraph (3), and

>> (II) the State did not respond to the request of the Indian tribe to negotiate such a compact or did not respond to such request in good faith,

> the burden of proof shall be upon the State to prove that the State has negotiated with the Indian tribe in good faith to conclude a Tribal-State compact governing the conduct of gaming activities.

> (iii) If, in any action described in subparagraph (A)(i), the court finds that the State has failed to negotiate in good faith with the Indian tribe to conclude a Tribal-State compact governing the conduct of gaming activities, the court shall order the State and the Indian Tribe to conclude such a compact within a 60-day period. In deter-mining in such an action whether a State has negotiated in good faith, the court—

>> (I) may take into account the public interest, public safety, criminality, financial integrity, and adverse economic impacts on existing gaming activities, and

>> (II) shall consider any demand by the State for direct taxation of the Indian tribe or of any Indian lands as evidence that the State has not negotiated in good faith.

> (iv) If a State and an Indian tribe fail to conclude a Tribal-State compact governing the conduct of gaming activities on the Indian lands subject to the jurisdiction of such Indian tribe within the 60-day period provided in the order of a court issued under clause (iii), the Indian tribe and the State shall each submit to a mediator appointed by the court a proposed compact that represents their last best offer for a compact. The mediator shall select from the two proposed compacts the one which best com-ports with the terms of this chapter and any other applicable Federal law and with the findings and order of the court.

> (v) The mediator appointed by the court under clause (iv) shall submit to the State and the Indian tribe the compact selected by the mediator under clause (iv).

> (vi) If a State consents to a proposed compact during the 60-day period beginning on the date on which the proposed compact is submitted by the mediator to the State under clause (v), the proposed compact shall be treated as a Tribal-State compact entered into under paragraph (3).

(vii) If the State does not consent during the 60-day period described in clause (vi) to a proposed compact submitted by a mediator under clause (v), the mediator shall notify the Secretary and the Secretary shall prescribe, in consultation with the Indian tribe, procedures—

(I) which are consistent with the proposed compact selected by the mediator under clause (iv), the provisions of this chapter, and the relevant provisions of the laws of the State, and

(II) under which class III gaming may be conducted on the Indian lands over which the Indian tribe has jurisdiction.

Initially, to trigger the state's duty to negotiate in good faith, the tribe must formally request that the state enter into compact negotiations. If 180 days pass without a response from the state, or without successful negotiation of a compact, then a cause of action accrues and the tribe may file suit against the state in federal district court. *Id.* § 2710(d)(7)(B)(i). To support its claim, the tribe must present evidence showing that the state did not respond to its request to enter into compact negotiations, or that the state and the tribe failed to reach a compact. Upon this prima facie showing, the burden of proof shifts to the state to establish that it in fact negotiated in good faith. *Id.* § 2710(d)(7)(B)(ii).

The court then must determine whether the state negotiated in good faith, considering the state's public interest as well as concerns about public safety, criminality, financial integrity, and adverse economic impacts on existing gaming. Any of these considerations might indicate that despite the failure to negotiate or to reach a compact, the state nevertheless fulfilled its good-faith duty. If, however, the state sought to tax the tribe, the court must consider that as evidence of bad faith on the part of the state. If the court finds that the state fulfilled its duty to negotiate in good faith, then it must decide the case in favor of the state. If the court finds that the state did not negotiate in good faith, then the court must order the state and the tribe to reach a compact within 60 days. *Id.* § 2710(d)(7)(B)(iii).

If, after the court-ordered negotiation period, the state and the tribe have not successfully negotiated a compact, the court will appoint a mediator and direct the state and the tribe each to submit proposed compacts—the state's and the tribe's "last best offer"— to the mediator. The mediator then will choose the proposed compact that "best comports with the terms of [IGRA] and any other applicable Federal law and with the findings and order of the court." *Id.* § 2710(d)(7)(B)(iv). After choosing between the state's and the tribe's proposed compacts, the mediator will forward the selected version to both the state and the tribe, who then have 60 days to consider it. If the state accepts the mediator's compact during that 60-day period, the compact is treated as though the state and the tribe successfully negotiated it and is submitted to the Secretary of the Interior for approval. *Id.* § 2710(d)(7)(B)(vi). If, however, the state does not agree to the mediator's version, the mediator will notify the Secretary of the state's disapproval. The Secretary then will consult with the tribe to draft a "compact" to govern the tribe's Class III gaming. In so doing, the Secretary will take into account the mediator's compact, IGRA's provisions, and state law. *Id.* § 2710(d)(7)(B)(vii). The Secretary has the power to sue in federal court to enforce the provisions of the administrative "compact." *Id.* § 2710(d)(7)(A)(iii).

The Interior Secretary has the power to approve or disapprove a tribal-state compact, whether reached through amicable negotiations between the state and the tribe or through the tribe's cause of action in federal court. The Secretary may disapprove a compact for any of three reasons: the compact violates one or more of IGRA's provisions; the compact violates federal law, other than the federal law allocating jurisdiction over gambling on reservation lands; or the compact violates the federal government's trust obligation to the tribes. *Id.* § 2710(d)(8). If the Secretary takes no action on a tribal-state compact within 45 days of its submission, the compact automatically will be approved. This "pocket" approval is limited to the extent that the compact's provisions comport with IGRA. *Id.* § 2710(d)(8)(C). Notices of approved tribal-state compacts are published in the Federal Register, and a compact becomes effective upon such publication. *Id.* §§ 2710(d)(8)(D), 2710(d)(3)(B).

In *Seminole Tribe v. Florida*, discussed below, the U.S. Supreme Court invalidated IGRA's primary enforcement mechanism for a state's failure to negotiate in good faith, the tribe's cause of action against the state. Nevertheless, the statutory cause of action remains relevant for at least two reasons. First, even after *Seminole Tribe*, a state may consent to suit under IGRA. Second, in the wake of *Seminole Tribe*, the Interior Secretary in 1999 promulgated regulations which in large part mimic IGRA's original procedures to effectuate Class III gaming when a state both fails to negotiate in good faith and refuses to submit to federal court jurisdiction. *See* 25 C.F.R. pt. 291.

As noted above, IGRA states that a compact may include provisions concerning (1) the application of the state's and the tribe's criminal and civil laws and regulations "that are directly related to, and necessary for, the licensing and regulation" of Class III games, (2) allocation of criminal and civil jurisdiction between the state and the tribe "necessary for the enforcement of such laws and regulations," (3) payments to the state to cover the state's costs of regulating the tribe's Class III games, (4) tribal taxation of Class III gaming, limited to amounts comparable to the state's taxation of similar activities, (5) remedies for breach of contract, (6) operating and facility maintenance standards, including licensing, and (7) "any other subjects that are directly related to the operation of gaming activities." 25 U.S.C. § 2710(d)(3)(C). IGRA expressly prohibits states from seeking to tax or charge the tribe a fee, other than the reimbursal of the state's regulatory costs, or refusing to negotiate on that basis. *Id.* § 2710(d)(4).

Although IGRA does not dictate that a tribal-state compact must provide for state regulation of Class III gaming, compacts typically have done so, though to widely varying extents. Some compacts merely incorporate particular aspects of state law, such as hours for serving alcohol, while others may assign primary regulatory authority over the tribal gaming operation to a state agency. The tribe retains the right to concurrent regulation of its Class III gaming, so long as tribal regulation is not inconsistent with or less stringent than the state's regulation as provided in the compact. *Id.* § 2710(d)(5).

Notes and Questions

1.   *Good faith duty, Indian tribes, and Indian lands.* Under IGRA, the state's good faith duty to negotiate a compact is triggered by a request from "[a]ny Indian tribe having jurisdiction over the Indian lands upon which a class III gaming activity is conducted, or is to be conducted." As mentioned in Chapter 3, the Sixth Circuit held that before a state's good-faith duty to negotiate a compact will be triggered, the tribe requesting negotiations must possess qualifying Indian lands; in other words, a state has no duty to negotiate with a tribe that lacks a reservation or other land constituting Indian lands under IGRA. *Match-E-Be-Nash-She-Wish Band of Pottawatomi Indians v. Engler*, 304 F.3d 616 (6th Cir. 2002). Similarly, the statutory language should require that a group qualify as an "Indian tribe" before the state will be required to enter into compact negotiations.

2. *State authority to negotiate.* In many states, the governor has power (sometimes formally delegated by the legislature) to negotiate a tribal-state compact, but the legislature retains authority to approve or reject the compact, as the decision to bind the state to the compact's terms invokes the legislative powers of law- or policymaking. The question of which branch of state government has the authority to negotiate a tribal-state compact has given rise to litigation in several states, including Michigan, New York, New Mexico, and Wisconsin. In state court, tribes may not be party to a lawsuit that will determine how and whether Indian gaming occurs. State court decisions therefore can bind tribes to state statutory and constitutional law without recourse. *See* Kathryn R.L. Rand, *Caught in the Middle: How State Politics, State Law, and State Courts Constrain Tribal Influence Over Indian Gaming*, 90 Marq. L. Rev. 971, 1007 (2007) ("Tribes' efforts to influence legal and political outcomes are limited by state politics and state court interpretation of state law. Tribes may not be able to meaningfully participate in the processes that determine outcomes."). If true, would this outcome be contrary to IGRA's intent? This issue is considered further in Chapter 8.

3. *Expansive compact negotiations.* Despite IGRA's enumeration of allowable compact provisions, the negotiation of tribal-state compacts has become more expansive in practice. An increasing number of compacts have included, with tribal approval, provisions authorizing direct payments or revenue sharing with the states. Some states and tribes have negotiated separate compacts for the state's fee or percentage take of the casino's profits to comply with the letter of IGRA. *See, e.g.,* Steven Andrew Light, Kathryn R.L. Rand, & Alan P. Meister, *Spreading the Wealth: Indian Gaming and Revenue-Sharing Agreements*, 80 N.D. L. Rev. 657 (2004). More controversially, some states have sought to include in tribal-state compacts provisions not expressly authorized by IGRA, such as restrictions on tribal hunting and fishing treaty rights. *See, e.g.,* Steven A. Light & Kathryn R.L. Rand, *Do "Fish and Chips" Mix? The Politics of Indian Gaming in Wisconsin*, 2 Gaming L. Rev. 129 (1998). As you read the tribal-state compacts from California and North Dakota, consider the categories of permissible provisions in § 2710(d)(3)(C).

Tribal-State Gaming Compact Between the [Insert *1], A Federally Recognized Indian Tribe, and the State of California

(1999)

This Tribal-State Gaming Compact is entered into on a government-to-government basis by and between the [insert *1], a federally recognized sovereign Indian tribe (hereafter "Tribe"), and the State of California, a sovereign State of the United States (hereafter "State"), pursuant to the Indian Gaming Regulatory Act of 1988 (P.L. 100-497, codified at 18 U.S.C. §§ 1166 et seq. and 25 U.S.C. §§ 2701 et seq.) (hereafter "IGRA"), and any successor statute or amendments.

Preamble

A. In 1988, Congress enacted IGRA as the federal statute governing Indian gaming in the United States. The purposes of IGRA are to provide a statutory basis for the operation of gaming by Indian tribes as a means of promoting tribal economic development, self-sufficiency, and strong tribal governments; to provide a statutory basis for regulation of Indian gaming adequate to shield it from organized crime and other corrupting influences; to ensure that the Indian tribe is the primary beneficiary of the gaming operation; to ensure that gaming is conducted fairly and honestly by both the operator and players; and to declare that the establishment of an independent federal regulatory authority for gaming on Indian lands, federal standards for gaming on Indian lands, and a National Indian Gaming Commission are necessary to meet congressional concerns.

B. The system of regulation of Indian gaming fashioned by Congress in IGRA rests on an allocation of regulatory jurisdiction among the three sovereigns involved: the federal government, the state in which a tribe has land, and the tribe itself. IGRA makes Class III gaming activities lawful on the lands of federally recognized Indian tribes only if such activities are: (1) authorized by a tribal ordinance, (2) located in a state that permits such gaming for any purpose by any person, organization or entity, and (3) conducted in conformity with a gaming compact entered into between the Indian tribe and the state and approved by the Secretary of the Interior.

C-1. The Tribe is currently operating a tribal gaming casino offering Class III gaming activities on its land. On September 1, 1999, the largest number of Gaming Devices operated by the Tribe was [insert *2].

C-2. [alternate paragraph] The Tribe does not currently operate a gaming facility that offers Class III gaming activities. However, on or after the effective date of this Compact, the Tribe intends to develop and operate a gaming facility offering Class III gaming activities on its reservation land, which is located in [insert *3] County of California.

D. The State enters into this Compact out of respect for the sovereignty of the Tribe; in recognition of the historical fact that Indian gaming has become the single largest revenue-producing activity for Indian tribes in the United States; out of a desire to terminate pending "bad faith" litigation between the Tribe and the State; to initiate a new era of tribal-state cooperation in areas of mutual concern; out of a respect for the sentiment of the voters of California who, in approving Proposition 5, expressed their belief that the forms of gaming authorized herein should be allowed; and in anticipation of voter approval of [Proposition 1A] as passed by the California legislature.

E. The exclusive rights that Indian tribes in California, including the Tribe, will enjoy under this Compact create a unique opportunity for the Tribe to operate its Gaming Facility in an economic environment free of competition from the Class III gaming referred to in Section 4.0 of this Compact on non-Indian lands in California. The parties are mindful that this unique environment is of great economic value to the Tribe and the fact that income from Gaming Devices represents a substantial portion of the tribes' gaming revenues. In consideration for the exclusive rights enjoyed by the tribes, and in further consideration for the State's willingness to enter into this Compact, the tribes have agreed to provide to the State, on a sovereign-to-sovereign basis, a portion of its revenue from Gaming Devices.

F. The State has a legitimate interest in promoting the purposes of IGRA for all federally recognized Indian tribes in California, whether gaming or non-gaming. The State contends that it has an equally legitimate sovereign interest in regulating the growth of Class III gaming activities in California. The Tribe and the State share a joint sovereign interest in ensuring that tribal gaming activities are free from criminal and other undesirable elements.

Section 1.0. Purposes and Objectives

The terms of this Gaming Compact are designed and intended to:

(a) Evidence the goodwill and cooperation of the Tribe and State in fostering a mutually respectful government-to-government relationship that will serve the mutual interests of the parties.

(b) Develop and implement a means of regulating Class III gaming, and only Class III gaming, on the Tribe's Indian lands to ensure its fair and honest operation in accordance with

IGRA, and through that regulated Class III gaming, enable the Tribe to develop self-sufficiency, promote tribal economic development, and generate jobs and revenues to support the Tribe's government and governmental services and programs.

(c) Promote ethical practices in conjunction with that gaming, through the licensing and control of persons and entities employed in, or providing goods and services to, the Tribe's Gaming Operation and protecting against the presence or participation of persons whose criminal backgrounds, reputations, character, or associations make them unsuitable for participation in gaming, thereby maintaining a high level of integrity in tribal government gaming.

Section 2.0. Definitions

2.1. "Applicant" means an individual or entity that applies for a Tribal license or State certification.

2.2. "Association" means an association of California tribal and state gaming regulators, the membership of which comprises up to two representatives from each tribal gaming agency of those tribes with whom the State has a gaming compact under IGRA, and up to two delegates each from the state Division of Gambling Control and the state Gambling Control Commission.

2.3. "Class III gaming" means the forms of Class III gaming defined as such in 25 U.S.C. §2703(8) and by regulations of the National Indian Gaming Commission.

2.4. "Gaming Activities" means the Class III gaming activities authorized under this Gaming Compact.

2.5. "Gaming Compact" or "Compact" means this compact.

2.6. "Gaming Device" means a slot machine, including an electronic, electromechanical, electrical, or video device that, for consideration, permits: individual play with or against that device or the participation in any electronic, electromechanical, electrical, or video system to which that device is connected; the playing of games thereon or therewith, including, but not limited to, the playing of facsimiles of games of chance or skill; the possible delivery of, or entitlement by the player to, a prize or something of value as a result of the application of an element of chance; and a method for viewing the outcome, prize won, and other information regarding the playing of games thereon or therewith.

2.7. "Gaming Employee" means any person who (a) operates, maintains, repairs, assists in any Class III gaming activity, or is in any way responsible for supervising such gaming activities or persons who conduct, operate, account for, or supervise any such gaming activity, (b) is in a category under federal or tribal gaming law requiring licensing, (c) is an employee of the Tribal Gaming Agency with access to confidential information, or (d) is a person whose employment duties require or authorize access to areas of the Gaming Facility that are not open to the public.

2.8. "Gaming Facility" or "Facility" means any building in which Class III gaming activities or gaming operations occur, or in which the business records, receipts, or other funds of the gaming operation are maintained (but excluding offsite facilities primarily dedicated to storage of those records, and financial institutions), and all rooms, buildings, and areas, including parking lots and walkways, a principal purpose of which is to serve the activities of the Gaming Operation, provided that nothing herein prevents the conduct of Class II gaming (as defined under IGRA) therein.

2.9. "Gaming Operation" means the business enterprise that offers and operates Class III Gaming Activities, whether exclusively or otherwise.

2.10. "Gaming Ordinance" means a tribal ordinance or resolution duly authorizing the conduct of Class III Gaming Activities on the Tribe's Indian lands and approved under IGRA.

2.11. "Gaming Resources" means any goods or services provided or used in connection with Class III Gaming Activities, whether exclusively or otherwise, including, but not limited to, equipment, furniture, gambling devices and ancillary equipment, implements of gaming activities such as playing cards and dice, furniture designed primarily for Class III gaming activities, maintenance or security equipment and services, and Class III gaming consulting services. "Gaming Resources" does not include professional accounting and legal services.

2.12. "Gaming Resource Supplier" means any person or entity who, directly or indirectly, manufactures, distributes, supplies, vends, leases, or otherwise purveys Gaming Resources to the Gaming Operation or Gaming Facility, provided that the Tribal Gaming Agency may exclude a purveyor of equipment or furniture that is not specifically designed for, and is distributed generally for use other than in connection with, Gaming Activities, if the purveyor is not otherwise a Gaming Resource Supplier as described by of Section 6.4.5, the compensation received by the purveyor is not grossly disproportionate to the value of the goods or services provided, and the purveyor is not otherwise a person who exercises a significant influence over the Gambling Operation.

2.13. "IGRA" means the Indian Gaming Regulatory Act of 1988 (P.L. 100-497, 18 U.S.C. §§1166 et seq. and 25 U.S.C. §§2701 et seq.) any amendments thereto, and all regulations promulgated thereunder.

2.14. "Management Contractor" means any Gaming Resource Supplier with whom the Tribe has contracted for the management of any Gaming Activity or Gaming Facility, including, but not limited to, any person who would be regarded as a management contractor under IGRA.

2.15. "Net Win" means "net win" as defined by American Institute of Certified Public Accountants.

2.16. "NIGC" means the National Indian Gaming Commission.

2.17. "State" means the State of California or an authorized official or agency thereof.

2.18. "State Gaming Agency" means the entities authorized to investigate, approve, and regulate gaming licenses pursuant to the Gambling Control Act (Chapter 5 (commencing with Section 19800) of Division 8 of the Business and Professions Code).

2.19. "Tribal Chairperson" means the person duly elected or selected under the Tribe's organic documents, customs, or traditions to serve as the primary spokesperson for the Tribe.

2.20. "Tribal Gaming Agency" means the person, agency, board, committee, commission, or council designated under tribal law, including, but not limited to, an intertribal gaming regulatory agency approved to fulfill those functions by the National Indian Gaming Commission, as primarily responsible for carrying out the Tribe's regulatory responsibilities under IGRA and the Tribal Gaming Ordinance. No person employed in, or in connection with, the management, supervision, or conduct of any gaming activity may be a member or employee of the Tribal Gaming Agency.

2.21. "Tribe" means [insert *1], a federally recognized Indian tribe, or an authorized official or agency thereof.

Section 3.0 Class III Gaming Authorized and Permitted

The Tribe is hereby authorized and permitted to engage in only the Class III Gaming Activities expressly referred to in Section 4.0 and shall not engage in Class III gaming that is not expressly authorized in that Section.

Section 4.0. Scope of Class III Gaming

4.1. Authorized and Permitted Class III gaming. The Tribe is hereby authorized and permitted to operate the following Gaming Activities under the terms and conditions set forth in this Gaming Compact:

(a) The operation of Gaming Devices.

(b) Any banking or percentage card game.

(c) The operation of any devices or games that are authorized under state law to the California State Lottery, provided that the Tribe will not offer such games through use of the Internet unless others in the state are permitted to do so under state and federal law.

(d) Nothing herein shall be construed to preclude negotiation of a separate compact governing the conduct of off-track wagering at the Tribe's Gaming Facility.

4.2. Authorized Gaming Facilities. The Tribe may establish and operate not more than two Gaming Facilities, and only on those Indian lands on which gaming may lawfully be conducted under the Indian Gaming Regulatory Act. The Tribe may combine and operate in each Gaming Facility any forms and kinds of gaming permitted under law, except to the extent limited under IGRA, this Compact, or the Tribe's Gaming Ordinance.

4.3. Authorized number of Gaming Devices

4.3.1. The Tribe may operate no more Gaming Devices than the larger of the following:

(a) A number of terminals equal to the number of Gaming Devices operated by the Tribe

on September 1, 1999; or

(b) Three hundred fifty (350) Gaming Devices.

4.3.2. Revenue Sharing with Non-Gaming Tribes. For the purposes of this Section 4.3.2 and Section 5.0, the following definitions apply: (i) A "Compact Tribe" is a tribe having a compact with the State that authorizes the Gaming Activities authorized by this Compact. Federally recognized tribes that are operating fewer than 350 Gaming Devices are "Non-Compact Tribes." Non-Compact Tribes shall be deemed third party beneficiaries of this and other compacts identical in all material respects. A Compact Tribe that becomes a Non-Compact Tribe may not thereafter return to the status of a Compact Tribe for a period of two years becoming a Non-Compact Tribe. (ii) The Revenue Sharing Trust Fund is a fund created by the Legislature and administered by the California Gambling Control Commission, as Trustee, for the receipt, deposit, and distribution of monies paid pursuant to this Section 4.3.2. (iii) The Special Distribution Fund is a fund created by the Legislature for the receipt, deposit, and distribution of monies paid pursuant to Section 5.0.

4.3.2.1. Revenue Sharing Trust Fund.

(a) The Tribe agrees with all other Compact Tribes that are parties to compacts having this Section 4.3.2, that each Non-Compact Tribe in the State shall receive the sum of $1.1 million per year. In the event there are insufficient monies in the Revenue Sharing Trust Fund to pay $1.1 million per year to each Non-Compact Tribe, any available monies in that Fund shall be distributed to Non-Compact Tribes in equal shares. Monies in excess of the amount necessary to $1.1 million to each Non-Compact Tribe shall remain in the Revenue Sharing Trust Fund available for disbursement in future years.

(b) Payments made to Non-Compact Tribes shall be made quarterly and in equal shares out of the Revenue Sharing Trust Fund. The Commission shall serve as the trustee of the fund. The Commission shall have no discretion with respect to the use or disbursement of the trust funds. Its sole authority shall be to serve as a depository of the trust funds and to disburse them on a quarterly basis to Non-Compact Tribes. In no event shall the State's General Fund be obligated to make up any shortfall or pay any unpaid claims.

4.3.2.2. Allocation of Licenses.

(a) The Tribe, along with all other Compact Tribes, may acquire licenses to use Gaming Devices in excess of the number they are authorized to use under Section 4.3.1, but in no event may the Tribe operate more than 2,000 Gaming Devices, on the following terms, conditions, and priorities:

(1) The maximum number of machines that all Compact Tribes in the aggregate may license pursuant to this Section shall be a sum equal to 350 multiplied by the number of Non-Compact tribes as of September 1, 1999, plus the difference between 350 and the lesser number authorized under Section 4.3.1.

(2) The Tribe may acquire and maintain a license to operate a Gaming Device by paying into the Revenue Sharing Trust Fund, on a quarterly basis, in the following amounts:

Number of Licensed Devices	Fee Per Device Per Annum
1–350	$0
351–750	$900
751–1250	$1950
1251–2000	$4350

(3) Licenses to use Gaming Devices shall be awarded as follows:

(i) First, Compact Tribes with no Existing Devices (i.e., the number of Gaming Devices operated by a Compact Tribe as of September 1, 1999) may draw up to 150 licenses for a total of 500 Gaming Devices.

(ii) Next, Compact Tribes authorized under Section 4.3.1 to operate up to and including 500 Gaming Devices as of September 1, 1999 (including tribes, if any, that have acquired licenses through subparagraph (i)), may draw up to an additional 500 licenses, to a total of 1000 Gaming Devices.

(iii) Next, Compact Tribes operating between 501 and 1000 Gaming Devices as of September 1, 1999 (including tribes, if any, that have acquired licenses through subparagraph (ii)), shall be entitled to draw up to an additional 750 Gaming Devices.

(iv) Next, Compact Tribes authorized to operate up to and including 1500 gaming devices (including tribes, if any, that have acquired licenses through subparagraph (iii)), shall be entitled to draw up to an additional 500 licenses, for a total authorization to operate up to 2000 gaming devices.

(v) Next, Compact Tribes authorized to operate more than 1500 gaming devices (including tribes, if any, that have acquired licenses through subparagraph (iv)), shall be entitled to draw additional licenses up to a total authorization to operate up to 2000 gaming devices.

(vi) After the first round of draws, a second and subsequent round(s) shall be conducted utilizing the same order of priority as set forth above. Rounds shall continue until tribes cease making draws, at which time draws will be discontinued for one month or until the Trustee is notified that a tribe desires to acquire a license, whichever last occurs.

(b) As a condition of acquiring licenses to operate Gaming Devices, a non-refundable one-time pre-payment fee shall be required in the amount of $1,250 per Gaming Device being licensed, which fees shall be deposited in the Revenue Sharing Trust Fund. The license for any Gaming Device shall be canceled if the Gaming Device authorized by the license is not in commercial operation within twelve months of issuance of the license.

4.3.2.3. The Tribe shall not conduct any Gaming Activity authorized by this Compact if the Tribe is more than two quarterly contributions in arrears in its license fee payments to the Revenue Sharing Trust Fund.

4.3.3. If requested to do so by either party after March 7, 2003, but not later than March 31, 2003, the parties will promptly commence negotiations in good faith with the Tribe concerning any matters encompassed by Sections 4.3.1 and Section 4.3.2, and their subsections.

Section 5.0 Revenue Distribution

5.1. (a) The Tribe shall make contributions to the Special Distribution Fund created by the Legislature, in accordance with the following schedule, but only with respect to the number of Gaming Devices operated by the Tribe on September 1, 1999:

Number of Terminals in Quarterly Device Base	Percent of Average Gaming Device Net Win
1–200	0%
201–500	7%
501–1000	7% applied to the excess over 200 terminals, up to 500 terminals, plus 10% applied to terminals over 500 terminals, up to 1000 terminals.
1000+	7% applied to excess over 200, up to 500 terminals, plus 10% applied to terminals over 500, up to 1000 terminals, plus 13% applied to the excess above 1000 terminals.

(b) The first transfer to the Special Distribution Fund of its share of the gaming revenue shall made at the conclusion of the first calendar quarter following the second anniversary date of the effective date of this Compact.

5.2. Use of funds. The State's share of the Gaming Device revenue shall be placed in the Special Distribution Fund, available for appropriation by the Legislature for the following purposes: (a) grants, including any administrative costs, for programs designed to address gambling addiction; (b) grants, including any administrative costs, for the support of state and local government agencies impacted by tribal government gaming; (c) compensation for regulatory costs incurred by the State Gaming Agency and the state Department of Justice in connection with the implementation and administration of the Compact; (d) payment of shortfalls that may occur in the Revenue Sharing Trust Fund; and (e) any other purposes specified by the Legislature. It is the intent of the parties that Compact Tribes will be consulted in the process of identifying purposes for grants made to local governments.

5.3(a) The quarterly contributions due under Section 5.1 shall be determined and made not later than the thirtieth (30th) day following the end of each calendar quarter by first determining the total number of all Gaming Devices operated by a Tribe during a given quarter ("Quarterly Device Base"). The "Average Device Net Win" is calculated by dividing the total Net Win from all terminals during the quarter by the Quarterly Terminal Base.

(b) Any quarterly contribution not paid on or before the date on which such amount is due shall be deemed overdue. If any quarterly contribution under Section 5.1 is overdue to the Special Distribution Fund, the Tribe shall pay to the Special Distribution Fund, in addition to the overdue quarterly contribution, interest on such amount from the date the quarterly contribution was due until the date such quarterly contribution (together with interest thereon) was actually paid at the rate of 1.0% per month or the maximum rate permitted by state law, whichever is less. Entitlement to such interest shall be in addition to any other remedies the State may have.

(c) At the time each quarterly contribution is made, the Tribe shall submit to the State a report (the "Quarterly Contribution Report") certified by an authorized representative of the Tribe reflecting the Quarterly Device Base, the Net Win from all terminals in the Quarterly Device Base (broken down by Gaming Device), and the Average Device Net Win.

(d) If the State causes an audit to be made pursuant to subdivision (c), and the Average Device Net Win for any quarter as reflected on such quarter's Quarterly Contribution Reports is found to be understated, the State will promptly notify the Tribe, and the Tribe will either accept the difference or provide a reconciliation satisfactory to the State. If the Tribe accepts the difference or does not provide a reconciliation satisfactory to the State, the Tribe must immediately pay the amount of the resulting deficiencies in the quarterly contribution plus interest on such amounts from the date they were due at the rate of 1.0% per month or the maximum rate permitted by applicable law, whichever is less.

(e) The Tribe shall not conduct Class III gaming if more than two quarterly contributions to the Special Distribution Fund are overdue.

Section 6.0. Licensing

6.1. Gaming Ordinance and Regulations. All Gaming Activities conducted under this Gaming Compact shall, at a minimum, comply with a Gaming Ordinance duly adopted by the Tribe and approved in accordance with IGRA, and with all rules, regulations, procedures, specifications, and standards duly adopted by the Tribal Gaming Agency.

6.2. Tribal Ownership, Management, and Control of Gaming Operation. The Gaming Operations authorized under this Gaming Compact shall be owned solely by the Tribe.

6.3. Prohibition Regarding Minors.

(a) Except as provided in subdivision (b), the Tribe shall not permit persons under the age of 18 years to be present in any room in which Class III Gaming Activities are being conducted unless the person is en-route to a non-gaming area of the Gaming Facility.

(b) If the Tribe permits the consumption of alcoholic beverages in the Gaming Facility, the Tribe shall prohibit persons under the age of 21 years from being present in any area in which Class III gaming activities are being conducted and in which alcoholic beverages may be consumed, to the extent required by the state Department of Alcoholic Beverage Control.

6.4. Licensing Requirements and Procedures.

6.4.1. Summary of Licensing Principles. All persons in any way connected with the Gaming Operation or Facility who are required to be licensed or to submit to a background investigation under IGRA, and any others required to be licensed under this Gaming

Compact, including, but not limited to, all Gaming Employees and Gaming Resource Suppliers, and any other person having a significant influence over the Gaming Operation must be licensed by the Tribal Gaming Agency. The parties intend that the licensing process provided for in this Gaming Compact shall involve joint cooperation between the Tribal Gaming Agency and the State Gaming Agency, as more particularly described herein.

6.4.2. Gaming Facility.

(a) The Gaming Facility authorized by this Gaming Compact shall be licensed by the Tribal Gaming Agency in conformity with the requirements of this Gaming Compact, the Tribal Gaming Ordinance, and IGRA. The license shall be reviewed and renewed, if appropriate, every two years thereafter. Verification that this requirement has been met shall be provided by the Tribe to the State Gaming Agency every two years. The Tribal Gaming Agency's certification to that effect shall be posted in a conspicuous and public place in the Gaming Facility at all times.

(b) In order to protect the health and safety of all Gaming Facility patrons, guests, and employees, all Gaming Facilities of the Tribe constructed after the effective date of this Gaming Compact, and all expansions or modifications to a Gaming Facility in operation as of the effective date of this Compact, shall meet the building and safety codes of the Tribe, which, as a condition for engaging in that construction, expansion, modification, or renovation, shall amend its existing building and safety codes if necessary, or enact such codes if there are none, so that they meet the standards of either the building and safety codes of any county within the boundaries of which the site of the Facility is located, or the Uniform Building Codes, including all uniform fire, plumbing, electrical, mechanical, and related codes then in effect provided that nothing herein shall be deemed to confer jurisdiction upon any county or the State with respect to any reference to such building and safety codes. Any such construction, expansion or modification will also comply with the federal Americans with Disabilities Act, P.L. 101-336, as amended, 42 U.S.C. § 12101 et seq.

(c) Any Gaming Facility in which gaming authorized by this Gaming Compact is conducted shall be issued a certificate of occupancy by the Tribal Gaming Agency prior to occupancy if it was not used for any Gaming Activities under IGRA prior to the effective date of this Gaming Compact, or, if it was so used, within one year thereafter. The issuance of this certificate shall be reviewed for continuing compliance every two years thereafter. Inspections by qualified building and safety experts shall be conducted under the direction of the Tribal Gaming Agency as the basis for issuing any certificate hereunder. The Tribal Gaming Agency shall determine and certify that, as to new construction or new use for gaming, the Facility meets the Tribe's building and safety code, or, as to facilities or portions of facilities that were used for the Tribe's Gaming Activities prior to this Gaming Compact, that the facility or portions thereof do not endanger the health or safety of occupants or the integrity of the Gaming Operation. The Tribe will not offer Class III gaming in a Facility that is constructed or maintained in a manner that endangers the health or safety of occupants or the integrity of the gaming operation.

(d) The State shall designate an agent or agents to be given reasonable notice of each inspection by the Tribal Gaming Agency's experts, which state agents may accompany any such inspection. The Tribe agrees to correct any Gaming Facility condition noted in an inspection that does not meet the standards set forth in subdivisions (b) and (c). The Tribal Gaming Agency and the State's designated agent or agents shall exchange any reports of an inspection within 10 days after completion of the report, which reports shall also be separately and simultaneously forwarded by both agencies to the Tribal Chairperson. Upon certification by the Tribal Gaming Agency's experts that a Gaming Facility meets applicable standards, the Tribal Gaming Agency shall forward the experts' certification to the State within 10 days of issuance. If the State's agent objects to that certification, the Tribe shall make a good faith effort to address the State's concerns, but if the State does not withdraw its objection, the matter will be resolved in accordance with the dispute resolution provisions of Section 9.0.

6.4.3. Suitability Standard Regarding Gaming Licenses. In reviewing an application for a gaming license, and in addition to any standards set forth in the Tribal Gaming Ordinance, the Tribal Gaming Agency shall consider whether issuance of the license is inimical to public health, safety, or welfare, and whether issuance of the license will undermine public trust that the Tribe's Gaming Operations, or tribal government gaming generally, are free from criminal and dishonest elements and would be conducted honestly. A license may not be issued unless, based on all information and documents submitted, the Tribal Gaming Agency is satisfied that the applicant is all of the following, in addition to any other criteria in IGRA or the Tribal Gaming Ordinance:

(a) A person of good character, honesty, and integrity.

(b) A person whose prior activities, criminal record (if any), reputation, habits, and associations do not pose a threat to the public interest or to the effective regulation and control of gambling, or create or enhance the dangers of unsuitable, unfair, or illegal practices, methods, or activities in the conduct of gambling, or in the carrying on of the business and financial arrangements incidental thereto.

(c) A person who is in all other respects qualified to be licensed as provided in this Gaming Compact, IGRA, the Tribal Gaming Ordinance, and any other criteria adopted by the Tribal Gaming Agency or the Tribe. An applicant shall not be found to be unsuitable solely on the ground that the applicant was an employee of a tribal gaming operation in California that was conducted prior to the effective date of this Compact.

6.4.4. Gaming Employees.

(a) Every Gaming Employee shall obtain, and thereafter maintain current, a valid tribal gaming license, which shall be subject to biennial renewal; provided that in accordance with Section 6.4.9, those persons may be employed on a temporary or conditional basis pending completion of the licensing process.

(b) Except as provided in subdivisions (c) and (d), the Tribe will not employ or continue to employ, any person whose application to the State Gaming Agency for a determination of suitability, or for a renewal of such a determination, has been denied or has expired without renewal.

(c) Notwithstanding subdivision (a), the Tribe may retain in its employ a person whose application for a determination of suitability, or for a renewal of such a determination, has been denied by the State Gaming Agency, if: (i) the person holds a valid and current license issued by the Tribal Gaming Agency that must be renewed at least biennially; (ii) the denial of the application by the State Gaming Agency is based solely on activities, conduct, or associations that antedate the filing of the person's initial application to the State Gaming Agency for a determination of suitability; (iii) the person is not an employee or agent of any other gaming operation; and (iv) the person has been in the continuous employ of the Tribe for at least three years prior to the effective date of this Compact.

(d) Notwithstanding subdivision (a), the Tribe may employ or retain in its employ a person whose application for a determination of suitability, or for a renewal of such a determination, has been denied by the State Gaming Agency, if the person is an enrolled member of the Tribe, as defined in this subdivision, and if (i) the person holds a valid and current license issued by the Tribal Gaming Agency that must be renewed at least biennially; (ii) the denial of the application by the State Gaming Agency is based solely on activities, conduct, or associations that antedate the filing of the person's initial application to the State Gaming Agency for a determination of suitability; and (iii) the person is not an employee or agent of any other gaming operation. For purposes of this subdivision, "enrolled member" means a person who is either (a) certified by the Tribe as having been a member of the Tribe for at least five (5) years, or (b) a holder of confirmation of membership issued by the Bureau of Indian Affairs.

(e) Nothing herein shall be construed to relieve any person of the obligation to apply for a renewal of a determination of suitability as required by Section 6.5.6.

6.4.5. Gaming Resource Supplier. Any Gaming Resource Supplier who, directly or indirectly, provides, has provided, or is deemed likely to provide at least twenty-five thousand dollars ($25,000) in Gaming Resources in any 12-month period, or who has received at least twenty-five thousand dollars ($25,000) in any consecutive 12-month period within the 24-month period immediately preceding application, shall be licensed by the Tribal Gaming Agency prior to the sale, lease, or distribution, or further sale, lease, or distribution, of any such Gaming Resources to or in connection with the Tribe's Operation or Facility. These licenses shall be reviewed at least every two years for continuing compliance. In connection with such a review, the Tribal Gaming Agency shall require the Supplier to update all information provided in the previous application. For purposes of Section 6.5.2, such a review shall be deemed to constitute an application for renewal. The Tribe shall not enter into, or continue to make payments pursuant to, any contract or agreement for the provision of Gaming Resources with any person whose application to the State Gaming Agency for a determination of suitability has been denied or has expired without renewal. Any agreement between the Tribe and a Gaming Resource Supplier shall be deemed to include a provision for its termination without further liability on the part of the Tribe, except for the bona fide repayment of all outstanding sums (exclusive of interest) owed as of, or payment for services or materials received up to, the date of termination, upon revocation or non-renewal of the Supplier's license by the Tribal Gaming Agency based on a determination of unsuitability by the State Gaming Agency.

6.4.6. Financial Sources. Any person extending financing, directly or indirectly, to the Tribe's Gaming Facility or Gaming Operation shall be licensed by the Tribal Gaming Agency prior to extending that financing, provided that any person who is extending financing at the time of the execution of this Compact shall be licensed by the Tribal Gaming Agency within ninety (90) days of such execution. These licenses shall be reviewed at least every two years for continuing compliance. In connection with such a review, the Tribal Gaming Agency shall require the Financial Source to update all information provided in the previous application. For purposes of Section 6.5.2, such a review shall be deemed to constitute an application for renewal. Any agreement between the Tribe and a Financial Source shall be deemed to include a provision for its termination without further liability on the part of the Tribe, except for the bona fide repayment of all outstanding sums (exclusive of interest) owed as of the date of termination, upon revocation or non-renewal of the Financial Source's license by the Tribal Gaming Agency based on a determination of unsuitability by the State Gaming Agency. The Tribe shall not enter into, or continue to make payments pursuant to, any contract or agreement for the provision of financing with any person whose application to the State Gaming Agency for a determination of suitability has been denied or has expired without renewal. A Gaming Resource Supplier who provides financing exclusively in connection with the sale or lease of Gaming Resources obtained from that Supplier may be licensed solely in accordance with licensing procedures applicable, if at all, to Gaming Resource Suppliers. The Tribal Gaming Agency may, at its discretion, exclude from the licensing requirements of this section, financing provided by a federally regulated or state-regulated bank, savings and loan, or other federally or state-regulated lending institution; or any agency of the federal, state, or local government; or any investor who, alone or in conjunction with others, holds less than 10% of any outstanding indebtedness evidenced by bonds issued by the Tribe.

6.4.7. Processing Tribal Gaming License Applications. Each applicant for a tribal gaming license shall submit the completed application along with the required information and an application fee, if required, to the Tribal Gaming Agency in accordance with the rules and regulations of that agency. At a minimum, the Tribal Gaming Agency shall require submission and consideration of all information required under IGRA, including [25 C.F.R. §556.4], for licensing primary management officials and key employees. For applicants who are business entities, these licensing provisions shall apply to the entity as well as: (i) each of its officers and directors; (ii) each of its principal management employees, including any chief executive officer, chief financial officer, chief operating officer, and general manager; (iii) each of its owners or partners, if an unincorporated business; (iv) each of its shareholders who owns more than 10 percent of the shares of the corporation, if a corporation; and (v) each person or entity (other than a financial institution that the Tribal Gaming Agency as determined does not require a license under the preceding section) that, alone or in combination with others, has provided financing in connection with any gaming authorized under this Gaming Compact, if that person or entity provided more than 10 percent of (a) the start-up capital, (b) the operating capital over a 12-month period, or (c) a combination thereof. For purposes of this Section, where there is any commonality of the characteristics identified in clauses (i) to (v), inclusive, between any two or more entities, those entities may be deemed to be a single entity. Nothing herein precludes the Tribe or Tribal Gaming Agency from requiring more stringent licensing requirements.

6.4.8. Background Investigations of Applicants. The Tribal Gaming Agency shall conduct or cause to be conducted all necessary background investigations reasonably required to determine that the applicant is qualified for a gaming license under the standards set forth in Section 6.4.3, and to fulfill all requirements for licensing under IGRA, the Tribal Gaming Ordinance, and this Gaming Compact. The Tribal Gaming Agency shall not issue other than a temporary license until a determination is made that those qualifications have been met. In lieu of completing its own background investigation, and to the extent that doing so does not conflict with or violate IGRA or the Tribal Gaming Ordinance, the Tribal Gaming Agency may contract with the State Gaming Agency for the conduct of background investigations, may rely on a state certification of non-objection previously issued under a gaming compact involving another tribe, or may rely on a State gaming license previously issued to the applicant, to fulfill some or all of the Tribal Gaming Agency's background investigation obligation. An applicant for a tribal gaming license shall be required to provide releases to the State Gaming Agency to make available to the Tribal Gaming Agency background information regarding the applicant. The State Gaming Agency shall cooperate in furnishing to the Tribal Gaming Agency that information, unless doing so would violate any agreement the State Gaming Agency has with a source of the information other than the applicant, or would impair or impede a criminal investigation, or unless the Tribal Gaming Agency cannot provide sufficient safeguards to assure the State Gaming Agency that the information will remain confidential or that provision of the information would violate state or federal law. If the Tribe adopts an ordinance confirming that Article 6 (commencing with § 11140) of Chapter 1 of Title 1 of Part 4 of the California Penal Code is applicable to members, investigators, and staff of the Tribal Gaming Agency, and those members, investigators, and staff thereafter comply with that ordinance, then, for purposes of carrying out its obligations under this Section, the Tribal Gaming Agency shall be considered to be an entity entitled to receive state summary criminal history information within the meaning of subdivision (b)(12) of § 11105 of the California Penal Code. The California Department of Justice shall provide services to the Tribal Gaming Agency through the California Law Enforcement Telecommunications System (CLETS), subject to a determination by the CLETS advisory committee that the Tribal Gaming Agency is qualified for receipt of such services, and on such terms and conditions as are deemed reasonable by that advisory committee.

6.4.9. Temporary Licensing of Gaming Employees. Notwithstanding anything herein to the contrary, if the applicant has completed a license application in a manner satisfactory to the Tribal Gaming Agency, and that agency has conducted a preliminary background investigation, and the investigation or other information held by that agency does not indicate that the applicant has a criminal history or other information in his or her background that would either automatically disqualify the applicant from obtaining a license or cause a reasonable person to investigate further before issuing a license, or is otherwise unsuitable for licensing, the Tribal Gaming Agency may issue a temporary license and may impose such specific conditions thereon pending completion of the applicant's background investigation, as the Tribal Gaming Agency in its sole discretion shall determine. Special fees may be required by the Tribal Gaming Agency to issue or maintain a temporary license. A temporary license shall remain in effect until suspended or revoked, or a final determination is made on the application. At any time after issuance of a temporary license, the Tribal Gaming Agency may suspend or revoke it in accordance with Sections 6.5.1 or 6.5.5, and the State Gaming Agency may request suspension or revocation in accordance with subdivision (d) of Section 6.5.6. Nothing herein shall be construed to relieve the Tribe of any obligation under [25 C.F.R. pt. 558].

6.5. Gaming License Issuance. Upon completion of the necessary background investigation, the Tribal Gaming Agency may issue a license on a conditional or unconditional basis. Nothing herein shall create a property or other right of an applicant in an opportunity to be licensed, or in a license itself, both of which shall be considered to be privileges granted to the applicant in the sole discretion of the Tribal Gaming Agency.

6.5.1. Denial, Suspension, or Revocation of Licenses

(a) Any application for a gaming license may be denied, and any license issued may be revoked, if the Tribal Gaming Agency determines that the application is incomplete or deficient, or if the applicant is determined to be unsuitable or otherwise unqualified for a gaming license. Pending consideration of revocation, the Tribal Gaming Agency may suspend a license in accordance with Section 6.5.5. All rights to notice and hearing shall be governed by tribal law, as to which the applicant will be notified in writing along with notice of an intent to suspend or revoke the license.

(b) (i) Except as provided in paragraph (ii) below, upon receipt of notice that the State Gaming Agency has determined that a person would be unsuitable for licensure in a gambling establishment subject to the jurisdiction of the State Gaming Agency, the Tribal Gaming Agency shall promptly revoke any license that has theretofore been issued to the person; provided that the Tribal Gaming Agency may, in its discretion, re-issue a license to the person following entry of a final judgment reversing the determination of the State Gaming Agency in a proceeding in state court conducted pursuant to § 1085 of the California Civil Code. (ii) Notwithstanding a determination of unsuitability by the State Gaming Agency, the Tribal Gaming Agency may, in its discretion, decline to revoke a tribal license issued to a person employed by the Tribe pursuant to Section 6.4.4(c) or Section 6.4.4(d).

6.5.2. Renewal of Licenses; Extensions; Further Investigation. The term of a tribal gaming license shall not exceed two years, and application for renewal of a license must be made prior to its expiration. Applicants for renewal of a license shall provide updated material as requested, on the appropriate renewal forms, but, at the discretion of the Tribal Gaming Agency, may not be required to resubmit historical data previously submitted or that is otherwise available to the Tribal Gaming Agency. At the discretion of the Tribal Gaming Agency, an additional background investigation may be required at any time if the Tribal Gaming Agency determines the need for further information concerning the applicant's continuing suitability or eligibility for a license. Prior to renewing a license, the Tribal Gaming Agency shall deliver to the State Gaming Agency copies of all information and documents received in connection with the application for renewal.

6.5.3. Identification Cards. The Tribal Gaming Agency shall require that all persons who are required to be licensed wear, in plain view at all times while in the Gaming Facility, identification badges issued by the Tribal Gaming Agency. Identification badges must display information including, but not limited to, a photograph and an identification number that is adequate to enable agents of the Tribal Gaming Agency to readily identify the person and determine the validity and date of expiration of his or her license.

6.5.4. Fees for Tribal License. The fees for all tribal licenses shall be set by the Tribal Gaming Agency.

6.5.5. Suspension of Tribal License. The Tribal Gaming Agency may summarily suspend the license of any employee if the Tribal Gaming Agency determines that the continued licensing of the person or entity could constitute a threat to the public health or safety or may violate the Tribal Gaming Agency's licensing or other standards. Any right to notice or hearing in regard thereto shall be governed by Tribal law.

6.5.6. State Certification Process.

(a) Upon receipt of a completed license application and a determination by the Tribal Gaming Agency that it intends to issue the earlier of a temporary or permanent license, the Tribal Gaming Agency shall transmit to the State Gaming Agency a notice of intent to license the applicant, together with all of the following: (i) a copy of all tribal license application materials and information received by the Tribal Gaming Agency from the applicant; (ii) an original set of fingerprint cards; (iii) a current photograph; and (iv) except to the extent waived by the State Gaming Agency, such releases of information, waivers, and other completed and executed forms as have been obtained by the Tribal Gaming Agency. Except for an applicant for licensing as a non-key Gaming Employee, as defined by agreement between the Tribal Gaming Agency and the State Gaming Agency, the Tribal Gaming Agency shall require the applicant also to file an application with the State Gaming Agency, prior to issuance of a temporary or permanent tribal gaming license, for a determination of suitability for licensure under the California Gambling Control Act. Investigation and disposition of that application shall be governed entirely by state law, and the State Gaming Agency shall determine whether the applicant would be found suitable for licensure in a gambling establishment subject to that Agency's jurisdiction. Additional information may be required by the State Gaming Agency to assist it in its background investigation, provided that such State Gaming Agency requirement shall be no greater than that which may be required of applicants for a State gaming license in connection with nontribal gaming activities and at a similar level of participation or employment. A determination of suitability is valid for the term of the tribal license held by the applicant, and the Tribal Gaming Agency shall require a licensee to apply for renewal of a determination of suitability at such time as the licensee applies for renewal of a tribal gaming license. The State Gaming Agency and the Tribal Gaming Agency (together with tribal gaming agencies under other gaming compacts) shall cooperate in developing standard licensing forms for tribal gaming license applicants, on a statewide basis, that reduce or eliminate duplicative or excessive paperwork, which forms and procedures shall take into account the Tribe's requirements under IGRA and the expense thereof.

(b) Background Investigations of Applicants. Upon receipt of completed license application information from the Tribal Gaming Agency, the State Gaming Agency may conduct a background investigation pursuant to state law to determine whether the applicant would be suitable to be licensed for association with a gambling establishment subject to the jurisdiction of the State Gaming Agency. If further investigation is required to supplement the investigation conducted by the Tribal Gaming Agency, the applicant will be required to pay the statutory application fee charged by the State Gaming Agency pursuant to California Business and Professions Code § 19941(a), but any deposit requested by the State Gaming Agency pursuant to § 19855 of that Code shall take into account reports of the background investigation already conducted by the Tribal Gaming Agency and the NIGC, if any. Failure to pay the application fee or deposit may be grounds for denial of the application by the State Gaming Agency. The State Gaming Agency and Tribal Gaming Agency shall cooperate in sharing as much background information as possible, both to maximize investigative efficiency and thoroughness, and to minimize investigative costs. Upon completion of the necessary background investigation or other verification of suitability, the State Gaming Agency shall issue a notice to the Tribal Gaming Agency certifying that the State has determined that the applicant would be suitable, or that the applicant would be unsuitable, for licensure in a gambling establishment subject to the jurisdiction of the State Gaming Agency and, if unsuitable, stating the reasons therefore.

(c) The Tribe shall monthly provide the State Gaming Agency with the name, badge identification number, and job descriptions of all non-key Gaming Employees.

(d) Prior to denying an application for a determination of suitability, the State Gaming Agency shall notify the Tribal Gaming Agency and afford the Tribe an opportunity to be heard. If the State Gaming Agency denies an application for a determination of suitability, that Agency shall provide the applicant with written notice of all appeal rights available under state law.

Section 7.0. Compliance Enforcement

7.1. On-Site Regulation. It is the responsibility of the Tribal Gaming Agency to conduct on-site gaming regulation and control in order to enforce the terms of this Gaming Compact, IGRA, and the Tribal Gaming Ordinance with respect to Gaming Operation and Facility compliance, and to protect the integrity of the Gaming Activities, the reputation of the Tribe and the Gaming Operation for honesty and fairness, and the confidence of patrons that tribal government gaming in California meets the highest standards of regulation and internal controls. To meet those responsibilities, the Tribal Gaming Agency shall adopt and enforce regulations, procedures, and practices as set forth herein.

7.2. Investigation and Sanctions. The Tribal Gaming Agency shall investigate any reported violation of this Gaming Compact and shall require the Gaming Operation to correct the violation upon such terms and conditions as the Tribal Gaming Agency determines are necessary. The Tribal Gaming Agency shall be empowered by the Tribal Gaming Ordinance to impose fines or other sanctions within the jurisdiction of the Tribe against gaming licensees or other persons who interfere with or violate the Tribe's gaming regulatory requirements and obligations under IGRA, the Tribal Gaming Ordinance, or this Gaming Compact. The Tribal Gaming Agency shall report significant or continued violations of this Compact or failures to comply with its orders to the State Gaming Agency.

7.3. Assistance by State Gaming Agency. The Tribe may request the assistance of the State Gaming Agency whenever it reasonably appears that such assistance may be necessary to carry out the purposes described in Section 7.1, or otherwise to protect public health, safety, or welfare. If requested by the Tribe or Tribal Gaming Agency, the State Gaming Agency shall provide requested services to ensure proper compliance with this Gaming Compact. The State shall be reimbursed for its actual and reasonable costs of that assistance, if the assistance required expenditure of extraordinary costs.

7.4. Access to Premises by State Gaming Agency; Notification; Inspections. Notwithstanding that the Tribe has the primary responsibility to administer and enforce the regulatory requirements of this Compact, the State Gaming Agency shall have the right to inspect the Tribe's Gaming Facility with respect to Class III Gaming Activities only, and all Gaming Operation or Facility records relating thereto, subject to the following conditions:

7.4.1. Inspection of public areas of a Gaming Facility may be made at any time without prior notice during normal Gaming Facility business hours.

7.4.2. Inspection of areas of a Gaming Facility not normally accessible to the public may be made at any time during normal Gaming Facility business hours, immediately after the State Gaming Agency's authorized inspector notifies the Tribal Gaming Agency of his or her presence on the premises, presents proper identification, and requests access to the non-public areas of the Gaming Facility. The Tribal Gaming Agency, in its sole discretion, may require a member of the Tribal Gaming Agency to accompany the State Gaming Agency inspector at all times that the State Gaming Agency inspector is in a non-public area of the Gaming Facility. If the Tribal Gaming Agency imposes such a requirement, it shall require such member to be available at all times for those purposes and shall ensure that the member has the ability to gain immediate access to all non-public areas of the Gaming Facility. Nothing in this Compact shall be construed to limit the State Gaming Agency to one inspector during inspections.

7.4.3. (a) Inspection and copying of Gaming Operation papers, books, and records may occur at any time, immediately after notice to the Tribal Gaming Agency, during the normal hours of the Gaming Facility's business office, provided that the inspection and copying of those papers, books or records shall not interfere with the normal functioning of the Gaming Operation or Facility. Notwithstanding any other provision of California law, all information and records that the State Gaming Agency obtains, inspects, or copies pursuant to this Gaming Compact shall be, and remain, the property solely of the Tribe; provided that such records and copies may be retained by the State Gaming Agency as reasonably necessary for completion of any investigation of the Tribe's compliance with this Compact.

(b)(i) The State Gaming Agency will exercise utmost care in the preservation of the confidentiality of any and all information and documents received from the Tribe, and will apply the highest standards of confidentiality expected under state law to preserve such information and documents from disclosure. The Tribe may avail itself of any and all remedies under state law for improper disclosure of information or documents. To the extent reasonably feasible, the State Gaming Agency will consult with representatives of the Tribe prior to disclosure of any documents received from the Tribe, or any documents compiled from such documents or from information received from the Tribe, including any disclosure compelled by judicial process, and, in the case of any disclosure compelled by judicial process, will endeavor to give the Tribe immediate notice of the order compelling disclosure and a reasonable opportunity to interpose an objection thereto with the court. (ii) The Tribal Gaming Agency and the State Gaming Agency shall confer and agree upon protocols for release to other law enforcement agencies of information obtained during the course of background investigations.

(c) Records received by the State Gaming Agency from the Tribe in compliance with this Compact, or information compiled by the State Gaming Agency from those records, shall be exempt from disclosure under the California Public Records Act. Sec. 7.4.4. Notwithstanding any other provision of this Compact, the State Gaming Agency shall not be denied access to papers, books, records, equipment, or places where such access is reasonably necessary to ensure compliance with this Compact.

7.4.5. (a) Subject to the provisions of subdivision (b), the Tribal Gaming Agency shall not permit any Gaming Device to be transported to or from the Tribe's land except in accordance with procedures established by agreement between the State Gaming Agency and the Tribal Gaming Agency and upon at least 10 days' notice to the Sheriff's Department for the county in which the land is located.

(b) Transportation of a Gaming Device from the Gaming Facility within California is permissible only if: (i) The final destination of the device is a gaming facility of any tribe in California that has a compact with the State; (ii) The final destination of the device is any other state in which possession of the device or devices is made lawful by state law or by tribal-state compact; (iii) The final destination of the device is another country, or any state or province of another country, wherein possession of the device is lawful; or (iv) The final destination is a location within California for testing, repair, maintenance, or storage by a person or entity that has been licensed by the Tribal Gaming Agency and has been found suitable for licensure by the State Gaming Agency.

(c) Gaming Devices transported off the Tribe's land in violation of this Section 7.4.5 or in violation of any permit issued pursuant thereto is subject to summary seizure by California peace officers.

Section 8.0. Rules and Regulations for the Operation and Management of the Tribal Gaming Operation

8.1. Adoption of Regulations for Operation and Management; Minimum Standards. In order to meet the goals set forth in this Gaming Compact and required of the Tribe by law, the Tribal Gaming Agency shall be vested with the authority to promulgate, and shall promulgate, at a minimum, rules and regulations or specifications governing the following subjects, and to ensure their enforcement in an effective manner:

8.1.1. The enforcement of all relevant laws and rules with respect to the Gaming Operation and Facility, and the power to conduct investigations and hearings with respect thereto, and to any other subject within its jurisdiction.

8.1.2. Ensuring the physical safety of Gaming Operation patrons and employees, and any other person while in the Gaming Facility. Nothing herein shall be construed to make applicable to the Tribe any state laws, regulations, or standards governing the use of tobacco.

8.1.3. The physical safeguarding of assets transported to, within, and from the Gaming Facility.

8.1.4. The prevention of illegal activity from occurring within the Gaming Facility or with regard to the Gaming Operation, including, but not limited to, the maintenance of employee procedures and a surveillance system as provided below.

8.1.5. The recording of any and all occurrences within the Gaming Facility that deviate from normal operating policies and procedures (hereafter "incidents"). The procedure for recording incidents shall: (1) specify that security personnel record all incidents, regardless of an employee's determination that the incident may be immaterial (all incidents shall be identified in writing); (2) require the assignment of a sequential number to each report; (3) provide for permanent reporting in indelible ink in a bound notebook from which pages cannot be removed and in which entries are made on each side of each page; and (4) require that each report include, at a minimum, all of the following:

(a) The record number.

(b) The date.

(c) The time.

(d) The location of the incident.

(e) A detailed description of the incident.

(f) The persons involved in the incident.

(g) The security department employee assigned to the incident.

8.1.6. The establishment of employee procedures designed to permit detection of any irregularities, theft, cheating, fraud, or the like, consistent with industry practice.

8.1.7. Maintenance of a list of persons barred from the Gaming Facility who, because of their past behavior, criminal history, or association with persons or organizations, pose a threat to the integrity of the Gaming Activities of the Tribe or to the integrity of regulated gaming within the State.

8.1.8. The conduct of an audit of the Gaming Operation, not less than annually, by an independent certified public accountant, in accordance with the auditing and accounting standards for audits of casinos of the American Institute of Certified Public Accountants.

8.1.9. Submission to, and prior approval, from the Tribal Gaming Agency of the rules and regulations of each Class III game to be operated by the Tribe, and of any changes in those rules and regulations. No Class III game may be played that has not received Tribal Gaming Agency approval.

8.1.10. Addressing all of the following:

(a) Maintenance of a copy of the rules, regulations, and procedures for each game as played, including, but not limited to, the method of play and the odds and method of determining amounts paid to winners;

(b) Specifications and standards to ensure that information regarding the method of play, odds, and payoff determinations shall be visibly displayed or available to patrons in written form in the Gaming Facility;

(c) Specifications ensuring that betting limits applicable to any gaming station shall be displayed at that gaming station;

(d) Procedures ensuring that in the event of a patron dispute over the application of any gaming rule or regulation, the matter shall be handled in accordance with, industry practice and principles of fairness, pursuant to the Tribal Gaming Ordinance and any rules and regulations promulgated by the Tribal Gaming Agency.

8.1.11. Maintenance of a closed-circuit television surveillance system consistent with industry standards for gaming facilities of the type and scale operated by the Tribe, which system shall be approved by, and may not be modified without the approval of, the Tribal Gaming Agency. The Tribal Gaming Agency shall have current copies of the Gaming Facility floor plan and closed-circuit television system at all times, and any modifications thereof first shall be approved by the Tribal Gaming Agency.

8.1.12. Maintenance of a cashier's cage in accordance with industry standards for such facilities.

8.1.13. Specification of minimum staff and supervisory requirements for each Gaming Activity to be conducted.

8.1.14. Technical standards and specifications for the operation of Gaming Devices and other games authorized herein to be conducted by the Tribe, which technical specifications may be no less stringent than those approved by a recognized gaming testing laboratory in the gaming industry.

8.2. State Civil and Criminal Jurisdiction. Nothing in this Gaming Compact affects the civil or criminal jurisdiction of the State under Public Law 280 (18 U.S.C. § 1162; 28 U.S.C. § 1360) or IGRA, to the extent applicable. In addition, criminal jurisdiction to enforce state gambling laws is transferred to the State pursuant to 18 U.S.C. § 1166(d), provided that no Gaming Activity conducted by the Tribe pursuant to this Gaming Compact may be deemed to be a civil or criminal violation of any law of the State.

8.3. (a) The Tribe shall take all reasonable steps to ensure that members of the Tribal Gaming Agency are free from corruption, undue influence, compromise, and conflicting interests in the conduct of their duties under this Compact; shall adopt a conflict-of-interest code to that end; and shall ensure the prompt removal of any member of the Tribal Gaming Agency who is found to have acted in a corrupt or compromised manner.

(b) The Tribe shall conduct a background investigation on a prospective member of the Tribal Gaming Agency, who shall meet the background requirements of a management contractor under IGRA; provided that, if such official is elected through a tribal election process, that official may not participate in any Tribal Gaming Agency matters under this Compact unless a background investigation has been concluded and the official has been found to be suitable. If requested by the tribal government or the Tribal Gaming Agency, the State Gaming Agency may assist in the conduct of such a background investigation and may assist in the investigation of any possible corruption or compromise of a member of the agency.

8.4. In order to foster statewide uniformity of regulation of Class III gaming operations throughout the state, rules, regulations, standards, specifications, and procedures of the Tribal Gaming Agency in respect to any matter encompassed by Sections 6.0, 7.0, or 8.0 shall be consistent with regulations adopted by the State Gaming Agency in accordance with Section 8.4.1. Chapter 3.5 (commencing with § 11340) of Part 1 of Division 3 of Title 2 of the California Government Code does not apply to regulations adopted by the State Gaming Agency in respect to tribal gaming operations under this Section.

8.4.1. (a) Except as provided in subdivision (d), no State Gaming Agency regulation shall be effective with respect to the Tribe's Gaming Operation unless it has first been approved by the Association and the Tribe has had an opportunity to review and comment on the proposed regulation.

(b) Every State Gaming Agency regulation that is intended to apply to the Tribe (other than a regulation proposed or previously approved by the Association) shall be submitted to the Association for consideration prior to submission of the regulation to the Tribe for comment as provided in subdivision (c). A regulation that is disapproved by the Association shall not be submitted to the Tribe for comment unless it is re-adopted by the State Gaming Agency as a proposed regulation, in its original or amended form, with a detailed, written response to the Association's objections.

(c) Except as provided in subdivision (d), no regulation of the State Gaming Agency shall be adopted as a final regulation in respect to the Tribe's Gaming Operation before the expiration of 30 days after submission of the proposed regulation to the Tribe for comment as a proposed regulation, and after consideration of the Tribe's comments, if any.

(d) In exigent circumstances (e.g., imminent threat to public health and safety), the State Gaming Agency may adopt a regulation that becomes effective immediately. Any such regulation shall be accompanied by a detailed, written description of the exigent circumstances, and shall be submitted immediately to the Association for consideration. If the regulation is disapproved by the Association, it shall cease to be effective, but may be re-adopted by the State Gaming Agency as a proposed regulation, in its original or amended form, with a detailed, written response to the Association's objections, and thereafter submitted to the Tribe for comment as provided in subdivision (c).

(e) The Tribe may object to a State Gaming Agency regulation on the ground that it is unnecessary, unduly burdensome, or unfairly discriminatory, and may seek repeal or amendment of the regulation through the dispute resolution process of Section 9.0.

Section 9.0. Dispute Resolution Provisions

9.1. Voluntary Resolution; Reference to Other Means of Resolution. In recognition of the government-to-government relationship of the Tribe and the State, the parties shall make their best efforts to resolve disputes that occur under this Gaming Compact by good faith negotiations whenever possible. Therefore, without prejudice to the right of either party to seek injunctive relief against the other when circumstances are deemed to require immediate relief, the parties hereby establish a threshold requirement that disputes between the Tribe and the State first be subjected to a process of meeting and conferring in good faith in order to foster a spirit of cooperation and efficiency in the administration and monitoring of performance and compliance by each other with the terms, provisions, and conditions of this Gaming Compact, as follows:

(a) Either party shall give the other, as soon as possible after the event giving rise to the concern, a written notice setting forth, with specificity, the issues to be resolved.

(b) The parties shall meet and confer in a good faith attempt to resolve the dispute through negotiation not later than 10 days after receipt of the notice, unless both parties agree in writing to an extension of time.

(c) If the dispute is not resolved to the satisfaction of the parties within 30 calendar days after the first meeting, then either party may seek to have the dispute resolved by an arbitrator in accordance with this section, but neither party shall be required to agree to submit to arbitration.

(d) Disagreements that are not otherwise resolved by arbitration or other mutually acceptable means as provided in Section 9.3 may be resolved in the United States District Court where the Tribe's Gaming Facility is located, or is to be located, and the Ninth Circuit Court of Appeals (or, if those federal courts lack jurisdiction, in any state court of competent jurisdiction and its related courts of appeal). The disputes to be submitted to court action include, but are not limited to, claims of breach or violation of this Compact, or failure to negotiate in good faith as required by the terms of this Compact. In no event may the Tribe be precluded from pursuing any arbitration or judicial remedy against the State on the grounds that the Tribe has failed to exhaust its state administrative remedies. The parties agree that, except in the case of imminent threat to the public health or safety, reasonable efforts will be made to explore alternative dispute resolution avenues prior to resort to judicial process.

9.2. Arbitration Rules. Arbitration shall be conducted in accordance with the policies and procedures of the Commercial Arbitration Rules of the American Arbitration Association, and shall be held on the Tribe's land or, if unreasonably inconvenient under the circumstances, at such other location as the parties may agree. Each side shall bear its own costs, attorneys' fees, and one-half the costs and expenses of the American Arbitration Association and the arbitrator, unless the arbitrator rules otherwise. Only one neutral arbitrator may be named, unless the Tribe or the State objects, in which case a panel of three arbitrators (one of whom is selected by each party) will be named. The provisions of § 1283.05 of the California Code of Civil Procedure shall apply; provided that no discovery authorized by that section may be conducted without leave of the arbitrator. The decision of the arbitrator shall be in writing, give reasons for the decision, and shall be binding. Judgment on the award may be entered in any federal or state court having jurisdiction thereof.

9.3. No Waiver or Preclusion of Other Means of Dispute Resolution. This Section 9.0 may not be construed to waive, limit, or restrict any remedy that is otherwise available to either party, nor may this Section be construed to preclude, limit, or restrict the ability of the parties to pursue, by mutual agreement, any other method of dispute resolution, including, but not limited to, mediation or utilization of a technical advisor to the Tribal and State Gaming Agencies; provided that neither party is under any obligation to agree to such alternative method of dispute resolution.

9.4. Limited Waiver of Sovereign Immunity.

(a) In the event that a dispute is to be resolved in federal court or a state court of competent jurisdiction as provided in this Section 9.0, the State and the Tribe expressly consent to be sued therein and waive any immunity there from that they may have provided that: (1) The dispute is limited solely to issues arising under this Gaming Compact; (2) Neither side makes any claim for monetary damages (that is, only injunctive, specific performance, including enforcement of a provision of this Compact requiring payment of money to one or another of the parties, or declaratory relief is sought); and (3) No person or entity other than the Tribe and the State is party to the action, unless failure to join a third party would deprive the court of jurisdiction; provided that nothing herein shall be construed to constitute a waiver of the sovereign immunity of either the Tribe or the State in respect to any such third party.

(b) In the event of intervention by any additional party into any such action without the consent of the Tribe and the State, the waivers of either the Tribe or the State provided for herein may be revoked, unless joinder is required to preserve the court's jurisdiction; provided that nothing herein shall be construed to constitute a waiver of the sovereign immunity of either the Tribe or the State in respect to any such third party.

(c) The waivers and consents provided for under this Section 9.0 shall extend to civil actions authorized by this Compact, including, but not limited to, actions to compel arbitration, any arbitration proceeding herein, any action to confirm or enforce any judgment or arbitration award as provided herein, and any appellate proceedings emanating from a matter in which an immunity waiver has been granted. Except as stated herein or elsewhere in this Compact, no other waivers or consents to be sued, either express or implied, are granted by either party.

Section 10.0. Public and Workplace Health, Safety, and Liability

10.1. The Tribe will not conduct Class III gaming in a manner that endangers the public health, safety, or welfare; provided that nothing herein shall be construed to make applicable to the Tribe any state laws or regulations governing the use of tobacco.

10.2. Compliance. For the purposes of this Gaming Compact, the Tribal Gaming Operation shall:

(a) Adopt and comply with standards no less stringent than state public health standards for food and beverage handling. The Gaming Operation will allow inspection of food and beverage services by state or county health inspectors, during normal hours of operation, to assess compliance with these standards, unless inspections are routinely made by an agency of the United States government to ensure compliance with equivalent standards of the United States Public Health Service. Nothing herein shall be construed as submission of the Tribe to the jurisdiction of those state or county health inspectors, but any alleged violations of the standards shall be treated as alleged violations of this Compact.

(b) Adopt and comply with standards no less stringent than federal water quality and safe drinking water standards applicable in California; the Gaming Operation will allow for inspection and testing of water quality by state or county health inspectors, as applicable, during normal hours of operation, to assess compliance with these standards, unless inspections and testing are made by an agency of the United States pursuant to, or by the Tribe under express authorization of, federal law, to ensure compliance with federal water quality and safe drinking water standards. Nothing herein shall be construed as submission of the Tribe to the jurisdiction of those state or county health inspectors, but any alleged violations of the standards shall be treated as alleged violations of this Compact.

(c) Comply with the building and safety standards set forth in Section 6.4.

(d) Carry no less than five million dollars ($5,000,000) in public liability insurance for patron claims, and that the Tribe provide reasonable assurance that those claims will be promptly and fairly adjudicated, and that legitimate claims will be paid; provided that nothing herein requires the Tribe to agree to liability for punitive damages or attorneys' fees. On or before the effective date of this Compact or not less than 30 days prior to the commencement of Gaming Activities under this Compact, whichever is later, the Tribe shall adopt and make available to patrons a tort liability ordinance setting forth the terms and conditions, if any, under which the Tribe waives immunity to suit for money damages resulting from intentional or negligent injuries to person or property at the Gaming Facility or in connection with the Tribe's Gaming Operation, including procedures for processing any claims for such money damages; provided that nothing in this Section shall require the Tribe to waive its immunity to suit except to the extent of the policy limits set out above.

(e) Adopt and comply with standards no less stringent than federal workplace and occupational health and safety standards; the Gaming Operation will allow for inspection of Gaming Facility workplaces by state inspectors, during normal hours of operation, to assess compliance with these standards, unless inspections are regularly made by an agency of the United States government to ensure compliance with federal workplace and occupational health and safety standards. Nothing herein shall be construed as submission of the Tribe to the jurisdiction of those state inspectors, but any alleged violations of the standards shall be treated as alleged violations of this Compact.

(f) Comply with tribal codes and other applicable federal law regarding public health and safety.

(g) Adopt and comply with standards no less stringent than federal laws and state laws forbidding employers generally from discriminating in the employment of persons to work for the Gaming Operation or in the Gaming Facility on the basis of race, color, religion, national origin, gender, sexual orientation, age, or disability; provided that nothing herein shall preclude the tribe from giving a preference in employment to Indians, pursuant to a duly adopted tribal ordinance.

(h) Adopt and comply with standards that are no less stringent than state laws prohibiting a gaming enterprise from cashing any check drawn against a federal, state, county, or city fund, including but not limited to, Social Security, unemployment insurance, disability payments, or public assistance payments.

(i) Adopt and comply with standards that are no less stringent than state laws, if any, prohibiting a gaming enterprise from providing, allowing, contracting to provide, or arranging to provide alcoholic beverages, or food or lodging for no charge or at reduced prices at a gambling establishment or lodging facility as an incentive or enticement.

(j) Adopt and comply with standards that are no less stringent than state laws, if any, prohibiting extensions of credit.

(k) Provisions of the Bank Secrecy Act, P.L. 91-508, October 26, 1970, 31 U.S.C. §§ 5311–5314, as amended, and all reporting requirements of the Internal Revenue Service, insofar as such provisions and reporting requirements are applicable to casinos.

10.2.1. The Tribe shall adopt and, not later than 30 days after the effective date of this Compact, shall make available on request the standards described in subdivisions (a)–(c) and (e)–(k) of Section 10.2 to which the Gaming Operation is held. In the absence of a promulgated tribal standard in respect to a matter identified in those subdivisions, or the express adoption of an applicable federal statute or regulation in lieu of a tribal standard in respect to any such matter, the applicable state statute or regulation shall be deemed to have been adopted by the Tribe as the applicable standard.

10.3 Participation in state statutory programs related to employment.

(a) In lieu of permitting the Gaming Operation to participate in the state statutory workers' compensation system, the Tribe may create and maintain a system that provides redress for employee work-related injuries through requiring insurance or self-insurance, which system must include a scope of coverage, availability of an independent medical examination, right to notice, hearings before an independent tribunal, a means of enforcement against the employer, and benefits comparable to those mandated for comparable employees under state law. Not later than the effective date of this Compact, or 60 days prior to the commencement of Gaming Activities under this Compact, the Tribe will advise the State of its election to participate in the statutory workers' compensation system or, alternatively, will forward to the State all relevant ordinances that have been adopted and all other documents establishing the system and demonstrating that the system is fully operational and compliant with the comparability standard set forth above. The parties agree that independent contractors doing business with the Tribe must comply with all state workers' compensation laws and obligations.

(b) The Tribe agrees that its Gaming Operation will participate in the State's program for providing unemployment compensation benefits and unemployment compensation disability benefits with respect to employees employed at the Gaming Facility, including compliance with the provisions of the California Unemployment Insurance Code, and the Tribe consents to the jurisdiction of the state agencies charged with the enforcement of that Code and of the courts of the State of California for purposes of enforcement.

(c) As a matter of comity, with respect to persons employed at the Gaming Facility, other than members of the Tribe, the Tribal Gaming Operation shall withhold all taxes due to the State as provided in the California Unemployment Insurance Code and the Revenue and Taxation Code, and shall forward such amounts as provided in said Codes to the State.

10.4. Emergency Service Accessibility. The Tribe shall make reasonable provisions for adequate emergency fire, medical, and related relief and disaster services for patrons and employees of the Gaming Facility.

10.5. Alcoholic Beverage Service. Standards for alcohol service shall be subject to applicable law.

10.6. Possession of firearms shall be prohibited at all times in the Gaming Facility except for state, local, or tribal security or law enforcement personnel authorized by tribal law and by federal or state law to possess fire arms at the Facility.

10.7. Labor Relations. Notwithstanding any other provision of this Compact, this Compact shall be null and void if, on or before October 13, 1999, the Tribe has not provided an agreement or other procedure acceptable to the State for addressing organizational and representational rights of Class III Gaming Employees and other employees associated with the Tribe's Class III gaming enterprise, such as food and beverage, housekeeping, cleaning, bell and door services, and laundry employees at the Gaming Facility or any related facility, the only significant purpose of which is to facilitate patronage at the Gaming Facility.

10.8. Off-Reservation Environmental Impacts.

10.8.1. On or before the effective date of this Compact, or not less than 90 days prior to the commencement of a Project, as defined herein, the Tribe shall adopt an ordinance providing for the preparation, circulation, and consideration by the Tribe of environmental impact reports concerning potential off-Reservation environmental impacts of any and all Projects to be commenced on or after the effective date of this Compact. In fashioning the environmental protection ordinance, the Tribe will make a good faith effort to incorporate the policies and purposes of the National Environmental Policy Act and the California Environmental Quality Act consistent with the Tribe's governmental interests.

10.8.2. (a) Prior to commencement of a Project, the Tribe will: (1) Inform the public of the planned Project; (2) Take appropriate actions to determine whether the project will have any significant adverse impacts on the off-Reservation environment; (3) For the purpose of receiving and responding to comments, submit all environmental impact reports concerning the proposed Project to the State Clearinghouse in the Office of Planning and Research and the county board of supervisors, for distribution to the public; (4) Consult with the board of supervisors of the county or counties within which the Tribe's Gaming Facility is located, or is to be located, and, if the Gaming Facility is within a city, with the city council, and if requested by the board or council, as the case may be, meet with them to discuss mitigation of significant adverse off-Reservation environmental impacts; (5) Meet with and provide an opportunity for comment by those members of the public residing off-Reservation within the vicinity of the Gaming Facility such as might be adversely affected by proposed Project.

(b) During the conduct of a Project, the Tribe shall: (1) Keep the board or council, as the case may be, and potentially affected members of the public apprised of the project's progress; and (2) Make good faith efforts to mitigate any and all such significant adverse off-Reservation environmental impacts.

(c) As used in Section 10.8.1 and this Section 10.8.2, the term "Project" means any expansion or any significant renovation or modification of an existing Gaming Facility, or any significant excavation, construction, or development associated with the Tribe's Gaming Facility or proposed Gaming Facility and the term "environmental impact reports" means any environmental assessment, environmental impact report, or environmental impact statement, as the case may be.

10.8.3. (a) The Tribe and the State shall, from time to time, meet to review the adequacy of this Section 10.8, the Tribe's ordinance adopted pursuant thereto, and the Tribe's compliance with its obligations under Section 10.8.2, to ensure that significant adverse impacts to the off-Reservation environment resulting from projects undertaken by the Tribe may be avoided or mitigated.

(b) At any time after January 1, 2003, but not later than March 1, 2003, the State may request negotiations for an amendment to this Section 10.8 on the ground that, as it presently reads, the Section has proven to be inadequate to protect the off-Reservation environment from significant adverse impacts resulting from Projects undertaken by the Tribe or to ensure adequate mitigation by the Tribe of significant adverse off-Reservation environmental impacts and, upon such a request, the Tribe will enter into such negotiations in good faith.

(c) On or after January 1, 2004, the Tribe may bring an action in federal court under 25 U.S.C. § 2710(d)(7)(A)(i) on the ground that the State has failed to negotiate in good faith, provided that the Tribe's good faith in the negotiations shall also be in issue. In any such action, the court may consider whether the State's invocation of its rights under subdivision (b) of this Section 10.8.3 was in good faith. If the State has requested negotiations pursuant to subdivision (b) but, as of January 1, 2005, there is neither an agreement nor an order against the State under 25 U.S.C. § 2710(d)(7)(B)(iii), then, on that date, the Tribe shall immediately cease construction and other activities on all projects then in progress that have the potential to cause adverse off-Reservation impacts, unless and until an agreement to amend this Section 10.8 has been concluded between the Tribe and the State.

Section 11.0. Effective Date and Term of Compact

11.1. Effective Date. This Gaming Compact shall not be effective unless and until all of the following have occurred:

(a) The Compact is ratified by statute in accordance with state law;

(b) Notice of approval or constructive approval is published in the Federal Register as provided in 25 U.S.C. § 2710(d)(3)(B); and

(c) [Proposition 1A] is approved by the California voters in the March 2000 general election.

11.2. Term of Compact; Termination.

11.2.1. Effective

(a) Once effective this Compact shall be in full force and effect for state law purposes until December 31, 2020.

(b) Once ratified, this Compact shall constitute a binding and determinative agreement between the Tribe and the State, without regard to voter approval of any constitutional amendment, other than [Proposition 1A], that authorizes a gaming compact.

(c) Either party may bring an action in federal court, after providing a sixty (60) day written notice of an opportunity to cure any alleged breach of this Compact, for a declaration that the other party has materially breached this Compact. Upon issuance of such a declaration, the complaining party may unilaterally terminate this Compact upon service of written notice on the other party. In the event a federal court determines that it lacks jurisdiction over such an action, the action may be brought in the superior court for the county in which the Tribe's Gaming Facility is located. The parties expressly waive their immunity to suit for purposes of an action under this subdivision, subject to the qualifications stated in Section 9.4(a).

Section 12.0. Amendments; Renegotiations

12.1. The terms and conditions of this Gaming Compact may be amended at any time by the mutual and written agreement of both parties.

12.2. This Gaming Compact is subject to renegotiation in the event the Tribe wishes to engage in forms of Class III gaming other than those games authorized herein and requests renegotiation for that purpose, provided that no such renegotiation may be sought for 12 months following the effective date of this Gaming Compact.

12.3. Process and Negotiation Standards. All requests to amend or renegotiate this Gaming Compact shall be in writing, addressed to the Tribal Chairperson or the Governor, as the case may be, and shall include the activities or circumstances to be negotiated, together with a statement of the basis supporting the request. If the request meets the requirements of this Section, the parties shall confer promptly and determine a schedule for commencing negotiations within 30 days of the request. Unless expressly provided otherwise herein, all matters involving negotiations or other amendatory processes under Section 4.3.3(b) and this Section 12.0 shall be governed, controlled, and conducted in conformity with the provisions and requirements of IGRA, including those provisions regarding the obligation of the State to negotiate in good faith and the enforcement of that obligation in federal court. The Chairperson of the Tribe and the Governor of the State are hereby authorized to designate the person or agency responsible for conducting the negotiations, and shall execute any documents necessary to do so.

12.4. The Tribe shall have the right to terminate this Compact in the event the exclusive right of Indian tribes to operate Gaming Devices in California is abrogated by the enactment, amendment, or repeal of a state statute or constitutional provision, or the conclusive and dispositive judicial construction of a statute or the state Constitution by a California appellate court after the effective date of this Compact, that Gaming Devices may lawfully be operated by another person, organization, or entity (other than an Indian tribe pursuant to a compact) within California.

Section 13.0 Notices

Unless otherwise indicated by this Gaming Compact, all notices required or authorized to be served shall be served by first-class mail at the following addresses:

Governor	Tribal Chairperson
State Capitol	[insert *1]
Sacramento, California 95814	[insert *4]

Section 14.0. Changes in IGRA

This Gaming Compact is intended to meet the requirements of IGRA as it reads on the effective date of this Gaming Compact, and when reference is made to the Indian Gaming Regulatory Act or to an implementing regulation thereof, the referenced provision is deemed to have been incorporated into this Compact as if set out in full. Subsequent changes to IGRA that diminish the rights of the State or the Tribe may not be applied retroactively to alter the terms of this Gaming Compact, except to the extent that federal law validly mandates that retroactive application without the State's or the Tribe's respective consent.

Section 15.0. Miscellaneous

15.1. Third Party Beneficiaries. Except to the extent expressly provided under this Gaming Compact, this Gaming Compact is not intended to, and shall not be construed to, create any right on the part of a third party to bring an action to enforce any of its terms.

15.2. Complete agreement; revocation of prior requests to negotiate. This Gaming Compact, together with all addenda and approved amendments, sets forth the full and complete agreement of the parties and supersedes any prior agreements or understandings with respect to the subject matter hereof.

15.3. Construction. Neither the presence in another tribal-state compact of language that is not included in this Compact, nor the absence in this Compact of language that is present in another tribal-state compact shall be a factor in construing the terms of this Compact.

15.4. Most Favored Tribe. If, after the effective date of this Compact, the State enters into a Compact with any other tribe that contains more favorable provisions with respect to any provisions of this Compact, the State shall, at the Tribe's request, enter into the preferred compact with the Tribe as a superseding substitute for this Compact; provided that the duration of the substitute compact shall not exceed the duration of this Compact.

15.6. Representations. By entering into this Compact, the Tribe expressly represents that, as of the date of the Tribe's execution of this Compact:

> (a) the undersigned has the authority to execute this Compact on behalf of his or her tribe and will provide written proof of such authority and ratification of this Compact by the tribal governing body no later than October 9, 1999;

> (b) the Tribe is (i) recognized as eligible by the Secretary of the Interior for special programs and services provided by the United States to Indians because of their status as Indians, and (ii) recognized by the Secretary of the Interior as possessing powers of self-government. In entering into this Compact, the State expressly relies upon the foregoing representations by the Tribe, and the State's entry into the Compact is expressly made contingent upon the truth of those representations as of the date of the Tribe's execution of this Compact. Failure to provide written proof of authority

to execute this Compact or failure to provide written proof of ratification by the Tribe's governing body will give the State the opportunity to declare this Compact null and void.

IN WITNESS WHEREOF, the undersigned sign this Compact on behalf of the State of California and the [insert *1].

Done at Sacramento, California, this 10th day of September 1999.

State of California   [insert *1]

By Gray Davis   By [insert *5]

Governor of the State of California   Chairperson of the [insert *1]

Amended Gaming Compact
Between the Spirit Lake Nation and the State of North Dakota
(1999)

The Amended Gaming Compact ("Amended Compact") is made and entered into this 29th day of September, 1999, by and between the Spirit Lake Tribe, formerly known as the Devils Lake Sioux Tribe (hereinafter referred to as the "Tribe"), and the State of North Dakota (hereinafter referred to as the "State").

I. Recitals

The Tribe is a federally recognized Indian Tribe, organized pursuant to the Constitution and By-Laws of the Spirit Lake Tribe, approved by the Commissioner of the Bureau of Indian Affairs, on February 14, 1946, as amended thereafter, and situated on its permanent homeland, with its headquarters at Fort Totten, North Dakota. Pursuant to Article VI of the Tribal Constitution, the Tribal Council is the governing body of the Tribe with constitutional and federal statutory authority to negotiate with state and local governments.

The State, through constitutional provisions and legislative acts, has authorized games of chance and other gaming activities, and the Congress of the United States, through the Indian Gaming Regulatory Act, Public Law 100-407, 102 Stat. 2426, 25 U.S.C. §§ 2701 et seq. (1988) (hereinafter referred to as the "IGRA"), has authorized the Tribe to operate Class III gaming pursuant to a tribal gaming ordinance approved by the National Indian Gaming Commission and a Compact entered into with the State for that purpose. Pursuant to its inherent sovereign authority and the IGRA, the Tribe intends to continue presenting Class III gaming, and the Tribe and State negotiated a Compact under the provisions of the IGRA to authorize and provide for the operation of such gaming. Said Compact was executed on October 7, 1992, by the then serving Tribal Chairman on behalf of the Tribe and the then serving Governor on behalf of the State and became effective when thereafter approved by the United States, Secretary of Interior and publicized in the Federal Register. Said Compact provides for Amendment upon agreement by both parties. The parties believe that amendment at this time would be appropriate.

NOW THEREFORE, in consideration of the covenants and agreements of the parties herein below, the Tribe and the State agree as follows:

II. Policy and Purpose

The Tribe and the State mutually recognize the positive economic benefits that gaming may provide to the Tribe and to the region of the State adjacent to Tribal lands, and the Tribe and, the State recognize the need to insure that the health, safety and welfare of the public and the integrity of the gaming industry of the Tribe and throughout North Dakota be protected. In the spirit of cooperation, the Tribe and the State hereby agree to carry out the terms of the IGRA regarding tribal Class III gaming.

The Tribal Gaming Code and regulations of the Tribal Gaming Commission (hereinafter referred to collectively as "Tribal Law"), this Compact, and the IGRA shall govern all Class III gaming activities, as defined in the IGRA. The purpose of this Compact is to provide the Tribe with the opportunity to license and regulate Class III gaming to benefit the Tribe economically.

III. Authorized Class III Gaming

3.1 Kinds of Gaming Authorized. The Tribe shall have the right to operate upon Tribal trust lands within the exterior boundaries of the Devils Lake Sioux Reservation, and the lands and waters identified in Section XXXIII below, the following Class III games during the term of this Compact, pursuant to Tribal Law and Federal Law, but subject to limitations set forth within this Compact.

A. Electronic games of chance with video facsimile displays. Machines featuring coin drop and payout, and machines featuring printed tabulations shall both be permitted;

B. Electronic games of chance with mechanical rotating reels whereby the software of the device predetermines the stop positions and the presence or lack thereof, of a winning combination and pay out, if any. Machines featuring coin drop and payout, and machines featuring printed tabulations shall both be permitted;

C. Blackjack; and similar banking card games;

D. Poker; including Pai Gai Poker and Caribbean Stud Poker;

E. Pari-mutuel and simulcast betting pursuant to the separate pari-mutuel horse racing addendum to Gaming Compact between the parties executed on April 8, 1993, and thereafter approved by the United States Secretary of Interior. This amended compact shall control any inconsistencies between the addendum and this compact;

F. Sports and Calcutta pools on professional sporting events as defined by North Dakota law, except as to bet limits and except that play may be conducted utilizing electronic projections or reproductions of a sports pool board;

G. Sports Book except as prohibited by the Professional and Amateur Sports Protection Act, P.L. 102-559; 28 U.S.C. Chap. 178, Pt. VI;

H. Pull-tabs or break-open tickets when not played at the same location where bingo is being played, subject to the limitations set forth at Section 3.4, below;

I. Raffles;

J. Keno;

K. Punchboards and jars;

L. Paddlewheels;

M. Craps and Indian Dice;

N. All games of chance and/or skill, other than those subject to Section 3.3 of this Compact, authorized to be conducted by any group or individual under any circumstances within the State of North Dakota, rules of play to be negotiated in good faith by the parties hereto;

O. Roulette, and similar games, whether played conventionally or electronically; and

P. Slot Tournaments, whether or not a fee is charged, in which players use designated electronic games of chance machines, whether equipped with video facsimile displays or mechanical rotating reels, that are equipped with special tournament EPROM chips, and are set to not receive coins during tournament play and which do not make printed tabulations during tournament play, in which the player competes against other players for a specified prize or prizes based on accumulated points as determined by the machine. The Tribe shall adequately account for slot tournament revenues.

3.2 Limits of Wagers. The Tribe shall have the right to operate and/or conduct authorized Class III gaming with individual bet maximum wagers to be set at the discretion of the Tribe, except that maximum wagers shall not exceed those set forth herein.

A. Wagers on blackjack may not exceed One hundred and no/100 dollars ($100.00) per individual bet. However, the Tribe may designate no more than two (2) tables on which wagers may not exceed Two Hundred Fifty and no/100 ($250.00) dollars per individual bet. Such tables shall be physically segregated, separately identified, and concurrently operative no more than twelve (12) hours per day.

B. Wagers on poker shall not exceed Fifty and no/100 dollars ($50.00) per individual bet per round, with a three raise maximum per round.

C. Bets on paddlewheels, whether individual or multiple, shall not exceed Fifty and no/100 dollars ($50.00) by any individual player per spin of the wheel.

D. Individual bets placed during the play of craps shall not exceed sixty and no/100 ($60.00) dollars per bet. A player may lay "true odds don't bets" to win no more than monies placed into play by the player during any individual game. Each game shall be attended by at least a two-person team, and normally by a three-person team, and overseen by at least one other non-participant supervisor who may oversee more than one game. Surveillance cameras shall not be considered a member of the three-person team.

E. The aggregate bets placed during the play of Indian dice shall not exceed an amount equal to One hundred and no/100 dollars ($100.00) multiplied by the number of players. Each game shall be attended by at least a two-person team, and normally by a three-person team, and overseen by at least one other non-participant supervisor who may oversee more than one game.

F. Electronic games of chance may not process individual bets in excess of Twenty-five and no/100 ($25.00) dollars per bet. However, play may be conducted upon individual machines which, process simultaneously any number of bets, so long as the total of all bets does not exceed Twenty-five and no/100 dollars ($25.00).

G. Bets on Roulette shall not exceed Fifty and no/100 dollars ($50.00) where a player places a single bet per spin of the wheel. Players may, however, place a series of non-duplicate individual bets of no more than Five and no/100 dollars ($5.00) each per spin of the wheel.

3.3 Availability of Additional Games and Bet Limits Legally Conducted by Other Tribes. All games and/or increased wager limits which any other Indian Tribe may legally conduct, or utilize, on trust lands located within North Dakota, whether by compact with the State, or through action by the United States Secretary of Interior, or determination of any court maintaining jurisdiction, shall be available for play by Tribe subject to the following: The State may condition play upon the provision by Tribe of consideration similar or equivalent to that provided by another compacting Tribe. Upon identification by Tribe of any such game, and written notice to State, the parties shall within fourteen (14) days commence good faith negotiations as to the inclusion of such additional game or games, consideration by the Tribe, if applicable, rules of play and presentation thereof. Such negotiations shall proceed with deliberate speed and attention.

3.4 Limits on Conduct of Pull-Tabs. Pull tabs and/or break-open tickets when conducted as Class III gaming shall be conducted in accordance with standards; and limitations then currently established under North Dakota State Law for the conduct of similar games, within the State of North Dakota. This Compact, as to pull-tabs and break-open games only, shall be deemed to be revised simultaneously with any revisions of North Dakota law as to the conduct of pull-tabs or break-open tickets to incorporate within the Compact, as applicable to Tribe, any such revisions.

Further, and in addition to the limitations set forth above, pull-tabs shall be dispensed only by machines that incorporate devices to tabulate machine activity.

The Tribe shall voluntarily comply with the above criteria in its conduct of all pull-tabs and break-open games. Should it not do so, it is agreed by the parties that the Tribe under the terms of this Agreement shall not be authorized to conduct any Class III pull-tabs or break-open ticket sales and shall not do so.

3.5 No Machine or Table Limit. There shall be no limit on the number of machines, tables, or other gaming devices which the Tribe may operate pursuant to this Compact, nor shall there be a limit as to number of sites on trust lands upon which gaming may be offered.

3.6 Technology Advancements. It is the desire of Tribe and of State to permit games authorized at Section 3.1 above to be conducted at the Tribe's option in a manner incorporating such advancement of technology as may be available. At the request of either party, State and Tribe shall meet to discuss such application.

3.7 New Games. At the request of either party, Tribe and State shall meet to discuss introduction of new games and appropriate rules of play along with the appropriateness and/or necessity of the Amendment of this Compact to permit such play.

3.8 Inflation or Deflation. At the request of either party, the Tribe and the State shall meet to discuss adjustment of betting limits to address economic inflation or deflation.

IV. Tribal Law

4.1 Gaming Code. The Tribe has adopted a Tribal Code, entitled "Gaming", and shall adopt regulations of the Tribal Gaming Commission pursuant thereto. Such Tribal Law shall be, and shall remain after any amendment thereto, at least as stringent as those specified in the Indian Gaming Regulatory Act and this Compact, and, with the exception of wagering limits and banking card games, those statutes and administrative rules adopted by the State of North Dakota to regulate those games of chance as may be authorized for play within the State of North Dakota, generally. The Tribe shall furnish the State with copies of such Tribal Law, including all amendments thereto.

4.2 Incorporation. The Gaming Code of the Tribe, as it may be from time-to-time amended, is incorporated by reference into this Compact.

V. Tribal Regulation of Class III Gaming

5.1 Tribal Council to Regulate Gaming. The Tribal Council of the Tribe ("the Council") shall license, operate and regulate all Class III gaming activities pursuant to Tribal Law, this Compact, and the IGRA, including, but not limited to, the licensing of consultants, primary management officials and key employees of each Class III gaming activity or operation, and the inspection and regulation of all gaming devices. Any discrepancies in any gaming activity or operation and any Violation of Tribal Law, this Compact or IGRA shall be corrected immediately by the Tribe pursuant to Tribal Law and this Compact.

5.2 Tribal Gaming Commission. The Tribal Gaming Commission, appointed pursuant to the Tribal Law and Order Code (hereinafter referred to as the "Tribal Commission"), shall have primary responsibility for the day-to-day regulation of all tribal gaming activities of operations, pursuant to delegation of authority by the Council, including licensing of all gaming employees.

5.3 Regulatory Requirements. The following regulatory requirements shall apply to the conduct of Class III gaming. The Tribe shall maintain as part of its lawfully enacted ordinances, at all times in which it conducts any Class III gaming, requirements at least as stringent as those set forth herein.

> A. Odds and Prize Structure. The Tribe shall publish the odds and prize structure of each Class Ill game, and shall prominently display such throughout every gaming facility maintained by the Tribe.
>
> B. No credit extended. All gaming shall be conducted on a cash basis. Except as herein provided, no person shall be extended credit for gaming by the gaming facility operated within the Reservation, and no operation shall permit any person or organization to offer such credit for a fee. This restriction shall not restrict the right of the Tribe or any other person or entity authorized by the Tribe to offer check cashing or to install or accept bank card, or credit card or automatic teller machine transactions in the same manner as would be normally permitted at any retail business within the State. The Tribe shall adopt check-cashing policies and advise the State of such policies.
>
> C. Age Restrictions. (i) No person under the age of 21, except for military personnel with military identification, may purchase a ticket, other than a raffle ticket, make a wager, or otherwise participate in any Class III game; provided that this section shall not prohibit a person 21 years old or older from giving a ticket or share to a person under the age of 21 as a gift. (ii) No person under the age of 21, except employees performing job-related duties, shall be permitted on the premises where any component of Class III gaming is conducted, unless accompanied by a parent, guardian, spouse, grandparent, or great-grandparent over the age of 21, sibling over the age of 21, or other person over the age of 21 with the permission of the minor's parent or guardian; provided that this subsection shall not apply to locations at which safe of tickets is the only component of Class III gaming. This section shall not limit the presence of individuals under the age of 21 within areas of gaming facilities conducting only Class II gaming, or exclusively providing activities other than Class III gaming such as food service, concerts, and gift items.
>
> D. Player Disputes. The Tribe shall provide and publish procedures for impartial resolution of a player dispute concerning the conduct of a game, which shall be made available to customers upon request.

VI. Compliance

6.1 Report of Suspected Violation by Parties. The parties hereto, shall immediately report any suspected violation of Tribal Law, this Compact, or the IGRA to the Tribal Gaming Commission and to such State official as the State may designate. If the Commission concludes that a violation has occurred, the violation will be addressed by the Commission within five (5) days after receipt of such notice. The Commission shall notify the State promptly as to such resolution.

6.2 Response to Complaints by Third Parties. The Tribe shall through its Gaming Commission arrange for reasonable and accessible procedures to address consumer complaints. The Commission shall submit to such State official as the State may designate, a summary of any written Complaint received which addresses a suspected violation of Tribal law, this Compact, or the IGRA, along with specification as to any action or resolution deemed warranted and/or undertaken.

6.3 Non-Complying Class III Games. The following are declared to be non-complying Class III Games:

A. All Class III games to which the agents of the State have been denied access for inspection purposes; and

B. All Class III games operated in violation of this Compact.

6.4 Demand for Remedies for Non-Complying Games of Chance. Class III games believed to be non-complying shall be so designated, in writing, by the agents of the State. Within five (5) days of receipt of such written designation, the Tribe shall either:

A. Accept the finding of non-compliance, remove the Class III games from play, and take appropriate action to ensure that the manufacturer, distributor, or other responsible party cures the problem; or

B. Contest the finding of non-compliance by so notifying the agents of the State, in writing, and arrange for the inspection of the contested game, by an independent gaming test laboratory as provided within ten (10) days or the receipt of the finding of non-compliance. If the independent laboratory finds that the Class III game or related equipment is non-complying, the non-complying Class III game and related equipment shall be permanently removed from play unless modified to meet the requirements of this Compact.

VII. Designated Usage of Funds

7.1 The Tribal Council of the Tribe has determined that it is in the interest of the Tribe that designated portions of revenue derived from gaming operations be guaranteed for usage within Tribal programs for economic development, other than gaming, and social welfare. In accordance therewith, at least ten (10%) percent of Net Revenues from Class III gaming operations must be directed to, and utilized within, economic development programs of the Tribe. Net Revenues shall be determined pursuant to the definition set forth within Section 4(9) of the Indian Gaming Regulatory Act according to Generally Accepted Accounting Principles (GAAP) as recognized by the American Institute of Certified Public Accountants.

7.2 The parties intend that set aside funds as described herein shall be used for the long-term benefit and improvement of the Tribe and its members and be directed towards long-term economic development activities that will produce lasting returns on usage of these funds.

7.3 Economic development funds shall be used consistent with the following criteria: (i) Purchase of supplies for the Tribes economic development programs. (ii) Purchase of equipment of fixtures for the economic development programs. (iii) Purchase, lease, or improvement of real estate for economic development operations or specific economic development projects. (iv) Capitalization for economic development projects being pursued by the Tribe. (v) Improvements to, or purchase towards tribal infrastructure (such as roads, buildings, water supply, waste water treatment, and similar efforts.) (vi) Funds shall not be used for salaries, or day-to-day operations, or for gaming activities, whether of debt service or otherwise. (vii) Planning and development of tribal businesses and other economic development activities. (viii) Economic development grants to tribal members.

7.4 Any member of the Tribe may inspect, during normal business hours, how economic development funds under this section have been used by the Tribe and to inspect annual audits. Such information shall be periodically distributed to the representative body of each District.

VIII. Licensing

8.1 Tribal License. All personnel employed or contractors engaged by the Tribe, and/or by any Management Agent under contract with the Tribe, whose responsibilities include the operation or management of Class III games of chance shall be licensed by the Tribe.

8.2 State License. All personnel employed or contractors engaged by the Tribe and/or by any Management Agent under contract with the Tribe, other and apart from Members of the Tribe, whose responsibilities include the operation or management of Class III games of chance, shall be licensed by the State, should the State maintain applicable licensure requirements.

IX. Background Investigation

9.1 Information Gathering. The Tribe, prior to hiring a prospective employee or engaging a contractor whose responsibilities include the operation or management of Class III gaming activities, shall obtain sufficient information and identification from the applicant to permit the conduct of a background investigation of the applicant.

9.2 Authorization of Background Investigation. Any person who applies for a tribal license pursuant to this Compact and Tribal law shall first submit an application to the Tribe which includes a written release by the applicant authorizing the Tribe to conduct a background investigation of the applicant and shall be accompanied by an appropriate fee for such investigation as determined by the Commission pursuant to Tribal law and this Compact.

9.3 Background Investigation by the Tribe. Upon receipt of the application and fee, the Commission shall investigate the applicant within thirty (30) days of the receipt of the application or as soon thereafter as is practical. The Commission shall utilize the North Dakota Bureau of Criminal Investigations (BCI) to assist in background investigations, but may utilize any other resource the Tribe determines appropriate.

9.4 Background Investigations by State Prior to Employment. The Tribe, prior to placing a prospective employee whose responsibilities include the operation or management of games of chance, shall obtain a release and other information from the applicant to permit the State to conduct a background check on the applicant. This information, along with the standard fee, shall be provided in writing to the state which shall report to the Tribe regarding each applicant within thirty (30) days of receipt of the request or as soon thereafter as is practical. The Tribe may employ any person who represents, in writing, that he or she meets the standards set forth in this section, but must not retain any person who is subsequently revealed to be disqualified. Criminal history data compiled by the State on prospective employees shall, subject to applicable state to federal law, be released to the Tribe as part of the reporting regarding each applicant. The background check of employees and contractors to be conducted pursuant to this paragraph shall be independent of any similar federal requirements.

9.5 Background Investigations of Employees During Employment. Each person whose responsibilities include the operation or management of Class III games shall be subject to periodic review by the Gaming Commission comparable to that required for initial employ-ment. This review shall take place at least every two years, commencing with the date of employment. Employees found to have committed disqualifying violations shall be dis-missed.

9.6 State Processing of Tribal Requests. The State shall process background investigation requests by the Tribe with equal priority as to that afforded requests for background in-vestigations by State Agencies.

9.7 Investigation Fees. The applicant shall reimburse the State for any and all reasonable expenses for background investigations required with this Compact.

X. Prohibitions in Hiring, Employment, and Contracting

10.1 Prohibitions. The Tribe may not hire, employ or enter into a contract relating to Class III gaming with any person or entity which includes the provision of services by any person who:

  A. Is under the age of 18;

  B. Has, within the immediate preceding ten (10) years, been convicted of, entered a plea of guilty or no contest to, or has been released from parole, probation or in-carceration, whichever is later in time; any felony, any gambling related offense, any fraud or misrepresentation offense; unless the person has been pardoned or the Tribe has made a determination that the person has been sufficiently rehabilitated.

  C. Is determined to have poor moral character or to have participated in organized crime or unlawful gambling, or whose prior activities, criminal record, reputation, habits, and/or associations pose a threat to the public interest or to the effective reg-ulation and control of gaming, or create or enhance the dangers of unsuitable, un-fair, or illegal practices, methods, and activities in the conduct of gaming, or as to the business and financial arrangements incidental to the conduct of gaming. De-terminations specified above will be disqualifying as to employment and/or con-tracting should such, be made by the Tribal Gaming Commission.

10.2 Dispensing of Alcoholic Beverages. Tribal employees will comply with State liquor laws with respect to the dispensing of alcoholic beverages.

XI. Employees

11.1 Procedural Manual. The Tribe shall publish and maintain a procedural manual for all personnel, which includes disciplinary standards for breach of the procedures.

11.2 Limitation of Participation in Games by Employees. The Tribe may not employ or pay any person to participate in any game (including, but not limited to, any shill or proposition player); except that an employee may participate, as necessary, to conduct a game as a dealer or bank.

XII. Management Agreements

12.1 Option for Tribe. The Tribe in its discretion may, but in no manner shall be required to enter into a management contract for the operation and management of a Class III gaming activity permitted under this Compact.

12.2 Receipt of Information by Tribe. Before approving such contract, the Tribe shall re-ceive and consider the following information:

  A. The name, address, and other additional pertinent background information on each person or entity (including individuals comprising such entity) having a direct financial interest in, or management responsibility for, such contract, and, in the case of a corporation, those individuals who serve on the board of directors of such corporation and each of its stockholders who hold (directly or indirectly) five (5%) percent or more of its issued and outstanding stock;

B. A description of any previous experience that each person listed has had with other gaming contracts with Indian Tribes or with the gaming industry generally, including specifically the game and address of any licensing or regulatory agency which has issued the person a license or permit relating to gaming or with which such person has had a contract relating to gaming; and

C. A complete financial statement of each person listed.

12.3 Provisions of Management Agreement. The Tribe shall not enter a management contract unless the contract provides, at least, for the following:

A. Adequate accounting procedures that are maintained, and for verifiable financial reports that are prepared, by or for the Tribe on a monthly basis;

B. Access to the daily operations of the gaming activities to appropriate officials of the Tribe, who shall also have a right to verify the daily gross revenues and income made from any such Tribal gaming activity;

C. A minimum guaranteed payment to the Tribe, that has preference over the retirement of development and construction costs;

D. An agreed ceiling for the repayment of development and construction costs;

E. A contract term not to exceed five (5) years, except that the Tribe may approve a contract term that exceeds five (5) years but does not exceed seven (7) years if the Tribe is satisfied that the capital investment required, and the income projections, for the particular gaming activity require the additional time;

F. A complete, detailed specification of all compensation to the Contractor under the contract;

G. Provisions for an early Tribal buy out of the rights of the Management Agent; and

H. Grounds and mechanisms for terminating such contract.

I. At least ten (10%) percent of net revenues, from Class III gaming operations shall be directed to, and utilized within, economic development programs of the Tribe other than gaming. Net Revenues shall be determined according to Generally Accepted Accounting Principles (GAAP).

12.4 Fee. The Tribe may approve a management contract providing for a fee based upon a percentage of the net revenues of a Tribal gaming activity, which shall not exceed thirty (30%) percent, unless the Tribe, determines that the capital investment required, and income projections, for such gaming activity, require an additional fee, which in no event shall exceed forty (40%) percent of net revenues of such gaming activity. A contract providing for a fee based upon a percentage of net revenues shall include a provision describing in detail how net revenues will be determined.

12.5 Background Check.

A. Prior to hiring a Management Agent for Tribal Class III games, the Tribal Gaming Commission shall obtain release and other information sufficient from the proposed Management Agent and/or its principals to permit the State to conduct a background check. All information requested will be provided in writing to this State which shall conduct the background check and provide a written report to the Tribe regarding each Manager applicant and/or its principals within thirty (30) days of receipt of the request or as soon thereafter as is practical. The background check to be conducted pursuant to this paragraph shall be in addition to any similar federal requirements.

B. The Tribe shall not employ a Management Agent for the Class III games if the State Gaming Commission determines that the Management Agent applicant and/or its principals are in violation of the standards set forth in Section X of this Compact.

XIII. Accounting and Audit Procedures

13.1 Accounting Standards. The Tribe shall adopt accounting standards, which meet or exceed those standards established in the IGRA.

13.2 Systems. All accounting records must be maintained according to Generally Accepted Accounting Principals (GAAP).

13.3 Audits. The Tribe shall conduct or cause to be conducted independent audits of every Class III gaming activity or operation. Audits will be conducted at least annually with copies all annual audits to be furnished to the State by the Tribe at no charge.

XIV. Tribal Record Keeping

14.1 Record Maintenance. The Tribe shall maintain the following records related to its gaming operations for at least three (3) years.

A. Revenues, expenses, assets, liabilities and equity for each location at which any component of Class III gaming is conducted;

B. Daily cash transactions for each game at each location at which Class III gaming is conducted including but not limited to transactions relating to each gaming table bank, game drop box and gaming room bank;

C. Individual and statistical game records to reflect statistical drop, statistical win, the statistical drop by table for each game, and the individual and statistical game records reflecting similar information for all other games;

D. Records of all tribal enforcement activities;

E. All audits prepared by or on behalf of the Tribe;

F. All returned checks which remain uncollected, hold checks or other similar credit instruments; and

G. Personnel information on all Class III gaming employees or agents, including time sheets, employee profiles and background checks.

14.2 Accounting Records and Audits Concerning Class III Gaming by Tribe. The Tribe shall provide a copy to the State of any independent audit report upon written request of the State. Any costs incidental to providing copies to the State will be borne by the Tribe.

XV. Access to Records

15.1 The Tribe shall permit reasonable access to review by the State of Tribal accounting and audit records associated with gaming conducted under this Compact. The State may copy such documents as it desires subject to the confidentiality provisions set forth herein below. Any costs incidental to such an inspection shall be covered from the Escrow Account for State Expenses established and maintained pursuant to Section XXV of this Compact.

15.2 The Tribe requires that its gaming records be confidential. Any Tribal records or documents submitted to the State, or of which the State has retained copies in the course of its gaming oversight and enforcement, will not be disclosed to any member of the public except as needed in a judicial proceeding to interpret or enforce the terms of this Compact, or except as may be required for law enforcement or tax assessment purposes. Such disclosure, however, shall be conditional upon: the recipient making no further disclosure absent authorization by the Tribe or under Court Order. This Compact is provided for by Federal law and therefore supersedes State records law to the contrary.

15.3 The Tribe shall have the right to inspect and copy all State records concerning the Tribe's Class III gaming unless such disclosure would compromise the integrity of an ongoing investigation.

XVI. Tax Reporting Matters

Whenever required by federal law to issue Internal Revenue Service Form W2G, the Tribe shall also provide a copy of the same to the State. In addition, the Tribe shall comply with employee income withholding requirements for all non-Indian employees and all Indian employees not living on the Reservation, who are not members of the Tribe.

XVII. Jurisdiction, Enforcement, and Applicable Law

17.1 Criminal Enforcement. Nothing in this Compact shall deprive the Courts of the Tribe, the United States, or the State of North Dakota of such criminal jurisdiction as each may enjoy under applicable law.

A. Nothing in this Compact shall be interpreted as extending the criminal jurisdiction of the State of North Dakota or the Tribe.

17.2 Civil Enforcement. Nothing in this Compact shall deprive the Courts of the Tribe, the United States, or the State of North Dakota of such civil jurisdiction as each may enjoy under applicable law. Nothing in this Compact shall be interpreted as extending the civil jurisdiction of the State of North Dakota or the Tribe.

XVIII. Sovereign Immunity

18.1 Tribe.

A. Nothing in this Compact shall be deemed to be a waiver of the sovereign immunity of the Tribe.

B. Sovereign immunity must be asserted by the Tribe itself and may not be asserted by insurers or agents. The Tribe waives sovereign immunity for personal injury arising out of its gaming activities, but only to the extent of its liability insurance coverage limits.

18.2 State. Nothing in this Compact shall be deemed to be a waiver of the sovereign immunity of the State.

XIX. Qualifications of Providers of Class III Gaming Equipment or Supplies

19.1 Purchase of Equipment and Supplies.

A. No Class III games of chance, gaming equipment or supplies may be purchased, leased or otherwise acquired by the Tribe unless the Class III equipment or supplies are purchased, leased or acquired from a manufacturer or distributor licensed by the Tribe to sell, lease, or distribute Class III gaming equipment or supplies, and further unless the gaming manufacturer is licensed to do business in one or more of the following states: Nevada, New Jersey, South Dakota, Colorado, and Mississippi. Should the Tribe wish to purchase equipment on supplies from a business not shown to be licensed to do business in one or more of the above mentioned States, the Tribe may petition the Office of the Attorney General for the State of North Dakota for review and approval of said manufacturer or supplier.

B. Should the State of North Dakota commence a comprehensive program of licensing the sale, lease, and/or distribution of Class III games of chance, gaming equipment, or supplies, no Class III games of chance, gaming equipment or supplies may be purchased, leased or otherwise acquired by the Tribe, after one year subsequent to the date of such enactment, except from a manufacturer or distributor licensed both by the Tribe and the State of North Dakota to sell, lease or distribute Class III gaming equipment or supplies, unless a manufacturer or distributor was licensed to do business in one of the States specified within Section 19.1.A, prior to the date of commencement of such licensing by the State of North Dakota.

19.2 Required Information. Prior to entering into any lease or purchase agreement for Class III gaming equipment or supplies, the Tribe's Gaming Commission shall obtain sufficient information and identification from the proposed seller or lessor and all persons holding any direct or indirect financial interest in the lessor or the lease/purchase agreement to permit the Tribal Gaming Commission to conduct a background check on those persons.

19.3 No Business Dealings with Disqualified Parties. The Tribe shall not enter into any lease or purchase agreement for Class III gaming equipment or supplies with any person or entity if the Tribal Gaming Commission or the State determines that the lessor or seller, or any manager or person holding a direct or indirect financial interest in the lessor/seller or the proposed lease/purchase agreement, has, been convicted (if a felony or any gambling related crime or whose gaming license has been suspended or revoked because of misconduct through administrative action in any other state or jurisdiction, within the previous five (5) years, or who is determined to have participated in or have involvement with organized crime.

19.4 Receipt of Gaming Equipment. All sellers, lessors, manufacturers and/or distributors shall provide, assemble and install all Class III games of chance, gaming equipment and supplies in a manner approved and licensed by the Tribe.

XX. Regulation and Play of an Electronic Game

20.1 Electronic Game — Definition. "Electronic Game" means a microprocessor-controlled device that allows a player to play games of chance, which the outcome may or may not be affected by the player's skill. A game is activated by inserting a token, coin, currency, or other object, or use of a credit, and which awards credit, cash, tokens, replays, or a written Statement of the player's accumulated credits and that is redeemable for cash.

20.2 Display. Game play may be displayed by video facsimile, or mechanical rotating reels that stop in positions that display the presence, or lack of, a winning combination and pay out and which are predetermined by the software of the game.

20.3 Testing.

A. Designation of a Gaming Test Laboratory. A Tribe may not operate an electronic game, including a bill acceptor, unless the game (or prototype) and bill acceptor have been tested and approved or certified by a gaming test laboratory as meeting the requirements and standards of this Compact. A gaming test laboratory is a laboratory agreed to and designated in writing by the State and Tribe as competent and qualified to conduct scientific tests and evaluations of electronic games and related equipment. A laboratory operated by or under contract with any State of the United States to test electronic games may be designated.

B. Providing Documentation and Model of an Electronic Game (or Prototype). As requested by a gaming test laboratory, a manufacturer shall provide the laboratory with a copy of an electronic game's (or prototype's) illustrations, schematics, block diagrams, circuit analyses, technical and operation manuals, program object and source codes, hexadecimal dumps (the compiled computer program represented in base-16 format), and any other information. As requested by the laboratory, the manufacturer shall transport one or more working models of the electronic game (or prototype) and related equipment to a location designated by the laboratory. The manufacturer shall pay for all costs of transporting, testing, and analyzing the model. As requested by the laboratory, the manufacturer shall provide specialized equipment or the services of an independent technical expert to assist the laboratory.

C. Report of Test Results. At the end of each test, the gaming test laboratory shall provide the State and Tribe a report containing the findings, conclusions, and a determination that the electronic game (or prototype) and related equipment conforms or does not conform to the hardware and software requirements of this Compact. If the electronic game (or prototype) or related equipment can be modified so it can conform, the report may contain recommended modifications. If the laboratory determines that an electronic game (or prototype) conforms, that determination will apply for all Tribes under this Compact.

D. Modification of an Approved Electronic Game. A Tribe may not modify the assembly or operational functions of an electronic game or related equipment, including logic control components, after testing and installation, unless a gaming test laboratory certifies to the State and Tribe that the modification conforms to the requirements and standards of this Compact.

E. Conformity to Technical Standards. A manufacturer or distributor shall certify, in writing, to the State and Tribe that, upon installation, each electronic game (or prototype): 1) conforms to the exact specifications of the electronic game (or prototype) tested and approved by the gaming test laboratory; and 2) operates and plays according to the technical standards prescribed in this section.

F. Identification. A non-removable plate(s) must be affixed to the outside of each electronic game. The plate must contain the machine's serial number, manufacturer, and a unique identification number assigned by the Tribe and date this number was assigned.

20.4 Tribal Reports to the State.

A. Installation of Electronic Game. At least forty-eight (48) hours before installing an electronic game at a gaming site, the Tribe shall report this information to the State for each game: (i) Type of game; (ii) Serial number; (iii) Manufacturer; (iv) Source from whom the game was acquired, how the game was transported into the State, and name and street address of the common carrier or person that transported the game; (v) Certification; (vi) Unique identification number and date assigned by the Tribe; (vii) Logic control component identification number; (vii) Gaming site where the game will be placed; and (ix) Date of installation.

B. Removal of Electronic Game. Upon removal of an electronic game from a gaming site, the Tribe shall provide the State, in writing: (i) Information for items i, ii, and iii of subsection A; (ii) Date on which it was removed; (iii) Destination of the game; and (iv) Name of the person to whom the game is to be transferred, including the person's street address, business and home telephone numbers, how the game is to be transported, and name and street address of the common carrier or person transporting the game.

20.5 Hardware Requirements.

A. Physical Hazard. Electrical and mechanical parts and design principles may not subject a player to physical hazards.

B. Surge Protector. A surge protector must be installed on the line that feeds electrical current to the electronic game.

C. Battery Backup. A battery backup or an equivalent must be installed on an electronic game for the game's electronic meters. It must be capable of maintaining the accuracy of all information required by this Compact for one hundred eighty (180) days after electrical current is discontinued. The backup device must be kept within the locked microprocessor compartment.

D. On/Off Switch. An on/off switch that controls the electrical current of an electronic game and any associated equipment must be located in a readily accessible place inside the machine.

E. Static Discharge. The operation of an electronic game should be protected from static discharge or other electromagnetic interference.

F. Management Information System. (i) The electronic game must be interconnected to a central on-line computer management information system, approved by the gaming test laboratory, that records and maintains essential information on machine play. This information must be retained for thirty (30) days. The State may inspect such records. (ii) An electronic game using a coin drop hopper is allowed, provided it is monitored by an on-line management information system, which has been approved by the gaming test laboratory. However, should the Tribe maintain individual or clusters of machines apart from a major casino location, all coin hoppers must be monitored by a computer. Data from the machines must be downloaded to the central on-line management information system daily. The system must generate, by machine, analytical reports of coins and currency in, coins out, actual hold and actual to theoretical hold percentages, and error conditions. The term "error conditions" includes any exterior or interior cabinet door openings, coin-in tilts, and hopper tilts. A Tribe shall prepare system reports at least on a monthly basis and retain the reports for at least three years. The State may inspect such records. (iii) The Tribe shall maintain accurate and complete records of the identification number of each logic control component installed in each electronic game. The State may inspect such records.

G. Cabinet Security. The cabinet or interior area of an electronic game must be locked and not readily accessible.

H. Repairs and Service. An authorized agent or employee of the Tribe may open a cabinet to repair or service the game, but may do it only in the presence of another Tribal agent or employee or when the access is recorded by a video surveillance system.

I. Microprocessor Compartment. Logic Boards and other logic control components must be located in a separate microprocessor compartment within the electronic game. This compartment must be sealed and locked with a key or combination different than the key or combination used for the main cabinet door and cash compartment. The microprocessor compartment may be opened only in the presence of a tribal official or security officer appointed by the Tribe. The key to the microprocessor compartment must be kept by the Tribe in a secure place. "Logic control components" means all types of program storage media used to maintain the executable program that causes the game to operate. Such devices include hard disk drives, PCMIA cards, EPROMs, EEPROMs, CD-ROMs and similar storage media. (i) The storage media must be disabled from being able to be written to by a physical or hardware write disable feature when it is in the machine. It must be impossible to write any contents to the storage media at any time, from an internal or external source. (ii) Sealing tape, or its equivalent, must be placed over areas that are access sensitive. The security tape must be numbered, physically secured, and available to only authorized personnel of the Tribe. (iii) Logic control components must be able to be inspected in the field. The components must be able to be verified for authenticity by using signatures, hash codes, or other secure algorithm, and must be able to be compared on a bit for bit basis. (iv) The supplier of an electronic game shall provide the State and Tribe with necessary field test equipment at no charge for carrying out tests required in (iii) above. Also, if requested by the State or Tribe, the supplier shall provide training on how to use the equipment.

J. Cash Compartment. The coin and currency Compartment must be locked separately from the main cabinet area, and secured with a key or combination different than the key or combination used for the main cabinet door. However, a separate cash compartment is not required for coins that are necessary to pay prizes through a drop hopper. The keys must be kept in a secure location. Except as provided in this section, the compartment into which coins and bills are inserted must be locked. An employee or official of the Tribe may open the cash compartment to collect the cash and shall record the amount collected.

K. Hardware Switches. No hardware switch may be installed on an electronic game or associated equipment that may alter the game's pay table or payout percentage. Any other hardware switch must be approved by the State and Tribe.

L. Printing of Written Statement of Credits. For an electronic game that awards credits or replays, but not coins or tokens, a player, on completing play may prompt the game to print a written statement of credits. The game's interior printer must retain an exact, legible copy of the statement produced within the game.

M. Network. A Tribe may operate an electronic game as part of a network of games with an aggregate prize; provided: (i) An electronic game capable of bi-directional communication with external associated equipment must use communication protocol, which ensures that erroneous data will not adversely affect the operation of the game. The local network must be approved a gaming test laboratory; and (ii) If the network links the Tribe's progressive electronic games to another Tribe's progressive games that are located on the other Tribe's Indian reservation, each participating Tribe must have a Class III gaming compact that authorizes the Tribe's gaming to be operated as part of a multi-location network. All segments of the network must use security standards agreed to between the State and Tribe and which are as restrictive as those used by the Tribe for its on-line games.

20.6 Software Requirements.

A. Randomness Testing. Each electronic game must have a true random number generator that will determine the occurrence of a specific card, symbol, number, or stop position to be displayed on a video screen or by mechanical rotating reels. An occurrence will be considered random if it meets all requirements: (i) Chi-Square

Analysis. Each card, symbol, number, or stop position, which is wholly or partially determinative, satisfies the 99 percent confidence limit using the standard chi-square analysis. (ii) Runs Test. Each card, symbol, number, or stop position does not, as a significant statistic, produce predictable patterns of game elements or occurrences. Each card, symbol, number, or stop position will be considered random if it meets the 99 percent confidence level with regard to the "runs test" or any generally accepted pattern testing statistic. (iii) Correlation Analysis. Each card, symbol, number, or stop position is independently chosen without regard to any other card, symbol, number or stop position, drawn within that game play. Each pair of card, symbol, number, or stop position is considered random if they meet the 99 percent confidence level using standard correlation analysis. (iv) Serial Correlation Analysis. Each card, symbol, number, or stop position is independently chosen without reference to the same card, number, or stop position in the previous game. Each card, number, or stop position is considered random if it meets the 99 percent confidence level using standard serial correlation analysis. (v) Live Game Correlation. An electronic game that represents a live game must fairly and accurately depict the play of the live game.

B. Software Requirements for Percentage Payout. Each electronic game must meet the following maximum and minimum theoretical percentage payouts. However, these percentages are not applicable to slot tournaments conducted pursuant to Section 3.1(d): (i) Electronic games that are not affected by player skill must pay out a minimum of eighty (80%) percent and no more than one hundred percent of the amount wagered. The theoretical payout percentage will be determined using standard methods of probability theory; and (ii) Electronic games that are affected by player skill, such as draw poker and twenty-one, must pay out a minimum of eighty-three (83 %) percent and no more than one hundred (100%) percent of the amount wagered. This standard is met when using a method of play that will provide the greatest return to the player over a period of continuous play. These percentages shall not be applicable to slot tournaments conducted pursuant to Section 3.1(d).

C. Minimum Probability Standard for Maximum Pay. Each electronic game must have a probability of obtaining the maximum payout, which is greater than 1 in 17,000,000 for each play.

D. Software Requirements for Continuation of Game After Malfunction. Each electronic game must be capable of continuing the current game with all the current game's features after a game malfunction is cleared. This provision does not apply if a game is rendered totally inoperable; however, the current wager and all player credits before the malfunction must be returned to the player.

E. Software Requirements for Play Transaction Records. Each electronic game must maintain an electronic, electro-mechanical, or computer system, approved by a gaming test laboratory, to generate external reports. The system must record and maintain essential information associated with machine play. This information must be retained for at least thirty days, regardless of whether the machine has electrical power.

F. No Automatic Clearing of Accounting Meters. No electronic game may have a mechanism by which an error will cause the electronic accounting meters to automatically clear.

G. Display of Information. The information displayed must be kept under glass or other transparent material. No sticker or other removable item may be placed on the machine face or cover game information.

H. Display of Rules. The machine must display: 1) the rules of the game before each game is played; 2) the maximum and minimum wagers, amount of credits which may be won for each winning hand or combination of numbers or symbols; and 3) the credits the player has accumulated. However, for an electronic game with a mechanical display, this information must be permanently affixed on the game in a conspicuous location.

XXI. Amendments to Regulatory and Technical Standards for Electronic Games of Chance

The State and the Tribe acknowledge the likelihood that technological advances or other changes will occur during the duration of this Compact that may make it necessary or desirable that the regulatory and technical standards set forth in Sections 20.5 and 20.6 for electronic games of chance be modified to take advantage of such advances or other changes in order to maintain or improve game security and integrity. Therefore any of the regulatory or technical standards set forth in Sections 20.5 and 20.6 may be modified for the purposes of maintaining or improving game security and integrity by mutual agreement of the North Dakota Attorney General and the Tribal Council or its Chairperson, upon the written recommendation and explanation of the need for such change made by either party.

XXII. Regulation and Play of Table Games

22.1 Gaming Table Bank. The Tribe shall maintain at each table a gaming table bank, which shall be used exclusively for the making of change or handling player buy-ins.

22.2 Drop Box. The Tribe shall maintain at each table a game drop box, which shall be used exclusively for rake-offs or other compensation received by the Tribe for maintaining the game. A separate game drop box shall be used for each shift.

22.3 Gaming Room Bank. The Tribe shall maintain, at each location at which table games are placed, a gaming room bank, which shall be used exclusively for the maintenance of gaming table banks and the purchase and redemption of chips by players.

22.4 Rules to be Posted. The rules of each game shall be posted and be clearly legible from each table and must designate:

A. The maximum rake-off percentage, time buy-in or other fee charged.

B. The number of raises allowed.

C. The monetary limit of each raise.

D. The amount of the ante.

E. Other rules as may be necessary.

XXIII. Minimum Internal Control Standards

Tribe shall abide with such Minimum Internal Control Standards as are adopted, published, and finalized by the National Indian Gaming Commission and as may be in current effect.

XXIV. Inspection

24.1 Periodic Inspection and Testing. Tribal officials, agents or employees shall be authorized to periodically inspect and test any tribally licensed electronic games of chance. Any such inspection and testing shall be carried out in a manner and at a time, which will cause minimal disruption of gaming activities. The Tribal Gaming Commission shall be notified immediately of all such inspection and testing and the results thereof.

24.2 Receipt of Reports of Non-compliance. The Tribe shall provide for the receipt of information by the State as to machines believed to not be in compliance with this Compact or not to be in proper repair. Upon its receipt of such information the Tribe shall reasonably inspect or arrange for the inspection of any identified machine and shall thereafter undertake and complete, or commission the undertaking and completion of such corrective action as may be appropriate.

24.3 State Inspection of Operations. Agents of the State of North Dakota, or their designated representatives, shall upon the presentation of appropriate identification, have the right to gain access, without notice during normal hours of operation, to all premises used for the operation of games of chance, or the storage of games of chance or equipment related thereto, and may inspect all premises, equipment, daily records, documents, or items related to the operation of games of chance in order to verify compliance with the provisions of this Compact. Agents of the State making inspection shall be granted access to non-public areas for observations upon request. The Tribe reserves the right to accompany State inspectors within non-public areas. The Tribe shall cooperate as to such inspections. Inspections will be conduct, to the extent practicable, to avoid interrupting normal operations. Any costs associated with such inspection will be covered from the Escrow Account for State Expenses established and maintained pursuant to Section XXV of this Compact.

24.4 Inspection of Electronic Games of Chance. The State may cause any electronic game of chance in play by the Tribe to be inspected by a Qualified Gaming Test Laboratory or examiner. Inspections shall be conducted, to the extent practicable, to avoid interrupting normal operations. Any costs associated with inspection shall be covered from the Escrow Account for State Expenses established and maintained pursuant to Section XXV of this Compact. The Tribe shall cooperate in such inspection. Upon completion of such testing, test results must be provided to both the State and the Tribe.

24.5 Removal and Correction. Any machine confirmed to be in non-compliance with this Compact shall be removed from play by the Tribe and brought into compliance before reintroduction.

XXV. Escrow Account for State Expenses

25.1 Escrow Fund. The Tribe shall establish an escrow fund at a bank of their choosing with an initial contribution of Fifteen Thousand and no/100 ($15,000.00) dollars to reimburse the State for the expenses specifically names for reimbursement in this Compact and for participation in legal costs and fees incurred in defending, with the concurrence of the Tribe, third party challenges to this Compact. The Tribe shall replenish the said escrow account as necessary and agree that the balance in the said escrow account will not drop below the sum of seven thousand five hundred and no/100 ($7,500.00) dollars.

25.2 Procedure. The payments referenced above shall be made to an escrow account from which the State may draw as hereinafter provided. The State shall bill the Tribe the reasonable, necessary, and actual costs related to obligations undertaken under this Compact. Unless unreasonable or unnecessary, the costs for such services shall be that established by state law. The State shall send invoices to the Tribe for these services and shall thereafter be permitted to withdraw the billed amounts from the escrow account under the circumstances provided in this section. The Tribe shall be advised in writing by the State of all withdrawals from the Escrow Account and as to the purpose of such withdrawal.

25.3 Tribal Challenge. Should the Tribe believe that any expenses for which the State has billed the Tribe under this section, or actions which the State proposes to undertake and charge the Tribe for, are unnecessary, unreasonable or beyond the scope authorized by this Compact, the Tribe may invoke any of the Dispute Resolution procedures specified in Section XXVII below. In such event, the provisions set forth above shall remain in full force and effect pending resolution of the complaint of the Tribe. Should, however, it be determined that any expense charged against the Tribe is not necessary, not reasonable and/or is not within the scope of this Compact, the State shall reimburse the Tribe any monies withdrawn from escrow to meet such expense.

25.4 Termination of Escrow. Any monies that remain on deposit at the time this Compact, including all extensions thereof, concludes, shall be reimbursed to the Tribe.

XXVI. IGRA Remedies Preserved

Nothing in this Compact shall be construed to limit the rights or remedies available to the parties hereto under the IGRA.

XXVII. Worker's Compensation and Unemployment Insurance

27.1 Unemployment Insurance. In order to provide protection to the employees of the Tribe from unemployment, the Tribe and the State agree that all employees engaged in gaming activities as provided herein, whose coverage would be mandated under North Dakota law in the case of a non-Tribal employer, shall be covered by the North Dakota Unemployment Insurance Fund, and to that extent, the Tribe agrees as an employer to participate in those funds as provided herein. The Tribe will pay premiums for such employees to the Fund as any other employer in the State of North Dakota. The Tribe and its employees that are employed in gaming activities shall have all rights and remedies, as any employer or employee covered by the Fund. To that end, the Tribe and the State agree that any dispute with respect to the aforementioned funds, the coverage and benefits provided thereby, and premiums assessed and collected, shall be in the Courts of the State of North Dakota, and for that limited purpose, the Tribe and the State, each respectively, make a limited waiver of sovereign immunity.

27.2 Worker's Compensation. In order to provide protection to the employees of the Tribe from injury, the Tribe and the State agree that all employees engaged in gaming activities, as provided herein, whose coverage would be mandated under North Dakota law in the case of a non-Tribal employer, shall be covered by worker's compensation insurance comparable to that provided under North Dakota state law to employees covered thereby. Tribe may elect to obtain coverage from the North Dakota Worker's Compensation Bureau or from one or more private insurers certified to provide insurance coverage for any purpose within the State of North Dakota. Should Tribe elect to obtain coverage from the North Dakota Worker's Compensation Bureau, the Tribe will pay premiums for such employees to the Bureau as any other employer in the State of North Dakota, with the Tribe and its employees that are employed in gaming activities having all rights and remedies as any employer covered under North Dakota state law. To that end, the Tribe and the State agree that any dispute with respect to the coverage and benefits provided under North Dakota state law and premiums assessed and collected by the North Dakota Worker's Compensation Bureau shall be in the courts of the State of North Dakota, and for that limited purpose, the Tribe and the State, each respectively, make a limited waiver of sovereign immunity.

XXVIII. Dispute Resolution

28.1 If either party believes that the other party has failed to comply with any requirement of this Compact, it shall invoke the following procedure:

A. The party asserting the non-compliance shall serve written notice on the other party. The notice shall identify the specific statutory, regulatory or Compact provision alleged to have been violated and shall specify the factual basis for the alleged non-compliance. The State and Tribe shall thereafter meet within thirty (30) days in an effort to resolve the dispute.

B. If the dispute is not resolved to the satisfaction of the parties within ninety (90) days after service of the notice set forth, either party may pursue any remedy which is otherwise available to that party to enforce or resolve disputes concerning the provisions of this Compact, including: (i) Arbitration pursuant to the specifications set forth in this section. (ii) Commencement of an action in the United States District Court for the District of North Dakota. (iii) Any remedy which is otherwise available to that party to enforce or resolve disputes concerning the provisions of this Compact.

28.2 In the event an allegation by the State asserting that a particular gaming activity by the Tribe is not in compliance with this Compact, where such allegation is not resolved to the satisfaction of the State within ninety (90) days after service of notice, the State may serve upon the Tribe a notice to cease conduct of such gaming. Upon receipt of such notice, the Tribe may elect to stop the gaming activity specified in the notice or invoke one or more of the additional dispute resolution procedures set forth, above and continue gaming pending final determination.

28.3 In the event an allegation by the Tribe is not resolved to the satisfaction of the Tribe within ninety (90) days after service of the notice set forth above, the Tribe may invoke arbitration as specified above.

28.4 Any arbitration under this authority shall be conducted under the rules of the American Arbitration Association, except that the arbitrators will be selected by the State picking one arbitrator, the Tribe a second arbitrator and the two so chosen shall pick a third arbitrator. If the third arbitrator is not chosen in this manner within ten (10) days after the second arbitrator is picked, the third arbitrator will be chosen in accordance with the rules of the American Arbitration Association.

28.5 Either party may initiate action in United States District Court to enforce an arbitration determination, or to pursue such relief as may be unavailable through arbitration.

XXIX. Cooperation by Parties

29.1 Gambling Addiction Programs. The parties hereto wish to proclaim their joint support of effective programs to address gambling addiction. Past donations in support of such efforts by Tribe are acknowledged. Tribe intends to continue such voluntary donations. State shall extend efforts to facilitate similar support from other gaming interests within North Dakota. The parties shall continue their joint efforts to most effectively support gambling addiction treatment, education and prevention programs, including completion of a study of gaming addiction in the State of North Dakota, to be completed by the start of the 2001 Legislative session.

29.2 Government-to-Government Issues. The parties acknowledge that there exist many Government-to-Government issues of concern between them and pledge to cooperate with each other in addressing such issues.

29.3 Local Jurisdictions. Tribe and Local Jurisdictions shall in good faith negotiate relative to the provision by the local jurisdiction of such services to the Tribe as may be requested by the Tribe, and as to a reasonable contribution from the Tribe for such services.

Tribe and Local Jurisdictions shall in good faith negotiate as to a reasonable contribution from the Tribe for services by local jurisdictions necessitated by the presence of a Tribal casino.

XXX. *Consultation*

Tribe and State shall in good faith periodically inform each other of issues associated with the implementation of this Compact and at the request of either party shall meet and discuss matters of concern. A status review meeting shall be had at least bi-annually in even numbered years between Tribe, other compacting Tribes within the state of North Dakota and state officials, including, but not limited to representatives of the Governor, Attorney General and legislative leaders. The State and the Tribe are concerned about the long term impact to the people of North Dakota (tribal and non-tribal alike) and are committed to implementing this Compact, making every effort during the term thereof, to provide economic opportunities and deal appropriately with any consequences resulting from gambling.

XXXI. *Effective Date*

This Amended Compact shall become effective, and shall supersede the terms of the parties initial Gaming Compact, upon execution by the Chairperson of the Tribe and the Governor of the State, approval by the Secretary of the Interior, and publication of such approval in the Federal Register pursuant to the IGRA.

XXXII. *Duration*

32.1 Term. This Compact shall be in effect, following its effective date, for a term consisting of the remaining period of the initial Class III Gaming Compact between Tribe and State (without any extensions) and hereafter for a period of ten (10) years.

32.2 Initial Renewal. This Compact shall, without action by either party, be extended for an additional five (5) year period beyond the term specified at Section 32.1 above, unless during the remaining period the initial Class III Gaming Compact between Tribe and State or during a subsequent period of seven (7) years thereafter, either party, believes that, the other has not been in substantial good faith compliance with the terms of this Compact and gives notice of non-compliance within the term herein specified. Such notice must be given in writing at least thirty (30) days prior to the conclusion of the above identified period ("Notice Date"). The Notice must be accompanied with specifications designating the manners the party is believed to have not been in good faith compliance. Failure by a party to give notice by the Notice Date as to activity by the other it views disfavor does not eliminate the ability of such party to arbitrate its concerns under Article XXVIII. If an arbitration panel, upon consideration of conduct occurring between the Notice Date and the end of the term specified at Section 32.1, determines that the Tribe has been in substantial non-compliance, the Governor within thirty (30) days of the determination may vacate the five (5) year extension provided therein. The parties may thereafter negotiate for a Successor Compact.

32.3 Automatic Extension. The duration of this Compact shall thereafter be automatically extended for terms of five (5) years upon written notice of renewal by either party on the other party during the final year of the original term of this Compact, inclusive of the initial renewal as specified applying both Section 32.1 and Section 32.2 or any extension thereof, unless the Tribe or the Governor serves written notice of non-renewal within thirty (30) days thereafter, or unless the North Dakota Legislature directs notice of non-renewal, by Bill or Resolution, passed with two-third (2/3) majority in each house during the legislative session immediately prior to the expiration of the Compact.

32.4 Operation. The Tribe may operate Class III gaming only while this Compact, including any amendment or restatement thereof is in effect.

32.5 Successor Compact. In the event that written notice of non-renewal of this Compact is given by one of the parties above, the Tribe may, pursuant to the procedures of the Indian Gaming Regulatory Act, request the State to enter into negotiations for a successor compact governing the conduct of Class III gaming activities to become effective following the expiration of this Compact. Thereafter the State shall negotiate with the Tribe in good faith concerning the terms of a successor compact (see § 11(d)(3)(A) of the Act).

32.6 Interim Operation. If a Successor Compact is not concluded by the expiration date of this Compact, or any extension thereof, and should either party request negotiation of a successor compact, then this Compact shall remain in effect until the procedures set forth in Section 11 (d)(7) of the Indian Gaming Regulatory Act are exhausted, including resolution of any appeal.

32.7 Cessation of Class III Gaming. In the event written notice of non-renewal is given by either party as set forth in this section, the Tribe shall cease all Class III gaming under this Compact upon the expiration date of this Compact, or upon the date the procedures specified above associated with a successor compact are concluded and a successor compact, if any, is in effect.

32.8 Pari-Mutuel Horse Racing Addendum. The duration specified above shall also be applicable to the pari-mutuel horse racing addendum to the Gaming Compact between Tribe and State pursuant to Section XVI of said Pari-mutuel Horse Racing Addendum that provides that the term of said Addendum shall be simultaneous with that of the Compact.

XXXIII. Geographic Scope of Compact

This compact shall only govern the conduct of Class III games by the Tribe on Tribal trust lands within the current exterior boundaries of the Spirit Lake Reservation, which are in compliance with the Indian Gaming Regulatory Act, at 25 U.S.C. § 2719, and waters adjacent thereto, together with such lands, and waters adjacent thereto, as may be acknowledged by the parties to be lands and waters of the Spirit Lake Tribe. The Tribe may conduct gaming on adjacent waters, limited to excursion boats offering food service, where passengers may board and unboard only from the Tribe's marina. This Amended Compact shall further govern such lands and waters as may be transferred to the Spirit Lake Tribe or acknowledged to be Tribal as a result of any Court determination or agreement between the parties in Devils Lake Sioux v. State of North Dakota, now pending in United States District Court, District of North Dakota, No. A286–87. The execution of this Compact shall not in any manner be deemed to have waived the rights of the State or the Tribe pursuant to the aforementioned section of the Indian Gaming Regulatory Act or as to the referenced pending litigation.

XXXIV. Amendment

The State or the Tribe may at any time and upon proper notification request amendment or negotiations for the amendment of this Compact. Both parties shall negotiate any requested amendment in good faith and reach a determination thereupon within ninety (90) days. Amendments to this Compact shall not become applicable until agreed to by both parties and, if necessary, approved by the United States Secretary of Interior.

XXXV. Notices

Unless a party advises otherwise in writing, all notices, payments, requests, reports, information or demand which any party hereto may desire or may be required to give to the other party hereto, shall be in writing and shall be personally delivered or sent by first class certified or registered United States mail, postage prepaid, return receipt requested, and sent to the other party at its address appearing below or such other address as any party shall hereinafter inform the other party hereto by written notice given as aforesaid:

Notice to the Tribe shall be sent to:

Spirit Lake Tribe
Fort Totten Community Center
PO Box 300
Fort Totten, ND 58335-0300

Notice to the State shall be sent to:

Governor, State of North Dakota
Office of the Governor
600 East Boulevard Avenue
Bismarck, ND 58505

Attorney General, State of North Dakota
Office of the Attorney General
600 East Boulevard Avenue
Bismarck, ND 58505

Each notice, payment, request, report, information or demand so given shall be deemed effective upon receipt, or if mailed, upon receipt or the expiration of the third day following the day of mailing, whichever occurs first, except that any notice of change of address shall be effective only upon receipt by the party to whom said notice is addressed.

XXXVI. Entire Agreement

This Compact is the entire agreement between the parties and supersedes all prior agreements whether written or oral, with respect to the subject matter hereof. Neither this Compact nor any provision herein may be changed, waived, discharged, or terminated orally, but only by an instrument in writing.

XXXVII. No Assignment

Neither the State nor the Tribe may assign any of its respective right, title, or interest in this Compact, nor may either delegate any of its respective obligations and duties except as expressly provided herein. Any attempted assignment or delegation in contravention of the foregoing shall be void.

XXXVIII. Severability

Each provision, section, and subsection of this Compact shall stand separate and independent of every other provision, section, or subsection. In the event that a court of competent jurisdiction shall find any provision, section, or subsection of this Compact to be invalid, the remaining provisions, sections and subsections of the Compact shall remain in full force and effect.

IN WITNESS WHEREOF, the parties hereto have caused this Compact to be executed as of the day and year first above written.

State of North Dakota
By: Edward T. Schafer, Governor
Dated this 29th day of September, 1999

Spirit Lake Nation
By: Phillip Longie, Chairman
Dated this 29th day of September, 1999

Department of the Interior
By: Kevin Gover, Assistant Secretary—Indian Affairs
Dated this 29th day of September, 1999

Notes and Questions

1. Different states, different tribes, different experiences. The North Dakota compact represents the compacts negotiated with each of the state's five gaming tribes in 1999; the California compact represents the "1999 Compacts" signed with 61 tribes in 1999 and 2000. The California and North Dakota compacts offer windows into very different experiences with Indian gaming. Along with Connecticut, California was one of the top two states in terms of tribal gaming revenue in 2006; together, the Indian gaming operations in those two states earned 40% of the industry's revenue. North Dakota, with its rural character and small market, is at the other end of the spectrum. California is home to over 100 federally recognized tribes, many of which are small rancherias with memberships of a few dozen to a few hundred. The five tribes with land in North Dakota range in size from about 5,000 to over 28,000 members. Tribes in North Dakota, as throughout the Great Plains, are "treaty tribes," each with a long history of government-to-government relations with the federal government and a strong tradition of tribal identity and sovereignty. California's 1999 model compact grew out of a dynamic and controversial legal and political environment as reflected in the condition of passage of Proposition 1A, a state constitutional amendment to allow tribes to conduct casino-style gaming. For more on California, see Roger Dunstan, *The Evolution and Impact of Indian Gaming in California*, 5 GAMING L. REV. 373 (2001) and Chad M. Gordon, *From Hope to Realization of Dreams: Proposition 5 and California Indian Gaming*, in INDIAN GAMING: WHO WINS? (Angela Mullis & David Kamper eds., 2000). North Dakota's compact was the result of relatively amicable and respectful negotiations. For more on North Dakota, see LIGHT & RAND, INDIAN GAMING AND TRIBAL SOVEREIGNTY, at 111–18.

2. Sample tribal-state compact provisions. Tribes in California and North Dakota have different histories and circumstances, tribal casinos in California are very different from those in North Dakota, and, generally speaking, North Dakota's public policy differs significantly from that of California. Where do you see these differences reflected in the tribal-state compacts entered into by each state? As noted above, IGRA provides a list of permissible compact provisions, including the catch-all "and any other subjects that are directly related to the operation of gaming activities." Do you see any provisions in the compacts that seem to fall outside of §2710(d)(3)(C)? Which provisions do you believe are most favorable to the tribes residing in each state? Which provisions do you believe are most favorable to the state? Which provisions appear to reflect shared public policy goals of both the tribe and the state? Under each compact, which entity has primary regulatory authority over the tribe's operation of Class III gaming? How would you sum up the scope and extent of state vs. tribal authority in each compact, and in comparison to one another?

3.   *Model compacts.* Some states, such as California, have used "model compacts." Consider the arguments raised in *Cheyenne River Sioux Tribe v. South Dakota*, 3 F.3d 273 (8th Cir. 1993):

> [After] the Cheyenne River Sioux Tribe requested the state to negotiate a tribal-state compact, five "official" negotiations between tribal and state officials [occurred, as did meetings between tribal officials and the governor]. The tribe alleges the state refused to negotiate in good faith because the state adopted a "rigid" negotiation strategy by offering the tribe the so-called "Flandreau compact," which the state used as a "model" in all subsequent tribal-state compact negotiations. [Under the terms of the "Flandreau compact," the tribe could operate a total of up to 250 slot machines, poker tables, or blackjack tables, which must comply with state regulations on hours of operation and pot, bet, and payout limits. The "Flandreau compact" also authorized state involvement in licensing and other civil and criminal matters.] If the tribe wanted more favorable terms than those in the Flandreau compact, the state demanded certain concessions, for example, expanded state criminal jurisdiction. The tribe contends the state refused to consider the particular circumstances and interests of the Cheyenne River Sioux Tribe. The tribe argues there are significant differences between the Cheyenne River Sioux and Flandreau Santee Sioux Tribes that make it unreasonable to impose the Flandreau compact on the Cheyenne River Sioux Tribe. The Cheyenne River Sioux reservation is about the size of Connecticut and is located in a remote western part of the state, far from population centers, which are located in the southeastern corner of the state (near the Iowa and Nebraska borders). The Cheyenne River Sioux Tribe has at least 10 times the members of the Flandreau Santee Sioux Tribe and, unlike the Flandreau Santee Sioux Tribe, has a mature tribal government, including tribal police and tribal courts.

Id. at 276–77. Does the state's good faith duty require it to tailor compacts to individual tribal circumstances? Or at least to be willing to negotiate individual compacts? Would a state that insisted on model compacts despite disparate tribal circumstances violate the duty to negotiate in good faith? What tribal circumstances would be relevant and why? In *Cheyenne River Sioux Tribe*, the state argued that because South Dakota already had entered into compacts with a number of tribes, it would be "unfair" to allow the Cheyenne River Sioux Tribe to operate any games not permitted by the other compacts. Would the same "fairness" argument hold for other compact terms, such as number of machines?

Seminole Tribe of Florida v. Florida
517 U.S. 44 (1996)

Chief Justice REHNQUIST delivered the opinion of the Court.

[Relying on its power under the Indian Commerce Clause, U.S. CONST. art. I, § 8, cl. 3,] Congress passed the Indian Gaming Regulatory Act in 1988 in order to provide a statutory basis for the operation and regulation of gaming by Indian tribes. Class III gaming — the type with which we are here concerned — is defined as "all forms of gaming that are not class I gaming or class II gaming," and includes such things as slot machines, casino games, banking card games, dog racing, and lotteries. It is the most heavily regulated of the three classes. The Act provides that class III gaming is lawful only where it is: (1) authorized by an ordinance or resolution that (a) is adopted by the governing body of the Indian tribe, (b) satisfies certain statutorily prescribed requirements, and (c) is approved by the National Indian Gaming Commission; (2) located in a State that permits such gaming for any purpose by any person, organization, or entity; and (3) "conducted in conformance with a Tribal-State compact entered into by the Indian tribe and the State under paragraph (3) that is in effect." § 2710(d)(1).

The "paragraph (3)" to which the last prerequisite of § 2710(d)(1) refers is § 2710(d)(3), which describes the permissible scope of a Tribal-State compact and provides that the compact is effective "only when notice of approval by the Secretary [of the Interior] of such compact has been published by the Secretary in the Federal Register." More significant for our purposes, however, is that § 2710(d)(3) describes the process by which a State and an Indian tribe begin negotiations toward a Tribal-State compact:

> Any Indian tribe having jurisdiction over the Indian lands upon which a class III gaming activity is being conducted, or is to be conducted, shall request the State in which such lands are located to enter into negotiations for the purpose of entering into a Tribal-State compact governing the conduct of gaming activities. Upon receiving such a request, the State shall negotiate with the Indian tribe in good faith to enter into such a compact.

The State's obligation to "negotiate with the Indian tribe in good faith" is made judicially enforceable by §§ 2710(d)(7)(A)(i) and (B)(i):

> (A) The United States district courts shall have jurisdiction over—
>
> (i) any cause of action initiated by an Indian tribe arising from the failure of a State to enter into negotiations with the Indian tribe for the purpose of entering into a Tribal-State compact under paragraph (3) or to conduct such negotiations in good faith....
>
> (B)(i) An Indian tribe may initiate a cause of action described in subparagraph (A)(i) only after the close of the 180-day period beginning on the date on which the Indian tribe requested the State to enter into negotiations under paragraph (3)(A).

Sections 2710(d)(7)(B)(ii)–(vii) describe an elaborate remedial scheme designed to ensure the formation of a Tribal-State compact. A tribe that brings an action under § 2710(d)(7)(A)(i) must show that no Tribal-State compact has been entered and that the State failed to respond in good faith to the tribe's request to negotiate; at that point, the burden then shifts to the State to prove that it did in fact negotiate in good faith. If the district court concludes that the State has failed to negotiate in good faith toward the formation of a Tribal-State compact, then it "shall order the State and Indian Tribe to conclude such a compact within a 60-day period." If no compact has been concluded 60 days after the court's order, then "the Indian tribe and the State shall each submit to a mediator appointed by the court a proposed compact that represents their last best offer for a compact." The mediator chooses from between the two proposed compacts the one "which best comports with the terms of [the Act] and any other applicable Federal law and with the findings and order of the court," and submits it to the State and the Indian tribe. If the State consents to the proposed compact within 60 days of its submission by the mediator, then the proposed compact is "treated as a Tribal-State compact entered into under paragraph (3)." If, however, the State does not consent within that 60-day period, then the Act provides that the mediator "shall notify the Secretary [of the Interior]" and that the Secretary "shall prescribe ... procedures ... under which class III gaming may be conducted on the Indian lands over which the Indian tribe has jurisdiction."

In September 1991, the Seminole Tribe of Florida, petitioner, sued the State of Florida and its Governor, Lawton Chiles, respondents. Invoking jurisdiction under 25 U.S.C. § 2710(d)(7)(A), petitioner alleged that respondents had "refused to enter into any negotiation for inclusion of [certain gaming activities] in a tribal-state compact," thereby violating the "requirement of good faith negotiation." Respondents moved to dismiss the complaint, arguing that the suit violated the State's sovereign immunity from suit in federal court. The District Court denied respondents' motion, and respondents took an interlocutory appeal of that decision.

The Court of Appeals for the Eleventh Circuit reversed the decision of the District Court, holding that the Eleventh Amendment barred petitioner's suit against respondents. 11 F.3d 1016 (1994). The court agreed with the District Court that Congress in § 2710(d)(7) intended to abrogate the States' sovereign immunity, and also agreed that the Act had been passed pursuant to Congress' power under the Indian Commerce Clause. The court disagreed with the District Court, however, that the Indian Commerce Clause grants Congress the power to abrogate a State's Eleventh Amendment immunity from suit, and concluded therefore that it had no jurisdiction over petitioner's suit against Florida. Finding that it lacked subject-matter jurisdiction, the Eleventh Circuit remanded to the District Court with directions to dismiss petitioner's suit.

We granted certiorari in order to consider two questions: (1) Does the Eleventh Amendment prevent Congress from authorizing suits by Indian tribes against States for prospective injunctive relief to enforce legislation enacted pursuant to the Indian Commerce Clause?; and (2) Does the doctrine of *Ex parte Young* permit suits against a State's Governor for prospective injunctive relief to enforce the good-faith bargaining requirement of the Act? We answer the first question in the affirmative, the second in the negative, and we therefore affirm the Eleventh Circuit's dismissal of petitioner's suit.

The Eleventh Amendment provides: "The Judicial power of the United States shall not be construed to extend to any suit in law or equity, commenced or prosecuted against one of the United States by Citizens of another State, or by Citizens or Subjects of any Foreign State." Although the text of the Amendment would appear to restrict only the Article III diversity jurisdiction of the federal courts, "we have understood the Eleventh Amendment to stand not so much for what it says, but for the presupposition ... which it confirms." That presupposition, first observed over a century ago in *Hans v. Louisiana*, 134 U.S. 1 (1890), has two parts: first, that each State is a sovereign entity in our federal system; and second, that "[i]t is inherent in the nature of sovereignty not to be amenable to the suit of an individual without its consent." For over a century we have reaffirmed that federal jurisdiction over suits against unconsenting States "was not contemplated by the Constitution when establishing the judicial power of the United States."

Here, petitioner has sued the State of Florida and it is undisputed that Florida has not consented to the suit. Petitioner nevertheless contends that its suit is not barred by state sovereign immunity, [because] Congress through the Act abrogated the States' sovereign immunity. Alternatively, petitioner maintains that its suit against the Governor may go forward under *Ex parte Young*. We consider each of those arguments in turn.

In order to determine whether Congress has abrogated the States' sovereign immunity, we ask two questions: first, whether Congress has "unequivocally expresse[d] its intent to abrogate the immunity," and second, whether Congress has acted "pursuant to a valid exercise of power." Congress' intent to abrogate the States' immunity from suit must be obvious from "a clear legislative statement." This rule arises from recognition of the important role played by the Eleventh Amendment and the broader principles that it reflects.

Here, we agree with virtually every other court that has confronted the question that Congress has in § 2710(d)(7) provided an "unmistakably clear" statement of its intent to abrogate. Section 2710(d)(7)(A)(i) vests jurisdiction in "[t]he United States district courts ... over any cause of action ... arising from the failure of a State to enter into negotiations ... or to conduct such negotiations in good faith." We think that the numerous references to the "State" in the text of § 2710(d)(7)(B) make it indubitable that Congress intended through the Act to abrogate the States' sovereign immunity from suit.

Having concluded that Congress clearly intended to abrogate the States' sovereign immunity, we turn now to consider whether the Act was passed "pursuant to a valid exercise of power." Petitioner argues that the abrogation power is validly exercised here because the Act grants the States a power that they would not otherwise have, viz., some measure of authority over gaming on Indian lands. It is true enough that the Act extends to the States a power withheld from them by the Constitution. See *California v. Cabazon Band of Mission Indians*, 480 U.S. 202 (1987). Nevertheless, we do not see how that consideration is relevant to the question whether Congress may abrogate state sovereign immunity. The Eleventh Amendment immunity may not be lifted by Congress unilaterally deciding that it will be replaced by grant of some other authority.

Thus our inquiry into whether Congress has the power to abrogate unilaterally the States' immunity from suit is narrowly focused on one question: Was the Act in question passed pursuant to a constitutional provision granting Congress the power to abrogate? Previously, in conducting that inquiry, we have found authority to abrogate under only two provisions of the Constitution. In *Fitzpatrick v. Bitzer*, 427 U.S. 445 (1976), we held that through the Fourteenth Amendment, federal power extended to intrude upon the province of the Eleventh Amendment and therefore that § 5 of the Fourteenth Amendment allowed Congress to abrogate the immunity from suit guaranteed by that Amendment. In only one other case has congressional abrogation of the States' Eleventh Amendment immunity been upheld. In *Pennsylvania v. Union Gas Co.*, 491 U.S. 1 (1989), a plurality of the Court found that the Interstate Commerce Clause, art. I, § 8, cl. 3, granted Congress the power to abrogate state sovereign immunity, stating that the power to regulate interstate commerce would be "incomplete without the authority to render States liable in damages."

[Relying on] the plurality decision in *Union Gas*, [petitioner] contends that "[t]here is no principled basis for finding that congressional power under the Indian Commerce Clause is less than that conferred by the Interstate Commerce Clause." Noting that the *Union Gas* plurality found the power to abrogate from the "plenary" character of the grant of authority over interstate commerce, petitioner emphasizes that the Interstate Commerce Clause leaves the States with some power to regulate, whereas the Indian Commerce Clause makes "Indian relations ... the exclusive province of federal law." *County of Oneida v. Oneida Indian Nation of N.Y.*, 470 U.S. 226 (1985). Contending that the Indian Commerce Clause vests the Federal Government with "the duty of protect[ing]" the tribes from "local ill feeling" and "the people of the States," *United States v. Kagama*, 118 U.S. 375 (1886), petitioner argues that the abrogation power is necessary "to protect the tribes from state action denying federally guaranteed rights."

Respondents dispute petitioner's analogy between the Indian Commerce Clause and the Interstate Commerce Clause, [arguing] that the two provisions are wholly dissimilar. Respondents contend that the Interstate Commerce Clause grants the power of abrogation only because Congress' authority to regulate interstate commerce would be "incomplete" without that "necessary" power. The Indian Commerce Clause is distinguishable, respondents contend, because it gives Congress complete authority over the Indian tribes. Therefore, the abrogation power is not "necessary" to Congress' exercise of its power under the Indian Commerce Clause.

Both parties make their arguments from the plurality decision in *Union Gas*, and we, too, begin there. We think it clear that Justice Brennan's opinion finds Congress' power to abrogate under the Interstate Commerce Clause from the States' cession of their sovereignty when they gave Congress plenary power to regulate interstate commerce. While the plurality decision states that Congress' power under the Interstate Commerce Clause would be incomplete without the power to abrogate, that statement is made solely in order to emphasize the broad scope of Congress' authority over interstate commerce. Following the rationale of the *Union Gas* plurality, our inquiry is limited to determining whether the Indian Commerce Clause, like the Interstate Commerce Clause, is a grant of authority to the Federal Government at the expense of the States. The answer to that question is obvious. If anything, the Indian Commerce Clause accomplishes a greater transfer of power from the States to the Federal Government than does the Interstate Commerce Clause. This is clear enough from the fact that the States still exercise some authority over interstate trade but have been divested of virtually all authority over Indian commerce and Indian tribes. We agree with petitioner that the plurality opinion in *Union Gas* allows no principled distinction in favor of the States to be drawn between the Indian Commerce Clause and the Interstate Commerce Clause.

Generally, the principle of *stare decisis*, and the interests that it serves, counsel strongly against reconsideration of our precedent. Nevertheless, we always have treated *stare decisis* as a principle of policy, and not as an inexorable command. When governing decisions are unworkable or are badly reasoned, this Court has never felt constrained to follow precedent. Our willingness to reconsider our earlier decisions has been particularly true in constitutional cases, because in such cases correction through legislative action is practically impossible.

The Court in *Union Gas* reached a result without an expressed rationale agreed upon by a majority of the Court. Since it was issued, *Union Gas* has created confusion among the lower courts that have sought to understand and apply the deeply fractured decision. The plurality's rationale also deviated sharply from our established federalism jurisprudence and essentially eviscerated our decision in *Hans*. Never before the decision in *Union Gas* had we suggested that the bounds of Article III could be expanded by Congress operating pursuant to any constitutional provision other than the Fourteenth Amendment. Indeed, it had seemed fundamental that Congress could not expand the jurisdiction of the federal courts beyond the bounds of Article III. *Marbury v. Madison*, 1 Cranch [5 U.S.] 137 (1803). *Fitzpatrick* was based upon a rationale wholly inapplicable to the Interstate Commerce Clause, viz., that the Fourteenth Amendment, adopted well after the adoption of the Eleventh Amendment and the ratification of the Constitution, operated to alter the pre-existing balance between state and federal power achieved by Article III and the Eleventh Amendment. In the five years since it was decided, *Union Gas* has proved to be a solitary departure from established law. We feel bound to conclude that *Union Gas* was wrongly decided and that it should be, and now is, overruled.

Petitioner argues that we may exercise jurisdiction over its suit to enforce § 2710(d)(3) against the Governor notwithstanding the jurisdictional bar of the Eleventh Amendment. Petitioner notes that since our decision in *Ex parte Young*, 209 U.S. 123 (1908), we often have found federal jurisdiction over a suit against a state official when that suit seeks only prospective injunctive relief in order to "end a continuing violation of federal law." The situation presented here, however, is sufficiently different from that giving rise to the traditional *Ex parte Young* action so as to preclude the availability of that doctrine.

Here, the "continuing violation of federal law" alleged by petitioner is the Governor's failure to bring the State into compliance with § 2710(d)(3). But the duty to negotiate imposed upon the State by that statutory provision does not stand alone. Rather, as we have seen, Congress passed § 2710(d)(3) in conjunction with the carefully crafted and intricate remedial scheme set forth in § 2710(d)(7). Where Congress has created a remedial scheme for the enforcement of a particular federal right, we have, in suits against federal officers, refused to supplement that scheme with one created by the judiciary. Here, of course, the question is not whether a remedy should be created, but instead is whether the Eleventh Amendment bar should be lifted, as it was in *Ex parte Young,* in order to allow a suit against a state officer. Nevertheless, we think that the same general principle applies. Therefore, where Congress has prescribed a detailed remedial scheme for the enforcement against a State of a statutorily created right, a court should hesitate before casting aside those limitations and permitting an action against a state officer based upon *Ex parte Young.*

Here, Congress intended § 2710(d)(3) to be enforced against the State in an action brought under § 2710(d)(7); the intricate procedures set forth in that provision show that Congress intended therein not only to define, but also to limit significantly, the duty imposed by § 2710(d)(3). For example, where the court finds that the State has failed to negotiate in good faith, the only remedy prescribed is an order directing the State and the Indian tribe to conclude a compact within 60 days. And if the parties disregard the court's order and fail to conclude a compact within the 60-day period, the only sanction is that each party then must submit a proposed compact to a mediator who selects the one which best embodies the terms of the Act. Finally, if the State fails to accept the compact selected by the mediator, the only sanction against it is that the mediator shall notify the Secretary of the Interior who then must prescribe regulations governing class III gaming on the tribal lands at issue. By contrast with this quite modest set of sanctions, an action brought against a state official under *Ex parte Young* would expose that official to the full remedial powers of a federal court, including, presumably, contempt sanctions. If § 2710(d)(3) could be enforced in a suit under *Ex parte Young,* § 2710(d)(7) would have been superfluous; it is difficult to see why an Indian tribe would suffer through the intricate scheme of § 2710(d)(7) when more complete and more immediate relief would be available under *Ex parte Young.*

Here, of course, we have found that Congress does not have authority under the Constitution to make the State suable in federal court under § 2710(d)(7). Nevertheless, the fact that Congress chose to impose upon the State a liability that is significantly more limited than would be the liability imposed upon the state officer under *Ex parte Young* strongly indicates that Congress had no wish to create the latter under § 2710(d)(3). Nor are we free to rewrite the statutory scheme in order to approximate what we think Congress might have wanted had it known that § 2710(d)(7) was beyond its authority. If that effort is to be made, it should be made by Congress, and not by the federal courts. We hold that *Ex parte Young* is inapplicable to petitioner's suit against the Governor of Florida, and therefore that suit is barred by the Eleventh Amendment and must be dismissed for a lack of jurisdiction.

Notes and Questions

1. **Ex parte Young.** In *Ex parte Young,* 209 U.S. 123 (1908), Minnesota had fixed railroad rates through state law. Railroad stockholders brought a shareholders' derivative suit in federal court under the Fourteenth Amendment, claiming the state law was confiscatory. The district court granted a preliminary injunction and enjoined Young, the

Minnesota Attorney General, from enforcing the statute or imposing penalties under it. Young ignored the court's injunction, however, and attempted to compel compliance with the state law. The federal court adjudged Young in contempt of the court's order. The Court held that the federal court's action was not in violation of the Eleventh Amendment. The state is presumed to act constitutionally, the Court reasoned, and so the unconstitutional acts of its officials were not protected by state sovereign immunity. "It is simply an illegal act upon the part of a state official.... If the act which the state Attorney General seeks to enforce be a violation of the Federal Constitution, the officer in proceeding under such enactment comes into conflict with the superior authority of the Constitution, and he is in that case stripped of his official or representative character and is subjected in his person to the consequences of his individual conduct." *Id.* at 159–60.

2. ***Implications for IGRA.*** In the immediate aftermath of the Court's decision, it was unclear as to whether the Court effectively had gutted IGRA in its entirety—or at least § 2710(d) in its entirety—by invalidating the enforcement mechanism for the state's good-faith duty, or whether instead the cause of action against the state was severable from the rest of the statute due to IGRA's severability clause in § 2721. This issue is discussed more fully below. Plainly, though, the Court's decision took the teeth out of the centerpiece of the legal and political compromises embodied in IGRA—Congress's careful balance of state and tribal authority. Recall the Senate Report's discussion of the state's good faith duty and the accompanying enforcement mechanism:

> Section [2710](d)(7) grants a tribe the right to sue a State if compact negotiations are not concluded. This section is the result of the Committee balancing the interests and rights of tribes to engage in gaming against the interests of States in regulating such gaming. Under this act, Indian tribes will be required to give up any legal right they may now have to engage in class III gaming if: (1) they choose to forgo gaming rather than to opt for a compact that may involve State jurisdiction; or (2) they opt for a compact and, for whatever reason, a compact is not successfully negotiated. In contrast, States are not required to forgo any State governmental rights to engage in or regulate class III gaming except whatever they may voluntarily cede to a tribe under a compact. Thus, given this unequal balance, the issue before the Committee was how best to encourage States to deal fairly with tribes as sovereign governments. The Committee elected, as the least offensive option, to grant tribes the right to sue a State if a compact is not negotiated and chose to apply the good faith standard as the legal barometer for the State's dealings with tribes in class III gaming negotiations.

The Court's decision in *Seminole Tribe* focused on the standard conception of federalism as the balance of authority between the federal government and the states. Did the Court overlook the "third sovereign" in the American political system? Did the Court read Congress's power too narrowly in the context of a statute intended to balance the authority of states and tribes?

3. ***Does IGRA violate the Tenth Amendment?*** In a footnote, the *Seminole Tribe* Court noted that

> [r]espondents also contend that the Act mandates state regulation of Indian gaming and therefore violates the Tenth Amendment by allowing federal officials to avoid political accountability for those actions for which they are in fact responsible. See *New York v. United States,* 505 U.S. 144 (1992). This argument was not

considered below by either the Eleventh Circuit or the District Court, and is not fairly within the question presented. Therefore we do not consider it here.

Seminole Tribe, at 60 n.10. For analysis of the Tenth Amendment's applicability to IGRA, see, e.g., *Ponca Tribe v. Oklahoma*, 37 F.3d 1422 (10th Cir. 1994), *judgment vacated by* 517 U.S. 1129 (1996), *and rev'd on other grounds*, 89 F.3d 690 (10th Cir. 1996); *Cheyenne River Sioux Tribe v. South Dakota*, 3 F.3d 271 (8th Cir. 1993). For an argument that IGRA violates the Tenth Amendment, see Neil Scott Cohen, Note, *In What Often Appears to be a Crapshoot Legislative Process, Congress Throws Snake Eyes When It Enacts the Indian Gaming Regulatory Act*, 29 HOFSTRA L. REV. 277 (2000). What do you think about this argument? How would you argue to the contrary?

4. ***Constitutional implications.*** Besides its effect on IGRA, the Court's decision in *Seminole Tribe* plainly is of constitutional import. For analysis of the case from a constitutional perspective, see, e.g., Laura S. Fitzgerald, *Beyond* Marbury: *Jurisdictional Self-Dealing in* Seminole Tribe, 52 VAND. L. REV. 407 (1999); Kit Kinports, *Implied Waiver After* Seminole Tribe, 82 MINN. L. REV. 793 (1998); Vicki C. Jackson, Seminole Tribe, *the Eleventh Amendment, and the Potential Evisceration of* Ex parte Young, 27 N.Y.U. L. REV. 495 (1997); Herbert Hovenkamp, *Judicial Restraint and Constitutional Federalism: The Supreme Court's* Lopez *and* Seminole Tribe *Decisions*, 96 COLUM. L. REV. 2213 (1996).

5. ***The "New Federalism" and the Rehnquist Court.*** In recent years, the Rehnquist Court favored a doctrine of new judicial federalism that protected state sovereignty from federal encroachment through judicially enforced constitutional limitations on national authority. Much of that jurisprudence stemmed from cases involving the Interstate Commerce Clause and the Tenth Amendment. *See, e.g., New York v. United States*, 505 U.S. 144 (1992); *United States v. Lopez*, 514 U.S. 549 (1995); *Printz v. United States*, 521 U.S. 898 (1997); *United States v. Morrison,* 529 U.S. 598 (2000). The Court used the Eleventh Amendment sovereign immunity defense to immunize states from individual suits for money damages in a number of policy arenas. *See, e.g., Alden v. Maine*, 527 U.S. 706 (1999); *Kimel v. Florida Board of Regents*, 528 U.S. 62 (2000); *Board of Trustees of the University of Alabama v. Garrett*, 531 U.S. 356 (2001). In its broad strokes, the *Seminole Tribe* decision could be seen as emblematic of that jurisprudence, as could the dissent in that case be perceived as illustrative of the "opposite" approach. *See, e.g.,* Ernest A. Young, *The Rehnquist Court's Two Federalisms*, 83 TEXAS L. REV. 1 (2004) (describing a "strong sovereignty" model often employed by the Rehnquist Court and a "weak autonomy" model sometimes used by Court members in dissent). For an argument that the Rehnquist Court's new federalism decisions effectively "eviscerated the powers of the U.S. Congress in favor of states' rights" across a wide range of legal and policy arenas, see, e.g., Norma M. Riccucci, *The U.S. Supreme Court's New Federalism and Its Impact on Antidiscrimination Legislation*, 23 REV. PUB. PERSONNEL ADMIN. 3 (2003).

D. Post-*Seminole* Environment

The Supreme Court's decision in *Seminole Tribe v. Florida* invalidated IGRA's centerpiece: the carefully constructed balance of tribal and state sovereignty. As the tribal industry continued to grow, the legal uncertainty created by *Seminole Tribe*'s impact on IGRA's tribal-state compacting process shaped compact negotiations. The Court's decision thus changed the politics of tribal gaming as well as the law.

1. Severability

A key question left unanswered by the Supreme Court was which of IGRA's provisions remained in effect: did the *Seminole Tribe* decision invalidate only the provisions setting forth the federal cause of action when a state refused to consent to suit, or did it invalidate § 2710(d) in its entirety? Perhaps more to the point, if a state refused to negotiate in good faith and refused to consent to suit, what alternatives were left for a tribe to exercise its right to conduct Class III gaming?

In a footnote, the *Seminole Tribe* Court noted that in affirming the Eleventh Circuit's decision, "[w]e do not here consider, and express no opinion upon, that portion of the decision below that provides a substitute remedy for a tribe bringing suit." *Seminole Tribe*, at 76 n.18. Unlike the Supreme Court, the Eleventh Circuit briefly grappled with the aftermath of invalidating IGRA's cause of action to enforce the state duty of good faith:

> As a result of our holding that the federal courts do not have jurisdiction to reach the issues brought by the tribes in these two suits, the procedures found in §§ 2710(d)(7)(A)(i) and (B)(i)–(vi) necessarily fail when an unconsenting state refuses to consent to suit.
>
> The final question we must resolve is whether all provisions for state involvement in class III gaming also fail, as the tribes contend. We hold that they do not. IGRA contains an explicit severability clause, [found in § 2721, which provides, "In the event that any section or provision of this chapter ... is held invalid, it is the intent of Congress that the remaining sections or provisions of this chapter ... shall continue in full force and effect"]; and we find no "strong evidence" to ignore that plain congressional directive. *See Alaska Airlines, Inc. v. Brock*, 480 U.S. 678, 686 (1987). Nevertheless, we are left with the question as to what procedure is left for an Indian tribe faced with a state that not only will not negotiate in good faith, but also will not consent to suit. The answer, gleaned from the statute, is simple. One hundred and eighty days after the tribe first requests negotiations with the state, the tribe may file suit in district court. If the state pleads an Eleventh Amendment defense, the suit is dismissed, and the tribe, pursuant to 25 U.S.C. § 2710(d)(7)(B)(vii), then may notify the Secretary of the Interior of the tribe's failure to negotiate a compact with the state. The Secretary then may prescribe regulations governing class III gaming on the tribe's lands. This solution conforms with IGRA and serves to achieve Congress' goals.

Seminole Tribe of Florida v. Florida, 11 F.3d 1016 (11th Cir. 1994). Is the answer to the question of what alternative a tribe may pursue when faced with an intransigent state as "simple" as the Eleventh Circuit concluded?

Alex Tallchief Skibine
Gaming on Indian Reservations:
Defining the Trustee's Duty in the Wake of Seminole Tribe v. Florida
29 Ariz. St. L.J. 121 (1997)

[Since IGRA's inception,] states have resisted signing Class III compacts with tribes. In 1996, they were finally rewarded in their struggle when the Supreme Court held in *Seminole Tribe v. Florida* that Congress did not have the power under the Indian Commerce Clause to abrogate the Eleventh Amendment sovereign immunity of a state. Therefore, IGRA could not grant a federal court jurisdiction over a state that did not consent to be sued by a tribe for a breach of good faith negotiation. The *Seminole* Court, however, refused to address the impact of its ruling on the remaining sections of the Act. This refusal has resulted in many legal uncertainties for Indian tribes confronting a state's invocation of sovereign immunity. Generally speaking, three possibilities confront these Indian tribes.

The first possibility, endorsed by the Eleventh Circuit and advocated by most tribes, is that a tribe faced with an Eleventh Amendment defense can directly ask the Secretary of the Interior to impose gaming procedures. There are two versions of this argument. Under the first version, the Secretary could issue his procedures pursuant to clause (vii) of §2710(d), which authorizes the Secretary to issue gaming procedures when a state refuses to cooperate. Under the second version, the Secretary could issue such gaming procedures pursuant to his general power to regulate Indian affairs under 25 U.S.C. §§2 and 9.

The second possibility, endorsed by most if not all of the states' attorneys general and governors, is that a tribe has no recourse once a state invokes its sovereign immunity.

A third possibility, endorsed by virtually no one but suggested by Justice Ginsburg during oral arguments in *Seminole*, is that all of §2710(d) should be considered stricken from the Act in cases in which a state raises its sovereign immunity defense. This would mean a return to the federal common law as enunciated in *California v. Cabazon Band of Mission Indians*.

It is impossible to decide the severability inquiry posed by *Seminole* without examining the law before the passage of IGRA and understanding the reasons IGRA was passed. Although various bills were introduced in Congress to regulate Indian gaming before 1988, the *Cabazon* decision provided the final and decisive incentive for congressional action. The findings and the declaration of policy contained in IGRA refer to a desire to promote tribal economic development, tribal self-sufficiency, and strong tribal governments, and to shield Indian gaming from organized crime. Yet the Indian tribes did not lobby Congress for the passage of gaming legislation. In fact, although the tribes did not have a unified view on IGRA, most of the tribes officially opposed the legislation at the time of passage.

The main reason for tribal opposition was IGRA's requirement of a tribal-state compact before any Class III gaming could be conducted. Most tribes considered any assertion of state jurisdiction inside their reservations as an intrusion on their right to self-government and viewed the tribal-state compact as bad precedent presaging further assumption of state jurisdiction in areas not related to gaming.

The enactment of IGRA is a landmark decision by Congress in the field of federal Indian law in two respects. The first one is the decision to venture at all into tribal-state civil jurisdictional conflicts and impose a federal statutory scheme in an area that had for some time been ruled by the federal common law. Besides the enactment of P.L. 280 in 1953 by a Congress bent on terminating the federal relationship between the Indian tribes and the federal government, Congress has never enacted a general law which has addressed the issue of state jurisdiction inside Indian reservations.

The second important aspect of IGRA is the decision to allow the tribes and the states to negotiate among themselves a solution to their jurisdictional disputes. In this respect, the requirement for a tribal-state compact represented a major step in the evolution of the trust relationship existing between the federal government and the tribes. The enactment of IGRA represented official congressional recognition that states and tribes do not have to be each other's "deadliest enemies" and that the states do have legitimate interests in sharing responsibilities for the regulation of gaming on Indian reservations. In effect, had the *Seminole* decision upheld its constitutionality, IGRA could have announced the beginning of the end of the exclusive federal role in regulating the relationship between the United States and the tribes.

Although IGRA recognized that the states should have an active and official role in this relationship, it did not represent an abdication of the federal government's trust responsibility to protect Indian interests. The tribes were not left to fend for themselves. Specifically, IGRA provided a mechanism to guarantee that tribes have judicial recourse to force the states to the negotiating table when the states failed to negotiate the compact in good faith. The traditional role of the trustee as protector of the tribal interests is also evident in the provision allowing the tribes to ask the Secretary of the Interior to promulgate gaming procedures when a state, which a [federal] court has found to have failed to negotiate in good faith, refuses to implement the solution recommended by a judicially appointed mediator.

The formulation of a policy coupling tribal-state compacts with a mechanism allowing the tribes to seek judicial review to ensure that states would negotiate in good faith was not a decision that Congress made lightly. It was made after five years of negotiation and consideration. In these years, Congress wavered between the idea of prohibiting Class III gaming, allowing it only under federal regulations, allowing it only under state regulations, or imposing a moratorium over it. In this respect, the scheme that the Supreme Court struck down in *Seminole* was a congressional recognition that it was time for the states and the tribes to resolve their problems by working together as equal partners without the federal government either dictating the relationship or preempting it altogether. Without the power to abrogate the Eleventh Amendment immunity of the states against suits brought by the tribes, however, it will be difficult for Congress to recognize the validity of the states' interests in Indian Country and at the same time strike a balance essential to the development of a tribal-state relationship based on mutual respect and equality.

The law on severability is both simple and problematic. The Supreme Court in its most recent opinion on the subject, *Alaska Airlines, Inc. v. Brock*, [480 U.S. 678 (1987),] enunciated four principles relevant to the severability inquiry. First, the Court reaffirmed the principle that "[a] court should refrain from invalidating more of the statute than is necessary." Second, the Court confirmed the role of congressional intent in the severability inquiry by reiterating that "unless it is evident that the Legislature would not have enacted those provisions which are within its power, independently of that which is not, the invalid part may be dropped if what is left is fully operative as a law." Third, the Court's inquiry focused on whether the remaining parts of the statute would remain fully operative after the removal of the unconstitutional provisions. "Congress could not have intended a constitutionally flawed provision to be severed from the remainder of the statute if the balance of the legislation is incapable of functioning independently.... The more relevant inquiry in evaluating severability is whether the statute will function in a manner consistent with the intent of Congress." Finally, the Court established a presumption of severability if the statute contains a severability clause. There is such a clause in [IGRA, found in §2721].

Once it is determined that part of IGRA can and has to be severed, the issue becomes how to sever. This is not an easy question. The severability analysis should focus on §2710(d)(7)(A)(i), the provision conferring federal court jurisdiction over tribal breach of good faith suits against states that the *Seminole* Court held unconstitutional, and the remainder of §2710(d)(7). The courts' reliance on legislative intent to determine severability has generated unpredictable results. There are three possible alternatives.

The first option is to strike [sub]sections (d)(7)(A)(i) and (B)(i)–(vi) but not (d)(7)(B)(vii), which is the clause allowing the Secretary of the Interior to impose regulations governing Class III gaming if the state refuses to accept the recommendations of the court-appointed mediator. The second option is to add clause (vii) to the language to be severed under the first option. This would mean that the Act would still require a tribal-state compact for Class III gaming but would not allow the tribes to go directly to the Secretary of the Interior once a state has invoked its sovereign immunity. This option would provide a state almost a veto power over Class III gaming. The third option is to sever all of § 2710(d), which requires a tribal-state compact for Class III gaming.

The unconstitutional part of the statute, § 2710(d)(7)(A)(i), appears to be so intertwined with § 2710(d)(7)(B) that the section cannot be considered "functionally independent" from the unconstitutional language and, therefore, should also be severed. Similarly, clause (vii) is so intertwined with the rest of § 2710(d)(7)(B) that it cannot survive on its own if the rest of the section is severed. Keeping clause (vii) would conform with the principle that "a court should refrain from invalidating more of the statute than is necessary." On the other hand, it is questionable whether clause (vii) can survive on its own when its very language refers to the lawsuits filed by the tribe. If the tribe cannot file the lawsuit, there can never be a mediator's report and, therefore, clause (vii) technically does not even take effect. In addition, under IGRA, the Secretary can only issue his gaming procedures once the federal district court has determined that the state has not negotiated in good faith. Congress has not delegated to the Secretary the power to determine whether a state has, in fact, failed to negotiated in good faith. Yet, for all practical purposes, this determination would have to be made by the Secretary before the gaming procedures can be imposed.

Once it is concluded that clause (vii) must also be severed from the Act, however, the severance of most of § 2710(d)(7) alters the substantive reach of the statute to such an extent that, arguably, the Act is not "functionally independent." Even if most of § 2710(d)(7) is determined to be functionally independent, [it is not clear that Congress would have enacted the rest of § 2710(d) without allowing a tribe to go directly to the Secretary of the Interior once a state had invoked its sovereign immunity]. It is difficult to believe that Congress would have passed an Act providing the tribes with no recourse. The Act and the Senate Report represent a strong endorsement of the right of tribes to engage in gaming activities. Although Congress at various points considered prohibiting Indian gaming or placing gaming under state regulations, it rejected these ideas. IGRA was passed in its present form because the tribes had enough advocates in Congress to prevent the enactment of legislation that would have allowed the states to veto any Class III gaming on Indian reservation. It seems that Congress would not have passed a statute which prohibited Class III gaming or made it subject to state consent.

Thus, a court could easily conclude that Congress would not have passed any portion of § 2710(d) if it knew that a state could veto Class III tribal gaming by simply invoking its sovereign immunity. Although this third option severs more provisions than the other two, it has the benefit of avoiding thorny questions concerning whether Congress would or would not have passed clause (vii) without the rest of § 2710(d)(7). Under this scenario, [in cases where the tribe and the state do not reach a compact and the state invokes its sovereign immunity to suit under § 2710(d)(7)(A)(i),] the law on Class III gaming would revert to *Cabazon*, [including the applicability of the Johnson Act in the absence of a tribal-state compact,] until such time as Congress once more addressed this issue.

Another solution, however, might allow most of § 2710(d), and even § 2710(d)(7), to remain operative. The court could determine that, even though the tribes cannot use clause (vii) alone after a state has invoked its sovereign immunity, the Secretary of the Interior could still issue gaming regulations using both IGRA and the Secretary's general power to regulate Indian affairs under 25 U.S.C. §§ 2 and 9. From a pure policy perspective, perhaps the best solution is to allow the Secretary to issue gaming procedures. Although the states have argued that the Secretary cannot be partial to their position because he is the trustee for the tribes, IGRA imposes on the Secretary the duty to consider the states' concerns. Nothing indicates that the Secretary could not be trusted, first, to make a fair determination that a state has not negotiated in good faith, and, second, to select an impartial mediator to resolve the dispute in the same fashion as originally envisioned under IGRA.

While it is impossible to know with certainty how the courts will rule on severability, it is clear that not allowing the tribes any recourse in cases of bad faith negotiations by a state would not have comported with the intent of Congress in enacting the Indian Gaming Regulatory Act.

United States v. Spokane Tribe of Indians
139 F.3d 1297 (9th Cir. 1998)

KOZINSKI, Circuit Judge.

The Spokane Tribe of Indians was operating a bingo hall and some card games at the time IGRA was passed but wanted to expand its operations. So the Tribe began to negotiate a compact with the State of Washington. Negotiations did not go well and broke down altogether after two years. As IGRA then allowed, the Tribe sued the State for failure to negotiate in good faith. Following the Supreme Court's decision in *Seminole Tribe,* the State invoked its newfound Eleventh Amendment immunity and brought the Tribe's suit to a sudden end. While its suit against the State was pending, the Tribe had stepped up its casino operations and started offering a wider range of games. Without a compact in place, the gaming operations violated IGRA and the United States brought this action to put a stop to them.

Does the Supreme Court's decision in *Seminole Tribe,* striking down another section of the same statute, affect the court's authority to enjoin Indian gaming thereunder? To answer this question we must first examine the history and structure of IGRA to determine the extent to which its parts are mutually dependent.

In 1987 the Supreme Court held that states were not authorized to regulate gambling in Indian country. States disliked *Cabazon* and so the following year Congress passed IGRA. The new law gave states considerable say over gambling in Indian country, but the Act was not an unmitigated defeat for tribes. Rather, the law closely balanced the interests of states and tribes. Under IGRA, class III activities — the most lucrative kind — must be authorized by a tribal ordinance approved by the National Indian Gaming Commission, permitted by the state for some person or organization, covered by a tribal-state compact. A different section of IGRA, [18 U.S.C. § 1166,] makes it a federal crime to violate state gambling law in Indian country unless authorized by a compact. The tribal-state compact is pivotal to the IGRA provisions governing class III gaming. Without a compact in place, a tribe may not engage in class III gaming. To guard against the possibility that states might choose not to negotiate, or to negotiate in bad faith, Congress included a complex set of procedures designed to protect tribes from recalcitrant states. In 1996, the Supreme Court [in *Seminole Tribe*] emasculated these procedures by holding that tribes are constitutionally precluded from bringing suit against recalcitrant states that do not consent to being sued. The Supreme Court did not consider whether the rest of IGRA survives.

IGRA does contain a severability clause, § 2721. This creates a presumption that if one section is found unconstitutional, the rest of the statute remains valid. But that presumption is not conclusive; we must still strike down other portions of the statute if we find strong evidence that Congress did not mean for them to remain in effect without the invalid section. The question we must ask is this: Would Congress have enacted IGRA had it known it could not give tribes the right to sue states that refuse to negotiate? If the answer is yes, then the rest of IGRA remains valid. If the answer is no, things become more complicated, as we must then ask which other provisions of IGRA are called into question, and under what circumstances.

Figuring out why Congress passed a piece of legislation is hard enough. Figuring out whether it would have passed that legislation in the absence of one of its key provisions is even harder. Yet, figure we must.

Under *Cabazon,* the states had little power to regulate gambling on tribal land. IGRA shifted power to the states — a major blow to tribal interests. Under IGRA states could effectively veto any class III gaming on Indian land simply by refusing to negotiate a compact. Section 2710(d)(7) restored some leverage to the tribes by giving them the right to sue recalcitrant states and thereby forcing them to enter into a compact. It is quite clear from the structure of the statute that the tribe's right to sue the state is a key part of a carefully crafted scheme balancing the interests of the tribes and the states. It therefore seems highly unlikely that Congress would have passed one part without the other, leaving the tribes essentially powerless.

IGRA's legislative history strongly supports this inference. The Senate report on S. 555, which became IGRA, repeatedly emphasizes that the bill balances the interests of tribes and states. *See, e.g.,* S.Rep. No. 100-446, at 1–2 ("[T]he issue has been how best to preserve the right of tribes to self-government while, at the same time, to protect both the tribes and the gaming public from unscrupulous persons."); *id.* at 5 ("[T]he Committee has attempted to balance the need for sound enforcement of gaming laws and regulations, with the strong Federal interest in preserving the sovereign rights of tribal governments[.]"); *id.* at 6 ("This legislation is intended to provide a means by which tribal and State governments can realize their unique and individual governmental objectives [.]"). In describing the balancing, the report refers specifically to the provision for suing states:

> Section [2710(d)(7)] grants a tribe the right to sue a State if compact negotiations are not concluded. This section is the result of the Committee balancing the interests and rights of tribes to engage in gaming against the interests of States in regulating such gaming.... [T]he issue before the Committee was how best to encourage States to deal fairly with tribes as sovereign governments. The Committee elected, as the least offensive option, to grant tribes the right to sue a State if a compact is not negotiated.

When the Eleventh Amendment became a concern after IGRA became law, Senator Daniel Inouye, chair of the Senate Committee on Indian Affairs and one of S. 555's authors, explicitly answered our question [during oversight hearings on IGRA's implementation]. He explained that Congress would not have passed IGRA in the form it did, had it known that tribes wouldn't be allowed to sue the states:

> Because I believe that if we had known at the time we were considering the bill — if we had known that this proposal of tribal state compacts that came from the States and was strongly supported by the States, would later be rendered virtually meaningless by the action of those states which have sought to avoid entering into compacts by asserting the Tenth and Eleventh Amendments to defeat federal court jurisdiction, we would not have gone down this path.

He [also] said, "If the courts rule that the Eleventh Amendment would prohibit the tribal governments from suing State officials, then you've got a piece of paper as a law."

IGRA as passed thus struck a finely tuned balance between the interests of the states and the tribes. Most likely it would not have been enacted if that balance had tipped conclusively in favor of the states, and without IGRA the states would have no say whatever over Indian gaming. In our case, the Tribe claims it attempted to negotiate in good faith, but that attempt failed because of bad faith on the part of the State. The Tribe thus fulfilled its obligation under IGRA. The Tribe then sued the State, as it was entitled to under the statute, but found it could not continue that suit after *Seminole Tribe*. As far as we can tell on the record before us, nothing now protects the Tribe if the State refuses to bargain in good faith or at all; the State holds all the cards (so to speak). Congress meant to guard against this very situation when it created IGRA's interlocking checks and balances.

Does this mean that the surviving portion of IGRA is invalid? Not quite. We deal here only with the narrow question presented by this interlocutory appeal: Is a preliminary injunction [against Class III gaming without a compact] authorized in these circumstances? We hold merely that the class III gaming provisions can't form the basis for an injunction against the Tribe on the record before us.

IGRA, however, remains valid and, under some circumstances, it may function close enough to what Congress had in mind to be enforceable by way of injunction. Most obviously, a state might waive sovereign immunity and allow a tribe to sue it in district court; IGRA would then function exactly as intended and there would be no reason not to give it full effect. Here, however, Washington invoked its rights under the Eleventh Amendment and caused the Tribe's suit to be dismissed, distorting the IGRA process. Or, the United States might sue on behalf of a tribe and force the state into a compact. If it did so, IGRA could work as intended and any IGRA violation by the tribe could be enjoined.

Other circumstances would present closer cases. Before *Seminole Tribe* reached the Supreme Court, the Eleventh Circuit anticipated the Eleventh Amendment problem. Unlike the Supreme Court, the circuit then considered what happens next. It held that if a tribe sues a state and the state pleads the Eleventh, the tribe may then notify the Secretary of the Interior, who may address the problem by regulation.

The Tribe here has already applied to the Secretary several times asking him to prescribe regulations, so far with no luck. The Department of the Interior has issued an advance notice of proposed rulemaking, suggesting it is busily considering what to do in situations such as these. The notice cites the Eleventh Circuit decision as authority supporting intervention by the Department. It also cites an earlier opinion of ours, *Spokane Tribe of Indians v. Washington*, 28 F.3d 991 (9th Cir. 1994), *vacated*, 517 U.S. 1129 (1996). There we considered the Eleventh Circuit's suggestion and said that "such a result would pervert the congressional plan," turning the Secretary of the Interior into "a federal czar." However, that was in the context of our (incorrect) assumption that tribes could sue states. We were pointing out that the Eleventh Circuit's suggestion would not be as close to Congress's intent as the scheme Congress in fact passed. True. But the Supreme Court has now told us that Congress's scheme is unconstitutional; the Eleventh Circuit's suggestion is a lot closer to Congress's intent than mechanically enforcing IGRA against tribes even when states refuse to negotiate. Whether or not such rulemaking would bring IGRA's operation close enough to Congress's intent to save the statute depends on the as yet undisclosed details of the proposed regulations.

None of the circumstances that might justify enforcing IGRA according to its terms appears to be present here. We are left, then, with a tribe that believes it has followed IGRA faithfully and has no legal recourse against a state that allegedly hasn't bargained in good faith. Congress did not intentionally create this situation and would not have countenanced it had it known then what we know now. Under the circumstances, IGRA's provisions governing class III gaming may not be enforced against the Tribe. However, because the court and the parties below operated under incorrect legal assumptions (largely because *Seminole Tribe* had not yet been decided), it's possible that there are facts of which we are ignorant. For instance, perhaps the Department of Justice had evidence that it was the Tribe that had failed to bargain in good faith. Or perhaps the Department of the Interior determined that no class III gaming should be allowed on the reservation because state law prohibits all such gambling. We cannot say with certainty that IGRA does not support an injunction against the Tribe; it simply doesn't on this record. If the United States persists in seeking relief, the district court will have to revisit the question and engage in a new factual investigation guided by a correct legal analysis.

Notes and Questions

1. *Severability.* Is Professor Skibine's analysis of the alternatives concerning IGRA's severability clause incontrovertible? Which alternative do you think best keeps to Congress's intent?

Skibine concluded that "[f]rom a pure policy perspective, perhaps the best solution is to allow the Secretary to issue gaming procedures." Why is this the best policy solution? In addition to the Interior Secretary's power under IGRA, Skibine referenced the Secretary's power under 25 U.S.C. §§ 2 and 9. Section 2 provides, "The Commissioner of Indian Affairs shall, under the direction of the Secretary of the Interior, and agreeably to such regulations as the President may prescribe, have the management of all Indian affairs and of all matters arising out of Indian relations." Section 9 authorizes the President to "prescribe such regulations as he may think fit for carrying into effect the various provisions of any act relating to Indian affairs, and for the settlement of the accounts of Indian affairs." How do these sections bolster the Secretary's power to promulgate gaming regulations? Does the Secretary have authority to make a determination whether the state has fulfilled its good-faith duty? These questions are addressed in the next section on administrative "compacts."

Do you agree with Skibine's conclusion that the Interior Secretary can fulfill the federal government's trust responsibility to tribes and still respect state sovereignty (or, put the other way, that the Secretary can respect state sovereignty and still fulfill the trust responsibility)? Does giving the Secretary authority to issue gaming regulations simply substitute the vagaries of federal politics for the vagaries of state politics? What would be the tribe's recourse if the Secretary refused to issue regulations?

Note that in *United States v. Spokane Tribe* the court limited its holding to precluding the federal government from shutting down the tribe's Class III operations in order to enforce IGRA's compact requirement. How did the court dodge the "big" question concerning the severability and the operations of the remainder of IGRA? Did the fact that the Interior Secretary was "busily considering" remedial administrative regulations play into the court's decision? Should it have?

2. **Seminole Tribe "*fixes.*"** In *United States v. Spokane Tribe*, the Ninth Circuit identified a number of possible "fixes" in the wake of *Seminole Tribe*:

> We note, however, that the courts aren't the only, or even the most appropriate, forum for solving the problems caused by *Seminole Tribe*. Several Executive

Branch agencies may be able to patch up the situation. The Department of the Interior, for example, might promulgate regulations that take the place of the compact process. Or, the Department of Justice might resuscitate the statute by prosecuting tribes only when it determines that the state has negotiated in good faith, or by suing states on behalf of the tribes when it determines that the states are refusing to comply with their obligations under IGRA. These alternatives, and others we haven't thought of, might provide avenues for salvaging IGRA. And, of course, Congress could return to the statute and come up with a new scheme that is both equitable and constitutional.

Spokane Tribe, 139 F.3d at 1302. Are the suggested avenues legally feasible? Politically feasible?

3.   **Chemehuevi Indian Tribe v. Wilson.** One of the possible "fixes" noted by the Ninth Circuit in *United States v. Spokane Tribe* was that the U.S. Department of Justice might sue states on behalf of tribes when the state refuses to negotiate a compact and to consent to suit. The district court in *Chemehuevi Indian Tribe v. Wilson*, 987 F. Supp. 804 (N.D. Cal. 1997), endorsed this approach. In that case, California Governor Pete Wilson refused to negotiate with seven tribes until he concluded a "model" compact with the Pala Band of Mission Indians. Wilson also demanded that the seven tribes cease all Class III gaming until a compact was concluded. The tribes requested the U.S. Attorney in the Northern District of California to bring suit on their behalf; when the U.S. Attorney declined and the Justice Department was unresponsive, the tribes sought a judgment declaring that the federal government has a mandatory duty to represent the tribes in their claim against the state. The court rejected the federal government's argument based on prosecutorial discretion, relying on the trust relationship between the U.S. and tribes, as well as 25 U.S.C. § 175, which provides, "In all States and Territories where there are reservations or allotted Indians the United States attorney shall represent them in all suits at law and in equity." The court reasoned,

> In the over 100 years of its existence, § 175 has been interpreted in only a handful of reported cases.... No reported case has relied on § 175 to order a United States Attorney to file suit on behalf of an Indian to avoid the government's breaching a fiduciary duty.

> The only case which analyzes the circumstances under which the United States Attorney might have a duty to sue on behalf of Indians is *Shoshone-Bannock Tribes v. Reno*, 56 F.3d 1476 (D.C. Cir. 1995). In affirming a lower court decision dismissing the Shoshone-Bannock Tribes' complaint, the Court of Appeals held that neither 25 U.S.C. § 175 nor the government's fiduciary relationship with the Tribes limited the Attorney General's discretion to refuse to assert the Tribes' claims to certain water rights. The Shoshone-Bannock Tribes had requested the United States to sue on their behalf to enforce certain water rights the Tribes claimed under the Treaty of Fort Bridger. After conducting an investigation, the Interior Department concluded that the Tribes' claims were not meritorious and recommended that the Justice Department not assert them. The Tribes then sued the Attorney General for declaratory and injunctive relief and for damages. [Though] troubled by the fact that § 175 lacked standards for evaluating the Attorney General's litigation decisions and terming the Shoshone-Bannock claims meritless, the Court concluded, "there is surely nothing in § 175, or any other federal statute, obligating government attorneys to file what they believe are meritless claims." The Court noted that the Tribes have "every right" to "pursue their claim on their own behalf."

The principal concerns which led the Court of Appeals to conclude § 175 did not provide a duty of representation for the Shoshone-Bannock compel the opposite conclusion here. The federal defendants here do not claim that the plaintiffs' claim is meritless. To the contrary, plaintiffs' claim that the State of California has violated IGRA by refusing to negotiate a compact as required by § 2710(d)(3)(A) appears supported by a literal reading of the statute. Far from having "every right" to pursue this claim on their own behalf, plaintiffs have no legal means to do so. A duty on behalf of the United States to sue the State to bring it to the bargaining table can certainly be implied from IGRA, since it appears that that is the only legal remedy available to the plaintiff Tribes to seek the benefits Congress intended them to have and to preserve the balance Congress carefully struck between the interests of the states and the tribes. Such a duty is also supported by the fiduciary relationship the federal defendants have with the plaintiffs. Whatever the full extent of the fiduciary relationship, it certainly should include a duty to represent the plaintiffs in a situation where, absent representation, the Tribes will have no legal remedy with which to bring the State to the bargaining table and obtain the benefits of IGRA as Congress intended.

The plaintiffs merely desire that the federal defendants sue the State to begin the almost mechanical process that will produce either a negotiated compact, a compact selected by a court-appointed mediator, or regulations permitting gaming promulgated by the Secretary of the Interior. Nothing in IGRA permits a state to set preconditions to compact negotiations with the Indian tribes.

Accordingly, the Court declares that the federal defendants have a mandatory duty to prosecute this action against the State of California on plaintiffs' behalf, to enforce plaintiffs' rights under IGRA to negotiate a compact.

Chemehuevi Indian Tribe, at 807–09. Similar to the Ninth Circuit, the district court concluded that IGRA's legislative history "compels the conclusion that a federal remedy is necessary to preserve Congress's balancing of tribal and state interests and to secure the benefits of IGRA to the tribes":

Congress recognized that for many tribes, gaming income "often means the difference between an adequate governmental program and a skeletal program that is totally dependent on Federal funding." Congress recognized the potential unfairness in the compacting process to the tribes and the potential for subjecting tribes to unwarranted state control. Congress concluded that giving a tribe a federal court remedy if a state refused to negotiate in good faith was essential to encouraging the states to deal fairly with the tribes. As Senator McCain stated: "As the debate unfolded, it became clear that the interests of the states and of the gaming industry extended far beyond their expressed concern about organized crime. Their true interest was protection of their own games from a new source of economic competition.... [T]he State [sic] and gaming industry have always come to the table with the position that what is theirs is theirs and what the Tribe [sic] have is negotiable." Denying the federal remedy Congress provided could produce the "unwarranted state control" Congress feared. It would permit states to exclude tribes, *de facto,* from class III gaming, or to subject the Indians to burdensome delay and economic hardship by controlling the timing and content of compact negotiations while state gaming activities continue.

Id. at 808 n.4. The court also noted that it wasn't entirely clear that the tribes could not conduct Class III gaming until a compact was in place, observing that § 2710(d)(3)(A) states, "Any Indian Tribe having jurisdiction over the Indian lands upon which a class III gaming activity *is being conducted,* or is to be conducted, shall request the State in which such lands are located to enter into negotiations for the purpose of entering into a Tribal-State compact governing the conduct of gaming activities" (emphasis added).

Is the *Chemehuevi* court's solution legally feasible? Politically feasible?

2. Administrative "Compacts"

Following the Supreme Court's decision in *Seminole Tribe,* the Interior Secretary promulgated regulations that allowed the Secretary to issue administrative rules governing Class III gaming when a tribe and state fail to voluntarily negotiate a compact and a state invokes its sovereign immunity from suit under IGRA. The regulations replicated the negotiation and mediation process set forth in IGRA, adjusted only to reflect tribes' inability to sue in federal court if a state refuses to waive its sovereign immunity. The regulations relied on the Secretary's authority under 25 U.S.C. §§ 2, 9, and 2710.

Class III Gaming Procedures
25 C.F.R. pt. 291

§ 291.1 Purpose and scope. The regulations in this part establish procedures that the Secretary will use to promulgate rules for the conduct of Class III Indian gaming when:

(a) A State and an Indian tribe are unable to voluntarily agree to a compact; and

(b) The State has asserted its immunity from suit brought by an Indian tribe under 25 U.S.C. 2710(d)(7)(B).

§ 291.2 Definitions

(a) All terms have the same meaning as set forth in the definitional section of IGRA, 25 U.S.C. section 2703(1)–(10).

(b) The term "compact" includes renewal of an existing compact.

§ 291.3 When may an Indian tribe ask the Secretary to issue Class III gaming procedures? An Indian tribe may ask the Secretary to issue Class III gaming procedures when the following steps have taken place:

(a) The Indian tribe submitted a written request to the State to enter into negotiations to establish a Tribal-State compact governing the conduct of Class III gaming activities;

(b) The State and the Indian tribe failed to negotiate a compact 180 days after the State received the Indian tribe's request;

(c) The Indian tribe initiated a cause of action in Federal district court against the State alleging that the State did not respond, or did not respond in good faith, to the request of the Indian tribe to negotiate such a compact;

(d) The State raised an Eleventh Amendment defense to the tribal action; and

(e) The Federal district court dismissed the action due to the State's sovereign immunity under the Eleventh Amendment.

§291.4 What must a proposal requesting Class III gaming procedures contain? A proposal requesting Class III gaming procedures must include the following information:

(a) The full name, address, and telephone number of the Indian tribe submitting the proposal;

(b) A copy of the authorizing resolution from the Indian tribe submitting the proposal;

(c) A copy of the Indian tribe's gaming ordinance or resolution approved by the NIGC in accordance with 25 U.S.C. 2710, if any;

(d) A copy of the Indian tribe's organic documents, if any;

(e) A copy of the Indian tribe's written request to the State to enter into compact negotiations, along with the Indian tribe's proposed compact, if any;

(f) A copy of the State's response to the tribal request and/or proposed compact, if any;

(g) A copy of the tribe's Complaint (with attached exhibits, if any); the State's Motion to Dismiss; any Response by the tribe to the State's Motion to Dismiss; any Opinion or other written documents from the court regarding the State's Motion to Dismiss; and the Court's Order of dismissal;

(h) The Indian tribe's factual and legal authority for the scope of gaming specified in paragraph (j)(13) of this section;

(i) Regulatory scheme for the State's oversight role, if any, in monitoring and enforcing compliance; and

(j) Proposed procedures under which the Indian tribe will conduct Class III gaming activities, including:

(1) A certification that the tribe's accounting procedures are maintained in accordance with American Institute of Certified Public Accountants Standards for Audits of Casinos, including maintenance of books and records in accordance with Generally Accepted Accounting Principles and applicable NIGC regulations;

(2) A reporting system for the payment of taxes and fees in a timely manner and in compliance with Internal Revenue Code and Bank Secrecy Act requirements;

(3) Preparation of financial statements covering all financial activities of the Indian tribe's gaming operations;

(4) Internal control standards designed to ensure fiscal integrity of gaming operations as set forth in 25 CFR Part 542;

(5) Provisions for records retention, maintenance, and accessibility;

(6) Conduct of games, including patron requirements, posting of game rules, and hours of operation;

(7) Procedures to protect the integrity of the rules for playing games;

(8) Rules governing employees of the gaming operation, including code of conduct, age requirements, conflict of interest provisions, licensing requirements, and such background investigations of all management officials and key employees as are required by IGRA, NIGC regulations, and applicable tribal gaming laws;

(9) Policies and procedures that protect the health and safety of patrons and employees and that address insurance and liability issues, as well as safety systems for fire and emergency services at all gaming locations;

(10) Surveillance procedures and security personnel and systems capable of monitoring movement of cash and chips, entrances and exits of gaming facilities, and other critical areas of any gaming facility;

(11) An administrative and/or tribal judicial process to resolve disputes between gaming establishment, employees and patrons, including a process to protect the rights of individuals injured on gaming premises by reason of negligence in the operation of the facility;

(12) Hearing procedures for licensing purposes;

(13) A list of gaming activities proposed to be offered by the Indian tribe at its gaming facilities;

(14) A description of the location of proposed gaming facilities;

(15) A copy of the Indian tribe's liquor ordinance approved by the Secretary if intoxicants, as used in 18 U.S.C. 1154, will be served in the gaming facility;

(16) Provisions for a tribal regulatory gaming entity, independent of gaming management;

(17) Provisions for tribal enforcement and investigatory mechanisms, including the imposition of sanctions, monetary penalties, closure, and an administrative appeal process relating to enforcement and investigatory actions;

(18) The length of time the procedures will remain in effect; and

(19) Any other provisions deemed necessary by the Indian tribe.

§ 291.5 Where must the proposal requesting Class III gaming procedures be filed? Any proposal requesting Class III gaming procedures must be filed with the Director, Indian Gaming Management Staff, Bureau of Indian Affairs, U.S. Department of the Interior, MS 2070-MIB, 1849 C Street NW, Washington, DC 20240.

§ 291.6 What must the Secretary do upon receiving a proposal? Upon receipt of a proposal requesting Class III gaming procedures, the Secretary must:

(a) Within 15 days, notify the Indian tribe in writing that the proposal has been received, and whether any information required under § 291.4 is missing;

(b) Within 30 days of receiving a complete proposal, notify the Indian tribe in writing whether the Indian tribe meets the eligibility requirements in § 291.3. The Secretary's eligibility determination is final for the Department.

§ 291.7 What must the Secretary do if it has been determined that the Indian tribe is eligible to request Class III gaming procedures?

(a) If the Secretary determines that the Indian tribe is eligible to request Class III gaming procedures and that the Indian tribe's proposal is complete, the Secretary must submit the Indian tribe's proposal to the Governor and the Attorney General of the State where the gaming is proposed.

(b) The Governor and Attorney General will have 60 days to comment on:

(1) Whether the State is in agreement with the Indian tribe's proposal;

(2) Whether the proposal is consistent with relevant provisions of the laws of the State;

(3) Whether contemplated gaming activities are permitted in the State for any purposes, by any person, organization, or entity.

(c) The Secretary will also invite the State's Governor and Attorney General to submit an alternative proposal to the Indian tribe's proposed Class III gaming procedures.

§ 291.8 What must the Secretary do at the expiration of the 60-day comment period if the State has not submitted an alternative proposal?

(a) Upon expiration of the 60-day comment period specified in § 291.7, if the State has not submitted an alternative proposal, the Secretary must review the Indian tribe's proposal to determine:

(1) Whether all requirements of § 291.4 are adequately addressed;

(2) Whether Class III gaming activities will be conducted on Indian lands over which the Indian tribe has jurisdiction;

(3) Whether contemplated gaming activities are permitted in the State for any purposes by any person, organization, or entity;

(4) Whether the proposal is consistent with relevant provisions of the laws of the State;

(5) Whether the proposal is consistent with the trust obligations of the United States to the Indian tribe;

(6) Whether the proposal is consistent with all applicable provisions of IGRA; and

(7) Whether the proposal is consistent with provisions of other applicable Federal laws.

(b) Within 60 days of the expiration of the 60-day comment period in § 291.7, the Secretary must notify the Indian tribe, the Governor, and the Attorney General of the State in writing that he/she has:

(1) Approved the proposal if the Secretary determines that there are no objections to the Indian tribe's proposal; or

(2) Identified unresolved issues and areas of disagreements in the proposal, and invite the Indian tribe, the Governor and the Attorney General to participate in an informal conference, within 30 days of notification unless the parties agree otherwise, to resolve identified unresolved issues and areas of disagreement.

(c) Within 30 days of the informal conference, the Secretary must prepare and mail to the Indian tribe, the Governor and the Attorney General:

(1) A written report that summarizes the results of the informal conference; and

(2) A final decision either setting forth the Secretary's proposed Class III gaming procedures for the Indian tribe, or disapproving the proposal for any of the reasons in paragraph (a) of this section.

§ 291.9 What must the Secretary do at the end of the 60-day comment period if the State offers an alternative proposal for Class III gaming procedures? Within 30 days of receiving the State's alternative proposal, the Secretary must appoint a mediator who:

(a) Has no official, financial, or personal conflict of interest with respect to the issues in controversy; and

(b) Must convene a process to resolve differences between the two proposals.

§ 291.10 What is the role of the mediator appointed by the Secretary?

(a) The mediator must ask the Indian tribe and the State to submit their last best proposal for Class III gaming procedures.

(b) After giving the Indian tribe and the State an opportunity to be heard and present information supporting their respective positions, the mediator must select from the two proposals the one that best comports with the terms of IGRA and any other applicable Federal law. The mediator must submit the proposal selected to the Indian tribe, the State, and the Secretary.

§ 291.11 What must the Secretary do upon receiving the proposal selected by the mediator? Within 60 days of receiving the proposal selected by the mediator, the Secretary must do one of the following:

(a) Notify the Indian tribe, the Governor and the Attorney General in writing of his/her decision to approve the proposal for Class III gaming procedures selected by the mediator; or

(b) Notify the Indian tribe, the Governor and the Attorney General in writing of his/her decision to disapprove the proposal selected by the mediator for any of the following reasons:

(1) The requirements of § 291.4 are not adequately addressed;

(2) Gaming activities would not be conducted on Indian lands over which the Indian tribe has jurisdiction;

(3) Contemplated gaming activities are not permitted in the State for any purpose by any person, organization, or entity;

(4) The proposal is not consistent with relevant provisions of the laws of the State;

(5) The proposal is not consistent with the trust obligations of the United States to the Indian tribe;

(6) The proposal is not consistent with applicable provisions of IGRA; or

(7) The proposal is not consistent with provisions of other applicable Federal laws.

(c) If the Secretary rejects the mediator's proposal under paragraph (b) of this section, he/she must prescribe appropriate procedures within 60 days under which Class III gaming may take place that comport with the mediator's selected proposal as much as possible, the provisions of IGRA, and the relevant provisions of the laws of the State.

§ 291.12 Who will monitor and enforce tribal compliance with the Class III gaming procedures? The Indian tribe and the State may have an agreement regarding monitoring and enforcement of tribal compliance with the Indian tribe's Class III gaming procedures. In addition, under existing law, the NIGC will monitor and enforce tribal compliance with the Indian tribe's Class III gaming procedures.

§ 291.13 When do Class III gaming procedures for an Indian tribe become effective? Upon approval of Class III gaming procedures for the Indian tribe under either § 291.8(b), § 291.8(c), or § 291.11(a), the Indian tribe shall have 90 days in which to approve and execute the Secretarial procedures and forward its approval and execution to the Secretary, who shall publish notice of their approval in the Federal Register. The procedures take effect upon their publication in the Federal Register.

§ 291.14 How can Class III gaming procedures approved by the Secretary be amended? An Indian tribe may ask the Secretary to amend approved Class III gaming procedures by submitting an amendment proposal to the Secretary. The Secretary must review the proposal by following the approval process for initial tribal proposals, except that the requirements of § 291.3 are not applicable and he/she may waive the requirements of § 291.4 to the extent they do not apply to the amendment request.

§ 291.15 How long do Class III gaming procedures remain in effect? Class III gaming procedures remain in effect for the duration specified in the procedures or until amended pursuant to § 291.14.

Notes and Questions

1.   The Secretary's authority to issue administrative Class III gaming rules. Some commentators have questioned the Interior Secretary's power under IGRA to issue administrative "compacts." As noted above, the Secretary relied on Congress's grant of authority through three federal statutes: 25 U.S.C. §§ 2, 9, and 2710.

Prior to the Secretary's promulgation of the rules, Professor Skibine defended the regulations as an appropriate response to *Seminole Tribe* and a valid exercise of both federal power and delegated administrative authority:

> In determining that he has the power to issue gaming procedures, the Secretary of the Interior does not have to rely exclusively on IGRA. He can also rely on 25 U.S.C. §§ 2 and 9. Under these sections, the Secretary has wide discretion to manage Indian affairs. Ever since these statutes were enacted in the 1830s, they have served as the source of the Secretary's administrative authority in discharging the federal government's trust obligations to Indians.

> While the Secretary could not issue gaming regulations pursuant to §§ 2 and 9 if his authority had been preempted by IGRA, IGRA only mandates that the Secretary act in accordance with the Act if a state consents to be sued under the Act. Once the state has invoked its sovereign immunity, IGRA's litigation mechanism to enforce a tribal-state compact no longer applies, and the Secretary should be able to act under other authority.

> The Secretary's authority under §§ 2 and 9 is not, however, plenary. The Secretary cannot issue a regulation in contravention of federal law, [or] that infringes on the tribes' power of self-government [without specific authorization]. Moreover, an argument can be made that unless authorized by other legislation, the Secretary cannot grant additional rights to Indians in contravention of state law solely on the basis of his authority under §§ 2 and 9. In issuing gaming regulations pursuant to §§ 2 and 9, however, the Secretary would not create new tribal rights in derogation of state law. The tribes have a right to good faith negotiations with the state and a right to conduct Class III gaming pursuant to secretarial regulations in the absence of such good faith negotiations. [Further], IGRA can be viewed as giving trust status to Indian gaming revenues so that they can be considered trust resources. IGRA is replete with congressional pronouncements expressing a desire to promote tribal self-sufficiency, economic development, and self-government through gaming opportunities.

Skibine, *Gaming on Indian Reservations*, at 142–43. Are you convinced by Skibine's reasoning?

2.   Administrative rules without a finding of bad faith? Though Part 291 tracks IGRA's cause of action, note that it allows secretarial action to be triggered by the state's assertion of sovereign immunity, not a finding that the state failed to negotiate in good faith, as required under IGRA. One criticism of the proposed regulations was that IGRA does not authorize the Secretary to determine that a state has failed to negotiate in good faith. The regulations as adopted sought to mitigate that concern by eliminating the requirement that the Secretary make a finding prior to issuing the administrative "compact" on whether the state negotiated in "good faith." U.S. Dep't of the Interior, *Fact Sheet on Indian Gaming and New Interior Regulations*, at http://www.doi.gov/news/ archives/fctgam.html.

Critics of the regulations contended that the regulations therefore remove the incentive for the *tribe* to negotiate in good faith. If a tribe brings suit against the state under

IGRA (assuming the state consents to suit), the tribe risks losing its claim—the federal court could find that despite the fact that a compact was not reached, the state fulfilled its duty to negotiate in good faith. Upon such a finding, under IGRA, the court should simply dismiss the tribe's suit. As a practical matter, presumably the onus would be on the tribe to reduce its bargaining demands in order for any compact negotiations to proceed. The risk of a finding that the state fulfilled its duty—and the resulting weakening of the tribe's bargaining position—serves as an incentive for tribes to negotiate with states rather than to sue on unsettled matters. By providing an administrative process and remedy where there may be no bad faith on the part of the state, the regulations arguably inappropriately increase tribes' bargaining position: if the state doesn't give into to the tribe's demands, the tribe will seek administrative rules from the Secretary. What are the arguments on the other side of this issue?

　　3.　　*The Secretary's impartiality.* Other challenges to the regulations have centered on whether the Secretary, presumably bound by the federal government's trust obligation to tribes, can be "fair" to state interests when setting rules for Class III gaming. *See, e.g.,* Rebecca S. Lindner-Cornelius, Comment, *The Secretary of the Interior as Referee: The States, Indian Nations, and How Gambling Led to the Illegality of the Secretary of the Interior's Regulations in 25 C.F.R. § 291,* 84 Marq. L. Rev. 685 (2001); Joe Lexague, Note, *Indian Gaming and Tribal-State Negotiations: Who Should Decide the Issue of Bad Faith?,* 25 J. Legis. 77 (1999). (One also might argue the opposite: that the federal government's trust obligation does not guarantee that the Interior Secretary will be above favoring state interests.)

　　4.　　**Texas v. United States.** *Texas v. United States,* 362 F. Supp. 2d 765 (W.D. Tex. 2004), involved the Kickapoo Traditional Tribe of Texas' efforts to negotiate a Class III gaming compact. After Texas refused to negotiate a compact, the tribe filed suit in federal court. While the case was pending, the Supreme Court decided *Seminole Tribe v. Florida,* and the case was dismissed on the state's motion. In 2003, the tribe filed an application for an administrative "compact" under 25 C.F.R. pt. 291. After determining that the tribe was eligible for an administrative "compact," the Interior Secretary invited Texas to provide comments on the proposed administrative rules or to submit an alternative proposal for the tribe's operation of Class III gaming. Instead, the state filed suit in federal court challenging the Secretary's authority to issue an administrative "compact" under Part 291.

　　The district court, though dismissing the state's challenge on ripeness grounds, opined that the Secretary's regulations were an appropriate exercise of authority granted through IGRA as well as 25 U.S.C. §§ 2 and 9:

> Under the two-step inquiry established in *Chevron,* courts must first ask whether Congress has spoken directly to the precise issue. In this case, there is no dispute that Congress has not addressed this issue. The second step then requires court to defer to the agency's interpretation if it is reasonable. . . .
>
> Section 9 of the general-authority statutes for the Bureau of Indian Affairs grants authority to the President of the United States to "prescribe such regulations as he may think fit for carrying into effect the various provisions of any act relating to Indian affairs." 25 U.S.C. § 9. Section 2 subdelegates this authority to the Commissioner of Indian Affairs. *Id.* at § 2. These provisions have been upheld by the courts as valid statutory grants of authority to the executive to manage Indian affairs and promulgate regulations. . . .
>
> This Court finds that IGRA vests the Secretary with the authority to promulgate the procedures governing Class III gaming on tribal land in light of her authority and trust responsibility under IGRA. Although Congress did not ex-

pressly grant authority to the Secretary to promulgate rules in the wake of the Supreme Court's *Seminole Tribe* decision, that grant of authority may be inferred from both the language in IGRA and the general-authority statutes. This inference is reasonable in light of IGRA's compacting and remedy provisions and the Secretary's general authority to implement regulations for acts related to Indian affairs. Therefore, this Court concludes that IGRA and the general-authority statutes provide the Secretary with the authority to promulgate the Gaming Procedures at issue in this case.

Id. at 770–71.

The Fifth Circuit reversed. After determining that the issue was ripe for review, the court held that Congress's intent was to "permit[] limited secretarial intervention only as a last resort, and only after the statute's judicial remedial procedures have been exhausted." The court explained,

In IGRA, Congress plainly left little remedial authority for the Secretary to exercise. The judicially managed scheme of good-faith litigation, followed by negotiation, then mediation, allows the Secretary to step in only at the end of the process, and then only to adopt procedures based upon the mediator's proposed compact. The Secretary may not decide the state's good faith; may not require or name a mediator; and may not pull out of thin air the compact provisions that he is empowered to enforce. To infer from this limited authority that the Secretary was implicitly delegated the ability to promulgate a wholesale substitute for the judicial process amounts to logical alchemy.

Texas v. United States, 497 F.3d 491, 503 (5th Cir. 2007).

In the alternative, the court held that even if Congress had not clearly spoken to the scope of the Secretary's authority, Part 291 was not a reasonable interpretation of IGRA:

The lynchpin of IGRA's balancing of interests is the tribal-state compact.... IGRA's legislative history amply demonstrates that Congress viewed the compact as an indispensable prerequisite to Class III gaming.... [T]he Secretarial Procedures contemplate Class III gaming in the absence of a tribal-state compact—directly in derogation of Congress's repeated and emphatic insistence.... [T]he Secretarial Procedures stand in direct violation of IGRA, the Johnson Act, and 18 U.S.C. § 1166 insofar as they may authorize Class III gaming without a compact.

Id. at 507.

Further, the court held that 25 U.S.C. §§ 2 and 9 did not provide "a general power to make rules governing Indian conduct," but instead only delegated authority to the Secretary to promulgate "regulations that implement specific laws and that are consistent with other relevant federal legislation." IGRA, said the court, "does not guarantee an Indian tribe the right to conduct Class III gaming"; rather it "grants tribes the right to negotiate the terms of a tribal-state compact." As a result, the court concluded, §§ 2 and 9 could not operate to grant authority to the Secretary to bypass the requirements of IGRA. *Texas v. United States*, at 509–11.

Do you agree with the Fifth Circuit's reasoning? Did the court correctly interpret Congress's intent? Did the court adequately address the import of Texas' unilateral ability to "stonewall" the Kickapoo by refusing to negotiate a compact and to consent to IGRA's good-faith cause of action? As the dissent noted,

The State of Texas permits certain types of gaming equivalent to Class III gaming as defined by IGRA. But Texas adamantly refuses to negotiate with the Kickapoo

Traditional Tribe towards a Class III gaming compact under IGRA and has blocked the tribe from seeking a remedy in federal court by invoking its right to Eleventh Amendment sovereign immunity from suit. Therefore, the tribe pursued its only alternative remedy of asking the Secretary of the Interior to issue Class III gaming procedures.... The Secretary requested comment from the State of Texas, but the state declined to comment [and instead] brought this action against the Secretary....

Id. (Dennis, J., dissenting).

If you were an attorney for the Kickapoo, what would you advise the tribe to do?

3. Law, Politics, and Negotiation

The Court's decision in *Seminole Tribe* not only changed the law of Indian gaming, it also changed the politics. As a result of the decision, states wielded greater political power over Class III compact negotiations, as a state could avoid the "referee" function of the federal court simply by asserting state sovereign immunity in the face of a tribe's challenge to the state's discharge of its good faith duty. Why the certainty that states would exploit their greater political power to disadvantage tribal interests? Drawing on the historical socio-legal context of tribal-state relations, Professor Tsosie criticized IGRA's compact requirement as favoring state sovereignty at the expense of tribal sovereignty. Her arguments take on even greater force in the state-dominated political environment after *Seminole Tribe*.

Rebecca Tsosie

Negotiating Economic Survival:
The Consent Principle and Tribal-State Compacts
Under the Indian Gaming Regulatory Act

29 Ariz. St. L.J. 25 (1997)

Historically, tribal-state relations have been rooted in adversity: adversity over land, over culture, over progress, over survival. This bitter adversity brewed between states and tribes in the expansion era, as the Supreme Court's 1886 decision in *United States v. Kagama* described: "[The tribes] owe no allegiance to the States, and receive from them no protection. Because of the local ill feeling, the people of the States where they are found are often their deadliest enemies." In truth, the brutal slaughter of Indian people by vengeful state militias, such as the massacre at Sand Creek in Colorado, proved the point: state growth and power during the expansion era depended on the destruction of tribal governments and cultures. In fact, the *Kagama* Court justified increased federal power over Indian affairs on the basis of the tribe's vulnerability to state hostility. Thus, rather than expecting states and tribes to resolve their disputes peacefully among themselves, the Court affirmed the necessity of an expansive federal power which would protect the Indian tribes as "wards" under a federal guardianship. In fighting the tribes, the state would be fighting the federal government — an intolerable prospect under principles of American federalism.

Although it has been over a century since the Supreme Court issued its opinion in *Kagama*, tribal-state hostilities continue to brew. The states, however, can no longer contemplate the removal of Indian tribes from their borders. The tribes have, after all, persisted as separate governments. Because tribes have now become incorporated within the national structure, state protests have shifted from requests for physical removal of tribes to requests for removal of tribal sovereignty and jurisdictional authority. To Indians, however, the nature of the adversity has changed little: they are still fighting for survival.

The latest grist for state protests is the Indian Gaming Regulatory Act, which authorizes Class III casino gaming on tribal lands under a tribal-state compact. The IGRA compacting provision is notable because it attempts to bridge the historical division between states and tribes through the use of alternative dispute resolution. Litigation is a last resort under the IGRA, used to correct bad faith conduct. Because the compact process is unconstrained by strict legal rules, the parties should be able to reach a mutually beneficial "sensible compromise" outside the adversarial context of the courtroom.

For all of its good intentions, the IGRA has frequently been unsuccessful in securing meaningful tribal-state agreements on disputed issues relating to Indian gaming. An initial problem concerns the motivation of the parties to enter negotiations. Both parties must feel that they have something to gain by negotiating a dispute, rather than litigating it. Thus, the initial bargaining positions of the parties must be roughly equivalent for the process to work appropriately. States generally have no incentive to enter into agreements with tribes unless they are convinced that the tribes have some right that will significantly compromise state interests.

IGRA fundamentally altered the motivations of the state and tribes to negotiate gaming compacts. In *Cabazon*, tribal rights to engage in gaming were litigated and the tribes prevailed. *Cabazon* also involved California, a P.L. 280 state in which civil and criminal jurisdiction had been delegated to the state. The sovereign rights of tribes in non-P.L. 280 states were not litigated in *Cabazon*, but these rights could only be more extensive because state criminal jurisdiction would not even apply to the reservation in a non-P.L. 280 state. Hence, in the post-*Cabazon* world, it was to the state's benefit to negotiate.

With the enactment of the IGRA, however, the states received a right to have a tribal-state compact in place before the tribes could commence Class III gaming. The IGRA's compact provision altered the balance of power that existed under *Cabazon* and made the tribe's sovereign right to engage in economic development contingent upon state consent. Because of the dismal history of tribal-state relationships, the IGRA attempted to preserve the balance of power between the parties by imposing a good faith standard and placing the burden on the state to prove good faith should the tribe bring suit to enforce this requirement in federal court. However, in *Seminole*, [the Court held that state sovereign immunity would bar the federal courts' enforcement of the states' obligation to negotiate in good faith].

The IGRA's compact provision places the tribes in a weak negotiating position because they may not engage in Class III gaming without a valid tribal-state compact in place. After *Seminole*, if the state refuses to negotiate a compact, the tribes have limited remedies. The states have made the most of their perceived victory in *Seminole*, with many states refusing to negotiate further tribal-state compacts.

The current conflicts between states and tribes regarding the obligation to negotiate a compact raise a serious issue: Can parties who have had a historically antagonistic relationship be expected to negotiate in good faith, particularly in cases where the state does not perceive Indian gaming as beneficial to its own interests? Tribal-state relations are rooted in a history of adversity, which has caused many tribes to see the states' main objective as "undermining ... the tribes' very existence." In the last few decades, states have litigated over tribal cigarette sales, tribal regulation of non-Indian owned fee land on the reservation, tribal taxation, and a host of other claims designed to impair tribal sovereignty and expand the scope of state power. This fact, combined with a history of racial animosity between Indian and non-Indian citizens, has caused the tribes to expect the worst in state relationships, and has tempted some state officials to disparage the separate status of tribal governments.

So long as the states can use political power to lobby Congress to divest the tribes of sovereignty or accomplish this by litigation, the states will continue to demonstrate a lack of respect for the sovereignty of the tribes and imply that the tribes are in a subordinate position to the states. The IGRA may even facilitate this result to the extent that tribal sovereignty is legislatively subordinated to state interests without hesitation, while state sovereignty is vindicated by decisions such as *Seminole*.

The tribes have several important interests at stake in gaming disputes. Reservation economies are directly impacted by the success or failure of the negotiations. Without a successful negotiation, there can be no Class III gaming, which is the most lucrative for the tribes. The tribes have endured nearly two centuries of severe economic deprivation and forced dependency. This has led to extreme poverty conditions on many reservations that are unrivaled in other parts of the country. Many tribes lack an adequate basis to gain revenue from taxation. Tribal members are generally quite poor and there is little industry on most reservations. Unemployment is rampant on reservations, and many tribal members must seek public assistance to survive.

Another important interest for the tribes is cultural survival. Although critics lampoon tribal casinos as an example of Indians adopting the white man's materialistic and exploitive values, this is a very superficial and misleading characterization. Native American cultural survival depends upon a rich notion of tribal self-determination and the financial resources to carry this out. The forced dependency of the last century is an intolerable reminder to Indian people of the brutal colonialism that divested them of their traditional economies, landbases, and political alliances. Gaming is a way for some tribes to gain the revenue and political clout necessary to achieve true self-determination and ensure cultural survival.

Finally, tribes have an essential interest in preserving their sovereignty and their right to decide what kind of economic development is best for their reservation and their members. Tribal sovereignty is not a negotiable item. One of the greatest injuries of the IGRA is that in many ways it tries to make tribal sovereignty negotiable, by, for example, specifying that tribes should give up the right to regulate less stringently than the state and that they should be willing to agree to share jurisdiction on the reservation with the states. Tribes perceive this as a threat to tribal sovereignty and as a fundamental abridgment of the federal government's trust duty to protect the tribes from state incursions.

At the root of the controversy over Indian gaming lies the historical conflict between states and tribes over tribal sovereignty and cultural survival. The states have historically failed to perceive any value in the continuation of tribal sovereignty and independence from state jurisdiction, while the tribes have been forced to recognize that expanded state jurisdiction often threatens to extinguish the separate cultural and political status that the tribes seek to preserve. Indian gaming encapsulates this long-standing political battle.

The political battles between states and tribes have engendered a continuing power imbalance that is intensified by the tribes' lack of representation in Congress, as well as the vehement promotion efforts of states' rights. This power imbalance also affects the negotiation process under the IGRA. Because the IGRA has been interpreted to uphold state sovereignty and subordinate tribal sovereignty, it is consistent with a tradition of American lawmaking that has disenfranchised indigenous rights. Congress's attempt to equalize the power imbalance by putting the burden on the state to prove good faith during the negotiation process became meaningless after the Supreme Court's decision [in *Seminole Tribe*] that tribes may not sue states in federal court absent state consent. In removing the tribes' ability to access the federal courts for enforcement authority, the Supreme Court appears to have irreparably altered the tenuous balance of power embedded in the IGRA. Today, the states have no incentive to bargain in good faith, and the unfortunate cycle of political disenfranchisement for Indian nations appears to have started anew.

Notes and Questions

1.   *The politics of compact negotiations after* **Seminole Tribe.** Professor Tsosie concluded, "The goal under the IGRA should be to reach an agreement that reflects an intercultural conception of justice. The preferences of the states to bring tribal gaming into accord with state policy should not be allowed to trump tribal rights to sovereignty and self-determination." Can this goal be achieved? How?

Light and Rand have argued that Indian gaming presents just such an opportunity, as tribal gaming has created a highly visible set of common interests shared by tribes and states in the continuation of Class III gaming. Acknowledging that the practical result of *Seminole Tribe* is an inappropriate state advantage in compact negotiations, they first proposed that Congress must "fix" IGRA:

> As legally enforceable rights and duties play a key role in equalizing political bargaining power and bringing parties to the table, it is imperative to reinstate IGRA's cause of action to enforce the state duty to negotiate tribal-state gaming compacts in good faith, whether in federal court or through federal administrative regulations, perhaps coupled with tools of alternative dispute resolution. Whatever form of corrective device Congress chooses, tribes must have a vehicle through which to enforce their rights and to bring states to the table. In addition to [an] enforcement mechanism, Congress should consider defining more clearly the state's duty to negotiate in good faith. Fundamentally, the state's good-faith duty should encompass state respect for tribal governments and tribes' inherent right of self-determination. Further, Congress might delineate in more detail appropriate topics for negotiation.

Light & Rand, Indian Gaming and Tribal Sovereignty, at 157–58. With a level bargaining table in place, they argued, tribal gaming is an opportunity for states and tribes to engage in cooperative policymaking:

> With a level playing field informed by tribes' inherent right of self-determination and firmly established through appropriate corrective mechanisms, Congress will have set the stage for fair and successful negotiations between tribes and states not only as mutual sovereigns, but as partners in cooperative policymaking. Indian gaming has the potential to induce both positive and negative socioeconomic impacts. The costs of tribal gaming should be an important part of any policy calculus. It is safe to say, however, that a substantial body of empirical research finds that Indian gaming produces net economic and social benefits that may outweigh its economic and social costs. Tribes arguably stand the most to gain, in terms of both quantifiable economic benefits like tribal government revenue and job creation and intangible social benefits like cultural preservation, spiritual self-determination, and strengthened tribal sovereignty. Non-tribal communities, however, also obtain a number of economic and social benefits from their proximity to tribal casinos, making them "natural allies" with gaming tribes. States, in turn, reap such substantial socioeconomic benefits as revenue sharing, job creation, and the

economic development of impoverished rural areas that include reservations and surrounding communities. These win-win outcomes suggest that "tribes and states need not be adversaries over compacting for casinos," or in other policy arenas in which balanced government-to-government relations stand to benefit all.

Id. at 159. The socioeconomic effects of Indian gaming are examined in Chapter 9.

Were Light and Rand overly optimistic? To date, Congress has not amended IGRA to reinstitute any mechanism to enforce the state's duty to negotiate in good faith. Are the Secretary's regulations in 25 C.F.R. pt. 291 sufficient? Why or why not?

2.   ***Expanded Class II gaming as an alternative.*** In the wake of *Seminole Tribe*, one option that a number of tribes have pursued is to turn their focus away from Class III gaming and its compact requirement in an attempt to make Class II gaming more profitable. For example, faced with state obstacles to compact renewal that would expand their Class III gaming operations, tribes such as the Confederated Salish and Kootenai in Montana have considerably expanded their Class II operations. Montana ranked last in the U.S. at $15.4 million in gaming revenue in 2006. Jodi Rave, *Tribes Place All Bets on Class II Gaming*, MONTANA BILLINGS GAZETTE (July 5, 2007). Does taking this route erect any of its own political roadblocks to the type of mutually beneficial outcomes posited by Tsosie or Light and Rand?

3.   ***"Buying" a Class III compact?*** As then-Acting Assistant Secretary for Indian Affairs Aurene M. Martin observed, "Another consequence of the Supreme Court's 1996 decision [in *Seminole Tribe*] is that more states have sought to include revenue-sharing provisions in Class III gaming compacts." Statement of Aurene M. Martin Before the U.S. Senate Committee on Indian Affairs (July 9, 2003). Are tribal-state revenue-sharing agreements mutually beneficial outcomes, or are states taking advantage of *Seminole Tribe* to demand concessions that would otherwise violate IGRA? How would Tsosie view such provisions? Revenue-sharing agreements are discussed in detail in Chapter 10.

Problem 5.1: Compacting Post-*Seminole Tribe*

1.   Consider the implications of *Seminole Tribe*. Imagine that you are the attorney for a tribe considering entering into Class III compact negotiations with a state. What would you advise the tribal government concerning the possible benefits and drawbacks of the compacting process?

2.   Now imagine that you are the attorney for the state. What would you advise the state government concerning the possible benefits and drawbacks of the compacting process?

3.   Consider the possible avenues available to a tribe that believes the state has not fulfilled its good faith duty, where the state refuses to consent to suit. What are the various alternatives, and what are the benefits and drawbacks of each?

E. State Public Policy and the Scope of Class III Gaming

Under IGRA, both Class II and Class III gaming are allowed only if "such" gaming "is located within a State that permits such gaming for any purpose by any person, organization or entity." 25 U.S.C. §§ 2710(b)(1)(A), 2710(d)(1)(B). If a state allows bingo, may a tribe operate all Class II games? If state law permits charitable or civic organizations to conduct "casino night" fundraisers, does that open the door to Class III gaming? If a state has authorized pari-mutuel wagering on horse races, but no other form of gambling, may a tribe conduct all Class III games on its reservation, or is it limited to pari-mutuel wagering? Interestingly, § 2710(b)(1)(A) refers to "such Indian gaming," while § 2710(d)(1)(B) refers to "such activities." Does the difference in statutory language lead to differing interpretations for the scope of gaming for Class II and Class III? Or does the fact that Congress took very different approaches to the regulation of Class II and Class III suggest that different interpretations of "permits such gaming" for each class are appropriate?

The answers to these questions are far from clear, and may not soon be clarified, at least by the federal courts. Another effect of *Seminole Tribe* was that fewer compacting disputes reached the federal courts, as they were resolved in the political arena, through state court decisions (as discussed in Chapter 8), or left unresolved. As a result, legal standards for issues surrounding the compacting process, perhaps particularly the scope of permissible gaming, effectively were halted mid-evolution.

The federal courts have taken two general approaches to the scope of gaming question. One approach is an expansive definition of "permits such gaming," under which state authorization of some games opens the door for a tribe to conduct additional games, even if not specifically permitted under state law. The expansive approach could put an entire class of games on the table so long as state law permits a single game within that class. If a state allows bingo, for example, then the tribe may conduct all Class II games, even if the state does not allow, say, pull-tabs. In this way, state law acts as a "floor" for Class III compact negotiations: the state will have to negotiate at least the games it specifically allows and may or must (depending on whether the court sees the expansive approach as permissive or mandatory) negotiate additional casino-style games.

The restrictive approach, on the other hand, limits "permits such gaming" to those games actually permitted under state law. If a state allows pull-tabs, for instance, IGRA does not automatically allow a tribe to operate bingo in the state. In this game-specific approach, state law acts as a "ceiling" for Class III compact negotiations. Depending on whether the court sees the expansive approach as permissive or mandatory, it may allow or compel a state not to negotiate any games other than those specifically allowed by state law.

1. Expansive Approaches

United States v. Sisseton-Wahpeton Sioux Tribe
897 F.2d 358 (8th Cir. 1990)

GIBSON, Circuit Judge.

[The Sisseton-Wahpeton Tribe opened a blackjack gaming enterprise on its South Dakota reservation in April 1988. Although IGRA excludes blackjack from its definition of Class II gaming, in § 2703(7)(C) Congress "grandfathered" into Class II card games in Michigan, Washington, North Dakota, and South Dakota "that were actually operated in such State by an Indian tribe on or before May 1, 1988." The grandfather provision presumably would apply only where the state "permits such gaming," because § 2710(b)(1)(A) makes that a prerequisite for Class II as a whole.]

Section 2710(b)(1)(A) permits a tribe to engage in class II gaming if "such Indian gaming is located within a State that permits such gaming for any purpose by any person, organization or entity." We believe that the legislative history reveals that Congress intended to permit a particular gaming activity, even if conducted in a manner inconsistent with state law, if the state law merely regulated, as opposed to completely barred, that particular gaming activity.

The statutory language in issue first appeared in H.R. 1920, the principal Indian gaming legislation considered by the 99th Congress. The Senate Report on this earlier measure noted that if state law completely barred class II gaming, then the Act would also bar such gaming. If the state permitted some form of class II gaming, however, then a tribe could engage in such gaming subject to the Act's requirements. [As the report stated,] "[T]ribes may conduct certain defined games (bingo, lotto and cards) under the Federal regulatory framework, provided the laws of the state allow such games to be played at all."

The Senate Report accompanying the bill ultimately enacted, S. 555, also discussed the difference between a state prohibiting, as opposed to merely regulating, a particular gaming activity:

> The phrase "for any purpose by any person, organization or entity" makes no distinction between State laws that allow class II gaming for charitable, commercial, or governmental purposes, or the nature of the entity conducting the gaming. *If such gaming is not criminally prohibited by the State in which tribes are located, then tribes, as governments, are free to engage in such gaming.*

S.Rep. No. 100-446, at 12 (emphasis added). The Senate Report is replete with explanations of the respective roles played by the tribes, federal government, and state government in regulating Indian gaming. In explaining the states' role under the Act, the Senate Report explains:

> The mechanism for facilitating the unusual relationship in which a tribe might affirmatively seek the extension of State jurisdiction and the application of state laws to activities conducted on Indian land is a tribal-State compact. *In no instance, does S. 555 contemplate the extension of State jurisdiction or the application of State laws for any other purpose.*

Id. at 6 (emphasis added).

One week after S. 555 was introduced, the Supreme Court decided *California v. Cabazon Band of Mission Indians.* In *Cabazon,* the Court utilized a prohibitory/regulatory distinction to determine whether California had criminal jurisdiction over offenses involving Indians under [Public Law 280], which authorized the transfer of criminal jurisdiction over Indians from the federal government to states in certain circumstances. The Court held in *Cabazon* that tribes have a right to conduct gaming on Indian lands without being subject to state regulation if located in a state which regulates but does not prohibit gaming. While *Cabazon* did not involve the gaming Act here, in developing the Act considered here, Congress adopted a modified version of the *Cabazon* test to aid in deciding whether "such Indian gaming is located within a State that permits such gaming for any purpose by any person, organization or entity," within the meaning of 25 U.S.C. § 2710(b)(1)(A):

> [T]he Committee anticipates that Federal courts will rely on the distinction between State criminal laws which prohibit certain activities and the civil laws of a State which impose a regulatory scheme upon those activities to determine whether class II games are allowed in certain States. This distinction has been discussed by the Federal courts many times, most recently and notably by the Supreme Court in *Cabazon.*

S.Rep. No. 100-446, at 6. Thus, as a court, our task is to assess whether South Dakota's gaming law is prohibitory or regulatory in nature in order to determine the effect, if any, of State law on the Tribe's blackjack operations.

This prohibitory/regulatory distinction is consistent with congressional perceptions of the relationship between Indian tribes, federal government, and state government. As explained by Senator Evans when S. 555 was considered, the Act must be construed in light of the following principle:

> When [Congress] has chosen to restrict the reserved sovereign rights of tribes, the courts have ruled that such abrogations of tribal rights must have been done expressly and unambiguously.... Therefore, if tribal rights are not explicitly abrogated in the language of this bill, no such restrictions should be construed. This act should not be construed as a departure from established principles of the legal relationship between the tribes and the United States. Instead, this law should be considered within the line of developed case law extending over a century and a half by the Supreme Court, including the basic principles set forth in the *Cabazon* decision.

The Government argues that Congress has simply assimilated state law here. We must reject this argument. The Act contains no explicit abrogation of the right of tribes to conduct gaming without being subject to state regulation if the tribe is located in a state which regulates but does not prohibit gaming. We must also be cognizant of the following principle, as expressed by Representative Udall during consideration of S. 555:

> [W]hile this legislation does impose new restrictions on tribes and their members, it is legislation enacted basically for their benefit. I would expect that the Federal courts, in any litigation arising out [of] this legislation, would apply the Supreme Court's time-honor[ed] rule of construction that *any ambiguities in legislation enacted for the benefit of Indians will be construed in their favor.* (Emphasis added.)

We now turn to the determinative issue of whether the South Dakota law governing blackjack activities is prohibitory, or merely regulatory, in nature. Subject to State regulation, South Dakota permits bingo, parimutuel horse and dog race betting, a State lottery, slot machines, and certain card games, including blackjack. At the time these actions were commenced, South Dakota prohibited card games "wherein anything valuable is wagered upon the outcome." Since the institution of these actions, South Dakota has amended its constitution to permit commercial card games, including blackjack, to be lawfully operated in the City of Deadwood, South Dakota.

Consistent with *Cabazon*, we conclude that South Dakota regulates, rather than prohibits, gambling in general and blackjack in particular. Therefore, the Act's requirement that class II gaming, such as the blackjack here, be "located within a State that permits such gaming for any purpose by any person, organization or entity," is fulfilled.

Mashantucket Pequot Tribe v. Connecticut
913 F.2d 1024 (2d Cir. 1990)

MAHONEY, Circuit Judge.

The Mashantucket Pequot Tribe seeks to operate casino-type games of chance on its reservation located in Ledyard, Connecticut, [specifically] Class III games of chance, such as those activities permitted by Connecticut law for certain nonprofit organizations during "Las Vegas nights," [including blackjack, poker, dice, roulette, and baccarat]. Conn.

Gen. Stat. §§ 7-186a to 7-186p (1989). [The State] advised the Tribe that the State would not negotiate concerning the operation of games of chance or "Las Vegas nights" on the reservation, since the Tribe only had a "right to conduct 'Las Vegas Nights' on the premises of the reservation subject ... to those restrictions contained in the Connecticut General Statutes," [but] was willing "to negotiate, in good faith, with the Tribe, concerning other permissible forms of gaming in Connecticut." After more than 200 days had elapsed since the Tribe requested negotiations, the Tribe filed its complaint in this action in the United States District Court for the District of Connecticut, invoking jurisdiction under § 2710(d)(7)(A)(i).

The State contends that the Class III gaming as to which the Tribe seeks to negotiate is not gaming that the State "permits ... for any purpose by any person, organization, or entity" within the meaning of § 2710(d)(1)(B). Specifically, the State argues that its limited authorization of the conduct of "Las Vegas nights" by nonprofit organizations does not amount to a general allowance of "such [casino-type] gaming" as the Tribe would institute; and further that such gaming activity is contrary to the State's public policy. Thus, the State urges, since the condition of subparagraph (B) of § 2710(d)(1) has not been satisfied, the State is not obligated to negotiate the tribal-state compact envisioned by subparagraph (C).

[According to Connecticut law,] the State sanctions "Las Vegas nights" conducted by "[a]ny nonprofit organization, association or corporation." Such entities "may promote and operate games of chance to raise funds for the purposes of such organization, association or corporation," subject to specified conditions and limitations as to, *inter alia,* the status of the sponsoring organization, size of wagers, character of prizes, and frequency of operations.

At the outset, we note the congressional "find[ing]," set forth in § 2701(5), that "Indian tribes have the exclusive right to regulate gaming activity on Indian lands if the gaming activity is not specifically prohibited by Federal law and is conducted within a State which does not, as a matter of criminal law and public policy, prohibit such gaming activity." This declaration is consistent with the Supreme Court's pre-IGRA ruling in *Cabazon,* [setting forth the distinction between criminal prohibitions and civil regulations].

Further, the Senate Report specifically adopted the *Cabazon* rationale as interpretive of the requirement in § 2710(b)(1)(A) that Class II gaming be "located within a State that permits such gaming for any purpose by any person, organization or entity," [as noted by the court in *United States v. Sisseton-Wahpeton Sioux Tribe,* 897 F.2d 358, 365 (8th Cir.1990)].

We deem this legislative history instructive with respect to the meaning of the identical language in § 2710(d)(1)(B), regarding Class III gaming, which we must interpret.* "It is a settled principle of statutory construction that when the same word or phrase is used in the same section of an act more than once, and the meaning is clear as used in one place, it will be construed to have the same meaning in the next place." Although the State correctly points out that this rule has its exceptions, none advanced by the State has any pertinence here.

The State's position is in direct opposition to the central premise of the IGRA with respect to Class III gaming. The heart of the ultimate legislative compromise regarding Class III gaming was described [by the Senate Report] in these terms:

---

* We agree with the district court that, contrary to the State's contention, no significance should be accorded to the modest difference between the introductory language of § 2710(b)(1) ("An Indian tribe may engage in, or license and regulate, class II gaming on Indian lands within such tribe's jurisdiction, if....") and § 2710(d)(1) ("Class III gaming activities shall be lawful on Indian lands only if....").

After lengthy hearings, negotiations and discussions, the Committee concluded that the use of compacts between tribes and states is the best mechanism to assure that the interests of both sovereign entities are met with respect to the regulation of complex gaming enterprises such as pari-mutuel horse and dog racing, casino gaming, jai alai and so forth. The Committee notes the strong concerns of states that state laws and regulations relating to sophisticated forms of class III gaming be respected on Indian lands where, with few exceptions, such laws and regulations do not now apply. The Committee balanced these concerns against the strong tribal opposition to any imposition of State jurisdiction over activities on Indian lands. The Committee concluded that the compact process is a viable mechanism for setting [sic] various matters between two equal sovereigns.

The compact process is therefore to be invoked unless, applying the *Cabazon* test, it is determined that the state, "as a matter of criminal law and public policy, prohibit[s] [Class III] gaming activity." Absent such a conflict, the interests of the tribe and state are to be reconciled through the negotiation of a compact, and, if negotiations fail to achieve a compact and it is determined that the state did not negotiate in good faith, through the litigation and mediation process prescribed by § 2710(d)(7)(A) and (B).

Under the State's approach, on the contrary, even where a state does not prohibit Class III gaming as a matter of criminal law and public policy, an Indian tribe could nonetheless conduct such gaming only in accordance with, and by acceptance of, the entire state corpus of laws and regulations governing such gaming. The compact process that Congress established as the centerpiece of the IGRA's regulation of class III gaming would thus become a dead letter; there would be nothing to negotiate, and no meaningful compact would be possible.

The district court concluded, after a careful review of pertinent Connecticut law regarding "Las Vegas nights," that Connecticut "permits games of chance, albeit in a highly regulated form. Thus, such gaming is not totally repugnant to the State's public policy. Connecticut permits other forms of gambling, such as a state-operated lottery, bingo, jai alai and other forms of pari-mutuel betting." We conclude, in agreement with the district court, that the Connecticut law applicable to Class III gaming is regulatory rather than prohibitive.

This ruling means only that the State must negotiate with the Tribe concerning the conduct of casino-type games of chance at the Reservation. We necessarily leave to those negotiations the determination whether and to what extent the regulatory framework under which such games of chance are currently permitted in the State shall apply on the Reservation.

Lac du Flambeau Band of Lake Superior Chippewa Indians v. Wisconsin

770 F. Supp. 480 (W.D. Wis. 1991)

CRABB, Chief District Judge.

[Shortly after IGRA's passage, the Lac du Flambeau Tribe of Lake Superior Chippewa Indians entered into compact negotiations with the state of Wisconsin. In the initial negotiations, the games covered by the draft compact included roulette, craps, house-banked card games, electronic games, and slot machines. At that point, the Wisconsin Lottery Board requested an opinion from state Attorney General Donald J. Hanaway on the legality of including games in the compact that were not expressly authorized by state law.

Hanaway concluded that with the exception of the state lottery and on-track pari-mutuel betting, casino games were prohibited under Wisconsin law. A subsequent Attorney General opinion reached a different conclusion, determining that the state constitution authorized the state legislature to permit any kind of gambling, though the legislature had chosen to permit only the state lottery and on-track betting. Relying on the Hanaway opinion, Governor Tommy G. Thompson refused to include Class III games other than lotteries and on-track betting in the compact with the Tribe.]

The issue between the parties centers on the provision in §2710(d)(1) that "Class III gaming activities shall be lawful on Indian lands only if such activities are.... (B) located in a State that *permits such gaming* for any purpose by any person, organization, or entity...." (Emphasis added.) Defendants argue that casino games, video games and slot machines are not permitted for any purpose by any person, organization or entity within Wisconsin; because they are not, the state is not required to bargain over these games. Defendants' position is that Congress meant "permits" to be given its usual dictionary meaning of formally or expressly granting leave; therefore, unless a state grants leave expressly for the playing of a particular type of gaming activity within the state, that activity cannot be lawful on Indian lands. Under this approach, the state is required to bargain only over gaming activities that are operating legally within the state.

Defendants' reading of "permits" ignores the other meanings assigned to the word, such as "[t]o suffer, allow, consent, let; to give leave or license; to acquiesce by failure to prevent, or to expressly assent or agree to the doing of an act." *Black's Law Dictionary* (5th ed.). More important, it ignores the Supreme Court's opinion in *California v. Cabazon Band of Mission Indians,* on which Congress relied in drafting [IGRA]. The Senate Report makes explicit reference to *Cabazon* in discussing Class II gaming, which has the same requirement as Class III gaming that the gaming activity be "located within a state that permits such gaming for any purpose by any person, organization or entity." The Senate committee stated that it anticipated that the federal courts would rely on the *Cabazon* distinction between regulatory gaming schemes and prohibitory laws. Under [the *Cabazon* Court's interpretation of] P.L. 280, a court looks at the civil-criminal distinction to determine whether a state can go onto an Indian reservation to enforce the state's criminal gambling laws; under [IGRA], the court looks at the distinction between the state's civil and criminal laws to determine whether the state permits gaming activities of the type at issue. Although the Senate committee was speaking of Class II activities, its comments are equally applicable to the requirement for Class III activities. *See Mashantucket Pequot Tribe v. Connecticut,* 913 F.2d 1024, 1030 (2d Cir.1990), *cert. denied,* 499 U.S. 975 (1991).

In addition, [IGRA's] congressional findings support the view that Congress did not intend the term "permits such gaming" to limit the tribes to the specific types of gaming activity actually in operation in a state: "Indian tribes have the exclusive right to regulate gaming activity on Indian lands if the gaming activity is not specifically prohibited by Federal law and is conducted within a State which does not, as a matter of criminal law and public policy, *prohibit* such gaming activity." [§2701(5).] (Emphasis added.) In light of the legislative history and the congressional findings, I conclude that the initial question in determining whether Wisconsin "permits" the gaming activities at issue is not whether the state has given express approval to the playing of a particular game, but whether Wisconsin's public policy toward class III gaming is prohibitory or regulatory.

The original Wisconsin Constitution provided that "[e]xcept as provided in this section, the legislature shall never authorize any lottery, or grant any divorce." For more than a century, this prohibition against "any lottery" was interpreted as prohibiting the operation or playing of any game, scheme or plan involving the elements of prize, chance and consideration. The prohibition against a "lottery" has been held to outlaw theater promotions, mercantile promotions, charitable bingo, and television games of chance. In 1965, however, the constitution was amended to allow Wisconsin citizens to participate in promotional sweepstakes (by defining "consideration" as not including listening to or watching a radio or television program or visiting a store or other place without being required to make a purchase or pay a fee). The constitution was amended again in 1973 to authorize bingo when played by charitable organizations, and in 1977 to allow raffles for charitable organizations. In 1987 the electorate approved two constitutional amendments: one authorized the state to operate a lottery, with the proceeds going to property tax relief; the second removed any prohibition on parimutuel on-track betting.

When the voters authorized a state-operated "lottery," they removed any remaining constitutional prohibition against state-operated games, schemes or plans involving prize, chance and consideration, with minor exceptions. The amendments to the Wisconsin Constitution evidence a state policy toward gaming that is now regulatory rather than prohibitory in nature. The fact that Wisconsin continues to prohibit commercial gambling and unlicensed gaming activities does not make its policy prohibitory.

Defendants argue that even if Wisconsin is viewed as having a regulatory policy toward Class III gaming activities in general, the state need not negotiate the specific activities in dispute because it does not permit expressly the type of gaming plaintiffs want to offer on their reservations. It is not necessary for plaintiffs to show that the state formally authorizes the same activities plaintiffs wish to offer. The inquiry is whether Wisconsin prohibits those particular gaming activities. It does not.

Defendants' assertion that they are required to negotiate only the identical types of games currently offered by the lottery board misconceives the point of [IGRA], as well as the holding in *Cabazon*. It was not Congress's intent that the states would be able to impose their gaming regulatory schemes on the tribes. The Act's drafters intended to leave it to the sovereign state and tribal governments to negotiate the specific gaming activities involving prize, chance and consideration that each tribe will offer under the terms of its tribal-state compact. Although defendants insist that their position is not that the tribes are limited to negotiating "the exact games" that the state lottery operates, they argue that Wisconsin law must give express authorization for a "gaming activity" before it can be a proper subject of negotiation. Defendants offer no authority for distinguishing between the state's current lottery games and the activities proposed for negotiation by the tribes. Instead, the state makes the bald statement that casino games "are of a wholly different character than a state lottery or on-track pari-mutual wagering." The state's current attorney general has rejected the imposition of artificial distinctions within the term lottery, so long as the activity involves the elements of prize, chance and consideration and is not addressed explicitly by the constitutional amendments. I find no reason to impose similarly artificial categories in applying the *Cabazon* test and in interpreting [IGRA].

I conclude that the state is required to negotiate with plaintiffs over the inclusion in a tribal-state compact of any activity that includes the elements of prize, chance and consideration and that is not prohibited expressly by the Wisconsin Constitution or state law.

Notes and Questions

1. **The expansive approach and state public policy.** How did the courts in *United States v. Sisseton-Wahpeton Sioux Tribe*, *Mashantucket Pequot Tribe v. Connecticut*, and *Lac du Flambeau Band v. Wisconsin* characterize a state's public policy? Is the "permits

such gaming" requirement in essence a codification of *Cabazon*'s "shorthand test" of state public policy? If so, then how should a court determine whether a state "permits such gaming"? If not, what is the appropriate test?

In a different context, the Ninth Circuit examined California's public policy toward gaming in *Sycuan Band of Mission Indians v. Roache*, 54 F.3d 535 (9th Cir. 1995). That case arose out of California's attempt to enforce state law against the Band's gaming operation. As discussed in Chapter 3, the court held that the state did not have authority to enforce its gaming laws against the tribe. In so holding, the court discussed the scope of inquiry regarding a state's public policy:

> In *California v. Cabazon Band of Mission Indians,* the Supreme Court made it clear that state law in a Public Law 280 state may be excluded from Indian country as "regulatory" even though the regulatory aspects of the law are enforced by criminal penalties. The key is "whether the conduct at issue violates the State's public policy." In *Cabazon,* the Supreme Court undertook this inquiry in regard to California's attempt to ban high-stakes bingo and certain card games in Indian country, and concluded that the State had no public policy against the gambling: it simply regulated it. Accordingly, California could not prohibit the games in issue, carried on by the Bands in Indian country.
>
> The State here points, however, to the Supreme Court's statement in *Cabazon* that "applicable state laws governing an activity must be examined in detail before they can be characterized as regulatory or prohibitory." The State argues that *Cabazon* does not control this case, because the issue here is not bingo or card games, but electronic machine gambling that California permits nowhere. We conclude, however, that the State's argument is useful only when applied to the distinctions between classes of gambling set up by IGRA. We express no opinion concerning Class III, but at least insofar as the State's argument is directed at Class II-type gaming, of the sort engaged in by the Tribes in *Cabazon,* the state cannot regulate and prohibit, alternately, game by game and device by device, turning its public policy off and on by minute degrees. *Cabazon* addressed the problem at a higher level of generality than that.... The [Court's] ruling, after careful analysis of particular laws, was generic: "California regulates rather than prohibits *gambling in general* and bingo in particular." The State has shown us no determinative changes in California public policy since *Cabazon,* and that decision controls.

Id. at 539. The *Sycuan Band* court stated that within a particular class, "the state cannot regulate and prohibit, alternately, game by game and device by device, turning its public policy off and on by minute degrees." Is the logical extension of the Ninth Circuit's statement that if the state allows any Class III game under any circumstances, then it regulates Class III gaming generally, so that the state must negotiate all Class III games? Do you agree that *Cabazon* supports that outcome? Does IGRA? Why or why not?

2. *The extent of the expansive approach.* What is the extent of the expansive approach taken by the courts in *United States v. Sisseton-Wahpeton Sioux Tribe, Mashantucket Pequot Tribe v. Connecticut,* and *Lac du Flambeau Band v. Wisconsin*? If a state allows any Class III games, must it *negotiate* over all Class III games, or *agree* to all Class III games? Does it matter whether the state expressly prohibits some Class III games? Are the expressly prohibited games "on the table" during negotiations?

If you answered that the expansive approach only requires a state to negotiate the entire class of games (rather than effectively gives the tribe the statutory "right" to conduct the entire class of games), what would be valid points of negotiation? What arguments could a state make to exclude a certain game from the compact while fulfilling its duty to negotiate in good faith? What arguments might evidence bad faith?

3.   *The expansive approach and Class II.* How does the expansive approach operate in Class II, where no tribal-state compact is required? If a state allows a single Class II game (say, bingo), may a tribe conduct all Class II games? If not, which games would be allowed? Are your answers to the questions regarding Class III consistent with your answers to the questions regarding Class II? Is there statutory support for treating Class II differently than Class III in the "scope of gaming" context?

2. Restrictive Approaches

Cheyenne River Sioux Tribe v. South Dakota
3 F.3d 273 (8th Cir. 1993)

McMILLIAN, Circuit Judge.

Since 1989, South Dakota has allowed state lotteries, video lottery, limited card games, slot machines, parimutuel horse and dog racing, and simulcasting. South Dakota has located within its boundaries nine federally recognized tribes. The first tribe to request negotiations toward a Class III gaming compact was the Flandreau Santee Tribe in 1989. Negotiations between the state and the Flandreau Santee Tribe broke down after about five months and the tribe sued South Dakota under the IGRA; however, the case was finally settled by the execution of a compact between the state and the tribe, approved by the [Interior Secretary in 1990].

Similar gaming compacts have been negotiated and executed between the state and five other tribes—the Sisseton-Wahpeton Sioux Tribe, March 1991; the Yankton Sioux Tribe, June 1991; the Lower Brule Sioux Tribe, September 1991; the Crow Creek Sioux Tribe, April 1992; and the Standing Rock Sioux Tribe, August 1992. The only other location in South Dakota to offer [non-tribal casino-style] gaming is the historic community of Deadwood.

[The state refused to negotiate games other than those permitted under the other tribal-state compacts, which allowed a limited number of slot machines and poker and blackjack tables, subject to existing state limits on the amount that a player could bet.] The tribe alleges the state [violated its duty to negotiate in good faith by refusing] to negotiate a tribal-state compact to include keno and other games permitted by state law, [as well as] higher bet limits. The district court found the state does not permit the traditional form of keno as a legalized form of gambling in South Dakota. The only form of keno permitted by the state is video keno; therefore, the district court concluded the state was required to negotiate only the subject of video keno and not traditional keno.

We agree with the state that it need not negotiate traditional keno if only video keno is permitted in South Dakota. The "such gaming" language of § 2710(d)(1)(B) does not require the state to negotiate with respect to forms of gaming it does not presently permit. Because video keno and traditional keno are not the same and video keno is the only form of keno allowed under state law, it would be illegal, in addition to being unfair to the other tribes, for the tribe to offer traditional keno to its patrons. Therefore, we agree with the district court that the state did not refuse to negotiate in good faith on the tribe's operation of traditional keno.

Coeur d'Alene Tribe v. Idaho
842 F. Supp. 1268 (D. Id. 1994)

RYAN, District Judge.

[Until 1988, the Idaho constitution prohibited the state legislature from authorizing "any lottery or gift enterprise under any pretense or for any purpose whatever." In 1988, the constitution was amended to allow pari-mutuel betting on horse, dog, and mule races, charitable gambling, and a state lottery. In 1992, the Coeur d'Alene, Nez Perce, and Kootenai tribes each formally requested that the state enter into compact negotiations for Class III gaming. Following the tribes' requests,] Idaho called a special session of its legislature, enacted legislation, and drafted a proposed constitutional amendment changing Idaho law regarding gaming. The Tribes contend that these actions were taken to prevent them from conducting certain Class III gaming activities on their reservations.

[The 1988 constitutional amendment provided]:

> No game of chance, lottery, gift enterprise or gambling shall be authorized under any pretense or for any purpose whatever, except for the following: (a) A state lottery which is authorized by the state if conducted in conformity with law; and (b) Pari-mutuel betting if conducted in conformity with law; and (c) Charitable games of chance which are operated by qualified charitable organizations in the pursuit of charitable purposes if conducted in conformity with law.

[The 1992 constitutional amendment modified the above provision to read]:

> (1) Gambling is contrary to public policy and is strictly prohibited except for the following: (a) A state lottery which is authorized by the state if conducted in conformity with enabling legislation; and (b) Pari-mutuel betting if conducted in conformity with enabling legislation; and (c) Bingo and raffle games that are operated by qualified charitable organizations in the pursuit of charitable purposes if conducted in conformity with enabling legislation.

> (2) No activities permitted by subsection (1) shall employ any form of casino gambling including, but not limited to, blackjack, craps, roulette, poker, [baccarat], keno and slot machines, or employ any electronic or electromechanical imitation or simulation of any form of casino gambling.

> (3) The legislature shall provide by law penalties for violations of this section.

After the voters passed the [1992 constitutional] amendment, the Nez Perce Tribe brought suit challenging that amendment on the grounds that the State failed to set forth an adequate and truthful statement of the purpose of the proposed amendment on the ballot as required under Idaho law. In a recent decision, the Idaho Supreme Court upheld the amendment, declaring that the statement of purpose placed on the ballot was sufficient and that the amendment was properly presented for voter approval on the November 3, 1992, election ballot. See *Nez Perce Tribe v. Cenarrusa*, 867 P.2d 911 (1993).

After numerous negotiation sessions, the Coeur d'Alene Tribe and the State entered into a partial compact in December 1992, covering all matters which could be agreed upon. No compacts have been entered into between the State and the Kootenai and Nez Perce Tribes. The present suit was filed because negotiations between the State and all three Tribes have reached an impasse regarding Class III gaming. The Tribes have expressed their intent to engage in extensive Class III gaming activities, including casino-style gambling, which the State contends are prohibited under Idaho law and public policy. Since negotiations began, the State has taken the position that it is only required to negotiate Class III activities permitted under Idaho law. Thus, the State has agreed to negotiate only as to a lottery and pari-mutuel betting on horse, mule, and dog races.

The State has consented to this suit and has waived any objection to jurisdiction based on immunity from suit under the Eleventh Amendment to the United States Constitution.

[Based on our analysis of *Cabazon* and IGRA's legislative history], it is clear that the prohibitory/regulatory analysis contained in *Cabazon* must guide the court in resolving this dispute. Therefore, the court must evaluate Idaho law and public policy on gambling.

The Tribes argue that the court must assess Idaho law and public policy as it was in the spring and summer of 1992, when the Tribes first requested negotiations on Class III gaming. The State contends that the laws now in effect should govern the compact negotiations. The Tribes base their argument on the following grounds: (1) IGRA does not allow a state to restrict Indian gaming by modifying its laws; (2) retroactive application of changes in state law cannot be allowed to deprive the Tribes of vested rights; and (3) the constitutional amendment ratified by the voters in 1992 is invalid because it was not adopted in accordance with Idaho law. The court need not address this third point because the Idaho Supreme Court has now upheld the amendment, and this court will defer to the findings and judgment of the Idaho Supreme Court as to the legality of the 1992 amendment process.

The Tribes [first] contend that Congress, in enacting IGRA, did not grant states authority to restrict Indian gaming by modifying their laws. The Tribes offer no authority to support their claim that IGRA precludes a state from changing its gaming laws prior to entering into a compact. IGRA is entirely silent on this issue. It appears that the basis of Tribes' argument is their feeling that the State has acted in an unfair and underhanded manner in changing its laws in 1992. The Tribes contend that they have been singled out for unfair treatment. The court does not agree. The 1992 changes in Idaho law apply equally to the State, to the Tribes, and to all other groups and individuals. The changes were made to make clear that only a lottery, pari-mutuel betting, and bingo and raffle games are permitted in Idaho, [as the 1992 amendment prohibited the charitable casino-style games allowed under the 1988 amendment]. All other forms of gambling are expressly prohibited to everyone, including both the State and the Tribes. It would be a much different question if Idaho had attempted to create a situation in which the State alone could engage in casino gambling and all other groups, including Indian tribes, could not. However, this is not the case. In fact, such a situation could never occur. Under IGRA, if the State were to engage in casino gambling, or permit any group or entity to do so, the Tribes could also engage in casino gambling.

Under IGRA, the law and public policy of the state set the scope of permissible Class III gaming on tribal lands. IGRA certainly does not command that a state may not change its gaming laws or amend its constitution prior to entering into a compact. There is nothing in IGRA which would prevent Idaho from abolishing and criminally prohibiting *all* Class III gaming entirely.

The Tribes also contend that the State could not change its gaming laws after compact negotiations were requested because to do so would deprive them of vested rights. At the time the Tribes requested compact negotiations, [the tribes argue,] they acquired a vested right to conduct any and all Class III gaming permitted under Idaho law at that time. Thus, the Tribes contend that to resolve this dispute under Idaho law as it now stands would mean giving retroactive effect to the 1992 changes in the law, depriving the Tribes of a vested right.

On the contrary, IGRA makes it clear that the Tribes have no right, vested or inchoate, to conduct Class III games until a compact has been negotiated with the state. Therefore, the only time an Indian tribe could arguably claim a vested right to conduct a particular form of Class III gaming would be after a compact between the tribe and state addressing the particular form of gaming had been entered into and finally approved. [Thus,] the proper scope of compact negotiations shall be determined by looking to Idaho law and public policy as they now stand, rather than reverting to Idaho law as it was at the time the Tribes first requested compact negotiations.

The State maintains that it is only required to negotiate with the Tribes with respect to the specific Class III gaming activities which are permitted under Idaho law. The Tribes contend that because Idaho permits some forms of Class III gaming, its policy toward Class III gaming as a class is regulatory rather than prohibitory, and therefore, the Tribes are free to engage in *all* forms of Class III gaming, including casino gambling and keno and slot machines, and the State must negotiate accordingly.

The Tribes rely primarily on *United States v. Sisseton-Wahpeton Sioux Tribe*, 897 F.2d 358 (8th Cir.1990); *Mashantucket Pequot Tribe v. Connecticut*, 913 F.2d 1024 (2d Cir.1990), *cert. denied*, 499 U.S. 975 (1991); [and] *Lac du Flambeau Band of Lake Superior Chippewa Indians v. Wisconsin*, 770 F. Supp. 480 (W.D. Wis.1991). The court has thoroughly reviewed these cases, [and] finds that all of the cases uniformly support the position taken by the State. All of the courts have followed the regulatory/prohibitory distinction established by the Supreme Court in *Cabazon*. In the cases relied on by the Tribes, the courts conducted a broad review of the laws and public policy of each state and concluded that the *specific* gaming activity at issue was permitted by the particular state.

The Idaho Constitution expressly declares that all gambling is contrary to public policy and is strictly prohibited, except for three carefully limited exceptions: the state lottery, pari-mutuel betting if conducted in conformity with enabling legislation, and bingo and raffle games that are operated by qualified charitable organizations in the pursuit of charitable purposes. In addition, the Idaho Constitution expressly forbids those engaging in the three carefully limited exceptions from employing any form of casino gambling including, but not limited to, blackjack, craps, roulette, poker, baccarat, keno and slot machines, or from employing any electrical or electromechanical imitation or simulation of any form of casino gambling. The Idaho Constitution further declares that the legislature shall provide for penalties for violation of the prohibition against gambling. Accordingly, [the Idaho code] provides that those who engage in gambling (other than participation in the three exceptions allowed under the Idaho Constitution) shall be guilty of a misdemeanor.

Based on the preceding discussion, the court finds that under the combined IGRA and *Cabazon* analysis, the State must negotiate with the Tribes only as to the conduct of a lottery and pari-mutuel betting on horse, mule, and dog races. The State is not required to negotiate as to any other forms of Class III gaming.

Panzer v. Doyle
680 N.W.2d 666 (Wis. 2004)

PROSSER, Justice.

This is an original action under Article VII, § 3(2) of the Wisconsin Constitution. The petitioners contend that the Governor exceeded his authority in 2003 when he agreed to certain amendments to the gaming compact our state has entered into with the Forest County Potawatomi (FCP) Tribe, a federally recognized Indian tribe indigenous to Wisconsin. They assert that the Governor improperly agreed to amendments that [*inter alia*] expand the scope of gaming by adding games that were previously not permitted for any purpose by any person, organization, or entity in Wisconsin.

To understand the factual and legal issues that affect our decision, we recapitulate our state's unique history with respect to legalized gambling.

Article IV, § 24, as part of the original constitution, prohibited the legislature from ever authorizing "any lottery." In all likelihood, the term "lottery" in this context was intended to apply to a particular species of gaming, inasmuch as contemporaneous legislation before and after the adoption of the constitution contained specific prohibitions against lotteries as well as separate prohibitions against other forms of gaming.

Over time, however, attorneys general and courts interpreted Wisconsin lottery statutes to prohibit any form of gaming that included the elements of prize, chance, and consideration. These statutory interpretations were linked eventually to the term "lottery" in Article IV, § 24, blurring the implicit limitations of the provision. Under this broad reading, the legislature could not authorize any gaming activities without amending [the state constitution]. The legislature enforced the public policy against gaming in the constitution by enacting criminal statutes.

Article IV, § 24 was amended five times between 1848 and 1987 to permit the legislature to authorize specific limited types of gaming. The first amendment (1965) modified the definition of "consideration" so that the legislature could authorize certain promotional contests. The second amendment (1973) authorized charitable bingo; the third (1977) authorized charitable raffles. In 1987 the constitution was amended twice more, to authorize pari-mutuel on-track betting and a state-operated lottery. The pari-mutuel betting amendment was the first to clearly depart from the historic concept of lottery. The state-operated lottery amendment soon prompted questions about its scope, and its ramifications have been the subject of controversy ever since.

The year 1987 was also a watershed year in the history of tribal gaming because of a decision by the United States Supreme Court. In *Cabazon*, the Court reaffirmed its earlier interpretation that distinguished between the effect of state criminal laws, which are fully applicable to certain reservations under Pub. L. 280, and state civil laws "applicable only as [they] may be relevant to private civil litigation in state court." The Court applied this criminal/prohibitory, civil/regulatory dichotomy in determining whether the state bingo regulations and county gambling restrictions in California were criminal or civil. "The shorthand test is whether the conduct at issue violates the State's public policy." Recognizing that the distinction between prohibiting and regulating "is not a bright-line rule," the Court concluded "that California regulates rather than prohibits gambling in general and bingo in particular." This conclusion was founded on a statutory scheme suggesting moderation rather than prohibition. The Court ultimately held that neither the state nor the county could enforce these particular gambling restrictions on tribal reservations.

Shortly after *Cabazon*, Congress enacted legislation to establish standards for the operation of gaming by Indian tribes. IGRA follows the spirit of *Cabazon* by making the permissibility of Class III games a function of state law. Section 2710(d) makes Class III gaming activities lawful on Indian lands *only if* such activities are "located in a State that permits such gaming for any purpose by any person, organization, or entity." § 2710(d)(1)(B).

As noted above, there was uncertainty in Wisconsin about the interpretation of the 1987 constitutional amendment authorizing a state-operated lottery. Confusion cropped up in the state's negotiations with the tribes under IGRA, with the state initially indicating a willingness to permit tribes to engage in a number of casino-type games. Contemporaneously, however, the new Wisconsin Lottery requested a formal opinion on the scope of gaming it could conduct. It also asked the Attorney General: "[I]f the Wisconsin Lottery cannot legally offer a particular type of gaming or gambling operation as part of the lottery, can such type of game or gambling operation be lawfully included in a state/tribal gaming compact" under IGRA? Because of IGRA's deference to state law on permissible Class III gaming and because the state would presumably negotiate compacts with tribes in conformity with the Attorney General's opinion, the answer to the Lottery's question was of critical importance to the future of Indian gaming in Wisconsin.

In February 1990 Attorney General Donald Hanaway concluded that the 1987 amendment authorizing the state to conduct a lottery did not, by its terms, permit the Wisconsin Lottery to engage in any casino-type games. Rather, the term "lottery" as it was used in the amendment, only referred to the narrow commonly understood meaning of lottery, which was a distinct type of gambling. At the same time, Attorney General Hanaway concluded that the Wisconsin Constitution did not prohibit casino-type games. These games, he said, were prohibited only by state criminal statutes. Consequently, the legislature could authorize casino-type games by changing the statutes, and could authorize casino-type gambling "just within Indian country." The Attorney General added: "[I]t is not my responsibility to establish the public policy on gambling in Wisconsin.... [The] policy as it relates to gambling is within the role, responsibility and ability of the Legislature to address."

The Hanaway opinion was a hot potato. It effectively precluded the state from agreeing to casino-type gambling for the tribes without explicit approval from the legislature. It simultaneously invited the legislature to approve casino-type gambling for Indians and non-Indians alike, or give the tribes a monopoly by approving casino-type gambling "just within Indian country." Either prospect was troubling to legislators opposed to expanded gambling in Wisconsin. A month later, the legislature approved a bill authored by Representative John Medinger giving the governor authority to negotiate and enter into gaming compacts with the tribes. The bill provided that "The governor may, on behalf of this state, enter into any compact that has been negotiated under 25 U.S.C. 2710(d)." Wis. Stat. § 14.035. By its terms, the Medinger bill anticipated compliance with IGRA but passed the negotiation and decision-making on gaming compacts to the governor. Before passage, both houses of the legislature rejected amendments requiring the legislature to ratify these compacts.

The Legislative Reference Bureau (LRB) attorney who drafted Representative Medinger's bill prepared a formal drafter's note in which he stated that any compact entered into must limit games to those authorized under ch. 945 of the Wisconsin Statutes, namely bingo, raffles, the lottery, pari-mutuel wagering, and "crane games" as well as other amusement devices. The LRB attorney disagreed with Attorney General Hanaway because he stated that Article IV, § 24 of the Wisconsin Constitution prohibited "casino-type gambling," and therefore no additional types of games could be authorized under ch. 945 without first amending the constitution.

In November 1990 Attorney General Hanaway was defeated for re-election. In May 1991 his successor, Attorney General James E. Doyle, issued a new opinion. The Attorney General wrote:

[T]he term "lottery" throughout article IV, section 24, refers to any game, scheme or plan comprising prize, chance and consideration.... Under the constitution, the legislature may authorize any type of state-operated lottery subject only to the advertising, use-of-revenue and off-track wagering restrictions. The Legislature may not, however, authorize such lotteries if they are not operated by the state, or fall within the bingo, raffle or on-track, pari-mutuel exceptions. Any other lottery requires an amendment to the constitution.

The effect of Attorney General Doyle's opinion was to lay the groundwork for casino-type gambling by a state-operated lottery *if* such gambling were authorized by the legislature, and for casino-type gambling by Indian tribes *if* such gaming were included in a legislatively authorized or approved compact.

Following the earlier Hanaway opinion, Governor Tommy Thompson had refused to bargain with the tribes over casino games, video games, and slot machines, offering only traditional lotteries and pari-mutuel on-track betting. This led to an impasse. Six weeks after Attorney General Doyle's opinion was issued, however, the District Court for the Western District of Wisconsin rendered a decision in a suit by two Chippewa bands challenging the state's refusal to bargain over casino games. *Lac du Flambeau Band of Lake Superior Chippewa Indians v. Wisconsin,* 770 F. Supp. 480 (W.D. Wis.1991). Judge Barbara Crabb held that the amendments to Article IV, § 24, in particular the 1987 amendment authorizing the state to operate a lottery, demonstrated "a state policy toward gaming that is now regulatory rather than prohibitory in nature." Judge Crabb's opinion drew upon the reasoning in the opinion of Attorney General Doyle. As noted, Attorney General Doyle theorized that when the voters of the state authorized the state to operate a "lottery," they removed any impediment to state operation of games involving the elements of prize, chance, and consideration. Thus, the state could potentially operate casinos. With this analysis at hand, Judge Crabb concluded that "the state is required to negotiate with plaintiffs over the inclusion in a tribal-state compact of any activity that includes the elements of prize, chance and consideration and that is not prohibited expressly by the Wisconsin Constitution or state law."

By June of 1992, Governor Thompson reached compact agreements with all eleven federally recognized tribes and bands in the state. Among these compacts was the 1992 compact with the FCP Tribe, which addressed Class III gaming in the following manner:

AUTHORIZED CLASS III GAMING

A. The Tribe shall have the right to operate the following Class III games during the term of this Compact but only as provided in this Compact:

1. Electronic games of chance with video facsimile displays;

2. Electronic games of chance with mechanical displays;

3. Blackjack; and

4. Pull-tabs or break-open tickets when not played at the same location where bingo is played.

B. The Tribe may not operate any Class III gaming not expressly enumerated in this section of this Compact unless this Compact is amended pursuant to section XXX [providing for amendment of the Compact].

In the meantime, work began in the legislature on a new amendment to the constitution to clarify the word "lottery." This amendment was passed by the legislature in 1992 and 1993, and approved by the people in April 1993. The opening sentence of Article IV,

§ 24, which had prohibited the legislature from authorizing any "lottery," was changed to provide that "[e]xcept as provided in this section, the legislature may not authorize *gambling* in any form" (emphasis added).

Further, the potential scope of the state-operated lottery was expressly narrowed. Subsection 6 of Article IV, § 24, which defines the parameters of the state-operated lottery, is now arguably the most detailed provision in the constitution. Subsection 6(a) [had been added in 1987 to authorize the state lottery]. The 1993 amendment added the following clarifying language:

> (b) The lottery authorized under par. (a) shall be an enterprise that entitles the player, by purchasing a ticket, to participate in a game of chance if: 1) the winning tickets are randomly predetermined and the player reveals preprinted numbers or symbols from which it can be immediately determined whether the ticket is a winning ticket entitling the player to win a prize as prescribed in the features and procedures for the game, including an opportunity to win a prize in a secondary or subsequent chance drawing or game; or 2) the ticket is evidence of the numbers or symbols selected by the player or, at the player's option, selected by a computer, and the player becomes entitled to a prize as prescribed in the features and procedures for the game, including an opportunity to win a prize in a secondary or subsequent chance drawing or game if some or all of the player's symbols or numbers are selected in a chance drawing or game, if the player's ticket is randomly selected by the computer at the time of purchase or if the ticket is selected in a chance drawing.

> (c) Notwithstanding the authorization of a state lottery under par. (a), the following games, or games simulating any of the following games, may not be conducted by the state as a lottery: 1) any game in which winners are selected based on the results of a race or sporting event; 2) any banking card game, including blackjack, baccarat or chemin de fer; 3) poker; 4) roulette; 5) craps or any other game that involves rolling dice; 6) keno; 7) bingo 21, bingo jack, bingolet or bingo craps; 8) any game of chance that is placed on a slot machine or any mechanical, electromechanical or electronic device that is generally available to be played at a gambling casino; 9) any game or device that is commonly known as a video game of chance or a video gaming machine or that is commonly considered to be a video gambling machine, unless such machine is a video device operated by the state in a game authorized under par. (a) to permit the sale of tickets through retail outlets under contract with the state and the device does not determine or indicate whether the player has won a prize, other than by verifying that the player's ticket or some or all of the player's symbols or numbers on the player's ticket have been selected in a chance drawing, or by verifying that the player's ticket has been randomly selected by a central system computer at the time of purchase; 10) any game that is similar to a game listed in this paragraph; or 11) any other game that is commonly considered to be a form of gambling and is not, or is not substantially similar to, a game conducted by the state under par. (a). No game conducted by the state under par. (a) may permit a player of the game to purchase a ticket, or to otherwise participate in the game, from a residence by using a computer, telephone or other form of electronic, telecommunication, video or technological aid.

The specificity of this language is self-evident.

The initial compacts were set to run out between February 1998 and March 1999. Governor Thompson reached agreements with the state's tribes to renew the compacts for five years. However, the 1998 amendments did not grant the FCP permission to operate additional *types* of games. [In] 2003, as the second term of the compact was nearing completion, Governor Doyle agreed to new amendments to the 1992 Gaming Compact (as amended in 1998) with the FCP Tribe. The Compact as amended clears the way for the FCP Tribe to conduct a number of casino games that have never been legal in Wisconsin, such as keno, roulette, craps, and poker.

The text of the constitution is absolutely clear: "Except as provided in this section, the legislature may not authorize *gambling* in any form." Nothing in § 24 authorizes electronic keno, roulette, craps, and poker. These games are specifically denied to the Wisconsin Lottery. Wis. Const. art. IV, § 24(6)(c).

Nonetheless, the Governor contends that state law is not the last word on permissible Class III gaming. State law, he argues, exerts only an indirect influence on Indian gaming, that being the games the state is *required* to negotiate. As we understand the Governor's position, he believes Congress has empowered states to agree to games beyond the games the state is required to negotiate.

Neither the "ceiling" view nor the "floor" view of IGRA authorizes *any* state actor to create a monopoly for Indian tribes by superseding, disregarding, or violating fundamental state law. The only *obligation* that states have under IGRA springs from 25 U.S.C. § 2710(d)(1)(B), which is the same provision setting forth the scope of lawful gaming activity on Indian lands. Section 2710(d)(1)(B) provides that "[c]lass III gaming activities *shall be lawful* on Indian lands *only if* such activities are [among other requirements] (B) located in a State that *permits such gaming* for any purpose by any person, organization, or entity." Thus, under IGRA, there are in essence two categories of Class III games: those over which a state *must* negotiate with a tribe and those that are illegal to negotiate. Those games over which a state *must* negotiate are games permitted "for any purpose by any person, organization, or entity," including games permitted, *by law*, exclusively for tribes.

Thus, regardless of how one frames the question, the ultimate inquiry focuses on the "permits such gaming" language in 25 U.S.C. § 2710(d) (1)(B). Until very recently, the *Lac du Flambeau* case was the only case concluding that, once a state regulates one form of Class III gaming, the state must negotiate over all forms of Class III gaming. *Compare Lac du Flambeau with Rumsey Indian Rancheria of Wintun Indians v. Wilson* ("IGRA does not require a state to negotiate over one form of Class III gaming activity simply because it has legalized another, albeit similar form of gaming."); *Cheyenne River Sioux Tribe v. South Dakota* ("The 'such gaming' language does not require the state to negotiate with respect to forms of gaming it does not presently permit."); *Coeur d'Alene Tribe v. Idaho* (holding that state was required to negotiate only with respect to specific Class III games that were permitted in the state). Accordingly, the continued vitality of *Lac du Flambeau's* holding is very doubtful, and the decision's statements regarding Wisconsin's policy toward gaming have been seriously undercut by the 1993 amendment to Article IV, § 24.*

---

* Other developments in this area of law contribute to the erosion of the legal and factual framework that existed in 1992 when Judge Crabb issued the *Lac du Flambeau* decision. For instance, in 1996, the United States Supreme Court handed down a landmark sovereign immunity decision in *Seminole Tribe v. Florida*. In that case, the Court held among other things that the Indian Commerce Clause, the authority under which Congress enacted IGRA, does not empower Congress to abrogate a state's Eleventh Amendment immunity. As a result, unless a state consents to suit, an Indian tribe may not enforce IGRA against states in federal court. This decision continues to color our understanding of the dynamics of federalism at play under IGRA.

Unlike the expansive interpretation of the term "lottery" that was at least plausible before 1993, our constitution is now quite clear that the legislature may not authorize any *gambling* except that permitted by Article IV, § 24, and is very clear that certain games do not fall under the term "lottery" in Article IV, § 24(6). The constitution is now specific about what the state-operated lottery may do and what it may not do. Blackjack and other varieties of banking card games, poker, roulette, craps, keno and slot machines are all games specifically outside the scope of § 24(6)'s authorized exception, and they do not come within any other exception. Thus, the legislature may not authorize new casino-type gambling in any form. No exception to the state constitution can be marshaled to support legislative authorization of new casino-type gambling to Indian tribes. The Tribe's existing games such as slot machines and blackjack must be sustained on the basis of the validity of the original compacts, which were negotiated pursuant to court order before the 1993 constitutional amendment, as well as constitutional and contract law.

Article IV, § 24 embodies a strong state policy against gambling. It prohibits the legislature from authorizing gambling in any form except as permitted in the constitution. Article V, § 4 of the constitution directs that the governor "take care that the laws be faithfully executed." Accordingly, we conclude that the Governor acted without authority by agreeing to games that are, as reflected in our state's criminal statutes and reinforced by its constitution, prohibited to everyone in the state. The new casino-style games the Governor agreed to in 2003 are expressly forbidden by statute. Thus, the Governor was without authority to agree, on behalf of the state, to add variations on blackjack, electronic keno, roulette, craps, poker, and other non-house banked card games under the 2003 Amendments to the FCP Gaming Compact. The governor may not carve out exceptions to the state's criminal statutes unilaterally. We are unable to conclude that the legislature delegated such power or could delegate such power in light of the 1993 constitutional amendment.

Our holding today raises inevitable questions about the validity of the original 1992 FCP Gaming Compact and the 1998 amendments thereto. Clearly, the 1992 Compact encompasses games that were and are precluded under our state's criminal statutes. Both the tribes and the state have relied on the validity of the original compacts. Any attempt at this point to impair these compacts would create serious constitutional questions. We do not believe the 1992 compact suffered from any infirmity under state law when it was entered into. Whether the 1992 compact is durable enough to withstand a change in state law that alters our understanding of what is "permitted" in Wisconsin is a separate question. The resolution of this question is likely to turn, at least in part, on the application of the impairment of contracts clauses in the United States and Wisconsin Constitutions as well as IGRA. Because these issues are not before us, and because they may turn in large measure on unresolved questions of federal law, our decision stops short of resolving these important questions.

Rumsey Indian Rancheria of Wintun Indians v. Wilson
64 F.3d 1250 (9th Cir. 1996)

O'SCANNLAIN, Circuit Judge.

[Several tribes in California wanted to conduct certain Class III games, including electronic games, such as video poker, and house-banked card games (the "Proposed Gaming Activities"). Governor Pete Wilson refused to negotiate with the tribes, asserting that the Proposed Gaming Activities were illegal under state law. California agreed not to assert its Eleventh Amendment immunity to suit under *Seminole Tribe* so that the impasse could be resolved by the federal court.]

The parties disagree as to whether California "permits" the Proposed Gaming Activities. The State's argument is straightforward: the Proposed Gaming Activities are illegal. California law prohibits the operation of a banked or percentage card game as a misdemeanor offense. In addition, according to the State, the stand-alone electronic gaming machines sought by the Tribes are electronic "slot machines" [also prohibited as a misdemeanor offense under state law]. The Tribes offer a broader reading of IGRA, claiming that a state "permits" a specific gaming activity if it "regulates" the activity *in general* rather than prohibiting it entirely as a matter of public policy. Under this approach, a specific illegal gaming activity is "regulated," rather than "prohibited," if the state allows the operation of similar gaming activities. The Tribes observe that video lottery terminals, parimutuel horse racing, and nonbanked, nonpercentage card gaming are legal in California. Because the Tribes view these activities as functionally similar to the Proposed Gaming Activities, they conclude that California regulates, and thus permits, these activities.

The [*Cabazon*] Court held that the fact that "an otherwise regulatory law is enforceable by criminal as well as civil means does not necessarily convert it into a criminal law within the meaning of Pub.L. 280." Instead, it explained [the distinction between state "criminal/prohibitory" laws and state "civil/regulatory" laws: criminal/prohibitory laws generally prohibit certain conduct, while civil/regulatory laws generally permit the conduct at issue, subject to regulation. The Court stated,] "*The shorthand test is whether the conduct at issue violates the State's public policy.*" The Tribes assert that IGRA codified *Cabazon*'s "criminal/regulatory" test. Under this approach, a court must determine whether a gaming activity, even if illegal, violates a state's public policy. If it does, then the activity is "criminally" prohibited. If it does not, then the activity is merely "regulated" and, thus, "permitted" for the purpose of applying IGRA.

We reject this reading of IGRA. Section 2710(d)(1)(b) is unambiguous. A dictionary definition of the term "permit" [is] "[t]o suffer, allow, consent, let; to give leave or license; to acquiesce, by failure to prevent, or to expressly assent or agree to the doing of an act" (quoting *Black's Law Dictionary*). Clearly, California does not allow banked or percentage card gaming. With the possible exception of video lottery terminals [which California operates through its state lottery], electronic gaming machines fitting the description of "slot machines" are prohibited.

The fact that California allows games that share some characteristics with banked and percentage card gaming—in the form of (1) banked and percentage games *other* than card games and (2) nonbanked, nonpercentage card games—is not evidence that the State permits the Proposed Gaming Activities. Nor is it significant that the state lottery, if not technically a slot machine, is functionally similar to one. We agree with the approach taken by the Eighth Circuit [in *Cheyenne River Sioux Tribe v. South Dakota*]. IGRA does not require a state to negotiate over one form of Class III gaming activity simply because it has legalized another, albeit similar form of gaming. Instead, the statute says only that, if a state allows a gaming activity "for any purpose by any person, organization, or entity," then it also must allow Indian tribes to engage in that same activity. In other words, a state need only allow Indian tribes to operate games that others can operate, but need not give tribes what others cannot have.

Because we find the plain meaning of the word "permit" to be unambiguous, we need not look to IGRA's legislative history. However, a brief examination helps to clarify why the word has different meanings with respect to Class II and Class III gaming. The primary source of IGRA's legislative history, the Senate Report accompanying its passage, does not describe the circumstances in which a state "permits" a gaming activity in the context of Class III gaming. The only relevant passages occur in the Senate Report's discussion of *Class II* gaming:

> [T]he Committee anticipates that Federal courts will rely on the distinction between State criminal laws which prohibit certain activities and civil laws of a State which impose a regulatory scheme upon those activities to determine whether class II games are allowed in certain States. This distinction has been discussed by the Federal courts many times, most recently and notably by the Supreme Court in *Cabazon*.

The Senate Report continues:

> The phrase "for any purpose by any person, organization or entity" makes no distinction between State laws that allow class II gaming for charitable, commercial, or governmental purposes, or the nature of the entity conducting the gaming. If such gaming is not criminally prohibited by the State in which tribes are located, then tribes, as governments, are free to engage in such gaming.

The Tribes point to those statements as evidence that Congress intended that *Cabazon*'s "criminal/regulatory" test govern for the purposes of determining whether a Class II gaming activity is permitted on Indian lands. The Tribes then observe that IGRA's Class II gaming provisions contain the same language used for Class III gaming: "An Indian tribe may engage in ... *class II* gaming on Indian lands ... if ... such Indian gaming is located within a State that *permits such gaming for any purpose by any person, organization or entity....*" Relying upon the maxim that identical language in a statute should be interpreted to have the same meaning, the Tribes infer that the Senate Report establishes the applicability of the *Cabazon* test to Class III gaming.

However, that inference is incorrect. Identical words appearing more than once in the same act, and even in the same section, may be construed differently if it appears they were used in different places with different intent. Such is the case for Class III gaming. The Senate Report repeatedly links the *Cabazon* test to Class II gaming while remaining silent as to Class III gaming—a fact that itself suggests that Class II and III provisions should be treated differently. Further, Congress envisioned different roles for Class II and Class III gaming. [As reflected in the Senate Report,] it intended that tribes have "maximum flexibility to utilize [Class II] games such as bingo and lotto for tribal economic development," and indicated that Class II gaming would be conducted largely free of state regulatory laws. Congress was less ebullient about tribes' use of Class III gaming, however, and indicated that Class III gaming would be more subject to state regulatory schemes, [as reflected in the Senate Report's discussion of the tribal-state compact requirement]. Even if we found it necessary to rely upon IGRA's legislative history, it supports the plain meaning of the term "permit" with regard to IGRA's Class III provisions.

With the possible exception of slot machines in the form of video lottery terminals, California has no obligation to negotiate with the Tribes on the Proposed Gaming Activities. We remand to the district court to consider the limited question of whether California permits the operation of slot machines in the form of the state lottery or otherwise.

CANBY, Circuit Judge, joined by PREGERSON, REINHARDT, and HAWKINS, Circuit Judges, dissenting from the denial of rehearing en banc:

> This is a case of major significance in the administration of the Indian Gaming Regulatory Act ("IGRA") and it has been decided incorrectly, in a manner that conflicts with the Second Circuit's interpretation of the same statutory language. The result is to frustrate the scheme of state-tribal negotiation that Congress established in IGRA. We should have granted rehearing en banc to prevent the near-nullification of IGRA in a circuit that

encompasses a great portion of the nation's Indian country. Our failure to do so may close the only route open to many tribes to escape a century of poverty.

Rumsey holds that California, which permits several varieties of Class III gambling, has no duty under IGRA to negotiate with the tribes over the tribes' ability to conduct any game that is illegal under California law. This ruling effectively frustrates IGRA's entire plan governing Class III Indian gaming. The primary purpose of IGRA, as set forth in the Act, is "to provide a statutory basis for the operation of gaming by Indian tribes as a means of promoting tribal economic development, self-sufficiency, and strong tribal governments." 25 U.S.C. § 2702(1). IGRA's otherwise drastic extension of state gaming law to Indian country (to be enforced only by the federal government) was modified by IGRA's process by which the states and tribes could arrive at compacts specifying what games might be allowed and who might have jurisdiction to enforce gaming laws. The whole idea was to foster these compacts. That goal is defeated if the details of the state's regulatory schemes, allowing some games and prohibiting others, apply if the state does nothing. Thus the Second Circuit, in arriving at a conclusion precisely opposite to that of *Rumsey,* stated:

> Under the State's approach, … even where a state does not prohibit class III gaming as a matter of criminal law and public policy, an Indian tribe could nonetheless conduct such gaming only in accord with, and by acceptance of, the entire state corpus of laws and regulations governing such gaming. The compact process that Congress established as the centerpiece of the IGRA's regulation of class III gaming would thus become a dead letter; there would be nothing to negotiate, and no meaningful compact would be possible.

Mashantucket Pequot Tribe v. Connecticut, 913 F.2d 1024, 1030–31 (2d Cir. 1990). The Second Circuit's fears of turning IGRA's compact process into a dead letter are well-founded. It is well to keep in mind that the issue here is not whether California must allow every game the tribes want to conduct; it is merely whether California has a duty to negotiate with the tribes to determine what games should be conducted, on what scale, and who has jurisdiction to enforce gaming laws. In passing IGRA, Congress knew that states and tribes both had important interests at stake. If a state has a genuine prohibitory public policy against all Class III gaming, as some states do, it can rest on that policy and not entertain the possibility of Indian Class III gaming within its borders. States like California that have no such wholesale public policy against Class III gaming must, under IGRA, reach an accommodation between their interests and the strong interests of the tribes in conducting such gaming. IGRA's method of reaching such an accommodation is by negotiation between the two affected groups. IGRA imposes on the states a duty to negotiate compacts in good faith. That duty is enforceable in federal court with the aid, if necessary, of a court appointed mediator to arrive at a compact and the Secretary of the Interior to dictate a compact if the parties do not accept the mediator's ruling. But under *Rumsey,* this whole process is nipped in the bud if the tribe seeks to operate games that state law, criminal *or* regulatory, happens to prohibit. The state has no duty to begin negotiations, even though under IGRA a compact may permit the tribe to operate games that state law otherwise prohibits. 18 U.S.C. § 1166(c)(2). The State thus has no incentive to negotiate, and there is no system to require negotiation. IGRA is rendered toothless.

Such a nullifying interpretation of IGRA might be understandable if it were required by the plain words of the statute, but it is not. *Rumsey* defeats the congressional plan for Class III gaming by a manifestly flawed interpretation of the statutory language. In deciding that California had no duty to negotiate with the plaintiff tribes, the *Rumsey* opinion asked and answered the wrong question. IGRA provides [that] "*Class III gam-*

ing activities shall be lawful on Indian lands only if such activities are … located in a State that *permits such gaming* for any purpose by any person, organization, or entity.…" Thus the state must negotiate with a tribe if the state "permits such gaming." The *Rumsey* opinion regards the key question as being whether the word "permits" is ambiguous; it holds that the word is not ambiguous, so the State need not bargain. But the proper question is not what Congress meant by "permits," but what Congress meant by "such gaming." Did it mean the particular game or games in issue, or did it mean the entire category of Class III gaming? The structure of IGRA makes clear that Congress was dealing categorically, and that a state's duty to bargain is not to be determined game-by-game. The time to argue over particular games is during the negotiation process.

The only natural reading of § 2710(d)(1)(B) is that, when Congress says "Class III gaming activities shall be lawful … if located in a State that permits such gaming," then "such gaming" refers back to the category of "Class III gaming," which is the next prior use of the word "gaming." *Rumsey* interprets the statutory language as if it said: "A Class III game shall be lawful … if located in a State that permits that game." But that is not what Congress said, and it is not a natural reading of the statutory language. The plain language cuts directly against *Rumsey;* Congress allows a tribe to conduct Class III gaming activities (pursuant to a compact) if the State allows Class III gaming by anyone.

Furthermore, Class II gaming is governed by virtually identical language in § 2710(b)(1)(A). A tribe may conduct and regulate *"Class II gaming* … if such Indian gaming is located within a State that *permits such gaming* for any purpose by any person, organization or entity.…" We have held [in *Sycuan Band*] that the state cannot allow or disallow Class II Indian gaming game-by-game. Our decision in *Sycuan Band* followed the reasoning of the Supreme Court in *Cabazon,* the seminal Indian gaming case that ultimately led to the passage of IGRA. In deciding for purposes of Public Law 280 whether California's prohibition of high-stakes bingo could be enforced against the Band, the Supreme Court noted that "[t]he shorthand test is whether the conduct at issue violates the State's public policy." After reviewing California's treatment of gambling, the Court stated, "In light of the fact that California permits a substantial amount of gambling activity, including bingo, and actually promotes gambling through its state lottery, we must conclude that California regulates rather than prohibits *gambling in general* and bingo in particular." Thus, *Cabazon* ascertained California's public policy at a level of generality far above that of the individual game in issue, and concluded that the Band could conduct high-stakes bingo even though California made that activity a misdemeanor. We applied a similarly broad and categorical approach to Class II gaming in *Sycuan Band.*

The *Rumsey* opinion refuses to apply the reasoning of *Cabazon* and *Sycuan Band,* and instead holds that a class-wide, categorical approach is precluded by the "unambiguous" plain words of section 2710(d)(1)(B), even though identical words in section 2710(b)(1)(A) require a contrary result for Class II gaming. The majority in *Rumsey* justifies its interpretation by referring to the Senate Committee Report on IGRA, which approves the approach of *Cabazon* for Class II gaming but says nothing about *Cabazon*'s applicability to Class III gaming. But we should not read a congressional negative into a committee report's failure to mention *Cabazon* in regard to Class III gaming. *Cabazon* dealt with games that IGRA placed in Class II, and that is explanation enough why the discussion of *Cabazon* in the Committee's report arose only in connection with Class II gaming. The fact remains that Congress wrote provisions of essentially identical wording and structure to govern both Class II and Class III gaming. We should give them both the same categorical meaning.

Rumsey has thus misconstrued IGRA's Class III gaming provisions, and has done so in a manner that defeats Congress's intention and causes great economic harm to numerous tribes. With all respect to the *Rumsey* panel, we dissent from the denial of rehearing en banc.

Notes and Questions

1.   *Distinguishing the restrictive approach.* In *Rumsey*, the Ninth Circuit distinguished its ruling in *Sycuan Band of Mission Indians v. Roache*:

> Our decision in *Sycuan Band of Mission Indians v. Roache* is not to the contrary. In *Sycuan Band,* this court held that California lacked jurisdiction to enforce its laws against certain Class III gaming activities on tribal lands because IGRA vests exclusive jurisdiction with the federal government. In the course of its analysis, the court also suggested that, even if the gaming devices at issue were Class II gaming, California would lack authority to enforce its law on tribal lands. The court relied on the statement in *Cabazon* that California "regulates rather than prohibits gambling in general and bingo in particular." The court interpreted this statement expansively to mean that California's gambling laws regarding Class II-type gaming fall on the civil/regulatory side of *Cabazon*'s test; thus, California lacked jurisdiction to enforce these laws on tribal lands.
>
> As an initial matter, the *Sycuan Band* court's analysis of *Cabazon Band* in the context of Class II gaming is dicta; the court expressly held that the gaming at issue was Class III gaming. Moreover, in its discussion of *Cabazon Band,* the *Sycuan Band* court expressed no opinion on its relevance for Class III-type gaming, the type of gaming at issue here. For the reasons expressed above, we have determined that the analysis of whether a type of gaming is permitted by a state under IGRA differs depending on the class of gaming involved.

Rumsey, at 1258. Are you persuaded by the court's reading of *Sycuan Band*? Do you agree that "the analysis of whether a type of gaming is permitted by a state under IGRA differs depending on the class of gaming involved"?

2.   *Recharacterization of expansive approach cases.* Recall that in *Coeur d'Alene v. Idaho,* the district court characterized several cases (presented above as illustrating an expansive approach) as supporting the state's position:

> The Tribes rely primarily on *United States v. Sisseton-Wahpeton Sioux Tribe,* 897 F.2d 358 (8th Cir.1990); *Mashantucket Pequot Tribe v. Connecticut,* 913 F.2d 1024 (2d Cir.1990), *cert. denied,* 499 U.S. 975 (1991); [and] *Lac du Flambeau Band of Lake Superior Chippewa Indians v. Wisconsin,* 770 F. Supp. 480 (W.D. Wis.1991). The court has thoroughly reviewed these cases, [and] finds that all of the cases uniformly support the position taken by the State. All of the courts have followed the regulatory/prohibitory distinction established by the Supreme Court in *Cabazon.* In the cases relied on by the Tribes, the courts conducted a broad review of the laws and public policy of each state and concluded that the *specific* gaming activity at issue was permitted by the particular state.

Do you agree? Consider the court's discussion of each of the cases excerpted above:

> In *United States v. Sisseton-Wahpeton Sioux Tribe,* the Indian tribe established a blackjack operation on its reservation in South Dakota. That case, like

the case at hand, turned on the proper interpretation of the phrase "permits such gaming for any purpose by any person, organization or entity." The Eighth Circuit addressed the case by focusing on the *particular gaming activity* — blackjack. The court did not hold that the case turned on whether or not a particular *class* of gaming was permitted by the state: "[W]e believe that the legislative history reveals that Congress intended to permit a *particular gaming activity*, even if conducted in a manner inconsistent with state law, if the state merely regulated, as opposed to completely barred, *that particular gaming activity*." The court went on to hold that because South Dakota permitted commercial card games, including blackjack, the Indian tribe could also conduct a blackjack operation. This decision is entirely consistent with the position advanced by Idaho in the case at hand. Idaho asks the court to focus not on whether Class III gaming as a *class* is permitted in Idaho, but rather on what *particular Class III gaming activities* are permitted under Idaho law, and compare that to the particular gaming activities sought to be conducted by the Tribes.

In *Mashantucket Pequot Tribe v. Connecticut,* the Indian tribe sought to conduct casino-type gaming activities on its reservation and the state refused to negotiate a compact regarding such activities. The court reviewed Connecticut law and noted that Connecticut allowed non-profit charitable organizations to conduct casino gambling on so-called "Las Vegas Nights" for charitable purposes. The court ruled that the state was required to negotiate with the tribe regarding the conduct of casino-type games of chance because the state permitted other organizations and entities to engage in such activities. The state would not have had to negotiate casino-type gaming had it prohibited such gaming to *all* persons, organizations, and entities within the state.

In *Lac du Flambeau Band of Lake Superior Chippewa Indians v. Wisconsin,* Indian tribes and the State of Wisconsin disagreed over whether the state was required to include casino games, video games, and slot machines in its negotiations with the tribes. As amended, the constitution authorized a state lottery and pari-mutuel betting and did not prohibit other forms of gaming involving the elements of prize, chance, and consideration. Thus, the court concluded that "the state is required to negotiate with plaintiffs over the inclusion in a tribal-state compact of any activity that includes the elements of prize, chance and consideration and *that is not prohibited expressly by the Wisconsin Constitution or state law.*" Given the broad definition of lottery and the fact that Wisconsin law no longer had any express prohibition against games involving the elements of prize, chance, and consideration, Wisconsin was required to negotiate regarding the games proposed by the tribes. The court in *Lac du Flambeau* took a more expansive view of the *Cabazon* decision than had previous courts. [Instead, the proper reading of] the thrust of *Cabazon* and its progeny requires a *particularized inquiry into the proposed gambling activity*. In addition, the *Lac du Flambeau* case is distinguishable from the case at hand because the Idaho Constitution *expressly prohibits* all forms of casino gambling and/or the electrical or electro-mechanical imitation or simulation of any form of casino gambling. The constitution also directs the legislature to provide criminal penalties for violation of this prohibition against such gaming.

Coeur d'Alene, at 1277–78. Do you agree with the *Coeur d'Alene* court's reading of the cases? How do you think the court would have read the Ninth Circuit's decision in *Sycuan Band*?

The Ninth Circuit similarly concluded that the Second Circuit's decision in *Mashantucket Pequot Tribe* was not inconsistent with its holding in *Rumsey*:

> The Tribes cite to *Mashantucket Pequot Tribe v. Connecticut* as authority for attributing the "Class II" legislative history to Class III. In *Mashantucket,* an Indian tribe sought to engage in "games of chance" that the State of Connecticut allowed charities to operate during "Las Vegas nights." Relying on the "Class II" legislative history, the court held that *Cabazon's* "criminal/regulatory" test applied to Class III gaming. It concluded that, because Connecticut permitted the games of chance to be operated by some persons in the state, the state had to negotiate over those games with the Tribes. While we disagree, for the reasons expressed above, with the *Mashantucket* court's use of the Class II legislative history to interpret IGRA's Class III provisions, we believe that the court nevertheless reached the correct result. As we have explained, IGRA's text plainly requires a state to negotiate with a tribe over a gaming activity in which the state allows others to engage, and no resort to legislative history is necessary to support this conclusion. Because Connecticut allowed charities to operate games of chance, it had to negotiate with the tribe over these games.

Rumsey, at 1259 n.6. Is the expansive approach merely a misreading of prior cases?

3. **The** Cabazon *"shorthand test" and scope of gaming.* The district court in *Coeur d'Alene* purported to apply *Cabazon's* distinction between state civil/regulatory and criminal/prohibitory laws. How did the district court's application of *Cabazon* differ from that of the courts in the expansive approach cases? Is there a difference between state public policy that "abolish[es] and criminally prohibit[s] *all* Class III gaming entirely" and state public policy that allows some forms of Class III gaming but not others? Is a tribe's operation of Class III gaming more abhorrent to the former state public policy?

The *Rumsey* court, on the other hand, rejected the *Cabazon* "shorthand test" of state public policy as inapplicable to Class III gaming. Why?

In his dissent, Judge Canby, a recognized expert in federal Indian law, argued that the "permits such gaming" requirement refers to the category of Class II or Class III gaming. Under this categorical approach, if a state permits any Class III games, then it is required to negotiate the entire range of Class III games. As Judge Canby explained it, "The structure of IGRA makes clear that Congress was dealing categorically, and that a state's duty to bargain is not to be determined game-by-game. The time to argue over particular games is during the negotiation process." *See also Yavapai-Prescott Indian Tribe v. Arizona,* 796 F. Supp. 1292 (D. Ariz. 1992) (stating that Congress intended the compact negotiation process to "facilitate the elimination of some areas of disagreement ... as to what forms of ... Class III gaming could be conducted under a compact"). Who has the better argument in *Rumsey*: the majority or the dissent? Why?

4. **The extent of the restrictive approach.** What is the extent of the restrictive approach taken by the courts in *Cheyenne River Sioux, Coeur d'Alene, Panzer,* and *Rumsey*? If a state allows a few Class III games, must it *negotiate* over those games, or *agree* to those games? May the state negotiate over other Class III games that are not specifically allowed under state law? Are prohibited games "on the table" during negotiations? Do different cases reach different conclusions on this point? What arguments support state law providing a "floor" for compact negotiations, and what arguments support state law providing a "ceiling"?

If the restrictive approach allows, but does not require, a state to negotiate the entire class of games, what would be valid points of negotiation? What arguments could a state make to exclude a certain game from the compact while fulfilling its duty to negotiate in good faith? What arguments might evidence bad faith?

If the restrictive approach limits compact negotiations to only those games specifically allowed under state law, is that in keeping with IGRA and Congress's intent? Why or why not?

5. *Changes in state law.* Idaho and Wisconsin share a similar history of the state constitution reflecting a clear public policy against gambling generally, modified by amendments in the 1970s and 1980s to allow some forms of gambling, including charitable gambling, pari-mutuel wagering, and state lotteries, and again modified in the early 1990s as Indian gaming expands under IGRA. Which court—*Lac du Flambeau, Coeur d'Alene,* or *Panzer*—has the best view of how such a history of state gambling policy should affect the scope of Indian gaming under IGRA? Are the courts' approaches similar or different, and how? What effect did Congress intend post-IGRA changes in state law to have on the scope of permitted tribal gaming?

6. *A matter of state constitutional law?* The Wisconsin Supreme Court's decision in *Panzer v. Doyle* further complicates the restrictive approach by characterizing it as a matter of state constitutional law. Are state courts in the best position to determine whether a state "permits such gaming"? Or is the question one of federal law?

3. Alternative Approaches

Are there workable alternatives to the expansive and restrictive approaches? Consider the suggestions of Professor Skibine.

Alex Tallchief Skibine
Scope of Gaming, Good Faith Negotiations and the Secretary of Interior's Class III Gaming Procedures: Is I.G.R.A. Still a Workable Framework After Seminole?
5 Gaming L. Rev. 401 (2001)

A slightly different, and in my mind improved, version of [the expansive approach] would be to interpret IGRA to create a presumption that tribes should be able to negotiate over all Class III games as long as the state allows some types of Class III games but allowing the state to rebut the presumption by demonstrating that a particular type of game is in fact against the public policy of the state. [The restrictive approach] seems too narrow because it could be interpreted as, for instance, allowing a state to select which house banked card games would be included in the tribal state compact negotiations by arbitrarily but specifically prohibiting some (baccarat for instance) while allowing others (such as blackjack) when in fact there are not apparent public policy reasons for making any such distinctions. A slightly modified and in my mind, more reasonable version [asks] "whether, in light or traditional understandings and the text and legislative history of the IGRA, the State has reasonably characterized the relevant state laws as completely prohibiting a distinct form of gaming." The Department of the Interior adopted [this] position, [explained] by the following hypothetical:

> If State law prohibits five-card stud poker but permits seven-card poker (or prohibits pari-mutuel wagering on dog racing, but not on horse racing), a question could arise as to whether that State law prohibits a distinct form of gaming known

as "five card stud poker" (or "dog racing"), or instead regulates the manner in which the permitted form of gaming known as "poker" (or "animal racing") may be conducted. If characterized in the former way, the State would have to negotiate concerning only seven-card draw poker (or horse racing); if characterized in the latter way, the State would have to negotiate over all poker games (or all animal racing).

Although the government's position is reasonable, one has to wonder why a state should ever be allowed to prohibit five card stud so as to prevent tribes from conducting that game when it allows seven card stud. Perhaps the government's position on the scope of gaming issue could be better conceptualized or perhaps refined by taking the position that the words "such gaming" refer to the words "gaming activity," but that the word "activity" should be understood to mean more than a specific form of game, [instead] encompassing all games sharing enough similarities so that players engaging in them can be considered to be engaged in the same type of gaming action.

Consistent with this position, if a state allowed any kind of casino games where the player plays against the house, it should be considered to have allowed all these types of casino games. If it allowed off track pari-mutuel betting, it should be considered to allow all off track pari-mutuel betting whether on horses, dogs, boxing matches or sports games. If any kind of lottery is allowed, all lottery type games should be subject to the negotiations. Same thing for any type of video gaming machine, or slot machines. The scope of games which can be grouped as belonging to a single type of "gaming activity" or "distinct form of game" should be defined by what makes sense from the point of view of the state's public policy. A state should not be able to withdraw a particular "game" from being considered in a tribal-state compact by specifically prohibiting such a game while still allowing other games which can be considered as belonging to the same type of gaming activity or form of gaming unless the state has carried its burden of demonstrating why such a prohibition is necessary under the public policy of the state.

Using this methodology, it would seem that while a state could put forth enough justification to prohibit gaming on dog racing while allowing it on horse racing, it would never be able to find enough public policy justification to treat five card and seven card poker differently so as to prevent tribes from negotiating over these two forms of poker. If properly conceptualized, [this approach] would be a reasonable compromise between the [expansive and restrictive approaches].

Notes and Questions

1. *"Compromise" approaches.* Is Skibine's practical approach to state public policy reasonable? Workable? Professor Washburn advocates a similar "compromise" approach to give effect to state public policy without merely subjecting tribes to the strictures of state law:

> At least in some circumstances, it seems clear that it is possible to divide the broad range of Class III gaming into portions that the state prohibits and portions that do not violate state policy. For example, if a state prohibits gambling on cock-fighting, it is doubtful that any court would hold the state liable for failing to negotiate in good faith regarding that activity. On the other hand, what if the state bans seven-card poker but allows five-card poker, or bans single-deck blackjack, but allows blackjack that is dealt out of a six-deck shoe? In such circumstances, it seems that the proper approach is a negotiation process in which

the state can explain its concerns about the particular evil that accompanies a particular game.

Kevin K. Washburn, *Recurring Issues in Indian Gaming*, 1 WYO. L. REV. 427 (2001).

   2.   The extent of the "compromise" approach. What is the extent of the compromise approach advocated by Skibine and Washburn? If a state allows, for example, blackjack, must it *negotiate* over all house-banked card games, or *agree* to all house-banked card games? What arguments could a state make to exclude a certain house-banked card game from the compact while fulfilling its duty to negotiate in good faith? What arguments might evidence bad faith?

   3.   Categorizing "distinct forms of gaming." In litigation over the permissible scope of gaming under Florida law, the federal government suggested that there were seven "distinct forms of gaming": lottery games (including scratch-off instant winner tickets and paper lottery games), house-banked casino games, non-house-banked card games, slot machines, off-track pari-mutuel betting, any games of skill whether or not machine operated, and sports betting. In determining whether a state "permits such gaming" under this approach, the court would decide whether each of these distinct forms of gaming was permitted or specifically prohibited under state law. Consider the courts' discussion of state law in each of the cases excerpted above. How would this approach operate if applied in *United States v. Sisseton-Wahpeton Sioux Tribe, Mashantucket Pequot Tribe v. Connecticut, Lac du Flambeau Band v. Wisconsin,* or *Sycuan Band of Mission Indians v. Roache?* How about in *Cheyenne River Sioux Tribe v. South Dakota, Coeur d'Alene Tribe v. Idaho, Panzer v. Doyle,* or *Rumsey Indian Rancheria of Wintun Indians v. Wilson?*

Problem 5.2: IGRA's "Permits Such Gaming" Requirement

   Consider the courts' interpretations of IGRA's requirement that tribes may conduct Class II and Class III gaming only in states that "permit[] such gaming for any purpose by any person."

For the cases adopting an expansive or categorical approach,

1.   How would you synthesize this set of cases to arrive at a legal standard?

2.   Should the legal standard be different for Class II and Class III gaming? Why or why not?

3.   Are the courts' holdings consistent with congressional intent?

4.   Are the courts' holdings consistent with the policy goals of Indian gaming?

5.   What do you see as the strengths and weaknesses of the expansive interpretation?

6.   What reforms would you suggest and why?

For the cases adopting a restrictive or game-specific approach,

1.   How would you synthesize this set of cases to arrive at a legal standard?

2.   Should the legal standard be different for Class II and Class III gaming? Why or why not?

3.   Are the courts' holdings consistent with congressional intent?

4.   Are the courts' holdings consistent with the policy goals of Indian gaming?

5.   What do you see as the strengths and weaknesses of the restrictive interpretation?

6.   What reforms would you suggest and why?

Is it possible to synthesize the entire set of cases? How would you do so? Which cases seem in line, and which seem to be "outliers"?

Part III

Government Authority over Indian Gaming

Under the federal regulatory scheme established by IGRA and explored in Part II, three levels of government have a hand in regulating Indian gaming: the federal government, tribal governments, and state governments. This Part explores the various institutions and officials with authority over Indian gaming. Chapter 6 details the federal government's extensive authority over tribal gaming, paying particular attention to the powers of the NIGC and the U.S. Secretary of the Interior. Other federal agencies, though not mentioned in IGRA, also play a part in the regulation of Indian gaming, including the Federal Bureau of Investigation and the U.S. Department of the Treasury. Chapter 7 explores tribal government authority over Indian gaming, including the primary role of tribal governments in regulating tribal casinos. Chapter 8 looks at state authority, including the role of the governor, the state legislature, and state courts.

As explained in Chapter 1, government regulation of legalized gambling addresses concerns that arguably are unique to the gaming industry, such as the potential for infiltration by organized crime and the need to protect the general public from the negative externalities of gambling. In its 1999 FINAL REPORT, the National Gambling Impact Study Commission outlined the policy rationales and challenges for government regulation:

> The gambling industry has emerged as an economic mainstay in many communities, and plays an increasingly prominent role in state and even regional economies. Although it could well be curtailed or restricted in some communities, it is virtually certain that legalized gambling is here to stay.

> Despite its increasing familiarity, nowhere is gambling regarded as merely another business, free to offer its wares to the public. Instead, it is the target of special scrutiny by governments in every jurisdiction where it exists, including even such gambling-friendly states as Nevada. The underlying assumption—whether empirically based or not—is that, left unregulated and subject only to market forces, gambling would produce a number of negative impacts on society and that government regulation is the most appropriate remedy. Thus, the authorization of legalized gambling has almost always been accompanied by the establishment of a corresponding regulatory regime and structure.

> Much of gambling regulation is focused on policing functions that differ little from community to community. The most immediate of these is ensuring the integrity of the games offered, a function often valued most by the propri-

etors of gambling establishments themselves. In the popular imagination, the "con" man forever hovers in the shadows of gambling; and in truth, without the stern presence of independent regulators, it would require little effort to conjure methods of conflating "games of chance" with outright deception. Thus, to the extent that governments assume a general responsibility to shield their populations from fraud, regulation is the most effective means of ensuring that such legal gambling as does exist is fair and honest.

A second area of government concern is crime, especially organized crime. Fairly or not, Nevada's casinos were once closely linked in the popular mind with organized crime, a bias given substance by repeated federal and state investigations and prosecutions of casino owners and operators. Because of the volume of cash transactions involved in casino gambling, and in order to minimize any resulting potential for money laundering, casinos must comply with requirements regarding the reporting of these transactions. All of the evidence presented to the Commission indicates that effective state regulation, coupled with the takeover of much of the industry by public corporations, has eliminated organized crime from the direct ownership and operation of casinos.

In addition to these relatively well-defined policing functions, a broader and far more important role for government regulation is determining the scope and manifestation of gambling's presence in society and thus its impact on the general public. In this sense, regulation can be broadly defined to include the political process by which the major decisions regarding legalized gambling are arrived at, the corresponding legislation and rules specifying the conditions of its operation, and the direction given to regulatory bodies. Through such means as specifying the number, location, and the size of gambling facilities; the types of games that can be offered; the conditions under which licensed facilities may operate; and so forth, governments have considerable control over the benefits and costs legalized gambling can bring with it. These measures can be as simple and straightforward as attempting to prevent underage gambling or as ambitious and contentious as promoting traditional social values.

If this basic responsibility is to be adequately met, government decisions regarding the introduction and regulation of legalized gambling would best be made according to a well-defined public policy, one formulated with specific goals and limits in mind. While governments have established a variety of regulatory structures, it is not at all clear that these have been guided by a coherent gambling policy or even that those making the decisions have had a clear idea of the larger public purpose they wish to promote. Generally, what is missing in the area of gambling regulation is a well thought-out scheme of how gambling can best be utilized to advance the larger public purpose and a corresponding role for regulation. Instead, much of what exists is far more the product of incremental and disconnected decisions, often taken in reaction to pressing issues of the day, than one based on sober assessments of long-term needs, goals, and risks.

There are a number of factors contributing to this gap between measures actually taken and any guiding public purpose, however conceived. One such factor is the existence of multiple decisionmakers: Federal, state, tribal, and local officials all have a say in gambling policy, and coordination among any of them is far more the exception than the rule. In addition, the gambling industry is not monolithic; each segment—lotteries, Native American casinos, convenience gambling, and so forth—comes with its own particular set of issues, concerns and interest groups, one result being that the respective regulatory structures and objectives often differ considerably from segment to segment. Further, the dynamism of the industry as a whole requires continuous adaptation on the part of regulation: In addition to a rapid pace of expansion, technology continues to produce new and different forms, often directly aimed at any weak links in government restrictions and regulation.

NGISC, Final Report, at 3-1 to 3-2.

As you read the chapters in this Part, consider first whether the gambling industry in fact raises unique legal and policy concerns requiring aggressive and multi-layered government regulation, and, second, whether those issues are any different in the context of Indian gaming. If the tribal gaming industry elicits its own unique concerns, how should federal, tribal, and state authority over Indian gaming mitigate them?

Chapter 6

Federal Authority

A. Overview

One of Congress's purposes in enacting IGRA was to

> declare that the establishment of independent Federal regulatory authority for gaming on Indian lands, the establishment of Federal standards for gaming on Indian lands, and the establishment of a National Indian Gaming Commission are necessary to meet congressional concerns regarding gaming and to protect such gaming as a means of generating tribal revenue.

25 U.S.C. §2702(3). IGRA assigns specific responsibilities to the NIGC as well as the U.S. Secretary of the Interior. Though not expressly included in IGRA, other federal agencies have a role in regulating Indian gaming as well. As the tribal gaming industry has grown and changed, so too has the real—and perceived—regulatory authority of the federal government.

B. National Indian Gaming Commission

1. Overview of NIGC Powers

Through IGRA, Congress established the NIGC, an independent federal regulatory agency in the U.S. Department of the Interior. The Commission's three members each serve three-year terms: a chair, appointed by the President with the advice and consent of the Senate, and two associate members, appointed by the Secretary of the Interior. The Commission selects one of the two associate members by majority vote to serve as Vice Chair. At least two commissioners must be enrolled members of a tribe, and no more than two commissioners may be members of the same political party. 25 U.S.C. §2704. In addition to the Commissioners, the NIGC is staffed by a General Counsel, as well as a Chief of Staff and an Office of Self Regulation Chief. *Id.* §2707. The Commission's Chief of Staff heads Directors of Enforcement, Congressional and Public Affairs, Audits, Contracts, and Administration, while the Director of Enforcement presides over investigators in six regional enforcement offices, located in Portland, Sacramento, Phoenix, Tulsa, St. Paul, and Washington, D.C.

The Commission's broad mission is "to regulate gaming activities on Indian lands for the purpose of shielding Indian tribes from organized crime and other corrupting influences; to ensure that Indian tribes are the primary beneficiaries of gaming revenue; and to assure that gaming is conducted fairly and honestly by both operators and players."

NIGC, *Mission and Responsibilities*, at http://www.nigc.gov/AboutUs/Missionand Responsibilities/tabid/72/Default.aspx. Along with other specified powers, the NIGC exercises broad authority to "promulgate such regulations and guidelines as it deems appropriate to implement [IGRA's] provisions." 25 U.S.C. §2706(b)(10). The Commission has issued a number of federal regulations, scattered throughout Title 25 of the Code of Federal Regulations, and located roughly in Parts 501 to 580. The Commission's decisions pursuant to 25 U.S.C. §§2710, 2711, 2712, and 2713 are final agency decisions and may be appealed in federal district court under the federal Administrative Procedure Act. *Id.* §2714.

The NIGC maintains a fairly comprehensive and informative Web site at http://www.nigc.gov/. In addition to the federal government's official gaming revenue reports, the site includes a database of final agency decisions, enforcement actions, game classification and Indian land opinions, approved gaming ordinances, and, of course, the Commission's existing and proposed regulations.

IGRA assigns some powers to the NIGC Chair, and others to the full Commission. Section 2705 details the powers of the Chair, which include authority to issue temporary closure orders (*see also* §2713(b)), to levy and collect civil fines (*see also* §2713), to approve tribal ordinances and resolutions (*see also* §2710(b) & (d)), and to approve management contracts (*see also* §§2710(d)(9), 2711). The Chair's decisions in these areas may be appealed to the full Commission. The Commission also may delegate additional authority to the Chair.

Section 2706 details the powers of the Commission:

(a) Budget approval; civil fines; fees; subpoenas; permanent orders. The Commission shall have the power, not subject to delegation—

(1) upon the recommendation of the Chairman, to approve the annual budget of the Commission as provided in section 2717 of this title;

(2) to adopt regulations for the assessment and collection of civil fines as provided in section 2713(a) of this title;

(3) by an affirmative vote of not less than 2 members, to establish the rate of fees as provided in section 2717 of this title;

(4) by an affirmative vote of not less than 2 members, to authorize the Chairman to issue subpoenas as provided in section 2715 of this title; and

(5) by an affirmative vote of not less than 2 members and after a full hearing, to make permanent a temporary order of the Chairman closing a gaming activity as provided in section 2713(b)(2) of this title.

(b) Monitoring; inspection of premises; investigations; access to records; mail; contracts; hearings; oaths; regulations. The Commission—

(1) shall monitor class II gaming conducted on Indian lands on a continuing basis;

(2) shall inspect and examine all premises located on Indian lands on which class II gaming is conducted;

(3) shall conduct or cause to be conducted such background investigations as may be necessary;

(4) may demand access to and inspect, examine, photocopy, and audit all papers, books, and records respecting gross revenues of class II gaming conducted on Indian lands and any other matters necessary to carry out the duties of the Commission under this chapter;

(5) may use the United States mail in the same manner and under the same conditions as any department or agency of the United States;

(6) may procure supplies, services, and property by contract in accordance with applicable Federal laws and regulations;

(7) may enter into contracts with Federal, State, tribal and private entities for activities necessary to the discharge of the duties of the Commission and, to the extent feasible, contract the enforcement of the Commission's regulations with the Indian tribes;

(8) may hold such hearings, sit and act at such times and places, take such testimony, and receive such evidence as the Commission deems appropriate;

(9) may administer oaths or affirmations to witnesses appearing before the Commission; and

(10) shall promulgate such regulations and guidelines as it deems appropriate to implement the provisions of this chapter.

Section 2706(c) also requires the Commission to submit a report, with minority views, to Congress every two years. As noted in §2706(a), other powers of the NIGC are scattered throughout IGRA, such as the power to issue a self-regulation certificate (§2710(c)) and the authority to issue subpoenas, order testimony, and take depositions (§2715).

As discussed in Chapter 4, under basic principles of separation of powers embodied in administrative law, courts accord considerable deference to regulations promulgated by agencies pursuant to their enabling legislation and their discretionary interpretation of relevant statutes. This principle applies to the NIGC's exercise of its powers authorized by Congress through IGRA. *See, e.g., Shakopee Mdewakanton Sioux Community v. Hope*, 16 F.3d 261 (8th Cir. 1994) ("Unless we find the Commission's classification of keno to be impermissible, we must uphold the Commission's interpretation of the ambiguous statutory provision."); *United States v. 103 Electronic Gambling Devices*, 223 F.3d 1091 (9th Cir. 2000) ("The NIGC's conception of what counts as bingo under IGRA is entitled to substantial deference."). In *Chevron, U.S.A., Inc. v. Natural Resources Defense Council, Inc.*, 467 U.S. 837, 843–44 (1984), the Supreme Court directed:

When a court reviews an agency's construction of the statute which it administers, it is confronted with two questions. First, always, is the question whether Congress has directly spoken to the precise question at issue. If the intent of Congress is clear, that is the end of the matter; for the court, as well as the agency, must give effect to the unambiguously expressed intent of Congress. If, however, the court determines Congress has not directly addressed the precise question at issue, the court does not simply impose its own construction on the statute, as would be necessary in the absence of an administrative interpretation. Rather, if the statute is silent or ambiguous with respect to the specific issue, the question for the court is whether the agency's answer is based on a permissible construction of the statute.

"The power of an administrative agency to administer a congressionally created ... program necessarily requires the formulation of policy and the making of rules to fill any gap left, implicitly or explicitly, by Congress." *Morton v. Ruiz*, 415 U.S. 199, 231 (1974). If Congress has explicitly left a gap for the agency to fill, there is an express delegation of authority to the agency to elucidate a specific provision of the statute by regulation. Such legislative regulations are given controlling weight unless they are arbitrary, capricious, or manifestly contrary to the statute. Sometimes the legislative delegation to an agency on a particular question is implicit rather than explicit. In such a case, a court may not substitute its own construction of a statutory provision for a reasonable interpretation made by the administrator of an agency.

> We have long recognized that considerable weight should be accorded to an executive department's construction of a statutory scheme it is entrusted to administer, and the principle of deference to administrative interpretations has been consistently followed by this Court whenever decision as to the meaning or reach of a statute has involved reconciling conflicting policies, and a full understanding of the force of the statutory policy in the given situation has depended upon more than ordinary knowledge respecting the matters subjected to agency regulations.

In addition to promulgating formal regulations, the NIGC also issues opinion letters and other informal interpretations of IGRA, typically signed by the NIGC's General Counsel or other staff. Under the Supreme Court's decision in *Skidmore v. Swift & Co.,* 323 U.S. 134 (1944), the weight to be afforded non-binding agency interpretations "will depend upon the thoroughness evident in its consideration, the validity of its reasoning, its consistency with earlier and later pronouncements, and all those factors which give it power to persuade, if lacking power to control." For a discussion of the distinction between the NIGC's advisory opinions and agency decisions, see *Cheyenne-Arapaho Gaming Commission v. NIGC,* 214 F. Supp. 2d 1155 (N.D. Okla. 2002).

The following case illustrates the application of the *Chevron* doctrine in the context of the NIGC's interpretation of IGRA.

Seneca-Cayuga Tribe of Oklahoma v. NIGC
327 F.3d 1019 (10th Cir. 2003)

HENRY, Circuit Judge.

[Recall from Chapter 4 that the Seneca-Cayuga Tribe of Oklahoma operated the Magical Irish Instant Bingo Dispenser System (the "Machine"). At the time, the Tribe had not entered into a Class III compact with Oklahoma, as state law allowed only Class II games. The tribe requested an administrative opinion from the NIGC regarding the classification of the Machine under IGRA. The resulting advisory opinion concluded that the game played with the Machine constituted unauthorized Class III gaming. The federal government then threatened the tribe with prosecution for the continued use of the machines, and the tribe brought this action. One of the issues in the case was the validity of one of the NIGC's regulations, 25 C.F.R. § 502.7, which included "pull tab dispensers and/or readers" in its definition of Class II technologic aids.]

With regard to classifying devices under IGRA, the NIGC's specialization warrants deference [under *Chevron*]. As the D.C. Circuit has noted, "Congress created the NIGC, headed by a Chair appointed by the President and confirmed by the Senate presumably for his or her expertise on Indian gaming." *Diamond Game Enter., Inc. v. Reno,* 230 F.3d 365, 369 (D.C. Cir. 2000). Congress intended that the NIGC would resolve difficult policy questions such as how to further the objective of allowing Indian tribes to use gaming as a means of "promoting tribal economic development, self-sufficiency, and strong tribal governments," while at the same time "shield[ing] [tribes] from organized crime and other corrupting influences," 25 U.S.C. §§ 2701–02, and from the risk of corruption or excessive gambling losses. Indeed, our circuit has held that we "afford the regulations promulgated by the [NIGC] and published in the Code of Federal Regulations the deference prescribed in *Chevron*." *U.S. v. 162 MegaMania Gambling Devices*, 231 F.3d 713, 718 (10th Cir. 2000). In reviewing the NIGC's interpretation of IGRA under *Chevron*, we ask two questions.

Chevron Step One. To determine "whether Congress has directly spoken to the precise question at issue," i.e., whether IGRA authorizes the use of technologic aids to pull-tabs, we employ "traditional tools of statutory construction." We turn to *Chevron's* second step only if "nothing in the statute directs" a clear answer.

We begin with the statutory text, [specifically IGRA's definition of Class II gaming]. Whether the authorization of the use of technologic aids extends to pull-tabs is not clearly resolved by the text of § 2703(7)(A)(i), which leaves ambiguous whether "technologic aids" parenthetical refers only to bingo, or also refers to the other games of chance authorized as Class II gaming in subsection (i)(III). [We are not aware of] any legislative history predating IGRA that speaks directly to the permissibility of Class II technologic aids for games other than bingo, or, for that matter, to the classification of pull-tab aids or dispensers in general.

Chevron Step Two: This step requires that we determine whether the NIGC's regulation stating that "pull tab dispensers and/or readers" are IGRA Class II "electronic, computer or other technologic aids," is a "permissible construction of the statute," or, instead, is "arbitrary, capricious, or manifestly contrary to the statute."

At least six factors support the reasonableness of the NIGC's construction as consistent with IGRA. First, the regulation represents a plausible reading of 25 U.S.C. § 2703(7)(A)(I)'s text. Second, as discussed above, the *ejusdem generis* ["of the same kind"] canon supports such a construction. Third, the NIGC's relatively inclusive reading of § 2703 has some support in IGRA's legislative history. *See* Committee Report, 1988 U.S.C.C.A.N. at 3079 ("The Committee specifically rejects any inference that tribes should restrict class II games to existing game sizes, levels of participation, or current technology. The Committee intends that tribes be given the opportunity to take advantage of modern methods of conducting Class II games and *the language regarding technology is designed to provide maximum flexibility*.") (emphasis supplied). Fourth, the NIGC's construction is not an unreasonable choice in the sense that the NIGC has adopted the reading of an ambiguous statute that is ostensibly more likely to expand the pool of tribal revenue through greater gaming variety and offerings.* Fifth, the NIGC may also wish to interpret ambiguities in IGRA so as to narrow its demanding oversight mandate. Finally, perhaps the best evidence of the reasonableness of the NIGC's construction is the favorable reception it has already received in the federal courts. *See, e.g., Diamond Game*; *Cabazon Band of Mission Indians v. NIGC*, 827 F. Supp. 26, 31 (D.D.C.1993) (noting that § 2703(7)(A) authorizes "the use of 'aids' for certain Class II *games*" (emphasis supplied)), *aff'd*, 14 F.3d 633 (D.C.Cir.1994)). *But see U.S. v. Santee Sioux Tribe of Nebraska*, 324 F.3d 607, 613 (8th Cir. 2003) (stating in dicta that "we believe that the phrase 'whether or not electronic, computer, or other technologic aids are used in connection therewith' applies only to bingo").

---

* *See* 25 U.S.C. § 2702 (stating that one of the purposes of IGRA was "to meet congressional concerns regarding gaming and to protect such gaming as a means of generating tribal revenue"); *see also, e.g.,* Kathryn R.L. Rand, *There Are No Pequots on the Plains: Assessing the Success of Indian Gaming*, 5 Chap. L. Rev. 47, 53 (2002) (surveying recent studies of tribal economic trends, and noting "marked improvements for many Native American communities, largely due to gaming revenue").

For these reasons, we hold that the NIGC's determination in 25 C.F.R. §502.7 that IGRA authorizes Class II technologic aids for pull-tabs is a "permissible construction of the statute," and we therefore accord it "controlling weight."

* * *

As you read through the following discussion of the NIGC's powers and its exercises of the same, consider whether the statutory language is clear on the extent and scope of authority assigned to the Commission. Viewing IGRA as enabling legislation, does it appear that Congress has given a broad mandate to the NIGC to exercise federal authority *over* Indian gaming, or a more limited mandate to *facilitate* federal policy goals for tribal gaming to accomplish what Congress intended? Does the NIGC's authority differ with regard to Class II or Class III gaming? Where do you see need for clarification or reform?

2. Defining Class II and Class III Gaming

One of the more pressing issues with which the NIGC has grappled is game classification. If a particular game falls within Class II, then it may be operated by a tribe without a tribal-state compact; if the game falls within Class III, however, legal operation requires a compact. IGRA's definitions do not offer much in the way of technical guidance. Class II gaming is defined as "bingo (whether or not electronic, computer or other technologic aids are used in connection therewith)," as well as some card games. Bingo is described in some detail in the statute as a game

(I) which is played for prizes, including monetary prizes, with cards bearing numbers or other designations,

(II) in which the holder of the card covers such numbers or designations when objects, similarly numbered or designated, are drawn or electronically determined, and

(III) in which the game is won by the first person covering a previously designated arrangement of numbers or designations on such cards, including (if played in the same location) pull-tabs, lotto, punch boards, tip jars, instant bingo, and other games similar to bingo....

25 U.S.C. §2703(7)(A)(i). Class II gaming specifically excludes house-banked card games and "electronic or electromechanical facsimiles of any game of chance or slot machines of any kind." *Id.* §2703(7)(B). Class III gaming is a residual category that includes all other forms of gaming (excepting, of course, Class I's traditional games). *Id.* §2703(8).

As discussed in Chapter 4, the NIGC's regulations in 25 C.F.R. pt. 502 attempt to provide additional guidance, including "plain language" restatements of the statutory definitions:

§502.3 Class II gaming. Class II gaming means:

(a) Bingo or lotto (whether or not electronic, computer, or other technologic aids are used) when players:

(1) Play for prizes with cards bearing numbers or other designations;

(2) Cover numbers or designations when object, similarly numbered or designated, are drawn or electronically determined; and

(3) Win the game by being the first person to cover a designated pattern on such cards;

(b) If played in the same location as bingo or lotto, pull-tabs, punch boards, tip jars, instant bingo, and other games similar to bingo....

§ 502.4 Class III gaming. Class III gaming means all forms of gaming that are not class I gaming or class II gaming, including but not limited to:

(a) Any house banking game, including but not limited to—

(1) Card games such as baccarat, chemin de fer, blackjack (21), and pai gow (if played as house banking games);

(2) Casino games such as roulette, craps, and keno;

(b) Any slot machines as defined in 15 U.S.C. § 1171(a)(1) and electronic or electro-mechanical facsimiles of any game of chance;

(c) Any sports betting and parimutuel wagering including but not limited to wagering on horse racing, dog racing or jai alai; or

(d) Lotteries.

§ 502.9 Other games similar to bingo. Other games similar to bingo means any game played in the same location as bingo (as defined in 25 U.S.C. § 2703(7)(A)(i)) constituting a variant on the game of bingo, provided that such game is not house banked and permits players to compete against each other for a common prize or prizes.

§ 502.11 House banking game. House banking game means any game of chance that is played with the house as a participant in the game, where the house takes on all players, collects from all losers, and pays all winners, and the house can win.

The most significant and enduring controversy stemming from IGRA's classification scheme has been the line between a Class II electronic bingo aid and a Class III electronic facsimile or slot machine. As discussed in Chapter 4, a by-product of IGRA is the creation of a Class II market: game manufacturers have invented machines meant to fall within Class II while supplying faster-paced play and entertaining displays. Fueling the controversy, electronic bingo machines often resemble slot machines, in that the display includes real or simulated spinning reels that visually reflect whether a player has won or not. Unlike slot machines, players actually win through their participation in a remote bingo game with multiple players competing against each other rather than through the random chance of lining up symbols on the reels. As Chapter 4 explains, as of this writing, the NIGC was in the midst of a prolonged process of promulgating regulations to provide extensive technical requirements for Class II aids. In the meantime, the NIGC continues to issue advisory opinions on game classification in accordance with current law, including its own regulations:

§ 502.7 Electronic, computer or other technologic aid.

(a) Electronic, computer or other technologic aid means any machine or device that:

(1) Assists a player or the playing of a game;

(2) Is not an electronic or electromechanical facsimile; and

(3) Is operated in accordance with applicable Federal communications law.

(b) Electronic, computer or other technologic aids include, but are not limited to, machines or devices that:

(1) Broaden the participation levels in a common game;

(2) Facilitate communication between and among gaming sites; or

(3) Allow a player to play a game with or against other players rather than with or against a machine.

(c) Examples of electronic, computer or other technologic aids include pull tab dispensers and/or readers, telephones, cables, televisions, screens, satellites, bingo blowers, electronic player stations, or electronic cards for participants in bingo games.

§ 502.8 Electronic or electromechanical facsimile. Electronic or electromechanical facsimile means a game played in an electronic or electromechanical format that replicates a game of chance by incorporating all of the characteristics of the game, except when, for bingo, lotto, and other games similar to bingo, the electronic or electromechanical format broadens participation by allowing multiple players to play with or against each other rather than with or against a machine.

National Indian Gaming Commission
Cadillac Jack "Triple Threat Bingo"
Advisory Game Classification Opinion
(2004)

Cadillac Jack offers "Triple Threat Bingo" as a linked bingo system using technological aids. Participation at the player level is accomplished through the use of multiple player stations. These may be established at multiple locations and the game linked between these locations. These Electronic Players Stations (EPS) communicate with a central server that provides a number of different services in order to create a game. These include a Linked Game Service (LGS) and a Game Management and Control System (GMCS). The LGS acts as a host for the bingo games and allows games to start and run independently from each other as players enter and play the games. The EPS are connected to the LGS and GMCS through an Ethernet LAN switch.

Game play is viewed on a video screen at the player terminal. It is a standard size video screen measuring approximately 19 inches along the diagonal. The game as presented to us is played using a 25 spot bingo card, in a five by five grid, displayed electronically on the video screen. Numbers or designations in the card spaces are not repeated on the same card. The game uses a non-replaceable pool of 75 numbered "balls" from which the numbers necessary to achieve designated prize patterns are randomly determined and used in the sequence they are selected.

The screen can also display spinning reel graphic icons, at the player's discretion. Cadillac Jack intends to offer the player an alternative of playing the game on a traditional bingo card that is the central feature of the video screen or in a version that would allow the player to switch back and forth between the traditional bingo card view and the spinning reels. The spinning reels do not affect the outcome of the game. When the spinning reels are displayed, a smaller bingo card, described below, will always be visible to the player during game play.

Bingo cards are distributed in micro-decks of up to 256 cards. The bingo cards are assigned by the LGS in such a manner as to insure that the cards that are distributed to the players are not duplicated for another player in the game. A player may select a new card before any game begins.

Participants are playing to achieve designated patterns on the bingo card based on the balls drawn for the game. Prizes in the form of game credits are awarded if a player covers, or daubs, the numbers on the card after the numbers are called and the numbers form one or more of the designated patterns. Credits translate to monetary value. The game will end when a player achieves a designated game-ending pattern and daubs this winning pattern. The game as submitted has a game-ending pattern comprised of a three-spot "V" pattern fixed at the center of the card. The game-ending pattern is always defined and designated in advance, and is never less than three spots. The prize for the game-ending pattern is structured so that the earlier the prize is awarded, the higher the prize may be for the player. In other words, the fewer the balls drawn to obtain the game-ending pattern, the higher the prize may be for the player.

The game may be displayed in two formats. One is a traditional bingo format where the cards are displayed, the balls selected are displayed on the screen and the numbers are daubed, winners and consolation prizes are determined, prizes are claimed and credits are issued. The second format uses alternative displays to illustrate amounts won in the bingo game. In this format the main area of the screen may contain a video simulation of spinning reels that start when the player joins the game by touching the "play" button. A smaller version of the Bingo card will always be visible when the alternative display appears, except during a graphical display that appears when bonus prizes of a certain value are being awarded. (In the version shown for this advisory opinion, the graphic featured mushrooms that when "opened" revealed a prize expressed in credits. This feature has no impact on the actual amount won and is for entertainment only.) In this second format, the Triple Threat Bingo card has an exterior dimension of 2 inches by 2 inches and an interior of just larger than 1 7/8 inches. The card is placed in the upper center of the screen. Play stops when the bingo card has been appropriately daubed and the prizes are awarded. The alternate spinning-wheel graphics do not affect the outcome of the game and are offered only as entertainment.

The first statutory criterion for bingo is that the game must be played for prizes on cards bearing numbers or other designations.

"Triple Threat Bingo" is a game played for prizes on cards bearing numbers. The "cards" in "Triple Threat Bingo" do not exist in a tangible medium but on a computer graphic at individual player stations. The game does not require paper cards. IGRA specifically permits the use of "technologic aids" in the play of bingo. The Commission's recent change to its definition of "technological aids" incorporated "electronic cards for participants in bingo games" as an example of a permitted technologic aid. 25 C.F.R. § 502.7(c).

The electronic cards in "Triple Threat Bingo" are provided to the player before actual game play begins. A player can change his card before entering a game. Card changes are not permitted once a game begins. Thus a player is actually playing the card and hoping to achieve a winning bingo pattern on the card when the numbers are drawn rather than buying a card with winning numbers pre-selected and hoping his purchase yielded a card containing a winning pattern.

The second statutory criterion from Section 2703(7)(A)(i) is that the holder of the card covers numbers or designations on the bingo card when objects, similarly numbered or designated, are drawn or electronically determined. Based on the game description, the "Triple Threat Bingo" game, as presented to the NIGC, meets the second requirement. A player "daubs" or covers the numbers on the player's card when the numbers are electronically determined. The numbers are determined in real time by a random number generator. The numbers are drawn in sets. When selected, the set of numbers is instantly conveyed to the EPS video screen. The selected numbers are indicated on the player's card by a small yellow dot. Once the player daubs, the yellow dot turns into a transparent red circle. The player is not relying on the machine itself to "daub" or cover the number. Rather, the player is actually performing some act to be involved in the play of the game of bingo.

The final element specified by Section 2703(7(A)(i) requires that players who enter bingo games compete to win by being the first person to cover a previously designated arrangement of numbers or designations on the card. As previously noted, in "Triple Threat Bingo," this previously designated arrangement, or winning pattern, is a three spot "V" pattern.

In evaluating the statutory criteria of Section 2703(7)(A)(i), we conclude that a basic premise of bingo is play and competition among others. The language, "won by the first person," set forth in 25 U.S.C. § 2703(7)(A)(i)(III), describes a contest or race among players to be the first to win. Numbers are drawn, players cover those numbers on their cards, more numbers are drawn, and so on until there is a winner. If all the balls necessary to produce a game-winning pattern are drawn and released at once, the game will likely end and someone will win with only one release of balls, thereby removing the contest element. In evaluating other electronic bingo games for advisory game classification opinion, we concluded that the method of play of the game of "bingo," as defined in IGRA, required that the game not be won in a single release of balls in the ball draw. There must be at least two ball draws or releases of electronically determined numbers before a player can win the game or any consolation or interim game. "Triple Threat Bingo" satisfies the requirement by providing multiple ball draws (electronic determinations) and releasing numbers in at least two sets as players compete for the prize won by the first player to obtain the designated game-ending bingo pattern. There are also corresponding daub opportunities or requirements following each set of balls released.

Because bingo is a game "won by being the first player to cover a previously designated arrangement of numbers" a player not attending to the game may "sleep" a bingo [meaning failing to cover a winning pattern or failing to claim a prize]. This is an important aspect of the "game of chance commonly known as bingo" and also to variations of that game. See 25 U.S.C. § 2703(7)(A)(i). "Triple Threat Bingo" provides this required feature. A player who fails to "daub" the game-winning (game-ending) pattern on his card within a configurable time "sleeps" the bingo and forfeits the prize. In "Triple Threat Bingo" all players continue in the game, and one or more additional bingo-numbers are drawn until another player obtains the game-winning (game-ending) pattern. A player who "slept" an earlier game-winning (game-ending) bingo pattern remains eligible to win a prize based on another pattern, but cannot win the game-ending prize because that pattern is assigned to a particular place on the card. The prize that is won by subsequent winning player is the same prize that would have been awarded to the player who obtained but slept the first winning bingo pattern.

The game will be displayed in two formats. One is a traditional bingo format where the cards are displayed, the balls selected are displayed on the screen and the numbers are daubed, winners and consolation prizes are determined, prizes are claimed and credits are issued. A second format uses alternative displays to illustrate amounts won in the bingo game but also has a prominently displayed card. The main area of the screen may contain a video simulation of spinning reels that start when the player joins the game by pressing "Play" and the stops when the bingo card has been daubed and the prizes are awarded. However, these graphics do not affect the outcome of the game and are important to the game only as entertainment.

We noted that in a previous advisory game classification opinion that while technical standards for electronic Class II bingo games and technologic aids may be developed in the future by the Commission, the current goal was to establish card size and visibility factors that made it easy for a bingo player to use and apparent that a player was actually engaged in the play of bingo. The Triple Threat Bingo card has an exterior dimension of 2 inches by 2 inches and an interior of just larger then 1 7/8 inches. The card is placed in the upper center of the screen. While not the dominant screen activity, a player is able to distinguish the card from other activity on the screen.

We also evaluated whether the player station terminal components for "Triple Threat Bingo" can be considered an "electronic, computer, or other technologic aid" to the play of bingo, a term defined in NIGC regulations, 25 C.F.R. § 502.7. The player station assists a player in the play of the common game. The electronic format of the "Triple Threat Bingo" game broadens participation in a common game and allows players to compete against one another. As such, the electronic characteristics of "Triple Threat Bingo" offered through its player stations are those of an "electronic, computer or other technologic aid."

First, to meet the requirements of the Commission definitions, the electronic format of the game must contain sufficient parameters to "allow" multiple players into the game. Conversely, we believe the format may not seek to limit player participation unnecessarily or in an overly restrictive manner. The fundamental idea is that the equipment and the electronic format "broaden" participation, not limit it. Second, in using the player terminal, the players must be playing with or against each other, in a contest of the game commonly known as bingo or a variant on that game.

Participation in any particular "Triple Threat Bingo" game is limited, in theory, only by the number of player stations available on the network and on which another game is not already in play. "Triple Threat Bingo" requires a minimum of two players for a game to begin. Additional players enter the game if they request participation within a set time period. The version shown at the NIGC allowed three (3) or more seconds for players to join. This meets our understanding of the minimum time for other players to join; however, a period less than two (2) seconds would not meet the minimum time. Our opinion is that the electronic format for "Triple Threat Bingo" does broaden participation among multiple players because the game format allows three seconds for additional players to enter after the first player enters the game. This time frame is a critical part of our overall opinion of the game.

"Triple Threat Bingo" in the form presented and described above, satisfies the criteria for a Class II game as that term is defined in IGRA and NIGC regulations.

Notes and Questions

1. ***"For entertainment only" displays.*** The NIGC's Cadillac Jack "Triple Threat Bingo" advisory opinion explains that game play may be illustrated in two formats on the video display. The first format roughly mimics traditional bingo play; the second uses "spinning-wheel graphics [which] do not affect the outcome of the game and are offered only as entertainment." The second format requires game manufacturers to use precise mathematical formulas to "reverse engineer" the representation of the game's outcomes so that the alternate display and the bingo card capture identical phenomena. Game manufacturers argue that all such games should be classified as Class II, since the "entertainment" value of the graphics never determines the game's outcomes. The game is won according to the live bingo game, not according to the result of a slot machine's random number generator. An assessment of the relative merits of this argument in large part drives the current controversies over game classifications that the NIGC is seeking to clarify through its proposed Definitions and Classification Standards and Technical Standards. Gaming experts generally support looking "behind the box" to classify such machines, while some policymakers employ a variation of "if it looks like a duck" logic: if the machines look and play like slots, then they must be slots. *See* Kathryn R.L. Rand & Steven Andrew Light, *Indian Gaming Law & Politics: Class II v. Class III Reforms*, CASINO LAWYER, Summer 2006, at 18–20.

2.   Testing labs. The NIGC frequently relies on third-party testing laboratories to assist in the process of determining how a game actually operates. As the above advisory opinion states,

> Cadillac Jack provided a report from Gaming Laboratories International (GLI) confirming that the "Triple Threat Bingo" game, Version V2.22.3, operates in the manner described in this opinion. The report also contains a signature for the key files so that verification may be obtained that the game in play in a gaming facility is the game considered in this classification opinion.

Why do you think independent game testing and verification is so important?

3.   Advisory opinions and technology. The "Triple Threat Bingo" NIGC advisory opinion is in the form of a letter from the NIGC Acting General Counsel to the Chief Technical Officer of the game manufacturer. If not final agency decisions, why are these advisory opinions so valuable to the manufacturers—and to tribes? What would happen if the NIGC issued new technical regulations concerning Class II gaming? Would the advisory opinion stand? Is it possible to legislate—or regulate—to stay ahead of technology?

3. Approval of Tribal Ordinances

Under IGRA, a tribe may not operate either Class II or Class III gaming in the absence of an authorizing tribal ordinance that has been approved by the NIGC Chair. *See* 25 U.S.C. § 2710(b)(1), (d)(1)(A). Section 2705 authorizes the Chair to approve or disapprove a tribal ordinance according to whether the ordinance contains provisions in compliance with 25 U.S.C. § 2710(b)(2) (e.g., sole proprietary interest, use of net revenues, annual outside gaming audits, independent audits of contracts, facility construction and maintenance, background investigations, and tribal licensing of management officials).

In addition to the statutory requirements governing the tribal ordinance provisions, the NIGC has adopted detailed submission requirements for approval in 25 C.F.R. pts. 522 (which applies to ordinances adopted after 1993) and 523 (which applies to existing ordinances). The submission requirements call for

(a) One copy on 8 1/2" x 11" paper of an ordinance or resolution certified as authentic by an authorized tribal official and that meets the approval requirements [outlined in 25 U.S.C. § 2710];

(b) A description of procedures to conduct or cause to be conducted background investigations on key employees and primary management officials and to ensure that key employees and primary management officials are notified of their rights under the Privacy Act as specified in § 556.2 of this chapter;

(c) A description of procedures to issue tribal licenses to primary management officials and key employees;

(d) Copies of all tribal gaming regulations;

(e) When an ordinance or resolution concerns class III gaming, a copy of the tribal-state compact or procedures as prescribed by the Secretary;

(f) A description of procedures for resolving disputes between the gaming public and the tribe or the management contractor;

(g) Designation of an agent for service … ; and

(h) Identification of a law enforcement agency that will take fingerprints and a description of procedures for conducting a criminal history check by a law enforcement agency. Such a criminal history check shall include a check of criminal history records information maintained by the Federal Bureau of Investigation.

25 C.F.R. § 522.2. IGRA requires the Chair to approve or disapprove a submitted ordinance within 90 days; if the Chair fails to take action in that time, the ordinance will be considered approved. 25 U.S.C. § 2710(e). Approved ordinances are published in the Federal Register; the Chair's disapproval may be appealed to the Commission. *See id.* § 2705; 25 C.F.R. § 524.1.

Tribal gaming ordinances are explored further in Chapter 7's discussion of tribal authority over Indian gaming.

4. Approval of Management Contracts

Section 2705 also authorizes the Chair to approve contracts for the management of Class II and Class III gaming facilities. Although IGRA requires that tribal casinos and other gaming establishments generally must be owned and operated by a tribe, a tribe may enter into a limited management contract with an outside party. *See* 25 U.S.C. §§ 2711(a) (Class II), 2710(d)(9) (Class III). The requirements for Class II and Class III management contracts differ; the entirety of § 2711 applies to Class II management contracts, while § 2710(d)(9) excepts Class III management contracts from the requirements of § 2711(a), (e), and (i).

In reviewing a proposed Class II management contract, the Chair is required to obtain background information on, and has the power to question, "each person or entity (including individuals comprising such entity) having a direct financial interest in, or management responsibility for" the proposed contract. *Id.* § 2711(a).

At a minimum, both Class II and Class III management contracts must provide:

(1) for adequate accounting procedures that are maintained, and for verifiable financial reports that are prepared, by or for the tribal governing body on a monthly basis;

(2) for access to the daily operations of the gaming to appropriate tribal officials who shall also have a right to verify the daily gross revenues and income made from any such tribal gaming activity;

(3) for a minimum guaranteed payment to the Indian tribe that has preference over the retirement of development and construction costs;

(4) for an agreed ceiling for the repayment of development and construction costs;

(5) for a contract term not to exceed five years, except that, upon the request of an Indian tribe, the Chairman may authorize a contract term that exceeds five years but does not exceed seven years if the Chairman is satisfied that the capital investment required, and the income projections, for the particular gaming activity require the additional time; and

(6) for grounds and mechanisms for terminating such contract, but actual contract termination shall not require the approval of the Commission.

Id. § 2711(b). Similar to the five-year time limit, IGRA also imposes a cap of 30 percent on management fees that are based on a percentage of net revenues (the cap may be increased to 40 percent where capital investments and income projections "require the additional fee"). *See id.* § 2711(c). Commission regulations further detail the required content of management contracts and procedures for submitting proposed management contracts to the Chair. *See* 25 C.F.R. pts. 531–539.

IGRA requires the Chair to disapprove a proposed Class II management contract if the Chair determines that

(1) any person [with a direct financial interest in or management responsibility for the proposed contract] —

(A) is an elected member of the governing body of the Indian tribe which is the party to the management contract;

(B) has been or subsequently is convicted of any felony or gaming offense;

(C) has knowingly and willfully provided materially important false statements or information to the Commission or the Indian tribe pursuant to this chapter or has refused to respond to questions propounded pursuant to subsection (a)(2) of this section; or

(D) has been determined to be a person whose prior activities, criminal record if any, or reputation, habits, and associations pose a threat to the public interest or to the effective regulation and control of gaming, or create or enhance the dangers of unsuitable, unfair, or illegal practices, methods, and activities in the conduct of gaming or the carrying on of the business and financial arrangements incidental thereto;

(2) the management contractor has, or has attempted to, unduly interfere or influence for its gain or advantage any decision or process of tribal government relating to the gaming activity;

(3) the management contractor has deliberately or substantially failed to comply with the terms of the management contract or the tribal gaming ordinance or resolution adopted and approved pursuant to this chapter; or

(4) a trustee, exercising the skill and diligence that a trustee is commonly held to, would not approve the contract.

25 U.S.C. § 2711(e). Interestingly, the Chair's review and approval of Class III management contracts are not governed by § 2711(e). *See id.* § 2710(d)(9).

Kevin K. Washburn
The Mechanics of Indian Gaming Management Contract Approval
8 GAMING L. REV. 333 (2004)

In the thirteen years that the NIGC has been in existence, the Commission has approved approximately forty-three gaming management contracts. The management contract review process at the NIGC is now routine. It proceeds roughly as follows.

The management contract review process begins when the parties submit a signed management contract for review. The time for NIGC review varies with the complexity of the management contract, the level of cooperation from the parties, and the scope of any necessary background investigations and environmental review.

Under the applicable regulations, the Chairman has only 180 days to review, and then approve or disapprove, a management contract. As a practical matter, this time limit is not a day-to-day concern for the NIGC. First, the Chairman may extend the deadline for 90 days at will as long as he notifies the parties that he is doing so. Second, the parties' primary means of enforcing the 180 day review requirement is an action in federal court to compel a decision by the Chairman. Obtaining judicial relief is likely to take a long time and might be met with hostility by Commission staff. Accordingly, parties regularly address NIGC delays with patience and cooperation. Finally, the NIGC has interpreted the law to mean that the 180-day time period does not begin to run until the NIGC receives a "complete submission." Because the NIGC staff will often require the parties to modify the contract and resubmit it, the clock usually is restarted at least once after initial submission.

Though the NIGC staff works diligently to process management contracts, the NIGC staff routinely advises parties that the contract review process takes from six to eighteen months. In recent years, the time required for approval has sometimes stretched out more than eighteen months, largely due to environmental compliance issues and issues related to Indian land acquisitions. Though some contract modifications or extensions are approved in as little as six months, it is probably more prudent to estimate twelve to thirty-six months from submission to approval for an entirely new contract. While environmental review and background investigations may occasionally cause delay, a common reason for delay is lack of cooperation or sophistication by parties to management contracts and lack of responsiveness to NIGC concerns.

In the history of the NIGC, probably no gaming management contract has ever been approved as submitted. The NIGC staff routinely raises dozens of questions and concerns and almost always requires the parties to amend the management contract, or at least provide additional clarification or justification for specific terms. The typical management contract submitted to the NIGC, though signed, may be intended primarily as an initial draft with the understanding that the parties will amend the contract as needed to obtain NIGC approval and possibly to address other matters of concern between the parties.

Following the initial submission of a gaming management contract, the NIGC Contracts Division usually responds with a letter detailing submission deficiencies, that is, an explanation of errors in submission and a list of additional information that must be submitted before formal contract review will begin.

Once the parties provide sufficient information for the NIGC staff to begin its review, NIGC staff in the Contracts Division will review the management contract submission and prepare an initial review memorandum setting forth potential problems and concerns and any remaining submission and content deficiencies. The memorandum prepared by NIGC staff at this stage typically will include the following information, among other things:

- a summary of any involvement thus far by the NIGC, including the date the contract was submitted, and any actions taken since submission such as summaries of meetings between the parties;
- a summary of the scope of the project, including general information, such as the square footage of the proposed casino, the type of gaming that may be involved, the names of the parties, and the estimated level of investment in the proposed casino (usually in the multiple millions of dollars);
- a summary of the proposed terms of the management contract;
- a justification for extraordinary terms (if the contract calls for a term in excess of five years or a fee in excess of thirty percent of gaming revenues);
- a summary of any collateral agreements and a description of their purposes;

- a summary of the status of any background investigations that lists the names of persons subject to investigation;
- a summary of the status of any environmental review;
- a description as to the status of the determination of whether the proposed project is on Indian lands;
- a statement as to whether there is an approved tribal gaming ordinance and the status of NIGC review of any proposed ordinance and/or the date the ordinance was approved by the NIGC;
- for Class III management contracts, a confirmation that the tribe has an approved tribal-state compact for Class III gaming and the date of approval;
- a lengthy list of issues and concerns that includes submission deficiencies, content deficiencies, and general concerns about the specific terms of the contract; and
- a recommendation by NIGC staff to the General Counsel and the Director of Contracts as to the proposed course of action, which at this stage usually involves a recommendation that the NIGC staff forward a letter to the parties detailing the problems and perhaps invites the parties to have a meeting with the parties and NIGC staff to go over problem areas.

The initial review memorandum, which summarizes the management agreement and addresses all the issues listed above, must be reviewed by a staff attorney in the Office of General Counsel and must be signed as "approved" by the General Counsel and the Director of the Contracts Division. This memo then serves as the basis for an initial deficiency letter to the parties, which will usually be prepared and signed by a financial analyst in the NIGC Contracts Division.

After the parties receive the initial deficiency letter, the parties will work to gather the new information and redraft and execute a new contract, if necessary, and then submit updated documents to the NIGC. When the additional information and, if necessary, a new version of the contract is submitted by the parties, the entire process repeats, with NIGC staff reviewing the information and creating another memorandum and a new deficiency letter to the parties.

Because the NIGC interprets [IGRA] as vesting with the NIGC the responsibility to insure that such contracts are "fair" to Indian tribes, the NIGC sometimes inserts itself into contract negotiations in an attempt to insure that the tribe obtains the maximum advantage from the gaming project. During discussions, the NIGC staff will sometimes meet with the tribe and its attorneys apart from the management contractor to discuss particular NIGC concerns and to insure that the NIGC can obtain the tribe's frank view of the contract outside the presence of the manager. Because a contract is void absent NIGC approval, the NIGC has tremendous informal authority at the pre-approval stage; each of the parties is usually strongly motivated to satisfy the concerns of NIGC staff, so that they can break ground on the project, even in circumstances when they believe that the NIGC is acting beyond the scope of its authority.

The principal decision maker at the NIGC is the Chairman. The entirety of the review process, including the discussions with the parties, is directed toward compliance with NIGC requirements so that the NIGC staff can recommend that the Chairman approve the management contract. The Chairman may disapprove a management agreement for a variety of reasons related to gaming regulatory concerns that are set forth in the regulations.

In addition, the Chairman must disapprove a management contract if he determines that a theoretical trustee for the tribe, acting with the prudence and diligence normally required of a trustee, would not approve the contract. This provision gives the Chairman the apparent discretionary power to second-guess business decisions by the tribe. However, because such action would not be consistent with current federal policies of treating tribes as self-governing sovereigns, disapproval on the basis of the trust responsibility is highly unusual. Though this "trust responsibility" therefore gives the NIGC staff some leverage to extract concessions from the management contractor, it does not, in practice, result in disapprovals of management contracts.

Rarely has a management contract been disapproved by the Chairman. Disapprovals are likely to occur where the parties lack sophistication to provide adequate "follow through" to complete the project approval process. If a contract is likely to be disapproved, members of the NIGC staff will communicate their concerns to the parties and encourage the parties to modify the contract to satisfy NIGC staff concerns or to withdraw the contract from NIGC review. Management contractors have a strong incentive to withdraw, rather than risk disapproval; disapproval by the NIGC may harm the party's reputation in the gaming industry and may have significant ramifications as to regulatory approvals with regard to other gaming jurisdictions. Moreover, although the parties have a right of appeal of a disapproval decision by the Chairman, parties are not likely to be willing to undergo the lengthy appeal process and the related opportunity costs, particularly in light of the unlikely result of prevailing on appeal.

Perhaps the most noteworthy content requirement is the compensation and length of term limitations. Under IGRA and NIGC regulations, a management contract generally may not be approved for a term exceeding five years, or for compensation in excess of thirty percent of net gaming revenues, absent extraordinary circumstances. The Chairman may approve a management contract term length in excess of five years (to a maximum term of seven years), or with a compensation term in excess of 30 percent of net gaming revenues (to a maximum of 40 percent), only if the Chairman is "satisfied that the capital investment required, and the income projections, for the gaming operation, require the additional time," or "the additional fee."

Neither IGRA nor the regulations provide further guidance as to what standards should be used to determine whether additional time or an additional fee is "required." The failure to define this term causes great difficulty and, frankly, great uncertainty in the management contract approval process. However, some rules of thumb have developed that are helpful in considering this question. First, because a management contract requires no justification if it is for no more than five years and calls for a management fee of no more than 30 percent of net gaming revenues, the NIGC generally considers the five year term and 30 percent management fee as both a safe harbor and a benchmark for comparison of any contract with terms in excess of the safe harbors. To establish a benchmark for review, the NIGC will routinely require financial projections for a hypothetical contract that would possess the 30 percent/five year safe harbor and that is otherwise ceteris paribus ["all other things being the same"]. The NIGC would then compare these financial projections to the projections for the contract under review. If the NIGC is able to determine that the contract under review to the tribe is more favorable to the tribe, the NIGC staff is likely to determine that the compensation term is "required" by the circumstances and recommend approval of the contract. Such circumstances may occur for example if the parties seek a length of term of six years, but call for compensation equal only to 25 percent of net gaming revenue.

In cases in which this method does not provide a definitive answer, the NIGC staff will consider a variety of ultimately uncertain variables including evidence that the project presents substantial risk to the management contractor, or that substantial revenues are not likely to exist in the early years, due to start up costs such as financing, marketing, training, and construction. Given the magnitude of costs in large projects, trying to pay all of these costs during a five-year term can impose serious burdens on a tribe, with the result that the tribe sees little or no revenue in the early years of a management contract. The tribe may very well wish to receive more revenue during the early years when the costs of repaying construction and startup costs are far greater as a percentage of overall revenue. If a contract calls for the term to be lengthened so that the tribe receives greater benefit in the early years, the NIGC staff may look more favorably on the excess terms, particularly if the agreement offers the tribe substantially greater revenue in the short term. Because many recent projects have involved construction costs in excess of $100 million, it is not unusual for parties to submit, and the NIGC to approve, management contracts with terms in excess of the safe harbors of five years/30 percent.

Notes and Questions

1.   Collateral and consulting agreements. Strictly speaking, IGRA authorizes the NIGC Chair to approve only management contracts. Typically, a management contract reflects just one aspect of the parties' relationship; the parties may have entered into other contractual agreements concerning, for example, financing or constructing the casino. Federal regulations define a "management contract" as "any contract, subcontract, or collateral agreement between an Indian tribe and a contractor ... if such contract or agreement provides for the management of all or part of the gaming operation." 25 C.F.R. §502.15. Collateral agreements are defined as

> any contract, whether or not in writing that is related, either directly or indirectly, to a management contract, or to any rights, duties or obligations created between the tribe (or any of its members, entities, or organizations) and a management contractor or subcontractor (or any person related to a management contractor or subcontractor).

Id. §502.5. Thus, a contract for the construction of the casino between the tribe and the management contractor could, as a collateral agreement, fall within the NIGC's definition of management contract and trigger the Chair's review under 25 U.S.C. §2711.

Consider Washburn's discussion of the NIGC's review of collateral agreements:

> Perhaps because of the perceived circularity of the definition, courts have shown some confusion as to the treatment of collateral agreements and have occasionally presumed that each document meeting the definition of collateral agreement is subject to approval by the NIGC. This approach is incorrect. As a practical matter, the NIGC does not take this view (and has not been a party to the decisions that have discussed the NIGC approval requirements). The NIGC has authority to approve a collateral agreement only if it also meets the definition of "management contract," that is, it provides for the "management of all or part of a gaming operation." In short, not all collateral agreements are management agreements. Those that do not meet the definition of "management contract" are not subject to NIGC review.
>
> That is not to say that the NIGC does not seek to review all collateral agreements. There are several reasons why it seeks to review such documents. First, the NIGC must make its own determination as to whether the collateral agreement is also a management contract. Upon request, the NIGC will review a contract and issue a letter indicating that the contract is not subject to the management

contract review and approval process. Second, the NIGC must look at collateral agreements as part of its review of the management contract. One concern is that parties might seek to evade [compensation] limits by hiding additional terms of compensation for management in other agreements that receive far less NIGC scrutiny.

Washburn, at 345. Despite the suggestion that collateral agreements may hide compensation terms that violate IGRA, tribes may resist NIGC review of collateral or consulting agreements for less nefarious reasons. As Washburn points out, the NIGC's review is a protracted and lengthy process, often taking one to three years to complete and resulting in significant delay—and lost profits—in opening the casino. Additionally, federal review of tribes' business agreements may be seen as paternalistic and, given increasing tribal savvy in the gaming industry, unnecessary. Regardless of the reasons cited, some tribes and contractors have sought to avoid NIGC review of collateral and consulting agreements, resulting in litigation. The next excerpt expands on this issue.

   2.   *Web resources.* The NIGC's Web site contains a number of resources to assist tribes in submitting management contracts for approval, including approved management contracts, checklists, and helpful hints. In 2007, the NIGC announced that it was considering amendments to update and streamline the management contract submission and approval process.

Heidi McNeil Staudenmaier
Negotiating Enforceable Tribal Gaming Management Agreements
7 Gaming L. Rev. 31 (2003)

Because of the length of time involved in obtaining NIGC approval of a management contract, many tribes and their business partners opt to enter into consulting agreements. The NIGC regulations are not clear as to what differentiates a consulting agreement from a management contract. Based on recent court decisions, it is strongly recommended that any agreement relating to a tribal gaming operation be submitted to the NIGC for review and the issuance of a declination letter. The NIGC warns that the "consequences are severe for a manager who mistakes his management agreement for a consulting agreement." Certainly, the losing parties in the *Catskill* and *Casino Magic* cases would likely concur with this NIGC warning.

By way of background, the St. Regis Mohawk Indian Tribe (Mohawk Tribe) retained Catskill Development (Catskill) for the purposes of developing, constructing and managing a casino on Mohawk land. Catskill (including its two subsidiaries, Mohawk Management and Monticello Raceway Development) entered into numerous agreements with the Mohawk Tribe, including a Management Agreement, a Development and Construction Agreement (DCA), and a Shared Facilities Agreement (collectively, the "Catskill Agreements"). A Land Purchase Agreement (LPA) was entered into between the Regis Mohawk Gaming Authority and Catskill (which had purchased the land for $10 million for the purpose of building the casino). There was also a Mortgage Leasehold Agreement executed between the Mohawk Tribe and a third-party mortgagee.

The Management Agreement was submitted to both the NIGC and the Bureau of Indian Affairs (BIA) for review and, where required, approval. Prior to receiving NIGC approval, Park Place Entertainment (Park Place) and the Mohawk Tribe entered into similar agreements, irrespective of the existing agreements between Catskill and the Mohawk Tribe. The Mohawk Tribe terminated the Catskill Agreements.

As a result of the termination, Catskill sued Park Place for tortious interference with contract. Park Place defended its actions by contending that, absent NIGC approval of the Catskill Agreements, there was no legitimately recognized contract between Catskill and the Mohawk Tribe.

In [*Catskill v. Park Place* (*Catskill I*), 144 F. Supp. 2d 215, (S.D.N.Y. 2001)], the Southern District Court of New York agreed with Park Place, holding that the Catskill-Mohawk Tribe Management Agreement was void for not having been approved by the NIGC. Likewise, the court found that the remaining Catskill Agreements were void as "collateral agreements" to the Management Agreement. The court stated:

> Collateral agreements executed in conjunction with gaming management contracts are included in the definition of management contracts, and thus are also void absent NIGC approval.... Each of the agreements executed by the parties relates either directly or indirectly to rights or obligations created between the Tribe and Catskill or one of its affiliates under the Management Agreement.

The court concluded that, because all the agreements were void as non-approved Management Agreements or collateral agreements, no enforceable contract existed and thus there was no basis for claiming tortious interference of contract.

Catskill sought a reversal of the decision that included the LPA as a collateral agreement. Pursuant to the LPA, Catskill purportedly spent $10 million for the purchase of land that was to be used for the casino site. In seeking reconsideration, Catskill asserted that the LPA was not void as a collateral agreement because 25 U.S.C. §2711(a)(3) applied only to Class II gaming. Catskill had sought approval from the NIGC of a Management Agreement for Class III gaming only. Catskill contended that 25 U.S.C. §2711(a)(3) therefore could not serve to bar validity of the collateral agreements, including the LPA.

Following an extensive review of the prior arguments, the court [in *Catskill II*, 154 F. Supp. 2d 696 (S.D.N.Y. 2001)] again concluded that the documents were collateral agreements. However, the court further determined that, because 25 U.S.C. §2711(a)(3) applied only to Class II gaming and not to Class III gaming, the collateral agreements were not void. As a result, the LPA was not void as a collateral agreement and was binding on both parties.

In *U.S. v. Casino Magic Corp.*, [293 F.3d 419 (8th Cir. 2002),] the Sisseton-Wahpeton Sioux Tribe entered into a Management Agreement with Casino Magic for the tribe's gaming operations. The parties also entered into a Secured Loan Agreement under which Casino Magic would lend the Sioux Tribe $5 million to start the casino project.

The two parties subsequently entered into a Consulting Agreement because the Management Agreement was never approved by the NIGC. Casino Magic submitted the Consulting Agreement to the NIGC for the issuance of a declination letter. The NIGC thereafter issued such a letter, stating that the Consulting Agreement did not need to be approved as it contained no management provisions.

Subsequently, the Sioux Tribe entered into a Construction and Term Loan Agreement with BNC under which BNC would provide $17.5 million if Casino Magic committed to contributing $5 million to the project. Casino Magic was not a party to the BNC Loan Agreement. BNC and Casino Magic did enter into a Participation Agreement to formalize Casino Magic's participation in the $5 million loan.

Thereafter, the Sioux Tribe terminated the Consulting Agreement with Casino Magic and also sent the Consulting Agreement and the BNC Loan Agreement to the NIGC for review. Notwithstanding the NIGC's prior declination letter regarding the Consulting

Agreement, the NIGC concluded that the two agreements "when considered as a whole, are management contracts," and therefore were void absent NIGC approval.

In the ensuing litigation, the South Dakota District Court disagreed with the NIGC's conclusion. The court held that the Sioux Tribe's agreement to "accept and comply with all recommendations made by the Consultant" in the BNC loan agreement was "insufficient to change Casino Magic's obligations to the Sioux Tribe from that of a consultant to that of a manager."

On appeal, the Eighth Circuit Court of Appeals found the lower court's reasoning "unpersuasive" and reversed. In so ruling, the Eighth Circuit relied on the NIGC decision and determined that the agreements, considered together, constituted a management agreement, thus requiring NIGC approval. The court reasoned that the BNC loan agreement transferred certain management responsibility to Casino Magic, even though Casino Magic was not a party to it. The court noted that Casino Magic was "aware of the combined effect of all agreements, and it assumed the risk of proceeding without having submitted all documents to the (NIGC) Chairman."

Based upon *Casino Magic*, Park Place sought reconsideration of *Catskill II*. Relying upon the reasoning in *Casino Magic*, Park Place urged that the collateral agreements relative to Class III gaming (and not just relative to Class II gaming) are subject to NIGC review and approval. Park Place argued that, contrary to the court's decision in *Catskill II*, the LPA was, in fact, a collateral agreement and should be deemed void and unenforceable. In essence, Park Place sought to have the court return to its original decision made in *Catskill I*.

[In *Catskill III*, 217 F. Supp. 2d 423 (S.D.N.Y. 2002)], the court agreed with Park Place, albeit on different grounds. The court noted that none of the parties (including the judge) had paid sufficient attention to the NIGC regulations applicable to the review of all management contracts. Specifically, the court focused on the NIGC's authority pursuant to 25 C.F.R. § 533.1 to review management contracts for both Class II and Class III gaming.

Based on its review of [the regulatory definitions of "management contract" and "collateral agreement"], the court concluded that the LPA fit squarely within the NIGC's definition of an agreement "collateral" to the management agreement. As a result, because the LPA had not received NIGC approval, the court held that it was void and of no effect.

What lessons can be learned from the *Catskill* and *Casino Magic* cases? Clearly, these decisions—albeit not binding on courts outside of New York or the Eighth Circuit—harshly underscore the need of parties pursuing any type of a business relationship with a tribal gaming operation to seek NIGC and BIA review of the transaction documents and, where appropriate, the issuance of a declination letter. Failure to obtain such assurances can lead to void and unenforceable agreements, without remedy or recourse. Further, the holding of the *Casino Magic* case counsels that, even if an agreement is initially found not to constitute a management agreement by the NIGC, if there are subsequent agreements negotiated which relate to the same transaction, it is wise to again confirm with the NIGC that the prior declination letter is still applicable (or seek a new declination letter covering the new documents).

Notes and Questions

1.   *Continued litigation in the* Catskill *and* Casino Magic *cases.* In 2004, the Eighth Circuit decided *Casino Magic II*, 384 F.3d 510 (8th Cir. 2004). Following its 2002 decision, the case was remanded to the district court to determine damages. Based on

the appellate court's decision that the contracts were invalid in the absence of NIGC approval, the federal government sought recovery of fees paid by the tribe for services rendered pursuant to the invalid contracts under 25 U.S.C. § 81, which allowed the U.S. to demand return of fees paid for illegal services (the statute has since been amended). The district court awarded $350,000 in damages to the federal government, the amount the tribe had paid to Casino Magic under the consulting agreement, and the Eighth Circuit affirmed.

In 2006, the federal district court issued another decision in the *Catskill* cases. In *deBary v. Harrah's Operating Co.*, 465 F. Supp. 2d 250 (S.D.N.Y. 2006), the court, on remand from the Second Circuit, dismissed Catskill's claim of tortious interference, relying on its reasoning in *Catskill III*. (Harrah's acquired Park Place in 2005 in its $9.4 billion buyout of Caesars Entertainment.) It is interesting to note that by the time of the court's decision in 2006, ten years had passed since the tribe and Catskill had begun the process of seeking regulatory approval of the parties' agreements.

The failed deal in the *Catskill* cases also gave rise to litigation in the St. Regis Mohawk Tribal Court, which in turned triggered a second line of litigation in federal court:

> At the time of these machinations [surrounding the tribe's termination of the Catskill agreements], the tribal chiefs were involved in a political struggle for control of the Tribe, which historically had been governed by a "Three Chiefs" system. In 1995, the Tribe held a referendum on whether to abandon the Three Chiefs system and to adopt a new Tribal Constitution, which would create three branches of tribal government, including a Tribal Court. The Constitution provided for its own adoption with 51% of the voting tribal members. The Tribal Clerk allegedly certified that 50.935093% of those voting were in favor of adopting the Constitution, yet certified that the Constitution was adopted by the requisite vote. In June 1996 the Tribal Council rescinded the certification of the Constitution following a second referendum. At the end of June, in a third referendum, the Tribe allegedly voted to elect Ransom, Smoke and Thompson in a "clean slate" of Chiefs, rather than retain the current Tribal Council officials. However, not all of the Tribe accepted the results of this referendum.

> On April 26, 2000, independent representatives of the Mohawk Tribe (including prior chiefs), filed a class action complaint in the St. Regis Mohawk Tribal Court against Park Place and the Three Chiefs who signed the agreement, asking the Court to nullify the agreement and seeking billions of dollars in damages. Soon after the complaint was filed, the Three Chiefs declared the Tribal Court invalid, raided the Court facilities, and removed the Court's computers and files. On June 2, 2000, Park Place brought suit in the Northern District of New York seeking: (1) an injunction against the Tribal Court proceeding and (2) a declaration that the Tribal Court was invalid and without authority to adjudicate the claims asserted. On September 18, 2000, Judge McAvoy dismissed Park Place's action for lack of subject matter jurisdiction. *See Park Place Entm't v. Arquette*, 113 F. Supp. 2d 322 (N.D.N.Y. 2000)....

> On March 20, 2001, the Mohawk Tribal Court entered a default judgment against Park Place and the other defendants in that case, and awarded $1.782 billion in actual damages and $5 million in punitive damages to plaintiffs. The Court set forth findings of fact and conclusions of law regarding the validity of the contracts and the actions of Park Place and Catskill. *See Arquette v. Park Place Entm't Corp.*, Case No. 00C10133GN, Mar. 20, 2001 (St. Regis Mohawk Tribal

Court, Hogansberg, NY). Park Place has advised the Court that it views this judgment as a nullity....

Catskill I, 144 F. Supp. 2d at 229. In mid-2007, the plaintiffs from the tribal court action (now organized as the Catskill Litigation Trust) announced that they would seek federal enforcement of the tribal court's nearly $1.8 billion judgment, as well as another $1 billion in interest on the judgment. *See* Arnold M. Knightly, *New York Tribe Seeks $3 Billion from Harrah's Entertainment*, LAS VEGAS REV.-J. (July 19, 2007).

2.   *Class II vs. Class III management contracts.* Recall that two separate provisions of IGRA deal with management contracts. In § 2711, titled "Management contracts," IGRA provides that "[s]ubject to the approval of the Chairman, an Indian tribe may enter into a management contract for the operation and management of a class II gaming activity...." Section 2711 also contains the requirements for approval and disapproval of management contracts. Strangely, the authorization for a tribe to enter into a management contract for a Class III facility is found elsewhere, in § 2710(d)(9), which states, "An Indian tribe may enter into a management contract for the operation of a class III gaming activity if such contract has been submitted to, and approved by, the Chairman." Section 2710(d)(9) goes on to require that the Chair's review and approval of Class III management contracts "shall be governed by the provisions of subsections (b), (c), (d), (f), (g), and (h) of section 2711," omitting subsections 2711(a), (e), and (i). Subsection (a) includes submission requirements, including the obligation of the tribe to disclose information on individuals with direct financial interest in or management responsibility for the contract; (e) outlines the circumstances under which the Chair must disapprove the contract; and (i) requires the NIGC to charge to the contractor the fees necessary to cover the cost of an investigation to determine whether any of the circumstances in (e) are present. As the *Catskill* cases indicate, the statutory requirements for Class III management contracts are less stringent than those for Class II management contracts. Why might Congress differentiate between Class II and Class III management contracts, and make it more difficult for a tribe to gain approval of a Class II management contract? Consider both that Congress was more concerned about Class III gaming, and that it created a role for state regulation through the compacting process.

3.   *Federal approval as a disincentive to doing business in Indian country.* Considering the bureaucratic "red tape" to seeking approval of management contracts as well as the danger of proceeding with an unapproved agreement, what effect does the approval requirement have on a tribe's ability to enter into an effective business partnership with a contractor? Are the practical realities of federal approval inconsistent with the federal government's goal of facilitating tribal economic development? Have tribes "outgrown" the need for federal oversight in their business dealings? Some policymakers have argued that the NIGC requires greater authority to review agreements related to Indian gaming. Do you agree? Given the difficulty in obtaining approval of management contracts, why would a tribe seek to have its gaming operation managed by an outside contractor?

5. Investigative and Enforcement Powers

The NIGC also exercises investigative and enforcement powers. The Commission's investigatory powers include oversight of tribal licensing of key employees and management officials, 25 U.S.C. § 2710(c), authority to conduct background investigations related to management contracts, *id.* § 2711(a), and power to issue subpoenas and conduct hearings, *id.* § 2715. NIGC regulations detail the content of background investigations for tribal licensing as well as the procedures for submitting proposed licenses to the Commission. *See* 25 C.F.R. pts. 556, 558. The Commission's oversight of tribal bingo operations includes the power to issue a "certificate of self-regulation" to a tribe under § 2710(c).

The Chair's powers include the authority to levy civil fines and to temporarily close a gaming facility; the Commission has power to make the Chair's temporary closure permanent. IGRA authorizes civil fines of up to $25,000 against tribal operators or management contractors for each violation of IGRA, NIGC regulations, or tribal gaming ordinances. 25 U.S.C. § 2713(a). Temporary closures may be ordered by the Chair for "substantial violation" of IGRA, NIGC regulations, or tribal gaming ordinances. *Id.* § 2713(b). Commission regulations also detail the NIGC's investigatory and enforcement powers. *See* 25 C.F.R. pts. 571–577.

Before exercising its enforcement powers, the NIGC must issue a written complaint alleging the violation in "common and concise language." 25 C.F.R. § 573.6(a) sets forth twelve specific substantial violations that may trigger the Chair's temporary closure:

(1) The respondent fails to correct violations within: (i) The time permitted in a notice of violation; or (ii) A reasonable time after a tribe provides notice of a violation.

(2) A gaming operation fails to pay the annual fee required by 25 CFR part 514.

(3) A gaming operation operates for business without a tribal ordinance or resolution that the Chairman has approved under part 522 or 523 of this chapter.

(4) A gaming operation operates for business without a license from a tribe, in violation of part 558 of this chapter.

(5) A gaming operation operates for business without either background investigations having been completed for, or tribal licenses granted to, all key employees and primary management officials, as provided in § 558.3(b) of this chapter.

(6) There is clear and convincing evidence that a gaming operation defrauds a tribe or a customer.

(7) A management contractor operates for business without a contract that the Chairman has approved under part 533 of this chapter.

(8) Any person knowingly submits false or misleading information to the Commission or a tribe in response to any provision of the Act, this chapter, or a tribal ordinance or resolution that the Chairman has approved under part 522 or 523 of this chapter.

(9) A gaming operation refuses to allow an authorized representative of the Commission or an authorized tribal official to enter or inspect a gaming operation, in violation of § 571.5 or § 571.6 of this chapter, or of a tribal ordinance or resolution approved by the Chairman under part 522 or 523 of this chapter.

(10) A tribe fails to suspend a license upon notification by the Commission that a primary management official or key employee does not meet the standards for employment contained in § 558.2 of this chapter, in violation of § 558.5 of this chapter.

(11) A gaming operation operates class III games in the absence of a tribal-state compact that is in effect, in violation of 25 U.S.C. § 2710(d).

(12) A gaming operation's facility is constructed, maintained, or operated in a manner that threatens the environment or the public health and safety, in violation of a tribal ordinance or resolution approved by the Chairman under part 522 or 523 of this chapter.

Upon the Chair's order of temporary closure, the tribe may demand a hearing before the Commission. The Commission must decide by majority vote whether to close the gaming operation permanently. The NIGC's order of permanent closure is reviewable in federal district court.

To levy a civil fine, the Chair reviews each violation and assesses a fine according to the economic benefit of noncompliance, the seriousness of the violation and the extent to which it threatens the integrity of Indian gaming generally, whether the operator has a history of violations, whether the violation is negligent or willful, and whether the operator made a good-faith effort to correct the violation after notification. *See* 25 C.F.R. §§ 575.4–.6. The tribe may appeal the Chair's fine to the Commission according to procedures set forth in 25 C.F.R. pt. 577. The NIGC's final decision on a civil fine levied by the Chair is reviewable in federal district court.

Notes and Questions

1.   *Scope of closure.* In *United States v. Seminole Nation of Oklahoma*, 321 F.3d 939 (10th Cir. 2002), the Tenth Circuit held that the Chair's power to order temporary closure is not limited to the offending games; the Chair may order the closure of a tribe's gaming operations in their entirety. The question arose because § 2713(b) refers to closure of "an Indian game." The court reasoned,

> While the narrow term "an Indian game" is used in § 2713(b)(1), when read as a whole IGRA unambiguously authorizes the NIGC Chairman to order the temporary closure of entire gaming operations. In § 2705(a)(1), the NIGC Chairman is authorized to "issue orders of temporary closure of gaming activities as provided in section 2713(b)." Accordingly, the phrases "gaming activities" and "an Indian game" are used interchangeably in reference to the NIGC Chairman's authority to issue temporary closure orders.

> Moreover, the NIGC is required by § 2713(b)(2) to review the NIGC Chairman's temporary closure order and either dissolve it or order "a permanent closure of the gaming operation." Because the NIGC can act to either dissolve or make permanent the Chairman's temporary order, the NIGC's permanent closure order is of the same scope as the NIGC Chairman's temporary closure order. The reference in § 2713(b)(2) to a "gaming operation," therefore, is substantially equivalent to the phrase "an Indian game" in § 2713(b)(1).

> Finally, the NIGC Chairman is obligated to approve tribal ordinances which, *inter alia*, provide for the protection of public health and safety at gaming facilities. The NIGC Chairman is authorized to enforce such tribal ordinances through the issuance of temporary closure orders. If the NIGC Chairman's authority to issue temporary closure orders was limited to the closure of individual games, he would be unable to carry out this obligation. Accordingly, when § 2710(b)(2)(E) and § 2713(b)(1) are read together, the NIGC Chairman's authority to issue temporary closure orders clearly includes the power to close entire gaming facilities.

Id. at 944–45.

2.   *Federal enforcement authority and* Seminole Tribe. The question of whether a tribe is operating Class III games in violation of IGRA is complicated somewhat by the U.S. Supreme Court's decision in *Seminole Tribe v. Florida*, 517 U.S. 44 (1996). After *Seminole Tribe*, a tribe may not sue a state without its consent for failure to negotiate in good faith a tribal-state compact. Because Class III gaming is illegal under IGRA (and, for

many casino-style games, also under the federal Johnson Act) in the absence of valid compact, a few tribes have responded to a state's alleged bad faith in failing to negotiate a compact by operating Class III gaming without a compact.

Just such a situation led to the litigation in *United States v. Santee Sioux Tribe of Nebraska*, 135 F.3d 558 (8th Cir. 1998) (*Santee I*). In 1996, after some three years of failed compact negotiations with the state, the Santee Sioux Tribe sued Nebraska for failure to negotiate in good faith. When the state did not consent to the suit, the district court dismissed it under *Seminole Tribe*. In the meantime, the tribe opened a casino, offering slot machines and video poker and blackjack. Shortly thereafter, the NIGC Chair entered an order of temporary closure. The tribe then appealed the order, first to the Commission and then to the district court, arguing that it was unfair to hold the tribe to the compact requirement where the state refused to enter into a compact and to allow a federal suit to resolve the deadlock. The Eighth Circuit first held that the U.S. Attorneys have authority to bring civil actions to enforce the NIGC's closure orders, reasoning that

> [b]ecause the IGRA is silent with respect to the authority to conduct litigation necessary to enforce the NIGC's closure orders in the event those orders are ignored or its assessments left unpaid by Indian Tribes engaging in gaming activities in violation of the Act, we must assume that Congress intended for the Attorney General to conduct this enforcement function on behalf of the agency.... We cannot imagine that Congress intended to vest in the Chairman and the NIGC the power to assess fines against the tribal operators of the facilities and to order temporary closures of Indian gaming facilities operating in violation of the IGRA without providing for a means to ensure compliance with those decisions.

Santee I, at 562.

Turning to the tribe's substantive argument, the court essentially decided that the state had negotiated in good faith. Nebraska law, concluded the court, prohibited slot machines and video games such as those offered by the tribe. "[T]he State is not required to negotiate for gambling that is illegal under Nebraska law," said the court, citing *Cheyenne River Sioux Tribe v. South Dakota* (discussed in Chapter 5). Following the Eighth Circuit's decision, the tribe voted to continue operating the Class III games while it pursued an administrative "compact" under 25 C.F.R. pt. 291. By 2001, the U.S. Secretary of the Interior had not issued an administrative compact, and the district court had assessed millions of dollars in fines against the tribe for its operation of illegal games. On the advice of the NIGC, the tribe replaced its Class III machines with "Lucky Tab II" electronic pull-tab machines, which the NIGC had classified as Class II machines. The Justice Department took a contrary position, however, arguing that the machines were Class III devices and, even if the machines fell within Class II, nevertheless were illegal gambling devices under the Johnson Act. In *Santee II*, 324 F.3d 607 (8th Cir. 2003) (excerpted in Chapter 4), the Eighth Circuit held that the Lucky Tab II machines were Class II machines and accordingly were not prohibited by the Johnson Act.

6. Minimum Internal Control Standards and NIGC Authority Over Class III Gaming

Perhaps the NIGC's most notable—and controversial—exercise of its power to promulgate regulations was its adoption of Minimum Internal Control Standards, or MICS, for tribal gaming operations. These highly detailed standards, found in 25 C.F.R. pt. 542, regulate the operation of specific games as well as cage and credit, internal audits, surveillance, information technology, and complimentary services and items.

For example, one of the shorter sets of standards included in the MICS is that governing pull-tabs:

(a) Computer applications. For any computer application utilized, alternate documentation and/or procedures that provide at least the level of control described by the standards in this section, as approved by the Tribal gaming regulatory authority, will be acceptable.

(b) Pull tab inventory.

(1) Pull tab inventory (including unused tickets) shall be controlled to assure the integrity of the pull tabs.

(2) Purchased pull tabs shall be inventoried and secured by a person or persons independent of the pull tab sales.

(3) The issue of pull tabs to the cashier or sales location shall be documented and signed for by the person responsible for inventory control and the cashier. The document log shall include the serial number of the pull tabs issued.

(4) Appropriate documentation shall be given to the redemption booth for purposes of determining if the winner purchased the pull tab from the pull tabs issued by the gaming operation. Electronic verification satisfies this requirement.

(5) At the end of each month, a person or persons independent of pull tab sales and inventory control shall verify the accuracy of the ending balance in the pull tab control by reconciling the pull tabs on hand.

(6) A monthly comparison for reasonableness shall be made of the amount of pull tabs sold from the pull tab control log to the amount of revenue recognized.

(c) Access. Access to pull tabs shall be restricted to authorized persons.

(d) Transfers. Transfers of pull tabs from storage to the sale location shall be secured and independently controlled.

(e) Winning pull tabs.

(1) Winning pull tabs shall be verified and paid as follows: (i) Payouts in excess of a dollar amount determined by the gaming operation, as approved by the Tribal gaming regulatory authority, shall be verified by at least two employees. (ii) Total payout shall be computed and recorded by shift. (iii) The winning pull tabs shall be voided so that they cannot be presented for payment again.

(2) Personnel independent of pull tab operations shall verify the amount of winning pull tabs redeemed each day.

(f) Accountability form.

(1) All funds used to operate the pull tab game shall be recorded on an accountability form.

(2) All funds used to operate the pull tab game shall be counted independently by at least two persons and reconciled to the recorded amounts at the end of each shift or session. Unverified transfers of cash and/or cash equivalents are prohibited.

(g) Standards for statistical reports.

(1) Records shall be maintained, which include win, write (sales), and a win-to-write hold percentage as compared to the theoretical hold percentage derived from

the flare, for each deal or type of game, for: (i) Each shift; (ii) Each day; (iii) Month-to-date; and (iv) Year-to-date or fiscal year-to-date as applicable.

(2) A manager independent of the pull tab operations shall review statistical information at least on a monthly basis and shall investigate any large or unusual statistical fluctuations. These investigations shall be documented, maintained for inspection, and provided to the Tribal gaming regulatory authority upon request.

(3) Each month, the actual hold percentage shall be compared to the theoretical hold percentage. Any significant variations (3%) shall be investigated.

(h) Electronic equipment.

(1) If the gaming operation utilizes electronic equipment in connection with the play of pull tabs, then the following standards shall also apply.

(i) If the electronic equipment contains a bill acceptor, then § 542.21(e) and (f), § 542.31(e) and (f), or § 542.41(e) and (f) (as applicable) shall apply.

(ii) If the electronic equipment uses a bar code or microchip reader, the reader shall be tested periodically to determine that it is correctly reading the bar code or microchip.

(iii) If the electronic equipment returns a voucher or a payment slip to the player, then § 542.13(n)(as applicable) shall apply.

(iv) If the electronic equipment utilizes patron account access cards for activation of play, then § 542.13(o) (as applicable) shall apply.

25 C.F.R. § 542.8. Longer sets of standards apply to bingo, table games, gaming machines, etc. The NIGC has "audit checklists" that break down applicable MICS into a set of questions. These checklists are available on the NIGC Web site.

Controversy over the MICS has stemmed from two overlapping issues: first, that tribes are able to develop MICS that are appropriate to their specific gaming operations without the imposition of federal standards, and second, that by applying the MICS to both Class II and Class III gaming, the NIGC exceeded its authority under IGRA. The latter issue, though arising in the context of the MICS, also raised the larger question about the NIGC's power to regulate Class III gaming generally.

Colorado River Indian Tribes v. NIGC
466 F.3d 134 (D.C. Cir. 2006)

RANDOLPH, Circuit Judge.

The issue is whether the Indian Gaming Regulatory Act gives the Commission authority to promulgate regulations establishing mandatory operating procedures for certain kinds of gambling in tribal casinos.

Congress enacted the Indian Gaming Regulatory Act in the wake of the Supreme Court's decision [in *Cabazon*] that state gaming laws could not be enforced on Indian reservations within states otherwise permitting gaming. The Act established the Commission as an agency within the Department of the Interior [and gave it] authority to investigate and audit certain types of Indian gaming, to enforce the collection of civil fines, and to "promulgate such regulations and guidelines as it deems appropriate to implement the provisions" of the Act.

The Tribe operates the BlueWater Resort and Casino on Indian lands in Parker, Arizona. The casino offers what the Act defines as "class II" and "class III" gaming. As to class

II gaming, the Commission and the tribes share regulatory authority: the tribes must enact a gaming ordinance applying the Act's minimum regulatory requirements, and the Commission's Chairman must approve the tribal ordinance before gaming may occur.

[U]nlike class II gaming, a tribe conducts class III gaming pursuant to a compact with the state. The Secretary of the Interior must approve any such compact before it may become effective. Thereafter, the "Tribal-State compact govern[s] the conduct of gaming activities," § 2710(d)(3)(A), and the tribe's class III gaming operations must be "conducted in conformance" with the compact, § 2710(d)(1)(C). Tribal-state compacts may contain provisions related to "standards for the operation of such activity" and "any other subjects that are directly related to the operation of gaming activities." § 2710(d)(3)(C)(vi), (vii). The Commission must approve any tribal ordinances for regulating and conducting class III gaming and any contracts the tribe enters into for the management of its class III gaming. § 2710(d)(1)(A)(iii), (d)(9).

The Colorado River Indian Tribes regulates gaming at its BlueWater casino pursuant to a tribal ordinance and rules contained in a tribal-state class III gaming compact with the State of Arizona. Both the ordinance and the compact contain their own internal control standards. The most recent version of the compact requires the Tribe's gaming agency to create standards governing operating procedures that are at least as stringent as those contained in [25 C.F.R. pt. 542]. The State of Arizona monitors the Tribe's compliance with the standards, for which the Tribe reimburses the state about $250,000 per year. The Tribe's gaming agency employs twenty-nine employees and has an annual budget of $1.2 million.

In 1999 the Commission promulgated regulations, which it termed "Minimum Internal Control Standards," governing class II and class III gaming. The regulations take up more than eighty pages in the Code of Federal Regulations. No operational detail is overlooked. The rules establish standards for individual games, customer credit, information technology, complimentary services, and many other aspects of gaming. To illustrate, tribes must establish "a reasonable time period" not to exceed seven days for removing playing cards from play, but "if a gaming operation uses plastic cards (not plastic-coated cards), the cards may be used for up to three (3) months if the plastic cards are routinely inspected, and washed or cleaned in a manner and time frame approved by the Tribal gaming regulatory authority." To take another example, coin drops are regulated differently according to the size of the gaming facility. There are rules prescribing the number and type of employees who must be involved in the removal of the coin drop, the timing of the removal of the coin drop, the tagging and transportation of the coin drop, the manner in which the coin drop must be housed while in the machine, and the purposes for which a coin drop may be used.

In January 2001, the Commission sought to audit the Tribe's class III gaming at the BlueWater casino in order to determine whether the Tribe was complying with the regulations. The Tribe protested on the ground that the rules exceeded the Commission's authority under the Act. The auditors departed and the Commission issued a notice of violation. After administrative hearings, the Commission fined the Tribe $2,000 for terminating the audit. The Commission denied the Tribe's objection, citing its authority to "promulgate such regulations and guidelines as it deems appropriate to implement the provisions" of the Act, among which is the provision stating that one of the Act's purposes is to protect the integrity of gaming revenue. The Commission located its power to audit the casino in § 2706(b)(4), which authorizes the Commission to "audit all papers, books, and records respecting gross revenues of class II gaming conducted on Indian lands and any other matters necessary to carry out the duties of the Commission under this chapter...." The Tribe brought an action in federal district court challenging the decision and the Commission's statutory authority to regulate class III gaming. The district court reached the "inescapable conclusion" that Congress did not intend to give such broad authority to the Commission, and therefore vacated the Commission's decision and declared the regulations unlawful as applied to class III gaming.

There was a time when the Commission agreed with the district court's view of the Act. The first Chairman of the Commission notified the Inspector General of the Department of the Interior in 1993 that "the regulation of class III gaming was not assigned to the Commission but was left to the tribes and the states...." Memorandum from Anthony J. Hope, Chairman, Nat'l Indian Gaming Comm'n to the Assistant Inspector General for Audits, Dep't of the Interior 2 (Oct. 18, 1993). He explained that this was why the Commission had not imposed "gaming control standards" on class III gaming: "the Act assigns those responsibilities to the tribes and/or the states." The Commission's Chairman took the same position when he testified before Congress the following year. *See Manner in which Gaming Activities Are Regulated by the Several States and the Role of the Federal Government in the Regulation of Indian Gaming Activities: Hearing Before the S. Comm. on Indian Affairs,* 103d Cong. 7-8 (1994) (testimony of Chairman Hope, Nat'l Indian Gaming Comm'n). Despite many legislative efforts since then, Congress has never amended the Act to confer any such express power on the Commission.

Even now the Commission concedes that no provision of the Act explicitly grants it the power to impose operational standards on class III gaming. Section 2706 grants the Commission authority over several aspects of class II regulation. Thus, the Commission "shall monitor class II gaming," and "inspect and examine all premises located on Indian lands on which class II gaming is conducted...." §2706(b)(1), (2). It "may demand access to and inspect, examine, photocopy, and audit all papers, books, and records respecting gross revenues of class II gaming conducted on Indian lands and any other matters necessary to carry out the duties of the Commission under this chapter...." §2706(b)(4). While the statute grants the Commission audit authority over "any other matters necessary to carry out [its] duties," the statute does not indicate that these duties extend to class III regulation. Instead, the main provision dealing with the regulation of class III gaming—§2710(d)—contemplates joint tribal-state regulation, [describing] tribal-state compacts as agreements "governing the conduct of [class III] gaming activities." A compact may contain provisions relating to "the application of the criminal and civil laws and regulations of the Indian tribe or the State that are directly related to, and necessary for, the licensing and regulation of" class III gaming, "standards for the operation of such activity," and "any other subjects that are directly related to the operation of [class III] gaming activities," §2710(d)(3)(C). That the Act sets up concurrent tribal-state regulation of class III gaming, not tribal-state-Commission regulation, is evident from §2710(d)(5): "Nothing in this subsection shall impair the right of an Indian tribe to regulate class III gaming on its Indian lands concurrently with the State, except to the extent that such regulation is inconsistent with, or less stringent than"—not Commission regulations, but—"the State laws and regulations made applicable by any Tribal-State compact entered into by the Indian tribe under paragraph (3) that is in effect." Contrast this provision with §542.4(c) of the regulations, which states that if a standard in the Commission's regulations is more stringent than a standard in a tribal-state compact, the Commission's regulation "shall prevail." There are other indications that Congress intended to leave the regulation of class III gaming to the tribes and the states, including the fact that the Secretary of the Interior—rather than the Commission—approves (or disapproves) tribal-state compacts regulating class III gaming.

As against this, the Commission offers three main arguments. One is that the Commission has "oversight" authority over class III gaming, that the dictionary defines "oversight" to mean "supervision," and that the Commission's regulation of class III gaming falls within that definition. The trouble is that the Act does not use the word "oversight." The Commission relies not on statutory language, but on a sentence from the Senate committee report on the Act: "The Commission will have a regulatory role for class II gaming and an oversight role with respect to class III gaming." But just two sentences before the "oversight" passage, the report states that the Senate bill "provides for a system for joint regulation by tribes and the Federal Government of class II gaming on Indian lands and a system for compacts between tribes and States for regulation of class III gaming." One might wonder why the Committee would rely on tribal-state compacts to regulate class III gaming. The report gives this explanation: "the Committee notes that there is no adequate Federal regulatory system in place for class III gaming, nor do tribes have such systems for the regulation of class III gaming currently in place. Thus a logical choice is to make use of existing State regulatory systems, although the adoption of State law is not tantamount to an accession to State jurisdiction. The use of State regulatory systems can be accomplished through negotiated compacts but this is not to say that tribal governments can have no role to play in regulation of class III gaming—many can and will." In addition to the point that a committee report is not law, it is perfectly clear that whatever the Senate committee thought "oversight" might entail, the committee did not foresee the Commission regulating class III gaming.

The Commission's other arguments proceed from the text of the Act. The Commission is funded by a percentage of each tribe's gross gaming revenues from class II and class III gaming. To this end, tribes must submit annual "outside audits" to the Commission of their class II and class III gaming operations. § 2710(b)(2)(C), (d)(1)(A)(ii). From this the Commission infers that it has the authority to regulate the handling and accounting of gaming receipts in order to ensure the integrity of audits. We cannot see how the right to receive an outside audit, presumably conducted in accordance with Generally Accepted Auditing Standards, translates into a power to control gaming operations. Under the Securities Exchange Act of 1934, public companies must file reports necessary to the protection of investors. If the public company happened to be in the casino business, such as Harrah's Entertainment, Inc., the Commission's logic here would entitle the SEC to dictate the details of how Harrah's conducts its casino operations because the SEC receives reports from the company. The SEC obviously has no such authority, and neither does the Commission.

This brings us to the Commission's third argument—namely, that its regulations are valid in light of its authority to "promulgate such regulations and guidelines as it deems proper to implement the provisions of [the Act]." *Mourning v. Family Publications Service, Inc.,* 411 U.S. 356 (1973), the Commission tells us, states a canon of statutory interpretation for general rulemaking provisions such as this—regulations promulgated pursuant to such statutes are valid so long as they are "reasonably related to the purposes of the enabling legislation." An agency's general rulemaking authority does not mean that the specific rule the agency promulgates is a valid exercise of that authority. So here.

In arguing that the regulations implement the provisions of the Act, the Commission points to § 2702, the Act's general declaration of policy, which it says embodies the congressional purpose to promote integrity in Indian gaming, a purpose the Commission's regulations further. But this cannot carry the Commission as far as it needs to go. The Commission is correct that Congress wanted to ensure the integrity of Indian gaming, but it is equally clear that Congress wanted to do this in a particular way. The declared policy is therefore not simply to shield Indian tribes "from organized crime and other corrupting influences" and "to assure that gaming is conducted fairly and honestly by both the operator and players," but to accomplish this through the "statutory basis for the regulation of gaming" provided in the Act. This leads us back to the opening question—what is the statutory basis empowering the Commission to regulate class III gaming operations? Finding none, we affirm.

Notes and Questions

1.   *The NIGC's authority over Class III gaming.* Is the D.C. Circuit's decision limited to the NIGC's authority to promulgate MICS or other operating standards for Class III gaming, or does it speak more broadly to the NIGC's general authority over Class III gaming? What powers regarding Class III gaming does IGRA specifically assign to the Chair and/or the Commission?

2.   *Class III MICS as "reasonably related" to IGRA's purposes.* The court disagreed with the NIGC's argument that pursuant to *Mourning v. Family Publications Service, Inc.*, 411 U.S. 356 (1973), and the canon of statutory interpretation for general rulemaking, the MICS should be presumed valid as long as they are "reasonably related to the purposes of the enabling legislation." Did the court effectively counter that argument? What additional points might you make to bolster the NIGC's position that the MICS are, in fact, "reasonably related" to IGRA's purposes?

3.   *Need for a "CRIT fix"?* Colorado River Indian Tribes v. NIGC (the "CRIT" case) may be one of the more significant court decisions concerning Indian gaming in recent years. Given the fact that the NIGC promulgated MICS in 1999, why did it take so long for this matter to be litigated? Should Congress amend IGRA to provide express authority over Class III gaming to the NIGC? Officials from some tribes claimed the outcome in the CRIT case as a victory, while those from other tribes expressed concern. Why the difference of opinion?

C. Secretary of the Interior

IGRA assigns specific duties to the Interior Secretary. Most notable, of course, is the Secretary's role in approving tribal-state compacts for Class III gaming under § 2710(d). IGRA also requires the Secretary to approve a tribe's plan for per capita distribution of gaming revenue under § 2710(b)(3) and to make a determination under the "best interests" exception (§ 2719(b)(1)(A)) to IGRA's general prohibition against gaming on newly acquired lands. The Secretary also has promulgated regulations directly related to its duties under IGRA. 25 C.F.R. pt. 290 details the approval process for per capita distribution plans, and 25 C.F.R. pt. 291 sets forth the process for an administrative "compact" when the state allegedly has failed to negotiate in good faith and refuses to consent to suit (recall Chapter 5's discussion of the Secretary's authority and the Fifth Circuit's decision regarding Part 291 in *Texas v. United States*).

The Office of Indian Gaming Management (OIGM), housed within the Bureau of Indian Affairs (BIA), is charged with implementation of the responsibilities assigned by IGRA to the Interior Secretary. The OIGM develops policies and procedures for review and approval of tribal-state compacts, per capita distributions of gaming revenue, and requests to take land into trust for the purpose of conducting gaming.

The Interior Secretary's influence over Indian gaming is greater than the duties contained in IGRA, however. The Interior Department is charged with fulfilling the federal government's trust responsibilities to tribes. The Assistant Secretary of the Interior for Indian Affairs heads the BIA and supervises other divisions and programs within the Department pertaining to tribes. With regard to Indian gaming, the Secretary performs two important "gatekeeping" functions through the power to take land into trust for the benefit of a tribe and the BIA's authority to administratively grant federal recognition to tribal groups. Chapter 3 provides an overview of these processes and their connection to tribal gaming; the political controversy over each is discussed in greater detail in Chapter 10.

D. Other Federal Agencies

As is apparent from the above discussion of the *Santee Sioux* litigation, other federal agencies, most notably the Department of Justice, are involved in the regulation of Indian gaming. As head of the Justice Department, the U.S. Attorney General is charged with the enforcement of federal laws, including IGRA and the Johnson Act. The Federal Bureau of Investigation (FBI) plays a key role in investigating criminal activity on tribal lands, including crimes related to Indian gaming. With the NIGC, the FBI created in 2003 the Indian Gaming Working Group, which reviews pending cases for "national importance," or significant impact on the tribal gaming industry, and coordinates federal resources in the investigation and prosecution of such cases. *See* Federal Bureau of Investigation, *Indian Gaming Investigations/The Indian Gaming Working Group*, at http://www.fbi.gov/hq/cid/indian/indgaming.htm.

In the Department of the Treasury, the Financial Crimes Enforcement Network (FinCEN) regulates financial transactions and assists in investigation of money laundering under the federal Bank Secrecy Act, 31 U.S.C. §§ 5311–5330, 12 U.S.C. §§ 1818(s), 1829(b), 1951–1959. Tribal casinos, like commercial casinos, are subject to the Act's money-laundering controls, including recordkeeping and reporting requirements for large transactions. Under the Act, casinos are required to report cash transactions of more than $10,000 and to record a number of other financial transactions. Additionally, the Internal Revenue Service (IRS) enforces civil regulations under the Bank Secrecy Act as well as federal tax laws and regulations that apply to tribal gaming operations. *See generally* Internal Revenue Service, *Tax Information for Indian Tribal Governments*, at http://www.irs.gov/govt/tribes.

Problem 6: The Federal Regulatory Role

In 2005, U.S. Senator John McCain (R-Ariz.), one of IGRA's architects, said, "Never in our wildest dreams at the time of the formulation of [IGRA] did we envision that Indian gaming would become the $19 billion-a-year enterprise that it is today." McCain also said, "[I]t's time we reviewed a 17-year-old piece of legislation … and make whatever necessary changes in order to deal [with] an … industry that none of us ever anticipated would reach this size when we passed the act in 1988." *See* Kathryn R.L. Rand & Steven Andrew Light, *How Congress Can and Should "Fix" the Indian Gaming Regulatory Act: Recommendations for Law and Policy Reform*, 13 Va. J. Soc. Pol'y & L. 396, 396–97 (2006).

Two years later, Indian gaming revenue surpassed $25 billion. Has the federal regulatory role as set by IGRA and other federal statutes kept up with the industry's growth? Is there a need to expand—or contract—the federal regulatory role? Why or why not? What reforms, if any, would you suggest, and why?

Chapter 7

Tribal Authority

A. Overview

Within the regulatory structure created by IGRA, tribes have significant regulatory authority over Indian gaming. Both Class II and Class III gaming are predicated on a tribal ordinance; though such tribal ordinances must comply with federal law, tribes also tailor gaming and related ordinances to their individual circumstances and needs. Even more fundamentally, of course, Indian gaming facilities are, by definition, located on Indian lands over which a tribe exercises governmental authority. *See* 25 U.S.C. § 2703(4).

This Chapter provides additional information about tribal government structure and specific information about tribal gaming commissions. We include several illustrative tribal court decisions relevant to Indian gaming.

B. Tribal Gaming Commissions

Like the NIGC or state gaming commissions, tribal gaming commissions are executive agencies that exercise delegated governmental authority. As such, tribal gaming commissions are part of tribal governments. In order to understand the scope and operation of tribal authority over Indian gaming, it is necessary to have some familiarity with the structure and powers of tribal governments.

Vine Deloria, Jr. & Clifford M. Lytle
American Indians, American Justice
99–105 (1983)

Modern tribal government can trace its inception, although not its fruition, back to the New Deal administration of Franklin Delano Roosevelt. When the federal government finally awakened to the fact that the Indian allotment policy had been a failure, resulting in the loss of a substantial portion of the Indian land estate and the impoverishment of the people, Congress, at the urging of the president and the secretary of the interior, Harold Ickes, initiated a new Indian policy by enacting the Indian Reorganization Act of 1934 (IRA). Part of the catalytic force behind this measure was the 1928 Meriam Report, which described the failure of the federal government to provide for Indians. The report mentioned the destructive impact that allotment had had on Indian life and culture and recommended major renovations in the federal bureaucracy.

The Indian Reorganization Act became important because it directed national policy from a deliberate effort to extinguish tribal governments and customs to a goal of establishing self-government and providing it with sufficient authority and powers to represent the reservation population in a variety of political and economic ventures.

The IRA, then, signaled an attitudinal change toward Indians and tribal governments. It provided an opportunity to revitalize tribal governments that had been submerged by the failure of either the legislative or the executive branches of the federal government to articulate the proper relationship that in fact existed between the Department of the Interior and the Bureau of Indian Affairs in their trustee capacity and the tribal governments, which, for better or for worse, were the successors to the gatherings of chiefs and headmen who had signed the treaties on behalf of their nations three-quarters of a century before. In addition to terminating the destructive allotment system, the IRA afforded tribes an opportunity to organize for their common welfare and to adopt written constitutions that would be formally approved by the secretary of the interior and that granted them status as federally chartered corporations. [Thus, the IRA laid] the foundation for a resurrection of tribal government and power. The bureaucratic stranglehold and paternalistic orientation of the BIA were substantially modified. Administrative centralization was replaced by decentralized power in tribal governments.

The political damage that had been inflicted upon tribal governments for so many decades in the past could not be undone overnight. The traditional forms of tribal government had been dormant for too long and much of the religious undergirding of the informal customs had been badly eroded. The format that emerged under the 1934 act was almost a carbon copy of the structured, legalistic European form of government. Since tribal governments were floundering, the Bureau of Indian Affairs seized the initiative and drafted a model constitution that could be used by tribes as a starting point for their written documents. This model constitution in most instances became the final product, which should not be surprising since Congress in passing the IRA required that all constitutions be approved by the secretary of the interior before becoming operational and homogeneity rather than usefulness consequently became the virtue.

The effort to revitalize tribal governments continued with limited success throughout the 1930s and 1940s. Although the exercise of power by tribal governments took on the appearance of increasing sophistication, these developments came at the expense of certain tribal traditions and informal customs that had served the communities well for nearly three-quarters of a century. Indians, consciously or not, were adopting the whites' legalistic perspective on government. The 1950s, however, posed a significant threat in tribal development. The Eisenhower administration initiated a policy of "termination," designed to eliminate the reservations and assimilate the Indians into the mainstream of the white social and economic systems.

In the overall scheme of things, however, the Eisenhower "termination" policy was but a momentary, though totally destructive, digression from the continuing resurgence of tribal government development. In the two decades following the Eisenhower years, tribes were once again placed in a position to seize the initiative that had begun in the 1930s to exercise self-governing powers. The social programs of the 1960s, the New Frontier and the Great Society social welfare legislation, enabled the tribal governments to be sponsors of federally funded programs, and tribal governments rapidly expanded to take advantage of these opportunities. Soon each tribe had developed its own massive bureaucracy to deal with the multitude of programs for which it was eligible. Although the IRA had enabled tribes to charter organizations for the purposes of economic development, few tribes had any experience in operating complicated subsidiaries. The first thought of many tribes during the 1960s was to designate the tribal council as the housing author-ity, the economic development corporation, and even sometimes the school board. But it was quickly apparent to both tribes and the federal funding agencies alike that this kind of institutional response was fraught with complications. Consequently, federal agencies required the tribal councils to charter separate housing authorities and nonprofit devel-opment corporations. In order to make certain that their people derived every possible service and program for which they were eligible, tribal governments were burdened with responsibilities far in excess of anything conceived during the IRA's formative years.

The Self-Determination and Education Assistance Act of 1975 created a statutory cli-mate for a real reawakening of tribal efforts. Among other things, this act authorized agencies of the federal government to contract with and make grants directly to Indian tribal governments for the delivery of federal services. The philosophy underlying this concept of tribal self-determination revolved around the vesting of both management and control of governmental service programs in the tribal governments on the theory that tribes knew best their own problems and could therefore allocate their resources and energies in the proper direction. This ideology assumed a sophistication that did not exist and generated tremendous expectations in Congress that the tribes would suddenly re-spond to new opportunities with the expertise of a modern corporation. When the tribes became bogged down in complicated management problems, some opponents of the pol-icy in the Bureau of Indian Affairs were quick to emphasize their inability to function in the white world. The experience of self-determination was therefore both good and bad. It allowed tribes to make some decisions without the pressure from bureaucrats to con-form to preexisting ideas but it also had pejorative effects when a project failed, further undermining the Indians' confidence in themselves.

During the years when tribal governments were weak, or even nonexistent, the BIA as-sumed almost total control and management of federal programs. Today the picture has changed significantly. Tribal governments, for the most part, have developed to the ex-tent that they can now undertake these management functions. Structurally, many tribal governments are composed of representative councils that perform legislative functions, professional bureaucrats charged with managing the administrative business of the tribe, tribal courts that handle the adjudicatory matters of a criminal and civil nature, and even special business councils that conduct the economic development activities on behalf of the reservation.

The metamorphosis that tribal government has experienced in the past decade from a latent governmental entity to a dynamic political force is not simply the result of such statutes as the Self-Determination Act. During the past decade other active elements on the reservations have worked to produce this change. Several decades ago the reservations were barren of attorneys. The infusion of attorneys on the reservations provided greater access to the courts and opened up an additional avenue to bring about needed procedural and substantive changes in Indian policy. Whereas the black community had embarked on its legal revolution in the 1930s and had seen its successful culmination in *Brown* and succeeding cases in the 1950s and 1960s, the Indian movement began its litigation activities during the 1970s. The use of the legal system as a pathway to strengthened tribal government to press for the restoration of Indian rights added an extra and important dimension to the poli-tics of Indian Country that heretofore had been dormant.

While the relationship between tribal governments and the BIA undoubtedly has changed over the past few years, it would be foolish to discount the agency as a constant visible entity in Indian political affairs. The BIA remains a formidable actor in the gov-ernmental process and one with which the tribes must continually reckon. Even in the age of self-determination the deep-seated belief held by federal employees that they must be involved in every activity undertaken by the tribes inevitably leads to a continuing irritation that cannot be easily resolved. In addition, the access of tribal officers to other federal agencies with a less rigid view of Indian matters and more willingness to become involved in difficult development projects has led to a sense of futility within the Bureau of Indian Affairs that often manifests itself in overzealous enforcement of the rules and regulations. Consequently, both tribal governments and the BIA, and ultimately the federal relationship itself, are in a state of rapid and unpredictable change.

David E. Wilkins
American Indian Politics and the American Political System
140–50 (2002)

It is important to note that the IRA had virtually no effect on the substantive powers already vested in the tribal nations, but added some powers and recognition of powers tribes could exercise without first securing secretarial approval: veto power over the dispensation of tribal funds or assets; the right to negotiate with federal, state, and local governments; and the right to be advised of all appropriation estimates affecting the tribe before these are submitted to Congress.

Finally, tribal governments were recognized as having the right to exercise all inherent "existing powers," [following] the premise that "those powers which are lawfully vested in an Indian tribe are not, in general, delegated powers granted by express acts of Congress, but rather inherent powers of a limited sovereignty which has never been extinguished."

Inherent powers included recognition of a tribe's right to choose its own form of government, the right to define the conditions for tribal citizenship, and the power to regulate and dispose of tribal property. In other words, tribes had been completely sovereign in the past, but in establishing their political relationship with the United States in various treaties surrendered some of their sovereignty, while retaining all other powers of sovereignty.

Tribal Councils (Legislative Functions)

A majority of tribal nations, particularly those organized under the IRA, vest legislative authority in a tribal council, although it is sometimes called something else. Tribal councils or business committees are usually fairly small, ranging from as few as five members up to eighteen. Tribal councils tend to be organized by districts, which in some cases date back to when reservations were divided into land management districts by agricultural and soil conservation agents in the New Deal era of the 1930s.

Council members, like U.S. or state legislators, generally serve for a specified period of time, usually two to four years. Satisfying the constitutional prerequisites for service in elected councils is not difficult. Generally, "they pertain only to minimum age, eighteen or twenty-one years; tribal membership; and being free of felonious convictions or indebtedness to the tribe. Otherwise it is left to the voters to decide whether the individual candidate is qualified for office. There are no other formal qualifications of an educational, occupational, or experiential sort."

Tribal councils, first of all, exercise those powers either stated or implied in the tribal constitution or other organic political documents. Typical of these broad powers or goals of governance are enacting ordinances and resolutions (the equivalent of congressional statutes), establishing justice, ensuring tranquility and enjoyment of the blessings of freedom and liberty, conserving tribal property, managing tribal business enterprises, establishing or modifying judicial systems, delegating powers to committees of its choice, and providing for the tribes' welfare. Nearly all major tribal ordinances or resolutions that have a substantial effect on tribal powers or resources are subject to review by the secretary of the interior.

It is important to recall, however, that tribal councils, acting for the tribal nation, derive their power to act from two other critical sources as well—inherent sovereignty and treaty rights. In fact, tribal constitutions themselves are, in some sense, a manifestation of tribal sovereignty, with treaties also being directly related since only sovereigns have the power to negotiate binding legal compacts.

Tribal Chairs (Executive Function)

Virtually all tribal constitutions provide for a tribal chairperson, who in some cases is called "president" or "governor." The chair performs the executive function of government, which involves the daily operations of administration, continual decision making, and setting up and overseeing systems that give tribal government law force and meaning. There are two basic components of the executive branch: the chief executive and the administration. Most tribal constitutions provide for at least four officers: the chair, the vice-chair, the tribal secretary, and the tribal treasurer.

The chair is head of the government. His or her powers are prescribed in the tribal constitution and by-laws. The chair also draws power from customs, tradition, personal charisma, and the prestige of the position. Powers and duties of a chair include seeing that the laws are being faithfully implemented; issuing directives and setting up administrative guidelines; handling negotiations with the BIA, Congress, local governments, and other tribes; presiding over all council meetings; and being responsible for the administration of the tribal bureaucracy.

In some tribes, the chair is elected by council vote. In other cases, he or she is directly chosen by the tribal electorate. These officers serve four-year terms. "The principal chief's responsibilities include organizing the executive department, overseeing tribal programs, preparing the annual budget, and informing the national council about the state of the nation's affairs." The principal chief, with the tribal council's concurrence, also selects the election board's members and a citizenship board, and he or she chooses the justice for the nation's supreme court.

Tribal Courts (Judicial Function)

The primary role of tribal government, at least historically and well into the contemporary era, was more judicial than legislative in nature. In other words, tribal leaders and governing structures functions primarily as adjudicatory bodies seeking to maintain harmony and balance and looking to amicably settle disputes when the arose. Notwithstanding this primordial and inherently judicial orientation, the inaccurate perception of most Europeans and Euro-Americans toward tribal nations was that they were largely lawless, anarchical societies lacking even rudimentary systems of law and order.

The reality, however, is that tribes have had their own very effective systems of law and order since long before European contact. Obviously, with so many indigenous communities, no two systems looked alike and certainly none bore much resemblance to those brought to North America by Europeans. While the passage of time, the force of Euro-American colonialism, tribal adaptations to that force, the litigious nature of Americans, and the enactment of laws like the IRA and the ICRA have led to the development of similarities in tribal judicial systems, it is still "in the operation of the judicial branch that one finds the most variety amongst tribal governments." This variety is intensified and complicated by the sheer volume of "law" that tribal courts must be aware of, and responded to, and that they also produce. Complicating matters even further are questions surrounding which entity or entities have jurisdiction over a specific dispute—tribal court, federal court, or state court.

At present there are three legal institutions that together compose the Indian judicial system—traditional courts, courts of Indian offenses (also known as Code of Federal Regulations [CFR] courts), and tribal (IRA) courts.

[Traditional] courts handle misbehavior through public scorn, the loss or restriction of certain privileges, or the payment of restitution to an injured party. In extreme cases, such as witchcraft, banishment from the nation might be called for. In traditional courts the values of the community dictated that compensation to victims and their families and resolution of problems "in such a manner that all could forgive and forget and continue to live within the tribal society in harmony with one another was of great importance."

[Courts of Indian Offenses], established by the secretary of the interior in the early 1880s, are also known as CFR courts because they operate under guidelines laid out under the Code of Federal Regulations (currently in Title 25). As tools of colonialism, the CFR courts were focused on imposing Western law and order on Indian communities. As a progressive mood emerged in the early twentieth century, out of which flowed developments that would culminate in the IRA and the modern tribal constitutions and tribal courts authorized under that act, the CFR courts began to be replaced. Many of them were phased out altogether, while others were folded into the constitutionally based tribal courts.

The tribal constitutions organized under the IRA and the court systems that followed were a vast improvement over the CFR courts, because tribal judges under the IRA constitutions were directly responsible for their tribe and not to the BIA. On the other hand, most tribal constitutions were, in fact, drafted by the BIA, based on a model constitution developed by that agency, and frequently reflected very little tribal input. More importantly, those constitutions "did not provide for any separation of powers and did not specifically create any court system." Nevertheless, despite the difficulties tribes had recovering from the previous decades of intense colonialism and the inherent flaws in the IRA system of Indian self-rule, tribal courts have grown and diversified tremendously over the last six decades. Although most tribal courts resemble their state or federal counterparts in structure and function, their jurisdiction has broadened from primarily criminal to include civil suits of increasing complexity.

Despite the fact that many tribal courts have assumed many of the forms and functions of Western-style governments, in part because of the anticipation of federal intrusion into tribal authority if they fail to do so, important differences remain between tribal courts and non-Indian courts.

In some tribes, tribal judges are popularly elected, while in most they are appointed by the tribal council or chairperson. Tribal judges usually are tribal members, though in some cases they are non-Indians or members of other tribal nations. Because of the doctrine of tribal sovereignty each tribe establishes its own qualifications for its judges, which may or may not include them being state-licensed attorneys. Judges typically serve a fixed term, usually two or four years.

Finally, many tribes have recently established appellate courts (usually consisting of three judges), though tribes are not required to have such a court. Some of the more developed tribal court systems, like that of the Navajo Nation, have appellate courts which sit permanently to hear appeals. Other tribes have established intertribal courts that hear appeals from a regional association of tribal councils. Still others have panels of judges who are assembled ad hoc for each appeal.

Notes and Questions

1.   Self-determination and IGRA. Deloria and Lytle wrote the above excerpt in the early 1980s, at a time when relatively few tribes were experimenting with high-stakes bingo halls and the vast majority were struggling with tremendous poverty, unemployment, and other socioeconomic challenges. They close with their sense that there was antipathy between tribal governments and the BIA, and that overall federal-tribal relations were in a state of flux. How do you think Deloria and Lytle would view IGRA and the creation of the NIGC?

2.   Functioning of tribal governments. The Deloria and Lytle excerpt, as well as the Wilkins excerpt, pointed out that tribal governments, whether or not resembling the Western-style tripartite system of government, have operated effectively throughout history. Have state and federal actors placed too much emphasis on how tribal governments are structured and too little emphasis on the effectiveness of their functions? Many tribal governments have preserved, revitalized, or incorporated traditional aspects in their present-day government institutions and functions. For more on tribal governments and their continuing evolution, see, e.g., Gavin Clarkson, *Reclaiming Jurisprudential Sovereignty: A Tribal Judiciary Analysis*, 50 U. KAN. L. REV. 473 (2002); Eric Lemont, *Developing Effective Processes of American Indian Constitutional and Governmental Reform: Lessons from the Cherokee Nation of Oklahoma, Hualapai Nation, Navajo Nation, and Northern Cheyenne Tribe*, 26 AM. INDIAN L. REV. 147 (2002).

3.   Tribal gaming commissions. Recall that IGRA requires a tribe to enact a gaming ordinance that must receive federal approval before the tribe can operate Class II or Class III gaming. Tribes typically create gaming commissions to implement, monitor, and enforce the gaming ordinance as well as ensure compliance with other relevant tribal ordinances or regulations, IGRA and federal regulations, and tribal-state compacts. A certificate of tribal self-regulation issued by the NIGC compels additional tribal responsibility for regulating Class II gaming. *See* 25 U.S.C. § 2710(c).

Tribal gaming commissions are intended to function as independent regulatory authorities within the executive branch. Commissioners may be elected or appointed. Typical responsibilities include monitoring and enforcement of employee background checks, compliance, licensing, surveillance, auditing, and inspection. Commissions are empowered to promulgate regulations and to hold hearings, and may have enforcement authority through fines or license suspension or revocation. Some tribes create appointive gaming review boards that approve regulations and hear appeals concerning licensing, fines, and patron disputes.

As Tracy Burris, a gaming commissioner with the Chickasaw Nation in Oklahoma, described, tribal gaming commissions administer a number of functions required by federal, tribal, and even state law:

1.   Develop licensing procedures for all employees of the gaming operation.

2.   Issue, suspend, revoke, and renew licenses of primary management officials and key employees upon completion of background investigations and after following [federal regulatory] procedures.

3. Conduct background investigations on primary management officials and key employees.

4. Forward completed employment applications for primary management officials and key employees to the NIGC.

5. Forward complete investigative reports on each background investigation for each primary management official or key employee to the NIGC prior to issuing a license.

6. Review a person's prior activities, criminal record, if any, and reputation, habits, and associations to make a finding concerning the eligibility of a key employee or primary management official for employment in a gaming operation.

7. Notify the NIGC if, after conducting a background investigation on a primary management official or key employee, the tribe does not license the individual.

8. Retain applications and reports of background investigations of primary management officials and key employees.

9. Issue separate licenses to each place, facility, or location on Indian lands where a tribe elects to allow gaming.

10. Ensure that gaming facilities are constructed, maintained, and operated in a manner that adequately protects the environment and the public health and safety.

11. Obtain annual independent outside audits [for] all gaming related contracts that result in purchases of supplies, services, or concessions for more than $25,000 in any year.

12. Ensure that net revenues from any gaming activities are used for the limited purposes set forth in the tribal gaming ordinance.

13. If the tribe authorizes individually owned gaming, issue licenses according to the requirements contained in the tribal gaming ordinance.

14. Promulgate tribal gaming regulations pursuant to tribal law.

15. Monitor gaming activities to ensure compliance with tribal law/regulations.

16. Interact with other regulatory and law enforcement agencies regarding the regulation of gaming.

17. Conduct investigations of possible violations and take appropriate enforcement action with respect to the tribal gaming ordinances and regulations.

18. Provide independent information to the tribe on the status of the tribe's gaming activities.

19. Take testimony and conduct hearings on regulatory matters, including matters related to the revocation of primary management official and key employee licenses.

20. Establish or approve minimum internal control standards or procedures for the gaming operation, including the operation's credit policies and procedures for acquiring supplies and equipment.

21. Establish any supplementary criteria for the licensing of primary management officials, key employees, and other employees that the tribe deems necessary.

22. Establish standards for and issue license or permits to persons and entities who deal with the gaming operation such as manufactures and suppliers of machines, equipment, and supplies.

23. Maintain records on licensees and on persons denied licenses including persons otherwise prohibited from engaging in gaming activities within the tribe's jurisdiction.

24. Perform audits of business transactions to ensure compliance with regulations and/or policy.

25. Establish or approve rules of various games, and inspect games, tables, equipment, machines, cards, dice, and chips or tokens used in the gaming operations.

26. Establish or approve video surveillance standards.

27. Establish standards/criteria for gaming machines and facilitate the testing of machines for compliance.

28. Resolve patron disputes, employee grievances, and other problems pursuant to the tribal gaming ordinance.

Tracy Burris, *How Tribal Gaming Commissions Are Evolving*, 8 Gaming L. Rev. 243, 245–46 (2004).

The NIGC urges tribes to take steps to ensure the independence of a tribal gaming commission, such as delegating to the commission the authority to promulgate and enforce gaming regulations, giving the commission unrestricted access to the gaming operation and relevant records, providing a permanent and stable funding source for the commission's functions, and establishing a fixed and sufficiently long term of office for commissioners. *See* NIGC Bulletin No. 99-3 (Independence of Tribal Gaming Commissions) (1999), at http://www.nigc.gov/ReadingRoom/Bulletins/BulletinNo19993/tabid/200/Default.aspx.

4. Critiques of tribal gaming commissions. Some critics of tribal regulation cite the regulatory improprieties of a particular tribal gaming commission or regulatory personnel, but otherwise believe that tribes are fully capable of regulating their own gaming enterprises. *See, e.g.*, Dave Palermo (special assistant to Hopi Tribe), *Chumash—A Tribal Gaming Nightmare*, Indian Country Today (Nov. 26, 2004) (describing criminal records of seven gaming commissioners of the Santa Ynez Band of Mission Indians in Santa Barbara County). Others, however, have suggested that tribal gaming commissions are, by their nature, corruptible or corrupt. In 2002, an exposé-style series on Indian gaming in *Time* magazine stated that tribal regulation of tribal gaming was "like Enron's auditors auditing themselves." *See* Donald L. Barlett & James B. Steele, *Playing the Political Slots*, Time, Dec. 23, 2002, at 59. Is the *Time* analogy a fair criticism of tribal gaming commissions? Is it a fair criticism of state lottery regulation by state lottery commissions? *Cf.* Palermo, *supra* ("I personally have found repulsive the repeated analogy by some members of the press and politicians that tribal regulations were tantamount to the 'fox watching the hen house.' That is racist. Do we assume state governments are incapable of regulating their lotteries and race tracks without federal oversight?").

Burris argues that tribal gaming commissions are "evolving," and that their effectiveness should be judged in the context of both the relative youth and unique nature of the Indian gaming industry:

The history of gambling policy in Indian country has been a conflict between two worlds: tribal culture and the modern world of business. It is said that gambling is morally and socially destructive for all people, but for the tribes it has been the best economic tool for expansion to other commerce for their tribal governments. They have some of the best gaming operations in the country due in part to their regulatory bodies. Although Nevada has had legalized gaming since 1869, it did not create the state gaming control board until 1959. Therefore, tribal governmental gaming and regulation should be given a reasonable timetable to be measured by.

Burris, at 245.

Kathryn R.L. Rand & Steven Andrew Light
How Congress Can and Should "Fix" the Indian Gaming Regulatory Act: Recommendations for Law and Policy Reform
13 Va. J. Soc. Pol'y & L. 396 (2006)

One of the largely untold success stories of Indian gaming is the role it has played in tribal institution building. The NIGC frequently is spotlighted as the agency "in charge" of regulating Indian gaming. This overly simplistic characterization overlooks both the more complex and far-reaching requirements for government regulation of Indian gaming under IGRA and the fact that each gaming tribe has created its own regulatory authorities that are responsible for administering the myriad regulatory challenges of Indian gaming. In assuming responsibility for gaming regulation, tribes determine the character and capacity of their own governmental institutions. Many tribal governments consciously have separated their political branches from regulatory and economic development commissions and boards. Tribal governments today are in a position to make continual and informed decisions about how to provide essential public services to their members, how to negotiate and contract with non-tribal commercial vendors, banks, and investors to determine the trajectory of economic development, and how to interact with state and local governments on a range of issues.

The tribal role in regulating Indian gaming has been instrumental in tribal government institution building. Not only have tribes created gaming commissions, but they have developed and enhanced other tribal government agencies to address issues related to gaming, such as law enforcement and court systems. Further, gaming revenue has allowed tribes to build schools, day care centers, health care clinics, elder care facilities, and community centers. These government-created institutions are direct evidence of strong tribal governments and increased self-sufficiency and self-determination. Tribal regulation of Indian gaming thus is a necessary exercise of tribal sovereignty that serves tribal and federal interests in building strong tribal governments and increasing tribal self-sufficiency.

We urge Congress to preserve or even enhance tribes' role in the direct regulation of Indian gaming. The best way to facilitate tribal government institution building while addressing the concerns raised in recent oversight hearings on Indian gaming is to couch any increased role for the federal government as one of *indirect* regulation — the *facilitation of sound and effective tribal regulation*, rather than the curtailment or replacement of tribal regulation with federal or state regulation. The former recognizes, protects, and strengthens tribal self-governance; the latter runs the risk of undermining it.

Additionally, we encourage Congress to continue and further other efforts to assist tribes in developing strong tribal governments. Congress should consider providing sufficient supplementary resources to the NIGC to expand its advisory and technical assistance role to tribes to help tribes share information, adopt appropriate tribal law and administrative regulations, and build effective regulatory agencies capable of effectively implementing the federal minimum internal control standards for Indian gaming operations. This in turn will assist the NIGC in fulfilling its own regulatory role — in the best interests of all involved. The NIGC can play a more effective role in enabling tribes to create responsive institutions while minimizing direct federal oversight or interference with tribal affairs, reinforcing the goals of federal Indian policy as well as IGRA.

Similarly, in the context of tribal use of gaming revenue, Congress should facilitate tribal government institution building to ensure that tribal members' concerns are adequately addressed at the tribal level. Elsewhere, we have recommended that states and tribes work together to ensure appropriate transparency to tribal members and state citizens. As the ordinary state political process should respond to state citizens' concerns about the use of state lottery revenue, for example, so should the tribal political process, rather than federal mandate, respond to tribal members' concerns about the use of tribal gaming revenue.

By continuing to encourage and assist tribes in developing effective and responsive tribal government institutions, Congress will address such concerns without undermining the federal goals of promoting strong tribal governments and tribal self-sufficiency.

Notes and Questions

1. *Legislative reform and tribal government.* Rand and Light called for Congress to exercise care if it opens up IGRA to amendment. Against the cacophonous background of repeated calls to reign in tribal gaming due to what some policymakers see as its unintended consequences, see generally *id.*, reminders about the importance of tribal government institution building may be drowned out. Government capacity can be increased through an influx of gaming or other revenue and other resources. With sufficient resources, tribal government decisions may be generated internally and with attention to tribal values and traditions, rather than through imposition by state, local, or federal officials or as a reflection of non-tribal public opinion. Rand and Light discussed the role of institution building as a vehicle for the creation of strong tribal governments — one of IGRA's stated policy goals — and a manifestation of tribal sovereignty and self-determination. But how should one measure or weigh the strength of government institutions?

2. *Tribal government institution building.* Professor Joseph Kalt has written extensively on the importance of tribal institution building by tribes, for tribes. *See, e.g.,* Joseph P. Kalt, *Constitutional Rule and the Effective Governance of Native Nations*, in American Indian Constitutional Reform and the Rebuilding of Native Nations (Eric D. Lemont ed., 2006). A recent comprehensive assessment, coordinated by Professor Kalt, of the status of tribal nations at the beginning of the twenty-first century carried this theme forward. The study found that in recent years, both gaming and non-gaming tribes have made noteworthy advances in the capacity of tribal governments to serve indigenous nations and their members. It further determined that both gaming and non-gaming tribes are experiencing economic growth at a rate three times that of the U.S. economy. Nevertheless tribal members living on reservations remain four times as likely to live in poverty as the "average" American. *See generally* Harvard Project on American Indian Economic Development, The State of the Native Nations: Conditions Under U.S. Policies of Self-Determination (2007).

C. Tribal Law

1. Gaming Ordinances

National Indian Gaming Commission
Model Gaming Ordinance

(revised 2005)

[From the accompanying NIGC Bulletin:] The Indian Gaming Regulatory Act (IGRA) requires each Tribe contemplating Class II or Class III gaming to adopt a tribal gaming ordinance. This ordinance must be approved by the Chairman of the National Indian Gaming Commission (NIGC) prior to the conduct of any Class II or Class III gaming on Indian lands.

To assist Tribes in meeting the ordinance requirements of the IGRA and the NIGC's regulations, the Commission has approved a Revised Model Gaming Ordinance. Many provisions of this Ordinance were taken from Tribal ordinances so that other Tribes may benefit from the knowledge and experience of Tribes sophisticated in gaming. As gaming Tribes review and amend their existing gaming ordinances, they may wish to consider adopting the Revised Model Gaming Ordinance or portions thereof. Several sections have different options so that Tribes may use what works best for them or get an idea of what they would like in their own ordinances.

The Revised Model Gaming Ordinance includes those requirements found in IGRA and NIGC's implementing regulations, incorporates guidance found in NIGC advisory bulletins, and includes other proposed language likely to assist Tribes in the development of their regulatory systems. The NIGC has found that well regulated Tribal gaming operations have included not only the requirements of IGRA and the implementing regulations in their ordinances, but have also incorporated matters from advisory bulletins. However, ordinances containing only the requirements found in IGRA and NIGC's implementing regulations remain acceptable. Tribes are encouraged to consult with legal counsel before adopting or amending a gaming ordinance to ensure that their ordinances do not conflict with a tribal-state compact or other applicable law.

Section 101. Purpose

The [Tribal Council or other authorized governing body] (Tribe), empowered by the [Tribe's Constitution or other governing authority] to enact ordinances, hereby enacts this ordinance in order to govern Class II [and Class III] gaming operations on the Tribe's Indian lands.

Section 102. Definitions

Unless a different meaning is clearly indicated in this Ordinance, the terms used herein shall have the same meaning as defined in the Indian Gaming Regulatory Act (IGRA), 25 U.S.C. § 2701 *et seq.*, and its regulations, 25 C.F.R. § 500 *et seq.* Specifically:

(a) Board of Directors means the Tribal Gaming Board of Directors, who shall serve as primary management officials in overseeing the General Manager and the day-to-day non-regulatory aspects of the gaming operation.

(b) Class I gaming means social games solely for prizes of minimal value or traditional forms of Indian gaming engaged in by individuals as a part of, or in connection with, tribal ceremonies or celebrations. *[25 U.S.C. § 2703(6); 25 C.F.R. § 502.2]*

(c) Class II gaming means:

(1) the game of chance commonly known as bingo (whether or not electronic, computer, or other technologic aids are used in connection therewith): (A) which is played for prizes, including monetary prizes, with cards bearing numbers or other designations, (B) in which the holder of the card covers such numbers or designations when objects, similarly numbered or designated, are drawn or electronically determined, and (C) in which the game is won by the first person covering a previously designated arrangement of numbers or designations on such cards, including (if played in the same location) pull-tabs, lotto, punch boards, tip jars, instant bingo, and other games similar to bingo, and

(2) card games that: (A) are explicitly authorized by the laws of the State, or (B) are not explicitly prohibited by the laws of the State and are played at any location in the State, but only is such card games are played in conformity with those laws and regulations (if any) of the State regarding hours or periods of operation of such card games or limitations on wagers or pot sizes in such card games.

(3) The term "class II gaming" does not include: (A) any banking card games, including baccarat, chemin de fer, or blackjack (21), or (B) electronic or electro-mechanical facsimiles of any game of chance or slot machines of any kind. *[25 U.S.C. §2703(7); 25 C.F.R. §502.3]*

(d) Class III gaming means all forms of gaming that are not class I gaming or class II gaming. *[25 U.S.C. §2703(8); 25 C.F.R. §502.4]*

(e) Commission means the Tribal Gaming Commission established to perform regulatory oversight and to monitor compliance with Tribal, Federal, and applicable State regulations.

(f) Commissioner means a Tribal Gaming Commissioner.

(g) Compact means a Tribal-State Compact concerning class III gaming approved by the Secretary of the Interior and published in the Federal Register pursuant to 25 U.S.C. §2710(d).

(h) Complimentary shall have the meaning as set forth in 25 C.F.R. §542.2(a).

(i) Directly related to means a spouse, child, parent, grandparent, grandchild, aunt, uncle, or first cousin.

(j) Director means a Member of the Tribal Gaming Board of Directors.

(k) Indian lands means:

(1) all lands within the limits of the Tribe's reservation;

(2) any lands title to which is either held in trust by the United States for the benefit of the Tribe or individual or held by the Tribe or individual subject to restriction by the United States against alienation and over which the Indian Tribe exercises governmental power; and

(3) for all lands acquired into trust for the benefit of an Indian tribe after October 17, 1988, the lands meet the requirements set forth in 25 U.S.C. §2719. *[25 U.S.C. §2703(4); 25 U.S.C. §2719; 25 C.F.R. §502.12]*

(l) Indian Tribe means the [name of the Tribe].

(m) Key Employee[1] means:

---

1. A Tribe may expand this definition, but not limit it.

(1) A person who performs one or more of the following functions: (A) Bingo caller; (B) Counting room supervisor; (C) Chief of security; (D) Custodian of gaming supplies or cash; (E) Floor manager; (F) Pit boss; (G) Dealer; (H) Croupier; (I) Approver of credit; or (G) Custodian of gambling devices including persons with access to cash and accounting records within such devices;

(2) If not otherwise included, any other person whose total cash compensation is in excess of $50,000 per year; or

(3) If not otherwise included, the four most highly compensated persons in the gaming operation. *[25 C.F.R. §502.14)]*

(n) Net Revenues means gross gaming revenues of an Indian gaming operation less

(1) Amounts paid out as, or paid for, prizes; and

(2) Total gaming-related operating expenses, excluding management fees. *[25 U.S.C. §2703(9); 25 C.F.R. §502.16]*

(o) Primary Management Official[2] means

(1) The person (s) having management responsibility for a management contract;

(2) Any person who has authority: (A) To hire and fire employees; or (B) To set up working policy for the gaming operation; or (C) The chief financial officer or other person who has financial management responsibility. *[25 C.F.R. §502.19]*

Section 103.   Gaming Authorized

Class II gaming is hereby authorized. [OR] Class II and Class III gaming are hereby authorized. *[25 C.F.R. §522.6(b)–(c)]*

Section 104.   Ownership of Gaming

The Tribe shall have the sole proprietary interest in and responsibility for the conduct of any gaming operation authorized by this ordinance. *[25 U.S.C. §2710(b)(2)(A); 25 C.F.R. §522.4(b)(1)]*

Section 105.   Use of Gaming Revenue[3]

(a) Net revenues from tribal gaming shall be used only for the following purposes:

(1) to fund tribal government operations and programs;

(2) to provide for the general welfare of the Tribe and its members;

(3) to promote tribal economic development;

(4) to donate to charitable organizations; or

(5) to help fund operations of local government agencies. *[25 U.S.C. §2710(b)(2)(B); 25 C.F.R. §522.4(b)(2)]*

Section 106.   Per Capita Payments

(a) "Per Capita Payment" means the distribution of money or other thing of value to all members of the Tribe, or to identified groups of members, which is paid directly from the net revenues of any tribal gaming activity. *[25 C.F.R. §290.2]*

---

2. A Tribe may expand this definition, but not limit it.

3. It is not necessary to have a provision allowing net gaming revenues to be used for payment of revenue-sharing provisions in Tribal-State compacts; these fall under promotion of tribal economic development because the Tribe must gain an economic benefit in return for the payments.

(b) If the Tribe elects to make per capita payments to tribal members from revenues derived from its gaming operations, it shall ensure that the following requirements of 25 C.F.R. Part 290 are met:

(1) The Tribe shall authorize and issue such payments only in accordance with a revenue allocation plan submitted to and approved by the Secretary of the Interior under 25 U.S.C. §2710(b)(3). *[25 U.S.C. §2710(b)(3); 25 C.F.R. §522.4(b)(2)(ii)]*

(2)The Tribe shall ensure that the interests of minors and other legally incompetent persons who are entitled to receive any per capita payments under a Tribal per capita payment plan are protected and preserved, and that the per capita payments are disbursed to the parents or legal guardian of such minors or legal incompetents in such amounts as may be necessary for the health, education, or welfare or the minor or other legally incompetent person, under a plan approved by the [Tribal governing body] and the Secretary of the Interior. The Tribe must also establish criteria and a process for withdrawal of funds by the parent or legal guardian. *[25 C.F.R. §290.12(b)(3)]*

(3) The [Tribal governing body] shall designate or create a Tribal court system, forum, or administrative process for resolution of disputes concerning the allocation of net gaming revenues and the distribution of per capita payments and will explain how it will correct deficiencies. *[25 C.F.R. §290.12(3)(iii), (b)(5); 25 C.F.R. §290.22]*

(4) The [Tribal governing body] shall ensure that the Tribal revenue allocation plan reserves an adequate portion of net gaming revenues from the tribal gaming activity to do one or more of the following purposes: fund Tribal government operations or programs; provide for the general welfare of the Tribe or its members; promote tribal economic development; donate to charitable organizations; or to help fund operations of local government. *[25 C.F.R. §290.12(b)(1)]*

(5) The [Tribal governing body] shall ensure that distributions of per capita payments are made according to specific eligibility requirements. *[25 C.F.R. §290.12(3)(iii), (b)(5)]*

(6)The [Tribal governing body] shall ensure that Tribal members are notified of the tax liability for per capita payments and how taxes with be withheld. *[25 C.F.R. §290.12(b)(4); 26 C.F.R. Part 31]*

Section 107.   Board of Directors[3]

(a) In addition to the General Manager for the facility, there shall be established a Tribal Gaming Board of Directors which shall serve in a management oversight role over the General Manager and the day-to-day operations of the gaming operation. In the event that the Tribe enters into a management contract approved by the NIGC, the Board may delegate some or all duties to the approved management contractor. The Board of Directors shall oversee all non-regulatory aspects of the gaming operation. Regulation of the gaming operation shall be the sole responsibility of the Tribal Gaming Commission.

(b) The Board of Directors shall consist of three (3) members; a Chairperson, Vice- Chairperson, and Director. Terms of office for members of the Tribal Gaming Board of Directors shall be as follows: the Chairperson shall serve an initial term of one year, with subsequent Chairpersons serving three-year terms. The Vice-Chairperson and other Director(s) shall serve an initial term of two years, with subsequent Vice-Chairpersons and

---

3. [sic] This provision is recommended, but not required.

Directors serving three-year terms. The members of the Board shall be subject to the same background requirements as key employees and primary management officials, and must be licensed accordingly. The minimum requirements for appointment as a member of the Board of Directors are as follows:[4]

One [or two] of the following:

- Degree in Business Administration, Accounting, Marketing, or an equivalent field;
- Minimum five (5) years experience in business management;
- Minimum two (2) years experience in casino management; or
- Demonstrated knowledge of federal Indian law, the Indian Gaming Regulatory Act, and related statutes and regulations.

[OR] A basic knowledge of gaming management, business, finance, or law.

[OR] [Insert Tribe's chosen criteria.]

(c) The Board of Directors shall perform the following duties:

(1) Monitor and oversee the day-to-day operations of the gaming facility, whether managed by a tribal employee or by an approved management contractor;

(2) Inspect and examine on a periodic basis all books, records, and papers of the gaming facility;

(3) Set hours of operation for the gaming facility;

(4) Set wager limits;

(5) Develop marketing plans;

(6) Oversee the interview, selection, and training of employees of the gaming operation;

(7) Establish employee policies, rates of pay, and hours of work;

(8) Adopt an annual operating budget, subject to Tribal Council approval;

(9) Enter into contracts on behalf of the gaming facility, subject to Tribal Council approval and NIGC review;

(10) Hold hearings on employee complaints, in compliance with procedures established in the gaming ordinance and other Tribal gaming regulations or personnel policies;[5] and

(11) Any other duties necessary to monitor and oversee the gaming operation.

(d) Board of Director positions shall be filled in the following manner: [Select one of the following options] Through election by the [Tribe's general voting body]. [OR] Through appointment by the [Tribe's governing body]. [OR] [Insert the Tribe's chosen method.]

(e) At least one member of the Board of Directors shall be a local business owner with no ties to or financial interest in the gaming operation.[6]

---

4. These requirements are possible qualifications. The Tribe may establish those qualifications it considers important. Generally, members who have some expertise in gaming or related areas tend to be the most effective.

5. The Tribe should only include this section if the personnel policy grievance procedure calls for the Board of Directors to hold hearings on employee complaints.

6. Optional.

(f) The Tribe recognizes the importance of an independent Tribal Gaming Board of Directors in maintaining a well-managed gaming operation. To avoid potential conflicts of interest between the operation and regulation of the gaming facility, the Tribe hereby finds that, at a minimum:

(1) No member of the Tribal Council or Tribal Gaming Commission may serve on the Board of Directors;

(2) No person directly related to or living with any Tribal Council member or Tribal Gaming Commissioner may serve on the Board of Directors;

(3) Members of the Board of Directors are prohibited from gambling in the facility; and

(4) Members of the Board of Directors are prohibited from accepting complimentary items from the gaming operation.

(g) Members of the Board of Directors may be removed from office by the Tribal Council prior to the expiration of their respective terms only for neglect of duty, misconduct, malfeasance, or other acts that would render the Director unqualified for his/her position. When the Tribal Council believes that a removal is appropriate, it shall so notify the Director(s) and hold a hearing on the matter. The Tribal Council may opt to preliminarily remove the Director pending the hearing. At the hearing the Director may provide evidence rebutting the grounds for his/her removal. A vote of the Tribal Council on the validity of the preliminary removal shall be final and not subject to further appeal. A finding by the Tribal Council that the preliminary removal was wrongful shall entitle the affected Director to compensation for expenses incurred in appealing the wrongful removal, and shall entitle the Director to any pay withheld.

(h) Members of the Tribal Gaming Board of Directors shall be compensated at a level determined by the Tribal Council.

Section 108.   Gaming Commission[7]

(a) The Tribe hereby establishes a Tribal Gaming Commission whose duty it is to regulate tribal gaming operations. The Tribal Gaming Commission shall consist of [insert chosen number: 3, 4 or 5] members. There shall be among them a Chairperson, Vice-Chairperson, and at least one additional Commissioner.

(b) The purpose of the Tribal Gaming Commission is regulatory, not managerial. The Commission will conduct oversight to ensure compliance with Tribal, Federal, and, if applicable, State laws and regulations. The Commission will serve as the licensing authority for individuals employed in the gaming operation and will administer background investigations as part of the licensing process. The Commission will also have a role in monitoring compliance with the internal controls for the gaming operation and in tracking revenues. In order to carry out its regulatory duties, the Commission shall have unrestricted access to all areas of the gaming operation and to all records. The Commission shall have authority to take enforcement actions, including suspension or revocation of an individual gaming license when appropriate.

(c) The Tribe recognizes the importance of an independent Tribal Gaming Commission in maintaining a well-regulated gaming operation. The Commission shall be and act independently and autonomously from the Tribal Council in all matters within its purview. No prior or subsequent review by the Tribal Council of any actions of the Commission

---

7. This provision is recommended, but not required.

shall be required or permitted except as otherwise explicitly provided in this Ordinance. To avoid potential conflicts of interest between the operation and regulation of the gaming facility, the Tribe hereby finds that, at a minimum:

(1) No member of the Tribal Council or Tribal Gaming Board of Directors may serve on the Gaming Commission;

(2) No member directly related to or living with any Tribal Council member or Tribal Gaming Board of Directors member may serve on the Gaming Commission;

(3) Members of the Gaming Commission are prohibited from gambling in the facility; and

(4) Members of the Gaming Commission are prohibited from accepting complimentary items from the gaming operation, excepting food and beverages valued at under five dollars.

(d) Tribal Gaming Commissioner positions shall be filled in the following manner: [Select one of the following options] Through appointment by the [Tribe's general voting body] pursuant to an election. [OR] Through appointment by the [Tribe's governing body]. [OR] [Insert the Tribe's chosen method.]

(e) Nominees for positions of Tribal Gaming Commissioner must satisfy the suitability standards set forth for key employees and primary management officials, found in Section XIII of this Ordinance. Such background investigations shall be performed under the direction of [office or entity outside the Tribe who will conduct the background investigations].

(f) The Tribal Gaming Commission shall:

(1) Conduct or cause background investigations to be conducted on, at a minimum, primary management officials and key employees;

(2) Review and approve all investigative work conducted;

(3) Report results of background investigations to the NIGC;

(4) Obtain and process fingerprints, or designate a law enforcement agency to obtain and process fingerprints;

(5) Make licensing suitability determinations, which shall be signed by the Chairman of the Gaming Commission;

(6) Issue gaming licenses to management officials and employees of the operation, consistent with the suitability determination;

(7) Establish standards for licensing Tribal gaming operations;

(8) Issue facility gaming licenses to Tribal gaming operations;

(9) Inspect, examine and monitor all gaming activities, and have immediate access to review, inspect, examine, photocopy and audit all records of the gaming establishment;

(10) Ensure compliance with all Tribal, State, and Federal laws, rules, and regulations regarding Indian gaming;

(11) Investigate any suspicion of wrongdoing associated with any gaming activities;

(12) Hold hearings on patron complaints, in compliance with procedures established in the gaming ordinance and other Tribal gaming regulations;

(13) Comply with any and all reporting requirements under the IGRA, Tribal-State compact to which the Tribe is a party, and any other applicable law;

(14) Promulgate and issue regulations necessary to comply with applicable internal control standards;

(15) Promulgate and issue regulations on the levying of fees and/or taxes associated with gaming license applications;

(16) Promulgate and issue regulations on the levying of fines and/or suspension or revocation of gaming licenses for violations of the gaming ordinance, or any other Tribal, Federal, or State, if applicable, gaming regulations; and

(17) Establish a list of persons not allowed to game in Tribal gaming facilities in order to maintain the integrity of the gaming;

(18) Establish a list of persons who have voluntarily asked to be excluded from Tribal gaming facility and create regulations for enforcing this exclusion;[8]

(19) Provide referrals and information to the appropriate law enforcement officials when such information indicates a violation of Tribal, Federal, or State statutes, ordinances, or resolutions;

(20) Create a list of regulatory authorities that conduct vendor background investigations and licensing which the Commission recognizes as trustworthy;

(21) Draft regulations exempting vendors from the licensing and/or background investigation requirements if they have received a license from a recognized regulatory authority;

(22) Perform such other duties the Commission deems appropriate for the proper regulation of the Tribal gaming operation.

(23) Promulgate such regulations and guidelines as it deems appropriate to implement the provisions of this Ordinance.

(g) The Gaming Commission shall ensure that all records and information obtained as a result of an employee background investigation shall remain confidential and shall not be disclosed to persons who are not directly involved in the licensing and employment processes. Information obtained during the course of an employee background investigation shall be disclosed to members of management, human resource personnel or others employed by the tribal gaming operation on a need-to-know basis for actions taken in their official capacities. This Section does not apply to requests for such information or records from any Tribal, Federal or State law enforcement or regulatory agency, or for the use of such information or records by the Commission and staff in the performance of their official duties.

(h) Terms of Office for Tribal Gaming Commissioners shall be as follows: the Chair shall serve an initial term of one year, with subsequent Chairs serving three-year terms. The Vice-Chair and Commissioner(s) shall serve an initial term of two years, with subsequent Vice-Chairs and Commissioners serving three-year terms.

(i) The following persons are not eligible to serve as Tribal Gaming Commissioners: Tribal Council members, while serving as such; employees of the gaming operation, while serving as such; gaming contractors (including any principal of a management or other contracting company); persons directly related to or sharing a residence with any of the above; persons ineligible to be key employees or primary management officials. Non-tribal members previously convicted of a felony, of embezzlement, of theft, or of any other money-

---

8. Examples of voluntary exclusion programs can be found in the codes of the states of Missouri, Illinois, Michigan, and New Jersey.

related crime or honesty-related crime (such as fraud) cannot serve as Tribal Gaming Commissioners. Tribal members previously convicted of a felony, of embezzlement, of theft, or of any other money-related crime or honesty-related crime (such as fraud) will only be allowed to serve as Tribal Gaming Commissioners if the [Tribe's governing body] specifically finds a significant amount of time has passed and that the person is now of trustworthy character. The Tribal Council shall require a criminal history check with appropriate law enforcement agencies and shall review this criminal history report and make an appropriate suitability determination before appointing an individual to a position as a Tribal Gaming Commissioner.

(j) The independence of the Tribal Gaming Commission is essential to a well-regulated gaming operation. For that reason, Commissioners may only be removed from office by the [Tribe's governing body] prior to the expiration of their respective terms for neglect of duty, misconduct, malfeasance, or other acts that would render a commissioner unqualified for his/her position. Any allegations of neglect of duty, misconduct, malfeasance, or other acts that would render him or her unqualified for his/her position must be substantiated by a preponderance of the evidence. Commissioners will be given an opportunity to provide evidence rebutting the grounds for their proposed removal before the removal is considered. A vote of the [Tribe's governing body] on the validity of the removal shall be final and not subject to further appeal. A wrongful removal shall entitle the affected Commissioner to compensation for expenses incurred in an appeal and any pay withheld.

(k) A majority of the Commission shall constitute a quorum. The concurrence of a majority of the members appointed to the Commission shall be required for any final determination by the Commission. The Commission may act in its official capacity even if there are vacancies on the Commission.

(l) Tribal Gaming Commissioners shall be compensated at a level determined by the Tribal Council. Commissioner compensation shall not be based on a percentage of gaming revenue to ensure the Commission is not improperly influenced.

(m) The Commission shall keep a written record of all its meetings.

Section 109.   Ethics[9]

(a) The Tribe recognizes that the duties of the Gaming Board of Directors and the Tribal Gaming Commission include making important decisions on highly sensitive issues. As such, the Tribe has determined that the Board of Directors and the Gaming Commission shall be held to extremely high ethical standards. Prior to taking their positions on the Board and the Commission (Members), the Members shall agree to be bound by the following principles:

(1) Members shall not hold financial interests that conflict with the conscientious performance of their duties as managers and regulators.[10]

(2) Members shall not engage in financial transactions using nonpublic information or allow the improper use of such information by others on their behalf to further any private interest.

(3) Members shall not solicit or accept any gift or other item of monetary value, including complimentary items or services (see Section 110, below), from any person

---

9. This provision is recommended, but not required.
10. Per Capita distributions are not considered financial interests that would conflict with the conscientious performance of duty by a manager or regulator.

or entity seeking official action or inaction from, doing business with, or conducting activities regulated by the member's organization, or whose interests may be substantially affected by the performance or nonperformance of the Members' duties.

(4) Members shall make no unauthorized commitments or promises of any kind purporting to bind the Tribe.

(5) Members shall not use their positions for private gain.

(6) Members shall act impartially, in accordance with all relevant Tribal, Federal, and State laws (where applicable), and shall not give preferential treatment to any private organization or individual, including to any persons related to Members.

(7) Members shall ensure that Tribal property and gaming assets shall be properly segregated and safeguarded, and that such property and assets shall not be used for unauthorized activities.

(8) Members shall not engage in outside employment or activities, including seeking or negotiating for future employment, which conflict with their official duties and responsibilities.

(9) Members shall disclose waste, fraud, abuse, and corruption to appropriate authorities.

(10) Members shall endeavor to avoid any actions creating the appearance that they are violating the law or the ethical standards listed herein.

(11) Members shall disclose any real or apparent financial or personal conflicts. If there is a real conflict or the appearance of one, the member shall not take part in any decision related to the conflict.

Section 110.   Complimentary Items[11]

(a) The use of complimentary items shall be governed by regulations established by the Tribal Gaming Commission.

(b) No Key Employee, Primary Management Official, Tribal Council member, member of the Gaming Board of Directors or Tribal Gaming Commission, or any person directly related to or sharing a residence with the persons, shall be authorized to receive complimentary items other than food and beverages valued at under five dollars, or, if at a public event held at the gaming facility, the free food and beverages offered to the general public.

(c) Complimentary Items shall be included in the annual budget for the gaming operation, with maximum limits specified, and shall be subject to approval by the Tribal Council.

Section 111.   Audit

(a) The Tribe shall cause an annual outside independent audit of gaming operations to be conducted, and shall submit the resulting audit reports to the National Indian Gaming Commission. *[25 U.S.C. § 2710(b)(2)(C); 25 C.F.R. § 522.4(b)(3)]*

(b) All gaming related contracts that result in the purchase of supplies, services, or concessions in excess of $25,000.00 annually, except contracts for professional legal and accounting services, shall be specifically included within the scope of the audit that is described in subsection (a) above. *[25 U.S.C. § 2710(b)(2)(D); 25 C.F.R. § 522.4(b)(4)]*

---

11. This provision is recommended, but not required.

Section 112.   Environment and Public Health and Safety

(a) Gaming facilities shall be constructed, maintained and operated in a manner that adequately protects the environment and the public health and safety. *[25 U.S.C. §2710(b)(2)(E); 25 C.F.R. §522.4(b)(7)]*

(b) [Insert the official title of a Tribal official or group] shall adopt standards that assure adequate protection of the environment and the public health and safety.[12]

Section 113.   Patron Dispute Resolution[13]

Patrons who have complaints against the gaming establishment shall have as their sole remedy the right to file a petition for relief with the Tribal Gaming Commission. Complaints shall be submitted in writing, and at the discretion of the Commission, the petitioner may be allowed to present evidence. The Gaming Commission shall hold a hearing within 30 days of receipt of petitioner's complaint. Petitioner may have counsel present at such hearing. The Commission shall render a decision in a timely fashion and all such decisions will be final when issued. Any patron complaint must be submitted to the Commission within thirty (30) days of the incident giving rise to the complaint. All claims by patrons shall be limited to a maximum recovery of [enter dollar amount] per occurrence, and a cumulative limit of [enter dollar amount] per patron in any twelve (12) month period, except disputes relating to a patron's entitlement to a game prize, which shall be limited to the amount of such prize. The Commission's decision shall constitute the complainant's final remedy.

Section 114.   Tribal Internal Control Standards

The Tribe shall adopt and implement Internal Control Standards (ICS) for the operation of its Tribal gaming operation in accordance with applicable law. The Tribe's ICS shall be set out in separate regulations to be reviewed and approved by the Tribal Council.

Section 115.   Facility Licenses[14]

(a) The Tribal Gaming Commission shall issue a separate license to each place, facility, or location on Indian lands where class II [and/or Class III] gaming is conducted under this ordinance. *[25 U.S.C. §2710(b)(1)(B); 25 C.F.R. §522.4(b)(6)]*

(b) The Tribal Gaming Commission shall issue a separate license to each place, facility, or location on Indian lands where Class II [and/or Class III] gaming is conducted under this ordinance once every [fill in number of years].[15] The Tribal Gaming Commission shall specify the form, conditions and content for the application for such licenses, which shall be submitted by the chief management official of the facility, and the initial application shall include a legal description of the lands whereon the facility is located, and a certification that said premises constitute "Indian lands" as specified in the Indian Gaming Regulatory Act, and shall identify the environmental, health, and public safety standards with which the facility must comply, and a certification that the facility is in compliance therewith. Each subsequent application for the renewal of such facility license shall identify any changes or additions to said legal description and applicable en-

---

12. The Tribe may wish to consult the interpretive rule put out at 67 Fed. Reg. 46109 (July 12, 2002) for guidance in creating environment and public health and safety standards.

13. This provision is recommended, but not required.

14. Subsection (a) is required by IGRA and the NIGC implementing regulations. Subsection (b) is recommended, but not required.

15. A period of one or two years is recommended for the term of a facility license.

vironmental, health and safety standards, and include current certifications of compliance therewith. The Tribal Gaming Commission shall only issue such licenses if the applications therefore include the required information and certifications and such further conditions as the Tribal Gaming Commission shall have specified.

Section 116.   Agent for Service of Process

The Tribe hereby designates [the Tribal Chair] as agent for service of process, who may be contacted at: [Physical Address where said official may be contacted] *[25 C.F.R. §519.1]*

Section 117.   Compliance with Federal Law[16]

The Tribe will comply with all applicable federal law, including the Bank Secrecy Act, 31 U.S.C. §5311 *et seq.*

Section 118.   Repeal[17]

To the extent that they are inconsistent with this ordinance, all prior gaming ordinances are hereby repealed.

Section 119.   Tribal Access to Financial Information[18]

A copy of the Tribal gaming operation annual audit will be made available for review, upon request, to: [Select one or more as appropriate] [The Tribe's Business Committee] [OR] [enrolled Tribal members] [OR] [desired Tribal group]

Section 201.   Licenses for Key Employees and Primary Management Officials

The Tribe shall ensure that the policies and procedures set out in this section are implemented with respect to key employees and primary management officials employed at any gaming enterprise operated on Indian lands. The Tribe will issue licenses and perform background investigations according to requirements at least as stringent as 25 C.F.R. Parts 556 and 558. *[25 U.S.C. §2710(b)(2)(F); 25 C.F.R. §558.3; 25 U.S.C. §522.4(b)(5)]*

Section 202.   License Application Forms

(a) The following notice shall be placed on the application form for a key employee or a primary management official:

> In compliance with the Privacy Act of 1974, the following information is provided: Solicitation of the information on this form is authorized by 25 U.S.C. 2701 et seq. The purpose of the requested information is to determine the eligibility of individuals to be employed in a gaming operation. The information will be used by the Tribe and the National Indian Gaming Commission members and staff who have need for the information in the performance of their official duties. The information may be disclosed to appropriate Federal, Tribal, State, local, or foreign law enforcement and regulatory agencies when relevant to civil, criminal or regulatory investigations or prosecutions or when necessary pursuant to a requirement by a Tribe or the National Indian Gaming Commission in connection with the hiring or firing of an employee, the issuance or revocation of a

---

16. This provision is recommended, but not required.
17. This provision is recommended, but not required
18. This provision is recommended, but not required.

gaming license, or investigation of activities while associated with a Tribe or a gaming operation. Failure to consent to the disclosures indicated in this notice will result in a Tribe being unable to hire you in a primary management official or key employee position. The disclosure of your Social Security Number (SSN) is voluntary. However, failure to supply a SSN may result in errors in processing your application. *[25 C.F.R. §556.2(a)]*

(b) The following additional notice shall be placed on the application form for a key employee or a primary official:

A false statement on any part of your application may be grounds for not hiring you, or for firing you after you begin work. Also, you may be punished by fine or imprisonment. (U.S. Code, Title 18, section 1001) *[25 C.F.R. §556.3(a)]*

(c) The Commission shall notify in writing existing key employees and primary management officials who have not completed an application containing the notices set forth above that they shall either:

(1) Complete a new application form that contains both the Privacy Act and false statement notices; or

(2) Sign a statement that contains the Privacy Act and false statement notices and consent to the routine uses described in that notice. *[25 C.F.R. §556.2(b); 25 C.F.R. §556.3(b)]*

Section 203. License Fees[19]

The Tribe may charge a license fee, to be set by the Tribal Gaming Commission, to cover its expenses in investigating and licensing Key Employees and Primary Management Officials of the gaming operation.

Section 204. Fingerprints[20]

Each applicant for a Key Employee or Primary Management Official shall be required to have fingerprints taken as part of the license application procedure. Fingerprints shall be taken by [Name of responsible law enforcement agency].[21] Fingerprints will then be forwarded to the NIGC for processing through the FBI and NCIC to determine the applicant's criminal history, if any. *[25 C.F.R. §522.2(h); 25 C.F.R. §556.4(a)(14)]*

Section 205. Background Investigations[22]

(a) The Tribal Gaming Commission is responsible for conducting background investigations and suitability determinations.

(b) The Tribal Gaming Commission shall request from each primary management official and from each key employee all of the following information:

(1) Full name, other names used (oral or written), social security number(s), birth date, place of birth, citizenship, gender, all languages (spoken or written);

---

19. This provision is recommended, but not required.

20. The Tribe may designate the Tribal regulatory authority as the law enforcement authority responsible for obtaining and forwarding or processing fingerprints.

21. The Tribe must choose a specific law enforcement agency to take fingerprints, and a specific entity to process the fingerprints or forward them to the NIGC for processing.

22. Unless a Tribal-State compact provides that a State has exclusive jurisdiction with respect to conducting background investigations and issuing licenses, the background investigation provisions apply to class III gaming.

(2) Currently and for the previous 5 years: business and employment positions held, ownership interests in those businesses, business and residence addresses, and drivers license numbers;

(3) The names and current addresses of at least three personal references, including one personal reference who was acquainted with the applicant during each period of residence listed under paragraph (b)(2) of this section;

(4) Current business and residence telephone numbers;

(5) A description of any existing and previous business relationships with Indian Tribes, including ownership interests in those businesses;

(6) A description of any existing and previous business relationships with the gaming industry generally, including ownership interests in those businesses;

(7) The name and address of any licensing or regulatory agency with which the person has filed an application for a license or permit related to gaming, whether or not such license or permit was granted;

(8) For each felony for which there was an ongoing prosecution or a conviction, within 10 years of the date of the application, the charge, the name and address of the court involved, and the date and disposition if any;

(9) For each misdemeanor conviction or ongoing misdemeanor prosecution (excluding minor traffic violations), within 10 years of the date of the application, the name and address of the court involved and the date and disposition;

(10) For each criminal charge (excluding minor traffic charges), whether or not there is a conviction, if such criminal charge is within 10 years of the date of the application and is not otherwise listed pursuant to paragraph (b)(8) or (b)(9) of this section, the criminal charge, the name and address of the court involved and the date and disposition;

(11) The name and address of any licensing or regulatory agency with which the person has filed an application for an occupational license or permit, whether or not such license or permit was granted;

(12) A photograph taken within the last year; and

(13) Any other information the Tribe deems relevant. *[25 C.F.R. §556.4]*

Section 206.   Procedures for Conducting a Background Check on Applicants[23]

(a) As part of its review procedure, the Commission or its agent shall employ or engage a private investigator to conduct a background investigation on each applicant sufficient to allow the Gaming Commission to make an eligibility determination under subsection G below. The investigator shall:

(1) Verify the applicant's identity through items such as a social security card, drivers license, birth certificate, or passport;

(2) Contact each personal and business reference provided in the License Application, when possible;

(3) Obtain a personal credit check;

(4) Conduct a civil history check;

---

23. This provision is recommended, but not required.

(5) Conduct a criminal history check via the submission of the applicant's fingerprints to the NIGC, and further obtain information from the appropriate court regarding past felony and/or misdemeanor convictions and criminal charges within the last ten years;

(6) Inquire into any previous or existing business relationships with the gaming industry and Indian tribes by contacting the entities or tribes;

(7) Verify the applicant's history and status with any licensing agency by contacting the agency; and

(8) Take other appropriate steps to verify the accuracy of the information, focusing on problem areas noted.

(b) The investigator shall create an investigative report noting the steps taken, information gained, potential problem areas, and disqualifying information.

(c) The Gaming Commission and its investigator shall promise to keep confidential the identity of each person interviewed in the course of the investigation, other than disclosure as required under Federal, Tribal, or State law.

Section 207.   Eligibility Determination

The Tribal Gaming Commission shall review a person's prior activities, criminal record, if any, and reputation, habits and associations to make a finding concerning the eligibility of a key employee or primary management official for employment in a gaming operation. If the Tribal Gaming Commission determines that employment of the person poses a threat to the public interest or to the effective regulation of gaming, or creates or enhances dangers of unsuitable, unfair, or illegal practices and methods and activities in the conduct of gaming, a tribal gaming operation shall not employ that person in a key employee or primary management official position. *[25 C.F.R. §558.2]*

Section 208.   Procedures for Forwarding Applications and Reports for Key Employees and Primary Management Officials to the National Indian Gaming Commission

(a) When a key employee or primary management official is employed to work at a gaming operation authorized by this ordinance, the Commission shall forward to the National Indian Gaming Commission a completed application for employment and conduct the background investigation and make the determination referred to in subsection D of this section. *[25 C.F.R. §558.3(a)]*

(b) The gaming operation shall not employ as a key employee or primary management official a person who does not have a license after 90 days. *[25 C.F.R. §558.3(b)]*

Section 209.   Report to the National Indian Gaming Commission

(a) The Tribal Gaming Commission shall prepare and forward a report on each background investigation to the National Indian Gaming Commission. An investigative report shall include all of the following:

(1) Steps taken in conducting a background investigation;

(2) Results obtained;

(3) Conclusions reached; and

(4) The bases for those conclusions. *[25 C.F.R. §556.5(a), (b)]*

(b) The Commission shall forward the completed investigative report to the National Indian Gaming Commission within 60 days after an employee begins work or within 60 days of the approval of this ordinance by the Chairman of the National Indian Gaming Commission. *[25 C.F.R. § 558.3(b)]*

(c) The Commission shall submit, with the investigative report, a copy of the eligibility determination, unless the NIGC shall have advised the Tribe that the submission of the eligibility determination is not necessary. This determination shall include a Statement describing how the information submitted by the applicant was verified; a Statement of results following an inquiry into the applicant's prior activities, criminal record, if any, and reputation, habits and associations; a Statement showing the results of interviews of a sufficient number of knowledgeable people (such as former employers, personal references, and others referred to by the applicant) in order to provide a basis for the Tribal Gaming Commission to make a finding concerning the eligibility for licensing required for employment in a gaming operation; and a Statement documenting the disposition of all potential problem areas noted and disqualifying information obtained.[24] *[25 C.F.R. § 556.5(c)]*

(d) If a license is not issued to an applicant, the Tribal Gaming Commission:

(1) Shall notify the NIGC; and

(2) Shall forward copies of its eligibility determination and investigative report (if any) to the NIGC for inclusion in the Indian Gaming Individuals Records System. *[25 C.F.R. § 556.5(d)]*

(e) With respect to all employees,[25] and in particular key employees and primary management officials, the Tribal Gaming Commission shall retain applications for employment and reports (if any) of background investigations for inspection by the Chairman of the NIGC or his or her designee for no less than three (3) years from the date of termination of employment. *[25 C.F.R. § 558.1(c)]*

Section 210.   Granting a Gaming License

(a) If, within a thirty (30) day period after the National Indian Gaming Commission receives a report, the National Indian Gaming Commission notifies the Tribe that it has no objection to the issuance of a license pursuant to a license application filed by a key employee or a primary management official for whom the Tribe has provided an application and investigative report to the National Indian Gaming Commission, the Tribal Gaming Commission, acting for the Tribe, may issue a license to such applicant. *[25 C.F.R. § 558.4(a)]*

(b) The Tribal Gaming Commission shall respond to a request for additional information from the Chairman of the National Indian Gaming Commission concerning a key employee or a primary management official who is the subject of a report. Such a request shall suspend the 30-day period under paragraph (a) of this section until the Chairman of the National Indian Gaming Commission receives the additional information. *[25 C.F.R. § 558.4(b)]*

(c) If, within the thirty (30) day period described above, the National Indian Gaming Commission provides the Tribe with a Statement itemizing objections to the issuance of

---

24. All that is required by 25 C.F.R. § 556.5(c) is that the Tribe include an eligibility determination with the report it furnishes to the NIGC. The suggested statements that might be included in an eligibility determination form provide information so that the Tribal Gaming Commission may make a fully informed decision.

25. The Tribe is only required to comply with the provisions of this section for the record of key employees and primary management officials. It is recommended that the Tribe maintain records on the applications of all employees.

a license to a key employee or to a primary management official for whom the Tribal Gaming Commission has provided an application and investigative report to the National Indian Gaming Commission, the Tribe shall reconsider the application, taking into account the objections itemized by the National Indian Gaming Commission. The Tribe shall make the final decision whether to issue a license to such applicant. *[25 C.F.R. § 558.4(b)]*

Section 211.   License Suspension

(a) If, after the issuance of a gaming license, the Tribal Gaming Commission receives from the National Indian Gaming Commission reliable information indicating that a key employee or a primary management official is not eligible for employment, the Tribal Gaming Commission shall suspend such license and shall notify in writing the licensee of the suspension and the proposed revocation. *[25 C.F.R. § 558.5(b)]*

(b) The Tribal Gaming Commission shall notify the licensee of a time and a place for a hearing on the proposed revocation of a license. *[25 C.F.R. § 558.5(c)]*

(c) After a revocation hearing, the Tribal Gaming Commission shall decide to revoke or to reinstate a gaming license. The Commission shall notify the NIGC of its decision. *[25 C.F.R. § 558.5(d)]*

Section 212.   Board of Review for Disputes[26]

The Tribe has determined that, in order to adhere to this Ordinance and all gaming regulations, there shall be established a Tribal Gaming Board of Review (Board of Review). The Board of Review shall serve as the final review body for employee disputes. Employee disputes shall include disputes with management, terminations, fines or other internal employee disputes, not to include actions taken by the Commission.

The Board of Review shall consist of five members. The membership shall be comprised of one member of the Tribal Gaming Commission, one member from the Tribal Council, one primary management official or key employee, one enrolled Tribal member not employed by the gaming operation, and one employee of the gaming operation.[27] The members from the Tribal Gaming Commission, Tribal Council, and gaming operation primary management official or employees shall be elected from their representative groups and the enrolled Tribal member shall be appointed by the [insert Tribal authority]. Board of Review members shall serve staggered terms. The two Tribal members shall serve three-year terms. The primary management official or key employee shall serve a two-year term. The members from the Tribal Gaming Commission and the Tribal Council shall serve one-year terms. The Board of Review members who are not employed by the Tribe in some other capacity shall be compensated at a rate of [enter dollar amount] per meeting or hearing, and shall be reimbursed for actual costs incurred during the scope of his/her duties as a member of the Board of Review. Compensation shall never be tied to tribal gaming revenues.

The Board of Review members shall elect a Chairperson from among them, whose duty it shall be to preside over all meetings and hearings. In addition, the members shall elect a Vice-Chair who shall be the custodian of any evidence submitted, and who shall preside in the Chairperson's absence. The Board of Review shall meet [enter frequency for meetings], shall keep official records of the meetings. No later than three working days

---

26. This provision is recommended, but not required.
27. The Tribe may adjust the membership of the Board of Review to fit its needs.

following a hearing on employee disputes, the Board of Review shall issue its findings. Findings of the Board shall be final when issued.

No Board of Review member shall be removed prior to the end of his/her term without cause. Removal shall be effectuated by a majority vote of the entire Board of Review, and shall be a final decision. A Board of Review member shall not review any decisions affecting himself/herself, or any person directly related to him or her.

Section 301. Licenses for Vendors[28]

(a) Vendors of gaming services or supplies with a value of $25,000[29] or more annually must have a vendor license from the Tribal Gaming Commission in order to transact business with the Tribal gaming operation. Contracts for professional legal and accounting services are excluded from this section.

(b) Gaming vendors are vendors who provide gaming supplies and services, including cash-related services.

(c) Non-gaming vendors provide services that do not have the ability to impact the integrity of the Tribal gaming operations, such as media advertising, facility maintenance workers, linen and laundry services, and food and beverage suppliers. The Tribal Gaming Commission shall create a regulation detailing which vendors fall into this category and shall maintain a register of the non-gaming vendors that it licenses. The regulation may exempt from licensing requirements non-gaming vendors who: 1) are a Tribal, Local, State, or Federal government agencies; 2) are regulated by the State of [fill in State] or the Tribe; or 3) will provide goods of insubstantial or insignificant amounts or quantities if the Tribal Gaming Commission determines that licensing of the vendor is not necessary to protect the public interest.

Section 302. Submission of a Vendor License Application[30]

In order to obtain a gaming vendor license, the business must complete a vendor application and submit to background checks of itself and its principals. Principals of a business include its officers, directors, management, owners, partners, non-institutional stockholders that either own 10% or more of the stock or are the 10 largest stockholders, and the on-site supervisor or manager under the agreement with the Tribe, if applicable.

Section 303. Contents of the Vendor License Application[31]

(a) Applications for gaming vendor licenses must include the following:

(1) Name of business, business address, business phone, federal tax ID number (or SSN if a sole proprietorship), main office address if different from business address, any other names the applicant has done business under, type of service applicant will provide;

(2) Whether the applicant is a partnership, corporation, limited liability company, sole proprietorship, or other entity;

---

28. This provision is recommended, but not required. The Tribe may leave this optional section in its ordinance or may create a vendor licensing regulation.
29. A Tribe may wish to evaluate the $25,000 minimum based on the size of the operation and the average amount of its contracts.
30. This provision is recommended, but not required.
31. This provision is recommended, but not required.

(3) If the applicant is a corporation, the state of incorporation, and the qualification to do business in the State of [insert State] if the gaming operation is in a different State than the State of incorporation;

(4) Trade name, other names ever used, names of any wholly owned subsidiaries or other businesses owned by the vendor or its principals;

(5) General description of the business and its activities;

(6) Whether the applicant will be investing in or loaning money to the gaming operation and, if so, how much;

(7) A description of any existing and previous business relationships with the gaming industry generally, including ownership interests in those businesses;

(8) A list of Indian tribes with which the vendor has an existing or previous business relationship, including ownership, financial, or management interests in non-gaming activities;[32]

(9) Names, addresses, and phone numbers of three business references with whom the company had regularly done business for the last five years;

(10) The name and address of any licensing or regulatory agency with which the business has filed an application for a license or permit related to gaming, whether or not such license or permit was granted;

(11) If the business has ever had a license revoked for any reason, the circumstances involved;

(12) A list of lawsuits to which the business has been a defendant, including the name and address of the court involved, and the date and disposition if any;

(13) List the business' funding sources and any liabilities of $50,000 or more.[33]

(14) A list of the principals of the business, their social security numbers, addresses and telephone numbers, title, and percentage of ownership in the company; and

(15) Any further information the Tribe deems relevant.

(b) The following notice shall be placed on the application form for a vendor and its principals:

Inclusion of false or misleading information in the vendor application may be grounds for denial or revocation of the Tribe's vendor license.

(c) A vendor may submit a copy of a recent license application to another jurisdiction if it contains the information listed above. The vendor will be required to submit in writing any changes in the information since the other license application was filed and any information requested by the Tribe not contained in the other application.

Section 304.   Vendor Background Investigation[34]

The Tribal Gaming Commission shall employ or otherwise engage a private investigator complete an investigation of the gaming vendor. This investigation shall contain, at a minimum, the following steps:

---

32. If the vendor has extensive interaction with Indian tribes, the Tribe may want to limit this list to the ten biggest contracts.

33. The Tribe may want to consider naming a higher amount for larger or publicly traded companies.

34. This provision is recommended, but not required.

(a) Verify of the business' incorporation status and qualification to do business in the State where the gaming operation is located;

(b) Obtain a business credit report, if available, and conduct a Better Business Bureau check on the vendor;

(c) Conduct a check of the business' credit history;

(d) Call each of the references listed in the vendor application; and

(e) Conduct an investigation of the principals of the business, including a criminal history check, a credit report, and interviews with the personal references listed.

Section 305.   Vendor License Fee[35]

The Tribe may charge a license fee, to be set by the Tribal Gaming Commission, to cover its expenses in investigating and licensing vendors of the gaming operation.

Section 306.   Vendor Background Investigation Report[36]

The private investigator shall complete an investigative report covering each of the steps taken in the background investigation of the gaming vendor and its principals and present it to the Tribal Gaming Commission.

Section 307.   Exemption for Vendors Licensed by Recognized Regulatory Authorities[37]

The Tribal Gaming Commission may adopt regulations naming specific licensing authorities that it recognizes and may authorize exemptions to the vendor licensing process for vendors which have received a license from one of the named regulatory authorities.

Section 308.   Licenses for Non-Gaming Vendors[38]

For non-gaming vendors, the Tribal Gaming Commission is authorized to create a less stringent vendor licensing process, including a due diligence check rather than a full background investigation as laid out in Section 304. The Gaming Commission may investigate such vendors when appropriate and may conduct audits in addition to monitoring Tribal purchases.

Notes and Questions

1.   *Tribal gaming commission functions.* Compare the list of tribal gaming commission functions provided by Burris in the Notes and Questions above, and the duties outlined in the NIGC model tribal gaming ordinance. Which duties would apply to all tribal gaming commissions, regardless of scope and size of the gaming operation? Which would vary?

2.   *Revenue sharing.* In reference to Section 105, Use of Gaming Revenue, in the model ordinance, the NIGC noted, "It is not necessary to have a provision allowing net gaming revenues to be used for payment of revenue-sharing provisions in Tribal-State compacts; these fall under promotion of tribal economic development because the Tribe must gain an economic benefit in return for the payments." In a single sentence, the NIGC

---

35. This provision is recommended, but not required.
36. This provision is recommended, but not required.
37. This provision is recommended, but not required.
38. This provision is recommended, but not required.

effectively shoehorned tribal-state revenue-sharing provisions into one of the permissible categories of compact provisions. Is this a reasonable interpretation of IGRA? Did Congress intend the category of "tribal economic development" to cover multi-million-dollar payments to states in exchange for some economic benefit? The NIGC's statement in the model ordinance reflected to some degree the Interior Secretary's position on revenue sharing. This issue is highly controversial and is discussed in detail in Chapter 10.

3.   Model ordinance. Recall Deloria and Lytle's discussion of the "model constitution" utilized under the IRA:

> The format that emerged under the 1934 act was almost a carbon copy of the structured, legalistic European form of government. Since tribal governments were floundering, the Bureau of Indian Affairs seized the initiative and drafted a model constitution that could be used by tribes as a starting point for their written documents. This model constitution in most instances became the final product, which should not be surprising since Congress in passing the IRA required that all constitutions be approved by the secretary of the interior before becoming operational and homogeneity rather than usefulness consequently became the virtue.

Deloria & Lytle, at 101–02. Does the NIGC model ordinance run the risk of valuing "homogeneity rather than usefulness"? Is there sufficient opportunity for tribes to tailor the required ordinance to meet their particular circumstances and needs?

2. Tribal Court Decisions

As explained at the start of this Chapter, many tribes have tribal courts or other justice systems for resolving disputes that fall within the tribe's jurisdiction. Besides federal law governing tribal jurisdiction, tribal-state Class III compacts may also assign jurisdiction over civil disputes or criminal matters. Tribal court decisions are an important source of law relevant to the operations of Indian gaming establishments. Here, we include a few examples of the types of cases a tribal court may decide and the sources of law on which it may rely. The cases also illustrate the varied disputes that arise in the factual and legal context of a tribal casino.

Kalantari v. Spirit Mountain Gaming, Inc.
Tribal Court for the Confederated Tribes
of the Grand Ronde Community of Oregon
(2003)

This case arises out of a collision between Plaintiff and a casino employee on the floor of the casino on February 13, 2001. Plaintiff has filed suit against the casino alleging that the employee was negligent in walking too fast, failing to keep a proper lookout, failing to maintain control of himself, and in carrying a container that partially blocked his vision. In discovery, Plaintiff sought any photographs or videotapes that Defendant had taken of her and of the accident. In response, Defendant produced a copy of all the known footage it had of Plaintiff. Plaintiff describes the one videotape given to her by Defendant as being "of poor viewing quality showing one view of the collision which took place."

Defendant has explained that it does not and cannot have any additional footage or videotapes of the accident. When an accident occurs on the casino gaming floor, a dub is made from the master tape and is retained, but the master tape is later reused. Plaintiff already has been given the only dubbed tape that shows the accident. Pursuant to customary casino policy, all other tapes have been recycled and reused.

At a pretrial conference held on March 14, 2003, the Court first ordered that Plaintiff's attorneys could view the surveillance room at the casino. Subsequently, Defendant's attorney sought reconsideration of that order. In its March 28, 2003, order, the Court adhered to its earlier decision and ordered again that Plaintiff's attorneys could view the surveillance room. The Court reasoned that Plaintiff had a strong interest in seeking to gather evidence and in demonstrating that relevant evidence might have been destroyed by Defendant.

Nevertheless recognizing that Defendant has a legitimate and significant concern with casino security, the Court imposed stringent limitations on Plaintiff's use of the information gleaned from its inspection. Those safeguards include: (1) the fact that only Plaintiff's attorneys, and not Plaintiff herself, can view the surveillance room, (2) that the attorneys cannot divulge to their client what they learned, (3) that any questions regarding the location and operation of the surveillance room and the equipment in it must be asked in a deposition only and without Plaintiff being present, unless Defendant's counsel agrees that the questions may be asked in some other forum, (4) that any tape or transcript of any such deposition is to be sealed by the Court and not revealed to Plaintiff, (5) that any testimony regarding the matter first be heard in chambers and remain under seal, unless the Court determines that the evidence is admissible, and (6) that Plaintiff's attorneys may not discuss with Plaintiff or anyone else what they learn in their inspection, except as absolutely necessary to prepare Plaintiff's case. In their response to Defendant's motion to amend the Court's earlier discovery order, Plaintiff's attorneys aver that, as officers of the Court, they agree at all times to abide by the "severe limitations" that the Court has imposed on the inspection that it has allowed.

Defendant now has moved to amend the Court's March 28, 2003, discovery order so as not to allow Plaintiff's attorneys, or anyone else acting on Plaintiff's behalf for that matter, to view the casino surveillance room. Plaintiff opposes that motion.

Defendant's motion to amend the Court's earlier discovery order is based on Fed. R. Civ. P. 60(b), which provides in part that "[o]n motion and upon such terms as are just, the Court may relieve a party or a party's legal representative from a final judgment, order, or proceeding" for certain reasons that are listed in the rule.[*] As Plaintiff notes, and as the word "final" indicates, the rule applies only to final decisions and not to interlocutory orders. *Prudential Real Estate Affiliates v. PPR Realty*, 204 F.3d 867, 860 (9th Cir. 2000); Wright, Miller and Kane, 11 Federal Practice and Procedure, §2852 at 233–34 & n.8 (2d ed. 1995).

That rule 60(b) does not apply here does not mean that the Court lacks authority to reconsider or to amend its earlier discovery order, however. Instead, the fact that "interlocutory judgments [or orders] are not brought within the restrictions of the rule" means that "they are left subject to the complete power of the court rendering them to afford such relief as justice requires." Wright, Miller and Kane, 11 Federal Practice and Procedure, §2852 at 233–34 n.8, quoting Advisory Committee Note to Rule 60(b). *See also John Simmons Co. v. Grier Brothers Co.*, 258 U.S. 82, 88, 475 (1922) ("at any time before final decree," a court may modify or rescind an interlocutory order). Thus, the Court has broad authority, constrained only by the proper exercise of its own discretion, to amend, re-

---

[*] This Court has adopted as its rules of procedure the Federal Rules of Civil Procedure.

scind, or modify its prior discovery orders. The question then becomes whether the Court should exercise that discretionary authority in this case and grant Defendant's motion. Having given due consideration to the arguments presented by both parties to this litigation, the Court adheres to its earlier order.

Fed. R. Civ. P. 26(b)(1) provides that, "[f]or good cause, the court may order discovery of any matter relevant to the subject matter involved in the action." Defendant contends, in effect, that Plaintiff has not made an adequate showing of good cause. In Defendant's view, Plaintiff does not need to view the surveillance room because she already has been given the only pertinent videotape that exists and because all other videotapes that might have shown anything else relevant to the case have long since been recycled and reused. Plaintiff responds that she needs to have her attorneys view the surveillance room because she believes that there may be other contiguous videotapes which were filmed from the surveillance room which would more clearly and extensively show the development of the incident and the incident itself. It is Plaintiff's contention that only an inspection of the surveillance room will assist Plaintiff's [attorneys] in evaluating the extent to which Defendant has disposed of evidence.

That issue is one that is or may be relevant in this case, at least for impeachment purposes and to contest what may be Defendant's eventual reliance on the one videotape that does exist. [U]nder Rule 26(b)(1), to be discoverable evidence need only be "relevant to the claim or defense of any party[.]" Here, the location of other video-recorders in the surveillance room, and the possibility that those recorders also might have taped the incident and that those tapes later were reused, is information that appears to be relevant both to Plaintiff's claims of negligence and to Defendant's denial of those allegations. To reiterate, Plaintiff's theory is that Defendant's reuse of the videotapes may suggest that "defendant has disposed of evidence." A party's destruction of relevant evidence may suggest a motive to do away with the evidence and prevent it from falling into the hands of the opposing party. And that, in turn, may suggest the party's awareness of its employee's fault in the matter, and of its own potential liability. Plaintiff avers that, as early as the day of the accident, Defendant's security staff was aware of the incident and suspected that a lawsuit might result.

Furthermore, even if the information gleaned from an inspection of the surveillance room led to the discovery of material that could be used only for impeachment of Defendant's witnesses, that would be enough under the rule to permit Plaintiff's inspection. 8 Federal Practice and Procedure § 2008, 2003 pocket part at 19, quoting Advisory Committee Note ("information that could be used to impeach a likely witness, although not otherwise relevant to the claims or defenses, might be properly discoverable" under Rule 26(b)). In sum, Plaintiff has shown a need for the inspection that is sufficient to warrant such pretrial discovery.

Defendant also suggests that it should not have to allow Plaintiff's attorneys into the surveillance room because the gaming compact between the Tribe and the state, and 25 C.F.R. § 542.43(c), prevent it from doing so. The compact provides that the state "acknowledges that the Tribe has voluntarily given the State access to ... information" regarding "sensitive financial, security and surveillance information that the Tribe considers confidential" and that "the Tribe otherwise would not be required by law" to disclose. Grand Ronde/State Class III Gaming Compact, section 9(2)(f). In the compact, the state also "acknowledges that this information should reasonably be considered confidential." However, the compact also provides unambiguously that nothing in section 9 "precludes the State or the Tribe from disclosing information pursuant to state, tribal or federal rules of civil procedure or evidence in connection with litigation, a prosecution or a criminal investigation." *Id.* section 9(3); *see also id.* section 13(E) ("This Compact is for the benefit of and governs only the respective authorities of and the relations between the Tribe and the State"). Thus, the compact does not support nondisclosure here. Instead, it simply does not apply.

The provision of the code of federal regulations on which defendant relies, 25 C.F.R. § 542.43(c), provides that: "Access to the surveillance room shall be limited to surveillance personnel, designated employees, and other persons authorized in accordance with the surveillance department policy. Such policy shall be approved by the Tribal gaming regulatory authority. The surveillance department shall maintain a sign-in log of other authorized persons entering the surveillance room."

Rather clearly the "policy" contemplated by this rule is one intended to cover the usual, day-to-day access to the surveillance room at a Tribal gaming site. The policy does not purport to cover all situations and it does not suggest that a court with jurisdiction over a civil suit cannot properly order access by persons other than those contemplated by the day-to-day policy. Indeed, it would be extraordinary if a mere administrative regulation could serve to deprive a court of competent jurisdiction of its authority and control over discovery matters in cases before it and of its ability to effect and enforce its own discovery orders. Nothing in the text of this administrative rule supports such an unlikely and extraordinary reading of it.

Defendant also emphasizes its legitimate and significant security concerns and its need to guard against undue disclosure of the location of its surveillance room and of the areas of the casino floor covered by the video-cameras in that room. In permitting Plaintiff's attorneys to view the surveillance room, the Court in no way doubts the validity of or diminishes the importance of those concerns. The Court has placed those weighty concerns in the balance, and it is those concerns that have prompted the Court to impose what Plaintiff accurately describes as "severe limitations on th[e] examination[.]" *See generally* 8 Federal Practice and Procedure § 2036, at 488 ("the rules ... permit the broadest scope of discovery and leave it to the enlightened discretion of the district court to decide what restrictions may be necessary in a particular case") (footnote omitted); *Patterson v. Avery Dennison Corp.*, 281 F3d 676, 681 (7th Cir. 2002) ("Before restricting discovery, [a] court should consider the totality of the circumstances, weighing the value of the material sought against the burden of producing it, and taking into account society's interest in furthering the truth-seeking function in the particular case before it") (internal quotation marks and citations omitted). The limitations imposed by the Court in this case are outlined above. In essence, those limitations mean that, although Plaintiff's attorneys can view the surveillance room, they cannot disclose what they have learned to anyone, or make any use of the information at trial without the Court's permission. Even deposition inquiries relating to the location and operation of the surveillance room and the surveillance equipment in it are to be conducted without Plaintiff being present, and the record then is to be sealed. These stringent limitations on Plaintiff's attorneys' use of what they see and what they learn during their inspection are designed to and should protect the security and integrity of casino security. Plaintiff's attorneys can look, but they can't tell.

In sum, having carefully considered and weighed the matter and after giving due regard to the arguments of both parties, the Court remains convinced that Plaintiff has a legitimate need to inspect the surveillance room, and that such an inspection involves a matter that is relevant to the claims and defenses of the parties. Because admittedly, on the other hand, Defendant's security concerns are both legitimate and significant, the Court has imposed extremely stringent limitations on Plaintiff's attorneys' use of what they see and learn. The Court has weighed the parties' interests and has struck a balance that serves the interests of both parties by giving Plaintiff the discovery to which she is entitled, while keeping Defendant's security secrets just that — secret.

In re the Class III-A Gaming License of Marc Joseph Eldridge, Licensee Tribal Court in and for the Puyallup Tribe

(2000)

FINDINGS OF FACT

The Licensee has worked as a security officer at the Emerald Queen Casino, since the latter part of 1998, and in the capacity of his job, he holds a Class III-A Gaming License, which is a prerequisite of his employment at the Casino.

On [January 20, 2000], an incident occurred at the Casino wherein the Licensee, acting in the capacity as a security guard employed by the Casino, subdued and handcuffed a patron of the Casino, one Mr. Owen J. Wood, hereinafter referred to as "Patron Wood." Further, during the same incident, the Licensee subdued, and later released, a friend of Patron Wood. During the incident, the Patron Wood was intoxicated and belligerent, and, as a result of the arrest perpetrated on the Patron Wood by the Licensee, the Patron Wood was subsequently arrested, prosecuted and convicted before the Tacoma Municipal Court for conduct related to the instant arrest.

[The following month,] the Licensee was "summarily suspended," on the basis of the Tribal Gaming Commission's finding that the Licensee used "excessive force" in detaining Patron Wood, during a situation wherein the Licensee used "overly aggressive action." In the [suspension] letter, the Commission notified the Licensee that he had to appear before the Commission and "show cause why the Commission should not revoke (the Licensee's) Class III-A gaming license." Further, the Commission wrote, "[A]t the hearing, the burden is on the licensee to show cause why the Commission should not revoke your Class III-A license." The Licensee, prior to [his] suspension, and at any time since, has not been provided a "complaint" by the Commission pertaining to the facts and circumstances relative to this litigation, pursuant to the mandate of Emergency Regulation 12.1, nor has the Licensee been afforded any of the other procedural safeguards promulgated in 12.1 et seq.

[The Licensee submitted to the Commission] a written request for discovery, which was denied. [T]he Licensee followed up the request for discovery with a personal visit to the Commission offices, at which time Ms. Ripley, an employee of the Tribe, told the Licensee that he could not see or receive any information that the Commission had concerning his case. The Licensee asked Ms. Ripley how, if it was his responsibility to show why his license should not be revoked, could he properly defend himself absent being given access to any discovery. In response, Ms. Ripley replied, "that would be like the prosecuting attorney giving the defense attorney all the information they had concerning the case." In response, the Licensee told Ms. Ripley that it was his understanding that they (i.e., prosecutors) did provide discovery consistent with the material he was requesting, and that the name of the requested material was called, in fact, "Discovery." In response, Ms. Ripley said, "well this isn't a court of law and we don't have to show you anything." Ms. Ripley further said, "Butch (Harry Dillon) made the decision to not show you anything. I already talked to him about it."

[On March 23, 2000, the Commission conducted a "Class III Show Cause Hearing" to review the Licensee's suspension. At the hearing,] despite not having been provided a complaint or discovery, the Licensee handed to the Commission on the occasion of his hearing a packet, [which] included material which would have refuted what he believed to be the charges against him, i.e., that he used excessive force against Patron Wood. Despite the Licensee's requests for discovery prior to the hearing, the Licensee was only provided discovery during the hearing, while being afforded a 5 to 10 minute recess to review the discovery, after which the hearing reconvened.

After the hearing, the Licensee asked Steve Koransky (Gaming Director) if he thought the Licensee's license would be revoked. Mr. Koransky said, "things should have been handled differently. Anytime you have to put your hands on someone, you've done something wrong." Mr. Koransky then proceeded to tell the Licensee that the Casino needed to adopt a policy, where the Security Officers were equipped with "Kubatons." (A Kubaton is a small baton/impact weapon with a flat end and a rounded point on the other, mostly used in martial arts). In response, the Licensee inquired as to the hypocrisy of Mr. Koransky's two statements (i.e., that a security guard should never put a hand on someone, as opposed to equipping a security force with Kubatons inferring hand to hand combat).

By Administrative Order issued by the Commission [after] the hearing, the Licensee's license was suspended. The Administrative Order, instead of dealing with the Patron Wood, dealt with two Casino Patrons, and it dealt with the use of insufficient force in releasing from custody the friend of Patron Wood after said friend had been temporarily apprehended, i.e., the Administrative Order made no finding of excessive force toward anyone, let alone the Patron Wood, but instead found that the Licensee used insufficient force in dealing with the friend of the Patron Wood.

[The matter proceeded to trial before the Puyallup Tribal Court.] [F]ollowing the start of trial, Mr. Koransky and Mr. Dillon, on behalf of the Commission, requested that the trial de novo be continued, claim[ing] that they were not aware that a trial de novo meant that they had to call witnesses and that they did not have any witnesses present, let alone had they yet hired a lawyer. [T]he Trial Judge denied the Commission's motion to continue [but] recessed to allow the parties sufficient time to attempt to settle the case in view of the developments.

When the Court reconvened, the Commission and the Licensee read into the record a settlement which had been reached, with only one contested point. The settlement consisted of the following: (1) the revocation of the Licensee's license would be immediately reversed; (2) the Commission would not oppose payment of all of the Licensee's back pay and back benefits for the work he missed as a result of the suspension or revocation of his license; (3) the Commission would expunge the Licensee's file regard[ing] the incident at bar; (4) the Commission guaranteed there would be no discrimination or harassment or prejudice shown toward the Licensee as a result of this settlement and after the Licensee's employment re-commenced at the Casino. The only point on which there was disagreement was whether the Casino should pay the Licensee's back wages, as contended by the Commission, or whether the Commission should pay the back wages of the Licensee, as argued by the Licensee.

[On the last point,] [t]he Trial Court found and ruled that the Commission had committed many grievous violations of its own regulations in prosecuting the case against the Licensee, up to and including the Commission's appearance on the date set for trial, when the Commission appeared unprepared to proceed. The Trial Court further stated that had this matter proceeded to trial, based on the numerous significant violations of its own regulations, resulting in numerous procedural and substantive due process violations of the rights of the Licensee, that the Trial Court would have "sanctioned" the Commission for its numerous violations. [Accordingly,] the Trial Court ruled that the Commission, not the Casino, would pay the Licensee's back wages [in the amount of $14,629.73].

CONCLUSIONS OF LAW

Pursuant to Section 2.27, of the Puyallup Tribe of Indians Tribal Gaming Code, the Commission shall promulgate regulations protecting due process rights of all individuals subject to the enforcement of this Code, and that such regulations shall provide, at a minimum fair notice and opportunity for hearing regarding any revocation or suspension of license, and regarding any enforcement action taken pursuant to this Code. Pursuant to Emergency Regulation 2.10,1.11, and 9.4, the Commission shall strictly follow the Emergency Regulations in all licensing matters, such as in the case at bar.

Throughout the process of the Commission's prosecution of this licensing action against the Licensee, the Commission violated many of its own regulations, resulting in many violations of the Licensee's right to substantive and procedural due process, which at least consisted of the following rights and violations:

> Pursuant to Emergency Regulation 12.1, the Commission was required to file against the Licensee a "complaint" which met with the mandate of Emergency Regulation 12.1. Not only did the Commission not file a complaint which met with the requirements of the statute, the Commission filed no complaint whatsoever.

> The Licensee was denied his procedural rights pursuant to Emergency Regulation 12.2 of the Emergency Regulations, to have the Commissioner or Executive Director examine the complaint, along with supporting documents, to determine the complaint's merits or frivolity, and to have the Executive Director dismiss the complaint if it does not establish sufficient grounds. The Licensee was denied this right.

> Pursuant to Emergency Regulation 12.8, the Licensee was entitled to file an answer to the Commission's complaint. The Licensee was denied this right.

> Pursuant to Emergency Regulation 12.11, the Licensee was entitled, after hearing the evidence and reaching a decision that the complaint has proven by a preponderance of the evidence, the Commission may revoke the license, may suspend the license for a particular period or time, or issue a public or private letter of reprimand to be placed in the file of the Licensee, or any combination thereof. Further, the Licensee is entitled to a dismissal of the complaint, in whole or part, in the event it has not been proven. In addition, the Licensee is entitled to the Commission viewing options apart from revocation of his license. The Licensee was denied all of these regulatory entitlements pursuant to Emergency Regulations 12.11, and, in fact, the burden was erroneously placed on the Licensee on the occasion of the hearing.

The actions of the Commission, in not following its own regulations, and in causing the Licensee to incur the above-mentioned due process violations, were severe enough to the extent that they were sanctionable. Due to the cumulative effect of the due process violations and regulatory shortcomings of the Commission, back pay and benefits shall be paid by the Tribe, as opposed to being paid by the Casino. Judgment shall enter against the Puyallup Tribe in the amount of $14,629.73.

Long v. Mohegan Tribal Gaming Authority
Mohegan Gaming Disputes Tribal Court of Appeals
(1997)

The Plaintiff has brought two actions against the Mohegan Tribal Gaming Authority, arising out of the alleged termination of his employment by the Defendant. The Plaintiff alleges that he was hired as Director of Craps on or about April 15, 1996, and on August 16, 1996 received a "Personnel Action Form" resulting in his termination effective August 30, 1996.

In each case, Plaintiff has alleged breach of express contract (Count One), breach of implied contract (Count Two), breach of implied covenant of good faith and fair dealing (Count Three), negligent misrepresentation (Count Four), a violation of the Mohegan Tribal Gaming Authority Ordinance No. 97-5 (Count Five), breach of contract as third party beneficiary (Count Six), statutory discrimination (Count Seven), and promissory estoppel (Count Eight). The Defendants Mohegan Tribal Gaming Authority and Mohegan Tribal Gaming Enterprise have moved to dismiss Plaintiff's claims in their entirety, on grounds that Count Five, alleging employment discrimination, is the only count cognizable by this court, and that as to that count, the Plaintiff lacks standing and that his claim is untimely filed. As to all other counts, the Defendants argue that it enjoys sovereign immunity from unconsented suit.

A. Claims Under the Mohegan Tribal Gaming Authority
Discriminatory Employment Practices Claims and Appeals Ordinance (TGA 97-5)

Article XIII of the Constitution of the Mohegan Tribe, Section I, grants to the Tribal Gaming Authority "all governmental and proprietary powers of The Mohegan Tribe over the development, construction, operation, promotion, financing, regulation and licensing of gaming, and any associated hotel, associated resort or associated entertainment facilities, on tribal lands." Such powers must be within the scope of the authority delegated by the Tribal Council to the Tribal Gaming Authority pursuant to Ordinance No. 95-2. The Constitution further provides as that "the Tribal Gaming Authority shall have the power to grant a limited waiver of sovereign immunity as to the Gaming matters." Mohegan Const., Art. XIII, Sec. 1.

Pursuant to this authority, the Mohegan Tribal Gaming Authority adopted Ordinance No. 97-5. This Ordinance contains a limited waiver of sovereign immunity "for the sole purpose of enabling an applicant for employment with the Gaming Enterprise or an employee or former employee of the Gaming Enterprise ... to file and process a claim or appeal in The Gaming Disputes Court in accordance with and subject to the specific provisions expressed in this Ordinance." Sovereign immunity is not waived for any other purpose, including the filing of claims or suits for any other adverse employment action, "including, but not limited to, any charge, claim, or suit complaining of wrongful discharge." TGA 97-5 §II (a).

The Mohegan Tribal Gaming Authority Discriminatory Employment Practices Claims and Appeals Ordinance is far from a general grant of authority for the bringing of actions for adverse employment decisions. Section XI specifically provides that all appeals and claims must be filed within the time limits provided, and any claim or appeal "which is not timely filed or fails to comply with the applicable provisions of this ordinance shall be dismissed." TGA 97-5 §XI (a, b). The Discriminatory Employment Practices Ordinance further establishes two types of matters which may be brought to The Gaming Disputes Court,

Claims and Appeals, and those qualified to file either one are strictly and narrowly defined. A claim may be filed only by two classifications of individuals: "Only individual applicants for employment who were denied or barred from employment ... and individuals employed or formerly employed by the Gaming Enterprise who have been suspended without pay or have had their employment terminated by the Gaming Enterprise prior to completion of their respective probationary periods of employment ..." TGA 97-5 §III (a)1.

The Ordinance further provides that the following classifications of individuals shall not have standing to file a claim pursuant to the Ordinance: "One who occupies or occupied a managerial position with The Gaming Enterprise"; "An applicant for a managerial position in The Gaming Enterprise"; [and] "An individual who has access to the grievance procedures set forth in The Gaming Enterprise Employment Policies or to the Board of Review." TGA 97-5.

The Defendants have challenged the standing of the Plaintiff to bring this claim, both on grounds that the Plaintiff does not fit into either of the two classifications of individuals eligible to file a claim, and that the Plaintiff occupied a managerial position and had access to appropriate grievance procedures, of which he did not avail himself.

In deciding jurisdictional issues raised by a pretrial Motion to Dismiss, the court must consider "the allegations of the complaint in their most favorable light." *Lemoine v. McCann*, 40 Conn. App. 460, 464, quoting *Reynolds v. Soffer*, 183 Conn. 67, 68 (1981). "A motion to dismiss admits all facts well pleaded and invokes any record that accompanies the motion, including supporting affidavits that contain undisputed facts." *Carl J. Herzog Foundation, Inc. v. University of Bridgeport*, 41 Conn. App. 790, 793 (1996). It is clear that the probationary status of the Plaintiff as of the time of his termination is in dispute. Similarly, whether the Plaintiff in fact occupied a managerial position cannot be determined from the record. Although the title of "Director of Craps" connotes supervisory authority, this court is not in a position to say whether the same equates with a "managerial position." (Cf. Connecticut General Statutes Section 5-270(g), defining "managerial employee," for purposes of collective bargaining, in terms of responsibility for direction, development, implementation and evaluation of goals and objectives, formulation of policy, etc.). In this case, the court is unable to make the necessary factual findings on these two issues from the affidavits, which findings are necessary to determine the existence of standing under TGA 97-5. Similarly, the issue of whether the Plaintiff had access to the grievance procedures or the Board of Review are clearly in dispute. The Connecticut Supreme Court has held it to be error for a trial court not to allow an evidentiary hearing where questions of fact relating to standing were raised. *Unisys Corp. v. Department of Labor*, 220 Conn. 689, 695–96 (1991).

The resolution of Defendants' Motion to Dismiss Count Five of Plaintiff's Complaint does not require such a hearing, however, in light of the court's ruling on the issue of Defendants' claim that the complaint was untimely filed. The Mohegan Tribal Gaming Authority Discriminatory Employment Practices Claims and Appeals Ordinance establishes strict time limits for the filing of claims thereunder: "A Claim may be filed directly with the Chief Clerk of the Court within thirty (30) days after the occurrence of the event of which such Claim arises, or within thirty (30) days after the Claimant first knew or, through the exercise of reasonable diligence should have known, of the occurrence of the event out of which such Claim arises. Any Claim filed more than thirty (30) days after the occurrence of the event out of which the Claim arises, or more than thirty (30) days after the Claimant first knew or, though the exercise of reasonable diligence should have known, of the occurrence of the event out of which such Claim arises, will be deemed untimely and will be subject to dismissal by the Court." The ordinance contains no provision allowing the court to vary the strict time limits set forth therein.

As already noted, the Plaintiff alleges that he was hired as Director of Craps on or about April 15, 1996. The complaint alleges conduct by the Defendants or by Plaintiff's supervisor indicative of a discriminatory employment practice that took place "throughout the Plaintiff's employment with Mohegan Sun," and which "created a hostile working environment for the Plaintiff in that it intentionally engaged in behavior to disrupt the Plaintiff's work, to make the Plaintiff feel uncomfortable, and to try to cause him to perform his job duties badly." These allegations, taken as a whole, clearly indicate that the conduct complained of was known to the Plaintiff, or discoverable in the exercise of reasonable diligence, at the time it took place. The Plaintiff has made no claim that he could not have reasonably known of the alleged behavior until a later date. On August 16, 1996, Plaintiff received a "Personnel Action Form" resulting in his termination effective August 30, 1996. Plaintiff's claim was not filed until May 9, 1997, well beyond the thirty day period allowed for the filing of claims.

In his Supplemental Memorandum, Plaintiff attacks Defendants' contention that this court lacks jurisdiction because the action was not brought within the time limits contained in TGA 97-5. Although Plaintiff is correct in asserting that in most cases the defense of statute of limitations is properly raised by a special defense, Connecticut Practice Book Section 164, where "a specific time limitation is contained within a statute that creates a right of action that did not exist at common law, then the remedy exists only during the prescribed period and not thereafter." *Ecker v. West Hartford*, 205 Conn. 219, 232 (1987). At issue is whether a time limitation contained within a statute is procedural, and thus subject to waiver, or is "rather is a limitation on the liability itself, and not of the remedy alone." *Ecker v. West Hartford, supra* at 232.

This particular issue has been extensively analyzed by the Mashantucket Pequot Tribal Court in *Jenkins v. Mashantucket Pequot Gaming Enterprise*, 1 Mash. 7 (1993), where the court, per Freeman, C.J., held that the time limitation contained in the Sovereign Immunity Waiver Ordinance, M.P.T.O. 100192-01, Sec. 11, is jurisdictional rather than procedural in nature. The holding in *Jenkins* followed the decision of the Connecticut Supreme Court in *Ecker v. West Hartford, supra*, that the time limitations contained in Connecticut General Statutes Section 52-555 (allowing actions for wrongful death) were a jurisdictional prerequisite that could not be waived, as well as the holdings of similar cases involving limited waivers of sovereign immunity as to the United States under the Federal Tort Claims Act, 28 USC Section 2671 et seq., and as to the State of Connecticut under Connecticut General Statutes Section 13a-144. These limitations were found to be jurisdictional and non-waivable.

In the instant case, TGA 97-5 leaves no doubt that the time limitations contained therein are jurisdictional and non-waivable. [The ordinance states,] "(a) All Appeals and Claims shall be filed within the time limits provided herein and in accordance with the applicable provisions of this ordinance. (b) Any Claim or Appeal which is not timely filed or fails to comply with the applicable provisions of this ordinance shall be dismissed."

Nevertheless, the Plaintiff has argued that the thirty-day statute of limitations contained in TGA 97-5 is void by operation of Section 702 of Ordinance 95-4, which establishes a general one year statute of limitations for actions against the Mohegan Tribe or Tribal Gaming Authority. M.T.O. 95-4, Art. VII, Sec. 702(1). While the language of Section 702 provides that the one year statute shall apply "unless otherwise specifically provided in this ordinance," there is no authority for holding that such a provision preempts the authority of the Mohegan Tribe or the Tribal Gaming Authority, as set forth in the Mohegan Constitution, to grant limited waivers of immunity at any time in the future under whatever limitations deemed appropriate. No authority has been cited that even suggests that this court should read into an ordinance any such limitation on the constitutional power of the Tribe or the Tribal Gaming Authority. "Later enactments are presumed to repeal [or be inapplicable to] earlier inconsistent ones to the extent of the conflict." *Plourde v. Liburdi*, 207 Conn. 412, 417 (1958), quoting *Keogh v. Bridgeport*, 187 Conn. 53, 65 (1982). A legislative body, in the enactment of statutes, "is always presumed to know all the existing statutes and the effect that its action or non-action will have upon any one of them. And it is always presumed to have intended that effect which its action or non-action produces." *Plourde v. Liburdi*, 207 Conn. at 417, quoting *State v. Staub*, 61 Conn. 553, 556 (1892). Clearly, the Mohegan Tribe and the Tribal Gaming Authority have the power by later enactment to modify the general statute of limitations contained in M.T.O. 95-4.

The court is aware that holding compliance with the thirty day statute of limitations to be a jurisdictional prerequisite, when viewed in the circumstances of this case, may seem unduly harsh, especially where the period of time by which the Plaintiff's claim did not comply with the strict time limits of TGA 97-5 is relatively short. Nevertheless, this court is bound by the strict, limited waiver of immunity contained in TGA 97-5 and is without authority to permit a deviation from the strict time limitations which are incorporated into the waiver of immunity.

The Defendants have moved to dismiss [the Plaintiff's remaining claims] on grounds that these counts are barred by the doctrine of sovereign immunity.

Absent "a clear waiver [of immunity] by the tribe or congressional abrogation," *Oklahoma Tax Commission v. Citizen Band Potawatomi Indian Tribe of Oklahoma*, 498 U.S. 505, 509 (1991), it is clear that Indian tribes possess the "common law immunity from suit traditionally enjoyed by sovereign powers." *Santa Clara Pueblo v. Martinez*, 436 U.S. 49, 58 (1978). The sovereignty of the Mohegan Tribe of Indians of Connecticut is further expressly set forth in the Mohegan Constitution, which provides that the Tribe shall have all the inherent sovereign rights and powers of an independent, indigenous sovereign nation. Mohegan Const., Art. II. While Indian Tribes can waive their sovereign immunity, "such waiver may not be implied, but must be expressed unequivocally." *McClendon v. United States*, 885 F.2d. 627, 629 (9th Cir. 1989). "The issue of tribal sovereign immunity is jurisdictional in nature." *Id.*

Section 502 of Mohegan Tribal Ordinance 95-4, which established the Gaming Disputes Court, specifies that nothing in the ordinance establishing the Gaming Disputes Court "shall be construed as a waiver of the sovereign immunity of the Tribe, the Authority or the Tribe's other enterprises or political sub-divisions, or its officers, agents, or employees, unless specifically denominated as such." M.T.O. 95-4, Art. V, Sec. 502. In support of his claim that, as to his contract of employment, the Defendant waived sovereign immunity, Plaintiff points to Article XIII, Section 1 of the Mohegan Constitution, dealing with the Tribal Gaming Authority, which provides in relevant part as follows:

> The Tribal Gaming Authority shall have the power to grant a limited waiver of sovereign immunity as to Gaming matters, to contracts relating to Gaming.... Nothing contained in this section shall limit the power of the Tribal Council to waive the sovereign immunity of The Mohegan Tribe as to Gaming or other matters, or with respect to other tribal revenues or assets. The Tribal Gaming Authority shall have the power to enter into contractual relationships which bind The Mohegan Tribe, provided that such contracts shall be within the scope of authority delegated by the Tribal Council to the Tribal Gaming Authority. Contracts of the Tribal Gaming Authority shall be the law of The Mohegan Tribe and shall be specifically enforceable in accordance with their terms.

At issue is whether the language quoted from Article XIII, Section I of the Constitution providing that contracts of the Tribal Gaming Authority "shall be specifically enforceable in accordance with their terms" constitutes the "clear waiver" of sovereign immunity, that "cannot be implied but must be unequivocally expressed." *Cherokee Nation of Oklahoma v. Babbitt*, 117 F.3d 1489, 1498 (D.C. Cir. 1997).

In interpreting the meaning of this constitutional provision, this court must recognize the "well established principle that statutes in derogation of sovereign immunity should be strictly construed." *White v. Burns*, 213 Conn. 307 (1990). The Connecticut Supreme Court has held "the state's sovereign right not to be sued without its consent is not to be diminished by statute, unless a clear intention to that effect on the part of the legislature is disclosed, by use of express terms." *White v. Burns*, 213 Conn. 307, 312 (1990), quoting *Murphy v. Ives*, 151 Conn. 259, 262–63 (1963).

The Plaintiff's construction of Article XIII, Section 1 of the Mohegan Constitution would interpret the phrase "shall be specifically enforceable in accordance with their terms" to waive the Tribe's and the Tribal Gaming Authority's sovereign immunity for every contract, whether dealing with employment or otherwise. As set forth above, such a broad waiver of sovereign immunity must be expressly stated, and cannot be implied. If Plaintiff's contention that Article XIII, Sec. 1 automatically inserts into every contract a waiver of sovereign immunity is correct, then the power expressly granted to the Tribal Gaming Authority to "grant a limited waiver of sovereign immunity ... to contracts relating to Gaming" is superfluous. "It is a basic tenet of statutory construction that the legislature did not intend to enact meaningless provisions." *State v. Szymkiewicz*, 237 Conn. 613, 621 (1996). The intent of the legislature is to be found "not in an isolated phrase or sentence, but rather, from the statutory scheme as a whole." *Figueroa v. C & S Ball Bearing*, 237 Conn. 1, 6 (1996), quoting *State v. Breton*, 235 Conn. 206, 226 (1995).

Taking Article XIII, Section 1 as a whole, the most logical construction, and the one requiring the "least change" in sovereign immunity, is that the Tribal Gaming Authority may, in its contracts, grant a limited waiver of sovereign immunity and may enter into contractual relationships which bind The Mohegan Tribe. These contracts are enforceable "in accordance with their terms," but any waiver of sovereign immunity must be an express term of the contract to be enforced.

The Plaintiff has not alleged, nor is the court aware of, any waiver of sovereign immunity contained in Plaintiff's contract, even if the same were interpreted to include the Mohegan Sun Employee Handbook and/or the Mohegan Sun Resort Policy and Procedure Manual. In the absence of a clear, unequivocal waiver of immunity by the Tribe or congressional abrogation, the [remaining] claims asserted by Plaintiff are barred by the Defendants' sovereign immunity. Accordingly, Defendants' motion to dismiss is hereby granted.

Notes and Questions

1. *Researching tribal court decisions.* Though an important source of law, tribal court decisions present legal research challenges, as they are not widely available through case reporters or electronic databases. The *Indian Law Reporter*, a subscription-based service, publishes selected tribal court opinions. Some useful Web resources include VersusLaw, a commercial searchable electronic database at http://www.versuslaw.com/, the National American Indian Court Judges Association's National Tribal Justice Resource Center at http://www.tribalresourcecenter.org/legal/opfolder/default.asp, and the Tribal Law and Pol-

icy Institute's Tribal Court Clearinghouse Project at http://www.tribal-institute.org/lists/decision.htm. The National Tribal Justice Resource Center maintains a tribal court directory that includes links to tribal constitutions at http://www.tribalresourcecenter.org/tribalcourts/directory/default.asp. Additionally, some tribal courts maintain their own electronic databases (for example, the Crow Tribe in Montana at http://www.littlehorn.com/CCA_Home.htm), and information about a tribe's court system often can be found on the tribal government Web site. Other useful resources include B.J. Jones, *A Primer on Tribal Court Civil Practice*, The Gavel, Sept. 1998, available at http://www.court.state.nd.us/court/resource/tribal.htm, and David Selden & Monica Martens, *Basic Indian Law Research Tips—Part II: Tribal Law* (2005), available at http://www.narf.org/nill/resources/basicguide.htm.

Problem 7: The NIGC Model Tribal Gaming Ordinance

1. You are the attorney for a large tribe in the Midwest. The tribe has entered into a tribal-state compact for a rural casino which will feature a dozen or so table games and about 250 slot machines. Which of the recommended provisions in the NIGC model ordinance would you advise the tribe to adopt and why? Which would you advise the tribe not to adopt and why? Are there other provisions you would suggest the tribe adopt?

2. You are the attorney for a small, newly federally recognized tribe on the Eastern seaboard. The tribe has entered into a tribal-state compact for a casino within a few hours' drive of several major metropolitan areas. The planned casino is a Las Vegas-style casino resort with over 1,000 slot machines, more than 100 table games, and two "high roller" rooms. Which of the recommended provisions in the NIGC model ordinance would you advise the tribe to adopt and why? Which would you advise the tribe not to adopt and why? Are there other provisions you would suggest the tribe adopt?

Chapter 8

State Authority

A. Overview

As discussed in Chapter 5, state law, though generally inapplicable to tribal governments, plays a significant role in Indian gaming regulation. State public policy determines whether either Class II or Class III gaming is permitted in a particular state in the first place. The state may assert greater or more extensive governmental authority over Class III gaming through the negotiation of a tribal-state compact. In this Chapter, we discuss state authority in the context of state political institutions, with specific attention to state gaming commissions (which may be charged with regulation under the terms of a tribal-state compact), state courts, and, in the context of separation of powers, state executive and legislative branches. We revisit the "scope of gaming" issue in relation to the question of whether the state constitutional authority to negotiate and enter into compacts lies with the governor, or with the legislature.

B. State Gaming Commissions

State gaming commissions regulate the general public policy environment in which legalized gambling occurs within a state. Although not granted formal authority over Class II gaming, in practice they exert some influence over that environment by implementing state gaming policy and promulgating regulatory requirements for state-licensed operators. IGRA's tribal-state compacting requirement created the opportunity for state gaming commissions to exercise significant regulatory authority—from licensing vendors to maintaining an on-site presence at tribal casinos—over Class III gaming in many states.

Sean McGuinness
They Call It Gaming ... and You Can Bet It's Changed a Lot
BUSINESS LAW TODAY (July/Aug. 2006)

Since 1988, the gaming industry has exploded in growth across the United States. Thirty years ago, only Nevada had legal casinos (and the voters in New Jersey had just adopted gaming by referendum). Today, legal casinos can also be found in states as varied and diverse as New Jersey, California, Louisiana, Indiana, Colorado, Michigan and Oklahoma—among others. Indeed, every state, except Utah and Hawaii, has some form of legalized gaming (that is, casino, bingo, lottery, racing, jai lai, pull tabs).

Casino operators as well as manufacturers of gaming devices are accustomed to operating in a highly regulated environment. Since many of these companies are publicly traded, there already are Securities and Exchange Commission requirements including Sarbanes-Oxley [Act of 2002]-related disclosures. More significant, however, are the regulatory bodies from which licenses and other approvals must be obtained and maintained in good standing in order to continue doing business. It is this gaming regulatory environment that affects many of the transactional documents and considerations when working on a gaming-related deal.

Today, gaming regulatory bodies in the United States are generally fairly consistent with licensing and operational requirements. While there are some differences from jurisdiction to jurisdiction, there are strong similarities among the Nevada State Gaming Control Board, the New Jersey Division of Gaming Enforcement, the Mississippi Gaming Commission, the Colorado Division of Gaming, and the National Indian Gaming Commission, for example, regarding how license investigations and approvals are handled.

Generally, there are two kinds of licensing that exist in every gaming jurisdiction: mandatory or discretionary licensing. For example, for privately held companies, every shareholder, every officer, every director and every key employee must be licensed. This means that long, detailed applications must be submitted (along with fingerprints). Then, the applicant pays for all of the investigative fees and costs (including but not limited to actual travel costs and expenses, an hourly rate for work on the file, and per diem—I have seen a Nevada investigation, for example, that cost in excess of $1 million and took more than a year to complete).

The gaming investigative process is very intrusive and has been likened to an unpleasant medical examination by some. That being said, licensees do appreciate the process in that it ensures the integrity of the industry. In addition to the criminal background and unsuitable associations review, [the investigators] will request copies of audited financials, tax returns, bank statements, copies of checks, escrow statements and the like, so as to track income and expenditures. They also inspect safe deposit boxes, home safes, travel records, litigation files, e-mails and computer usage. It is important to note that the burden is on the applicant at all times to prove suitability and not on the regulators to establish unsuitability. Failure to fully cooperate can result in license denial.

The mandatory licensure standard for public company applicants is different. Generally, every 5 percent or greater shareholder, every officer, every director and every key employee must be licensed. The less than 5 percent shareholders are in the discretionary license category, which means that the gaming authorities can exercise their right to call them forward to be licensed. In addition, there are change-of-control provisions in the gaming laws as to public companies so that prior licensing and approval of the gaming agency is required for a change in control of a licensed public company.

In addition, most publicly traded companies involved in gaming now have gaming compliance committees, which are different from typical compliance committees. The Nevada Gaming Commission started this trend by requiring its registered public companies to adopt gaming compliance committee programs. In some instances, private companies have these programs as well. The purpose of these committees is to require gaming licensees to conduct requisite due diligence in all of their activities (even nongaming related) so as to ensure that they do not unwittingly associate with unsuitable individuals or otherwise become involved in an activity that could prove detrimental to the gaming industry.

Slot machines and other gaming devices, as well as software that tracks gaming revenue, are required to be inspected and approved by gaming laboratories. The purpose of the testing is threefold: to make sure that the game is fair and operates in a manner that cannot be manipulated or altered; to ensure that the game itself is authorized by the applicable statutes and regulations for the jurisdiction in question; and to confirm that revenue will be properly tracked and accounted for so that all taxes are paid. Some states have their own state-run labs: Nevada, New Jersey and Michigan, for example. Other states have entered into contracts with third-party gaming laboratories and the costs are paid by the game manufacturers seeking approval.

[In addition to the state gaming commissions' regulatory authority over licensing and gaming devices,] the statutory and regulatory framework also frequently applies to the transactional realm applicable to business lawyers. [Some examples include:]

Federal maritime law—Even though a dockside or riverboat casino can have extensive land-based improvements and amenities, a major portion of a riverboat or dockside casino's assets for collateral purposes are located on casino vessels or casino barges, which are subject to provisions of federal maritime law. [For example,] in order for a lender to perfect a lien on these assets, a preferred ship's mortgage needs to be property filed with the U.S. Coast Guard.

Private placements and public offerings—Gaming applicants and licensees need to properly consider and address gaming law disclosures and the approval process when working on a private placement or public offering. In many jurisdictions, the prior approvals of the applicable gaming regulatory agencies are required for private placements and public offerings. In addition, most jurisdictions also require a disclaimer be placed on the cover page to affirmatively state that the accuracy of the offering has not been endorsed by any gaming jurisdiction and any representation to the contrary is unlawful.

Loans to licensee reporting—Many jurisdictions require licensees to report loans that they receive. This would include providing the applicable gaming regulatory agency with details of the loan transaction, the terms, the parties, personal information of individuals (officers, directors, key employees) and copies of all loan-related documentation. In Nevada and Mississippi, for example, the gaming regulatory agencies reserve the power to order that a loan be rescinded. As such, it is important in loan transactions involving gaming companies to have specific language and provisions to adequately address applicable gaming law requirements for the jurisdictions involved.

Stock pledges and negative covenants—According to gaming law requirements in most states, prior approval must first be obtained from the applicable gaming regulatory agencies before a stock pledge and certain negative covenants are deemed to be enforceable. Failure to get these approvals renders the purported stock pledge or negative covenants void and ineffectual. Accordingly, when drafting documents, it is prudent to add a provision where the parties agree to apply for these approvals on an expeditious basis and to fully cooperate with the applicable gaming regulatory agencies, as well as acknowledging that these provisions will not be enforceable unless and until all required approvals are received.

Gaming device collateral and bankruptcy related considerations—In order for a lender to take possession and foreclose on gaming collateral (that is, slot machines) as a remedy of default, in some jurisdictions it is first necessary for the lender to apply for and receive a license to dispose of the gaming devices. The investigative process is very lengthy, expensive and burdensome for an unlicensed lender. Likewise, an individual or company cannot be placed in control of a casino's operations without first having obtained a license or other approval from the applicable gaming regulatory agency. That is why it is rare to see court-appointed receivers or bankruptcy trustees taking control of casino operations, except for those rare instances where there are significant operational matters facing the property (that is, the debtor walking away). It is much more common to allow the casino to be operated by the debtor-in-possession, while working toward either an auction sale or plan of reorganization.

Notes and Questions

1.   State regulation as model. Compare McGuinness' description of the background investigations conducted by state gaming commissions to those conducted by tribal gaming commissions and the NIGC. The specific requirements in the NIGC's regulations are modeled after state gaming regulations, drawing on the experience of states with longer histories of legalized gambling. McGuinness' list of additional regulatory implications that may arise in the course of representing clients in the gaming industry also applies to companies doing business in tribal gaming. That is, the publicly traded status of many commercial gaming companies subjects them to regulatory requirements that may not be applicable to tribal governments due to tribal sovereignty and their status as governments (think state lottery); however, the requirements will apply to those companies that do business *with* tribes. Indeed, the tripartite nature of Indian gaming regulation (tribal, state, federal) means that attorneys must be cognizant of the implications of additional layers of regulation.

2.   States as primary regulators? Based on IGRA's language and legislative history, particularly the different treatment of Class II and Class III gaming, it may be fair to say that Congress assumed that state gaming commissions would serve as primary regulators of casino-style Indian gaming. Because IGRA leaves the scope and extent of state regulation to states and tribes to negotiate in the context of a Class III compact, the state role varies with each compact. Under some compacts, state gaming commissions serve as the primary regulatory authority for tribal casinos; other compacts make some state law requirements applicable to tribal casinos but leave direct regulation to the tribal gaming commission and the NIGC. Professor Washburn has suggested that this lack of uniformity has undermined IGRA's regulatory framework. He argued that Congress should consider amending IGRA to create a tribal/federal regulatory model for Class III gaming. *See* Hearing Before the S. Comm. on Indian Affairs, 109th Cong. (Sept. 21, 2005) (statement of Professor Kevin K. Washburn).

C. State Law

Kathryn R.L. Rand
Caught in the Middle: How State Politics, State Law, and State Courts Constrain Tribal Influence Over Indian Gaming
90 Marq. L. Rev. 971 (2007)

Since *Seminole Tribe* [*v. Florida*, 517 U.S. 44 (1996)], the terms of casino-style gaming on reservations increasingly have been determined by state politics. With reference only to the "State," IGRA's compact requirement does not establish which branch of state government is responsible for the negotiations. In many states, this authority is exercised by the governor, who serves as a gatekeeper for Class III gaming. The political culture of a state has become a key factor in compact negotiations. The governor's own attitudes toward legalized gambling and Indian gaming, as well as her political viability, may determine the governor's posture toward the compacting process and thus the nature of the compact negotiations. By extension, the transition to a new governing regime may change the state's position on the existing compact.

Without prescribed authority in IGRA, the state legislature's role in the compacting process is left to state law, which may require legislative approval before a tribal-state compact takes effect or may relegate the legislature to political criticism or support of the governor's compact negotiations. Legislative activity at the state level reflects a range of influence over the politics of tribal gaming. State legislatures have passed laws specifically intended to limit the scope or extent of Indian gaming, participated in the policy debates over Indian gaming's social and economic effects on tribal and non-tribal communities, and encouraged governors to pressure tribes to renegotiate existing tribal-state compacts and incorporate revenue-sharing agreements to "level the playing field" and "spread the wealth" with state and local governments. Similarly, state courts do not exercise a prescribed role under IGRA. Instead, the authorized statutory causes of action all fall under federal jurisdiction.

Yet state legislatures and state courts increasingly have asserted their influence over state policy toward Indian gaming. The sometimes contentious politics of legislative delegation of the authority to negotiate compacts to the executive branch or a governor's unilateral assumption of that power have resulted in litigation. State courts have been asked to answer important questions related to separation of powers and other dimensions of state constitutional law and public policy, including the scope of gaming permitted by the state.

[*Seminole Tribe's*] invalidation of IGRA's legal cause of action against a state hindered the development of a legal standard to determine whether a state has fulfilled its duty to negotiate in good faith, as well as a uniform approach to the scope of gaming permitted under state law. As a practical result, for a state that refuses to consent to suit, good faith may equate simply to the state's posture toward Indian gaming: what the governor is willing to negotiate, the state legislature to approve, or the state courts to uphold. The increasing political and legal influence of state government in delimiting Indian gaming is manifest in two highly controversial areas: the scope of tribal gaming and tribal-state revenue sharing.

The burgeoning role of state courts in setting the terms for tribal gaming was not anticipated by Congress, as it had carefully designed a federal cause of action to resolve Class III compacting disputes. IGRA's tribal-state compact requirement, in its reference to the "State," presumably left it to state political branches to decide how to negotiate and approve compacts. The sometimes contentious state politics over Indian gaming have resulted in litigation—not between a tribe and state in federal court, as IGRA authorized and Congress envisioned, but between state political actors in state court.

1. State Public Policy

As discussed in Chapter 5, IGRA provides that "Class III gaming activities shall be lawful on Indian lands only if such activities are ... located in a State that permits such gaming for any purpose by any person, organization, or entity...." 25 U.S.C. § 2710(d)(1)(B). Federal courts are split on the proper interpretation of the "permits such gaming" requirement as either treating each class of gaming as a category, or authorizing only the specific games permitted under state law. Here, we focus on the authority of state actors—particularly state courts—to determine the scope of gaming permitted by state public policy. As you read the decisions of the Wisconsin Supreme Court, consider the difference between a federal court decision and a state court decision on the issue. Would the courts' analysis or outcome be any different? If not, does the mere fact of the forum matter?

Panzer v. Doyle
680 N.W.2d 666 (Wis. 2004)

PROSSER, Justice.

This is an original action under Article VII, § 3(2) of the Wisconsin Constitution. The petitioners are Mary Panzer, personally and in her capacity as the Majority Leader of the Wisconsin Senate, John Gard, personally and in his capacity as Speaker of the Wisconsin Assembly, and the Joint Committee on Legislative Organization (collectively referred to as the petitioners). The respondents are James E. Doyle, in his official capacity as Governor of Wisconsin, and Marc J. Marotta, in his official capacity as Secretary of Administration (collectively referred to as the Governor).

The supreme court hears original actions in cases that involve substantial legal questions of more than ordinary importance to the people of the state. Normally, these questions require prompt and authoritative determination. This case presents questions about the inherent and delegated power of Wisconsin's governors to negotiate gaming compacts with Indian tribes.

The petitioners contend that the Governor exceeded his authority in 2003 when he agreed to certain amendments to the gaming compact our state has entered into with the Forest County Potawatomi (FCP) Tribe, a federally recognized Indian tribe indigenous to Wisconsin. They assert that the Governor improperly agreed to amendments that [*inter alia*] expand the scope of gaming by adding games that were previously not permitted for any purpose by any person, organization, or entity in Wisconsin.

To understand the factual and legal issues that affect our decision, we recapitulate our state's unique history with respect to legalized gambling. [This portion of the court's opinion is reprinted in Chapter 5.]

The initial compacts were set to run out between February 1998 and March 1999. Governor Thompson reached agreements with the state's tribes to renew the compacts for five years. However, the 1998 amendments did not grant the FCP permission to operate additional *types* of games. [In] 2003, as the second term of the compact was nearing completion, Governor Doyle agreed to new amendments to the 1992 Gaming Compact (as amended in 1998) with the FCP Tribe. The Compact as amended clears the way for the FCP Tribe to conduct a number of casino games that have never been legal in Wisconsin, such as keno, roulette, craps, and poker.

Several amicus curiae have filed briefs stressing the positive impact of Indian gaming on Wisconsin tribes as well as local economies and local governments. All the parties acknowledge that the amended FCP Gaming Compact is projected to generate additional revenue for the state at a time when additional revenue is needed.

This court does not decide cases on these grounds. Our duty is to interpret and apply the law. It is for the legislature "to make policy choices, ours to judge them based not on our preference but on legal principles and constitutional authority."

This is not to say that the legal and practical consequences of our opinions are not considered. We are mindful that this decision will require both a renegotiation of certain compact terms and a reconsideration of the Wisconsin state budget. We would be derelict if we were to reject a legitimate request to maintain the proper balance of power between and among the branches of our state government simply because of short-term consequences. In the end, fundamental questions about Wisconsin constitutional law ought to be decided in Wisconsin's highest court.

The petitioners assert that the Governor, the chief constitutional officer of Wisconsin's executive branch, was without authority to agree to games prohibited by the 1993 amendment to the Wisconsin Constitution. Originally, petitioners argued that the Governor, acting alone, could not agree to the expansion of games in the FCP Gaming Compact. This was a traditional separation of powers argument. They expressly declined to take a position on whether the legislature alone, or acting in concert with the Governor, could have agreed to games prohibited to the Wisconsin Lottery under the 1993 constitutional amendment. Petitioners' reluctance to take a position prompted us to request additional briefs on the question whether Article IV, § 24 made certain games uncompactable as a matter of Wisconsin law, thereby prohibiting *any* Wisconsin actor from agreeing to such games in an Indian gaming compact. Petitioners now concede that Article IV, § 24 acts as a limitation on both the legislature and the governor, so that if one is prohibited by the provision, so is the other.

The text of the constitution is absolutely clear: "Except as provided in this section, the legislature may not authorize *gambling* in any form." Nothing in § 24 authorizes electronic keno, roulette, craps, and poker. These games are specifically denied to the Wisconsin Lottery. Wis. Const. art. IV, § 24(6)(c).

Neither the "ceiling" view nor the "floor" view of IGRA authorizes *any* state actor to create a monopoly for Indian tribes by superseding, disregarding, or violating fundamental state law. The only *obligation* that states have under IGRA springs from 25 U.S.C. § 2710(d)(1)(B), which is the same provision setting forth the scope of lawful gaming activity on Indian lands. Section 2710(d)(1)(B) provides that "[c]lass III gaming activities *shall be lawful* on Indian lands *only if* such activities are [among other requirements] (B) located in a State that *permits such gaming* for any purpose by any person, organization, or entity." Thus, under IGRA, there are in essence two categories of Class III games: those over which a state *must* negotiate with a tribe and those that are illegal to negotiate. Those games over which a state *must* negotiate are games permitted "for any purpose by any person, organization, or entity," including games permitted, *by law,* exclusively for tribes.

Thus, regardless of how one frames the question, the ultimate inquiry focuses on the "permits such gaming" language in 25 U.S.C. § 2710(d) (1)(B). Until very recently, the *Lac du Flambeau* case was the only case concluding that, once a state regulates one form of Class III gaming, the state must negotiate over all forms of Class III gaming. *Compare Lac du Flambeau with Rumsey Indian Rancheria of Wintun Indians v. Wilson* ("IGRA does not require a state to negotiate over one form of Class III gaming activity simply because it has legalized another, albeit similar form of gaming."); *Cheyenne River Sioux Tribe v. South Dakota* ("The 'such gaming' language does not require the state to negotiate with respect to forms of gaming it does not presently permit."); *Coeur d'Alene Tribe v. Idaho* (holding that state was required to negotiate only with respect to specific Class III games that were permitted in the state). Accordingly, the continued vitality of *Lac du Flambeau's* holding is very doubtful, and the decision's statements regarding Wisconsin's policy toward gaming have been seriously undercut by the 1993 amendment to Article IV, § 24.

Unlike the expansive interpretation of the term "lottery" that was at least plausible before 1993, our constitution is now quite clear that the legislature may not authorize any *gambling* except that permitted by Article IV, § 24, and is very clear that certain games do not fall under the term "lottery" in Article IV, § 24(6). The constitution is now specific about what the state-operated lottery may do and what it may not do. Blackjack and other varieties of banking card games, poker, roulette, craps, keno and slot machines are all games specifically outside the scope of § 24(6)'s authorized exception, and they do not come within any other exception. Thus, the legislature may not authorize new casino-type gambling in any form. No exception to the state constitution can be marshaled to support legislative authorization of new casino-type gambling to Indian tribes. The Tribe's existing games such as slot machines and blackjack must be sustained on the basis of the validity of the original compacts, which were negotiated pursuant to court order before the 1993 constitutional amendment, as well as constitutional and contract law.

Article IV, § 24 embodies a strong state policy against gambling. It prohibits the legislature from authorizing gambling in any form except as permitted in the constitution. Article V, § 4 of the constitution directs that the governor "take care that the laws be faithfully executed." Accordingly, we conclude that the Governor acted without authority by agreeing to games that are, as reflected in our state's criminal statutes and reinforced by its constitution, prohibited to everyone in the state. The new casino-style games the Governor agreed to in 2003 are expressly forbidden by statute. Thus, the Governor was without authority to agree, on behalf of the state, to add variations on blackjack, electronic keno, roulette, craps, poker, and other non-house banked card games under the 2003 Amendments to the FCP Gaming Compact. The governor may not carve out exceptions to the state's criminal statutes unilaterally. We are unable to conclude that the legislature delegated such power or could delegate such power in light of the 1993 constitutional amendment.

Our holding today raises inevitable questions about the validity of the original 1992 FCP Gaming Compact and the 1998 amendments thereto. Clearly, the 1992 Compact encompasses games that were and are precluded under our state's criminal statutes. Both the tribes and the state have relied on the validity of the original compacts. Any attempt at this point to impair these compacts would create serious constitutional questions. We do not believe the 1992 compact suffered from any infirmity under state law when it was entered into. Whether the 1992 compact is durable enough to withstand a change in state law that alters our understanding of what is "permitted" in Wisconsin is a separate question. The resolution of this question is likely to turn, at least in part, on the application of the impairment of contracts clauses in the United States and Wisconsin Constitutions as well as IGRA. Because these issues are not before us, and because they may turn in large measure on unresolved questions of federal law, our decision stops short of resolving these important questions.

ABRAHAMSON, Chief Justice, BRADLEY, J., and CROOKS, J., dissenting.

The sum total of the majority opinion is to deliver the following bad news to the people of the State: all bets are off. Or at least, all new bets in the 2003 amendments are off.

As a result of the majority opinion, the Tribe's payment to the State of $34.125 million due on June 30, 2004, need not be paid. Almost $207 million of direct tribal payments to the State, upon which the legislature relied in adopting the budget, are in jeopardy, as is approximately $100 million annually thereafter. Employment in the State will also be dramatically affected by the majority opinion. The Tribe estimates that gaming compacts have created 35,000 jobs in the State to date and that the 2003 amendments will add 20,000 more jobs and a billion dollars in new investments. The majority opinion's ruling against Indian gaming not only will have an enormous effect on the state and local economies but also will interfere with federal and state policies promoting the economic welfare of the Indian tribes and Indian education.

In sum, the majority's analysis cannot withstand scrutiny. Why is it unconstitutional for Governor Doyle to negotiate the 2003 amendments authorizing games outlawed by the 1993 Wisconsin constitutional amendment and yet it was constitutional for Governor Thompson to have negotiated the 1998 amendments authorizing games similarly outlawed? In light of the majority opinion, if any Indian gaming whatsoever is to be permitted in Wisconsin in the future, it may be only because of the intervention of the federal courts.

Section XXVI of the 1992 compact states the following: "To the extent that State law or Tribal ordinances, or any amendments thereto, are inconsistent with any provision of this Compact, this Compact shall control." In clear and simple language, the parties expressed their intent to be bound by the laws as they were in 1992. Regardless of future laws or amendments to preexisting laws, the parties agreed to let the terms of the compact control their relationship. In holding that the amendment to Article IV, § 24 of the Wisconsin Constitution barred the Class III games that the parties agreed to in 2003, the majority opinion takes a position that clearly violates Section XXVI of the compact, and, therefore, runs afoul of the impairment of contract clauses of the United States and Wisconsin Constitutions.

While the amendment to Article IV, § 24 did change Wisconsin's law with respect to gaming, it did not affect the compact before us. Any Class III games that would be outlawed by Article IV, § 24 could be negotiated for and permitted in an amended compact, given Section XXVI of the 1992 compact. This provision overrides any subsequent changes in state law, including those brought about by the amendment to Article IV, § 24. The changes to the compact made in the 1998 and 2003 amendments are permissible given the fact that they involve automatic extensions as well as amendments to the 1992 compact. That compact, in Section XXVI, clearly states that the provisions of the compact apply over any changes in state or tribal law. A conclusion to the contrary patently ignores the basic provisions contracted for by the parties involved.

We also recognize that federal preemption is involved in determining whether an impairment of contract would result by declaring the 2003 amendments unauthorized. Here, the compacts are between two sovereigns, the State and the Tribe, and are created under federal law with federal government approval. The compacts unquestionably have federal preemptive force. Because the State and Tribe entered into a valid compact in 1992, their agreement is insulated from further changes in Wisconsin's gaming laws. Section XXVI of the 1992 compact clearly reflects the intentions of the State and Tribe that changes in state law would not affect the compact's provisions. We conclude that any attempt to read Article IV, § 24 as altering the types of games that may be negotiated for under the compact would impair the compact to which the parties agreed, and would, therefore, run afoul of the United States and Wisconsin constitutional clauses against impairment of contract.

The *Cabazon* and *Lac du Flambeau* decisions together with IGRA permitted the parties to negotiate for the inclusion of *any Class III games* in a compact between the Tribe and the State of Wisconsin, and a change in Wisconsin law cannot alter that fact. The claim that some Class III games are "grandfathered in," while others are not permitted because of the 1993 constitutional amendment, is not only illogical, it is nonsensical.

The conclusion of the majority is that the Governor violated state law by authorizing the disputed new games. That conclusion misses the mark because it rests on an erroneous assumption that states can directly regulate Indian gaming, independent of IGRA. They cannot. Under IGRA, state law can only indirectly affect Indian gaming, and only through compact negotiations. Outside of that process, state law does not apply to Indian gaming. Instead of recognizing this limitation to its jurisdiction, however, the majority proceeds to analyze IGRA, going so far as to call *Lac du Flambeau's* holding into doubt. By doing so, the majority flouts Congress' clear intent to preclude state courts from adjudicating the rights of Indian tribes to engage in on-reservation activities.

In the wake of *Cabazon Band,* states increasingly expressed their desires to be factored into Indian gaming regulation. Congress responded with the passage of IGRA in 1988. Through IGRA, Congress performed the necessary balancing of states' interest in regulating high stakes gambling within their borders and the Indians' resistance to state intrusions on their sovereignty. The essential feature of IGRA is the Tribal-State compact process. By enacting IGRA, Congress created a "carefully crafted and intricate remedial scheme," which cannot be augmented by the courts. That scheme contemplates actions only in federal — not state — courts. Every reference to court action in IGRA specifies federal court jurisdiction. State courts are never mentioned.

If the majority's approach was a sound one, Congress' strict limits on the means to enforce IGRA would be easily evaded by restyling collateral attacks on compacts as claims that the state is not bound by a particular compact because the state's agent exceeded his or her authority. The preemptive force of IGRA was designed to prevent such an evasion.

IGRA is not the only reason why this case belongs in federal court. Compacts entered into under IGRA are agreements between sovereigns, not private parties. Indeed, the governmental nature of compacts makes such agreements analogous to interstate compacts.

In the end, the majority's formulation of the scope-of-gaming issues as state law cannot mask the obvious federal nature of the case. Here, the petitioners have sought a declaratory judgment centered on the meaning and application of a federal statute and the validity of a federally approved compact. Accordingly, this court lacks jurisdiction to adjudicate the dispute.

Dairyland Greyhound Park, Inc. v. Doyle
719 N.W.2d 408 (Wis. 2006)

BUTLER, Justice.

We conclude that the 1993 Amendment to Article IV, Section 24 of the Wisconsin Constitution does not invalidate the Original Compacts. Because the Original Compacts contemplated extending the Compacts and amending the scope of Indian gaming within the Compacts, we further conclude that the parties' right of renewal is constitutionally protected by the Contract Clauses of the Wisconsin and United States Constitutions, and that amendments to the Original Compacts that expand the scope of gaming are likewise constitutionally protected by the Contract Clauses of the Wisconsin and United States Constitutions. We withdraw any language to the contrary in *Panzer v. Doyle* that would limit the State's ability to negotiate for Class III games under the Original Compacts. Accordingly, gaming can be expanded to the extent that the State and Tribes negotiate for additional Class III games.

The essence of what is at issue here is whether Wisconsin should break treaties with Tribes by walking away from its contractual obligations. Rules of contract interpretation and the Contract Clauses of the United States and Wisconsin Constitutions [U.S. Const. art. I, § 10 ("No state shall ... pass any bill of attainder, ex post facto law, or law impairing the obligation of contracts...."); Wis. Const. art. I, § 12 ("No bill of attainder, ex post facto law, nor any law impairing the obligation of contracts, shall ever be passed....")] compel us to conclude that the State must honor its contractual obligations in their entirety.

This case stems from allegations by Dairyland that the 1993 Amendment deprives the Governor of the authority to permit Wisconsin Tribes to continue conducting casino-type gaming in Wisconsin. Dairyland alleges that it began to lose revenue due to the Class III games allowed on Tribal land. Dairyland first filed this action against then-Governor Scott McCallum on October 23, 2001, claiming that the Governor was not authorized to extend the gaming compacts with the Tribes in light of the 1993 Amendment. Dairyland sought an injunction preventing the Governor from entering into any future compacts and directing the Governor to serve a timely notice of nonrenewal to the Tribes for the existing compacts. Dairyland asserts that Article IV, Section 24 of the Wisconsin Constitution renders all types of Class III gaming illegal, except for certain games that are specifically exempted under the Wisconsin Constitution. Therefore, according to Dairyland, Class III games that are not specifically exempted under the constitution are not lawful subjects of the State-Tribal Compacts.

In *Panzer,* this court concluded that the Original Compacts were lawfully entered into and that the question of the Compacts' durability after the 1993 Amendment was a question that may require an analysis under the impairment of Contract Clauses under the United States and Wisconsin Constitutions, as well as under the Indian Gaming Regulatory Act ("IGRA"). The *Panzer* majority, however, declined to resolve these questions. We now address the impairment of contracts issues raised by the Original Compacts and the 1993 change to the Wisconsin Constitution.

In 1989, the Wisconsin Legislature granted the Governor the authority to enter into compacts with the Tribes located in Wisconsin, pursuant to IGRA. By 1992, Wisconsin's Governor entered into the Original Compacts on behalf of the State, thereby creating a contractual relationship between the State and all 11 federally recognized Tribes and bands located within the State borders. These compacts were validly executed prior to the change in Wisconsin law under the 1993 Amendment. The parties do not dispute that the Original Compacts were valid when they were entered into in 1991 and 1992. The parties dispute, however, whether the 1993 Amendment changes the terms agreed to in the Original Compacts. The Governor contends that the 1993 Amendment does not impact the terms of the Original Compacts. In contrast, Dairyland asserts that the 1993 Amendment precludes the State from renewing or amending the compacts.

Whether the 1993 Amendment retrospectively invalidates the Original Compacts or any provisions contained therein, raises questions of constitutional interpretation and contract impairment.

The Amendment clearly states: "the legislature may not authorize gambling in *any* form." These words can be construed to mean, simply, that *all* Class III games in Wisconsin, excluding the specific games enumerated in the Amendment, were made unconstitutional by the 1993 Amendment. Because the Amendment did not explicitly exclude Tribal gaming, the Class III games on Tribal land are, arguably, unconstitutional.

On the other hand, constitutional amendments that deal with the substantive law of the State are presumed to be prospective in effect unless there is an express indication to the contrary. Because the 1993 Amendment is silent with regard to the issue of the pre-existing Tribal gaming compacts, the Amendment is not retrospective in operation.

We conclude that the 1993 Amendment's failure to explicitly address the Original Compacts creates an ambiguity as to whether the compacts fall within the Amendment's reach.*

A review of the drafting files for the constitutional amendment indicates that the legislators intended to preserve the Original Compacts as they existed at the time. The legislative records also reveal that Wisconsin's legislators were uniformly informed that the amendment would not affect the Original Compacts. These records clearly demonstrate that the legislators voted to pass the constitutional amendment with the understanding that the Original Compacts would survive the amendment. We thus conclude that the Wisconsin Legislature did not intend the 1993 Amendment to invalidate the Original Compacts.

Wisconsin citizens voted to ratify the 1993 Amendment to Article IV, Section 24 on April 6, 1993. Public statements and news accounts leading to the April 6 vote demonstrate that voters were informed that the 1993 Amendment would not affect the Original Compacts, and polls released days prior to the April 6, 1993, vote indicate that most voters did not want to make the Tribal gaming casinos illegal. We conclude that the vast number of news articles, which informed voters that the amendment would not impact the existing Indian gaming, clearly demonstrates that the voters who ratified the constitutional amendment were informed that the ratification of the 1993 Amendment would not affect the Original Tribal Gaming Compacts.

We also find that subsequent laws enacted immediately following passage of the 1993 Amendment clearly relied on the continuation of the existing Indian gaming compacts. The [1993] Budget Act, [for example], relied on funds from the Class III games authorized by the Original Compacts. Of significance, the legislature passed 1993 Wisconsin Act 406, enacted on April 21, 1994, which explicitly validated any contract between the State and a federally-recognized Indian Tribe that was entered into prior to May 6, 1994. This statute, passed one year after the voters ratified the 1993 Amendment, "signal[s] legislative approval of the original compacts."

In sum, based on the 1993 Amendment's history and the earliest legislative interpretations of that Amendment, we conclude that the 1993 Amendment was not intended to preclude the Tribes from conducting Class III games pursuant to the Original Compacts. Because the Original Compacts are not invalidated by the 1993 Amendment, the terms agreed to in the Original Compacts remain in full effect.

Both the Wisconsin and the United States Constitutions prohibit states from impairing their contractual obligations. We recognize that the Contract Clause does not place an absolute barrier to a state's power to modify its own contracts. To demonstrate that a contract has been unconstitutionally impaired, a complaining party must first establish beyond a reasonable doubt that the legislature changed the law after the formation of the contract and that the operation of the contract is substantially impaired by this change. Second, if a law substantially impairs an already existing contractual relationship, the state, in justification, must have a significant and legitimate public purpose for the legislation. Finally, if a significant and legitimate public purpose exists for the legislation, the question becomes whether the legislature's impairment of contract is reasonable and necessary to serve that purpose.

In the present case, the State of Wisconsin and the 11 Tribes have had an ongoing relationship since the parties entered into the Original Compacts more than a decade ago.

---

* We therefore disagree with the *Panzer* holding that "[t]he text of the constitution[al amendment] is absolutely clear." Any language in *Panzer* to the contrary is hereby withdrawn.

Because we have concluded that the 1993 Amendment does not invalidate the Original Compacts, whether the 1993 Amendment applies to renewals of the Original Compacts depends upon whether the "renewal" constitutes a new contract or a continuation of the pre-existing contractual relationship. This is because, in general, the laws in existence at the time of the contract are incorporated into that contract. Subsequent changes to a law will not interfere with an existing contract. When a law changes, however, contracts entered into after the date of a change in law are subject to the new law.

Each of the Original Compacts contains a provision that addresses Tribal ordinances and State law: "To the extent that State law or Tribal ordinances, or any amendments thereto, are inconsistent with any provision of this Compact, this Compact shall control." Under the plain terms of the Original Compacts, therefore, changes in State law do not impact the compacts. The parties clearly intended to preserve the law as it existed in 1991–92, and to prevent the application of changes to the State's or Tribes' laws to the Original Compacts. In addition, because the 1993 Amendment did not apply to the Original Compacts, the Amendment does not apply to continuations or extensions of the Original Compacts.

We have already concluded that the 1993 Amendment does not invalidate the Original Compacts, extensions, or continuations thereof. Therefore, the terms agreed upon in the Original Compacts, and the laws in effect at the time the contract was entered into, control the Tribal casinos operating under the authority of Original Compacts. Nevertheless, according to Dairyland, because the 1993 Amendment makes the Class III games currently operated at the Tribal casinos unconstitutional, even if the 1993 Amendment does not apply to the Original Compacts, the State cannot continue to operate under a contract that is in violation of the constitution and, therefore, the State must exercise its right of nonrenewal.

Assuming that the 1993 Amendment precludes those Class III games explicitly prohibited by Art. IV, sec. 24 in any compact negotiated after 1993, no Class III casino game can be the proper subject of any new compact negotiation, save the few specifically exempted Class III games: bingo games operated by charitable and religious organizations, raffle games operated by charitable and religious organizations, pari-mutuel on-track betting, and the state-operated lottery. As a result, forcing the State to exercise its right of nonrenewal, thereby forcing the State to negotiate new compacts, would remove the State's authority to negotiate for any Class III games, except the limited games specifically authorized by the Constitution.

[Because] the operation of Class III games on Tribal land was a material consideration in the compact negotiations, forcing nonrenewal, thereby requiring the parties to negotiate for new compacts under which most forms of Class III games are non-negotiable, would therefore constitute a "severe disruption of contractual expectations." Forcing the State to negotiate new compacts would thus severely impair, indeed eliminate, the State's contractual rights to continue any Class III games excluded by the Amendment.

Under the impairment of contracts analysis, the State is not prohibited from passing a law that substantially impairs an existing contractual obligation as long as the impairment is justified under a significant and legitimate public purpose, and the constitutional amendment is reasonable and appropriate to advance that purpose. We note that the State's interests are less compelling when the inquiry involves Tribal sovereigns because state laws and policies do not extend to Tribal lands unless authorized by Congress. Congress passed IGRA to establish federal standards for gaming on Indian lands, and to allow state involvement through compacts with regard to Class III gaming. However, IGRA blocks the operation of state policy with regard to a valid compact once that compact has been executed under IGRA's authority. *See Gaming Corp. of Am. v. Dorsey & Whitney*, 88 F.3d 536, 544–45 (8th Cir. 1996). Moreover, without a valid compact, state laws have no regulatory power over gaming on Tribal land, and states have no authority to police Tribal casinos.

We recognize that regulation of gambling is a legitimate public purpose. We also recognize that this Amendment could be construed as a strong state policy against all gaming. *See Panzer*. However, the purpose of the 1993 Amendment was to make only *some* forms of Class III games unconstitutional in Wisconsin, but excluded pari-mutuel on-track betting, the state lottery, and Class III games operated pursuant to the Original Compacts. Neither the legislature nor Wisconsin's citizens intended the 1993 Amendment to invalidate the games operated pursuant to the Original Compacts. Therefore, even if the Amendment embodies a strong public policy against some games, it does not embody a public policy against the games operated by the Tribes under the authority of the Original Compacts. Although Wisconsin was not precluded from doing so, the State did not exercise its sovereign police power in an effort to ban gaming under the Original Compacts. Wisconsin did not abrogate its sovereign police powers with regard to gaming; the State simply decided to exclude the Original Compacts from the constitutional prohibition on gaming.

We further conclude that it would be unreasonable for the 1993 Amendment to interfere with the provision that allows for extending or continuing the Original Compacts. To a certain extent, because gaming had been regulated in the past, it was not entirely unforeseeable that the State might regulate gaming in the future. Yet, the parties anticipated future regulations on Tribal gaming and negotiated to exclude changes in State and Tribal law from impacting the Original Compacts: "To the extent that State law or Tribal ordinances, or any amendments thereto, are inconsistent with any provision of this Compact, this Compact shall control." It was *not* foreseeable, however, that the 1993 Amendment would invalidate the future operations of the Tribal casinos. The parties' actions demonstrate that there was little doubt as to the continued legality of the casino gaming pursuant to the Original Compacts. The State has continued to rely on revenue from the compacts, and the Tribes have continued to invest in and operate the casinos.

Therefore, although the prohibition of casino gaming can be a significant and legitimate State interest, we conclude that the State's interest in prohibiting gaming does not pass the heightened scrutiny test.

Because the 1993 Amendment does not apply to the Original Compacts, the terms of the compacts control whether the parties can amend the compact to expand the scope of Class III gaming. Each of the 11 compacts states: "The Tribe may not operate any Class III gaming not expressly enumerated in this section of this Compact unless this Compact is amended pursuant to section XXX." This language clearly reveals that the Compacts allow the parties to agree to amend the scope of Class III games. These provisions create a contractual obligation to allow new games should the parties agree to amend the scope of gaming.

In addition, even if we determined that these provisions are indefinite, the parties' subsequent conduct clearly evinces their intent to amend the scope of gaming. Moreover, because the scope of gaming is a material provision in the compacts, if we were to find these material provisions to be indefinite, the compacts would be void and unenforceable. Instead, we conclude that, should the parties agree to amend the scope of gaming, the compacts clearly obligate the parties to abide by such amendments. Furthermore, the parties negotiated for the amendment provision under the auspices of the law as interpreted by the court in *Lac du Flambeau*, under which all Class III games are negotiable.

Justice Prosser, in his concurrence/dissent, contends: "if state law prohibits a Class III gaming activity, the governor's power to negotiate that activity is circumscribed." Justice Prosser summarizes his conclusion: "[T]he Wisconsin state government, including Wisconsin governors, may agree to amendments of gaming compacts to add forms of gaming activity that are permitted by state law 'for any purpose by any person, organization, or entity,' but may not add forms of gaming activity that are prohibited by state law for all purposes to all persons, organizations, and entities."

Justice Prosser's arguments regarding the scope of gaming are structurally unsound. Under the analysis proposed by Justice Prosser, if the amendment applies to the scope of gaming, then blackjack, slot machines, and video gaming machines included in the Original Compacts are now unconstitutional. Either the Original Compacts are fully in force or they are not — it cannot be both ways.

Because we conclude that the Original Compacts were not invalidated by the 1993 Amendment, and that the compacts have been lawfully extended, the Original Compacts are in full force. The Original Compacts specifically contemplated amending the compacts, including the type of Class III games that can be conducted on Tribal land. In addition, the law at the time the Original Compacts were entered into controls the compacts. The parties negotiated under the *Lac du Flambeau* decision, under which all Class III games were negotiable. Therefore, the Class III games that the State and Tribes agreed to in their compact extension negotiations are lawful. We withdraw any language to the contrary in *Panzer* that would limit the State's ability to negotiate for Class III games under the Original Compacts.

Notes and Questions

1.   *What about the 2003 amendments?* In *Dairyland*, the court concluded that the 1993 state constitutional amendment did not affect the original compacts, including subsequent renewal of the compacts (i.e., the 1998 amendments). Doesn't that logically lead to the conclusion that the 2003 amendments likewise are not affected, contrary to the court's holding in *Panzer*? In a footnote, the *Dairyland* court explained,

> In the present case, we reach the question as to the scope of gaming provisions in the Original Compacts because this issue is "of sufficient public interest," and because the parties have explicitly asked the courts to review the scope of gaming issue. In its court of appeals brief, Dairyland asserted that the Governor had no authority to amend or extend compacts authorizing casino gambling in 1998 or 2003. The Governor argued that the original compacts, including the scope of gaming provisions, continued until they were terminated. We note that the Class III games added in 2003 include: roulette, big wheel and other wheel games, craps, poker and similar non-house banked card games, games played at blackjack-style tables, such as Let-It-Ride, Casino Stud, and Casino War, electronic keno, pari-mutuel wagering on live simulcast, horse, harness and dog racing events, including participation in interstate betting pools, all other banking, percentage and pari-mutuel card games, all other banking and non-banking dice games, Wheel of Fortune, Baccarat, chemin de fer, all finite lottery and lottery games, any other game whether played as a table game or played on an electronic or mechanical device, including devices that operate like slot machines, which consist of the elements of prize, chance and consideration, Caribbean Stud Poker, Let-It-Ride, and Pai-Gow Poker.

In its briefs to this court, Dairyland asserted that the amendments in 2003 are invalid. The Governor advocated that this court overrule the portion of *Panzer* dealing with the scope of permissible Tribal gaming in Wisconsin. In addition, at oral argument Dairyland asserted that the issue and focus of this case was "how can a governor in the year 2003 and also in 1998, how can that governor authorize casino gaming for anybody when the casino gambling had been expressly prohibited by Article IV, Section 24 of the Wisconsin Constitution when it was amended in 1993?" When asked to clarify which compact extensions Dairyland wanted addressed, Dairyland stated: "The one in 1998. I think more importantly, the one in 2003." Later, Dairyland also asserted that the 1998 amendments were not valid, but that they were not as important as the 2003 amendments.

Justice Prosser [in his dissent] similarly asserts that the 1998–99 amendments were not substantial enough to be unconstitutional, and advocates for the conclusion that the 2003 extensions are unlawful because the amendments went too far, observing that the games that were added in 2003 are explicitly listed in the constitution as prohibited forms of gaming under Article IV, section 24, clauses 3 to 6. Justice Roggensack [in her dissent] asserts that "[t]he majority opinion concludes that the games added to the compacts in 2003 do not violate Wisconsin law." That is incorrect. We do not reach the 2003 gaming compacts. While we recognize these arguments, we are simply ruling on the scope of gaming provisions contracted for in the Original Compacts.

Dairyland, at 438 n.61. Do you find the court's explanation persuasive? Is there a sound basis for reaching different conclusions as to the legality of the 1998 and 2003 compact amendments?

2.   State courts and policy judgments. As *Panzer* and *Dairyland* illustrate, state courts can markedly influence the scope of Indian gaming allowed in a state. In another footnote, the *Dairyland* court commented on the court's role in this regard:

Justice Prosser [in his dissent] asserts that this decision opens the door to an explosion of gaming. We share Justice Prosser's concern regarding the potential for the expansion of gaming in this State. However, it is up to the Governor and the legislature to determine the amount of gaming as they see fit. Gaming can be expanded only to the extent that the State and Tribes negotiate for additional Class III games. Therefore, the "explosion" will only expand as far as the State and Tribes permit. This court cannot impose its judgment regarding what Class III games we believe the State should allow. This would place the court in the activist position of imposing our policy judgments over those of the Governor, the legislature and the Wisconsin citizens. We refuse to do so. This determination is for the State and the Tribes.

Dairyland, at 443 n.73. Did the *Panzer* court impose its policy judgment over those of the governor, legislature, and citizens of Wisconsin? Did the *Dairyland* court? Can a court interpret state law to determine the scope of gaming allowed under IGRA in a way that does not impose the court's policy judgment? Is the point whether the court's decision undermines *state* policy, or whether it undermines *federal* policy as reflected in IGRA? Does it matter whether the court is a federal court or a state court?

3.   Critique of **Panzer** *and* **Dairyland.** Consider Rand's critique of *Panzer* and *Dairyland*:

As the *Panzer* court observed, after the U.S. Supreme Court's decision in *Seminole Tribe*, disputes between tribes and states are "more likely to be resolved in a state court," as the availability of a federal forum depends upon state consent. Once in state court, not surprisingly, cases like *Panzer* and *Dairyland* are "dominated by questions of state law, which the Wisconsin Supreme Court has the right and duty to resolve." The Wisconsin case study demonstrates how state courts influence the ability of political actors to set the terms of debate and of public policy. Though state court constraints on the *state's* political actors — here, Wisconsin's governor — most certainly are appropriately determined under state law, the same cannot be said of tribes. Tribal sovereignty, alongside the tenet of federal Indian law that states generally may not exercise authority over tribes, makes problematic the Wisconsin Supreme Court's insistence that state law, as interpreted by state courts, was wholly determinative of the issues raised in the cases.

IGRA's "permits such gaming" and tribal-state compact requirements reflect Congress's intent to balance the authority of two sovereigns — state and tribal governments. In practical terms, the appropriate balance for any particular state and tribe would be struck either by a successfully negotiated compact or by a suit in federal court to enforce the state's good faith duty. Through the enforcement of IGRA, federal courts would perform a referee function to effect Congress's intent. The federal court would consider the scope of gaming permitted under state law and the state's reasons for refusing to agree to compact terms, and it also would consider federal law — namely IGRA. The tribe, as the plaintiff, would have an opportunity to argue its position, in terms of proper interpretation of both state and federal law, as well as in terms of its status as a sovereign government.

In state court, however, no balance is struck between state and tribal authority. Instead, tribal authority and tribal interests typically are literally absent, as the availability of a state forum usually does not turn on tribal consent. State law and state power are determinative and thus the only issues the court need address.

The blanket and controlling authority of state law also speaks to tribes' ability to meaningfully participate in state court adjudication of their interests. The *Panzer* court indicated that it would have welcomed the tribe's intervention in the suit, but what would there have been for the tribe to say? The tribe likely would have found itself taking sides in arguing over the proper interpretation of Wisconsin's state constitution, rather than asserting its own interests. The tribe was treated no differently than any other potential intervener, despite its status as a government. Even when present, a tribe's interests may be "shelved" through the court's consideration of state law issues.

Although not acknowledged by the court, the tribe had good reason not to intervene. First, of course, tribal intervention would have submitted the tribe's interests to adjudication in the Wisconsin court, akin to Wisconsin volunteering to have its interests litigated in Illinois state court. The tribe's participation is particularly problematic in state court, because states, unlike the federal government, generally have no authority over tribal governments. Second, the court made clear that in its opinion, state law and state interests were determinative. The court's approach did not afford much if any room for tribal interests to impact the court's reasoning: "The Tribe's decision not to participate as a party cannot deprive this court of its own core power to interpret the Wisconsin Constitution and resolve disputes between coequal branches of state government."

Despite the relatively favorable outcome in *Dairyland*, the case turned on the legally binding nature of the compacts as contracts — again, without regard to the government-to-government negotiation of tribal-state compacts. Although the *Dairyland* court characterized the "essence" of the issue as "whether Wisconsin should break treaties with Tribes," the court's reasoning treated the compact terms simply as contractual obligations subject to state law.

Although Congress delegated some authority over Indian gaming to states through IGRA, the post-*Seminole Tribe* environment has resulted in state power eclipsing tribal authority. Wisconsin's roller coaster ride reveals the extent to which state law sets — and can change — the terms of Indian gaming.

Rand, at 1005–1007. Is Rand correct that in state court, "no balance is struck between state and tribal authority"? Was that the case in *Panzer* and *Dairyland*? What about in *Lac du Flambeau Band*? Why does the fact that the *Dairyland* court treated the compact terms as equivalent to contractual obligations trouble Rand? Are state courts simply unable to interpret state law in a manner that is fair to tribes? Is it enough that a tribe can choose to intervene in a state court action?

2. State Separation of Powers

The Wisconsin Supreme Court decisions in *Panzer* and *Dairyland* raise issues of state constitutional law as well as state statutory law and state public policy. Controversy over the terms of tribal-state compacts, usually negotiated between tribal leaders and the state's governor, has fueled challenges to the validity of the compacts in state court, often on state constitutional grounds. Such challenges raise the issue of the governor's ability to bind the state to the compact generally or, as seen in *Panzer* and *Dairyland*, to specific terms.

As a first principle of the separation of powers, one branch cannot assume the constitutionally delegated functions of another. Hence the executive branch cannot, in theory, engage in law- or public policymaking. In practice, however, the distinctions among the functions of the political branches have blurred, in part as legislatures have delegated discretionary authority to the executive branch, primarily in the form of executive agencies but sometimes directly to the chief executive. Still, a legislature cannot delegate too much of its core authority to the executive branch. The separation of powers limitations on legislative authority to delegate are known as the delegation doctrine, or in the negative, the non-delegation doctrine.

IGRA does not specify which branch of state government is authorized to negotiate tribal-state compacts, but in most states, the governor has assumed (or been delegated by the legislature) this authority. State legislatures — or more accurately, some state legislators — and other interested officials and organizations have entreated the courts to interpret the state constitution as well as federal law on the question of whether the negotiation of compacts does, in fact, fall under the ambit of state executive authority.

New Mexico ex rel. Clark v. Johnson
904 P.2d 11 (N.M. 1995)

MINZNER, Justice.

Petitioners [including two state legislators] filed [an original action] for writ of mandamus or writ of prohibition and declaratory judgment from this Court directed at Respondent, who is the Governor of the State of New Mexico. Attached to the petition was a copy of the "Compact and Revenue Sharing Agreement" entered into by the Governor of New Mexico with the Governor of Pojoaque Pueblo. The petition alleges that the Governor of New Mexico has entered into similar compacts and revenue-sharing agreements with the Presidents of the Jicarilla and Mescalero Apache Tribes, as well as the Governors of Acoma, Isleta, Nambe, Sandia, Santa Ana, Santa Clara, San Felipe, San Ildefonso, San Juan, Taos, and Tesuque Pueblos pursuant to the Indian Gaming Regulatory Act (the Act or the IGRA).

Petitioners generally contend that the Governor of New Mexico lacked the authority to commit New Mexico to these compacts and agreements, because he attempted to exercise legislative authority contrary to the doctrine of separation of powers expressed in the state Constitution. Petitioners sought an order that would preclude the Governor of New Mexico from implementing the compacts and revenue-sharing agreements he has signed.

[In 1995, when Gary Johnson took office as governor of New Mexico], he appointed a negotiator to meet with various Indian tribal representatives to develop compacts and revenue-sharing agreements. [The compacts were approved by the U.S. Secretary of the Interior.] The compact with Pojoaque Pueblo is representative of the other compacts and agreements [entered into by the governor]. The Recitals in the Compact indicate that both the State and Tribal Governors believed that the Governor of New Mexico was authorized to bind the State of New Mexico with his signature.

We initially consider whether, in light of the procedural posture of this case, [an original action for] a writ of mandamus is an appropriate remedy. The issues presented are of "great public interest and importance." Petitioners assert in the present proceeding that the Governor has exercised the state legislature's authority. Their assertion presents issues of constitutional and fundamental importance; in resolving those issues, we will contribute to this State's definition of itself as sovereign. Moreover, an early resolution of this dispute is desirable. The Governor asserts, and it has not been disputed, that several of the compacting tribes are in the process of establishing and building gambling resorts and casinos. These projects entail the investment of large sums of tribal money. Capital financing for these projects may well depend upon resolution of the issue presented in this case. Accordingly, we conclude that the exercise of our original constitutional jurisdiction is appropriate in this case.

The final procedural issue is whether mandamus, which normally lies to compel a government official to perform a non-discretionary act, is a proper remedy by which to enjoin the Governor from acting unconstitutionally. Although it is not within the province of this Court to evaluate the wisdom of an act of either the legislature or the Governor, it certainly is our role to determine whether that act goes beyond the bounds established by our state Constitution.

The Governor has argued that the Tribes and Pueblos with whom he signed the compacts and agreements are indispensable parties to this proceeding. We disagree. In a mandamus case, a party is indispensable if the "performance of an act [to be compelled by the writ of mandamus is] dependent on the will of a third party, not before the court." That is not the case here. Petitioners seek a writ of mandamus against the Governor of New Mexico, not against any of the tribal officials. Resolution of this case requires only that we evaluate the Governor's authority under New Mexico law to enter into the compacts and agreements absent legislative authorization or ratification.

The compact authorizes all forms of "casino-style" gaming. Although not stated in the compact, we assume this might include such games as blackjack and poker in all its forms, keno, baccarat, craps, roulette, or any other form of gambling wherein the award of a prize is determined by some combination of chance or skill. The Governor states that New Mexico permits charities to conduct all forms of gaming, including "casino-style" gaming, under the provisions of the permissive lottery exception to New Mexico's gambling laws. *See* [New Mexico Statutes] § 30-19-6. [While the scope of gaming permitted by state law] is ultimately a federal question [under IGRA], it depends on an interpretation of New Mexico's gambling laws.

We do not agree with the Governor's broad assertion that any and all forms of "casino-style" gaming, such as the ones we have described, would be allowed under Section 30-19-6, [which] allows charitable and other non-profit organizations to operate a "lottery" twice a year and requires that the revenue derived be used for the benefit of the organization or for public purposes. [This Court has not decided] specifically what forms of gaming or gambling the legislature may have intended to allow under this provision, and we will not undertake the task of attempting to catalogue those games now, [as] its resolution is unnecessary to our decision in this case.

It is true, as the Governor has asserted, that the statutory definition of a "lottery" is extremely broad: "an enterprise wherein, for a consideration, the participants are given an opportunity to win a prize, the award of which is determined by chance, even though accompanied by some skill." [The general criminal prohibition against lotteries does not apply to section 30-19-6's authorization of charitable lotteries, but] the exception to hold a lottery for charitable purposes would in no way exempt the organization involved from other prohibitions against gambling in the [state] Criminal Code. The general criminal prohibition against gambling is applicable to both "making a bet" and participating in or conducting a lottery. Like the term "lottery," the term "bet" is also defined broadly as it relates to gambling: "a bargain in which the parties agree that, dependent upon chance, even though accompanied by some skill, one stands to win or lose anything of value specified in the agreement."

We think that most of the forms of "casino-style" games we have described could just as easily fall within the definition and prohibition against "betting" as within the broad definition of "lottery." The question, as we see it, would be whether that form of gaming or gambling is more like "making a bet" or conducting or participating in a "lottery." If it was the former, the activity would still be illegal in all circumstances despite the effect of the permissive lottery statute.

Moreover, we think the term "lottery" as used in Section 30-19-6 should not receive an expansive definition and should be narrowly construed. New Mexico law has unequivocally declared that all *for-profit* gambling is illegal and prohibited, except for licensed pari-mutuel horse racing. The permissive lotteries allowed by Section 30-19-6 include church fair drawings, movie theater prize drawings, and county fair livestock prizes, as well as the twice-a-year provision for nonprofit organizations on which the Governor's argument depends. We think that any expansive construction of the term "lottery" that would authorize any of these organizations to engage in a full range of "casino-style" gaming would be contrary to the legislature's general public policy against gambling.

We have no doubt that the compact and agreement authorizes more forms of gaming than New Mexico law permits under any set of circumstances. We need not decide which forms New Mexico permits. The legislature of this State has unequivocally expressed a public policy against unrestricted gaming, and the Governor has taken a course contrary to that expressed policy. That fact is relevant in evaluating his authority to enter into the compacts and revenue-sharing agreements, [to which we now turn.]

The New Mexico Constitution vests the legislative power in the legislature and the executive power in the governor. The Constitution also explicitly provides for the separation of governmental powers: "The powers of the government of this state are divided into three distinct departments, the legislative, executive and judicial, and no person or collection of persons charged with the exercise of powers properly belonging to one of these departments, shall exercise any powers properly belonging to either of the others, except as in this constitution otherwise expressly directed or permitted...." This provision reflects a principle that is fundamental in the structure of the federal government and the governments of all fifty states.

Our task, then, is to classify the Governor's actions in entering into the gaming compacts. If the entry into the compacts reasonably can be viewed as the execution of law, we would have no difficulty recognizing the attempt as within the Governor's authority as the State's chief executive officer. If, on the other hand, his actions in fact conflict with or infringe upon what is the essence of legislative authority—the making of law—then the Governor has exceeded his authority.

We have no doubt that the compact with Pojoaque Pueblo does not execute existing New Mexico statutory or case law, but that it is instead an attempt to create new law. However, that in itself is not dispositive. The test is whether the Governor's action disrupts the proper balance between the executive and legislative branches.

One mark of undue disruption would be an attempt to foreclose legislative action in areas where legislative authority is undisputed. The terms of the compact with Pojoaque Pueblo give the Tribe a virtually irrevocable and seemingly perpetual right to conduct any form of Class III gaming permitted in New Mexico on the date the Governor signed the agreement. Arguably, even legislative change could not affect the Tribe's ability to conduct Class III gaming authorized under the original compact. The compact is binding on the State of New Mexico for fifteen years, and it is automatically renewed for additional five-year periods unless it has been terminated by mutual agreement. Any action by the State to amend or repeal its laws that had the effect of restricting the scope of Indian gaming, or even the attempt to directly or indirectly restrict the scope of such gaming, terminates the Tribe's obligation to make payments to the State of New Mexico under the revenue-sharing agreement separately entered into between the Governor and Pojoaque Pueblo. [Further,] the compact strikes a detailed and specific balance between the respective roles of the State and the Tribe in such important matters as the regulation of Class III gaming activities, the licensing of its operators, and the respective civil and criminal jurisdictions of the State and the Tribe necessary for the enforcement of state or tribal laws or regulations. All of this has occurred in the absence of *any* action on the part of the legislature. While negotiations between states and Indian tribes to address these matters is expressly contemplated under the IGRA, we think the actual balance that is struck represents a legislative function. While the legislature might authorize the Governor to enter into a gaming compact or ratify his actions with respect to a compact he has negotiated, the Governor cannot enter into such a compact solely on his own authority.

Moreover, it is undisputed that New Mexico's legislature possesses the authority to prohibit or regulate all aspects of gambling on non-Indian lands. Pursuant to this authority, our legislature has, with narrow exceptions, made for-profit gambling a felony, and thereby expressed a general repugnance to this activity. The compact signed by the Governor, on the other hand, authorizes Pojoaque Pueblo to conduct "all forms of casino-style games;" that is, virtually any form of commercial gambling. By entering into such a permissive compact with Pojoaque Pueblo and other Indian leaders, we think that the

Governor contravened the legislature's expressed aversion to commercial gambling and exceeded his authority as this State's chief executive officer.

The Governor argues that he possesses the authority, as a matter of *federal law*, to bind the State to the terms of the compact, irrespective of whether he has the authority as a matter of state law. We find the Governor's argument on these points to be inconsistent with core principles of federalism. The Governor has only such authority as is given to him by our state Constitution and statutes enacted pursuant to it. We entertain no doubts that Congress could, if it so desired, enact legislation legalizing all forms of gambling on all Indian lands in whatever state they may occur. That is, however, not the course that Congress chose. Rather, Congress sought to give the states a role in the process. It did so by permitting Class III gaming only on those Indian lands where a negotiated compact is in effect between the state and the tribe. To this end, the language of the IGRA provides that "Any State ... may enter into a Tribal-State compact governing gaming activities on the Indian lands of the Indian Tribe." 25 U.S.C. § 2710(d)(3)(B). The only reasonable interpretation of this language is that it authorizes state officials, acting pursuant to their authority held under state law, to enter into gaming compacts on behalf of the state. It follows that because the Governor lacked authority under New Mexico law to enter into the compact with Pojoaque Pueblo, the State of New Mexico has not yet entered into any gaming compact that the Governor may implement.

Kansas ex rel. Stephan v. Finney

836 P.2d 1169 (Kan. 1992)

PER CURIAM.

This is an original action in mandamus and quo warranto wherein the Attorney General of Kansas challenges the authority of the Governor of Kansas to negotiate and enter into a binding tribal-state compact under the Indian Gaming Regulatory Act (IGRA). The compact in issue authorizes casino gambling on the Kickapoo Indian Reservation located within the State of Kansas, said gambling operation to be monitored by the State of Kansas.

[In 1992, the Kickapoo Nation and then-Governor Joan Finney signed a Class III gaming compact. While the compact was before the U.S. Interior Secretary for approval, the state legislature considered, but did not pass, a concurrent resolution urging the Secretary to Department of Interior to withhold approval based on the governor's failure to obtain legislative ratification of the compact. On the heels of that effort, two other bills were introduced in the state legislature: one that would have authorized the governor to enter into tribal-state compacts on behalf of the state, and another that would have created a state Legislative Commission on State-Indian Affairs charged with negotiating gaming compacts. Both bills failed to pass. Around the same time, the state attorney general, Robert T. Stephan, brought this action against the governor. In the meantime, the Interior Secretary required a revision to the compact to reduce the amount the tribe would pay to the state. After the governor and tribe submitted a revised compact, the Secretary advised the tribe that it would approve the compact if the state supreme court determined that "the Governor is authorized to bind the State to the compact." The tribe and the governor then filed an action in federal district court to compel the Secretary's approval of the compact, arguing that 25 U.S.C. § 2710(d)(8)(C) required the Secretary to take action within 45 days of submission.]

In this action [it is alleged that the governor] has exceeded the constitutional authority granted that office and usurped the constitutional power granted to the legislative branch of government. The subject of the alleged usurpation is neither minor nor inconsequential. The compact in question, if approved by the Secretary of the Interior, contains provisions which would require the State to expend substantial sums of money in hiring and training new personnel as well as accomplishing a multitude of changes in existing law.

Clearly, this is a matter of great statewide concern. Additionally, to those directly involved the matter demands immediate settlement. It would be no service to the Kickapoo Nation or other tribes such as the Sac and Fox Nation and the Prairie Band of Potawatomi Indians, who are seeking negotiations with the State of Kansas leading to tribal-state compacts, to leave the matter unresolved and let those involved proceed at the peril of subsequent invalidation of the negotiations. In view of the position of the Department of Interior, the whole question of tribal-state compacts could just hang in limbo were we not to determine the issue raised.

We have no hesitancy in concluding that an actual controversy of great public importance and concern exists and that the essential purpose of the proceeding is to obtain an authoritative interpretation of the law for the guidance of public officials in the administration of the public business. The mandamus/quo warranto proceeding herein is an appropriate vehicle for the resolution of the issue.

The Kansas Constitution provides: "Lotteries and the sale of lottery tickets are forever prohibited." The court has considered on several occasions what constitutes a lottery and has construed the term broadly to include any act of gaming which includes the elements of consideration, prize, and chance. Amendments to the state constitution allowed charitable bingo, pari-mutuel betting on horse and dog races, and a state lottery.

The Governor is declared by the Kansas Constitution to be the supreme executive power of Kansas: "The governor shall transact all the business of the state, civil and military, with the general government, except in cases otherwise specially provided by law." [The governor argues that this power includes authority to enter into tribal-state compacts on behalf of the state:] "General government" means the federal government, and the negotiation of tribal-state compacts under IGRA is a matter of federal law. [Further, the governor asserts that] it is neither practical nor feasible for the legislature to negotiate or participate in the negotiation or execution of such compacts by virtue of the [180-day] time limitation contained in [25 U.S.C. 2710(d)(7)(B)] as the legislature is only in session a small percentage of the year, and by its very nature, the legislature is wholly unsuited to the negotiation process.

The compact herein and negotiations leading thereto are between the Governor and the Kickapoo Nation—not the federal government. Further, the transaction of business connotes the day-to-day operation of government under previously established law or public policy. The implementation of law and policy rather than the enactment of law and the determination of public policy constitutes the transaction of business between Kansas and the federal government. The *carte blanche* interpretation asserted by the Governor herein is massive in its implication and, additionally, would have serious problems if challenged on grounds that it constitutes an impermissible delegation of the legislature's law-making powers.

In determining whether or not the head of the executive branch has the authority to negotiate and bind the State to the compact, some examination of the terms of the compact is necessary in order to establish the nature of the obligations undertaken. Under the compact, the State is granted the authority to monitor the casino gaming operation [through a] "State Gaming Agency," [identified as] "the Kansas Lottery or a division thereof or such other agency of the State as the Governor may from time to time designate as responsible for oversight of Class III Gaming as authorized by this Compact." The compact would thus create a State Gaming Agency. Such agency does not now exist and has never been authorized by the legislature. The duties undertaken will require the hiring, training, and supervision of new state employees. The legislature has not authorized such and the same has not been budgeted. A whole new function would be engrafted upon an existing agency, the Kansas Lottery (or some other agency if the Governor so designated), requiring new personnel, policies, procedures, rules and regulations. The creation of a state agency is clearly a legislative function and cannot be accomplished by the executive branch under the guise of merely adding a new function to an existing agency.

Other provisions in the compact are also clearly legislative in nature, [such as the requirement that] the Kansas Bureau of Investigation (KBI) do a background investigation on each prospective gaming employee and provide a written report thereof to the tribe, the Tribal Gaming Agency, and the State Gaming Agency. A substantial new function is thus added to that agency.

[While] we find no constitutional impediment to the Governor's authority to enter into negotiations with the Kickapoo Nation, the power to bind the State to the compact is another matter.

Saratoga County Chamber of Commerce, Inc. v. Pataki
798 N.E.2d 1047 (N.Y. 2003)

ROSENBLATT, Justice.

On this appeal we address the authority of the Governor to enter into agreements with Indian tribes to permit casino gaming on Indian reservations. Plaintiffs are legislators, organizations and individuals opposed to casino gambling. In challenging the Governor's authority, they contend that by negotiating and signing the agreements without legislative authorization or approval, Governor Mario M. Cuomo in 1993 and Governor George E. Pataki in 1999 violated the principle of separation of powers under the State Constitution.

[In 1993, the St. Regis Mohawk Tribe and Governor Cuomo entered into a compact. The tribe was permitted to operate baccarat, blackjack, craps and roulette, and the tribe and state shared oversight and law enforcement authority. The compact was approved by the U.S. Interior Secretary. The tribe did not open its casino until 1999, the same year that Governor Pataki agreed to an amendment to the 1993 compact allowing electronic Class III games, including video keno, for one year. Shortly after the 1999 amendment, plaintiffs filed this suit challenging both the amendment and the original compact.]

The State claims that the nearly six-year delay between the effective date of the 1993 compact and the start of this suit has prejudiced the Tribe. Nowhere in the present case, however, is there any indication that the delay in bringing this action has caused the slightest harm to the Tribe. Plaintiffs point out that the Tribe has been operating the casino—and presumably profiting from it—during the entire pendency of this suit. True enough, had the casino been shut down on its grand opening, the investment would have been lost. But the casino has been operating for four years, and there is nothing on this record to indicate how much money the casino has made during the pendency of this action. While the casino is presumably expected to make large sums over the next several years, and while plaintiffs' suit threatens that source of revenue, the prejudice caused by a loss of expected profits based on a predictably vulnerable compact is not the sort of prejudice that supports a defense of laches. Were it otherwise, very few suits would proceed past laches analysis, and certainly no suits seeking to invalidate illegal contracts could ever proceed.

The Tribe is not a party to this action. Although its interests are certainly affected by this litigation, the Tribe has chosen not to participate. Not only will these plaintiffs be stripped of a remedy if we hold that the Tribe is an indispensable party, but no member of the public will ever be able to bring this constitutional challenge. In effect, the Executive could sign agreements with any entity beyond the jurisdiction of the Court, free of constitutional interdiction. The Executive's actions would thus be insulated from review, a prospect antithetical to our system of checks and balances. While sovereign immunity prevents the Tribe from being forced to participate in New York court proceedings, it does not require everyone else to forego the resolution of all disputes that could affect the Tribe. While we fully respect the sovereign prerogatives of the Indian tribes, we will not permit the Tribe's voluntary absence to deprive these plaintiffs (and in turn any member of the public) of their day in court.

The State Constitution vests the Senate and the Assembly with the legislative power of the State, [and] the executive power in the Governor. It falls to the courts, and ultimately to this Court, to determine whether a challenged gubernatorial action is "legislative" and therefore ultra vires. In this case we have no difficulty determining that the Governor's actions were policy-making, and thus legislative in character.

Initially, we hold that IGRA does not preempt state law governing which state actors are competent to negotiate and agree to gaming compacts. IGRA imposes on "the State" an obligation to negotiate in good faith, but identifies no particular state actor who shall negotiate the compacts; that question is left up to state law.

IGRA itself contemplates that states will confront several policy choices when negotiating gaming compacts. Congress provided that potential conflicts may be resolved in the compact itself, explicitly noting the many policies affected by tribal gaming compacts. Indeed, gaming compacts are laden with policy choices, as Congress well recognized. Compacts addressing these issues listed in 25 U.S.C. § 2710(d)(3)(c) necessarily make fundamental policy choices that epitomize "legislative power." Decisions involving licensing, taxation and criminal and civil jurisdiction require a balancing of differing interests, a task the multimember, representative Legislature is entrusted to perform under our constitutional structure.

Additionally, the compacts require the State Racing and Wagering Board to adopt new regulations for carrying out its casino oversight responsibilities. The choice of *which* agency shall regulate an activity can be as fundamental a policy decision as choosing the substance of those regulations. For that reason, and because agencies are creatures of the Legislature, the Constitution requires that agencies carry out only those duties assigned them by the Legislature expressly or by necessary implication. There is no legislative authorization for state agencies to promulgate regulations for the oversight of casino gambling. The compacts therefore have usurped the Legislature's power.

The State argues that by passing certain appropriation bills, the Legislature has signaled its approval of the compact. We disagree. Those enactments are no substitute for approval or total ratification. The Legislature has been free to ratify the compact but, as yet, has not done so.

Unsurprisingly, every state high court to consider the issue has concluded that the state executive lacks the power unilaterally to negotiate and execute tribal gaming compacts under IGRA. Today we join those states in a commitment to the separation of powers and constitutional government.

Taxpayers of Michigan Against Casinos v. Michigan

685 N.W.2d 221 (Mich. 2004)

CORRIGAN, Chief Justice.

In this declaratory action, we must determine whether the Legislature's approval by resolution of tribal-state gaming compacts constituted "legislation" and therefore violated [the state constitution].

[In 1997, then-Governor John Engler entered into Class III compacts with the Little Traverse Bay Band of Odawa Indians, the Pokagon Band of Potawatomi Indians, the Little River Band of Ottawa Indians, and the Nottawaseppi Huron Potawatomi. Each compact provided that it would take effect after "[e]ndorsement by the Governor of the State and concurrence in that endorsement by resolution of the Michigan Legislature." The compacts were amended in 1998; that same year, the state legislature passed a resolution, House Concurrent Resolution 115, approving the amended compacts. Under Michigan law, while a majority of the full legislature must vote in favor of a legislative bill, a resolution may be passed by a majority vote of those legislators present at the time, provided a quorum is present. HCR 115 passed by a vote of 48 to 47 in the house and 21 to 17 in the senate.]

Resolution of whether HCR 115 constituted legislation necessarily turns on the definition of "legislation." Plaintiffs argue that the Legislature's approval of the compacts must be legislation because HCR 115 had the effect of altering legal rights and responsibilities. We find this definition of "legislation" overly simplistic. Although it is true that legislation alters legal rights and responsibilities, not everything that alters legal rights and responsibilities can be considered legislation. A more accurate definition of "legislation" is one of unilateral regulation. The Legislature is never required to obtain consent from those who are subject to its legislative power. This unilateral action distinguishes legislation from contract, [which requires the consent of both parties to the contract].

Here, the Legislature was required to approve the compacts only as the result of negotiations between two sovereigns: the Legislature could not have unilaterally exerted its will over the tribes involved. Because the tribes' consent is required by federal law, the compacts can only be described as contracts, not legislation.

In order to understand the contractual nature of the compacts, it is essential to understand the state's limited role under federal law generally, as well as IGRA. Through IGRA, Congress has permitted the states to negotiate with the tribes through the compacting process to shape the terms under which tribal gaming is conducted. The states have no authority to regulate tribal gaming under the IGRA unless the tribe explicitly consents to the regulation in a compact.

Although [IGRA] provides that class III gaming activities are only lawful if conducted in conformance with a tribal-state compact, that does not mean the states have any authority to regulate class III gaming activities in the absence of a compact. States may not enforce the terms of IGRA; rather, the only enforcement provided for in the IGRA is through the federal government. In other words, although it may be "unlawful" for the tribes to engage in class III gaming absent a compact, the Legislature is powerless to regulate or prohibit such gaming. State legislatures have no regulatory role under IGRA aside from that negotiated between the tribes and the states.

IGRA only grants the states bargaining power, not regulatory power, over tribal gaming. The Legislature is prohibited from unilaterally imposing its will on the tribes; rather, under IGRA, it must negotiate with the tribes to reach a mutual agreement. As noted above, the hallmark of legislation is unilateral imposition of legislative will. Such a uni-lateral imposition of legislative will is completely absent in the Legislature's approval of tribal-state gaming compacts under IGRA.

Further, the compacts approved by HCR 115 do not apply to the citizens of the state of Michigan as a whole; they only bind the two parties to the compact. Legislation "looks to the future and changes existing conditions by making a new rule to be applied there-after to all or some part of those subject to its power." Here, the compacts approved by HCR 115 have no application to those subject to legislative power; rather, they only set forth the parameters within which the tribes, as sovereign nations, have agreed to oper-ate their gaming facilities.

The compacts do not create any state agencies or impose any regulatory obligation on the state. The state also has no responsibility to enforce the compacts' requirements. In this way, the compacts here can be distinguished from those at issue in the cases relied upon by plaintiffs. In *Kansas v. Finney,* the compact at issue created a state gaming agency re-sponsible for monitoring the tribe's compliance with the contract, and the compact was not submitted to the legislature for any form of approval. Unlike the compact in *Finney,* however, the compacts at issue here do not create any state agencies and were presented to the Legislature for approval. Similarly, in *New Mexico v. Johnson,* the compacts au-thorized more forms of gaming than were otherwise permitted in New Mexico. Unlike the compacts in *Johnson,* the compacts here do not create new forms of gaming and were presented to the Legislature for approval. Thus, the compacts do not impose new oblig-ations on the citizens of the state subject to the Legislature's power; they simply reflect the contractual terms agreed to by two sovereign entities.

Unlike the federal constitution, our Constitution is not a grant of power to the legis-lature, but is a limitation upon its powers. Therefore, the legislative authority of the state can do anything which it is not prohibited from doing by the people through the Con-stitution of the State or the United States. We have held that our Legislature has the gen-eral power to contract unless there is a constitutional limitation. It is acknowledged by all that our Constitution contains no limits on the Legislature's power to bind the state to a contract with a tribe; therefore, because nothing prohibits it from doing so, given the Legislature's residual power, we conclude that the Legislature has the discretion to ap-prove the compacts by resolution.

Notes and Questions

1.   State courts' application of state constitutional principles. Does the court's rea-soning in *Taxpayers of Michigan* cast any doubt on the courts' decisions in *Johnson, Finney,* or *Saratoga County*? If Class III compacts are a creation of federal law—that is, states may exercise authority over Indian gaming only through the power delegated to them by Congress in IGRA—does it make sense that the operation of state law could "undo" a duly negotiated compact? Are you persuaded by the Michigan Supreme Court's empha-sis on the factual distinction between *Taxpayers of Michigan* and *Johnson*? If Governor Engler had agreed to games not expressly permitted under Michigan law, how would that change the court's analysis of the compacts' validity?

2.   Federal preemption of state law. On the question of the interaction of state law and IGRA, recall that the Senate Report states, "[IGRA] is intended to expressly preempt the field in the governance of gaming activities on Indian lands. Consequently, Federal courts should not balance competing Federal, State, and tribal interests to determine the extent to which various gaming activities are allowed." S. Rep. No. 446, 100th Cong., 2d Sess., *reprinted in* 1988 U.S.C.C.A.N. 3071, 3076. Consider the Eighth Circuit's reasoning in *Gaming Corp. of America v. Dorsey & Whitney*, 88 F.3d 536, 545 (8th Cir. 1996), which arose out of the tribal gaming commission's refusal to issue a gaming license to a management company. The company sued the tribe's law firm in Minnesota state court, alleging a number of state law claims as well as claims under IGRA. The case was removed to federal district court, where the court remanded the case to state court on the ground that IGRA did not completely preempt the application of state law. The Eighth Circuit reversed, holding that IGRA completely preempts state law:

> Examination of the text and structure of IGRA, its legislative history, and its jurisdictional framework indicates that Congress intended it to completely preempt state law. There is a comprehensive treatment of issues affecting the regulation of Indian gaming.... The only avenue for significant state involvement is through tribal-state compacts covering class III gaming....

> Every reference to court action in IGRA specifies federal court jurisdiction. State courts are never mentioned.... Congress apparently intended that challenges to substantive decisions regarding the governance of Indian gaming would be made in federal courts....

> Congress thus left states with no regulatory role over gaming except as expressly authorized by IGRA, and under it, the only method by which a state can apply its general civil laws to gaming is through a tribal-state compact. Tribal-state compacts are at the core of the scheme Congress developed to balance the interests of the federal government, the states, and the tribes. They are a creation of federal law, and IGRA prescribes the permissible scope of a Tribal-State compact. Such compacts must also be approved by the Secretary of the Interior....

> The conclusion that IGRA completely preempts state law is reinforced when the statute is viewed in the context of Indian law.... A long line of Supreme Court decisions illustrates the importance of the federal and tribal interests in Indian cases and the authority of Congress to protect those interests.

Id. at 544–47. The court went on to state, "Potentially valid claims under state law [related to Indian gaming] are those which would not interfere with the [tribe's] governance of gaming, [such as] a violation of a duty owed to one of the management companies because of an attorney-client relationship." *Id.* at 550. Compare the federal district court's decision remanding *Kansas ex rel. Stephan v. Finney*, 1993 WL 192809 (D. Kan. 1993), to state court on the ground that the permitted scope of gaming is a question of state law that may be resolved without reference to IGRA, and the *Johnson* court's statement that while scope of gaming "is ultimately a federal question, it depends on an interpretation of [state] gambling laws." Under *Gaming Corp.*'s reasoning, is the validity of a tribal-state compact—or a specific provision of the compact—a question of federal law?

Are state court decisions about the governor's ability to bind the state to a compact under state constitutional law essentially the state "apply[ing] its general civil laws to [tribal] gaming" in contravention of IGRA and *Cabazon*? How should IGRA's compacting and "permits such gaming" requirements operate to preserve both tribal sovereignty and Congress's intent?

Given the lack of clarity on state separation of powers and tribal-state compacting, could the U.S. Interior Secretary promulgate a regulation that assigns to state governors the authority to bind the state through a tribal-state compact? What constitutional issues might that raise? Is there another alternative?

3.   ***Tribes as indispensable parties.*** Note that in none of the cases excerpted in this section were the affected tribes party to the suit. Recall the reasoning of the New York court in *Saratoga County Chamber of Commerce v. Pataki*:

> The Tribe is not a party to this action. Although its interests are certainly affected by this litigation, the Tribe has chosen not to participate. Not only will these plaintiffs be stripped of a remedy if we hold that the Tribe is an indispensable party, but no member of the public will ever be able to bring this constitutional challenge. In effect, the Executive could sign agreements with any entity beyond the jurisdiction of the Court, free of constitutional interdiction. The Executive's actions would thus be insulated from review, a prospect antithetical to our system of checks and balances. While sovereign immunity prevents the Tribe from being forced to participate in New York court proceedings, it does not require everyone else to forego the resolution of all disputes that could affect the Tribe. While we fully respect the sovereign prerogatives of the Indian tribes, we will not permit the Tribe's voluntary absence to deprive these plaintiffs (and in turn any member of the public) of their day in court.

Was the absence of the tribe from the litigation problematic? Why or why not? For more on tribes as indispensable parties, see Matthew L.M. Fletcher, *The Comparative Rights of Indispensable Sovereigns*, 40 Gonz. L. Rev. 1 (2004–2005) (discussing in detail cases involving Indian gaming and courts' consideration of tribes as indispensable parties).

4.   ***Practical implications of "undoing" compacts.*** Practically speaking, what should happen when a state court holds that a duly negotiated — and often federally approved — tribal-state compact is invalid under state law? Is the compact simply void? Must the tribe and the state renegotiate the compact from scratch? Recall that in the New Mexico case, the tribes had relied on the compacts to begin construction on new casinos. How did the state court's decision affect the tribes' ability to comply with the financing and construction agreements into which they may have entered? If a tribe already operates a casino, must it stop operating the games authorized by the compact? In New York, the state court decision came a decade after the St. Regis Mohawk Tribe signed a compact with Governor Cuomo and four years after it opened its casino.

Problem 8: "Undoing" Compacts

Consider IGRA's "permits such gaming" and compacting requirements for Class III gaming. Does invalidating a compact based on the scope of gaming allowed under state law have a stronger basis in IGRA than does invalidating a compact based on lack of state legislative approval or other state constitutional requirements? Referencing the case law from this Chapter as well as appropriate state constitutional principles, lay out the best arguments on either side.

Part IV
Policy Implications

In the introduction to its 1999 FINAL REPORT, the National Gambling Impact Study Commission (NGISC) bemoaned the lack of accurate and complete information about the socioeconomic impacts and policy implications of legalized gambling.

> Presumably, many of the debates [over the spread of legalized gambling] could be settled if either the benefits or costs of gambling could be shown to be significantly greater than the other. But such a neat resolution has evaded would-be arbiters. Efforts to assess the various claims by proponents and opponents quickly encounter [one of] gambling's ... defining characteristic[s], the lack of reliable information. Regarding gambling, the available information on economic and social impact is spotty at best and usually inadequate for an informed discussion let alone decision. On examination, much of what Americans think they know about gambling turns out to be exaggerated or taken out of context. And much of the information in circulation is inaccurate or even false.... Add to this the fact that many of the studies that do exist were contracted by partisans of one point of view or another and uncertainty becomes an understandable result. Nevertheless, decisions must be made and governments have shown little hesitation in making them.

> The problem is not simply one of gathering information. Legalized gambling on a wide scale is a new phenomenon in modern America and much of the relevant research is in its infancy. Many phenomena are only now beginning to be recognized and defined, a prerequisite to gathering useful information. And many of the key variables are difficult to quantify: Can the dollar costs of divorce or bankruptcy adequately capture the human suffering caused by problem gambling? The more difficult the measurement; the more the weighing of competing claims retreats from science to art or, with even greater uncertainty, to politics. Nevertheless, the lack of information will not reduce the pressures on governments to make decisions.

NGISC, FINAL REPORT, at 1-6.

As the Commission noted, the scarcity of quality information has not stopped governments from making policy decisions, many of which likely are informed more by politics (or ideology) than by research.

The Commission's observations about the lack of scientific research on the social and economic effects of legalized gambling, as well as the fact that policy decisions are made without useful or even necessary information, remain as salient today as they were nearly a decade ago. Indeed, they are more relevant in the area of Indian gaming than ever. One might argue that the law and policy that govern tribal gaming are developed in more of an information vacuum, and are guided more by the politics of misinformation, than any other form of legalized gambling.

In this Part, we first examine what the existing research has to say about the social and economic impacts of Indian gaming before exploring some of the key legal and political issues that have arisen. In Chapter 9 we include materials addressing whether Indian gaming is, in fact, achieving IGRA's policy goals in terms of assisting tribes to develop their economies and achieve self-sufficiency. Is Indian gaming the solution to, or the cause of, various social ills that beset tribal communities? What are Indian gaming's spillover effects on non-tribal communities near reservations? We then examine the challenges and opportunities of economic development and diversification in Indian country. There are numerous obstacles to commercial enterprise which tribes must surmount. These hurdles to capital acquisition and investment differ substantially from the legal and regulatory requirements for tribal gaming discussed in prior Chapters, yet they are no less important determinants of success.

At the conclusion of its FINAL REPORT, the NGISC recommended:

> [G]ambling tribes, states, and local governments should recognize the mutual benefits that may flow to communities from Indian gambling. Further, the Commission recommends that tribes should enter into reciprocal agreements with state and local governments to mitigate the negative effects of the activities that may occur in other communities and to balance the rights of tribal, state and local governments, tribal members, and other citizens.

Id., at 6-23.

The Commission's recommendations stem from its recognition that Indian gaming generates significant socioeconomic benefits as well as costs, and vital imperatives as well as opportunities for productive intergovernmental relations. Political scientist Steven Light discusses the necessity for policymakers and practitioners alike to understand the mechanisms underlying such relations, as well as their significance.

> Despite their recognized political status and long history of interactions with other governments, American Indian tribal governments are the "often-overlooked third sovereign in the American political system." Contemporary understanding of intergovernmental relations (IGR) in the United States reflects the interactions of national, state, and local governments. The place of tribal governments in relation to theoretical and empirical understandings of IGR remains a relative conceptual enigma.

> Indian gaming is opening a new window in IGR. Subject to an elaborate federal, state, and tribal regulatory scheme mandated by federal law, Indian gaming reflects a complex nexus of interactions among numerous governments and policymakers. As the industry has emerged and matured as a means of self-determination and economic development for tribes across the United States—and as the associated economic stakes because of the real and perceived success of tribal casinos have increased dramatically—tribal-state interactions have increased in scope and intensity. Tribal political behavior is changing, too, as tribes are using gaming revenue to participate in state and local politics, both to mold public policy to their interests and to defend those interests against economic competition or threats to tribal sovereignty. Increasingly a story is told in which tribal political clout is on the rise. In short, Indian gaming has generated an unprecedented era of IGR in which nontribal governments pay attention to tribes.

Within a framework of tribal-state IGR in which tribes are an "intergovernmental partner in the federal system," it is critical to assess whether and under what conditions tribal governments can in fact participate *fully* and *effectively* within that system. Given their political behavior, are gaming tribes best understood as governments that adopt interest group strategies to cope with state political systems? And if so, what are the normative implications of such empirical findings? Although evidence is building, the jury remains out on how best to understand tribal political behavior as well as the full implications of Indian gaming for a broadened theoretical understanding of IGR. It is clear, however, that tribal gaming's socioeconomic effects and political ramifications are increasingly significant for state, local, and tribal communities throughout the United States. As tribes and states negotiate the legal, political, and economic dynamics of Indian gaming, it is important to understand how tribal-state IGR generates opportunities for and constraints on potential political partnerships.

Steven Andrew Light, *Indian Gaming and Intergovernmental Relations: State-Level Constraints on Tribal Political Influence Over Policy Outcomes*, 38 AM. REV. PUB. ADMIN. (2008).

There is no doubt that the Indian gaming industry is subject to a wide array of legal and political forces that manifest and change on a daily basis. In Chapter 10 we lay out several of the most critical issues with which tribal, federal, state, and local governments grapple. We begin with tribal land acquisition and Indian gaming on "newly acquired lands," a topic that is in the news somewhere in the U.S. nearly every day. We then examine the impetus behind and legality of the revenue-sharing agreements that have become part and parcel of many tribal-state compacts. After tackling how Indian gaming has become a lightning rod for controversy over the BIA's acknowledgment process for tribal groups seeking federal recognition, we turn to the intriguing questions presented by employment law and its application in Indian country.

This Part concludes our examination of Indian gaming law, and yet is far from the last word on a dynamic and fascinating area of the law that is subject to so many legal, political, and policy developments that we could not possibly hope to contain them all between the covers of this casebook.

Chapter 9

Socioeconomic Impacts of Indian Gaming

A. Overview

The law and policy of Indian gaming anticipate and acknowledge that legalized gambling has social and economic costs and benefits both on and off the reservation. As IGRA states, the policy rationale for Indian gaming in large part rests on the goal of facilitating tribal economic development as a means to achieving tribal self-sufficiency. The regulatory scheme established pursuant to IGRA, including numerous federal, state, and tribal agencies and officials, seeks to provide a framework for the lawful collection and distribution of gaming revenue to tribal governments and assist in maximizing gaming's socioeconomic benefits while minimizing its negative externalities. As we have seen in prior Chapters, numerous court decisions take the socioeconomic impacts of Indian gaming into account when interpreting federal, state, or tribal law.

Government institutions and public officials act on their sense of the social and economic impacts of Indian gaming, sometimes informed by public opinion and the will of the electorate, other times by advocacy groups or lobbyists. But how much do we really know about the effects of Indian gaming?

In its 1999 overview of the socioeconomic impacts of Indian gaming, the NGISC surveyed the existing research concerning legalized gambling. It found that

> [w]hat is ... astonishing is how little is known and has been studied regarding the social and economic impacts of this diverse industry upon our nation. Despite the growing magnitude of the industry and the widespread involvement of a significant portion of the population, there is a paucity of research in this field. Much of what does exist is flawed because of insufficient data, poor or undeveloped methodology, or researchers' biases.
>
> It is evident to this Commission that there are significant benefits and significant costs to the places, namely, those communities which embrace gambling and that many of the impacts, both positive and negative, of gambling spill over into the surrounding communities.... In an ideal environment, citizens and policy-makers consider all of the relevant data and information as part of their decisionmaking process. Unfortunately, the lack of quality research and the controversy surrounding this industry rarely enable citizens and policymakers to truly determine the *net* impact of gambling in their communities, or, in some cases, their backyards.

NGISC, Final Report, at 7-1. In regard to Indian gaming, the Commission noted that

> [o]nly a limited number of independent studies exist regarding the economic and social impact of Indian gambling. Some have found a mixture of positive and

negative results of the impact of gambling on reservations, whereas others have found a positive economic impact for the tribal government, its members and the surrounding communities.

Id. at 6-14.

Nearly a decade later, the NGISC's conclusions about the state of research on legalized gambling and Indian gaming remain strikingly on the mark. Given the magnitude of the attention paid to Indian gaming by journalists, policymakers, and the public in recent years, one may be surprised by the relative lack of high-quality information available as a foundation for the informed assessment of the socioeconomic effects of tribal gaming. And yet, there have been significant advances made in the field since the Commission issued its FINAL REPORT. In this Chapter, we "assess the assessments" of Indian gaming's economic and social impacts with an overview of some of the best research to date and the methodology such studies employ.

B. Economic Impacts

A critical part of the foundation for Indian gaming law and policy rests on its assumed value to tribal as well as non-tribal economies. Equally important is the assumption that any negative externalities of Indian gaming do not outweigh the positive ones. But how do we measure these economic impacts *empirically*? Social-scientific research presents unique methodological challenges in this regard, particularly as they apply to understanding the effects of Indian gaming.

1. Methodology

Steven Andrew Light & Kathryn Rand
Indian Gaming and Tribal Sovereignty: The Casino Compromise
77–80 (2005)

In states where tribes operate casinos, policy debates over Indian gaming revolve around assessments of its socioeconomic impacts. Researchers frequently distinguish between the economic and social effects of tribal gaming while seeking to quantify each and assess their net impact on communities. Policymakers often weigh against each other various social and economic outcomes generated by Indian gaming. With the continued rapid growth of the Indian gaming industry, the National Gambling Impact Study Commission's (NGISC) 1999 report on gambling's social and economic impacts was at the forefront of researchers' efforts to facilitate greater understanding of the empirical impacts of gambling generally and tribal gaming specifically. Perhaps needless to say, the data, and its interpretation, have painted a mixed portrait of those social and economic effects. Although many of tribal gaming's socioeconomic effects are intertwined and some are potentially unquantifiable, we take the categorical distinctions between economic and social impacts as our starting point in assessing whether anyone is winning from Indian gaming.

Some economists have argued that gambling inherently "produces ... no new wealth" and thus "makes no genuine contribution to economic development." On the other hand, it appears difficult to argue with the proposition that gambling creates both positive and negative externalities—benefits as well as costs—that flow from gambling transactions. The impacts of these externalities ripple outward beyond any one individual's decision, rational or otherwise, to drop a quarter into an electronic slot machine, and the resultant payout—or, more likely, disappointment.

The methodologies underpinning studies of Indian gaming's economic impacts vary somewhat, but ultimately boil down to estimations relying on similar types of data and modeling techniques. Data quality and methodological sophistication matter and do indeed vary, but arguably the real distinctions among studies result from how the data is used in relation to what questions are asked: the quality of analysis, biases reflected in conclusions, and whether policy prescriptions simply make sense all speak to that critical issue. In this section we discuss the methodological approaches employed by those researching the socioeconomic impacts of Indian gaming. We attempt to synthesize these approaches into broad and understandable categories, starting with economic impact estimation.

Researchers employ different economic impact estimation methodologies, but virtually all studies of Indian gaming's economic effects share the same basic goal of modeling its costs and benefits to a given economy (tribal, local, state, or national) and assessing the net economic effects. Representative major studies of Indian gaming exemplify researchers' use of similar methodological approaches but differing impact estimation models and distinct terminology.

One common approach to economic impact estimation is input-output economic and fiscal impact analysis. Standard input-output models allow one to trace the secondary economic effects generated by direct expenditures in a particular industry. The input, or direct effect, of Indian gaming consists of consumer gaming and non-gaming expenditures (primarily spending on food, beverages, hotel, retail, and entertainment) at tribal gaming operations. This spending has secondary effects; that is, each dollar spent at a slot machine sends additional dollars rippling throughout the economy in the form of indirect and induced effects. Indirect effects result from business-to-business purchases of goods and services. That is, to serve meals at a tribal casino's all-you-can-eat buffet, the tribe must contract with local or regional food goods and services suppliers. These vendors in turn purchase goods from their own regional suppliers, who themselves contract with larger agribusiness concerns and trucking firms located throughout the nation. Induced effects stem from the wages that are directly or indirectly earned by employees of tribal gaming facilities, the numerous industries that interact with the tribal gaming industry, and the public sector, such as regulators or law enforcement personnel. Input-output analysis produces three major categorical measures of economic activity: output, wages, and jobs. Output measures the dollar value of production. Wages encompass household income and the dollar value of employee benefits. Jobs are quantified by person-years of employment as a measure of those who are fully employed as a result of the Indian gaming industry. Fiscal impact analysis measures the financial impacts of Indian gaming in two forms: tax revenue and revenue sharing by tribes. Tribal casinos generate corporate profits taxes, income tax, sales tax, property tax, and excise and licensing fees and fines. Under the terms of negotiated revenue-sharing agreements, tribes directly contribute gaming revenue to state and local governments and special distribution funds.

A second common approach to economic impact estimation seeks to model tribal gaming's direct impacts, gross impacts, and net impacts. Direct economic impacts include job creation and employment, payment of wages and salaries, purchase of supplies and services, revenue transfers to government, and taxes paid or withheld. Gross impacts model the ripple effects of spending on goods and services as well as those flowing from other direct impacts. Net impacts derive from "but-for" analysis: but for tribal casinos, what would the area's economy look like? As in input-output analysis, this type of impact estimation model incorporates economic multiplier effects. Each dollar a consumer spends at the casino generates additional expenditures: the casino's infrastructure must in the first place be built, parking lots and roads paved, food and other goods and services purchased from vendors, utilities purchased from public or private suppliers, labor costs and taxes paid, and so forth. One can calculate a standardized economic multiplier to account for these transactions. Ultimately, researchers assess the larger policy question of whether tribal casinos produce a net positive or net negative impact on the area's economy.

Data, method, or analysis may affect a given study's validity as well as its contributions to policy debates. Data insufficiencies, limitations of impact estimation modeling, and the possibility of ideological bias stemming from the polarizing nature of the debate between perceived "proponents" and "opponents" of tribal gaming or legalized gambling more generally are among the difficulties inherent to systematically quantifying the economic impacts of tribal gaming in a manner that satisfies either scholars or policymakers. Many studies of gaming's economic impacts are conducted by private consulting firms or commissioned by organizations that may have a vested interest in the outcome of an economic impact study. Some have suggested that such research may suffer from poor design or bias. [S]tudies of Indian gaming's economic impacts generally use some variant of cost-benefit analysis that itself raises issues of methodological and interpretive accuracy.

Notes and Questions

1. *The modeling process.* As Professors Light and Rand explained, economists use specialized statistical modeling to estimate the economic and fiscal impacts of Indian gaming. The modeling process captures the complexities of numerous interrelationships that occur behind the scenes in an identified economy, such as a city, county, state, or reservation. The three most common models are IMPLAN (IMpact Analysis for PLANning), an input-output framework originally developed for use by various federal agencies and widely used since 1979; the U.S. Department of Commerce Regional Input-Output Modeling System (RIMS II); or an econometric model, such as that developed by Regional Economic Models, Inc. (REMI). *See* Adam Rose et al., *The Regional Economic Impacts of Casino Gambling: Assessment of the Literature and Establishment of a Research Agenda* (Report to the National Gambling Impact Study Commission) 9–13 (1998).

Economic impact models can be used for basic or applied research, or for commercial purposes. Professors Shields and Deller explained an additional rationale for the modeling process, assisting policymakers in informed decision making:

> Local leaders and citizens increasingly face difficult questions about the impacts of changes such as business growth, the decline of traditional industry, and evolving land uses.... To fully understand the effects of economic change, citizens and officials must first understand the local economic structure. Unfortunately, many communities lack the resources to examine the consequences of change. As a result, important decisions too often are made with limited information and understanding and, in some cases, misinformation.
>
> Economic impact models can help officials and citizens address these concerns. These models focus on how a local economy functions, how various elements of the local economy are interrelated, and how a change in one element

may affect the others. These relationships can help predict important aspects of economic change, including employment and unemployment, commuting and migration, and projected changes in government and school district revenues and spending.

Martin Shields & Steven C. Deller, *Using Economic Impact Models as an Educational Tool in Community Economic Development Programming: Lessons from Pennsylvania and Wisconsin*, 41 J. EXTENSION (2003), available at http://www.joe.org/joe/2003june/ent.shtml#a4.

The complexity of identifying the linkages in the modeling process stems in large part from the fact that

> [i]n every local economy, businesses, governments, and consumers conduct thousands of seemingly unrelated transactions each day. But from an economic perspective, all of these transactions are interrelated. Businesses sell goods and services to households and other businesses, households sell resources (such as their labor) to businesses, and governments collect taxes from both to pay for public services. Because of these interrelationships, changes in one sector often affect other sectors. For example, when a local business expands, the increase in jobs and income can substantially affect the housing market, the demand for government services, and retail sales, as well as other local businesses.

Id.

Given all of the variables, the input specification process into a model is as much art as science. For a readable explanation of how the IMPLAN model has been used to calculate the national economic impacts of Indian gaming, see ALAN P. MEISTER, INDIAN GAMING INDUSTRY REPORT 7–9 (2007–2008 ed.).

2.   *Data availability.* One of the greatest methodological difficulties in economic impact estimation concerning Indian gaming is the lack of data available to independent researchers. Historically, data collected by the BIA, Census Bureau, and other federal agencies on tribes and tribal members has been incomplete and of inconsistent quality. *See* Jonathan B. Taylor, Matthew B. Krepps, & Patrick Wang, *The National Evidence on the Socioeconomic Impacts of American Indian Gaming on Non-Indian Communities* 4 (2000). Perhaps more significantly in terms of modeling the dynamic Indian gaming industry, tribes are not subject to federal and state public information disclosure requirements because of their status as political sovereigns. Reliable data on economic impacts thus may be difficult for researchers or policymakers unaffiliated with tribal governments to obtain. Accordingly, some have called for Congress to remove IGRA's exemption from the federal Freedom of Information Act, 5 U.S.C. §552. *See, e.g.*, William N. Thompson, *Economic Issues and Native American Gaming*, WISCONSIN INTEREST 5 (Fall/Winter 1998). Others have suggested that the "imperatives of data gathering and analysis as a precursor to informed policymaking"—for tribes as much if not more than for non-tribal governments—merit a full-scale national study of Indian gaming's impacts supported by tribal data but underwritten with a federal guarantee of respect for tribal sovereignty. LIGHT & RAND, INDIAN GAMING AND TRIBAL SOVEREIGNTY, at 152–55.

2. Impacts

As one might imagine, public officials and community members are not always sold on the idea that a tribal casino has positive economic impacts that extend off the reservation. Perhaps the tribal gaming facility simply "captures" dollars through a substitution effect, in which dollars are spent on gambling that otherwise would be spent at, say, the local movieplex. Perhaps a casino exports economic costs, not benefits; for instance, the increased costs of local law enforcement. And what about the fact that there is no direct state sales tax on the reservation? A key question for many policymakers is whether dollars spent on the reservation exclusively circulate there, or throughout broader economies. Read the excerpt from the following study with an eye toward the methodological complexities of identifying and disaggregating the economic impacts of Indian gaming on reservations from those on surrounding non-Indian communities.

Jonathan B. Taylor, Matthew B. Krepps, & Patrick Wang
The National Evidence on the Socioeconomic Impacts of American Indian Gaming on Non-Indian Communities
5–9 (2000)

This paper takes advantage of a comprehensive dataset constructed by the National Opinion Research Center (NORC) at the University of Chicago on behalf of the National Gambling Impact Study Commission (NGISC). The dataset was originally constructed to assess the effect of casino introductions on communities of 10,000 persons or larger which witnessed a casino introduction of any kind within 50 miles. We analyze the data to determine whether differential effects can be measured for communities that witnessed Indian casino introductions, in particular. None of the 100 communities studied are Indian communities; nonetheless, our statistical analysis affords preliminary answers to empirical questions raised in policy debates around the country, particularly regarding the exportation of harmful social consequences to non-Indian communities.

The economic impacts of Indian casinos are helpfully divided into five categories. Table 1 lists them and presents their expected effect on the reservation economy and the economy surrounding the reservation.

Table 1: Categories of Indian Casino Economic Impacts

	Expected Effect on the:	
	Reservation	**Surrounding Community**
Destination Effects	Positive	Positive
Substitution Effects	Positive	Negative
Cannibalization Effects	Positive	Negative
Multiplier Effects	Modest or None	Positive
Intensity Effects	Positive	Positive

Given that many Indian reservations are in relatively remote areas, creating an Indian casino has the potential to make the region more attractive to in-state and out-of-state tourists. This *destination effect* has the potential thereby to improve the fortunes both of the tribes and of the surrounding communities, as out-of-region casino patrons spend their money at hotels, gas stations, and other establishments in the region.

However, the potential exists that the establishment of an Indian casino would create competition with local entertainment establishments and the restaurant and hotel sector and that, therefore, the jobs created by a casino are not net new jobs that encourage migration or decrease the ranks of the unemployed. The aforementioned blandishments offered to casino patrons are a regular feature of Nevada and New Jersey casinos, and a number of Indian casinos have offered the same, possibly pulling customers from other establishments in the area. As a result, the potential exists that Indian casinos have a *substitution effect* on the local leisure and hospitality sector that improves tribal fortunes at the expense of the off-reservation economy.

This substitution effect on surrounding communities could be exacerbated by a *cannibalization effect*, depending on the availability of other gambling opportunities within the region of analysis. If tribal casinos cause gamblers to substitute their products for another locally available gambling product (e.g., dog tracks, non-Indian casinos, or lotteries), then tribal casinos would exert a negative or cannibalization, effect on the off-reservation economy to the benefits of the tribal economy.

Combining the three aforementioned effects results in a net direct impact on the regional, off-reservation economy. That net direct effect is associated with additional *multiplier effects* that ripple outward through the economy. If a tribal casino introduces a net increase in the consumption of food, bedding, labor, and asphalt, the gross regional product of the regions supplying the goods will potentially rise. These indirect effects are properly attributed to the casino and, generally speaking, will favor the off-reservation economy more as tribes are not generally capable of autarky—economic self-sufficiency and non-reliance on imports. Thus, the multiplier effects are likely to be *de minimis* on the reservation and substantial off the reservation.

Finally, there is an *intensity effect* that captures the impact of the casino on consumer decisions to alter their spending in the leisure sector. A casino may prompt consumers to shift spending from non-leisure categories (e.g., a second car) toward the leisure category. Much of this shift is likely to be a benign change in consumer behavior, and as such, the introduction of the casino improves consumer wellbeing by increasing the diversity of spending choices. The intensity effect may also be associated with pathology, for example with a shift away from spending on children's clothing. Nonetheless, so long as the social costs are also tallied and weighed against the economic effects, it is proper here to add an estimate of the intensity effect to the economic side of the cost-benefit analysis.

Of course, relative to creating this classification, the task of accurately measuring the effects is quite difficult. Heretofore, most research has approached the task from the bottom upwards—i.e., from the casino level. Typically, the studies tally jobs created, construction multipliers, tax withholdings, restaurant closings, and the like. However, very little of this research employs techniques that can conclusively assert that the effects would not have taken place, but for the introduction of the casino. Thus, for example, assertions that restaurants have closed because of the introduction of an Indian casino have not really been approached with dispositive evidence one way or the other. The problem is even more acute on the social side.

* * *

Chapter 1's overview of the current state of the Indian gaming industry included economic impact analysis from several sources, including the annual report by economist Alan Meister. Here we revisit that report. Consider the different categorical measures of the national economic impacts of Indian gaming in view of the methodological challenges presented by input-output modeling and IGRA's policy goals.

Alan P. Meister
Indian Gaming Industry Report
3–5 (2007–2008 ed.)

Indian gaming continued to exhibit strong growth in calendar year 2006. There were 228 tribes operating 423 gaming facilities in 28 states. In total, these gaming facilities generated approximately $25.5 billion in gaming revenue, an 11 percent increase over the $23.0 billion generated in 2005. Total non-gaming revenue rose approximately 12 percent, from about $2.2 billion in 2005 to $2.5 billion in 2006.

Total jobs and wages also increased substantially in the industry. Indian gaming facilities, including non-gaming operations, directly supported approximately 327,000 jobs and provided about $11.3 billion in wages in 2006. In 2005, the industry supported 301,000 jobs and provided $10.4 billion in wages.

On the whole, Indian gaming continued to play a significant role in the gaming industry. In 2006, Indian gaming facilities generated 42 percent of all U.S. casino gaming revenue (i.e., gaming revenue generated at Indian gaming facilities, commercial casinos, and racinos). And while commercial casinos still led the way with a market share of 52 percent, Indian gaming continued to gain ground.

In terms of performance by type of gaming, Class III continues to generate the vast majority (93 percent) of gaming revenue at Indian gaming facilities nationwide. In 2006, the five states with *only* Class II gaming (Alabama, Alaska, Florida, Nebraska, and Texas) generated just over $1.7 billion in gaming revenue. Of this amount, approximately 91 percent, or $1.6 billion, was generated in Florida alone. The remaining 23 states with at least some Class III Indian gaming generated approximately $23.7 billion.

Despite its smaller size, Class II gaming generally grew at a faster rate than Class III gaming. In 2006, gaming revenue grew a total of 20 percent for Class II only states and 10 percent for Class III states. The growth of the Class II only states was largely driven by strong growth in Florida (22 percent). However, a number of Class II only states experienced sizable growth. In fact, of all 28 states with Indian gaming, the three fastest growing states in terms of gaming revenue were Class II only states (Nebraska, Alaska, and Texas). Interestingly enough, though, Class II only states included the two lowest and four of the eight lowest in terms of gaming revenue generation.

On the whole, Indian gaming continues to make significant contributions to the U.S. economy. It has stimulated economic activity, created jobs, and provided wages— all of which generated tax revenue to federal, state, and local governments. In 2006, it is estimated that Indian gaming directly and indirectly led to:

- $80.7 billion in output;
- 703,000 jobs;
- $27.8 billion in wages; and
- $11.7 billion in federal, state, and local tax revenue.

This reflects a considerable increase over the estimated contribution of Indian gaming in 2005, which included $74.2 billion in output, 646,000 jobs, $25.5 billion in wages, and $10.7 billion in tax revenue.

The fiscal benefits of Indian gaming go beyond just tax revenue from secondary economic activity. Many tribes also made direct payments to federal, state, and local governments, including payments to defray regulatory costs, revenue sharing with local governments, and revenue sharing with states. In 2006, the total of all identifiable direct payments to federal, state, and local governments was $1.2 billion. This included: $51.5 million in payments to defray federal and state regulatory costs; $136.2 million in local revenue sharing, and $1.0 billion in state revenue sharing. In total, direct payments by tribes to federal, state, and local governments were up 9.5 percent from $1.1 billion in 2005. Overall, the total fiscal benefit of Indian gaming, including tax revenue and all direct payments by tribes to other governments, was $12.9 billion in 2006.

Notes and Questions

1. **Indian gaming and "new wealth."** Some economists have argued that as gambling involves only the transfer of wealth from consumer to casino, it creates no new wealth, and thus "makes no genuine contribution to economic development." *See* Paul H. Brietzke and Teresa L. Kline, *The Law and Economics of Native American Casinos*, 78 NEB. L. REV. 263, 268 (1999) (quoting economist Jack Van Der Slik). Brietzke and Kline criticized this view as "wrong or at least badly overdrawn." They explained,

> As "entertainment," $100 sunk into a slot machine is (a little) more likely to provide a financial payoff than $100 sunk into an opera ticket. Both provide psychic payoffs, or else there would be no repeat gambling or opera customers, and it can be thought a matter of "taste" for the customer or policymaker to prefer one payoff over the other. Both opera and gambling are produced with varying combinations of land, labor, capital, technology, entrepreneurship, and a host of "political" resources: chiefly legitimacy and philanthropic subsidies for opera, and regulation and often-hidden political subsidies for gambling. These resources are valuable only because of how people use them; owners are compensated according to (and sometimes beyond) their resource's "opportunity costs"; and any profits the activity generates reflect peoples' values by definition. These payoffs constitute "new money," and "new wealth" for someone.

Id.; see also, e.g., William R. Eadington, *The Economics of Casino Gambling*, 13 J. ECON. PERSPECTIVES 173 (1999); William R. Eadington, *Contributions of Casino-Style Gambling to Local Economies*, 556 ANNALS AM. ACAD. POL. & SOC. SCI. 53 (1998).

2. **Indian gaming and taxes.** Despite the widespread perception among non-Native people that tribes and tribal members do not pay any federal, state, or local taxes, there are only three circumstances in which this occurs: tribes do not pay corporate income taxes on gaming revenues, tribal members who live and work on a reservation are exempt from state income or property taxes, and tribal members do not pay state or local sales or excise taxes for purchases made on reservations. Yet, as Meister's study indicates, tribal gaming operations contribute a substantial amount in state and federal tax revenue. For more on tribal gaming and taxes, see Scott A. Taylor, *Federal and State Income Taxation of Indian Gaming Revenues*, 5 GAMING L. REV. 383 (2001).

3. **Economic benefits of Indian gaming.** In light of Meister's industry figures for Indian gaming's direct economic effects in 2006, Indian gaming appears to have some positive economic effects on and off reservations, even taking into account possible substitution and cannibalization effects. The question typically posed by policymakers and others is whether the economic benefits outweigh the perceived social costs. As Light and Rand noted,

There is general consensus among a number of influential studies that Indian gaming generates economic benefits for tribes, as well as for local and state governments. There is some divergence, however, about the extent of these economic benefits. More fundamental disagreements arise over the appropriate weight to be assigned to tribal gaming's economic benefits during the policymaking process.

LIGHT & RAND, INDIAN GAMING AND TRIBAL SOVEREIGNTY, at 83. We next turn to Indian gaming's social impacts.

C. Social Impacts

1. Methodology

Steven Andrew Light & Kathryn R.L. Rand
Indian Gaming and Tribal Sovereignty: The Casino Compromise
80–83 (2005)

The question of whether tribal gaming produces a net economic benefit or detriment to a state frequently is accompanied by inquiry into whether tribal gaming results in unacceptable social costs either to non-Native communities that surround reservations or to the state as a whole. Accordingly, research on Indian gaming also seeks to measure its social impacts. Although social impacts are perhaps distinct from economic impacts, the two are difficult to isolate. For example, although problem and pathological gambling results in social costs, including divorce and domestic abuse, it also imposes direct economic costs, such as treatment costs. Recognizing the overlap between social and economic impacts, many studies attempt to express social impacts in dollar amounts, but the usual focus appears to be on social costs rather than social benefits. This oversight yields an inherently one-sided analysis, as researchers and policymakers attempt to weigh economic benefits against social costs in an artificial dichotomy. Reservation communities stand the most to gain from tribes' decisions to open casinos. With great poverty comes great opportunity in terms of measurable socioeconomic gains. Although often overlooked, particularly in studies of states and non-tribal communities, the social impacts of Indian gaming include social benefits as well as social costs. Further complicating the equation, both social costs and social benefits may be difficult to quantify, and there may be social impacts that do not lend themselves to an easily reduced cost-benefit calculation.

Yet many studies employ a cost-benefit evaluation of casino gambling, summing the economic benefits and costs as well as social costs expressed in dollar amounts (negative or "real-resource-using harmful externalities") to compare individual consumer utility with and without the introduction of casinos. One method of estimating social costs is to identify the average individual costs of problem and pathological gamblers, multiplied by the prevalence of problem and pathological gamblers in the general population. Another method is to measure the impact of casinos on a particular variable, such as crime rates. The first approach, by itself, accounts only for social costs of problem and pathological gambling. It does not undertake to measure and weigh any possible social benefits or other social costs. Although the second approach may measure both positive and negative effects on a particular variable, its methodological difficulty lies in isolating the impact of casino gambling. The typical cost-benefit analysis, incorporating one or both of the basic methodological approaches, struggles with the problems inherent to each.

Critics suggest that a number of economic impact studies either overlook social costs and benefits to tribal communities or disaggregate their analysis of benefits accruing to tribes from their assessment of how Indian gaming affects the state in which those tribes are located. The NORC study, for example, did not include any tribal communities in its sample. Statewide studies rarely isolate effects on tribal communities, choosing instead to focus on impacts affecting the state's residents as a whole. The net assessment of gaming thus appears to turn on its benefits or costs to non-tribal communities. Still others suggest that cost-benefit impact analysis ultimately seems artificially sterile and divorced from the complex social realities of public policymaking, particularly as they relate to tribes.

Many of the social benefits to Indian gaming are most readily apparent in tribal communities. The creation of new jobs on reservations may be the most basic economic benefit that directly translates to social benefits for tribal members and others. Beyond that, "[t]ribes have invested in economic development; basic infrastructure; police, fire, and emergency services; health, housing, and social programs; education; natural resource management; language retention; Indian material and cultural heritage; land base re-acquisition; and individual member incomes." These benefits need not be conceived as exclusive to the tribe; a healthy reservation economy ultimately benefits both surrounding non-tribal communities and the state.

The near absence of tribal communities in research on the socioeconomic effects of casino gambling is perhaps justified by the small population size of Native communities (in a statewide cost-benefit analysis, for example, any impacts on a tribal community should be considered only relative to the community's size), the general methodological difficulties in breaking out statewide impact analysis to the community level, and the practical difficulties in acquiring data specific to tribal communities.

[Nevertheless,] studies accounting for gaming's impacts on tribal communities only according to their population size inappropriately minimize the impacts of Indian gaming on its intended beneficiaries—tribal governments and tribal members—and overlook IGRA's specific policy goals. Given the limited availability of comprehensive quantitative data concerning Indian gaming's impacts on reservation life, accounts of tribal gaming's socioeconomic impacts frequently are multi-methodological and may be historically grounded and thick with qualitative and anecdotal evidence. Such research serves the important role of incorporating the experiences and perspectives of tribes and tribal members into the public discourse over casino gambling. Too, it reveals possible social benefits not accounted for in the usual statistical modeling methods, such as strengthening tribal governments and realizing tribal self-determination.

Jonathan B. Taylor, Matthew B. Krepps, & Patrick Wang
The National Evidence on the Socioeconomic Impacts of American Indian Gaming on Non-Indian Communities
9–13 (2000)

Often in debates on the merits of introducing non-Indian casinos, the social side of the impacts question focuses entirely on costs. From these debates, one could get the impression that on the one side there are economic benefits and on the other, social costs. However, the status of reservation Indians as America's poorest minority—a group also suffering from a multitude of social pathologies associated with poverty—means that Indian casino introductions also bring potentially substantial social gains. Thus, analysis of the social impacts in the context of Indian casino introductions properly takes into account both social benefits and social costs.

The largest social benefits of Indian casinos redound to the tribes themselves. The casinos operate on the Indian society by raising employment in the most chronically poor class of Americans—on reservation Indians. Moreover, tribal ownership of the casinos implies that casino profits are a source of fiscal strength for tribal governments. To be sure, there is a great deal of heterogeneity of tribal spending policies (just as among states); however, the general pattern across Indian Country is that these fiscal resources go to strengthening tribal community. Indications are that this social investment is beginning to turn around the fortunes of Indians across such diverse measures of community health as ambulance response times, migration back to the reservation, and Indian language retention among high school students. Off-reservation, there are frequently community benefits where tribes contribute to charitable and civic organizations ranging from the little league, to the Victory Games for the Disabled, to local government treasuries.

Balanced against these social benefits are social costs. On the reservations, casino revenues have raised the stakes of political discourse, occasionally with deleterious consequences to the reservation community. A relatively benign feature of the strengthening of tribal treasuries has been the migration of members who had to leave in the past to find employment. This reversal of earlier emigration—particularly when combined with the issuance of large per capita revenue distributions—has heightened the tension over the question of who is and who is not appropriately a member of the tribe. Moreover, by effectuating a quantum change in tribal governmental discretion over spending, gaming revenue has intensified political debates within tribes. Among a handful of tribes, political tensions have surpassed the capacity of tribal institutions of governance to contain and resolve conflict, and in those tribes, what had been a relatively modest social friction erupted into civil violence.

On the off-reservation social cost side, the primary focus of attention has been pathological or compulsive gambling. Indian casinos may induce both Indian and non-Indian customers to gamble to a level that is detrimental to themselves and to others. Thus, a summation of the associated costs of their compulsive or pathological gambling (e.g., the cost of bankruptcy, child neglect, suicide) is properly weighed against the social benefits and net economic benefits in the overall cost-benefit analysis.

As on the economic side, the evaluators of Indian casino social benefits and costs have generally approached the problem from the micro level. Indian gaming benefits have been studied at the tribal and state level and across only one national sample of five tribes. Thus, on the benefits side, little comprehensive national data exist on tribal employment and spending patterns or their effects. Similarly, pathological gambling cost analysis typically began (until recently) with the basic arithmetic of multiplying the measured costs of an individual pathological gambler by estimates of the number of problem gamblers. This bottom-up approach to social benefits and costs is one of the major shortcomings of these policy debates. The Indian data are impressionistic, and the gambling pathology analysis focuses on proximate measures of social cost (the prevalence of the problem gambler) rather than ultimate consequences (rates of suicide, bankruptcy, etc.). A much more fruitful approach, particularly in the realm of Indian gambling (where pathologies such as suicides could as easily be decreasing due to community development as increasing due to problem gambling), would entail a comprehensive top-down approach to ultimate social consequences with controls to measure departures from the counterfactual but-for-the-casino world.

Notes and Questions

1. *Impacts on Tribal Communities.* Light and Rand argued that many studies fail to measure or assess the socioeconomic impacts of Indian gaming on tribal communities. *See also* Steven Andrew Light & Kathryn R.L. Rand, *Reconciling the Paradox of Tribal Sovereignty: Three Frameworks for Developing Indian Gaming Law and Policy*, 4 NEV. L.J. 262 (2004); Kathryn R.L. Rand, *There Are No Pequots on the Plains: Assessing the Success of Indian Gaming*, 5 CHAPMAN L. REV. 47 (2002); Kathryn R.L. Rand & Steven Andrew Light, *Raising the Stakes: Tribal Sovereignty and Indian Gaming in North Dakota*, 5 GAMING L. REV. 329 (2001). Would it surprise you to learn that most impact studies focus on the effects of legalized gambling generally on non-Indian communities and populations, and not on the effects of tribal casinos on American Indian communities and populations specifically?

Some research, however, has focused intentionally on tribal communities. For instance, affiliates of the Harvard Project on American Indian Economic Development have sought to document the socioeconomic effects of tribal gaming in particular, rather than legalized gambling in general. *See, e.g.,* Cabazon, *The Indian Gaming Regulatory Act, and the Socioeconomic Consequences of American Indian Governmental Gaming*, at http://www.ksg. harvard.edu/hpaied/pubs/cabazon.htm; see also Stephen Cornell et al., *American Indian Gaming Policy and its Socio-Economic Effects: A Report to the National Gambling Impact Commission* (1998).

2. *Economic costs of social impacts.* As Light and Rand noted, cost-benefit analysis of legalized gambling often involves translating negative social effects, such as problem and pathological gambling, into economic costs. The study conducted by the National Opinion Research Center for the NGISC (the NORC study) described its methodological approach to assigning economic costs to the prevalence of problem and pathological gambling:

> Problem and pathological gamblers experience excessive rates of adverse consequences that have tangible economic costs. Further consequences experienced by these gamblers that are quite real (e.g., broken relationships and families), although not readily amenable to having price tags attached, are often termed "intangible" costs. Another dimension of gambling consequences is that their impact is usually spread across an entire community. While costs begin with the gambler, they spill over to the household, other family members, friends, employers, creditors, and the community as a whole.

> In this analysis, our basic strategy is to compare rates (and costs) of specific adverse consequences associated with problem and pathological gambling for each of our designated gambling types. For examples, problem and pathological gamblers (and perhaps those considered at risk as well) are believed to experience higher rates of personal bankruptcy (primarily attributed to their problems with gambling) than persons who are otherwise similar but do not gamble or at lower risk gamblers. Obviously, there are reasons unrelated to gambling for individuals to experience bankruptcy.

> The analysis thus attempts to ascertain whether the bankruptcy rates (and other negative consequences) of problem and pathological gamblers are greater than bankruptcy rates of other gambling types who are otherwise similar, and to determine whether the difference is larger than might be expected due to chance. The bankruptcy cost attributed to problem and pathological gambling adjusts for "expected" rates of bankruptcy. Thus, the estimates are of "excessive" costs (be it for bankruptcy, job loss, health problems, etc.) experienced by problem and pathological gamblers.

There have been several prior efforts at describing the economic impacts of problem and pathological gambling. The critical contribution of these studies has been the identification of consequences and impacts of problem and pathological gambling that have economic implications, and the efforts made to develop estimates of these costs. Among the obvious financial consequences these studies have examined are gambling-attributed bankruptcy, dissipation of assets, debt, and theft. Other impacts studied are missed work or lateness to work, lost employment, stress and impaired physical and mental health, suicidal ideation, and alcohol- and drug-related disorders. Families and personal relationships usually are adversely affected, with associated conflict and strife, with divorce frequently the result.

For the most part, the existing body of research examines persons in treatment for a gambling disorder. Data on gamblers in treatment probably describe the most severely impacted individuals — the tail of the distribution in terms of severity and number of impacts. We expect that the general population survey will identify individuals who have not reached this extreme level of severity.

Since the problems often attributed to problem and pathological gambling are also experienced by many people whether or not they gamble, we adjusted for whether a problem or pathological gambler has other characteristics or behaviors that might contribute to the consequence in question. For example, if those who gamble also have alcohol and drug problems, ignoring these other problems might result in attributing an inaccurately high consequence rate to problem and pathological gambling.

Our analysis used logistical regression to control for the following sociodemographic factors: age, gender, ethnicity, educational attainment, residence with one's children, and use/abuse of alcohol and illicit drugs. In general, these factors were generally strongly predictive of whether individuals had experienced the costly consequences identified above.

Dean Gerstein et al., *Gambling Impact and Behavior Study: Report to the National Gambling Impact Study Commission* 38–42 (1999). The study's analysis of problem and pathological gambling is excerpted below.

    3.   Problem and pathological gambling. Problem and pathological gambling often are cited as the most serious social cost of legalized gambling. The American Psychiatric Association's *Diagnostic and Statistical Manual of Mental Disorders* (DSM-IV) classifies pathological gambling as an impulse control disorder. The diagnostic criteria are (1) preoccupation with gambling, (2) a need to gamble with increasing amounts of money to achieve the desired excitement, (3) restlessness or irritability associated with abstinence from gambling, (4) use of gambling as a means of escape from problems, (5) "chasing" losses with more gambling, (6) dishonesty to conceal gambling, (7) repeated unsuccessful attempts to stop gambling, (8) committing crimes to finance gambling, (9) placing a significant relationship, or a career or educational opportunity, in jeopardy because of gambling, and (10) reliance on others to provide a financial "bail out" necessitated by gambling. *See* NGISC, Final Report, at 4-2 (Table 4-1). Pathological gamblers meet at least five of the ten criteria, while problem gamblers meet fewer than five criteria.

The NORC study used five terms to describe varying degrees of the prevalence of gambling among Americans: "non-gamblers," or those who have never gambled; "low-risk gamblers," or those who have gambled but never lost more than $100 in a single day or year; "at-risk gamblers," or those who have lost more than $100 in a single day or year and meet one or two of the DSM-IV criteria; "problem gamblers," or those who have lost more than $100 in a single day or year and meet three or four of the DSM-IV criteria; and "pathological gamblers," or those who have lost more than $100 in a single day or year and meet five or more of the DSM-IV criteria. Gerstein et al., at 21 (Table 3).

The NGISC FINAL REPORT cited estimates that in 1998, between 1.2 and 1.5 percent of the adult population in the U.S. (or approximately 3 million people) were pathological gamblers at least at some point during their lives, while another 1.5 to 3.9 percent of adults (or between 3 and 7.8 million people) were problem gamblers. NGISC, FINAL REPORT, at 4-1. The Commission noted that "it is possible that the numbers [from the two studies cited in the NGISC report] may understate the extent of the problem," as one aspect of problem and pathological gambling is concealing the extent of one's gambling. *Id.* at 4-9. The Commission further categorized problem and pathological gamblers as either "lifetime" (those who have met the criteria at any point in their lifetime) or "past year" (those who have met the criteria in the past twelve months) gamblers. *Id.* at 4-4. Because pathological gambling is characterized as a chronic disorder, the "lifetime" prevalence rates seem to be most relevant as measures, as the diagnostic criteria do not require that a person meet the criteria within a specific timeframe, such as one year.

4.   The NORC study on casino proximity. The NORC study, commissioned by the NGISC, is one of a handful of systemic national assessments of the socioeconomic impacts of legalized gambling. The study's design attempted to minimize the problem of isolating the impact of casinos on communities through the use of multilevel regression. The NORC study examined social and economic changes attributed to a community's "casino proximity," defined in the study as one or more casinos operating within 50 miles of a community.

The NORC study included 100 randomly selected sample communities over the period of 1980 to 1997. In 1980, five of the sample communities were located near casinos; by 1997, 45 sample communities were near casinos. Thus, the study compared both communities with and without a nearby casino, and the years before and after a casino opened near a sample community. To measure social effects of casino proximity, the NORC study selected several specific indicators, including crime rates, health indices, and employment and income data. These indicators were standardized across the sample communities by calculating per capita rates based on permanent resident population. The study tested the association of the introduction of a casino with changes in the socioeconomic variables.

A multilevel model reflected comparisons both of sample communities and of years within a specific sample community, and controlled for changes in communities that occurred independently of casino proximity. Multilevel regression allows measurement of effects on two levels; the NORC study compared communities that experienced the introduction of a nearby casino with those that did not, and also compared the years before and after a casino was opened in those communities that experienced the introduction of a nearby casino. Each of the socioeconomic variables (and per capita casino spending) was a response variable in a pair of multilevel regressions.

As noted above, the NORC study did not include any tribal communities in its sample; the next excerpt from the NORC study is followed by an excerpt from the study conducted by Taylor, Krepps, and Wang utilizing the NORC data to examine the social effects of Indian gaming.

2. Impacts

Dean Gerstein et al.
Gambling Impact and Behavior Study:
Report to the National Gambling Impact Study Commission
42–55 (1999)

It is important to note that many of the costs often associated with problem and patho-logical gambling are not unique to persons who gamble or who might need help for gam-bling problems. Thus, our analysis examines the following questions:

- To what extent did the problem and pathological gamblers surveyed experience a certain consequence?
- To what extent did they attribute the consequence to their gambling?
- What plausible economic costs can be associated with higher than expected rates of this consequence?

Based on these questions, we concluded that the major findings are as follows:

- Problem and pathological gamblers have significantly higher rates of costly con-sequences than otherwise similar persons do.
- Problem and pathological gamblers experience or impose thousands of dollars of economic costs per year on society.
- Problem and pathological gamblers rarely directly attributed these costly prob-lems to their gambling behaviors or difficulties.

Adverse financial consequences are the crux of the issue for problem and pathological gambling. While there are obviously other manifestations and consequences that can and often do arise, the financial problems are generally thought to underlie these in some way. One potential mechanism through which gambling might bring adverse consequences is for the gambler to lose too much money relative to her or his earning capacity and/or wealth.

Another mechanism for adverse consequences is for one to engage in gambling at times and places that are inappropriate given one's responsibilities; adverse outcomes could in-clude a decline in job performance and additional costs to employers, job loss, lost wages, and reliance on Unemployment Insurance and/or other social welfare programs.

The data reveal somewhat complex patterns regarding employment. For example, pathological gamblers had relatively high employment (76.3 percent) at the time of the survey. However, among those that had worked in the past year, we found a slightly higher (but not statistically significant) rate of working less than a full year (about 26.6 percent, versus 18.6 percent for low-risk gamblers). Still, the pathological gamblers who had worked in the prior 12 months were significantly more likely to have lost/been fired from a job (13.8 percent versus 4 percent for low-risk gamblers). However, they were not sig-nificantly more likely to have been earning a wage below $10 per hour than others. The mean household income for pathological gamblers was about 15 percent lower than for low-risk gamblers, but this difference was not statistically significant.

Problem gamblers, in contrast, were significantly more likely to have been unemployed or at least not working at the time of their interview. However, those who did work were employed for as much of the year as low-risk gamblers. Their rate of having lost or been fired from a job was also higher (10.8 percent compared to 2.6 percent for nongamblers). Wage rates did not appear to be impaired in this group.

The most unambiguous measure of employer dissatisfaction with employee performance (productivity) is to fire an employee. Employers incur search and training costs assumed equal to 10 percent of the annual salary for each employee replaced. Since pathological gamblers in our sample earned about $18 per hour, or $40,000 per year, firing an employee costs an employer an average of $4,000. Since pathological gamblers had a job loss rate of 13.8 percent, versus the expected rate of 5.8 percent, their "excess" rate of job loss was 8 percent. Therefore, the average pathological gambler costs his or her employer 8 percent of $4,000, or about $320. The costs of the excess job loss for each problem gambler was $200. Even though problem and pathological gamblers have elevated rates of job loss, there is no systematic indication that they earned less than otherwise similar individuals due to either excess unemployment or lower wages.

Pathological gamblers have clearly elevated rates of indebtedness, both in an absolute sense and relative to their income. Indebtedness per person is 25 percent greater than that of low-risk gamblers and about 120 percent greater than that of nongamblers. However, the disparity is even greater when debt is compared to income: pathological gamblers owe $1.20 for every dollar of annual income, while low-risk and nongamblers only owe $0.80 and $0.60 respectively. In accord with their higher debt, pathological gamblers have significantly elevated rates of having ever declared bankruptcy: 19.2 percent, versus 5.5 percent and 4.2 percent for low-risk and nongamblers. Again, for problem gamblers the story is not as clear. Their average level of indebtedness is actually the lowest of any type of gambler; however, they still have an elevated rate of bankruptcy (10.3 percent), but this is only marginally statistically significant when compared to the rate among nongamblers.

On average, excess lifetime losses involved with bankruptcy are about $3,300 for pathological gamblers and $1,600 for problem gamblers. Almost 19 percent of pathological gamblers have ever declared bankruptcy, versus an expected 10.8 percent, given their personal characteristics. For problem gamblers, their 10 percent rate compares to an expected rate of 6.3 percent. Personal bankruptcies result in an average of $39,000 in losses to creditors, although one should keep in mind that there are major differences between Chapter 7 and 13 filings.

Pathological and problem gamblers in treatment populations often reveal that they have stolen money or other valuables in order to gamble or pay for gambling debts. Although we asked study participants if they had ever stolen money in order to gamble or pay a gambling debt, the reported frequency was too low to measure, or at least to report in this study. Still, to the extent that problem and pathological gamblers have rates of arrest and imprisonment that are greater than low-risk gamblers and nongamblers, it is possible to infer that the difference may be related to gambling behaviors and problems (although the direction of causality may be open to debate). About one-third of problem and pathological gamblers reported having been arrested, compared to 10 percent of low-risk gamblers and only 4 percent of nongamblers. About 23 percent of pathological gamblers and 13 percent of problem gamblers have ever been imprisoned. Again, these rates are much higher than rates for low-risk gamblers and nongamblers (4 and 0.3 percent, respectively).

For this analysis, we performed tests to establish the probability that these differences were not primarily associated with other characteristics of the respective gambler types (e.g., age, gender, alcohol, and drug problems) and were not observed due to chance. The arrest and imprisonment rates of problem and pathological gamblers were highly significant. Pathological and problem gamblers account for about $1,000 each ($1,250 and $960, respectively) in excess lifetime police costs. Pathological gamblers are estimated to have $1,700 in lifetime corrections costs, with problem gamblers having $670 in costs.

Family problems are one of the primary concerns associated with problem and patho-logical gambling. While this type of consequence is difficult to measure and to assign value to, the number of resulting divorces can be measured, and legal fees can be esti-mated. One measure of gambling as a factor in divorce is that respondents representing about 400,000 adults pointed to their own gambling as a cause or factor in a past divorce, and respondents representing 2 million adults identified a spouse's gambling as a signif-icant factor in a prior divorce.

The analysis estimates that the average pathological gambler has accumulated $4,300 more than expected for legal fees involved with excess divorces (measured rate of 53.5 percent, versus an expected rate of 33.4 percent). Low-risk gamblers and nongamblers have lifetime divorce rates of 30 and 18 percent, respectively. Problem gamblers have losses of $1,950 in lifetime excess divorce legal fees. Their reported divorce rate was 39.5 percent, compared to a rate of 31 percent expected for persons otherwise similar with-out gambling problems. The economic consequences of divorce are actually much greater than the direct value of the associated legal costs. The major economic conclusion from the divorce literature is that the economic well-being of children and the mother usually significantly falls, while that of males increases materially. Thus, there is a tragic winner-loser scenario, where the values are somewhat offsetting. These costs are clearly to be dif-ferentiated from the emotional costs that [are] borne by all of those involved. The ability to calculate these economic costs in the present study is limited, however, because the costs are quite complicated.

Several studies have suggested that pathological and problem gambling is correlated with a decline in health and elevated rates of illness—either physical or mental. It is unclear how gambling problems would cause adverse impacts on health, although such impacts are be-lieved to be a function of stress and strain. In our survey, 33.8 percent of pathological gam-blers reported that they were in poor or only fair health, while only 14 percent of low-risk gamblers reported poor or fair health. We estimated that annual health care expenditures were elevated by about $750 for pathological gamblers, with an estimated annual expendi-ture of about $3,800 per capita. Based on their other characteristics, absent the effect of gambling, we expected significantly fewer pathological gamblers to be in poor or fair health—about 17 percent, with personal health expenditures of about $3,000 per capita.

Pathological and problem gamblers had annual mental health expenditures about $330 and $360 greater than expected, respectively. About 13 percent of these two groups reported past-year use of mental health services, while our analyses projected use by only about 6 percent. Utilization of mental health services was just under 7 percent for low-risk and nongamblers. Therefore, an excess of 7 percent of problem and pathological gamblers had mental health problems, at an average cost of $5,000 per year, which yields the esti-mated cost per problem and pathological gambler of about $350 per year.

About 3 percent of pathological gamblers seek care [for their gambling problems] in a given year, with an average cost per person of $1,000. If one uses these data to estimate the cost of treatment in a year, then the annual treatment cost per pathological gambler is about $30. It is assumed that most problem gamblers do not seek treatment unless or until they advance to pathological.

Annual costs of lifetime pathological gamblers are estimated at $1,195, compared to $715 for lifetime problem gamblers. However, substantial additional costs are present that can only be estimated on a lifetime basis, as they did not occur frequently enough in the past year to be estimated with the current sample size. Lifetime impacts were $10,550 and $5,130 for pathological and problem gamblers.

The costs of problem and pathological gambling minus transfers are $1,050 and $560 per year, and $10,550 and $5,130 per lifetime, respectively. When these sums are multiplied by the estimated prevalence of pathological and problem gamblers, they translate into annual costs of about $4 billion per year, and $28 billion on a lifetime basis. If transfers to the gambler from creditors and other taxpayers are included, the costs rise to about $5 billion per year and $40 billion per lifetime.

The findings of this part of the report directly raise the question of the extent to which problem gambling behavior is the cause of the higher rates of consequences. This analysis cannot rule out the possibility that the gambling problems are actually reflective of certain underlying inclinations or values of these persons, such as a reduced willingness to abide by social norms or an inclination to take extra risks (not simply in gambling). To the extent that this is true, the gambling problems are as much symptomatic of the other characteristics or issues as causes of difficulties in the life of gamblers and their families.

While the conclusions of this analysis are relatively robust, they must be tempered by several factors. The small sample size was a limiting factor in the analysis. There were too few problem and pathological gamblers in the survey, even after the random digit dial and the patron surveys were combined and weighted to generate cost estimates for consequences that were directly attributed by interviewees to "gambling problems." All of the costs that have been estimated are associated with excess rates of consequences that can be caused by factors in addition to problem and pathological gambling. Analyses have been done to adjust for selected other factors such as alcohol and drug use, age and educational attainment. Adjustment for these factors does result in smaller estimates of costs than would otherwise result simply by comparing problem and pathological gamblers to nongamblers and those with no problems.

Finally, the costs that we measured are tangible and relatively amenable to economic analysis. However, many of the human burdens of pathological and problem gambling are not so readily quantifiable into dollars, for conceptual and practical reasons. Without a substantially greater research case on the characteristics and consequences of pathological and problem gambling, it is impossible to say with precision where the upper bound or midpoint of economic impact would lie.

Notes and Questions

1. *The costs of problem gambling.* As noted, the risk of increased problem and pathological gambling often is raised as the most serious social cost of legalized gambling. There seems little doubt that problem and pathological gambling carries with it both tangible economic costs and less tangible "human burdens," as Gerstein et al. put it. Problem and pathological gambling certainly is not alone in terms of human behavior that creates costs to society:

> The annual cost estimate for pathological and problem gambling in 1998 of $5 billion compares with 1995 estimates for drug abuse of $110 billion and alcohol abuse of $166.5 billion. Motor vehicle crashes in 1992 cost $71 billion. The most recent estimates for other major health problems such as diabetes [$92 billion], stroke [$30 billion], and heart disease [$125 billion], have been compiled and compared by the National Institutes of Health (1997). The current economic impact of problem and pathological gambling, in terms of population or cost per prevalent case, appears smaller than the impacts of such lethal competitors as alcohol abuse and heart disease.

Gerstein et al., at 53. How should the relative costs of various public health problems be weighed by policymakers? Can the social costs of problem and pathological gambling be countered by social benefits, such as increased employment or reduced reliance on public entitlements?

For more on the costs of problem and pathological gambling, see Henry R. Lesieur, *Costs and Treatment of Pathological Gambling*, 556 ANNALS AM. ACAD. POL. & SOC. SCI. 153 (1998); RACHEL A. VOLBERG, WHEN THE CHIPS ARE DOWN: PROBLEM GAMBLING IN AMERICA (2001).

Jonathan B. Taylor, Matthew B. Krepps, & Patrick Wang
The National Evidence on the Socioeconomic Impacts of American Indian Gaming on Non-Indian Communities
16–29 (2000)

Clearly, Indian gaming is a tool tribes can use to improve their own fortunes. The evidence suggests that tribes have understood this possibility and may have embraced it, particularly those most in need of economic development. Among the 75 largest tribes in the country, 17 of the poorest 20 opened casinos. Moreover, tribes that eventually compacted for casino gaming by 1996 reported 24% *higher* unemployment at the time of IGRA's passage (1988) than those that did not eventually develop casinos. By 1995, these gaming tribes reported 12% *lower* unemployment rates than their non-compacting counterparts. Thus, the tribes that adopted gaming started the period 1988–1995 with higher unemployment and finished the period with lower unemployment than their peers. More generally, the reservations with casinos saw employment, income, and government revenues rise substantially since the advent of casino gaming.

A more open question concerns the "Surrounding Community" effects[;] i.e., whether Indian gaming's cannibalization and substitution effects make Pyrrhic victories for non-Indian communities of the destination, multiplier, and intensity effects.

To capture the Indian effects and to distinguish between large and small markets, we elaborate upon Gerstein et al. by adding two variables to account for the proximity of a tribal casino and a large casino market. The results indicate a pattern of distinguishable Indian casino effects consistent with the notion that destination effects more than offset substitution and cannibalization effects for off-reservation communities outside of large market areas. While estimated casino spending in communities witnessing the introduction of an Indian casino is statistically indistinguishable from casino spending in communities witnessing non-Indian casino introductions, the income effects are quite different. [Our model] indicates that a discernible 3% increase in total income ($485 per capita) and a 5% increase in net earnings ($549 per capita) are visited upon non-Indian communities when an Indian casino is introduced nearby.

These increases in total income and total net earnings come despite declines in income associated with income maintenance programs and from transfer payments. Casinos generally could be expected to have a 6% decrease in income from income maintenance programs, whereas Indian casinos precipitate a more profound 32% decline.

Not only do Indian casinos help the poorer of the tribes move ahead vis-à-vis their counterparts with respect to employment, but also this evidence indicates Indian casinos have accomplished the same for proximate non-Indian communities with respect to income maintenance programs.

While net earnings are positively affected by the introduction of an Indian casino, the picture is not consistently positive through the categories of income we examined. On the one hand, earnings in the recreation sector rise by 55% for casinos generally; however, Indian casinos appear to precipitate only a net increase of 17%. On the other hand, local government earnings decline by 4% for casinos generally; however, they rise by 6% in communities where proximate Indian casinos are introduced.

On the social side, we find discernible effects in the crime categories of motor vehicle theft and robbery. Gerstein et al. found no statistically significant results for any crime variables, yet our [model] indicates communities witnessing the introduction of proximate Indian casino experience a substantial net decline in auto theft and robbery. We found no statistically discernible effects for larcenies, burglaries, assaults, and the crime indexes.

The data on auto theft and robberies are consistent with the hypothesis that casino introductions in depressed regions would reduce the existing propensity to commit crime more than introducing new levels of crime. Nonetheless, the silence of our results on the other dimensions of crime and on infant mortality underscores the difficulty of picking up statistically discernible social effects. As Gerstein et al. point out, the net effects could be there but too small to register in the "wash of the statistics" or self-cancelled by virtue of offsetting costly and beneficial consequences.

The overall picture indicates Indian casinos in more rural and poorer markets have a net positive impact on the surrounding communities. Gross incomes rise and certain crime rates fall when Indian casinos are introduced near non-Indian communities. As a result, the income gap between communities that witnessed a non-Indian casino introduction and those that saw a proximate Indian casinos introduction closed. In addition, the average per capita income derived from income maintenance programs in communities proximate to Indian casinos (outside of large market areas) dropped from above comparable community averages to below. Moreover, no detectable increase in social pathology is visible in, e.g., infant mortality and crime increases. Thus, this evidence would tend to allay the policy concern that, while Indian gaming may be a boon to tribes, it could come at the expense of the surrounding communities. Indeed, it suggests exactly the opposite, i.e., that Indian gaming is not only a development tool that poorer-than-average tribes have used to pull ahead in their cohort, it is a tool of development by which tribes have improved the economic lot of their non-Indian neighbors as well.

Notes and Questions

1. Comparing results. Taylor, Krepps, and Wang summarized the results of Gerstein et al.'s study of the effects of casino proximity as follows:

They find no statistically significant impact of casinos on such social cost outcomes as bankruptcy filings, crime, and infant mortality. As they note, there is a marked reduction in unemployment and a reduction in personal income derived from income maintenance, unemployment insurance, and other transfer programs. Interestingly, retail trade employment, local government employment, and private earnings in the restaurant and bar sector decline, yet total income is statistically unchanged by a casino introduction. Gains are made in construction employment and earnings and in hotel/lodging and recreation/amusement earnings. Gerstein et al. conclude: "The net picture in the economic ... data is on the positive side, but not in an overwhelming way. There appears to be more of a shift in the types and locations of work, and perhaps the overall number of workers, than a rise in per capita earnings."

Using the same dataset but modeling the specific impacts of Indian casinos on surrounding communities, Taylor, Krepps, and Wang compared their results with those of Gerstein et al.:

> While we concur generally, we also note that while total income is statistically unchanged by casinos, the reductions in unemployment and welfare income lend some credence to the widely held notion that casinos are a useful economic development strategy for reducing poverty. These effects are even more pronounced for the communities that witness the introduction of an Indian casino.

Taylor, Krepps, & Wang, at 13–14.

Does it surprise you that tribal casinos might have a greater net positive impact on unemployment and welfare income rates than do commercial casinos? Does it make sense that this would occur on the reservation as well as in surrounding non-tribal communities?

National Gambling Impact Study Commission Final Report
6-6 to 6-16 (1999)

The poor economic conditions in Indian country have contributed to the same extensive social ills generated in other impoverished communities including high crime rates, child abuse, illiteracy, poor nutrition, and poor health care access.

But with revenues from gambling operations, many tribes have begun to take unprecedented steps to begin to address the economic as well as social problems on their own. For example, through gambling tribes have been able to provide employment to their members and other residents where the federal policies failed to create work. This has resulted in dramatic drops in the extraordinarily high unemployment rates in many, though not all, communities in Indian country and a reduction in welfare rolls and other governmental services for the unemployed.

Tribes also use gambling revenues to support tribal governmental services including the tribal courts, law enforcement, fire protection, water, sewer, solid waste, roads, environmental health, land-use planning and building inspection services, and natural resource management. They also use gambling revenues to establish and enhance social welfare programs in the areas of education, housing, substance abuse, suicide prevention, child protection, burial expenses, youth recreation, and more. Tribes have allocated gambling funds to support the establishment of other economic ventures that will diversify and strengthen the reservation economies. Gambling revenues are also used to support tribal language, history, and cultural programs. All of these programs have historically suffered from significant neglect and underfunding by the federal government. Although the problems these programs are aimed at reducing continue to plague Indian communities at significant levels, gambling has provided many tribes with the means to begin addressing them. There was no evidence presented to the Commission suggesting any viable approach to economic development across the broad spectrum of Indian country, in the absence of gambling.

Only a limited number of independent studies exist regarding the economic and social impact of Indian gambling. Some have found a mixture of positive and negative results of the impact of gambling on reservations, whereas others have found a positive economic impact for the tribal governments, its members and the surrounding communities. This is an area greatly in need of further research. However, it is clear that the revenues from Indian gambling have had a significant—and generally positive—impact on a number of reservations.

According to the Chairman of the National Indian Gaming Commission, many tribes have used their revenues "to build schools, fund social services, provide college scholarships, build roads, provide new sewer and water systems, and provide for adequate housing for tribal members."

Many tribes are providing more basic services. One example is the Prairie Island Indian Community. Their representative testified before the Commission's Subcommittee on Indian Gambling that:

> We no longer rely on government funding to pay for the basics. We have used gaming proceeds to build better homes for our members, construct a community center and an administration building, develop a waste water treatment facility and build safer roads. We are also able to provide our members with excellent health care benefits and quality education choices.... We are currently working with the [Mayo Clinic] on a diabetic study of Native Americans. We can provide chemical dependency treatment to any tribal member who needs assistance. And our education assistance program allows tribal members to choose whatever job training, college, or university they wish to attend.

A representative of the Viejas Band of Kumeyaay Indians also testified that:

> Our gaming revenues provide such government services as police, fire, and ambulance to our reservation, neighbors and casino. Earnings from gaming have paved roads, provided electricity, sewage lines, clean water storage, recycling, trash disposal, natural habitat replacement, and watershed and other environmental improvements to our lands.

Other tribal governments report the development of sewage management projects, energy assistance, housing, job training, conservation, education, native language programs, and many other services that previously were absent or poorly funded before the introduction of gambling. There also has been an emphasis by many tribes on using gambling revenues for preserving cultural practices and strengthening tribal bonds.

For some, Indian gambling provides substantial new revenue to the tribal government. For others, Indian gambling has provided little or no net revenue to the tribal government, but has provided jobs for tribal members.

Although the impact varies greatly, tribal gambling has significantly decreased the rates of unemployment for some tribes. For example, the Subcommittee received testimony that stated that, for the Mille Lacs Band of Ojibwes in Minnesota, unemployment has decreased from about 60 percent in 1991 to almost zero at present. For the Oneida Tribe of Wisconsin, the unemployment rate dropped from nearly 70 percent to less than 5 percent after their casino opened. Representatives from the Gila River Indian Community testified that unemployment on their reservation has decreased from 40 percent to 11 percent since the introduction of gambling. The Coeur d'Alene Tribe reported a decrease in the unemployment rate from 55 percent to 22 percent. A number of other tribes have reported similar results.

The Subcommittee also heard much testimony about the pride, optimism, hope and opportunity that has accompanied the revenues and programs generated by Indian gambling facilities. As one tribal representative stated:

> Gaming has provided a new sense of hope for the future among a Nation that previously felt too much despair and powerlessness as a result of our long term poverty ... and a renewed interest in the past. The economic development generated by gaming has raised our spirits and drawn us close together.

* * *

As the quote that closes the above excerpt suggests, while job creation and poverty reduction are highly desired outcomes of tribal economic development, there is more to it than that. Read the following discussions of tribal economic development with an eye toward the goals and strategies that underlie tribes' efforts to leverage gaming into more fully diversified economies and a richer quality of life for tribal members.

D. Indian Gaming and Reservation Economic Development

Robert L. Gips
Current Trends in Tribal Economic Development
37 New Eng. L. Rev. 517 (2003)

In 1983, having finished law school and a clerkship, I joined two lawyers who had just completed Mashantucket Pequot Indian Land Claims Settlement Act, which awarded $900,000 to the Mashantucket Pequot Tribe. I was assigned to represent the Mashantucket Pequot Tribe, and I have continued to do so since 1983. It has been an interesting vantage point from which to participate in and watch the course of tribal economic development.

Starting from 1983 and looking forward to the present, what has happened in Indian economic development is quite remarkable. What little development was occurring on reservations in the early 1980s primarily involved mining or energy production on reservations with natural resources, like coal, gas, or uranium. Aside from a few scattered businesses designed to take advantage of minority preference provisions, there was little other significant economic development occurring anywhere in Indian country.

One reason for this lack of economic development was access to capital, which was a major problem. Each time tribes attempted to borrow money, they faced numerous problems, as multiple legal issues needed to be resolved. These legal issues included questions about the ability of tribes to waive sovereign immunity, the validity of tribal consent to state court jurisdiction, questions about the exhaustion of tribal court remedies, and uncertainty concerning the enforceability of security agreements involving cash and personal property collateral. Further compounding these problems was a third-party lack of understanding of tribal governments, tribal decision-making, and tribal courts. In addition, a lack of tribal experience and sophistication in dealing with capital markets and businesses also impacted a tribe's ability to borrow the needed funds. As a result, almost no lending occurred in Indian country.

Loans, when they did occur, generally took one of two forms—they were either guaranteed by the federal government or fully cash collateralized by the tribe itself. A cash collateralized loan, however, was not really a loan. Rather, it was a mechanism whereby banks re-loaned to tribes the tribes' own money. Further, the loan guarantee program for Indian tribes was, and remains today, woefully inadequate in scope. The entire Bureau of Indian Affairs (BIA) loan guarantee program for Indian tribes in the mid-eighties was only about $60 million, and the program's funding is not, I believe, much greater than that today. With over 500 tribes, this amount obviously is not going to leverage significant capital or catalyze significant economic development in Indian country.

When we first attempted to finance the Mashantucket Pequot Tribe's bingo hall in 1985, we needed a little over $4 million. Jim Sappier was the Governor of the Penobscot Nation, which had agreed to manage the facility for the Mashantucket Pequots. The Penobscots were able to put approximately $700,000 toward the venture, and we were able to win a federal economic development grant for $300,000. However, even with a million dollars of equity, not a single bank would loan the tribe the remainder of the money. Fortunately, the firm I worked with, Tribal Assets Management, eventually located one bank that was willing to finance the bingo hall with a federal loan guarantee. I believe this transaction was the first bank-financed Indian gaming facility in the country. Due to this financing, the bingo hall was built and, since then, has performed extremely well.

Despite this success, in the early 1990s, when we decided to create and open Foxwoods and Tribal Assets Management approached approximately thirty-five lenders in this country and around the world, not a single bank or institutional investor would finance the project. For that reason we ended up turning to private lenders from Malaysia, who believed in what we were trying to do and were willing to take risks that others perceived to be insurmountable. The initial Foxwoods financing was about $60 million—an amount that would have subsumed almost the entire Indian loan guarantee budget for the year, had it been guaranteed—and this loan was the largest Indian gaming financing that had occurred up until that point.

Fortunately, Foxwoods was an immediate success and became the most profitable gaming facility—Indian or non-Indian—in the world. The facility's success helped to pave the way for the dramatic change in the way lenders and developers perceived Indian country gaming projects. The Mashantucket Pequot Tribal Nation now issues investment-grade bonds and has raised over one billion dollars through multiple financings. More importantly, the Tribe's success has been duplicated by other tribes around the country, and the revenues created by successful tribal gaming facilities are fueling the potential for a renaissance in tribal economic development.

The capital access problems faced by Indian country in the 1980s have been solved and good projects in Indian country generally—though not always—can be financed today. Yet putting together good projects and promoting successful tribal economic development continues to be challenging. The vexing problems all new businesses face are only amplified on Indian reservations. Not only is capital needed, but experienced entrepreneurs and managers, trained laborers, and sound business plans are essential as well. Having access to debt markets does not mean that one has equity to put into projects, and many tribes, particularly those without gaming revenues, lack equity capital. Experienced tribal entrepreneurs and managers are still in short supply and often have more attractive job opportunities outside of Indian country.

In addition, tribes are governments, and governments generally have problems running businesses. Similar to other governments that run businesses, tribes must address political interference with business decision-making and micromanagement by tribal governing bodies. The governmental need for funds often means that the surplus created by a prof-

itable tribal business is stripped off for distribution to members or governmental programs rather than reinvested, as would happen in other businesses. Additionally, governmental employee work and incentive structures are often not the same as those required
in a competitive business. Finally, governmental decision-making timetables are often
much slower and more protracted than the business world tolerates.

However, these are solvable problems. Tribes are learning to separate their business
entities from their political entities and are becoming more successful at doing so. Lack
of capital and experienced management also may be solved through joint ventures and
management agreements. Yet, in such arrangements, tribes must overcome their suspicion that they will not be treated fairly—though this is a well-grounded suspicion stemming from Indian country's unfortunate historical experience with hustlers and shills
promoting self-serving and flawed projects.

One very positive trend is an increase in tribal focus on areas of tribal strategic advantage. Gaming is a prime example of this; tribes have a strategic advantage in gaming
due to the preemption of state regulatory laws in that field. This often leads to a relative
tribal monopoly; that is, at least for as long as states do not legalize gaming generally.

[Another] example of this is a resurgence of energy deals on tribal lands. Companies
are interested in working with tribes because while federal regulatory laws are still applicable, cumbersome and time-consuming state regulatory laws and permitting schemes
are preempted, and tribes are adopting streamlined tribal permitting systems.

Similarly, in real estate development, where local zoning laws are inapplicable, tribes
can set up their own zoning laws, and, since local property taxes are preempted, this gives
tribes a competitive advantage. There is an increasing interest in tribal real estate and
commercial development, often ancillary to casino facilities. If you go into Mohegan Sun,
for example, you will see leased space, just like in a mall.

Another area where tribes are making tremendous strides is through the adoption of
tribal laws relating to commercial and economic development activity. For example, the
Mashantucket Pequot Tribal Nation has adopted its own workers' compensation system,
which has saved the Tribe money and has preempted the state workers' compensation
system. Tribes also are adopting their own health, safety, and environmental laws, and we
are seeing numerous tribes adopting uniform commercial codes and secured transaction
codes. Tribes are dealing with issues that concern lenders, such as the fact that absent a
provision in a tribal constitution, the Fifth Amendment impairment of contracts clause
will not apply to tribes. Some tribes are addressing this problem through constitutional
reforms.

Similarly, tribes are moving to create their own business and corporation laws. Tribes
face complicated questions when considering whether to operate a business under a corporate structure, as an arm of the tribal government, or as a tribal authority; but increasingly tribes are developing the infrastructure to create corporate structures under
tribal regulatory regimes. For example, outside of Indian country, limited liability companies are probably the most common structure for business formation today. The key
advantages offered by limited liability companies—limited liability along with an absence of corporate level taxation—are equally attractive to tribally-owned businesses,
and in certain instances it is advantageous for a tribe to create a limited liability company
formed under tribal law rather than state law. As a result, we are working with tribes that
are creating their own limited liability company codes. Similarly, tribes are instituting
their own taxes, which can be an important factor in balancing test cases concerning the
preemption of state taxes.

Another encouraging trend involves inter-tribal agreements to promote economic development. One of the projects that I have been involved with, through representation of the Mashantucket Pequot Tribal Nation, has been the creation over the past several years of the Native American National Bank. The formation of this bank involves twelve tribes from around the country, each putting up a million dollars in capital to create a bank designed to serve Indian country.

[While] problems remain, and successful economic development remains difficult to achieve, a tremendous amount of exciting activity is occurring, and I believe we are on the cusp of a renaissance in economic activity in Indian country.

Notes and Questions

1.   *Critiquing the Pequots.* In light of Gips' account, it is interesting to note that the Mashantucket Pequots have been roundly criticized for a host of issues, including being "inauthentic" Indians who, in the eyes of some, have capitalized on federal recognition to become absurdly wealthy. *See, e.g.,* Jeff Benedict, Without Reservation: The Making of America's Most Powerful Indian Tribe and Foxwoods, the World's Largest Casino (2000); Brett D. Fromson, Hitting the Jackpot: The Inside Story of the Richest Indian Tribe in History (2003); *see also* Light & Rand, Indian Gaming and Tribal Sovereignty, at 108–10 (describing and assessing various critiques). Gips referenced the fact that the Pequots obtained some $58 million in venture capital and a $175 million line of credit from Malaysian construction magnate Lim Goh Tong to construct the Foxwoods Resort and Casino. This, too, has been critiqued on the basis of Tong's foreign status, as well as for the Pequots "being taken advantage of" by agreeing to pay Tong 10 percent of the casino's adjusted gross income until 2016. Gips, by contrast, indicated the tribe at the time had virtually no other options to obtain the necessary capital. Indian gaming was relatively new (and was unprecedented in Connecticut), and other investors were unwilling to assume the risk in financing what few knew would become one of the most lucrative casinos in the world. The tribe, therefore, presumably entered into its contract with Tong with eyes wide open.

2.   *Competitive advantage.* Gips discussed areas in which tribes may create a competitive advantage for business by adopting a less burdensome regulatory scheme than exists under state law, either for tribally owned businesses (e.g., a tribal ordinance allowing the tribe to operate high-stakes bingo where state law limits bingo jackpots) or to attract private business (e.g., a streamlined energy permit process under tribal law where the state permit process may be more time-consuming). A classic example is tribal sale of cigarettes at a lower price than the state cigarette tax would require. States, too, pass laws meant to attract business; in 1980, for example, South Dakota eliminated its strict usury laws to entice Citibank's credit card division to relocate from New York to South Dakota. Just as South Dakota took advantage of its governmental authority to create a business-friendly regulatory environment, the competitive advantages described by Gips rely on tribal sovereignty. What are the legal and political advantages and disadvantages to such strategies? (A short time after South Dakota changed its usury laws, a handful of other states followed suit, including Delaware. Said former South Dakota governor Bill Janklow, "[W]e thought we were going to get them all. Chase, Manufacturer's Hanover, Chemical—they all went to Delaware. They were coming here. The tragedy to me is that if Delaware would have waited one year [before changing its usury laws], we would have had 20,000 more jobs in this state today." *See* Robin Stein, *The Ascendancy of the Credit Card Industry* (Nov. 23, 2004), available at http://www.pbs.org/wgbh/pages/frontline/shows/ credit/more/rise.html.)

Miriam Jorgensen & Jonathan B. Taylor
What Determines Indian Economic Success?
Evidence from Tribal and Individual Indian Enterprises
4–12 (2000)

Essentially, poverty in Indian Country is a political problem—not an economic one. There has been a substantial supply of labor in Indian Country for decades, yet scores of economic development plans have been unable to tap that supply on a sustained basis and thereby improve the fortunes of Indian households. Likewise, tribes possessing natural or capital resources have not uniformly led the vanguard of development. While a lack of resources can hamper tribes, and certain systemic features of Indian Country confound investment (for example, the difficulty of collateralizing trust lands), the real deficiency in Indian Country is a shortage of safe havens for capital. The ability to create these safe havens is largely a matter of tribal political and institutional effectiveness.

The research of the [Harvard Project on American Indian Economic Development] repeatedly uncovers the long-term importance of profitability as a goal for tribal enterprises. While tribal governments often view employment as the immediate problem to solve, Project research shows that managing tribal enterprises primarily as job engines is a recipe for on-going subsidization or for failure. Long-term enterprise health depends on profitability: if an enterprise is minding its profitability, then employment will take care of itself.

Having downplayed the importance of employment as a measure of success, we acknowledge that employment is nonetheless one of the ultimate goals of both federal policy and tribal economic development activity. Indeed, consultation with tribal leaders and Indian entrepreneurs confirmed to [National Congress of American Indians] researchers that employment ought to be a key ingredient in any evaluation of Indian enterprise success. Thus, we examine both profitability *and* employment trend.

Before identifying the determinants of success, it is important to take account of variation in the data that results from factors beyond tribal control. This is variation that affects a firm's success, but cannot reasonably be a policy variable with which tribes could hope to influence success. For example, a firm's location may be strongly correlated with the success measure used here, but "relocate" is not useful advice to an enterprise manager committed or required to stay on or near a particular reservation. Our question should be, *given* an enterprise's location, what other factors affect its success?

Our analysis yielded three strong findings: (1) Firms with outstanding technical assistance (TA) needs tend to perform more poorly; (2) Firms with non-politicized boards of directors tend to perform better; and (3) Firms that were tribally owned tend to perform more poorly.

The fact that many Indian-owned enterprises appear to have remaining needs for technical assistance—despite the fact that many of them *do* receive TA—indicates that available assistance fails to meet these needs. Because Indian enterprises in the sample report unmet technical assistance needs in high correlation with diminished enterprise success, the real need may be for linked financial and managerial capital investments—that is, targeted, firm-specific TA, arranged in conjunction with capital investment. In fact, in the international arena, development institutions are already making this course correction. They are turning away from "aid capital" (i.e., foreign aid) and toward the development of private capital markets, particularly venture capital. The advantage of such markets is that they result in an alignment of investors' and firm managers' incentives—venture capitalists find it in their best interest to do all they can to facilitate appropriate knowledge transfers, minimize capital risk, and increase returns from start-up enterprises. Thus, the data appear to indicate that policy toward Indian enterprises ought to mimic venture capital models in at least one way—the combination of financial investment with knowledge transfer. Nonetheless, if we take the federal "aid capital" as a given, the survey data indicate that, to ensure a good return on investment, tribal enterprises also must have adequate access to technical and managerial skill development resources.

Additionally, the results underscore the importance of enterprise and tribal institutions. In our statistical tests, enterprises with corporate boards did not perform markedly differently than enterprises without corporate boards. Instead, it was the existence of a *non-politicized* board that mattered to success. A board that serves as a buffer between the (inherently) political tasks of setting tribal direction and strategy and the more specialized and technical tasks of managing enterprises contributes to success. This result from the statistical data is congruent with the results from NCAI's case studies, which indicate that keeping political actors and their constituents' immediate concerns out of business decisions is beneficial to enterprise health.

Also of note, tribal ownership of enterprises is correlated with reduced enterprise success, even after accounting for the independence of boards. As discussed above, tribally owned enterprises face competing pressures (as do all government-owned enterprises): the pressure to raise profits for the community (that is, to be accountable to shareholders) and the pressure to meet other community needs such as employment training (that is, to provide benefits to constituents). These dual pressures and the always-present possibility that elected leaders can interfere in the day-to-day running of businesses in the name of constituent service place an extra burden on tribally owned enterprises. Thus, while independent boards may provide an increase in profitability, our data indicate there is an additional premium on good institutions of government where tribally owned enterprises are concerned.

Notes and Questions

1.   *"Keys" to tribal economic development.* Drawing on prior work of the Harvard Project, Jorgensen and Taylor concluded that there are three "keys" to successful tribal economic development. The first is that "sovereignty matters," meaning that tribes should exercise their power of self-determination in adopting economic development strategies. "Because tribes bear the consequences of their governments' decision-making, whereas the Bureau of Indian Affairs, non-tribal developers, state governments, and other outsiders do not, tribes that make their own development decisions do better." The second is that "culture matters," meaning that tribes should tailor economic development strategies to their unique cultures and norms. "Not only does [Indian] culture itself provide important institutional resources, but so does a congruence between the institutions of government and the views of the governed about what *appropriate* government is also matters to success. Cultural norms and resources support, complement, and sometimes even serve as appropriate institutions of government." The third key is that "institutions matter," meaning that successful economic development requires strong and well functioning tribal government institutions. "[S]uccessful tribal governments…. settle disputes fairly, separate the functions of elected representation and business management, and successfully implement tribal policies that advance tribal strategic goals." Jorgensen & Taylor, at 3–4. How do each of these "keys" relate to successful Indian gaming operations?

2.   Variables influencing the success of a tribal casino. Do the variables Jorgensen and Taylor identified that influence the success of a tribal enterprise (technical assistance, non-politicized boards of directors, and tribal ownership) apply in the context of tribally owned gaming facilities? Given these findings, what specific advice would you give to a tribe that is pursing a casino development opportunity?

Robert J. Miller
Economic Development in Indian Country: Will Capitalism or Socialism Succeed?
80 Or. L. Rev. 757 (2001)

Economic development in Indian country has received considerable attention in the last few decades, and for very good reason. American Indians suffer from the highest rates of poverty, unemployment and substandard housing of any group in the United States. The basic services and infrastructure that Americans take for granted are absent on most reservations. Moreover, American Indians own private businesses at a much lower rate per capita and the businesses they own produce less income on average than all other racial groups.

Attempts to address these economic problems, however, have largely focused on tribal governments. The majority of the public and private efforts to create and sustain economic development on Indian reservations have dealt with tribal governments funding, starting, and operating business activities. Today, Indian tribes organize, fund, and, in many instances, operate or direct the day-to-day affairs of many of the businesses and the majority of the economic activity in Indian country. This situation is a result of, or an "accident" caused by, federal control over Indians and Indian tribes, federal funding of tribal operations, and over two hundred years of Federal Indian law and policy. It has resulted to a large degree in the formation of what looks to the untrained eye to be socialistic economies in Indian country because the federal and tribal governments control most of the economic activity and jobs.

In contrast, the United States economy is based on the principle of trying to keep government out of private business and free enterprise, and allegedly of allowing the nation's economy to develop and grow on its own. The government concentrates on fostering an economy where private investors and entrepreneurs pursue their own property interests and profit motives by operating private businesses. This theory has worked to the point that the American economy is dominated by small privately owned businesses. This form of capitalism allows individual economic self-interest and initiative to fuel the American economy. In Indian country, however, the opposite paradigm prevails because federal policy has allowed and actively encouraged tribes to organize and operate businesses. The results reveal that this policy is not succeeding in developing strong and diverse economies on Indian reservations. In fact, the opposite has occurred because tribally operated or controlled businesses fail regularly or function poorly. In addition, as pointed out above, poverty is still the norm on most reservations and the economic condition of Indian people is the worst of any ethnic or racial group in America. Far more important than the abstract failure of economic policies and programs is that reservation economies and Indian people cannot afford lost economic opportunities. Reservation populations desperately need economic development, jobs and diverse economies. However, reservations have not prospered because the federal policy of assisting and encouraging tribes to control and operate the majority of the economic activity in Indian country has been a failure.

The potential for developing the economy and private business sector on Indian reservations is almost unlimited. Regrettably, that is because the economic conditions on most reservations are so poor and Indians as a group place last in the United States in the number of privately owned businesses and business income per capita. The good news, however, is the potential for growth which is demonstrated by the encouraging increase in individual Indian ownership of private businesses in the last three decades. The number of Indian-owned private businesses on and off reservations has grown from 3,000 in 1969 to 13,000 in 1982, which generated about $5 million in revenues, to 197,300 in 1997, which generated more than $34 billion in revenues. Even after this improvement, though, Indians still rank last in per capita business ownership. Thus, there continues to be a great opportunity for enormous growth in the number of Indian-owned businesses. Indians, their families, reservations and tribal governments will all benefit from this increased economic activity.

Indian reservations need an active small business environment so that the consumption that reservation Indians engage in will be done on reservations with Indian businesses and not miles away at the nearest non-Indian town. In the United States, it is considered desirable for money to circulate up to five to seven times in a local economy before it spins out of the area. However, very few, if any, Indian tribes in the United States have fully integrated economies in which reservation residents can be employed, cash checks, and spend money for necessities and luxuries all on the reservation. Thus, this spending occurs off reservations. This loss or "leakage" of reservation residents' income and the economic activity and benefits it represents occurs because of the absence of private small businesses on reservations where people can spend their money on goods and services. On most reservations there are, for example, no movie theaters, motels, video stores, larger grocery stores, clothing stores, restaurants, or even bank branches where residents can cash their checks. Consequently, on the vast majority of the more than three hundred Indian reservations in the United States, reservation residents have to travel to off-reservation, non-Indian cities to cash their checks and spend their money. This leads to the loss of an enormous amount of economic activity and employment which should occur in Indian country.

The solution to this problem seems to be for tribal and federal governments to encourage individuals and corporate entities to develop and operate businesses on reservations so that money can be spent and circulated between reservation consumers, businesses, and employees. This will increase the standard of living for all residents, create more economic activity by circulating dollars around the reservation, and give reservation Indians the option to participate in a capitalist economy to the extent they desire.

A diversified economy of small and large tribal and private businesses is more recession proof and will give needed economic stability to reservations. Significantly, a very positive social and cultural benefit has already begun for tribes where economic activity is increasing and jobs are available on reservation: tribal members are moving back to their reservations. An increasing population and the return of more families and family members will be a major boost for reservation societies and cultures.

Tribal governments will also benefit economically from increasing sources of taxation if reservation economies grow. In general, tribes lack adequate funding to operate their services and to develop needed infrastructure. Few tribes have access to substantial sources of taxation because of a lack of economic activity. Thus, a wider range of private businesses functioning on reservations would give tribes a broader tax base to utilize for funding social and cultural programs.

Increased economic activity on reservations will also have a beneficial effect on many tribal social issues. Increased income and living standards for Indian families should ameliorate some of the social problems affecting reservation populations. Tribes would thus be faced with fewer welfare and criminal problems if there were more jobs and income on reservations. In addition, most tribes have already been using their increased income from tribal casinos and businesses to build infrastructure such as roads, health clinics, day care centers, and housing, which helps social and cultural aspects of tribal life. Tribes could expand these types of programs by accessing an improved tax base if diversified tribal economies are created.

Tribal governments, like all governments, will also benefit from increasing economic activity as they gain increased spending power, governmental authority and the ability to protect their sovereign rights. Tribes with money to invest and to affect public policy are becoming influential players on the American economic and political scene. Successful and active reservation economies will also add to tribal and Indian political and social clout as tribal and reservation based businesses hire non-Indian employees. As tribes and private Indian businesses hire even more non-Indians and have an ever greater impact on county and state economies, tribal influence in the political arena will increase and tribes and Indians will be better able to manage their destinies. Significantly, tribes have also used improved economic situations to increase or consolidate reservation land holdings. This has a very beneficial political, social and cultural value to tribes and their citizens.

Federal and state governments also have much to gain from increased economic activity by individual Indians on and off reservations, and from a reduction in poverty levels and the resulting social issues. The federal government will benefit by collecting income taxes on increased economic activity by Indians on reservations and off, and states will receive increased income and sales taxes to the extent Indians operate businesses off reservation and perhaps also for some on-reservation activity. The federal and state governments already benefit significantly from the spillover effect of different aspects of economic activity in Indian country. That is because reservation activities such as tourism and gaming have benefited states as tourists travel to visit Indian country or tribal casinos, and the federal government has received increased tax revenues and seen social conditions improve. The United States and the individual states have also benefited from major increases in non-Indian employment in tribal businesses because the majority of employees at most tribal casinos are non-Indians, and these governments could expect to see increased private business ownership by individual Indians resulting in more employment of Indians and non-Indians, thus lowering the unemployment rates. States will also benefit from an increase in the number of Indian-owned private businesses because it has been estimated that states have lost hundreds of millions of dollars in economic activity due to the underrepresentation and underproduction of Indian private business owners.

The majority of commentators agree that tribal economies need certain specific items to grow to their potential. In general, the recommendations are: (1) tribes need to develop sources of financial capital to help both tribes and individual Indians to start new businesses; (2) tribes need to develop the human capital of their workforce by education, work experience, motivation and training; (3) tribes need to free themselves of federal bureaucratic involvement; and (4) reservation land ownership problems from the Allotment Era which negatively affect economic growth must be addressed. A recent study conducted with tribal chairs of one-third of American tribes revealed their opinions of the top five obstacles to tribal economic development: (1) lack of capital; (2) lack of economic resources and the ability to obtain capital; (3) lack of natural resources; (4) lack of trained management; and (5) lack of trained personnel.

Indian people have little exposure to successful entrepreneur role models and private business owners since Indians have such a low incidence of business ownership. Thus, most Indians do not have models from which they can learn or be inspired and they rarely even consider the possibility of owning their own business. Tribes can take steps to remedy this problem. Most tribes have economic development departments which could establish or participate in mentoring and training programs to develop entrepreneurs and to help Indians start new businesses. Various private organizations already provide business development training for individual Indians and Indians can also access training programs from the U.S. Small Business Administration (SBA).

Tribally operated businesses and governmental programs also play an important role in being the training ground for tribal members to gain experience as employees and to learn work habits and management skills. In addition, tribes have the opportunity to direct all the tribal business they can to privately owned Indian businesses to assist them to get started and to be successful.

Besides training and education issues, it is universally accepted that one of the main reasons for the very low rate of private business ownership among Indians is the lack of capital. Most private non-Indian businesses are started with family money, oftentimes accumulated over several generations, by borrowing money through normal credit avenues or by using home equity. Indians as a group, however, have very little access to these three prime ways of raising funds to start a new business. Due to the history of poverty in Indian country, most Indians lack access to family money and rarely have built up home equity due to the absence of mortgage home ownership in Indian country and a nearly non-existent appreciating private housing market. In addition, Indians have little access to the usual credit channels. Consequently, Indians need access to seed money, which could be provided by tribal, private, state, and federal loan funds, to help alleviate this funding problem for starting new privately owned businesses. There are a few options already available to Indians through tribes, non-profit organizations and some banks for microloans of start-up money. However, tribes and other governments need to work diligently to address this problem because it seriously hampers the creation of new Indian-owned private businesses.

Tribal governments have an extremely important role to play in reservation economic activity and in the development of a capitalist private business sector. By no means does this Article discount the importance of tribes in developing and assisting economic activity and in increasing private business ownership by Indians on reservations. In fact, there are no purely capitalist economies in the world because every government takes some role in managing their economy and trying to see that businesses are created and flourish. Moreover, governments act as the watchdog to protect the public interest, keep their economy in balance, and see that fair and true competition continues. All governments also play a crucial part in a healthy economic environment by enacting laws and regulations, maintaining law and order, enforcing contracts, defining property rights, and establishing court systems and procedures that enforce economic rights. The stability provided by governments encourages people to work to secure commercial rights and to risk investments of their capital and effort. Tribal governments have this same important role on reservations.

As with all governments, tribes need to create a business-friendly political environment by supporting the creation and operation of private businesses on reservations. Businesses locate and are created where they can be profitable and where the laws and governmental regulations will be fairly and evenly applied. Tribes need to work on this aspect of attracting businesses to locate in Indian country and even to make reservation inhabitants feel confident that they will reap the benefits from their hard work if they start new businesses. Tribes can help improve the reservation as a business-friendly location by reviewing and adopting as necessary laws and regulatory codes that help businesses function and that protect business and property rights. Tribes also must insure that their court systems are impartial, free of political influence, and evenly and fairly protect business and personal property rights.

If Indian tribes are to break out of the cycle of poverty and the absence of business activity on reservations, tribes need to use every possible economic tool and all the options and resources at their disposal to develop diverse economies. Private business ownership for individual Indians, on and off reservations, capitalism if you will, is an idea whose time has come for modern day American Indians. Moreover, a private free market economy looks well suited to the history and cultures of most tribes; better in fact than does the "socialism" of tribal governments monopolizing and directing business activity in Indian country. The bottom line tells us that tribal governments, reservation inhabitants, and federal and state governments need to emphasize, encourage and support the creation and operation of privately owned free market businesses on reservations to increase the diversity of economic activity and employment available on reservations.

Notes and Questions

1. Capturing dollars. Professor Miller explained that dollars tend not to circulate and recirculate on the reservation; instead, they are externalized. This is because there typically are fewer on-reservation businesses at which to spend. Based on the analysis you have read throughout this Chapter, can tribal casinos help to "capture" these dollars? Suppose you are an economist who has been asked to explain to a lay audience how this phenomenon works. Now suppose you also have to convince non-tribal members who live off the reservation how, despite the fact that more dollars will be captured by expanded reservation economies, a tribal casino also would help non-tribal communities.

2. Economic diversification. Miller advocated for diversified tribal economies with specific focus on privately owned small businesses, a shift from the "socialism" of tribally owned businesses (as IGRA generally requires for Class II and Class III gaming enterprises). Professor Ansson and attorney Oravetz described the successful diversification of government-owned business ventures of the Mississippi Band of Choctaw Indians:

> Shortly after the nation created its industrial park in 1979, it landed a contract with General Motors to assemble automotive harness wires. Thereafter, the nation began landing one contract after another. Today, the nation operates a 42,000 square foot plant that assembles harness wires for General Motors and Ford, with annual sales in excess of $100 million; a 60,000 square foot plant that produces speakers for Ford, Chrysler, and McDonnell-Douglas, with annual sales close to $30 million; a plant that produces cables for Ford and Chrysler, and circuit boards and other electronic units for AT&T, Xerox, Westinghouse, and Navistar; a plant that assembles cards for American Greetings; and a 72,000 square foot printing press.
>
> In all, the tribe has an annual payroll of $105 million. Furthermore, it employs over 6,000 individuals, 3000 of whom are non-Indian, making it among the ten largest employers in the state of Mississippi. Finally, tribal unemployment, which 20 years ago stood at 75 percent, now stands at four percent.
>
> The tribe has used the revenues generated from their businesses to provide traditional government services to tribal members and to provide capital for new

tribal enterprises. The Choctaw tribal government has used the funds to provide numerous traditional government services to its members, including a court system; a fire department; a police force; a reservation-based school system; a gaming commission; a housing authority; a utility commission; an economic agency; and an integrated health care system which includes an accredited hospital, field clinic, nursing home and kidney dialysis center.

Richard J. Ansson & Ladine Oravetz, *Tribal Economic Development: What Challenges Lie Ahead for Tribal Nations as They Continue to Strive for Economic Diversity?*, 11 Kan. J.L. & Pub. Pol'y 441, 445–46 (2002). The Mississippi Band of Choctaw Indians also operates the Pearl River Resort, featuring the Silver Star and Golden Moon casinos, near Philadelphia, Mississippi.

As Ansson and Oravetz explained, gaming revenue can fund economic diversification. Many tribes have opened businesses related to gaming enterprises, such as gift shops, restaurants, hotels, golf courses, and gas stations. Others have leveraged gaming profits to diversify beyond a casino resort or other tourism-based ventures. The Oneida Nation of Wisconsin, for example, opened a Radisson hotel and conference center next to its Oneida Bingo and Casino in Green Bay, Wisconsin, and also leveraged gaming proceeds to invest in a wide array of enterprises:

> Oneida Nation Electronics, a joint venture with a Wisconsin corporation to manufacture printed circuit assemblies for a variety of customers and industries; ... Airadigm Communications, Inc., a company that is a personal communications service provider; ... a 32-acre retail park with stores such as Sam's Wholesale, Wal-Mart, and Festival Foods; a limited liability corporation to develop, hold, and oversee commercial properties for the tribe; a number of other businesses, including Oneida Printing, Oneida Nation Farms, Oneida Productions, and three self service gas stations; Baybank, a locally-owned, full service bank located on the Oneida Reservation; and the Oneida Small Business Development Center, which provides loans, counseling, training, and technical support for the creation of small businesses on tribal lands.

Id. at 448. The Oneida Nation and Forest County Potawatomi Community of Wisconsin, along with the San Manuel Band of Mission Indians and the Viejas Band of Kumeyaay Indians in California, are partners in Four Fires, LLC. Four Fires, in turn, partnered with Marriott to open the $43 million Marriot Residence Inn Capitol in Washington, D.C., near the Smithsonian's Museum of the American Indian. The Oneida Nation also is a major shareholder in the Native American Bank. Owned by a group of 26 tribal nations and corporations, the Bank holds some $85 million in assets and focuses on large business loans, agricultural operations, and community development. In 2002, the Oneida Nation entered into a ten-year partnership agreement with the Green Bay Packers, which includes the Nation's sponsorship of the "Oneida Nation Gate," a grand stairway entrance gate to the renovated Lambeau Field.

3.   *Waving a magic wand.* Echoing some of the recommendations made by Jorgensen and Taylor, Professor Miller suggested a wide range of individual and government-sponsored strategies to foster tribal economic development opportunities, including fostering business-friendly legal environments and developing a well-trained work force. *See also* Ansson & Oravetz. Suppose you were asked to recommend and justify three specific strategies that would have the greatest immediate or long-term impact on reservation quality of life, and your recommendations would be implemented tomorrow. Which would you choose, and why?

4. Gaming, economic development, and socioeconomic impacts. In 1990, just two years after IGRA's passage and less than two decades after the federal policy of tribal self-determination and self-sufficiency encouraged tribes to aggressively pursue economic development, American Indians living on reservations experienced extraordinarily high rates of poverty (per capita income was less than one-third of the U.S. average) and unemployment (three times the national average). The 2000 Census provided an opportunity to measure whether a decade of Indian gaming and other forms of economic development changed reservation life. Economist Jonathan Taylor and Professor Joseph Kalt compiled 1990 and 2000 Census data on fifteen measures, including per capita income, poverty rates, unemployment rates, and housing conditions. Their findings indicated marked improvement in living conditions for Native Americans residing on reservations:

- [B]etween 1990 and 2000, real (inflation-adjusted) per capita Indian income rose by about one-third. For both gaming and non-gaming tribes, the overall rate of income growth substantially outstripped the 11% increase in real per capita income for the U.S. as a whole.

- From 1990 to 2000, family poverty rates dropped by seven percentage points or more in non-gaming areas, and by about ten percentage points in gaming areas. U.S. family poverty dropped eight-tenths of a percentage point.

- Unemployment rates dropped by about two-and-a-half percentage points in non-gaming areas and by more than five percentage points in gaming areas. U.S. unemployment dropped by half a percentage point.

- Housing overcrowding decreased during the decade, particularly in Indian areas without gaming. The percentage of American Indians living in homes with plumbing increased markedly in both gaming and non-gaming areas.

Jonathan B. Taylor & Joseph P. Kalt, *American Indians on Reservations: A Databook of Socioeconomic Change Between the 1990 and 2000 Censuses* i (2005). What do the results of this study suggest about whether or not Indian gaming is "working" as public policy?

Taylor and Kalt also isolated the impact of gaming by comparing reservations with and without tribal casinos. They concluded,

The results are remarkable. In all but two categories, Census-measured socioeconomic improvement is greater for gaming reservations than for non-gaming reservations. At the same time, the measures also indicate substantial improvement for the latter, especially when compared against the changes experienced by the U.S. population overall. Indeed, the progress evident among *non-gaming* tribes in the 1990s suggests that it is not so much gaming that is driving the socioeconomic changes evident across Indian America as it is a broader policy of Indian self-government. Jurisdiction over the gaming choice is part, but hardly the entirety, of that policy.

Id. at xi. In view of what you have read throughout this as well as other Chapters, what do you think Taylor and Kalt mean by their conclusion about the key role played by a "broader policy of Indian self-government"? If the authors are correct, how should this finding inform the policy debate over Indian gaming? What does the conclusion suggest about the importance of encouraging cooperation and achieving congruence among tribal, federal, and state governments concerning the underlying goals for gaming and economic development law and policy in Indian country?

Problem 9: Research Design

The NGISC "urge[d] policymakers at all levels of government to accept our challenge to evaluate and to critically test both the economic and social costs and benefits associated with the introduction of, or continuation of, or restriction of gambling activities within their communities." NGISC FINAL REPORT, at 7-4. The NGISC continued,

> the real question—the reason gambling is an issue in need of substantially more study—is not simply how many people work in the industry, nor how much they earn, nor even what tax revenues flow from gambling. The central issue is whether the net increases in income and well-being are worth the acknowledged social costs of gambling.

Id. at 7–29.

Suppose you have been asked by the NGISC to design and execute an empirical study to carefully measure and critically assess the social and economic benefits and costs of a tribal casino for a reservation and the two non-tribal communities located nearby. What methodology would you use? What data would you need to collect? How would you assess whether the net benefits of Indian gaming exceed the net costs? How would you foster tribal participation? Safeguard tribal sovereignty? Ensure the study was used wisely by local, tribal, and state policymakers?

Chapter 10

Recurring Legal and Political Issues

A. Overview

As should be apparent by now, Indian gaming is a product of the confluence of law and public policy that sanction and govern the industry at the tribal, state, federal, and local levels. With so much at stake for so many stakeholders, it is no surprise that the resultant politics of tribal gaming is complex and controversial. With over 225 tribes operating some 400 gaming facilities around the U.S., numerous issues that affect Indian gaming arise on a daily basis.

These matters have become increasingly complex due to the politics of implementing IGRA's tribal-state compact provisions in the aftermath of *Seminole Tribe v. Florida*. For instance, beyond the specific provisions authorized by IGRA, states post-*Seminole Tribe* have sought to negotiate over issues that arguably are beyond the scope of IGRA's catch-all of "any other subjects that are directly related to the operation of gaming activities." 25 U.S.C. § 2710(d)(3)(C)(vii). Mandated revenue sharing with state and local governments or among tribes is one such example. IGRA's prerequisites for Indian gaming — that it must be conducted by an "Indian tribe," *id.* § 2703(5), on "Indian lands," *id.* § 2703(4) — are linked to ongoing controversies over the federal government's tribal acknowledgment process and, pursuant to other IGRA provisions, tribes' attempts to acquire new lands for the purpose of gaming. Additionally, as we discuss below, the applicability of federal labor laws to tribal casinos and other tribally owned enterprises versus tribes' assertion of jurisdiction over employment-related decisions generates friction among tribal governments, labor unions, and state and local policymakers.

In this Chapter we focus on the complications presented by these key recurring issues that will continue to shape the law, politics, and public policy of Indian gaming.

B. Gaming on Newly Acquired Lands

1. Overview

In § 2719 (sometimes referred to as "Section 20," in reference to the numbering of the statutory sections in bill form), IGRA sets forth a general prohibition against tribal gaming on trust lands acquired after IGRA's date of enactment: "Except as provided in subsection (b) of this section, gaming regulated by this chapter shall not be conducted on lands acquired by the Secretary in trust for the benefit of an Indian tribe after October 17, 1988...." Such lands are commonly referred to as "newly acquired" or "after acquired" lands. There are, however, a number of general and state- and tribe-specific exceptions.

§ 2719. Gaming on lands acquired after October 17, 1988

(a) Prohibition on lands acquired in trust by Secretary. Except as provided in subsection (b) of this section, gaming regulated by this chapter shall not be conducted on lands acquired by the Secretary in trust for the benefit of an Indian tribe after October 17, 1988, unless—

(1) such lands are located within or contiguous to the boundaries of the reservation of the Indian tribe on October 17, 1988; or

(2) the Indian tribe has no reservation on October 17, 1988, and—

(A) such lands are located in Oklahoma and—

(i) are within the boundaries of the Indian tribe's former reservation, as defined by the Secretary, or

(ii) are contiguous to other land held in trust or restricted status by the United States for the Indian tribe in Oklahoma; or

(B) such lands are located in a State other than Oklahoma and are within the Indian tribe's last recognized reservation within the State or States within which such Indian tribe is presently located.

(b) Exceptions.

(1) Subsection (a) of this section will not apply when—

(A) the Secretary, after consultation with the Indian tribe and appropriate State and local officials, including officials of other nearby Indian tribes, determines that a gaming establishment on newly acquired lands would be in the best interest of the Indian tribe and its members, and would not be detrimental to the surrounding community, but only if the Governor of the State in which the gaming activity is to be conducted concurs in the Secretary's determination; or

(B) lands are taken into trust as part of—

(i) a settlement of a land claim,

(ii) the initial reservation of an Indian tribe acknowledged by the Secretary under the Federal acknowledgment process, or

(iii) the restoration of lands for an Indian tribe that is restored to Federal recognition.

. . . .

(c) Authority of Secretary not affected. Nothing in this section shall affect or diminish the authority and responsibility of the Secretary to take land into trust.

25 U.S.C. § 2719.

First, a tribe may conduct gaming on newly acquired lands that are located within the tribe's existing reservation or that are contiguous to the reservation's boundaries. *Id.* § 2719(a)(1). Seven tribal casinos currently operate under this exception.

Second, for tribes without reservations as of October 17, 1988, gaming is not prohibited on newly acquired lands if the lands are within the tribe's last recognized reservation and within the state in which the tribe currently resides. *Id.* § 2719(a)(2)(B). A special exception applies to tribes without reservations that have acquired trust lands in Oklahoma. Gaming is allowed on newly acquired lands in Oklahoma if the lands are within the tribe's former reservation or if the lands are contiguous to the tribe's current trust or restricted lands. *Id.* § 2719(a)(2)(A).

Third, an exception is made when gaming on newly acquired lands is "in the best interest of the tribe and its members, and would not be detrimental to the surrounding community." *Id.* § 2719(b)(1)(A). We call this the "best interests" exception; others refer to it as the "two-part determination." Specifically, the Secretary of the Interior must first consult with the tribe, the state, local officials, and officials of nearby tribes, and then determine that gaming on the newly acquired lands would be in the best interest of the tribe and its members and would not be detrimental to the surrounding community. Importantly, the state's governor must concur in the Secretary's determination—essentially providing veto power over tribal gaming under this exception. The consultation and governor's concurrence requirements create potential political obstacles to the likelihood that a tribe may conduct gaming on newly acquired lands under the "best interests" exception. Only three tribes currently operate gaming on newly acquired lands under this exception: the Keweenaw Bay Indian Community of the Lake Superior Bands of Chippewa Indians operate a casino in Choclay Township, outside of Marquette, Michigan; the Forest County Potawatomi operate a casino in Milwaukee, Wisconsin; and the Kalispell Tribe conducts gaming in Airway Heights, Washington.

The constitutionality of the governor's concurrence requirement was challenged in *Confederated Tribes of Siletz Indians v. United States*, 110 F.3d 688 (9th Cir. 1997). There, the Interior Secretary had disallowed a tribal casino on newly acquired lands near Salem, Oregon, because Governor Barbara Roberts refused to agree that gaming on the lands was in the best interest of the tribe and not detrimental to the surrounding community. The tribe contended that the concurrence requirement violated both the Appointments Clause in Article II of the U.S. Constitution, because the governor was exercising authority without being duly appointed to a federal post, and separation of powers principles, because the concurrence requirement reassigned authority from the Interior Secretary to state governors. The court rejected both arguments, holding that IGRA does not give governors "primary authority" to determine applicability of the exception and that Congress appropriately conditioned the Secretary's delegated power to take land into trust on state concurrence.

The Seventh Circuit reached a similar conclusion in *Lac Courte Oreilles Band v. United States*, 367 F.3d 650 (7th Cir. 2004) (excerpted below). There, the Interior Secretary had determined that an off-reservation casino near Hudson, Wisconsin, would be in the best interests of the tribes and would not be detrimental to the surrounding community. Governor Scott McCallum refused to concur in the Secretary's determination, defeating the tribes' proposal. The tribes challenged the governor's authority under 25 U.S.C. § 2719(b)(1)(A) on a number of grounds, including the separation of powers doctrine, nondelegation doctrine, Appointments Clause, state sovereignty, and the federal government's trust obligation to the tribes. None of these arguments persuaded the Seventh Circuit that the provision was unconstitutional. The cases also suggest that IGRA does not place any limits on the governor's reason for not concurring; it appears that the governor may "veto" tribal gaming under this exception for any reason or no reason at all.

Fourth, gaming is allowed on newly acquired lands when the lands are placed in trust as a settlement of a land claim, or as the initial reservation of a federally recognized tribe, or as the restoration of lands for a tribe whose federal recognition is restored. *Id.* § 2719(b)(1)(B). These, too, are controversial exceptions, despite the fact that relatively few tribal casinos operate under them: currently, four casinos operate on settlement lands (all stemming from the Seneca Tribe of New York's land claim), three on initial reservations, and twelve on restored reservations. Accusations of "reservation shopping" abound, and as of this writing Congress was considering limiting these exceptions to lands to which the tribe could demonstrate a historical nexus and which were located in the same state as the tribe currently resides.

Though the term "off-reservation gaming" often is used to refer to gaming under any of the § 2719 exceptions, the Interior Department generally uses the term "off-reservation" to refer to land that is neither within or contiguous to existing reservation boundaries. Further, the "best interests" exception is the sole exception that does not require some historical tie or legal claim to the land in question.

Finally, IGRA includes specific exceptions for the St. Croix Chippewa Indians in Wisconsin and the Miccosukee Tribe of Indians in Florida. *Id.* § 2719(b)(2). These tribe-specific exceptions also reference particular lands.

The exceptions to the general rule prohibiting gaming on newly acquired lands obviously implicate the Interior Secretary's power to take land into trust for the benefit of a tribe. Generally speaking, the Secretary may exercise discretion whether to grant or deny an application to take land into trust for a tribe. (Some acquisitions by the Secretary are nondiscretionary, such as those mandated by a federal statute or court decision directing the Secretary to place land into trust.) The Secretary has promulgated regulations governing both on-reservation and off-reservation land acquisitions, which require consideration of the impact on local and state governments as well as opportunity for public comment.

In addition to meeting the requirements of IGRA's § 2719, the tribe also must satisfy the requirements of the land-into-trust process. The primary purposes for which the Secretary might approve a trust application are to facilitate tribal government services, for economic development, and for housing. Gaming falls within economic development. *See* Larry E. Scrivner, *Acquiring Land Into Trust for Indian Tribes*, 37 New Eng. L. Rev. 603, 606 (2003). As Scrivner, then-Acting Director of the BIA's Office of Trust Responsibilities, explained,

> Gaming is how the land is used and is not a part of the process of acquiring land. Sometimes, these two things come together in one application because the tribe wants the land in trust and, as soon as they succeed in obtaining trust status for the land, they develop it for gaming purposes. These two actions are often processed simultaneously, even though the land must first be placed into trust before it can be developed. [The process of approving gaming on the newly acquired land] is a whole different process from acquiring land into trust.

Id. It is important to keep in mind that § 2719 does not authorize the Interior Secretary to take land into trust; instead, it creates a separate requirement that a tribe must meet independent of the land-into-trust process before the tribe may conduct gaming on land taken into trust.

Changes in land use are not prohibited, as the federal government does not permit deed restrictions to be attached to government-owned land such as land held by the U.S. in trust for the benefit of a tribe. Nevertheless, tribes are "discouraged" from submitting a land-into-trust application for a non-gaming purpose and later changing the use of the land to gaming. If a tribe wants to conduct gaming on any land acquired after 1988, it must satisfy all of IGRA's requirements. As George T. Skibine, Acting Deputy Assistant Secretary for Policy and Economic Development for Indian Affairs, explained,

It should be stressed that Section 20 prohibits all Indian gaming on land acquired after October 1988, and this prohibition applies regardless of the original purpose for which the land was acquired.... It is also important to emphasize that before trust land can be used for gaming, even if acquired for another purpose, it must meet other requirements of IGRA, which include a determination that the land in question is "Indian land" over which the tribe exercises jurisdiction and over which it exercises governmental power; receive approval of a gaming ordinance by the Chairman of the National Indian Gaming Commission; and receive approval of a tribal/state gaming compact by the Secretary if the tribe is seeking to engage in class III gaming activities on the land.

George T. Skibine, Statement Before the U.S. Senate Committee on Indian Affairs Concerning Taking Land Into Trust (May 18, 2005).

Typically, the review of a tribe's application to take land into trust for gaming purposes occurs simultaneously with review of the applicability of one of § 2719's exceptions. The Secretary's land acquisition regulations describe the first step of placing the land into trust.

§ 151.10 On-reservation acquisitions. Upon receipt of a written request to have lands taken in trust, the Secretary will notify the state and local governments having regulatory jurisdiction over the land to be acquired, unless the acquisition is mandated by legislation. The notice will inform the state or local government that each will be given 30 days in which to provide written comments as to the acquisition's potential impacts on regulatory jurisdiction, real property taxes and special assessments. If the state or local government responds within a 30-day period, a copy of the comments will be provided to the applicant, who will be given a reasonable time in which to reply and/or request that the Secretary issue a decision. The Secretary will consider the following criteria in evaluating requests for the acquisition of land in trust status when the land is located within or contiguous to an Indian reservation, and the acquisition is not mandated:

(a) The existence of statutory authority for the acquisition and any limitations contained in such authority;

(b) The need of the individual Indian or the tribe for additional land;

(c) The purposes for which the land will be used;

(d) If the land is to be acquired for an individual Indian, the amount of trust or restricted land already owned by or for that individual and the degree to which he needs assistance in handling his affairs;

(e) If the land to be acquired is in unrestricted fee status, the impact on the State and its political subdivisions resulting from the removal of the land from the tax rolls;

(f) Jurisdictional problems and potential conflicts of land use which may arise; and

(g) If the land to be acquired is in fee status, whether the Bureau of Indian Affairs is equipped to discharge the additional responsibilities resulting from the acquisition of the land in trust status.

(h) The extent to which the applicant has provided information that allows the Secretary to comply with 516 DM 6, appendix 4, National Environmental Policy Act Revised Implementing Procedures, and 602 DM 2, Land Acquisitions: Hazardous Substances Determinations....

§ 151.11 Off-reservation acquisitions. The Secretary shall consider the following requirements in evaluating tribal requests for the acquisition of lands in trust status, when the land is located outside of and noncontiguous to the tribe's reservation, and the acquisition is not mandated:

(a) The criteria listed in § 151.10 (a) through (c) and (e) through (h);

(b) The location of the land relative to state boundaries, and its distance from the boundaries of the tribe's reservation, shall be considered as follows: as the distance between the tribe's reservation and the land to be acquired increases, the Secretary shall give greater scrutiny to the tribe's justification of anticipated benefits from the acquisition. The Secretary shall give greater weight to the concerns raised pursuant to paragraph (d) of this section.

(c) Where land is being acquired for business purposes, the tribe shall provide a plan which specifies the anticipated economic benefits associated with the proposed use.

(d) Contact with state and local governments pursuant to § 151.10 (e) and (f) shall be completed as follows: Upon receipt of a tribe's written request to have lands taken in trust, the Secretary shall notify the state and local governments having regulatory jurisdiction over the land to be acquired. The notice shall inform the state and local government that each will be given 30 days in which to provide written comment as to the acquisition's potential impacts on regulatory jurisdiction, real property taxes and special assessments.

25 C.F.R. pt. 151.

The Interior Department's Office of Indian Gaming Management (OIGM) has produced a "Checklist for Gaming Acquisitions, Gaming-Related Acquisitions, and IGRA Section 20 Determinations" for gaming-related land acquisitions based on the requirements of 25 U.S.C. § 2719, 25 C.F.R. pt. 151, and federal environmental laws. The checklist details the submission process for an acquisition request, including explanations of the supporting documentation required for each of the exceptions. Though BIA Regional Directors may approve land-into-trust applications for non-gaming purposes, all gaming-related applications must pass through the OIGM and be approved by the Assistant Secretary for Indian Affairs. The tribe's application first goes to the BIA Regional Director, who will review it for compliance with the requirements of 25 C.F.R. pt. 151 and request from OIGM a determination whether the land in question will qualify for one or more of § 2719's exceptions. The Regional Director also will consult with state and local officials in accordance with 25 C.F.R. pt. 151. The public has an opportunity to comment during the process required by the National Environmental Policy Act, which includes review of socioeconomic impacts of taking the land into trust for gaming. The Regional Director submits its recommendation on the tribe's application to the OIGM, which in turn provides a final recommendation to the Assistant Secretary for Indian Affairs.

Applications falling under the "best interests" exception follow a slightly different process. Review of whether the tribe has met the requirements of the exception occurs prior to the decision of whether to take the land into trust. The Regional Director will make factual findings regarding whether gaming on the land is "in the best interest of the tribe and its members, and would not be detrimental to the surrounding community." 25 U.S.C. § 2719(b)(1)(A). The Regional Director's factual findings are forwarded to the OIGM for further review; ultimately, if the Secretary agrees with a positive recommendation, he will ask the state's governor to concur. Without the governor's concurrence, gaming cannot be conducted on the land under the "best interests" exception, and the tribe's application to take the land into trust for the purpose of gaming will be denied without further review. We discuss the "best interests" exception in more detail in the next section.

2. Exceptions to IGRA's General Prohibition Against Gaming on Newly Acquired Land

a. The "Best Interests" Exception

As noted above, gaming-related land-into-trust applications falling under IGRA's "best interests" exception involve off-reservation lands (land within or contiguous to a tribe's reservation fall within §2719's other exceptions). Unlike other "off-reservation" exceptions under §2719, the "best interests" exception does not require any historical ties or legal claim to the land in question. Not surprisingly, such applications are highly controversial and involve a much greater level of state and local input and control, including the governor's power to effectively "veto" a tribe's attempt to conduct gaming on newly acquired lands under this exception.

Heidi McNeil Staudenmaier

Off-Reservation Native American Gaming:
An Examination of the Legal and Political Hurdles

4 Nev. L.J. 301 (2004)

Generally, the land-into-trust process is governed by the rules and regulations promulgated pursuant to 25 C.F.R. Part 151. The land-into-trust process can be quite lengthy, even if the acquisition is not for a gaming purpose and there is no controversy surrounding the particular piece of land being taken into trust. The greatest controversy — from both a legal and political perspective — involves land-into-trust acquisitions for gaming purposes pursuant to the 25 U.S.C. §2719(b)(1)(A) exception of IGRA.

For land sought for gaming purposes pursuant to the 25 U.S.C. §2719(b)(1)(A) exception, the Secretary must make a two-part determination: (1) the gaming operation will be in the "best interest of the Indian tribe and its members" and (2) the gaming operation will "not be detrimental to the surrounding community." In addition to this two-part determination, the governor of the state in which the land is located must concur in the determination.

The initial determination is made by the BIA Regional Director, who is responsible for consulting with the applicant tribe, the state (including the governor), and local and other nearby tribal officials. Typically, the Regional Director will issue consultation letters and provide at least 30 days or longer for comments and responses to the letter. In determining whether the land acquisition is in the "best interest" of the tribe, the OIGM Checklist provides that the tribe must submit the following information for review by the BIA:

1. Projections of income statements, balance sheets, fixed assets accounting, and cash flow statements for the gaming entity pursuant to Generally Accepted Accounting Principles ("GAAP") and the National Indian Gaming Commission ("NIGC") standards for at least a three-year period;

2. Projected tribal employment, job training, and career development;

3. Projected benefits to tribe from tourism and the basis for this projection;

4. Projected benefits to the tribe and its members from the proposed uses of the increased tribal income;

5.   Projected benefits to the relationship between the tribe and the surrounding community;

6.   Possible adverse impacts on the tribe and plans for dealing with these impacts; and

7.   Any other information for the acquisition demonstrating it is in the best interest of the tribe.

In determining whether the acquisition will be detrimental to the surrounding community, the OIGM Checklist provides that consulted officials and the tribe must submit the following information:

1.   Evidence of the environmental impact and plans for mitigating this adverse impact;

2.   Reasonably anticipated impact on social structure, infrastructure, services, housing, community character, and land use patterns of the surrounding community;

3.   Income and employment of the surrounding community and the impact on the economic development of the community;

4.   Costs of impact to the surrounding community and sources of revenue to accommodate them;

5.   Proposed programs for compulsive gamblers and source of funding; and

6.   Any other information showing that acquisition is not detrimental to the surrounding community.

Given the complex web of federal, state, local, and tribal interests involved, the land-into-trust process under 25 U.S.C. § 2719(b)(1)(A) is long and arduous. A tribe must overcome a number of obstacles before securing the Secretary's approval for off-reservation gaming.

Although local communities are statutorily powerless under 25 U.S.C. § 2719, "their support can make or break attempts to establish new Indian lands for gaming where none existed before." A tribe must demonstrate that taking land into trust will not negatively impact the community's social structure, services, economic development, housing, and community character. According to George Skibine, Director of the OIGM, "[w]hat we've found is that the tribes that have done their homework show they've gained community support." Gaining local support begins with choosing a location that satisfies the most people in the community. Most communities are concerned with the crowds and traffic that a casino would invariably attract.

In determining whether the land acquisition is in the "best interest" of the tribe, the tribe must demonstrate that it and its members will reap benefits from the gaming operation. Benefits include tribal employment, job training, and development. Further, the Secretary will closely scrutinize casino profit distribution. Pursuant to the OIGM Checklist, the BIA will review projections of income statements, balance sheets, fixed assets accounting, and cash flow statements of the gaming entity for at least three years. The BIA will also review projected benefits to the tribe and its members from the proposed uses of the increased tribal income.

Tribes with existing casinos sometimes oppose other tribes seeking to establish nearby gaming facilities. There are instances of rival tribes vying to acquire the same piece of land. For example, the Chemehuevi Indians of Needles, California, and the Los Coyotes Band of Cahuilla both want to secure an off-reservation casino site in Barstow, California. Los Coyotes won the city's blessing to build a $150 million hotel-casino. Nevertheless, the Chemehuevi have asserted they have aboriginal ties to the area and therefore should have priority rights to use the land at issue.

With the change in administration after the Fall 2000 election, the Secretary has grown progressively more hostile towards off-reservation gaming. In a letter last year to New York Governor George Pataki, pertaining to the approval of certain tribal-state compacts in New York, Secretary Gale Norton said she was bothered that "tribes are increasingly seeking to develop gaming facilities in areas far from their reservations." In the last year, the Secretary refused to approve a tribal-state compact between the Jena Band of Choctaws and Louisiana, in large part because the proposed casino was 150 miles from the tribe's ancestral base.

Even when a tribe obtains approval from the Secretary, the governor of the affected state, ultimately, has veto power. For instance, both the Sault St. Marie Tribe of Chippewa Indians of Michigan and the St. Regis Band of Mohawk of New York met the Secretary's two-part test, but the respective governors did not concur. Consequently, the tribes were unable to open off-reservation gaming operations.

Notes and Questions

1.   Cobell *litigation.* As tribal gaming attorney Staudenmaier detailed, the OIGM plays a primary role in the land-into-trust process. Interestingly, despite its presumed importance, the OIGM's Checklist for Gaming Acquisitions is not widely available to the public. *See* Office of Indian Gaming Management, U.S. Dep't of the Interior, Checklist for Gaming Acquisitions Gaming-Related Acquisitions and IGRA Section 20 Determinations (Oct. 2001), available by calling OIGM at 202-219-4066. Nor is very much information available online about the OIGM itself. *See* http://www.doi.gov/bia/indiangaming.html. This likely in part is due to the ongoing *Cobell* litigation (*Cobell v. Kempthorne*, previously titled *Cobell v. Norton* and *Cobell v. Babbit*), a class action suit against the federal government concerning alleged mismanagement of Individual Indian Monies (IIM) trust accounts. As a result of the litigation, the BIA has been under a federal court order since December 2001 to shut down portions of its Web site and e-mail servers. For more on the *Cobell* litigation, see the Web site maintained by lead plaintiff Elouise Cobell, at http://www.indiantrust.com/. The NIGC's Web site remains the best federal government source of information on Indian gaming, though it does not include the OIGM Checklist.

2.   *Going local.* How important is it for a tribe to "go local," Steven A. Light & Kathryn R.L. Rand, *Are All Bets Off? Off-Reservation Indian Gaming in Wisconsin*, 5 GAM-ING L. REV. 351 (2001), and acquire up front community political support for a proposed land-into-trust application? Will the support of local officials make any difference to the Interior Secretary?

3.   *Casinos operating under the "best interests" exception.* As Staudenmaier noted, very few tribes have successfully negotiated all of the legal and political hurdles of the "best interests" exception. Only three tribal casinos currently operate under this exception. According to Acting Deputy Assistant Secretary George Skibine,

> Since 1988, state governors have concurred in only three positive two-part determinations for off-reservation gaming on trust lands: the Forest County Potawatomi gaming establishment in Milwaukee, Wisconsin; the Kalispel Tribe gaming establishment in Airway Heights, Washington; and the Keweenaw Bay Indian Community gaming establishment near Marquette, Michigan. During this Administration, the Secretary has made two such affirmative determinations: One for three Wisconsin tribes seeking a gaming establishment in Hudson, Wisconsin, and the other for the Jena Band of Choctaw seeking a gaming

establishment in Logansport, Louisiana. In both cases, the governors of the affected states have refused to concur in the Secretary's determinations. Currently, there are eleven applications for two-part determinations under section 20(b)(1)(A) pending with the Bureau of Indian Affairs for sites in New York, Wisconsin, Michigan, California, and Oregon. Of these, only one concerns the proposed acquisition of land in a state other than where the tribe is currently located. However, more applications are rumored to be in development for cross-state acquisitions, including potential applications in Ohio, Colorado, Illinois, and New York. It is within the context of this emerging trend that Secretary Norton has raised the question of whether Section 20(b)(1)(A) provides her with sufficient discretion to approve or disapprove gaming on off-reservation trust lands that are great distances from their reservations, so-called "far-flung lands."

George T. Skibine, Statement Before the U.S. Senate Committee on Indian Affairs Concerning Taking Land Into Trust (May 18, 2005). As Skibine's testimony indicates, applications involving "far-flung lands" or land in another state raise significant political, if not legal, issues.

George T. Skibine
Statement Before the U.S. Senate Committee on Indian Affairs Concerning Taking Land into Trust
(May 18, 2005)

Good morning, Mr. Chairman and Members of the Committee. My name is George Skibine, and I am the Acting Deputy Assistant Secretary for Policy and Economic Development for Indian Affairs at the Department of the Interior. I am pleased to be here today to discuss the role of the Department in taking land into trust and the procedures used when the land is for gaming purposes.

The Department manages approximately 46 million acres of land held in trust for Indian tribes. The basis for the administrative decision to place land into trust for the benefit of an Indian tribe is established either by a specific statute applying to a tribe, or by Section 5 of the Indian Reorganization Act of 1934 (IRA), which authorizes the Secretary to acquire land in trust for Indians "within or without existing reservations." Under these authorities, the Secretary applies her discretion after consideration of the criteria for trust acquisitions in our "151" regulations (25 CFR Part 151), unless the acquisition is legislatively mandated. The regulations, first published in 1980, provide that upon receipt of an application to acquire land in trust the Bureau of Indian Affairs (BIA) will notify state and local governments having regulatory jurisdiction over the land of the application and request their comments concerning potential impacts on regulatory jurisdiction, real property taxes, and special assessments. In reviewing a tribe's application to acquire land in trust, the Secretary considers the need; purposes; statutory authority; jurisdictional and land use concerns; the impact of removing the land from the tax rolls; the BIA's ability to manage the land; and compliance with all necessary environmental laws.

The ["151"] regulations impose additional requirements for approval of tribal off-reservation acquisitions. The Secretary is required to consider the location of the land relative to state boundaries; distance of the land from the tribe's reservation; business plan; and state and local government impact comments. In doing so, the Secretary "shall give greater scrutiny to the tribe's justification of anticipated benefits from the acquisition ...

[and] greater weight to the concerns raised" by the local community the farther the proposed acquisition is from the tribe's reservation.

We have spent substantial effort examining the overall statutory scheme that Congress has formulated in the area of Indian self-determination and economic development. This includes a careful examination of what Congress intended when it enacted Section 20(b)(1)(A). Our review suggests that Congress sought to establish a unique balance of interests. The statute plainly delineates the discretion of the Secretary, limiting her focus to two statutory prongs. Also, by requiring that the Governor of the affected state concur in the Secretary's determination, the statute acknowledges that in a difference of opinion between a sovereign tribe and an affected state, the state prevails. Further, at least on its face, Section 20(b)(1)(A) does not contain any express limitation on the distance between the proposed gaming establishment and the tribe's reservation, nor is the presence of state boundaries between the proposed gaming establishment and the tribe's reservation a factor.

Our review indicates that the role of the Secretary under section 20(b)(1)(A) is limited to making objective findings of fact regarding the best interests of the tribe and its members, and any detriment to the surrounding community. Therefore, while the trust acquisition regulations provide broader discretion, Section 20(b)(1)(A) does not authorize the Secretary to consider other criteria in making her two-part determination, thus limiting her decision-making discretion to that degree. It should be noted that neither this Administration, nor previous ones, have ever approved a two-part determination under Section 20(b)(1)(A) of IGRA that would authorize a tribe to engage in gaming activities on land located in a state other than where the tribe is presently located. Although off-reservation acquisitions for gaming under Section 20(b)(1)(A) are subjected to a very lengthy approval process, potential ventures between tribes and their financial partners keep emerging because neither IGRA nor the main land acquisition authority in the Indian Reorganization Act, or regulations promulgated thereunder, close the door on these projects. In our view, Section 20 of IGRA reflects Congressional intent to impose a prohibition on gaming on lands acquired in trust after enactment of the statute. Section 20 does contain a series of exceptions discussed above, but we do not believe that it was the intent of Congress that the exceptions swallow the rule.

Taking land into trust is an important decision not only for the tribe seeking the determination but for the local community the land is located in. The regulations seek to ensure that the local community is kept informed and allowed to participate in the process. Any community comments received are considered before a determination is made whether to take the land into trust. The tribe and the public are also given an opportunity to appeal to federal court.

In addition, the Department recognizes the growing concerns about land venue shopping by tribes, especially for gaming purposes, and the concerns some have expressed about efforts to take developed (or land with development potential) land into trust. We are evaluating closely the expansion of tribal interests in filing fee-into-trust applications for sites ever more distant from current geographic locations or for sites with significant implications for state and local jurisdictions.

Notes and Questions

1.   *Which exception?* Interestingly, the OIGM Checklist does not require a tribe to specify under which § 2719 exception it is proceeding. Instead, the OIGM reviews the

parcel identified by the tribe and makes a determination whether the land falls within one of the exceptions. Presumably, the OIGM will apply the "best interests" exception only where the land in question does not fall into one of the other exceptions in § 2719.

2.   *§ 2719(b)(1)(A) vs. 25 C.F.R. pt. 151.* Consider the various submission requirements in the OIGM Checklist for an application under the "best interests" exception. How do they differ from the requirements in 25 C.F.R. pt. 151? Are the extra steps justified? On what basis? For more on the mechanics and politics of this exception, see LIGHT & RAND, INDIAN GAMING AND TRIBAL SOVEREIGNTY, at 63–65; KATHRYN R.L. RAND & STEVEN ANDREW LIGHT, INDIAN GAMING LAW AND POLICY 156–61 (2006).

3.   *Need to amend IGRA.* Several members of Congress have asserted that the process of taking land into trust for the purpose of gaming threatens to allow numerous such acquisitions, particularly across state lines, that will (perhaps improperly) fuel the widespread growth of Indian gaming. Given the statutory and administrative requirements, including the Checklist, and the resulting political hurdles, as well as the small number of tribes that actually have succeeded in clearing them, does Congress need to amend IGRA to make it more difficult for a tribe to conduct gaming on trust lands acquired after 1988?

4.   *Purpose of the "best interests" exception.* Although IGRA's legislative history does not provide much insight into Congress's intent in enacting § 2719(b)(1)(A), one likely possibility is that Congress was cognizant of the fact that not all tribes had lands in areas amenable to profitable gaming enterprises. Tribes with reservations near metropolitan areas obviously would see more financial success than tribes in more remote locales. Congress may have intended that tribes in rural areas could acquire land for the purpose of taking fuller advantage of Indian gaming (i.e., tapping into a larger customer base) with, of course, strict state controls. *See* Kathryn R.L. Rand & Steven Andrew Light, *How Congress Can and Should "Fix" the Indian Gaming Regulatory Act: Recommendations for Law and Policy Reform*, 13 VA. J. SOC. POL'Y & L. 396, 465–69 (2006).

Lac Courte Oreilles Band of Lake Superior Chippewa Indians of Wisconsin v. United States
367 F.3d 650 (7th Cir. 2004)

Plaintiffs are three federally recognized Indian Tribes with reservations in sparsely populated areas of northern Wisconsin ("the Tribes"). While each of the Tribes operates a casino on reservation land, these casinos do not generate income comparable to casinos operated by tribes who have reservations near Wisconsin's urban centers or destination resorts. Seeking to advance their tribal and economic development, the Tribes joined together for the purpose of establishing a jointly owned and operated off-reservation gaming facility in a lucrative location.

The Tribes found a struggling pari-mutuel greyhound racing facility in Hudson, Wisconsin that they wished to acquire and convert into a casino gaming facility. Hudson was attractive to the Tribes because they believed its proximity to the metropolitan areas of Minneapolis and St. Paul and easy accessibility to Interstate Highway 94 would ensure a broad customer base. In October 1992 the Tribes formally submitted their application under the Indian Gaming Regulatory Act ("IGRA") to the Department of the Interior seeking to have the Hudson property taken into trust for their benefit for the purpose of operating a casino gaming facility.

The Tribes hoped that their application would be favorably received pursuant to 25 U.S.C. § 2719(b)(1)(A), [the "best-interests"] exception to IGRA's general ban on gaming on after-acquired lands. The Department of the Interior initially denied the Tribes' application, but later vacated the rejection following a lawsuit and settlement. In February 2001, the Department of the Interior issued findings that the proposal was in the best interests of the Tribes and would not be detrimental to the surrounding community. The Department of the Interior sent the matter to then Governor of Wisconsin Scott McCallum for his concurrence. In May 2001, Governor McCallum issued a letter declining to concur in the Secretary's findings, citing Wisconsin's general disapproval of off-reservation gaming and public policy of permitting only "limited exceptions to the general prohibition against gambling." Governor McCallum opined that the public interest would not be served by the addition of another major casino gaming facility to the seventeen casino gaming facilities already operating in Wisconsin. In June 2001, the Department of the Interior issued a final decision denying the Tribes' application on the grounds that, absent the Governor's concurrence, the exception provided in 25 U.S.C. § 2719(b)(1)(A) did not apply and 25 U.S.C. § 2719(a) precluded the acquisition of the land for the purposes of gaming.

The Tribes assert that the gubernatorial concurrence provision of § 2719(b)(1)(a) violates the separation of powers doctrine because it prevents the Executive Branch from executing the laws. In their view, § 2719(b)(1)(A) unconstitutionally diverts to the Governors of the 50 States the final decisional authority delegated by IGRA to the Secretary of the Interior. The Tribes submit that § 2719(b)(1)(A) requires a governor to review the Secretary of the Interior's analysis of the two factual predicates and empowers the governor to "veto" the Secretary of the Interior's conclusion by withholding concurrence. The Tribes cite *INS v. Chadha*, 462 U.S. 919 (1983), for the proposition that Congress cannot confer upon itself or an actor external to the federal Executive Branch the power to veto the President's execution of federal law.

At issue in *Chadha* was Section 244(c)(2) of the Immigration and Nationality Act, which authorized either House of Congress, by resolution, to veto the Attorney General's decision to suspend the deportation of a particular alien. The Supreme Court noted that the one-House veto served an "essentially legislative ... purpose and effect," and was therefore subject to the procedural requirements for enacting legislation set forth in the Constitution: bicameral passage, and presentment to the President.

Unlike the one-House veto provision at issue in *Chadha*, the gubernatorial concurrence provision does not prevent the Executive Branch from accomplishing its delegated function under IGRA. Section 2719(b)(1)(A) assigns the Secretary of the Interior two responsibilities: (1) to evaluate whether gaming on the proposed trust land would be in the best interest of the applicant tribe and not detrimental to the surrounding community; if so, then (2) to ascertain whether the Governor of the State where the proposed trust land is located concurs with his or her favorable determination. A governor's concurrence is no less a precondition to the Executive Branch's authority to waive IGRA's general prohibition of gaming on after-acquired lands than are the factual circumstances that give rise to Secretary of the Interior's conclusion that gaming on the proposed trust land would be in the Indian tribe's best interests and would not be detrimental to the surrounding community. Unless and until the appropriate governor issues a concurrence, the Secretary of the Interior has no authority under § 2719(b)(1)(A) to take land into trust for the benefit of an Indian tribe for the purpose of the operation of a gaming establishment.

The power delegated to the Attorney General in *Chadha* had no similar contingency predicate to the Attorney General's statutory authority to execute the law. The one-House veto wrested final decision-making power away from the Executive Branch over an issue that had been legislatively entrusted to the Attorney General and thereby directly impeded the Attorney General from accomplishing the function delegated: to determine whether to suspend, and to suspend, the deportation of a particular alien. In contrast, after the two preconditions to the Secretary of the Interior's authority are met—i.e., the two factual predicates exist and the governor issues a concurrence—the Secretary of the Interior's decision to execute § 2719(b)(1)(A) by taking the proposed land into trust is not subject to review.

We agree with the Ninth Circuit that § 2719(b)(1)(A) is an example of contingent legislation, wherein Congress restricted the authority to execute federal legislation contingent upon the approval of an actor external to the federal Executive Branch. *Confederated Tribes of Siletz Indians of Oregon v. United States,* 110 F.3d 688, 694–95 (9th Cir. 1997). Congress may place "a restriction upon its own regulation by withholding its operation" unless a specified percentage of those affected by the regulation agree to submit to it. Moreover, Congress may condition the operation of federal law on the approval of a state official. This condition does not impermissibly interfere with the Executive Branch's execution of federal law, so much as its occurrence is a prerequisite to the Executive Branch's authority to act pursuant to § 2719(b)(1)(A).

The Tribes contend that the contingent legislation rationale is an inappropriate analogy to § 2719(b)(1)(A) because that Section empowers governors to impose the force of law on Indian Tribes, who they characterize as "unwilling third parties," whereas contingent legislation typically empowers the decision-maker to submit only itself to regulation.

According to the Tribes, § 2719(b)(1)(A) regulates Indian tribes with reservations encompassed by the state where the proposed trust land is located. We disagree. The object of regulation under § 2719(b)(1)(A) is land that the Secretary of the Interior has taken into trust for Indians for the purpose of operating a gaming establishment. Before the land is taken into trust, it is within the jurisdiction of a state and is not yet subject to federal regulation under IGRA. Therefore, while the Secretary of the Interior investigates whether gaming on the proposed trust land "would be in the best interest of the Indian tribe" and "would not be detrimental to the surrounding community," the proper spokesperson for the land in question is necessarily a representative of the state where the land is located. It is only after the Secretary of the Interior determines that the proposed trust land meets the factual requirements of § 2719(b)(1)(A), the governor issues a concurrence, and the Secretary executes the federal law by taking the land into trust, that the Tribe enjoying that trust land becomes its appropriate representative. Thus, conditioning the Secretary of the Interior's power on the assent of the relevant governor is not unlike other contingent legislation in that the proper spokesperson of the object of regulation—the land—is empowered to invite, or refuse, federal regulation.

We find that the remaining separation of powers issues illustrated by the one-House veto in *Chadha* are not present here. The gubernatorial concurrence provision does not aggrandize the power of the Legislative Branch at the expense of the Executive Branch. The Secretary of the Interior would have no authority to permit gaming on after-acquired trust lands absent the power delegated by Congress in IGRA. Congress may, consistent with the doctrine of separation of powers, condition that delegation on the approval of an actor external to the Executive Branch. Congress has not wrongfully enhanced its power by the use of the contingent legislation mechanism; whether the governor concurs and thereby triggers the Secretary of the Interior's power under § 2719(b)(1)(A) is a circumstance outside of Congress's influence or control. *See Morrison v. Olson,* 487 U.S. 654 (1988) (holding that the independent counsel provisions of the Ethics in Community Government Act do not violate separation of powers principles by impermissibly interfering with the functioning of the Executive Branch, when "Congress retained for it-self no powers of control or supervision over an independent counsel").

Finally, the Tribes argue that §2719(b)(1)(A) violates the separation of powers doctrine because it transfers control over the execution of federal law from the Executive Branch to the Governors of the 50 States, citing *Printz v. United States*, 521 U.S. 898 (1997). In *Printz*, at issue were certain interim provisions of the Brady Handgun Violence Prevention Act ("Brady Act"), which obliged state law enforcement officers to conduct background checks of prospective handgun purchasers until a national system became operative. The Supreme Court held that the interim provisions unconstitutionally transferred the responsibility of the President to "take Care that the Laws be faithfully executed," to the law enforcement officers of the 50 States, "who are left to implement the program without meaningful Pres-idential control." The *Printz* Court noted that, by accomplishing the execution of the law through state officers, Congress had denigrated the President's power by circumventing the Executive Branch and had weakened the accountability and vigor of that Branch.

Unlike the Brady Act's requirement that state officers temporarily execute federal law by performing background checks, the gubernatorial concurrence provision does not re-quire or even permit any governor to execute federal law. The execution of §2719(b)(1)(A) occurs when the Secretary of the Interior takes land into trust for the benefit of Indians for the purpose of operating a gaming establishment. IGRA does not empower any gov-ernor to perform that function. For example, even if a governor believed that taking land into trust for an Indian tribe for the purpose of gaming "would be in the best interest of the Indian tribe" and "would not be detrimental to the surrounding community," if the Secretary of the Interior disagreed, the governor would be unable to execute §2719(b)(1)(A) by taking the land into federal trust.

As only the Secretary of the Interior may execute the §2719(b)(1)(A) exception to IGRA's general prohibition of gaming on after-acquired land, the Executive Branch retains control over IGRA's execution, and therefore there is no *Printz* separation of powers problem. In conclusion, we hold that the contested provision of IGRA does not violate the separation of powers doctrine by interfering with the Executive Branch's execution of federal law.

We now turn to the Tribes' argument that Congress violated a related branch of the sep-aration of powers jurisprudence: the nondelegation doctrine. In the Tribes' view, if §2719(b)(1)(A) does not require a governor to decide whether to concur based on his or her analysis of the two factual predicates that bind the Secretary of the Interior's de-termination, but instead directs each governor to select any standard on which to base the decision, then Congress has abdicated its duty to guide the execution of the law. Ac-cording to the Tribes, Congress failed to adequately constrain the discretion of the Gov-ernors, and §2719(b)(1)(A) therefore requires the Governors to establish Congressional policy, in violation of U.S. Const. Art. 1, §1.

The Supreme Court has explained that the nondelegation doctrine generally prohibits Congress from delegating its legislative power to another Branch of the federal govern-ment. We conclude that the nondelegation doctrine is not implicated by the provision at issue because §2719(b)(1)(A) does not delegate any legislative power to the Governors of the 50 States. When Congress enacts contingent legislation, it does not "abdicate, or ... transfer to others, the essential legislative functions with which it is vested by the Con-stitution." There is no "delegation of legislative authority" to the actor whose assent is a precondition to the execution of the law.

Congress exercised its legislative authority by enacting IGRA's general prohibition of gaming on after-acquired land, creating an exception to that rule in §2719(b)(1)(A), and dictating the prerequisites for the application of that exception. A governor does not enact federal policy by issuing a concurrence, but instead merely waives one legislatively enacted restriction on gaming. Nor does a governor impact federal policy by declining to concur; in that event, IGRA's policy of prohibiting gaming on after-acquired lands remains in force.

During oral argument, it became evident that the Tribes' concern is not so much the unconstrained discretion that Congress permitted the Governors of the 50 States to exercise under § 2719(b)(1)(A), but that Congress had delegated any power to the Governors at all. The Tribes conceded that they would not have objected on nondelegation grounds had Congress conditioned the Secretary's power to take land into trust not upon the concurrence of a governor, but rather upon the majority vote of the Indian tribes with reservations encompassed by the state where the proposed trust land is located. In the Tribes' view, the Governor of Wisconsin is an improper delegatee because his administration oversees the Wisconsin State Lottery, which they maintain is in competition with the casinos subject to regulation under IGRA. The Tribes rely on *Carter v. Carter Coal Co.*, 298 U.S. 238 (1936), for the proposition that Congress may not delegate to a private party the power to regulate an industry when the delegatee has "interests [that] may be and often are adverse to the interests of others in the same business."

At issue in *Carter* were certain provisions of the Bituminous Coal Conservation Act of 1935. Under that Act, the largest producers of coal were delegated the power to establish the maximum hour and minimum wage terms that controlled the entire coal industry. In striking down the provision, the Supreme Court was troubled that the statute did not empower "an official or an official body, presumptively disinterested," but instead empowered "private persons whose interests may be and often are adverse to the interests of others in the same business." The Supreme Court concluded that the Act denied the smaller coal producers their "rights safeguarded by the due process clause of the Fifth Amendment," and therefore invalidated the provision at issue.

We conclude that the gubernatorial concurrence provision does not raise the concerns presented in *Carter*. The Governors of the 50 States are politically accountable to their constituencies and will therefore be motivated to maximize the public good, contrary to the chief coal producers in *Carter*, whose relationship with minor coal producers was "conflicting and even antagonistic," and whose motivations were self-serving. Even if a particular governor might enjoy ultimate authority over a state lottery or gaming system, that role will surely be eclipsed by the governor's responsibility to regulate the broader state economy.

In conclusion, we find that § 2719(b)(1)(A) does not violate the nondelegation doctrine because it does not entrust to the Governors of the 50 States any legislative power, nor does it violate the principles of *Carter* by wrongfully authorizing a self-interested leader of private industry to regulate its competitors.

Notes and Questions

1.   Other challenges. The Seventh Circuit addressed and rejected a number of other arguments raised by the tribes. One was the tribes' argument that § 2719(b)(1)(A)'s gubernatorial concurrence requirement violated the Appointments Clause, which requires the President to appoint "Officers of the United States," or relatively high-level officials who exercise significant federal authority. U.S. Const. art. II, § 2, cl. 2. The court concluded,

> Nor is the governor's role under § 2719(b)(1)(A) significant enough to merit the title of an Officer of the United States. An Officer of the United States enjoys

more than a merely "temporary, episodic" opportunity to act pursuant to federal law, and instead enjoys a somewhat regular opportunity to issue enforceable decisions. Not only is a governor unable to issue the Secretary of the Interior's final decision regarding an Indian tribe's application under § 2719(b)(1)(A), a governor's opportunity to participate in the administration of IGRA will arise irregularly, if it materializes at all. Moreover, the influence of any one governor is temporary and limited to the particular application under review.

Lac Courte Oreilles, 367 F.3d at 661.

The tribes also challenged the gubernatorial concurrence requirement as violating the federal government's trust responsibility. This argument contended that Congress's power under the Indian Commerce Clause is limited by the trust doctrine, so that all legislation relying on the clause must be rationally related to serving the federal government's obligations under the doctrine. The Seventh Circuit refused to invalidate § 2719(b)(1)(A) on this ground:

> The Supreme Court has not yet invalidated a federal statute on the ground that it did not advance the federal government's trust obligation to Indian tribes. Indeed, even after concluding that an Act of Congress failed to comport with Congress's fiduciary responsibility to Indians, the Supreme Court refrained from acknowledging a cause of action on that ground. *See United States v. Sioux,* 448 U.S. 371 (1980). In *Sioux,* the Sioux Nation challenged the Congressional Act of February 28, 1877 ("the 1877 Act") which had authorized the confiscation of lands that had been pledged by treaty to the Sioux Nation. Before evaluating the Sioux Nation's claim, the Supreme Court sought to answer a preliminary question: had Congress enacted the 1877 Act in its capacity as trustee and guardian of tribal property, or had Congress instead passed the 1877 Act in exercise of its power of eminent domain? The *Sioux* Court endorsed the following test for distinguishing between the two types of Congressional action. If Congress had "made a good faith effort to give the Indians the full value of their lands," then Congress had acted in its fiduciary capacity. In the event that it had not attempted to adequately compensate the Sioux, however, then Congress had exercised its power of eminent domain and effecting a taking for which just compensation was due under the Fifth Amendment. Notably, the Supreme Court did not hold that Congress violated the trust doctrine by failing to make a "good faith effort" to "transmut[e]" the Sioux Nation's property for property of equal value, even though it acknowledged that a trustee would ordinarily be required to do so when dispensing of the property of her ward. The Sioux Nation prevailed in *Sioux,* but singularly on the ground that 1877 Act effected a taking under the Fifth Amendment. Thus, *Sioux* establishes that, in the context of congressional management of Indian land, the trust doctrine imposes no restriction on Congress beyond compliance with the constitutional restrictions which would otherwise constrain Congress's power.

Id. at 667.

Is the gubernatorial concurrence requirement legally sound? Even if so, is it unproblematic?

b. *Other Exceptions*

As one might expect, the politics of taking land into trust for the purpose of gaming has proved controversial in practice. Litigation has ensued over IGRA's various exceptions to the general prohibition on gaming on newly acquired land, often the result of a state challenging a determination in favor of a tribe. As you read the following cases, consider what Congress intended when it created the exceptions.

Due in part to the complexities of the historical relationship of tribes to the U.S., including the various eras of federal Indian policy, it is not always clear under which of the exceptions to IGRA's prohibition on gaming on newly acquired lands a tribe — or the Interior Secretary — is proceeding. As noted above, a tribe may submit a land-into-trust application without specifying which §2719 exception it believes applies to the land in question. Recall that §2719(b)(1)(B) exempts lands taken into trust as part of the "settlement of a land claim," "the initial reservation of an Indian tribe acknowledged by the Secretary," or the "restoration of lands for an Indian tribe that is restored to federal recognition." The following challenge concerns the interpretation of IGRA's "restoration of lands" exception under §2719(b)(1)(B)(iii).

City of Roseville v. Norton
348 F.3d 1020 (D.C. Cir. 2003)

The Auburn Indian Band is a small tribe, numbering somewhere around 247 members, most of whom live near the village of Auburn in central California, not far from Sacramento. The Auburn Band currently has no reservation; in fact, the Auburn Tribe had no federally recognized existence between 1967 and 1994. The Band appears to have been formed when several surviving families of the Maidu and Meiwok Tribes, both devastated by the settlement policies of the nineteenth century, grouped into a small community that survived much of the depredation that came with the settlement of California. In 1917, the federal government provided the Auburn Tribe with a small 20-acre reservation, which was expanded to 40 acres in 1953, known as the Auburn "Rancheria." As part of then-prevailing policies on Indian assimilation, however, Congress withdrew the Auburn Tribe's recognition and terminated its reservation in 1967, distributing most of the Rancheria land in fee to individual holders, pursuant to the terms of the Rancheria Act, Pub. L. No. 85-671 (1958). The policy of attempting to assimilate Indians by terminating federal trust responsibilities has since been repudiated by the President and Congress, and many tribes terminated as part of those policies have now been restored to federal recognition.

Congress restored the Auburn Band's rights as a federally recognized tribe in 1994 and authorized the Secretary of the Interior to take land into trust to serve as the Auburn Tribe's reservation. [The Auburn Indian Restoration Act, 25 U.S.C. §§ 1300http://www.west-law.com/Find/Default.wl?rs=dfa1.0&vr=2.0&DB=1000546&DocName=25USCAS50&FindType=Ll-1300l-7 (2003) ("AIRA")] directs the Secretary to accept lands located on the Tribe's former reservation into trust, but also authorizes the Secretary to accept other unencumbered lands located elsewhere in Placer County. AIRA also references the Secretary's authority, pursuant to the Indian Reorganization Act, to take additional land into trust within the tribe's "service area," which includes several neighboring counties. Under AIRA, all land taken into trust pursuant to its terms "shall be part of the Tribe's reservation."

Rather than apply to the Secretary to re-establish their reservation on the Rancheria, most of which land was unavailable because held in fee by individual Indians or non-Indians, the Auburn Tribe applied for three separate parcels of land: one for residential and community use, one for commercial use as a gaming casino, and a third, containing a church within the boundaries of the old reservation, for community use. The Tribe submitted a revised application in 2000, however, to request only the gaming site, reserving the other two sites for later applications. The gaming site consists of 49.21 acres located in an unincorporated portion of Placer County, California, and photographs of the area indicate that the land is flat, barren, and virtually uninhabited. The parties disagree over how far the land is from the Auburn Tribe's Rancheria, but it is at least clear that the land is neither on nor close to the Tribe's former reservation, and is possibly as far as 40 miles away. What is clear, however, is that the land is close to the Cities [of Roseville and Rocklin].

In response to the Bureau of Indian Affairs' notice and request for comments, the Cities opposed the Auburn Tribe's application, arguing that the casino would increase crime in their communities and interfere with planned residential developments nearby, as well as with the family-oriented nature of the area. Moreover, they argued that because the proposed gaming was to take place on land acquired after the IGRA's effective date of October 17, 1988, the Secretary was not authorized to permit gaming on the land unless she made a threshold determination under § 2719(b)(1)(A), that the proposed gaming activity "would not be detrimental to the surrounding communities" and obtained the concurrence of the Governor. The Bureau, relying on opinions of two Associate Solicitors of the Interior Department, took the position that the land was exempt from the threshold no-community-detriment finding normally applicable to Indian lands acquired after 1988 because AIRA brought the Auburn Tribe's land within IGRA's exception for a "restoration of lands" to a restored tribe under § 2719(b)(1)(B)(iii). The Cities' objections based on local community detriment were therefore not legally relevant, as IGRA does not require a no-community-detriment finding on lands that are part of a "restoration of lands" before the Secretary can authorize gaming. The Cities' objections were not entirely irrelevant, however, because the Bureau considered the Tribe's land a "discretionary" acquisition, and Interior Department regulations, see 25 C.F.R. pt. 151, require the Secretary to consider potential land use conflicts and jurisdictional problems. Additionally, the Secretary must balance the need of a tribe for additional land, the use to which the land will be put, and the distance of the land from the tribe's reservation, before exercising discretion to take new land into trust for Indians. The Bureau found that the balance of these factors favored the Auburn Tribe's planned use of the land for gaming. Ultimately, the Secretary, through her designees, agreed with the legal and factual determinations and approved the Tribe's application. Notice was published in the Federal Register of the Secretary's intent to take the land into trust.

Section 2719 creates a prohibition: gaming is not permitted on Indian land taken into trust by the Secretary after IGRA's effective date, October 17, 1988, unless the land borders an existing reservation or is within the last recognized reservation of a tribe that was landless at the time IGRA was enacted (unless the tribe is in Oklahoma, in which case lands bordering its former reservation are exempted as well). This prohibition is subject to two exceptions. The first, § 2719(b)(1)(A), allows the Secretary of the Interior to override the general prohibition and permit gaming on a newly acquired parcel when, "after consultation with the Indian tribe and appropriate State and local officials" the Secretary "determines that a gaming establishment ... would be in the best interest of the Indian tribe and its members, and would not be detrimental to the surrounding community, but only if the Governor of the State ... concurs...." The second, § 2719(b)(1)(B), exempts lands taken into trust as part of the "settlement of a land claim," "the initial reservation of an Indian tribe acknowledged by the Secretary," or the "restoration of lands for an Indian tribe that is restored to federal recognition." The IGRA does not define a "restoration of lands."

The Cities do not challenge the Secretary's authority under AIRA to take the land into trust for the Tribe. Nor do they contend on appeal that the Secretary's decision to accept the Tribe's application improperly balanced the factors set forth in the Department's regulations, 25 C.F.R. pt. 151, by failing to give adequate weight to the Cities' concerns. Thus, the Cities' appeal presents a single question of statutory interpretation. They contend that the Secretary violated IGRA because the Auburn Tribe's acquisition of the 49.21 acres cannot be a "restoration of lands" as the Tribe never owned those acres in the past as part of its former reservation, the Rancheria, and the tract of land is too different from the Rancheria to be a "restoration" of it. IGRA therefore forbids gaming on the land absent a finding by the Secretary, concurred in by the Governor, that gaming will not have a detrimental effect on the local community—a finding the Secretary did not make. The Cities maintain that the "restoration of lands" exception can bear only one meaning, namely, that lands must be either identical or almost identical to those previously owned in order to be a "restoration," and that that reading is necessitated by the IGRA's overall policy of limiting the expansion of Indian gaming.

All parties urge plain meaning constructions of the exception, albeit with different nuances. The Cities, citing Webster's Dictionary, urge the narrowest construction of the word "restoration" as "bring[ing] back to an original state," in light of their view that IGRA is designed to restrict gambling on Indian reservations and to protect surrounding communities. The Secretary and the Tribe, also referring us to the dictionary, urge an interpretation of the word "restoration" that encompasses the concept of "restitution." The Tribe also points to this meaning of the word in ancient times as encompassing a broader concept of compensation. The Book of Exodus, for instance, at Chapter 22, Verse 1, requires that someone guilty of killing or selling another's stock must "restore five oxen for an ox, and four sheep for a sheep."

No circuit court of appeals has yet had occasion to address the scope of IGRA's "restoration of lands" exception under § 2719(b)(1)(B)(iii), and district courts have assumed that lands are "restored" when included in a tribe's restoration act. When the exception has been litigated, the question has usually been whether there can be a "restoration of lands for an Indian tribe restored to federal recognition" even though the recognition of the Tribe and the land grant did not occur as a result of the same statute—implying that when they do it is the paradigm "restoration of lands." For example, in *Confederated Tribes of Coos v. Babbitt*, 116 F. Supp. 2d 155, 161–65 (D.D.C. 2000), the court rejected the Secretary's interpretation, since modified, that the "restoration of lands" exception applies only to lands taken into trust pursuant to a statute restoring a tribe to federal recognition, and held that lands a tribe acquires by other means might also qualify under certain circumstances. Even assuming the instant case is not at the center of the paradigm because the AIRA does not identify these particular 49 acres in Placer County, the term "restoration" can nonetheless readily be construed to include lands acquired pursuant to the restoration statute (AIRA) from within the restored tribe's service area designated in the AIRA.

Because the Auburn Tribe's land is located in Placer County, which was a designated area in the AIRA, and thus became, by operation of law, the Tribe's reservation, the court has no occasion to decide whether land obtained by a tribe other than through the tribe's restoration act is the "restoration of lands" for IGRA purposes, nor whether "restored" tribes include those whose termination or recognition has not been the result of congressional action. Instead, the court must decide the ancillary question presented by the Cities' appeal of whether lands identified in a tribe's restoration act as its reservation must meet the additional qualification of prior tribal ownership before the land can be considered a "restoration of lands for an Indian tribe that is restored to federal recognition."

The Cities contend that the plain meaning of the term "restoration of lands" cannot encompass lands over which a tribe did not exert prior ownership, or which are dissimilar from those the tribe previously owned. Because to "restore" something means to "bring [it] back to an original state," they maintain that the only lands that can be "restored" to the Auburn Tribe are those on its prior reservation, the Rancheria, or lands sufficiently similar in nature that they can be said to bring the reservation back to its "original" state. Other land acquired pursuant to AIRA, such as the 49 acres that the Secretary has agreed to take into trust, are simply "lands acquired by the Secretary in trust for the benefit of an Indian Tribe after October 17, 1988" for which the Auburn Tribe, like any other tribe that acquires new land, must meet the requirements of § 2719(b)(1)(A) before the land can be used for commercial gaming. The Cities maintain that the narrow reading of the word "restore" is supported by IGRA's general ban on Indian gaming because if a "restoration" of lands is allowed to encompass lands to which a tribe does not demonstrate a prior connection, such as prior ownership, the exception will swallow the rule. However, the Secretary and the Tribe respond with dictionary definitions of their own, contending that "restoration" encompasses the concept of "restitution," such that it can be a "restoration" to give the Auburn Tribe lands to make restitution for past wrongs. They point out that this meaning of the word, even if less common in everyday parlance, is also included in the dictionary, fits far better with the structure of IGRA and the remedial purposes of AIRA, and is supported by AIRA's provision that all lands taken into trust pursuant to the act "shall be part of the Tribe's reservation."

There is much to commend the interpretation of the Secretary and the Auburn Tribe regarding the scope of the "restoration of lands" exception. The IGRA plainly includes exceptions to its general prohibition of gaming on off-reservation sites, and Congress' purpose in enacting IGRA includes the promotion of tribal economic self-sufficiency, a purpose with which Congress' enactment of AIRA is entirely consistent. Moreover, the syntax of the statute, which discusses not simply the restoration of the lands themselves, but their restoration "for an Indian tribe," fits more comfortably with the concept of restitution. Even the definitions of "restore" the Cities quote in their own brief include the notion of restitution. But, for the reasons advanced by the Cities, a narrower construction of the exception is not without a measure of plausibility. In sum, neither side can prevail by quoting the dictionary.

We turn, therefore, to context, for the court is to "consider not only the bare meaning of the word but also its placement and purpose in the statutory scheme." The force of the Cities' interpretation fades upon closer analysis, particularly in light of the general environment in which IGRA was enacted, its structure and general purpose. Even assuming that the Cities' definition of "restore" as to "bring back to an original state" is the more common meaning of the word, the statutory context makes broader readings of § 2719(b)(1)(B)(iii) more plausible. That a "restoration of lands" could easily encompass new lands given to a restored tribe to re-establish its land base and compensate it for historical wrongs is evident here, where much of the Auburn Tribe's Rancheria is, as a practical matter, unavailable to it. Further, even under the Cities' definition of "restore" as to "bring back to an original state," there would appear to be no reason to limit the "original state" to 1967, rather than the earlier period before the Tribe was granted only a 40-acre reservation. Section 2719(b)(1)(B)(iii) refers to the restoration of "lands," not the restoration of a "reservation." The Maidu and Meiwok Tribes from which the Auburn Tribe descended once occupied much of central California. For the Cities to now argue that the 49 acres are a windfall, as if the Tribe's ancestors had never possessed any more, is ahistorical. Given the history of Indian tribes' confinement to reservations, it is not reasonable to suppose that Congress intended "restoration" to be strictly limited to land constituting a tribe's reservation immediately before federal recognition was terminated.

The Cities' interpretation is also difficult to reconcile with IGRA's other provisions. Limiting a "restoration of lands" to the return of lands on a tribe's prior reservation practically reads the "restoration of lands" provision out of existence. As one of the exemptions the "restoration of lands" in §2719(b)(1)(B)(iii), unless it is surplusage, must exempt some land that would otherwise fall within the gaming prohibition of §2719(a). But the general prohibition explicitly excludes the "last recognized reservation" of a tribe that "has no reservation on October 17, 1988." Under the Cities' plain meaning interpretation whereby the only lands that can be part of a "restoration" are those in a tribe's former reservation, the exception would be virtually bereft of meaning because gaming on such lands is not prohibited in the first place. If the Auburn Tribe had reacquired some of the land on its former reservation, the Rancheria, it would have no need to look to the "restoration of lands" exception in order to use the land for commercial gaming because §2719(a)(2)(B) would have excluded its Rancheria from the general ban on gaming. While a few scenarios might exist where §2719(b)(1)(B)(iii) would remain applicable under the Cities' interpretation (such as in the case of tribes who held other reservations prior to their "last recognized reservation"), the scope of the exemption would be substantially diminished in a manner that would appear inconsistent with Congress' general goal under IGRA of "promoting tribal economic development" and "self-sufficiency." The difficulty of reassembling a former reservation as a result of the passage of substantial periods of time between the loss of federal recognition and its restoration is illustrated by the experience of the Auburn Tribe: its Rancheria is largely held in fee by individuals and unavailable as a practical matter more than a quarter of a century later. To be given meaningful effect, then, a "restoration of lands" would seem to encompass more than only the return of a tribe's former reservation.

The Cities contend, as a fallback position, that, at the very least, land cannot be considered brought "back to its original state" unless it is at least similar to the reservation it replaces. Indeed, the Cities' view that the Secretary violated IGRA by failing to make a factual determination that the accepted tract of land was substantially identical to the old Rancheria depends on their view that the 49.21 acres cannot meet this standard because is too geographically distant, considerably more valuable, and to be put to commercial rather than residential use. But to the extent the Cities rely on the notion that the Auburn Tribe's new land cannot be a "restoration" because it is not being used residentially, like the old Rancheria was, their argument is nonsensical. The point of the "restoration of lands" exception is that such lands may be used for gaming; it would make no sense if a tribe's use of land for gaming could defeat the land's eligibility for gaming. Moreover, these considerations undermine the Cities' plain meaning interpretation by admitting that a "restoration of lands" to a tribe can include different lands than those on its former reservation, as occurred here.

Essentially, the Cities maintain that the "restoration of lands" exception cannot be read in a manner that would allow the Auburn Tribe to put together a new reservation that an "established" tribe would not be permitted to acquire, namely, a gaming parcel separate from its residential and community areas. This explains the Cities' reasoning that a broad reading of the exception would swallow the rule. Because the Tribe would not have been permitted to acquire the 49 acres for gaming if its federal recognition had never been terminated, its "restoration" should not allow it greater rights than it otherwise would have enjoyed as a chronologically continuous tribe. This approach is problematic for several reasons. Had the Auburn Tribe never been terminated, it would have had opportunities for development in the intervening years, including the possible acquisition of new land prior to the effective date of IGRA. A "restoration of lands" compensates the Tribe not only for what it lost by the act of termination, but also for opportunities lost in the interim.

Even assuming the policy underlying IGRA §2719(a) does support a narrow reading of the "restoration of lands" exception, the exceptions as well as AIRA itself all embody policies counseling for a broader reading. The general purpose of IGRA is "promoting tribal economic development" and "self-sufficiency." A reading allowing the Auburn Tribe to participate in that economic base furthers this purpose of IGRA while a reading that confines "restoration of lands" to the old reservation, the Rancheria, (most of which is now in the hands of homeowners, many non-Indian, and hence unavailable for development) would likely deny the Tribe this opportunity. The same objective is apparent in AIRA, which directs the Secretary to consult with the tribe regarding a plan for economic development. AIRA's purpose of reestablishing the Auburn Tribe as an economically viable entity would be served by considering the new reservation established under the Restoration Act a "restoration of lands" allowing it to operate a gaming facility.

Finally, were there any remaining doubt that Congress intended IGRA's "restoration of lands" exception to be read broadly, to encompass more than a tribe's former reservation as of the date of the termination of its federal recognition, the Cities appear to appreciate that their interpretation would not prevail. The Indian Canon of statutory construction would resolve any doubt. The Supreme Court has on numerous occasions noted that ambiguities in federal statutes are to be read liberally in favor of the Indians. *See generally County of Yakima v. Confederated Tribes & Bands of Yakima Indian Nation*, 502 U.S. 251 (1992); *Montana v. Blackfeet Tribe*, 471 U.S. 759 (1985). IGRA is designed to promote the economic viability of Indian Tribes, and AIRA focuses on ensuring the same for the Auburn Tribe. In this context, the Indian canon requires the court to resolve any doubt in favor of the tribe.

Wyandotte Nation v. NIGC
437 F. Supp. 2d 1193 (D. Kan. 2006)

This matter is before the Court upon plaintiff Wyandotte Nation's ("the Tribe" or "Wyandotte") challenge to the final agency decision of the National Indian Gaming Commission ("NIGC") concluding that plaintiffs may not lawfully conduct gaming on the Shriner Tract, a parcel of land that the United States holds in trust for the benefit of plaintiffs.

The Tribe's ancestors, known as the Huron, originally resided in Canada, eventually moving south to the area around Detroit and into what is presently Ohio and western Pennsylvania, becoming known as the Wyandotte. In a series of treaties between 1795 and 1832, the Tribe ceded to the United States all of its interest in approximately six million acres of land in the present states of Ohio and Michigan. In 1842, the Tribe entered into a treaty with the United States ceding its remaining Ohio and Michigan lands to the United States in exchange for an unidentified 148,000-acre tract of land located west of the Mississippi River. The Tribe then negotiated to purchase land from the Shawnee Tribe located near Westport, Missouri.

The Tribe moved westward to the Town of Kansas in 1843, and originally took up residence on a strip of federal land between the Missouri border and the Kansas River. Shortly thereafter, the Tribe learned that the Shawnee Tribe would not complete the sale of the Westport lands and that the United States would not honor its 1842 Treaty commitment to provide the Tribe with a 148,000-acre reserve. On December 14, 1843, the Tribe entered into an agreement with the Delaware Nation to acquire land in the Kansas Territory. Under that agreement, the Delaware Nation gifted to the Tribe three sections of land, each comprising 640 acres, situated in the Kansas Territory at the confluence of the Kansas and Missouri Rivers. The Delaware Nation also sold the Tribe an additional thirty-six sections of land, located west of the gifted land. The United States Senate ratified the 1843 Agreement between the Tribe and the Delaware Nation on July 25, 1848.

Between 1843 and 1855, the Tribe was instrumental in founding and platting Wyandotte City, later renamed Kansas City, Kansas. In 1855, the Tribe entered into a Treaty with the United States ceding the thirty-six sections of land that it had purchased from the Delaware Nation to the United States. Specifically reserved from the Treaty cession were three parcels, one of which was the Huron Parcel, which was and remains adjacent to the "Shriner Tract"—the parcel at issue in this case. The Treaty of 1855 also offered the Tribe's members the option of becoming United States citizens or maintaining their tribal affiliation and relocating to the present State of Oklahoma. In 1857, 200 tribal members who had elected to maintain their tribal affiliation were removed to the Indian Territory in Oklahoma. The Wyandotte eventually received their own reservation in the Indian Territory pursuant to the Omnibus Treaty of 1867. In 1893, the Tribe's reservation was allotted to individual tribal members.

Pursuant to the Oklahoma Indian Welfare Act of 1936, the Wyandotte adopted a Constitution and By-Laws, which were ratified on July 24, 1937. In 1956, the United States terminated federal supervision over the Tribe; the termination attempt was never completed because it was conditioned upon the United States purchasing the Huron Cemetery from the Wyandotte—an event that never occurred. Congress restored the Wyandotte as a federally recognized Indian Tribe in 1978. The Tribe's Revised Constitution was approved in 1985. The United States has held the Huron Parcel in trust for the benefit of the Tribe from 1855 to the present day. The Tribe contends that the Huron Parcel and land surrounding that parcel, including the Shriner Tract, are of "tremendous historical significance" to the Tribe.

During the 1950's, the Wyandotte filed several actions against the United States with the Indian Claims Commission (the "ICC") involving title determination of the Tribe's claims to land. The ICC entered judgment for the Tribe. The judgments were compensation for lands in Ohio that the Wyandottes had ceded to the United States in the 1800's. To effectuate the judgment, Congress enacted Public Law 98-602 that, *inter alia,* mandated that a portion of the judgment funds be used for the purchase of real property, which the Secretary of the Interior was required to take into trust for the benefit of the Tribe.

In 1994 and 1995, as part of its efforts to develop a gaming facility in Wyandotte County, Kansas, the Tribe negotiated the purchase of several properties adjacent to the Huron Cemetery. In January 1996, the Tribe submitted an application to the Bureau of Indian Affairs ("BIA") requesting that the United States accept title to these parcels, including the "Shriner Tract," in trust for the Tribe's benefit, citing the mandatory acquisition provision contained in Pub.L. 98-602. In memoranda dated February 13, 1996 and May 16, 1996, the Associate Solicitor for Division of Indian Affairs at the Department of Interior concluded that: (1) Pub.L. 98-602 mandated that the Secretary of the Interior acquire the Shriner Tract in trust for the Wyandotte and (2) the Huron Parcel was Wyandotte reservation land on October 17, 1988, and that because the proposed trust parcels were contiguous to the Tribe's reservation, the parcels qualified for gaming under § 2719(a)(1). On or about June 12, 1996, the Assistant Secretary for Indian Affairs ("Assistant Secretary") published a Notice in the Federal Register stating that the BIA intended to accept title to the Shriner Tract into trust for the benefit of the Wyandotte for gaming purposes.

On July 12, 1996, the Governor of the State of Kansas and four other Indian tribes located in the State of Kansas filed suit against the Assistant Secretary, seeking to enjoin the trust acquisition of the Shriner Tract. After an injunction was entered against the United States, the Wyandotte took an emergency appeal to the Tenth Circuit Court of Appeals; on July 15, 1996, the Tenth Circuit vacated the injunction, and that same day, the Secretary accepted title to the Shriner Tract in trust for the Wyandotte's benefit.

The case found its way back to the Tenth Circuit, which concluded that Pub.L. 98-602 is a mandatory trust acquisition statute, that the Secretary had no discretion in accepting title to the Shriner Tract in trust for the Tribe, and that neither National Environmental Policy Act of 1969 (NEPA) nor National Historic Preservation Act (NHPA) analyses were required for the non-discretionary decision to take the property into trust. The court remanded the case to the district court with instructions to remand to the Secretary to determine whether the Shriner Tract was purchased with only Pub.L. 98-602 funds.

The Circuit refused to give deference to the Secretary's determination that the Shriner Tract was contiguous to the Wyandotte reservation as of October 17, 1988. The court held that the Secretary lacked authority to interpret the term "reservation" under an exception to the general prohibition against gaming contained in Section 2719 of the IGRA. As such, the court concluded that because the Huron Cemetery was not a reservation, the Shriner Tract was not contiguous to the Wyandotte's reservation. Congress reacted to this part of the court's determination, however, by passing legislation declaring the authority to determine whether a specific area of land is a "reservation" for purposes of IGRA was delegated to the Secretary of the Interior on October 17, 1988.

On remand, the Secretary confirmed that the Shriner Tract was, in fact, purchased with only Pub.L. 98-602 funds and on March 11, 2002, published a Notice in the Federal Register, concluding the same. Plaintiffs challenged the agency decision pursuant to the Administrative Procedure Act; this Court recently entered an Order affirming the Secretary's decision on remand.

In this case, the Tribe submitted a Class II Gaming Ordinance to the NIGC, which the NIGC Chairman approved on June 29, 1994. On June 19, 2002, the Tribe submitted an Amended Gaming Ordinance to the NIGC, which specifically stated that Class II gaming would be conducted on the Shriner Tract. The Tribe also submitted documentation to support its assertion that the Shriner Tract met three separate exceptions to IGRA's prohibition of gaming on lands acquired after October 17, 1988. When the NIGC indicated that it needed more time to decide if the Shriner Tract was eligible for gaming, the Tribe withdrew the Amended Gaming Ordinance, and subsequently advised the NIGC that it did not intend to game on the Shriner Tract after all.

One year later, on August 28, 2003, the Tribe commenced gaming at a small Class II gaming facility on the Shriner Tract. The gaming consisted of approximately fifty Class II gaming devices located in temporary trailers. Approximately forty-eight persons were employed at the Tribe's gaming facility. On September 10, 2004, the NIGC issued a final agency decision and order finding that the Tribe may not lawfully game on the Shriner Tract, based on its determination that none of the exceptions to IGRA's general prohibition were applicable.

Under the Administrative Procedures Act ("APA"), "[a] person suffering legal wrong because of agency action, or adversely affected or aggrieved by agency action within the meaning of a relevant statute, is entitled to judicial review thereof." The APA authorizes the reviewing court to "compel agency action unlawfully withheld" and to "hold unlawful and set aside agency actions, findings, and conclusions" that the court finds to be, as plaintiffs allege here, "arbitrary, capricious, an abuse of discretion, or otherwise not in accordance with law."

The appropriate framework for analysis is *Chevron, U.S.A., Inc. v. Natural Resources Defense Council*, 467 U.S. 837 (1984). *Chevron* requires a two-step analysis. The first question "always, is … whether Congress has directly spoken to the precise question at issue." But if the statute is silent or ambiguous, the Court is generally required to defer to the agency's interpretation "if it is based on a permissible construction of the statute." More specifically, if the Court finds "an express delegation of authority to the agency to elucidate a specific provision of the statute by regulation," we must accept the agency's interpretation unless it is "arbitrary, capricious, or manifestly contrary to the statute." Alternatively, if the Court does not find an express delegation by Congress, but nevertheless perceives an implicit delegation to the agency on the particular question, it must accept a "reasonable interpretation made by the administrator of [the] agency."

Complicating the matter, the Tenth Circuit has held that the canon of construction that ambiguities are to be resolved in favor of Native Americans may control over the deference otherwise afforded administrative agencies under *Chevron*. The canon only has a role in the interpretation of an ambiguous statute.

The Tribe argues that three exceptions to the general prohibition on gaming on after-acquired lands apply to the Shriner Tract: (1) the Shriner Tract is within the Tribe's last reservation; (2) the Shriner Tract was taken into trust as part of a settlement of a land claim; and (3) the Shriner Tract was taken into trust as a part of the restoration of their lands. The Court addresses each of these exceptions in turn.

The "last reservation exception" provides that gaming may be conducted on lands acquired after October 17, 1988, provided that: (1) the tribe had no reservation on October 17, 1988; (2) the lands are located in a state other than Oklahoma; and (3) the lands are located "within the Indian tribe's last recognized reservation within the State or States within which such Indian tribe is presently located." The first two parts of this exception are met: the Tribe had no reservation on October 17, 1988, and the Shriner Tract is in Kansas, not Oklahoma. The Court thus turns its attention to the remaining issue: whether the land at issue is within the Tribe's last recognized reservation within the State or States within which the Tribe is presently located.

This issue turns on the scope and meaning of the term "presently located," which is not defined by the IGRA. Both parties urge plain meaning constructions of the exception, albeit with different results. The dictionary definition of "presently" is "at the present time." The word "located" means "to establish oneself or one's business" or "to set or establish in a particular spot." The NIGC defines "presently located" to mean where the tribe physically resides; to determine where this is, the NIGC looks to the seat of tribal government and population center in concluding that the Tribe is presently located in Oklahoma.

The Tribe argues that a plain reading of section 2719(a)(2) evinces that there is no requirement that the Tribe's seat of government and population center must be located in the state where the land taken into trust is located. By determining that the Tribe is not presently located in Kansas because its population center and seat of government are located in Oklahoma, the Tribe asserts that the NIGC read the phrase "or States" out of section 2719(a)(2)(B).

The NIGC counters that the phrase "State or States within which such tribe is presently located" is Congress' acknowledgment that there are many tribes whose reservations span several states; for example, the Navaho reservation spans the borders of Arizona, New Mexico and Utah. The parties dispute, however, whether such tribes are required to have a seat of government in more than one state, or merely a "major governmental presence" on their reservations in those states. If the former, the Tribe contends that the NIGC rendered the phrase "or States" superfluous, and thus its final decision is inconsistent with the plain meaning of the statute. The Tribe argues that none of the tribes listed by the NIGC by way of example have their seat of government in more than one state. If the NIGC applied the same "major governmental presence" test to the Wyandotte as it did for those tribes, the Tribe contends that it would certainly qualify for the exception, as the Wyandotte exercises governmental authority over the Shriner Tract.

The Court agrees with the Tribe that the NIGC's decision appears to nullify the term "or States." By defining the term "presently located" to mean where a tribe's seat of tribal government is located, the NIGC decision only permits a tribe to qualify for the exception in a single state. This definition contradicts the plain language of the statute, which expressly applies the last reservation exception to "State or States" where the Indian tribe is presently located. The Tribe seems to accept a less restrictive definition of "presently located" put forward by the NIGC in its brief, i.e., where a tribe has its population center and *"major governmental presence."* The Court agrees that this is a reasonable interpretation in light of the plain meaning of the phrase "presently located," and adopts the same.

The Court thus turns to the issue of application of the phrase "presently located" to the Tribe in this case. The Tribe asserts that it exercises governmental authority over the Shriner Tract, as determined by the NIGC in its original Opinion Letter. In addition, the Tribe maintains that it had a major governmental presence in Kansas by virtue of the Tribal Gaming Commission, which exercised jurisdiction over the Tribe's gaming activities, albeit unauthorized. The Tribe also asserts that the Huron Cemetery has been held in trust for the Tribe's benefit since 1855 and the record indicates the existence of an intergovernmental agreement with Kansas City, Kansas providing for the maintenance and security of the cemetery. Finally, the Tribe stresses that approximately 100 of its members reside and work in Wyandotte County.

The Court concludes that, even applying the less restrictive "major governmental presence" definition, the Tribe does not qualify for the last reservation exception. Although there appears to be no dispute that the Tribe exercises governmental *power* over the Shriner Tract, the Court does not agree that this constitutes a major governmental *presence* in Kansas. On the contrary, it appears that the Wyandottes' governmental power was primarily exercised from Oklahoma. While the Tribe has an inter-governmental agreement with Kansas City providing for the maintenance and security of the Huron Cemetery, there is nothing in the record that indicates the Tribe performs any of this oversight. Nor is there anything in the record to support the Tribe's assertion that the Tribal Gaming Commission constituted a major governmental presence, through regular meetings or inspections by the commission. Thus, the Tribe's governmental presence in Kansas appears to be peripheral rather than major.

The Court also rejects the Tribe's assertion that approximately 100 members constitutes a "population center." These tribal members resided in Wyandotte County at the time of the NIGC decision and shortly after the gaming activities were shut down by the Attorney General of Kansas. Although the Tribe may have a presence in Kansas, its population center is Oklahoma. Accordingly, the Court finds that the Shriner Tract does not meet the last reservation exception, and the NIGC's decision is upheld on this issue.

The Tribe argues that the NIGC ignored the plain language of IGRA in concluding that the Shriner Tract did not qualify for gaming under the "settlement of a land claim" exception in Section 2719(b)(1)(B)(i). That section provides for an exception to the general prohibition on gaming on land taken into trust after 1988 if the land was taken into trust "as part of a settlement of a land claim." Specifically, the Tribe argues that the Shriner Tract was taken into trust as part of the settlement of a land claim because the Wyandotte acquired the land pursuant to a settlement of its title claims against the United States, filed with the ICC. In those proceedings, the Wyandotte, along with other tribal signatories to the Treaty of Greenville, asserted claims for the tribal land cessions to the United States under the Treaty of Fort Industry of 1805 and the Treaty of September 29, 1817, respectively. The claims asserted by the Wyandotte involved determinations of (1) whether the tribes held recognized title to the property, and (2) if so, what percentage interest each tribe held. The United States disputed that the Treaty of Greenville granted recognized title to the tribes. The ICC held that the Tribe was granted recognized title to what was known as the Royce Areas 53 and 54 by virtue of two treaties and that the ICC had to apportion interest in the areas among various tribal signatories to the treaties before the ICC could evaluate damages. The Tribe asserts that a claim requiring a determination of ownership of title to land is a "land claim" within the meaning of the exception. After considering these arguments, the NIGC concluded that the "land claims" exception did not apply because the ICC granted the Tribe a money judgment.

As with the "last reservation" exception, the interpretation of the land claims settlement exception must begin with the language of the statute itself. The initial question to be addressed is whether the Tribe's ICC claims were "land claims" within the meaning of section 2719(b)(1)(B)(i), which does not define the term. As with the last reservation exception, both parties contend that the term "land claim" is clear and unambiguous, with divergent results. There is no dispute about the meaning of the word "land," which Webster's defines as "the solid ground of the earth." The Black's Law Dictionary definition of "claim" is "[t]he aggregate of operative facts giving rise to a right enforceable by a court," or "assertion of an existing right." Webster's defines "claim" as "a demand for something as rightful or due."

The NIGC asserts that a claim for land clearly means a claim for a *return* of land, not a *monetary* award, which is what the Tribe received. The NIGC focused on the nature of the claim brought by the Tribe and the resulting award to the Tribe, stating that the Tribe brought claims before the ICC and Claims Court exclusively for money damages, not over title to land itself, and that the award was limited to money damages.

In other words, as articulated by counsel at oral argument, in order to qualify for the exception a claim must be related to the land itself, rather than a wrong committed over the land.

This approach is problematic. The plain meaning of "land claim" does not limit such claim to one for the return of land, but rather, includes an assertion of an existing right to the land. As the Tribe points out, the word "land" modifies the word "claim," not "settlement," and thus a "land claim" means that the operative facts giving rise to a right arise from a dispute over land, not that the land claim be resolved by the return of land. Thus, the plain language of section 2719(b)(1)(B)(i) does not preclude the land claim brought before the ICC in this case from falling within that exception.

By restricting its interpretation of "land claim" to mean only a claim for the return of land, the NIGC appears to have focused on the remedy sought by a tribe rather than the substantive claim itself. Until 1946, Indian tribes could not litigate claims against the United States unless they obtained specific permission from Congress. The Indian Claims Commission Act ("ICCA") was enacted that year, creating a quasi-judicial body to hear and determine all tribal claims against the United States that accrued before August 13, 1946. The period for filing tribal claims with the ICC was limited to five years. The ICCA limited the scope of relief for tribes to an award of monetary compensation rather than the return of disputed lands or the confirmation of title. Federal courts, including the Tenth Circuit, have held that the ICC was the exclusive forum for Indian land claims, including claims such as the Wyandottes' to litigate the validity of title to lands that were ceded to the United States and to be recompensed for government actions inconsistent with those titles. Thus, the NIGC's characterization of the nature of the ICC case as one "exclusively" for money damages ignores the fact that this was the exclusive remedy for a tribe bringing a land claim under the ICC.

The NIGC's focus on the ICC money judgment might pass muster if the Tribe had merely purchased the Shriner Tract with money received from a claim brought before the ICC. That is not the case, however, because Congress mandated that $100,000 of the Tribe's ICC judgment funds be utilized to purchase land to be taken into trust for the benefit of the Tribe as a means of effectuating a judgment that resolved the Tribe's land claims. The Wyandotte used the funds appropriated by Congress in satisfaction of the ICC judgment to acquire the Shriner Tract, and the Secretary, based upon the mandate of Pub.L. 98-602, accepted title to the Shriner Tract in trust for the Tribe.

In this case, the NIGC's focus on the monetary nature of the ICC judgment and its dismissal of Pub.L. 98-602 as merely a "mechanism" with which to distribute judgment funds awarded to the Tribe, leads the Court to conclude that the NIGC failed to consider an important aspect of a factor upon which it relied in making its decision. That the remedy for a land claim is monetary, rather than specific relief, is irrelevant where, as here, Congress *mandated* that the monetary remedy be utilized to purchase land to be held in trust for the benefit of the Tribe. The Court therefore concludes, after much reflection, that the NIGC's articulated reason for its interpretation is arbitrary, capricious and unsupported by law.

The Court also finds that the NIGC's decision is at odds with a determination by the Secretary of the Interior that certain Seneca Nation lands were acquired as part of the settlement of a land claim. The Seneca Nation, like the Wyandotte, sought to game on a parcel of land that was taken into trust after October 17, 1988, and asserted that gaming should be allowed on its after-acquired land because the land fell within the "settlement of land claim" exception. The Seneca based its assertion that the exception was applicable because the land was purchased with funds obtained from the "Seneca Nation Settlement Act of 1990" (the "Settlement Act"). Pursuant to the Settlement Act, the Secretary of the Interior and the State of New York paid the Seneca Nation a total of $60 million; there was no "claim for return of land." Congress declared that a portion of that $60 million be used "for economic or community development," and that the Seneca Nation "may" acquire "[l]and within its aboriginal area in the State or situated within or near proximity to former reservation land...."

After comparing the facts of this case with the Seneca Nation, the Court finds that the NIGC's reasoning was internally contradictory, further supporting its finding that the Final Determination in this case is arbitrary and capricious. Specifically, the NIGC's reasoning required the Wyandotte to establish "a claim for the return of land," whereas the Seneca Nation was required [only] to establish a claim for compensation for a breached lease. The NIGC has required the Wyandotte to meet criteria that it has not required in other cases, and the Secretary of the Interior has allowed lands to qualify for the settlement of lands exception in circumstances at least as suitable as the case at bar. Because the agency's action was internally inconsistent, it was not founded on a reasoned evaluation of the relevant factors and must be set aside.

The Tribe argues that the NIGC applied inappropriate criteria when analyzing whether the Tribe met the "restored lands" exception to IGRA's general prohibition of gaming on land acquired in trust after October 17, 1988. Section 2719(b)(1)(B)(iii) provides that the prohibition will not apply when lands are taken into trust as part of "the restoration of lands for an Indian tribe that is restored to Federal recognition." This analysis requires a two-part determination: (1) that the Tribe is a "restored" tribe, and (2) that the Shriner Tract was taken into trust as part of a "restoration" of lands to such restored tribe. The parties agree that the Tribe is a restored tribe. Thus, the Court turns its attention to whether the Shriner Tract was taken into trust as part of a restoration of land.

IGRA does not define "restored" and "restoration." Thus, this court must give the words "their ordinary, contemporary, common meaning, absent an indication Congress intended them to bear some different import." Several courts have had occasion to address the "restoration of lands" exception, and have concluded that the term "restoration" has a plain meaning that may be applied.

As noted by the NIGC, the court in *Grand Traverse Band of Ottawa and Chippewa Indians v. U.S. Attorney*, 198 F. Supp. 2d 920 (W.D. Mich. 2002) (*Grand Traverse II*), aff'd, 369 F.3d 960 (6th Cir. 2004), has suggested a three-part test to determine what land qualifies under the "restoration of lands" exception:

> Given the plain meaning of the language, the term "restoration" may be read in numerous ways to place belatedly restored tribes in a comparable position to earlier recognized tribes while simultaneously limiting after-acquired property in some fashion. For example, land that could be considered part of such restoration might appropriately be limited by *the factual circumstances of the acquisition, the location of the acquisition, or the temporal relationship of the acquisition to the tribal restoration.*

This interpretation was adopted by the court in *Confederated Tribes of Coos v. Babbitt*, 116 F. Supp. 2d 155 (D.D.C. 2000), which noted that such limitations would avoid a result that "any and all property acquired by restored tribes would be eligible for gaming." The NIGC adopted the *Grand Traverse II* factors and used them in its analysis of the restoration of lands exception.

The factual circumstances of the acquisition are not at issue. Under this factor, the factual circumstances of the acquisition must provide indicia of restoration. The Tribe was restored to federal recognition on May 14, 1978; the Secretary of Interior approved the Revised Constitution on May 30, 1985. The Tribe negotiated the purchase of the Shriner Tract in 1994 and 1995, and thereafter submitted an application to the BIA requesting the United States accept the Shriner Tract into trust. This factor appears to be neutral, and will be construed in the Tribe's favor.

The second, and arguably most important, component of the test for the restoration of land exception relates to the location of the land in relation to the tribe's historical location. Courts [including the D.C. Circuit in *City of Roseville v. Norton*] have been careful to observe that the restoration of lands encompasses more than simply the return of a tribe's former reservation, although "placement within a prior reservation of the [tribe] is significant evidence that the land may be considered ... restored."

The NIGC began its analysis by evaluating the physical location of the Shriner Tract, which is located in Kansas City, Kansas. The NIGC noted however, that the seat of the Wyandotte Tribal government, its present trust lands and its population center are in Wyandotte, Oklahoma, a distance of approximately 175 miles from Kansas City. The Tribe's convenience store, daycare center, seniors program and educational assistance programs are also located in Wyandotte, Oklahoma. It was clear to the NIGC that the Shriner Tract is situated far from where the Tribe is actually located in Wyandotte, Oklahoma. This contrasts significantly from the other Indian lands cases analyzing the restoration of lands exception. As the NIGC discussed in depth in its opinion, the other tribes had occupation centers near the proposed gaming cites and had not left the areas since aboriginal times. While the NIGC declined to establish a standard for determining what is a reasonable distance for purposes of the restoration of lands analysis, it concluded that in this case, a distance of 175 miles between the parcel and the tribal center is not close enough to establish a geographical connection.

The NIGC also concluded that the Tribe does not have a sufficient historical nexus to the Shriner Tract to qualify it as restored land. The NIGC noted that the Tribe was transient for much of its history, making its way from Huronia to Michigan, Pennsylvania, Missouri, Ohio and Kansas before reaching its present location of Oklahoma. The Tribe occupied the Shriner Tract area from 1843 to early 1855 — only eleven full years. By contrast, the NIGC noted that in all of the cases that have analyzed the restored lands exception, there was a "significant, longstanding historical connection to the land-sometimes even an ancient connection." The NIGC declined to find that occupation of land for a period of eleven years, despite that "significant roots" were put down, rises to the level of an historical connection. To so find, the NIGC would conceivably be bound to find that the Tribe also had an historical nexus to Michigan, Ohio, Pennsylvania and Missouri, and that if land were taken into trust in those locations, the Tribe could game there.

The Tribe takes great issue with the NIGC's apparent emphasis on the physical distance between the Shriner Tract and the Wyandotte's seat of government, noting that the federal government forced the Wyandotte to uproot to Oklahoma. Moreover, the Tribe contends, the Wyandotte has maintained a significant presence in the State of Kansas. The Tribe attempts to distinguish itself from prior agency decisions, in particular the land determination regarding the Mechoopda, where the existence of an historic tribal trail across the parcel and the parcel's location one mile from three buttes that were prominent in a tribal myth were important to the determination. The Tribe finds it difficult to comprehend how a trail elevates the land at issue in Mechoopda to a higher significance than the Shriner Tract, which is adjacent to the Huron cemetery where the Tribe's ancestors are buried and which the Tribe has held since the mid-1800's. This, the Tribe argues, constitutes an attempt by the NIGC to impose a novel and arbitrary present-use occupation requirement upon the Wyandotte.

The Court disagrees. As stated previously, the Court's role in reviewing the NIGC's decision in applying the three prongs of the restoration analysis is not to inject its own views or pick sides, but rather, to ascertain whether the NIGC examined the relevant data and articulated a rational connection between the facts found and the decision made. A careful examination of the record reflects the NIGC has examined the relevant data regarding the location factor and there is a rational connection between the facts found and the NIGC's decision that the Tribe did not meet this aspect of the "restored lands" exception. In evaluating the Tribe's historical nexus to the Shriner Tract, the NIGC cited to its *Grand Traverse II* opinion for its finding that restoration was shown by "substantial evidence tending to establish that the ... site has been important to the tribe throughout its history and remained so immediately on resumption of federal recognition." The NIGC also cited to previous opinions involving the Mechoopda Indian Tribe and the Bear River Band of Rohnerville Rancheria, noting that the longstanding historical and cultural connections those tribes had to the acquired trust lands. The NIGC then evaluated the Tribe's historical nexus to the Shriner Tract, and concluded that the Tribe had not shown a sufficient historical nexus. The Court finds nothing infirm about the manner in which the NIGC evaluated the historical nexus and agrees with the NIGC that in order to evaluate this issue fully, the agency must evaluate the present circumstances of the Tribe and its relationship with the land at issue. It cannot be said that the NIGC clearly erred in this regard.

Moreover, the Shriner Tract significantly differs from the trust lands at issue in previous opinions in terms of geographical distance from the Tribe's occupation area in Oklahoma. As the NIGC discussed in depth in its opinion, the other tribes had occupation centers near the proposed gaming sites and had not left the areas since aboriginal times. The NIGC recognized that the Wyandottes' unfortunate history of forced relocation left the Tribe in a different position with regard to historical occupation than the other tribes, but concluded nonetheless that the Shriner Tract's distant location and relatively minor place in the Tribe's history militates against applying language another court used in a different context. Additionally, prior agency opinions have emphasized trust land's significance to a tribe. In this case, the NIGC concluded that the Shriner Tract, while of importance to the Tribe, does not have the continuing significant presence in the Tribe's history as the parcels in prior land opinions, having spent less than twelve years in Kansas before ceding the land and moving to Oklahoma. Although the significance of the Huron Cemetery to the Wyandottes cannot be denied, key to the location factor is the historical significance of the Shriner Tract; the fact that the tract is adjacent to this non-reservation, isolated burial ground does not render the agency's conclusion arbitrary. Again, the Court cannot conclude that the NIGC clearly erred in this regard.

Because the Court finds that the NIGC's final decision that the Tribe does not meet the settlement of a land claim exception to the general prohibition on gaming is arbitrary, capricious and otherwise not in accordance with the law, it reverses the NIGC's September 10, 2004 decision and remands the matter to the agency for proceedings consistent with the terms of this order.

Notes and Questions

1. *"[A] procedural history as complex as a random maze."* As the court noted in *Wyandotte Nation v. NIGC*, protracted litigation and administrative decisions have surrounded the tribe's efforts to conduct gaming on the Shriner Tract. (For a full recap through 2001, see *Sac & Fox Nation v. Norton*, 240 F.3d 1250, 1253–58 (10th Cir. 2001).) After the Interior Secretary took the parcel into trust, the tribe sought NIGC approval to conduct gaming on the land. Frustrated with delays in the administrative approval process, the tribe opened a relatively modest Class II operation on the parcel. In the words of the Tenth Circuit, the tribe's casino "set off a furious round of legal maneuvering." *Wyandotte Nation v. Sebelius*, 443 F.3d 1247, 1251 (10th Cir. 2006). The NIGC, prompted by Kansas' governor, notified the tribe that it could not conduct gaming on the land. The tribe filed suit in federal district court seeking review of the NIGC's decision. While the tribe's suit was pending, state officials, armed with a search warrant obtained in state court, stormed the tribe's casino, confiscating some $1.25 million in cash and equipment and arresting the casino's general manager for violation of state gambling laws. (The state court later dismissed the charges for lack of state jurisdiction on the Shriner Tract.) The tribe then successfully sought a federal court order requiring state officials to return the casino's property. The federal court went a bit further than the tribe intended, however, and also enjoined the tribe from conducting gaming on the land. Shortly before the district court issued its opinion in *Wyandotte Nation v. NIGC*, the Tenth Circuit vacated the preliminary injunction against the tribe on the ground that it was granted without sufficient notice or appropriate justification. *Wyandotte Nation v. Sebelius*, 443 F.3d at 1251.

Said the court, "This long battle [between the Wyandotte Nation, Kansas, and the U.S.] has produced a procedural history as complex as a random maze." *Id.* at 1249. In 2007, the tribe opened the Wyandotte Nation Casino, the "Bellagio of this area," on tribal land in Oklahoma.

2.   *Gaming under § 2719's exceptions.* In 2005, Deputy Assistant Secretary George Skibine testified before the U.S. Senate Committee on Indian Affairs regarding the Interior Department's approval of gaming on newly acquired lands:

> Since 1988, the Secretary has approved 26 trust acquisitions for gaming that have qualified under the five Section 20 exceptions:
>
> - seven gaming acquisitions under the exception in Section 20(a)(1)—four on-reservation acquisitions, two contiguous acquisitions, and one that contained land that was partly on-reservation, and partly contiguous to the reservation;
>
> - four gaming acquisitions under the "settlement of a land claim" exception contained in Section 20(b)(1)(B)(i), although all four parcels are contiguous to each other and are all for the Seneca Tribe of New York;
>
> - three gaming acquisitions for Indian tribes under the "initial reservation" exception contained in Section 20(b)(1)(B)(ii);
>
> - twelve gaming acquisitions for Indian tribes under the "restored land for a restored tribe" exception contained in Section 20(b)(1)(B)(iii); and
>
> - no gaming acquisitions under the exception contained in Section 20(a)(2)(B), the "last recognized reservation" exception.

George T. Skibine, Statement Before the U.S. Senate Committee on Indian Affairs on Section 20 of the Indian Gaming Regulatory Act (July 25, 2005). Considering that there are more than 560 federally recognized tribes and the Interior Department manages approximately 46 million acres of trust land, is the relatively small number of tribal gaming establishments operating on newly acquired lands surprising? What do the Interior Department's approvals (and, for the "best interests" exception, governors' concurrences) reveal about whether § 2719 currently functions consistent with Congress's intent?

3.   *Pending federal regulations.* In early 2007, the Interior Secretary re-opened the comment period on its proposed regulations governing gaming on newly acquired lands, originally published in the Federal Register in October 2006. The proposed regulations formalize some of the requirements of the OIGM Checklist, as well as provide definitions and specific requirements for meeting the various exceptions.

Problem 10.1: Gaming on Newly Acquired Lands

Suppose you are a tribal official charged with serving as an intergovernmental liaison to a nearby city government. You are appearing before the mayor and city council, along with the city administrator and other city planning officials. What points would you make to convince city government that it should pass a resolution of support for your efforts to take a 25-acre parcel of land on the outskirts of the city into trust for the purpose of opening a casino and hotel development that will include an amphitheater, golf course, and waterpark? Now suppose you are meeting with officials of a tribe located 50 miles away that has its own casino on reservation lands. How would you convince them not to oppose your efforts?

C. Tribal-State Revenue-Sharing Agreements

IGRA explicitly prohibits states from imposing direct taxes or fees on tribal casinos as a precondition for signing a tribal-state compact:

> (4) Except for any assessments [to defray regulatory costs] that may be agreed to under paragraph (3)(C)(iii) of this subsection, nothing in this section shall be interpreted as conferring upon a State or any of its political subdivisions authority to impose any tax, fee, charge, or other assessment upon an Indian tribe or upon any other person or entity authorized by an Indian tribe to engage in a class III activity. No State may refuse to enter into the [Class III compact] negotiations described in paragraph (3)(A) based upon the lack of authority in such State, or its political subdivisions, to impose such a tax, fee, charge, or other assessment.

25 U.S.C. § 2710(d)(4). Additionally, in the context of an action to enforce the state's duty to negotiate compacts in good faith, IGRA provides that "[i]n determining ... whether a State has negotiated in good faith, the court ... shall consider any demand by the State for direct taxation of the Indian tribe or of any Indian lands as evidence that the State has not negotiated in good faith." *Id.* § 2710(d)(7)(b)(iii). While IGRA's plain language suggests that states cannot condition compact negotiations on mandatory tribal payments, in practice § 2710(d)(4) has provided ample wiggle room for states and tribes to enter into a wide range of revenue-sharing agreements.

1. Interior Secretary's Interpretation of IGRA

Despite IGRA's prohibition on the imposition on tribes of taxes, fees, charges, or other assessments, the U.S. Secretary of the Interior has interpreted the section as allowing tribes to make payments to states in return for additional benefits beyond the right to operate Class III gaming. As the following excerpt explains, if the state provides to the tribe a "valuable economic benefit," typically "substantial exclusivity" in the market, a revenue-sharing agreement presumably will not run afoul of IGRA under the Secretary's interpretation.

Aurene M. Martin
Statement Before the U.S. Senate Committee on Indian Affairs
on the Indian Gaming Regulatory Act
(July 9, 2003)

Good morning, Mr. Chairman and members of the Committee. My name is Aurene Martin, Acting Assistant Secretary for Indian Affairs. I am pleased to be here today to discuss the role of the Department of the Interior in reviewing revenue-sharing provisions included in Class III tribal-state gaming compacts submitted to the Department for approval under [25 U.S.C. § 2710(d)].

IGRA provides that Class III gaming activities are lawful on Indian lands only if they are, among other things, conducted in conformance with a tribal-state compact entered into by an Indian tribe and a state and approved by the Secretary. The Secretary may only disapprove a compact if the compact violates (1) any provision of IGRA; (2) any other provision of Federal law that does not relate to jurisdiction over gaming on Indian lands; or (3) the trust obligations of the United States to Indians. Under this statutory scheme, the Secretary must approve or disapprove a compact within 44 days of its submission, or the compact is considered to have been approved, but only to the extent the compact is consistent with the provisions of IGRA. A compact takes effect when the Secretary publishes notice of its approval in the Federal Register.

Since IGRA was passed in 1988, nearly 15 years ago, the Department of the Interior has approved approximately 250 Class III gaming compacts between states and Indian tribes in 24 states. These compacts have enabled many Indian tribes to establish Class III gaming establishments. These establishments have helped reduce tribes' reliance on Federal dollars and enabled them to implement a variety of tribal initiatives in furtherance of Congress' intent in IGRA "to provide a statutory basis for the operation of gaming by Indian tribes as a means of promoting tribal economic development, self-sufficiency, and strong tribal governments." The Department supports lawful and regulated tribal gaming under IGRA because it has proved to be an effective tool for tribal economic development and self-sufficiency.

[A] consequence of the Supreme Court's 1996 decision in *Seminole Tribe v. State of Florida* is that more states have sought to include revenue-sharing provisions in Class III gaming compacts, resulting in a discernable increase in such provisions in the past seven years. In general, the Department has attempted to apply the law to limit the circumstances under which Indian tribes can make direct payments to a state for purposes other than defraying the costs of regulating Class III gaming activities. To date, the Department has only approved revenue-sharing payments that call for tribal payments when the state has agreed to provide valuable economic benefit of what the Department has termed "substantial exclusivity" for Indian gaming in exchange for the payment. As a consequence, if the Department affirmatively approves a proposed compact, it has an obligation to ensure that the benefit received by the state under the proposed compact is appropriate in light of the benefit conferred on the tribe. Accordingly, if a payment exceeds the benefit received by the tribe, it would violate IGRA because it would amount to an unlawful tax, fee, charge, or assessment. While there has been substantial disagreement over what constitutes a tax, fee, charge or assessment within this context, we believe that if the payments are made in exchange for the grant of a valuable economic benefit that the governor has discretion to provide, these payments do not fall within the category of prohibited taxes, fees, charges, or other assessments.

Since 1988, the Department has approved, or deemed approved, revenue-sharing provisions between Indian tribes and the following States: Connecticut, New Mexico, Wisconsin, California, New York, and Arizona. In addition, four Michigan Indian tribes are making revenue-sharing payments to the State of Michigan under compacts that became effective by operation of law. Other Michigan tribes have made revenue-sharing payments to the State of Michigan under a court-approved consent decree, but these tribes stopped making the payments when Michigan authorized non-Indian casinos in Detroit.

Notes and Questions

1. *The Secretary's interpretation.* Is the Secretary's interpretation of IGRA to allow revenue-sharing agreements reasonable, in light of the statutory language and congressional intent? Why or why not?

2. *Is a revenue-sharing "agreement" always voluntary?* What is the significance of a tribe's complicity on revenue sharing? Does the fact that a tribe can "agree" to revenue

sharing obviate the argument that the state is "imposing" a tax or fee? Is this argument always a legitimate one, given *Seminole Tribe*'s extraction of IGRA's teeth? That is, in the absence of IGRA's cause of action for a state's failure to negotiate in good faith, if a tribe has no other leverage to bring a state to the table *other* than to offer up revenue sharing, is there any guarantee that it is in fact a free-will offering? Are such concerns mitigated by the promulgation of the 1999 regulations empowering the Secretary to impose an "administrative compact," discussed in Chapter 3? What other authority may the Secretary exercise to ensure that states do not negotiate revenue-sharing agreements in bad faith, especially after *Seminole Tribe*?

2. Revenue-Sharing Agreements

Steven Andrew Light, Kathryn R.L. Rand, & Alan P. Meister
Spreading the Wealth:
Indian Gaming and Revenue-Sharing Agreements
80 N.D. L. REV. 657 (2004)

Indian gaming clearly is a tool of tribal economic development. For many tribes, gaming is a significant source of government revenue, catalyzing a renaissance of sorts on reservations throughout the United States. But Indian gaming's beneficiaries are not limited to tribes; non-tribal jurisdictions benefit from tribal casinos, as well. On balance, states with Indian gaming operations, as well as the numerous non-reservation communities located near tribal casinos, have realized extensive economic and social benefits from tribal gaming operations, ranging from increased tax revenues to decreased public entitlement payments to the disadvantaged. Tribal gaming assists states by promoting economic development in underdeveloped rural areas while leveraging growth and development in surrounding non-tribal communities. Increasingly though, states are attempting to acquire a direct share of Indian gaming revenue through revenue-sharing agreements with gaming tribes.

To some, revenue sharing is political coercion at tribes' expense. The state simply wields its greater political clout, flouting tribal rights and federal law. To others, tribal-state revenue-sharing agreements represent cooperative economic development between tribes and states. The state, through compact negotiations and state public policy, facilitates successful Indian gaming within its borders, while the tribe pays the state a "fair share" of the resulting revenue. We argue, however, that the issue does not necessarily lend itself to a single, right-or-wrong answer. Revenue-sharing agreements may be right for some tribes, but not for others. Such agreements are strategic decisions made within a broad and complex context by both tribal and state actors that have both short-term and long-term economic and public policy impacts.

As the Indian gaming industry continues to grow, and a few tribal casinos find extraordinary financial success near the nation's population centers, an increasing number of states have negotiated revenue-sharing provisions as part of Class III compacts. In a revenue-sharing agreement, a tribe commits to paying a portion of its gaming revenues to the state in exchange for the right to conduct casino-style gaming in the state, sometimes including a guarantee of exclusivity. The Mashantucket Pequots and Connecticut reached the first revenue-sharing agreement in 1992, in which the tribe agreed to pay the state twenty-five percent of its slot revenues in exchange for the exclusive right to operate slot machines in the state.

Through the mid-1990s, revenue-sharing provisions were a rarity, perhaps limited to the nearly unparalleled market of the Pequots' Foxwoods and the peculiarities of Connecticut's gambling laws. Following the Supreme Court's decision in *Seminole Tribe*, which coincided with both steadily increasing Indian gaming profits and state budget crises, more states, including Wisconsin, New Mexico, New York, and California, have sought their "fair share" of tribal casino profits. Without the ability to challenge a state's demand for revenue sharing in federal court under IGRA (unless, of course, the state consents to suit, as has California), the danger for tribes is that states can simply charge tribes what, in practice, amounts to a multi-million-dollar fee to conduct Class III gaming, in direct contravention to tribes' sovereign right under *Cabazon* and Congress's intent under IGRA. At the same time, the Court's decision in *Seminole Tribe* as a practical matter arguably gave states and tribes greater flexibility in tailoring compacts to meet individualized needs and concerns. The United States Secretary of the Interior's position on revenue sharing reflects this confidence in the "give and take" nature of compact negotiations. Although IGRA prohibits state taxation of tribal casinos as a condition of signing a tribal-state compact, as interpreted by the Interior Secretary, tribes can make payments to states in return for additional benefits beyond the right to operate Class III gaming. Tribes thus have agreed to make "exclusivity payments," in which they pay a percentage of casino revenues to the state in return for the exclusive right to operate casino-style gaming.

The majority of revenue-sharing payments are based on a percentage of gaming revenue. Some tribes pay a fixed percentage directly to the state, like Connecticut's twenty-five percent take of slot revenue. Other tribes make payments based on a sliding percentage scale contingent upon varying criteria. For example, as of 2003, California tribes made payments to the state ranging from zero to thirteen percent of gaming machine revenue based on number of operational gaming devices, while New Mexico tribes currently pay three to eight percent of gaming machine revenue, dependent upon Class III gaming machine revenue. In New York, tribal payments begin at eighteen percent of electronic gaming revenue and top out at twenty-five percent after the current compact's seventh year. A small and decreasing number of compacts require tribes to make fixed annual payments to the state; for instance, until a number of Wisconsin tribes renegotiated their tribal-state compacts in 2002 and agreed to make payments based on annual revenue, each of the state's eleven gaming tribes made flat annual payments.

A growing number of tribes have signed revenue-sharing agreements with local governments, and some also contribute to special community funds. Tribes in Arizona, California, Louisiana, Michigan, and Washington make payments directly to local governments. After Idaho voters approved a ballot initiative containing a tribal-state revenue-sharing agreement, tribes agreed to contribute five percent of gaming revenue to local schools and education programs. Tribes in Oregon pay between five and six percent of net gaming revenue to a community benefit fund. Tribes also contribute to state and local programs seeking to lessen the effects of problem and pathological gambling. Arizona's tribes, for instance, contributed approximately $760,000 to the state's Department of Gaming — more than double the amount contributed by the Arizona Lottery.

Depending on the type of agreement and, most importantly, the amount of gaming revenue tribes realize, annual revenue payments to state and local governments can add up rapidly, contributing significant revenue to state coffers. Tribes provided $759 million to state and local governments in 2003, nearly a one-third increase over the prior year. Connecticut tribes paid the state about $400 million, and California tribes provided approximately $132 million, while Arizona tribes paid roughly $43 million, and Michigan tribes provided about $32 million to state and local governments. Following a protracted tribal-state compact renegotiation process, Wisconsin tribes in early 2004 agreed to a five-fold increase in annual revenue payments to the state, from $20 million to more than $100 million, in return for exclusivity and the ability to operate additional casino-style games.

Clearly, a growing number of states have requested that tribes interested in operating gaming facilities share gaming revenue or have sought to renegotiate existing compacts or revenue-sharing agreements to provide larger revenue transfers from gaming tribes. California, in many respects, exemplifies recent trends.

With over 100 federally recognized tribes and some 35 million residents, California boasts both more tribes and more people than any other state in the continental United States and, as such, represents a vast potential market for the continued expansion of Indian gaming. Generating $4.7 billion in revenue in 2003, Indian gaming in California, conducted by fifty-four tribes, far outpaces other states, earning as much as a third of the Indian gaming industry's total revenue and ranking California's total gambling revenue third after only that of Nevada and New Jersey. California, along with Connecticut, also leads the nation in setting precedents for tribal-state political interactions over gambling, particularly with regard to revenue sharing. Two gubernatorial administrations, two ballot initiatives, and two key court decisions resulted in tribal-state compacts in California with two revenue-sharing provisions. In exchange for allowing tribes the exclusive right to conduct casino-style gambling in the state, the tribes agreed to make payments to two funds under then-Governor Gray Davis's model tribal-state compact. A third gubernatorial administration under current Governor Arnold Schwarzenegger changed all that.

Under the newly authorized Davis compacts, tribes agreed to make payments to two funds. The first of these, the Special Distribution Fund, is available for appropriation by the state legislature for a number of gaming-related purposes and essentially is a limited-purpose revenue-sharing agreement with the state. Under the terms of the model compact, tribes pay a graduated percentage of gaming machine revenue, up to thirteen percent, based on the number of machines operated by the tribe prior to September 1999.

The second fund into which the tribes are required to pay is the Revenue Sharing Trust Fund. This fund is unique in that it established "tribe-to-tribe" revenue sharing. Tribes pay a per-machine licensing fee into the fund. The fee structure ranges from $900 to $4,350 per machine annually, depending on the number of slot machines operated by the tribe. For a tribe operating 2,000 slot machines prior to September 1999, the maximum number of machines allowed under the model compact, the licensing fee would be just under $4.6 million each year. With the fees paid into the Revenue Sharing Trust Fund, each non-gaming tribe in California is paid up to $1.1 million each year. In 2003, gaming tribes in California paid about $130 million into the two funds.

Indian gaming under the Davis compacts appeared secure for at least the next two decades, the minimum duration of the model compact. But just two years later, faced with a budget shortfall of nearly $35 billion, Davis proposed renegotiating the tribal-state compacts. Looking to examples like Connecticut, where the state's two tribal casinos pay the state an estimated $400 million per year, Davis offered to consider increasing the maximum number of slot machines a tribe could operate at its casinos in exchange for annual revenue payments to the state of $1.5 billion. Davis also required tribes entering into new compacts to agree to make payments directly to the state treasury, bypassing the use limitations of the model compact's Special Distribution Fund. Not surprisingly, Davis' suggestion was ill-received by the tribes. By mid-2003, Davis had reduced his revenue-sharing proposal to $680 million per year, but in the meantime, his political viability was fading fast. Republicans and others dissatisfied with Davis' performance had successfully initiated a fall recall election, and Hollywood actor Arnold Schwarzenegger entered the race.

Schwarzenegger launched a series of attacks on tribal casinos during his campaign, criticizing California's gaming tribes for being "special interests" who should "pay their fair share," which he estimated as similar to Connecticut's twenty-five percent take of the Pequots' and Mohegans' slot revenues, to help reduce the state's enormous budget deficit. In California, a quarter of tribal gaming revenue could amount to more than $1 billion in annual payments to the state. Davis lost the recall election, and Schwarzenegger became the new governor of California. Schwarzenegger soon sought to renegotiate compacts that would have been in effect for twenty years with a few tribes. At the time of this writing, Schwarzenegger and five tribes had reached agreements in renegotiating their compacts. The new compacts remove the existing limit on the number of slot machines in exchange for increased contributions to the state, including additional licensing fees for all new machines and substantial annual payments. "What's changed [since the negotiation of Davis's model compact]?" asked a gaming consultant about the state's demands for higher payments. "The state economy is in the toilet and Indians have stuff."

In the absence of federal action to clarify what is permissible, whether through congressional amendment of IGRA to provide guidelines for the negotiation and realization of revenue-sharing agreements, or through a formal legislative ruling by the Secretary of the Interior regarding the legality of revenue sharing under IGRA's existing provisions, new permutations of revenue-sharing agreements will continue to arise on a case-by-case basis, contingent on the economic and political circumstances particular to a given situation.

In Massachusetts, for example, the state has agreed to limit, but not prohibit, commercial casino gambling in exchange for annual payments of $90 million from the Wampanoag Tribe's planned casino. The Interior Secretary's position on revenue sharing appears to allow a state to offer a tribe less than total exclusivity, but just how much less is not clear. With revenue sharing occupying a decidedly gray area of the law, it seems likely that in negotiating such agreements, states will push the envelope on how much they should get in return for granting tribes absolute or more limited exclusivity. Some tribes may be willing to agree to pay the states higher percentages of gaming revenue in return for absolute exclusivity, or to concede to qualified exclusivity in return for a successfully negotiated compact.

The decade-old experiences of tribes and the state of Connecticut continue to pave the way for the future of tribal-state revenue sharing. While the revenue-sharing agreements negotiated first by the Pequots and then by the Mohegans obviously have been extremely lucrative for the tribes, Connecticut's willingness to "give up" absolute exclusivity to the tribes benefited the state in three major ways: the state negotiated a then-unprecedented twenty-five-percent share of tribal gaming revenue, the grant of absolute exclusivity placed the state on the safest footing with the Secretary of the Interior in its interpretation of the permissibility of revenue sharing under IGRA, and the state managed to preserve the politically popular appearance of opposing the expansion of legalized gambling. Although Californians appear to favor public policy supporting gambling more than Connecticut voters, the state is fairly typical of those with minimal legalized gambling outside of Indian gaming facilities. In such states, it most likely will prove politically viable for the state to use the negotiation of revenue-sharing agreements to strike the balance between fostering Indian gaming as a means of tribal economic development and self-determination and controlling the spread of legalized gambling generally.

Recent tribal-state interactions in California hint at their potential for establishing the benchmark for the negotiation and realization of new revenue-sharing agreements. The key shift in the developing revenue-sharing paradigm has been the move to renegotiate existing tribal-state compacts. By renegotiating existing compacts to pursue greater revenue payments from tribes, the actions of the Schwarzenegger administration, as a follow-up to prior events during the Davis regime, demonstrate how compacts can become impermanent manifestations of changing state political goals rather than codified tribal-state agreements negotiated to further common interests and in recognition of tribes' sovereign status.

Kris Olson, the chair of the Board of Trustees of Oregon's Spirit Mountain Community Fund, recently bemoaned a "cookie-cutter approach" to negotiating new tribal-state compacts in that state. A similar one-size-fits-all approach by other states in seeking to negotiate new compacts or to renegotiate existing compacts to institute "fair-share" agreements may constitute short-sighted public policy.

First, this approach undercuts stated goals of federal Indian policy, decreasing tribal economic development opportunities (and by extension, those of surrounding non-tribal communities and the state) and threatening the long-term viability of Indian gaming. The cookie-cutter approach is of particular concern to tribes in rural locales with limited gaming markets, such as North Dakota. Tribes in that state use their relatively modest casino profits to fund tribal government operations and programs and to create employment opportunities on the reservation. Should the state follow California's lead and demand a revenue-sharing agreement from the tribes, the result could endanger the viability of the five tribal casinos in the state. This would impact not only the tribes' ability to provide essential government services on the reservation, but also the continued positive economic impacts of the casinos felt both on and off the reservation.

Second, the cookie-cutter approach banks on Indian gaming revenue as a short-term means to make up for state budgetary shortfalls that must be addressed instead through long-term planning. Gambling policy is dynamic and unpredictable; even in Connecticut, where tribal gaming has helped to reinvigorate the state's economy, Indian gaming remains highly controversial and politically charged. As tribes are often cautioned, states should be wary of overdependence on gaming profits to support their economies.

In view of the stated long-term goals of federal Indian policy and the law governing Indian gaming of maximizing tribal self-governance, self-determination, and economic self-sufficiency, one might caution that short-term revenue-sharing agreements may be negotiated at the expense of tribal economic development and even of tribal sovereignty. Moreover, states themselves may lose out in the long run from short-sighted public policy driven by an overreliance on tribal gaming revenues. By contrast, recognition of shared political and economic interests generated by Indian gaming creates potential win-win outcomes for tribes and states alike.

Notes and Questions

1.   The first revenue-sharing agreement. When the Pequots first approached Connecticut to negotiate a compact, the state took the position that although it allowed charities to operate casino-style gaming for "Las Vegas Night" fund-raisers, Class III games, and especially slot machines, were contrary to state public policy. Accordingly, Connecticut refused to negotiate a compact to allow the tribe to operate such games. The Pequots sued under IGRA's then-valid cause of action (*Seminole Tribe v. Florida*'s invalidation of a tribe's right to sue did not come until 1996). The Second Circuit, after examining the Las Vegas Nights law, determined that casino-style gaming was not against Connecticut's public policy, thus obligating the state to negotiate a compact with the tribe. *See Mashantucket Pequot Tribe v. Connecticut*, 913 F.2d 1024, 1026–32 (2d Cir. 1990) (excerpted in Chapter 5). Because slot machines were not allowed under state law and were not specifically addressed by the court's decision, Connecticut and the Pequots reached the revenue-sharing compromise, which gave the tribe the exclusive right to operate slot machines in exchange for a state cut of the slot revenue. The Pequots subsequently agreed to abrogate exclusivity to allow the Mohegan Tribe to build the Mohegan Sun Casino, which became one of the world's largest casinos, along with the Pequots' own Foxwoods Resort and Casino.

2. *Recent revenue sharing figures.* The Light, Rand, and Meister article provided 2003 figures for revenue sharing; the amounts have steadily increased since then. In 2006, tribes paid over $1 billion in revenue-sharing payments to states, and another $136.2 million in payments to local governments. In Connecticut, tribes paid the state over $433 million, and tribes in California paid the state more than $270 million. Tribal payments in New York, Arizona, and Wisconsin also continued to increase in 2006, reaching approximately $97 million, $82 million, and $75 million respectively. ALAN P. MEISTER, INDIAN GAMING INDUSTRY REPORT 5, 45 (2007–2008 ed.).

3. *Trends in revenue sharing.* As Light, Rand, and Meister noted, the legal limits of revenue sharing are very much a grey area of the law. The political trend, though, seems to be toward increasing state demands, as exemplified by their account of California's demands. What happens when the state wants to negotiate over the inclusion of a revenue-sharing provision in a tribal-state compact and the tribe does not wish to do so? IGRA requires the state to engage in good-faith negotiations, and provides direction to a reviewing court in making a determination of what exactly is "good faith" under such a circumstance. Read the following case with an eye toward how much flexibility the court employs in interpreting both the good-faith requirement and its own duty under IGRA's requirements.

In re Indian Gaming Related Cases
331 F.3d 1094 (9th Cir. 2003)

The Coyote Valley Band of Pomo Indians ("Coyote Valley") contends that the State of California ("the State") has refused to negotiate in good faith with the tribe to conclude a Tribal-State compact, as required by 25 U.S.C. § 2710(d)(3)(A), and moved in the district court for an order that would require it to do so, § 2710(d)(7)(B)(iii). In a carefully considered decision, the district court denied the motion and entered judgment for the State. We agree with the district court that the State has negotiated in good faith within the meaning of IGRA.

After IGRA's enactment, certain California tribes (including Coyote Valley) sought to negotiate compacts with the State permitting the operation of class III games on their respective reservations. Among the class III games over which these tribes sought to negotiate were live banked or percentage card games and stand-alone electronic gaming machines (similar to slot machines). These particular games were not permitted under California law, but the State did allow other forms of class III gaming, such as non-electronic keno and lotto.

During the Administration of Governor Pete Wilson, the State refused to negotiate with the tribes with respect to the class III games they sought to conduct. In the State's view, because it did not permit live banked or percentage card games or slot machine-like devices, it had no duty to negotiate with respect to them. In the tribes' view, because the State permitted other types of class III games, it could not refuse to negotiate over the subset of class III games that they sought to conduct.

We rejected the tribes' construction of § 2710(d)(1)(B) in 1994 in *Rumsey Indian Rancheria of Wintun Indians v. Wilson*, 64 F.3d 1250 (9th Cir. 1994). We held that IGRA does not require a state to negotiate over one form of Class III gaming simply because it has legalized another, albeit similar form of gaming. Instead, the statute says only that, if a state allows a gaming activity "for any purpose by any person, organization, or entity," then it also must allow Indian tribes to engage in that same activity. § 2710(d)(1)(B). In other words, a state need only allow Indian tribes to operate games that others can operate, but need not give tribes what others cannot have.

Our decision in *Rumsey* meant that the State had no obligation to negotiate with tribes over the most lucrative forms of class III gaming. The Wilson Administration also refused to negotiate compacts covering class III games that the State *did* permit, unless and until the tribe requesting such negotiations ceased engaging in unlawful class III gaming—Class III gaming conducted in the absence of a valid Tribal-State compact as required by § 2710(d)(1)(C). Because IGRA grants the federal government exclusive jurisdiction to prosecute any violations of State gambling laws in Indian country, the State's refusal to engage in negotiations was one of the few forms of leverage it possessed to force tribes to comply with IGRA's compacting requirement. In light of the Supreme Court's ruling in *Seminole Tribe,* the tribes could not challenge the legitimacy of this position under IGRA absent State consent to suit, and such consent was not forthcoming. (Governor Wilson did offer to waive the State's sovereign immunity to suits brought by tribes pursuant to IGRA, but only if and when he received written certification that the tribes had ceased all illegal class III gaming.)

Rather than give up the ongoing class III gaming operations on which many tribes had come to rely, the tribes went directly to the people of California. A coalition of California tribes drafted and put on the November 1998 State ballot Proposition 5, a statutory initiative containing a model compact. The proposition, which amended state law but not the State constitution, required the state to enter into a model "Tribal-State Gaming Compact" with Indian tribes to allow certain class III gambling activities, such as banked card games and slot machines.

Relevant to this appeal, Proposition 5's model compact created three funds to which compacting tribes would contribute a set percentage of their net wins from tribal gaming terminals: (1) a "Nongaming Tribal Assistance Fund," from which distributions were to be made to non-gaming tribes to fund social services; (2) a "Statewide Trust Fund," from which distributions were to be made to counties in California to supplement emergency medical care and to establish or supplement programs addressing compulsive and addictive gambling; and (3) a "Local Benefits Grant Fund," from which distributions were to be made to address the needs of the cities or counties within the boundaries of which tribal gaming facilities were located. Under the terms of the model compact, the tribes' obligation to contribute to these funds was expressly conditional:

> The parties acknowledge that the operation of Tribal gaming terminals authorized under this Gaming Compact is expected to occupy a unique place in gaming within the State that is material to the ability of the Tribe and other tribal governments operating under similar compacts to achieve the economic development and other goals intended by IGRA. The Tribe therefore agrees to make

the contributions to the trust funds described [herein], only for as long as it and other tribes that have entered into Gaming Compacts are not deprived of that unique opportunity.

In other words, the tribes' obligation to contribute to these funds lasted only so long as they maintained their monopoly in the State over the operation of slot machines. Proposition 5 also included an explicit waiver of the State's sovereign immunity to suits brought against it pursuant to IGRA.

Proposition 5 passed by a wide margin. Shortly after its passage, however, the Hotel Employees and Restaurant Employees International Union (the "Union") and others filed a petition in the California Supreme Court seeking to prevent the Governor from implementing Proposition 5 because, they argued, it violated Article IV, Section 19(e) of the California Constitution. *Hotel Employees & Rest. Employees Int'l Union v. Davis*, 981 P.2d 990 (Cal. 1999). Section 19(e), added to California's Constitution in 1984, provides that the "Legislature has no power to authorize, and shall prohibit casinos of the type currently operating in Nevada and New Jersey."

On August 23, 1999, the California Supreme Court held, in agreement with the Union, that the gaming rights conferred on tribes by Proposition 5 violated the California Constitution. "Because Proposition 5, a purely statutory measure, did not amend section 19(e) or any other part of the Constitution, and because in a conflict between statutory and constitutional law the Constitution must prevail," the court invalidated the proposition in its entirety, save the final sentence of Cal. Gov.Code § 98005, containing the State's consent to federal suits brought by California tribes pursuant to IGRA.

Before the California Supreme Court ruled in *Hotel Employees,* the new Davis Administration had sought to engage tribes in compact negotiations, despite its limited obligations under our decision in *Rumsey.* Among other things, Governor Davis was concerned about the effect an adverse decision in *Hotel Employees* could have on tribes then engaged in (and dependent on revenue from) unlawful class III gaming operations. Depending on the scope of the opinion, the decision could completely prohibit the State from entering compacts to legitimize that gaming, thus leaving these tribes vulnerable to federal prosecution.

In March 1999, Governor Davis appointed a Special Counsel for Tribal Affairs to lead the State's negotiating team, and on April 9th he met personally with tribal leaders to introduce his appointee. At that meeting, which was attended by a representative of Coyote Valley, the State's lead negotiator asked that the tribes organize themselves into one or more negotiating teams to provide structure to the compact discussions. The tribes agreed, and subsequently formed three groups: (1) the United Tribe Compact Steering Committee ("UTCSC"); (2) the Desert Six group; and (3) the Pala Tribe group. Coyote Valley joined the UTCSC negotiating group, but reserved its right to withdraw at any time. In May and June 1999, Governor Davis convened initial rounds of compact negotiations with the tribal groups.

Negotiations commenced again at the end of August. Two significant events occurred at about this time. First, the California Supreme Court announced its decision in *Hotel Employees.* The State already had no *obligation* to conclude compacts with tribes permitting slot machines and banked card games, *see Rumsey,* [and] the decision meant it now also lacked *the authority* to do so. To address this problem, the Davis Administration proposed an amendment to Section 19 of Article IV of the California Constitution that would exempt tribal gaming from the prohibition on Nevada-style casinos, effectively granting tribes a constitutionally protected monopoly on most types of class III games in California. Although the voters would not have the opportunity to ratify the proposed amendment ("Proposition 1A") until March of 2000, the parties nonetheless determined to keep working to conclude a Tribal-State compact that would be conditional on that ratification. Second, the United States Department of Justice announced that it planned to proceed with enforcement actions against certain California tribes engaged in un-compacted class III gaming if those tribes did not enter compacts with the State before October 13, 1999.

The State delivered a new draft compact to the tribes on August 27, 1999. A third round of negotiations then took place in Sacramento from August 30 until September 3, and again from September 6 to September 10. At a meeting conducted on August 31, attended by each of the tribal negotiating groups, the tribes expressed [their] primary concerns with the August 27 draft circulated by the State. [One concern was] that the required contributions to the compact's revenue-sharing funds were overly burdensome.

The State responded by circulating a revised draft on September 7 and a final offer on September 9. The final draft included several changes from the August 27 draft, the most significant of which was an expansion of the types of games that tribes were permitted to conduct. Each of the previous drafts (indeed, even Proposition 5's model compact), had permitted only gaming devices and banked card games that paid prizes in accordance with a "players' pool prize system." By contrast, the final State proposal, in a major concession, permitted the tribes to operate real Las Vegas-style slot machines and house-banked blackjack.

According to Coyote Valley, the State delivered this final offer at approximately 8:00 p.m. and required that the tribes respond by 10:00 p.m. that same night if they wished to accept. A representative from Coyote Valley went to the Governor's office during this two hour interval to discuss the tribe's concerns with the proposed compact, but the State's negotiating team was inaccessible. Several tribal leaders and attorneys sought to meet with the Governor's negotiating team at this same time. The Governor's negotiating team met with one tribal employee and one tribal attorney, neither of whom represented Coyote Valley. The remaining people were escorted from the Governor's reception room.

That night, 57 tribes (including Coyote Valley) signed letters of intent to enter the compact. Only one tribe initially refused, and it signed the letter a few days later with slight modifications to the compact. That tribe was the Agua Caliente Band of Cahuilla Indians of Palm Springs ("Agua Caliente"). Frustrated with the lull in negotiations in June, July, and early August, Agua Caliente had begun a campaign to place Proposition 5 (and its model compact) back on the ballot, this time as a constitutional amendment. Agua Caliente had gathered enough signatures to qualify the initiative for the April 2000 ballot when Governor Davis made the unexpected concession offering tribes the right to operate real Las Vegas style slot machines as well as house-banked blackjack. In response, Agua Caliente withdrew its initiative petition. Agua Caliente signed a letter of intent to enter the Davis Compact on September 14, 1999.

The core of the negotiated compact (the "Davis Compact") is that the State granted the tribes the exclusive right to conduct lucrative Las Vegas-style class III gaming, free from non-tribal competition in the State. In return, the tribes agreed to a number of restrictions and obligations concerning their gaming enterprises. Specifically, the tribes agreed to three provisions that Coyote Valley contends in this suit are impermissible and whose inclusion in the ultimate compact demonstrates the bad faith of the State. These challenged provisions are: (1) the Revenue Sharing Trust Fund provision; and (2) the Special Distribution Fund provision.

The Revenue Sharing Trust Fund: The preamble to the Davis Compact recites that the "State has an interest in promoting the purposes of IGRA for all federally recognized Indian tribes in California, whether gaming or non-gaming." In furtherance of this interest, Section 4.3.2.1 of the compact creates a Revenue Sharing Trust Fund (the "RSTF") that grants a maximum of $1.1 million dollars to each of the State's non-gaming tribes each year. The idea of gaming tribes sharing gaming revenue with non-gaming tribes originated in Proposition 5's "Nongaming Tribal Assistance Fund," and this idea had been incorporated into the UTCSC discussion draft of June 17. Under Section 4.3.2.2 of the Davis Compact, gaming tribes fund the RSTF by purchasing "licenses" to acquire and maintain gaming devices in excess of the number they are authorized to use under Section 4.3.1. The cost of a license is graduated: $900 per year per machine for the first 400 machines in excess of 350; $1950 per year per machine for the next 500 machines in excess of 750; and $4350 per year per machine for the next 750 machines in excess of 1250. In no event can a tribe acquire licenses for more than 2000 machines. In addition, for each license tribes are required to pay into the RSTF a one-time fee of $1250. According to the State, the purpose of the progressive fee structure is to ensure that tribes with the largest, and therefore most lucrative, gaming establishments will pay a relatively greater share in supporting other California tribes in return for the right to operate additional licensed machines. The progressive fee structure also assists in achieving the State's objective of limiting the expansion of gaming facilities.

The Special Distribution Fund: The preamble to the compact also recites that "the exclusive rights that Indian tribes in California will enjoy under this Compact create a unique opportunity for the Tribe to operate its Gaming Facility in an economic environment free of competition from the Class III gaming referred to in Section 4.0 of this Compact on non-Indian lands in California. The parties are mindful that this unique environment is of great economic value to the Tribe and the fact that income from Gaming Devices represents a substantial portion of the tribes' gaming revenues. In consideration for the exclusive rights enjoyed by the tribes, and in further consideration for the State's willingness to enter into this Compact, the tribes have agreed to provide the State, on a sovereign-to-sovereign basis, a portion of its revenue from Gaming Devices."

Pursuant to this part of the preamble, the compact provides in Section 5 for the creation of a Special Distribution Fund ("SDF"), to be financed out of the tribes' net win from the operation of their gaming devices. As provided in Section 5.1, the amount that goes to the fund is to be calculated as 0% of the net win for the first 200 terminals, 7% of the net win for the next 300 terminals, 10% of the net win for the next 500 terminals, and 13% of the net win for any additional terminals above 1000. Section 5.2 provides that the revenue deposited in the SDF is available for appropriation by the Legislature for the following specified purposes: (a) grants for programs designed to address gambling addiction; (b) grants for the support of state and local government agencies impacted by tribal gaming; (c) compensation for regulatory costs incurred by the State Gaming Agency and the state Department of Justice in connection with the implementation and administration of the compact; (d) payment of shortfalls that may occur in the RSTF; and (e) "any other purposes specified by the legislature." The compact states that it "is the intent of the parties that Compact Tribes will be consulted in the process of identifying purposes for grants made to local governments."

Coyote Valley initially signed a letter of intent stating that it accepted the Davis Compact, including the provisions it now challenges. However, when the time came actually to execute the compact, Coyote Valley refused. In a letter dated October 13, 1999, Coyote Valley informed the State that before it would agree to sign, it needed to meet with State representatives to discuss "various issues and concerns" regarding certain provisions in the Davis Compact. The State replied in a letter dated October 18, 1999. The State did not respond to the tribe's request for a meeting, but instead emphasized the numerous negotiating opportunities the tribe had had, and highlighted the fact that the tribe had already signed a letter of intent to enter the Davis Compact. The tribe responded by letter on October 20, again requesting a meeting with the State on an individual tribal basis to discuss its concerns. The State replied on October 25, asking that Coyote Valley submit in writing any proposed changes or modifications to the Davis Compact for consideration.

Coyote Valley submitted its proposed changes to the State on November 12. In addition to several other modifications, the tribe sought: (1) the complete elimination of the RSTF provision; and (2) a limitation of its obligation to contribute to the SDF to only those amounts necessary to reimburse the costs to the State of regulating activities at Coyote Valley's gaming facility. In an accompanying cover letter, Coyote Valley indicated that it was only proposing changes "to the provisions of the Compact that it views as irreconcilable with IGRA."

The State indicated that it would be willing to meet with the tribe's representative to discuss the State's position and to allow the tribe an opportunity to discuss its position. No such meeting ever occurred.

Section 11.1(c) of the Davis Compact provides that it will not take effect "unless and until" Proposition 1A is approved by California voters. On September 10, 1999, the State Legislature passed Proposition 1A; the voters of California ratified it on March 7, 2000. On May 5, 2000, the United States Secretary of the Interior approved, the Tribal-State compacts entered into between the State and 60 tribes. Because Coyote Valley had refused to sign the compact, it was not among those tribes.

IGRA provides that, in determining whether a State has negotiated in good faith, a court "(I) may take into account the public interest, public safety, criminality, financial integrity, and adverse economic impacts on existing gaming activities, and (II) shall consider any demand by the State for direct taxation of the Indian tribe or of any Indian lands as evidence that the State has not negotiated in good faith." § 2710(d)(7)(B)(iii). "[U]pon the introduction of evidence by an Indian tribe that ... the State ... did not respond to [the request of the Indian tribe to negotiate a compact] in good faith, the burden of proof shall be upon the State to prove that the State has negotiated with the Indian tribe in good faith to conclude a Tribal-State compact governing the conduct of gaming activities." § 2710(d)(7)(B)(ii). *See* S.Rep. No. 100-446, at 15 (1988), *reprinted in* 1988 U.S.C.C.A.N. 3071, 3085 ("The Committee notes that it is States not tribes, that have crucial information in their possession that will prove or disprove tribal allegations of failure to act in good faith. Furthermore, the bill provides that the court, in making its [good faith] determination, may consider any of the number of issues listed in this section, including the State's public interest and other claims. The Committee recognizes that this may include issues of a very general nature and, and course [sic], trusts that courts will interpret any ambiguities on these issues in a manner that will be most favorable to tribal interests consistent with the legal standard used by courts for over 150 years in deciding cases involving Indian tribes.").

Section 2710(d)(3)(C) provides that any Tribal-State compact negotiated under § 2710(d)(3)(A) may include provisions relating to:

> (i) the application of the criminal and civil laws and regulations of the Indian tribe or the State that are directly related to, and necessary for, the licensing and regulation of [gaming] activity;

> (ii) the allocation of criminal and civil jurisdiction between the State and the Indian tribe necessary for the enforcement of such laws and regulations;

(iii) the assessment by the State of such activities in such amounts as are necessary to defray the costs of regulating such activity;

(iv) taxation by the Indian tribe of such activity in such amounts comparable to amounts assessed by the State for comparable activities;

(v) remedies for breach of contract;

(vi) standards for the operation of such activity and maintenance of the gaming facility, including licensing; and

(vii) any other subjects that are directly related to the operation of gaming activities.

§ 2710(d)(3)(C). Section 2710(d)(4) provides that except for any assessments that may be agreed to under paragraph (3)(C)(iii), "nothing in this section shall be interpreted as conferring upon a State or any of its political subdivisions authority to impose any tax, fee, charge, or other assessment upon an Indian tribe or upon any other person or entity authorized by an Indian tribe to engage in a class III activity."

IGRA's legislative history gives guidance to courts deciding whether a party has negotiated in good faith. Because of the scant authority interpreting or applying IGRA's good faith requirement, we set forth a somewhat lengthy excerpt from the Senate Committee Report:

> In the Committee's view, both State and tribal governments have significant governmental interests in the conduct of class III gaming. States and tribes are encouraged to conduct negotiations within the context of the mutual benefits that can flow to and from tribe and States [sic]. This is a strong and serious presumption that must provide the framework for negotiations. A tribe's governmental interests include raising revenues to provide governmental services for the benefit of the tribal community and reservation residents, promoting public safety as well as law and order on tribal lands, realizing the objectives of economic self-sufficiency and Indian self-determination, and regulating activities of persons within its jurisdictional borders. A State's governmental interests with respect to class III gaming on Indian lands include the interplay of such gaming with the State's public policy, safety, law and other interests, as well as impacts on the State's regulatory system, including its economic interest in raising revenue for its citizens. It is the Committee's intent that the compact requirement for class III gaming not be used as a justification by a State for excluding Indian tribes from such gaming or for the protection of other State-licensed gaming enterprises from free market competition with Indian tribes....
>
> The terms of each compact may vary extensively depending on the type of gaming, the location, the previous relationship of the tribe and State, etc. Section [2710(d)(3)(C)] describes the issues that may be the subject of negotiations between a tribe and a State in reaching a compact. The Committee recognizes that subparts of each of the broad areas may be more inclusive. For example, licensing issues under clause vi may include agreements on days and hours of operation, wage and pot limits, types of wagers, and size and capacity of the proposed facility. A compact may allocate most or all of the jurisdictional responsibility to the tribe, to the State or to any variation in between. The Committee does not intend that compacts be used as a subterfuge for imposing State jurisdiction on tribal lands....
>
> Finally, the bill allows States to consider negative impacts on existing gaming activities. That is not to say that the bill would allow States to reject Indian gam-

ing on the mere showing that Indian gaming will compete with non-Indian games. Rather, the States must show that economic consequences will be severe and that they will clearly outweigh positive economic consequences.

S. Rep. 100-446, at 13–14 (1988), *reprinted in* 1988 U.S.C.C.A.N. 3071, 3083–84.

Coyote Valley makes two kinds of arguments. The first is procedural. The tribe contends that the State's conduct during negotiations—specifically its dilatory tactics over the course of a seven-year period—constitutes bad faith. The second is substantive. The tribe contends that the RSTF and SDF provisions of the Davis Compact fall outside the list of appropriate topics for Tribal-State compacts set forth in § 2710(d)(3)(C), and that the State therefore acted with "per se bad faith" when it demanded that these provisions be included in any compact it entered with the tribe. The tribe also contends that the State's insistence on the RSTF and SDF provisions constitutes a "demand by the State for direct taxation of the Indian tribe," giving rise to a statutory presumption that the State has not negotiated in good faith. § 2710(d)(7)(B)(iii)(II).

We cannot conclude from the history of negotiations recounted above that, as a procedural matter, the State has refused to negotiate in good faith. It is clear that the Wilson Administration was not sympathetic to tribal gaming and was exceedingly reluctant to reach any agreement that the tribes considered acceptable. But the gravamen of Coyote Valley's amended complaint is that the Davis Administration, rather than the Wilson Administration, has refused to negotiate in good faith; and it is against the Davis Administration that Coyote Valley seeks injunctive relief.

On the record before us, it appears that the Davis Administration has actively negotiated with Indians tribes, including Coyote Valley, concerning class III gaming, and that it has negotiated despite the absence of any legal obligation to do so. Until Proposition 1A was ratified in March of 2000, the State had no obligation to negotiate with Coyote Valley over the types of class III games covered in the Davis Compact. *See Rumsey.* Moreover, at the time Coyote Valley filed its amended complaint with the district court, alleging bad faith by the Wilson and Davis Administrations, the State remained willing to meet with the tribe for further discussions. To the extent that Coyote Valley may have a valid objection to negotiations by the Davis Administration, it is not an objection to the timing and procedures of those negotiations. It is, rather, an objection to the substance of the provisions of the Davis Compact to which Coyote Valley specifically objects.

We do not believe that the challenged provisions are categorically forbidden by the terms of IGRA. Nor do we believe on the facts of this case that the State's insistence on their inclusion in the compact demonstrates a lack of good faith.

Coyote Valley first argues that the Revenue Sharing Trust Fund, which requires that gaming tribes share gaming revenues with non-gaming tribes, is impermissible under IGRA. Coyote Valley takes the position that except for "assessment[s] by the State ... in such amounts as are necessary to defray the costs of regulating" tribal gaming activities, § 2710(d)(3)(C)(iii), a provision in a Tribal-State compact requiring that the tribe pay a "tax, fee, charge, or other assessment" to the State or a third party is categorically prohibited, § 2710(d)(4). The tribe relies on § 2710(d)(4) and § 2710(d)(7)(B)(iii)(II), and emphasizes Congress's concern that States would use the negotiation process as a means of extracting forbidden taxes from tribes. *See Oklahoma Tax Comm'n v. Chickasaw Nation,* 515 U.S. 450 (1995) (explaining that absent express Congressional permission, a State is without power to tax reservation lands and reservation Indians). Because the RSTF provision requires payments from compacting tribes that go beyond amounts necessary to defray the costs incurred by the State in regulating class III gaming, Coyote Valley contends that the provision cannot properly be included in a Tribal-State compact. By insisting that this forbidden provision be included in the compact, the tribe argues, the State failed to negotiate in good faith.

As explained more fully below, we hold that §2710(d)(3)(C)(vii) authorizes the RSTF provision and that the State did not lack good faith when it insisted that Coyote Valley adopt it as a precondition to entering a Tribal-State compact. In so holding, we do not interpret IGRA as "conferring upon a State or any of its political subdivisions *authority to impose* any tax, fee, charge or other assessment upon an Indian tribe." Given that the State offered meaningful concessions in return for its demands, it did not "impose" the RSTF within the meaning of §2710(d)(4). To the extent that the State's insistence on the RSTF provision constitutes a "demand by the State for direct taxation of the Indian tribe," §2710(d)(7)(B)(iii)(II), which we do not decide, the State has successfully rebutted any inference of bad faith created thereby.

Section 2710(d)(3)(C)(vii) explicitly provides that a "Tribal-State compact ... may include provisions relating to ... subjects that are directly related to the operation of gaming activities." It is clear that the RSTF provision falls within the scope of paragraph (3)(C)(vii). Congress sought through IGRA to "promot[e] tribal economic development, self-sufficiency, and strong tribal governments." §2702(1). The RSTF provision advances this Congressional goal by creating a mechanism whereby *all* of California's tribes—not just those fortunate enough to have land located in populous or accessible areas—can benefit from class III gaming activities in the State. Moreover, the provision accomplishes this in a manner directly related to the operation of gaming activities.

Coyote Valley asks us to read §2710(d)(3)(C)(vii) narrowly and to hold that it does not encompass a provision like the RSTF. The tribe invokes the Senate Committee's statement that we should "interpret any ambiguities on these issues in a manner that will be most favorable to tribal interests." Even with the assistance of this language from the legislative history, we do not agree with Coyote Valley's reading of paragraph (3)(C)(vii). First, we believe that the paragraph is not ambiguous and that the RSTF provision clearly falls within its scope. Second, we do not believe that Coyote Valley's preferred reading of paragraph (3)(C)(vii) as forbidding revenue-sharing with non-gaming tribes is the interpretation "most favorable to tribal interests." Third, it is clear from the legislative history that by limiting the proper topics for compact negotiations to those that bear a direct relationship to the operation of gaming activities, Congress intended to prevent compacts from being used as subterfuge for imposing State jurisdiction on tribes concerning issues unrelated to gaming. In advocating the inclusion of the RSTF, the State has not sought to engage in such a subterfuge.

We also reject Coyote Valley's argument that, regardless of whether the RSTF provision would otherwise fall within§2710(d)(3)(C)(vii), it cannot in good faith be included in a Tribal-State compact because it violates §2710(d)(4). The plain language of this paragraph forbids us from construing anything in §2710 as conferring upon the State an "authority to impose" taxes, fees, charges, or other assessments on Indian tribes. However, our interpretation of paragraph (3)(C)(vii) as authorizing the RSTF provision does not run afoul of this prohibition.

We do not hold that the State could have, *without offering anything in return*, taken the position that it would conclude a Tribal-State compact with Coyote Valley only if the tribe agreed to pay into the RSTF. Where, as here, however, a State offers meaningful concessions in return for fee demands, it does not exercise "authority to impose" anything. Instead, it exercises its authority to negotiate, which IGRA clearly permits. Depending on the nature of both the fees demanded and the concessions offered in return, such demands might, of course, amount to an attempt to "impose" a fee, and therefore amount to bad faith on the part of a State. If, however, offered concessions by a State are real, §2710(d)(4) does not categorically prohibit fee demands. Instead, courts should consider the totality of that State's actions when engaging in the fact-specific good-faith inquiry IGRA generally requires. *See* §2710(d)(7)(B)(iii).

In this case, Coyote Valley cannot seriously contend that the State offered no real concessions in return for its insistence on the RSTF provision. Under our holding in *Rumsey*, the State had no obligation to enter any negotiations at all with Coyote Valley concerning most forms of class III gaming. Nor did the State have any obligation to amend its constitution to grant a monopoly to tribal gaming establishments or to offer tribes the right to operate Las Vegas-style slot machines and house-banked blackjack. As part of its negotiations with the tribes, the State offered to do both things. We therefore reject the tribe's challenge to the RSTF premised on §2710(d)(4).

Finally, Coyote Valley relies on §2710(d)(7)(B)(iii)(II), which provides that courts "shall consider any demand by the State for direct taxation of the Indian tribe or of any Indian lands as evidence that the State has not negotiated in good faith." We need not decide whether the fee structure used to fund the RSTF constitutes a "direct tax"; nor need we determine whether the State "demanded" it. Even if we assume that both are true, we would still find that the State did not negotiate in bad faith by taking the position that any compact it would enter with Coyote Valley must include the RSTF provision. Paragraph (7)(B)(iii)(II) provides only that a court "shall consider any demand by the State for direct taxation of the Indian tribe or of any Indian lands as *evidence* that the State has not negotiated in good faith." Coyote Valley would have us read "evidence" to mean "conclusive proof." This we cannot do. Not only does the plain language of the paragraph forbid such a construction, but IGRA's legislative history also makes clear that the good faith inquiry is nuanced and fact-specific, and is not amenable to bright-line rules. *See* S. Rep. No. 100-446, at 14 (1988), *reprinted in* 1988 U.S.C.C.A.N. 3071, 3084 ("The terms of each compact may vary extensively depending on the type of gaming, the location, the previous relationship of the tribe and State, etc.").

On the facts of this case, we do not find that the State's demands regarding the RSTF provision amount to bad faith. That provision does not put tribal money into the pocket of the State. Rather, it redistributes gaming profits to other Indian tribes. The idea of gaming tribes sharing revenue with non-gaming tribes traces its origins not to a State-initiated proposal, but rather to tribe-drafted and tribe-sponsored Proposition 5. Moreover, the UTCSC, of which Coyote Valley was a member, suggested in its discussion draft of June 17 that just such a provision be included in the Davis Compact. Every other compacting tribe in California has agreed to the provision.

Given that the State offered significant concessions to tribes during the course of negotiations in return for the RSTF provision, that the provision originated in proposals by the tribes and now has strong support among the tribes, and that Coyote Valley was not excluded from the negotiations that shaped the RSTF provision, we hold that the State did not act in bad faith by refusing to enter a compact with Coyote Valley that did not include this provision.

Unlike contributions to the RSTF, money that goes into the Special Distribution Fund *does* go into the pocket of the State. But it does not go into just any pocket. Although at the outset of compact negotiations with the UTCSC the State sought unrestricted access to a percentage of the tribes' net win from gaming devices, the SDF provision ultimately incorporated into the Davis Compact is much more restrictive. It provides that money from the SDF may be appropriated by the Legislature for only the following purposes:

(a) grants for programs designed to address gambling addiction;

(b) grants for the support of state and local government agencies impacted by tribal gaming;

(c) compensation for regulatory costs incurred by the State Gaming Agency and the state Department of Justice in connection with the implementation and administration of the compact;

(d) payment of shortfalls that may occur in the RSTF; and

(e) any other purposes specified by the legislature.

The district court interpreted subsection (e) under the *ejusdem generis* principle to be "limited to purposes that, like the first four enumerated purposes, are *directly related* to gaming." The State does not contest that construction on appeal, and we adopt it here.

Coyote Valley raises objections to the SDF provision similar to those it raised against the RSTF provision. Specifically, it argues that the SDF provision both falls outside the proper scope for compact negotiations set forth in § 2710(d)(3)(C) and constitutes a direct tax within the meaning of § 2710(d)(7)(B)(iii)(II). We first consider whether a requirement that tribes fund any or all of the items listed in the SDF provision falls within the permissible scope of a Tribal-State compact pursuant to § 2710(d)(3)(C). We can quickly approve the funding specified in subsection (c) of the SDF provision ("compensation for regulatory costs incurred by the State Gaming Agency and the state Department of Justice in connection with the implementation and administration of the compact"). Pursuant to § 2710(d)(3)(C)(iii), assessments on tribes designed to cover the State's costs of regulating Indian gaming are clearly appropriate, and by demanding such assessments the State does not act in bad faith. We can likewise easily dispose of the tribe's challenge to subsection (d) ("payment of shortfalls that may occur in the [RSTF]"); its inclusion in the Davis Compact does not demonstrate a lack of good faith for the same reasons that the inclusion of the RSTF provision did not demonstrate a lack of good faith. That leaves subsections (a) ("grants for programs designed to address gambling addiction"), (b) ("grants for the support of state and local government agencies impacted by tribal gaming"), and (e) ("any other purposes [directly related to gaming] specified by the legislature"). Although these provisions do not fit comfortably within paragraph (3)(C)(iii), it cannot seriously be doubted that each are "directly related to the operation of gaming activities" and are thus permissible under paragraph (3)(C)(vii). Coyote Valley argues that to interpret § 2710(d)(3)(C)(vii) as encompassing these provisions violates § 2710(d)(4), but we reject this argument for the reasons stated in the previous section.

We next determine whether the State acted in bad faith by insisting on the inclusion of the SDF provision in the Davis Compact. Even if the State's insistence on this provision was indeed a "demand" for a "direct tax" (which we do not decide), we hold that circumstances exist in this case to justify the State's conduct. As explained above, a State's demand for direct taxation of an Indian tribe constitutes only "evidence" of bad faith that courts "shall consider." This evidence is not conclusive, and on the facts of this case the State's demands do not establish bad faith. As noted above, the terms of the compact restrict what the State can do with the money it receives from the tribes pursuant to the SDF provision, and all of the purposes to which such money can be put are directly related to tribal gaming. While the contributions tribes must make to the SDF are significant, the tribes receive in exchange an exclusive right to conduct class III gaming in the most populous State in the country. We do not find it inimical to the purpose or design of IGRA for the State, under these circumstances, to ask for a reasonable share of tribal gaming revenues for the specific purposes identified in the SDF provision.

Congress did not intend to allow States to invoke their economic interests "as a justification ... for excluding Indian tribes from" class III gaming; nor did Congress intend to permit States to use the compact requirement "as a justification ... for the protection of other State-licensed gaming enterprises from free market competition with Indian tribes." By the same token, however, Congress also did not intend to require that States ignore their economic interests when engaged in compact negotiations. Indeed, §2710(d)(7)(B)(iii)(I) expressly provides that we may take into account the "financial integrity" of the State and "adverse economic impacts on [the State's] existing gaming activities" when deciding whether the State has acted in bad faith, and IGRA's legislative history explains that a "State's governmental interests with respect to class III gaming on Indian lands include ... its economic interest in raising revenue for its citizens."

Here the State did not use compact negotiations to protect "other State-licensed gaming enterprises from free market competition with Indian tribes." Instead, the State proposed a constitutional amendment protecting tribal gaming enterprises from free market competition by the State, even though it had no obligation to do so. We conclude that for the State to demand that Coyote Valley, in exchange for these exclusive gaming rights, accede to the limited revenue sharing required in the SDF provision does not constitute bad faith. The tribes who drafted and placed Proposition 5 on the ballot thought such an exchange was fair. The Proposition 5 model compact required that tribes, in exchange for exclusive rights to conduct certain class III games in the State, contribute funds to counties in California to supplement emergency medical care and programs on addictive gambling and to address the needs of the cities or counties within the boundaries of which tribal gaming facilities are located. The former Secretary of the Interior also appears to believe such an exchange is fair, given that he approved the Davis Compact in May 2000.

Notes and Questions

1. *"Fee demands" as permissible under IGRA?* Recall the Ninth Circuit's reasoning in holding that the Davis compact's revenue-sharing provisions did not violate IGRA:

> We do not hold that the State could have, *without offering anything in return*, taken the position that it would conclude a Tribal-State compact with Coyote Valley only if the tribe agreed to pay into the RSTF. Where, as here, however, a State offers meaningful concessions in return for fee demands, it does not exercise "authority to impose" anything. Instead, it exercises its authority to negotiate, which IGRA clearly permits. Depending on the nature of both the fees demanded and the concessions offered in return, such demands might, of course, amount to an attempt to "impose" a fee, and therefore amount to bad faith on the part of a State. If, however, offered concessions by a State are real, §2710(d)(4) does not categorically prohibit fee demands. Instead, courts should consider the totality of that State's actions when engaging in the fact-specific good-faith inquiry IGRA generally requires.

Are you persuaded by the court's analysis? What's the difference between the "authority to impose" and the "authority to negotiate"? Did California *negotiate* the revenue-sharing provisions with the Coyote Valley Band? Why or why not?

IGRA mandates that a court examining whether a state has negotiated in good faith "shall consider any demand by the State for direct taxation of the Indian tribe or of any

Indian lands as evidence that the State has not negotiated in good faith." 25 U.S.C. §2710(d)(7)(B)(iii). The court emphasized that the statutory language only requires that the state's demand is "evidence" of the state's failure to negotiate in good faith, rather than "conclusive evidence" of the same. Is the court correct that a state could demand direct taxation while meeting its obligation to negotiate in good faith? Note that §2710(d)(4) states, "No state may *refuse to enter into the [compact] negotiations ...* based upon the lack of authority ... to impose such a tax, fee, charge, or other assessment." (Emphasis added.) Does a state that refuses to negotiate entirely violate its good faith duty? Would a state that treats revenue sharing as a "deal breaker" during negotiations meet its good faith duty? What's the difference between the two scenarios?

2.   **In re Gaming Related Cases** *and the Secretary's interpretation.* In essence, the *In re Gaming Related Cases* court seemed to adopt the approach of the Interior Secretary by relying on California's "meaningful concessions" to the tribes to characterize the revenue-sharing provisions as something other than a "tax, fee, charge, or other assessment upon an Indian tribe." The court stated that "[d]epending on the nature of both the fees demanded and the concessions offered in return, such demands might, of course, amount to an attempt to 'impose' a fee, and therefore amount to bad faith on the part of a State." What exactly were California's meaningful concessions in this case? Generally speaking, what will constitute a meaningful concession? Does it depend on the amount of revenue sharing demanded? If so, what is the relationship between the concession requirement and the size of the state's demand?

In addition to the state's concessions, the court also emphasized that California's Special Distribution Fund (SDF) has designated uses related to gaming. In a footnote, the court distinguished the SDF from revenue-sharing payments paid to a state's general fund:

> The SDF provision in the Davis Compact differs in this respect from the revenue-sharing provisions found in Tribal State compacts entered into by the States of Connecticut, New Mexico, and New York, for example. In these States, revenue derived from tribal gaming goes into the States' general funds. The legality of such compacts is not before us, and we intimate no view on the question.

In re Gaming Related Cases, at 1115 n.17. Is the distinction between California's SDF and other states' general funds significant? Would the court have found the SDF revenue-sharing provision in violation of IGRA if tribal payments were made to the state's general fund? What other factors related to the "nature of both the fees demanded and the concessions offered in return" would be relevant? How would you articulate the standard adopted by the Ninth Circuit? How would you synthesize the Ninth Circuit's opinion and the Secretary's interpretation?

3.   *State leverage.* After *Cabazon*, California does not have authority to enforce state regulatory law on tribal lands. And, as the Ninth Circuit held in *Sycuan Band of Mission Indians v. Roache*, 54 F.3d 535 (9th Cir. 1995), the federal government has exclusive authority to enforce IGRA's provisions. Noting the same, the Ninth Circuit in *In re Gaming Related Cases* construed the state's refusal to negotiate under the Wilson administration as "one of the few forms of leverage it possessed to force tribes to comply with IGRA's compacting requirement." Is that a fair reading of the intent behind IGRA's good faith requirement? Why does the state need leverage to force tribes to comply with IGRA's compacting requirement? Recall that one of the pressures on the tribes to agree to the Davis compact was the federal government's threat to proceed with enforcement actions under IGRA and the Johnson Act.

4.   *A roller-coaster ride.* The court's detailed narrative of the varied responses of the Wilson and Davis administrations illustrates how the complicated politics of Indian gam-

ing in California, perpetuated under the Schwarzenegger administration, are nothing short of a "roller-coaster ride." *See* LIGHT & RAND, INDIAN GAMING AND TRIBAL SOVEREIGNTY, at 66–72. For more on Indian gaming in California, see, for example, Roger Dunstan, *The Evolution and Impact of Indian Gaming in California*, 5 GAMING L. REV. 373 (2001); Chad M. Gordon, *From Hope to Realization of Dreams: Proposition 5 and California Indian Gaming*, in INDIAN GAMING: WHO WINS? (Angela Mullis & David Kamper, eds., 2000).

5.   *Pushing the revenue sharing envelope.* During California's 2004 recall campaign, gubernatorial candidate Arnold Schwarzenegger promised that he would require tribal casinos to pay their "fair share," or 25 percent of gambling revenue—an estimated $1.25 billion annually—to the state. After his election, Schwarzenegger set about keeping his promise by renegotiating the compacts. To meet the standard set by the Interior Secretary and the Ninth Circuit, the state offered to increase the number of slot machines allowed in exchange for a larger share of tribal gaming revenue. (In negotiating the Davis compact, tribes cited what they saw as unreasonably low limits on the number of slot machines as one primary objection to the draft compact.) During the renegotiations, commercial gaming interests sought passage of a ballot initiative that would require all tribes with casinos to pay 25 percent of slot revenue to the state. If any tribe refused, the initiative then would allow commercial race tracks and card rooms to offer slot machines (under Proposition 1A's state constitutional amendment, only tribes enjoyed an exception to California's general prohibition against Las Vegas-style casinos). Some tribes countered with a ballot initiative that would set the rate for tribal payments at the amount of the state's corporate tax rate, or just under nine percent of gambling revenue. Both proposals ultimately were rejected by California voters. In the meantime, Schwarzenegger successfully negotiated new compacts with five tribes. The new compacts required the tribes, in exchange for unlimited slot machines, to make an initial payment to the state of $1 billion, and additional annual payments estimated to range between $150 million and $275 million. Schwarzenegger continued to negotiate new or amended compacts in 2006 and 2007, generally seeking increased revenue sharing in exchange for higher limits on slot machines. Under California law, all new and amended compacts must be approved by the state legislature, which, at the time of this writing, continued to debate the merits of approval.

In mid-2007, the Rincon Indian Band filed suit in federal court alleging that Schwarzenegger's revenue-sharing demands were in bad faith. Under its 1999 compact, the Band currently operates 1,600 slot machines, which according to the state, enjoy the highest profit per machine in the state. The Band sought renegotiation to increase its slot limit to 2,500, but challenged California's demand for increased revenue sharing to be paid into the state's general fund. One financial expert estimated that the additional slot machines would bring in another $39 million to the Band in annual profits; after paying the state's revenue-sharing demands the Band's new annual profits would drop to $1.7 million. How should the standards employed by the Ninth Circuit and the Interior Secretary apply to the Band's suit?

Problem 10.2: Negotiating a Revenue-Sharing Agreement

You have been appointed by the governor of a Midwestern state to renegotiate existing compacts with tribes in the state. There are two tribes with casinos in the state, one in the rural northern reaches and one in the southern half near the metropolitan state capital. The northern tribal casino is marginally profitable, and the tribe uses its gaming revenue to provide modest government services to its 5,000 members. The casino's estimated annual net revenue is approximately $5 million. The southern tribal casino is very lucrative, allowing the tribe to donate over $1 million annually to various non-profit organizations in the state, and to make per capita payments of about $10,000 a year to each of its 500 members. Its estimated annual net revenue is approximately $25 million. The northern casino employs about 200 workers, mostly tribal members; the southern casino employs about 2,000 workers, mostly non-Indians. Both casinos currently operate under identical compacts which allow them to operate unlimited table games and 1,000 slot machines. Each casino operates the maximum number of slot machines; the southern casino is larger and operates twice as many table games as the northern casino. Under the current compacts, the tribes reimburse the state for its regulatory costs, about $500,000 annually. The smaller northern casino pays about one-third of this amount, while the larger southern casino pays two-thirds. The renegotiation of the compacts was initiated by the governor, who is looking for revenue to assist the state in a budget crisis. The governor wants the two tribes to pay a total of $10 million annually to the state. In exchange for the state's share in tribal casino revenue, the governor is willing to increase the number of slot machines to 1,500 in each casino.

What would you propose to each tribe as a draft revenue-sharing provision? How would you justify its terms to each tribe? How would you ensure that it meets IGRA's requirements?

D. Federal Tribal Recognition

1. The Federal Tribal Recognition Process

Congress's authority in relation to tribes has been interpreted by the U.S. Supreme Court to encompass the power to formally acknowledge or "recognize" groups of American Indians as "tribes." (Originally, this occurred as part of the treaty-making process and other alliances between various Indian tribes and European nations and later the U.S.) Federal acknowledgment recognizes a tribal government's authority over its own people and establishes the framework for government-to-government relations with the U.S. It also entitles the tribe to certain programs, services, and benefits under federal law. Congress sometimes exercises its power to recognize tribes through federal legislation, but also has delegated authority to the Department of Interior and the BIA to promulgate and implement administrative regulations and procedures governing federal acknowledgment. *See* 25 U.S.C. §§ 2, 9.

In 1978, the federal government changed its practice of ad hoc determinations and adopted detailed administrative regulations and procedures for tribal recognition, found in 25 C.F.R. pt. 83. The group seeking acknowledgement is required to formally petition the BIA's Office of Federal Acknowledgment (OFA), formerly known as the Branch of Acknowledgment and Research, for recognition. Federal researchers review a group's petition and supporting documentation to determine if the group meets seven mandatory criteria. The OFA's determinations are appealable to the Interior Board of Indian Appeals.

§ 83.7 Mandatory criteria for Federal acknowledgment. The mandatory criteria are:

(a) The petitioner has been identified as an American Indian entity on a substantially continuous basis since 1900. Evidence that the group's character as an Indian entity has from time to time been denied shall not be considered to be conclusive evidence that this criterion has not been met. Evidence to be relied upon in determining a group's Indian identity may include one or a combination of the following, as well as other evidence of identification by other than the petitioner itself or its members.

(1) Identification as an Indian entity by Federal authorities.

(2) Relationships with State governments based on identification of the group as Indian.

(3) Dealings with a county, parish, or other local government in a relationship based on the group's Indian identity.

(4) Identification as an Indian entity by anthropologists, historians, and/or other scholars.

(5) Identification as an Indian entity in newspapers and books.

(6) Identification as an Indian entity in relationships with Indian tribes or with national, regional, or state Indian organizations.

(b) A predominant portion of the petitioning group comprises a distinct community and has existed as a community from historical times until the present.

(1) This criterion may be demonstrated by some combination of the following evidence and/or other evidence that the petitioner meets the definition of community set forth in § 83.1:

(i) Significant rates of marriage within the group, and/or, as may be culturally required, patterned out-marriages with other Indian populations.

(ii) Significant social relationships connecting individual members.

(iii) Significant rates of informal social interaction which exist broadly among the members of a group.

(iv) A significant degree of shared or cooperative labor or other economic activity among the membership.

(v) Evidence of strong patterns of discrimination or other social distinctions by non-members.

(vi) Shared sacred or secular ritual activity encompassing most of the group.

(vii) Cultural patterns shared among a significant portion of the group that are different from those of the non-Indian populations with whom it interacts. These patterns must function as more than a symbolic identification of the group as Indian. They may include, but are not limited to, language, kinship organization, or religious beliefs and practices.

(viii) The persistence of a named, collective Indian identity continuously over a period of more than 50 years, notwithstanding changes in name.

(ix) A demonstration of historical political influence under the criterion in § 83.7(c) shall be evidence for demonstrating historical community.

(2) A petitioner shall be considered to have provided sufficient evidence of community at a given point in time if evidence is provided to demonstrate any one of the following:

(i) More than 50 percent of the members reside in a geographical area exclusively or almost exclusively composed of members of the group, and the balance of the group maintains consistent interaction with some members of the community;

(ii) At least 50 percent of the marriages in the group are between members of the group;

(iii) At least 50 percent of the group members maintain distinct cultural patterns such as, but not limited to, language, kinship organization, or religious beliefs and practices;

(iv) There are distinct community social institutions encompassing most of the members, such as kinship organizations, formal or informal economic cooperation, or religious organizations; or

(v) The group has met the criterion in §83.7(c) using evidence described in §83.7(c)(2).

(c) The petitioner has maintained political influence or authority over its members as an autonomous entity from historical times until the present.

(1) This criterion may be demonstrated by some combination of the evidence listed below and/or by other evidence that the petitioner meets the definition of political influence or authority in §83.1.

(i) The group is able to mobilize significant numbers of members and significant resources from its members for group purposes.

(ii) Most of the membership considers issues acted upon or actions taken by group leaders or governing bodies to be of importance.

(iii) There is widespread knowledge, communication and involvement in political processes by most of the group's members.

(iv) The group meets the criterion in §83.7(b) at more than a minimal level.

(v) There are internal conflicts which show controversy over valued group goals, properties, policies, processes and/or decisions.

(2) A petitioning group shall be considered to have provided sufficient evidence to demonstrate the exercise of political influence or authority at a given point in time by demonstrating that group leaders and/or other mechanisms exist or existed which:

(i) Allocate group resources such as land, residence rights and the like on a consistent basis.

(ii) Settle disputes between members or subgroups by mediation or other means on a regular basis;

(iii) Exert strong influence on the behavior of individual members, such as the establishment or maintenance of norms and the enforcement of sanctions to direct or control behavior;

(iv) Organize or influence economic subsistence activities among the members, including shared or cooperative labor.

(3) A group that has met the requirements in paragraph 83.7(b)(2) at a given point in time shall be considered to have provided sufficient evidence to meet this criterion at that point in time.

(d) A copy of the group's present governing document including its membership criteria. In the absence of a written document, the petitioner must provide a statement describing in full its membership criteria and current governing procedures.

(e) The petitioner's membership consists of individuals who descend from a historical Indian tribe or from historical Indian tribes which combined and functioned as a single autonomous political entity.

(1) Evidence acceptable to the Secretary which can be used for this purpose includes but is not limited to:

(i) Rolls prepared by the Secretary on a descendancy basis for purposes of distributing claims money, providing allotments, or other purposes;

(ii) State, Federal, or other official records or evidence identifying present members or ancestors of present members as being descendants of a historical tribe or tribes that combined and functioned as a single autonomous political entity.

(iii) Church, school, and other similar enrollment records identifying present members or ancestors of present members as being descendants of a historical tribe or tribes that combined and functioned as a single autonomous political entity.

(iv) Affidavits of recognition by tribal elders, leaders, or the tribal governing body identifying present members or ancestors of present members as being descendants of a historical tribe or tribes that combined and functioned as a single autonomous political entity.

(v) Other records or evidence identifying present members or ancestors of present members as being descendants of a historical tribe or tribes that combined and functioned as a single autonomous political entity.

(2) The petitioner must provide an official membership list, separately certified by the group's governing body, of all known current members of the group. This list must include each member's full name (including maiden name), date of birth, and current residential address. The petitioner must also provide a copy of each available former list of members based on the group's own defined criteria, as well as a statement describing the circumstances surrounding the preparation of the current list and, insofar as possible, the circumstances surrounding the preparation of former lists.

(f) The membership of the petitioning group is composed principally of persons who are not members of any acknowledged North American Indian tribe. However, under certain conditions a petitioning group may be acknowledged even if its membership is composed principally of persons whose names have appeared on rolls of, or who have been otherwise associated with, an acknowledged Indian tribe. The conditions are that the group must establish that it has functioned throughout history until the present as a separate and autonomous Indian tribal entity, that its members do not maintain a bilateral political relationship with the acknowledged tribe, and that its members have provided written confirmation of their membership in the petitioning group.

(g) Neither the petitioner nor its members are the subject of congressional legislation that has expressly terminated or forbidden the Federal relationship.

Given the administrative regulations and procedures detailed in 25 C.F.R pt. 83, the federal recognition process has required tribal groups to retain teams of experts, including cultural anthropologists, genealogists, historians, and, of course, attorneys. The typical administrative record resulting from the process can exceed 100,000 pages. For more on the federal recognition process generally, see MARK EDWIN MILLER, FORGOTTEN TRIBES: UNRECOGNIZED INDIANS AND THE FEDERAL ACKNOWLEDGMENT PROCESS (2004); Roberto Iraola, *The Administrative Tribal Recognition Process and the Courts*, 38 AKRON L. REV. 867 (2005); Mark D. Myers, *Federal Recognition of Indian Tribes in the United States*, 12 STAN. L. & POL'Y REV. 271 (2001).

2. Indian Gaming and Recognition

Many tribes have long histories of federal recognition dating back to treaties and other interactions with the newly formed U.S. that are akin to the federal government's recognition of foreign nations. However, many other tribes have been subject to broken treaties, armed conflict, forced relocation, and other dimensions of federal Indian policy, such as allotment and termination, that led to the disintegration of tribal communities and tribal governmental authority. Some tribal groups have been recognized only by states or have organized—or more accurately, reorganized—in the modern era of tribal self-determination. As the federal government's rules and procedures for tribal groups to obtain recognition have been promulgated and clarified, an increasing number of tribal groups are seeking federal acknowledgment.

As mentioned above, federal acknowledgment recognizes a tribe's governmental authority—its sovereignty—and entitles the tribe to access various programs and services and claim certain benefits under federal law. In the last two decades, one highly significant ramification is a newly recognized tribe's potential ability to operate gaming enterprises under IGRA. (Recall that only "Indian tribes" may conduct Class II and Class III gaming under IGRA.) The tremendous growth of Indian gaming has fueled concerns that tribal groups are seeking federal acknowledgement for the sole purpose of opening a casino, sometimes resulting in a process corrupted by political or financial influence. Consider the following testimony of Mary Kendall, Deputy Inspector General in the Interior Department.

Mary L. Kendall
Statement Before the U.S. Senate Committee on Indian Affairs on Federal Recognition of Indian Tribes
(May 11, 2005)

I am here today to testify about the Office of Inspector General's oversight activities concerning the federal acknowledgment process administered by the Department of the Interior. As you know, the Office of Inspector General has oversight responsibility for all programs and operations of the Department. However, because, the Inspector General Act specifically precludes the Office of Inspector General from exercising any programmatic responsibility, we cannot—and do not—substitute our judgment for substantive decisions or actions taken by the Department or its bureaus. This is especially true in the area of federal acknowledgment, which typically involves the review and evaluation of evidence by professional historians, genealogists and cultural anthropologists. Therefore, when we undertake to address concerns—whether those concerns are raised on our own accord or through another body such as Congress—about the operation or management of a DOI program, we first look at the established processes by which decisions or actions in that particular program take place and the controls over those processes. After we determine what the established process is to address the issue at hand, we then look to see whether there has been any deviation from that process. If we determine that deviation occurred, we will go on to attempt to determine the impact of that deviation on the resulting decision or action and whether any inappropriate behavior was involved by either Department employees and/or external participants.

As you know, the tribal recognition, or federal acknowledgement process at the Department of the Interior is governed by regulations that set forth the process by which groups seeking federal acknowledgment as Indian tribes are handled. While this process has been harshly criticized for its lack of transparency, based on our experience, it is, relatively speaking, one of the more transparent processes in DOI. The process follows the requirements of the Administrative Procedures Act, which include notice, an opportunity to comment, and an appeal or review mechanism. When we conduct any kind of inquiry, my office is always advantaged if a program has the backdrop of a well-established process with documented requirements and guidelines.

When conducting an investigation of a program such as federal acknowledgment, we also identify all the key participants and endeavor to strategically interview as many of these individuals as possible. This includes not only DOI personnel, but other interested parties outside of the Department as well. In federal acknowledgment matters, this may include other parties identified by the Office of Federal Acknowledgment (OFA) or parties who have expressly signaled an interest in the acknowledgment process, such as an affected State Attorney General.

Accordingly, when we conduct interviews in a given federal acknowledgment process, we typically begin with those OFA research team members who are charged with the petition review process. By beginning at this level, we have had some historical success at discovering irregularities at the very heart of the process. For example, in our 2001 investigation of six petitions for federal acknowledgment, we discovered that pressure had been exerted by political-decision makers on the OFA team members who were responsible for making the federal acknowledgment recommendations. The OFA research team members who reported this pressure were, at the time, courageous in their coming-forward, as my office had not yet established our now well-known Whistleblower Protection Program. At the time, we had to assure each individual who came forward that we would do everything necessary to protect them from reprisal; today, however, we have a recognized program in place which publicly assures DOI employees that we will ensure their protection. In other cases, we have had considerable success in obtaining candid information from lower-level employees intent on telling the Office of Inspector General their concerns. Therefore, given their track record in our 2001 investigation and our now-two-year-old Whistleblower Protection Program, we feel confident that if any inappropriate pressure is being applied we will hear that from the members of the OFA team.

In 2001, we did find that there was some rather disturbing deviation from the established process during the previous Administration. At that time, several federal acknowledgment decisions had been made by the acting Assistant Secretary for Indian Affairs, which were contrary to the recommendations of the OFA research team. In several instances, the OFA research team felt so strongly that they issued memoranda of nonconcurrence, at some risk to their own careers.

Although any Assistant Secretary for Indian Affairs has the authority to issue his or her decision even if contrary to OFA's recommendation, we found in those particular instances that significant pressure had been placed on the OFA research teams to issue predetermined recommendations, that the decisions were hastened to occur prior to the change in Administration, and that all decision documents had not been properly signed. In fact, we even found that one of these decisions had been signed by the former acting Assistant Secretary after leaving office.

When we reported our findings in February 2002, the new Assistant Secretary for Indian Affairs undertook an independent review of the petitions. This action alleviated many of our concerns about the procedural irregularities we identified in our report. In

March 2004, we were asked by Senator Christopher Dodd to investigate the Schaghticoke Tribal Nation acknowledgment decision. Subsequent to Senator Dodd's request, the Secretary of the Interior, Gale A. Norton, specifically requested that we to give this matter high priority. In conducting this investigation, we interviewed OFA staff, research team members, and senior Department officials to determine if undue pressure may have been exerted. We also spoke to the Connecticut Attorney General and members of his staff, as well as affected citizens, to ascertain their concerns. In this case, as we have in all other such investigations, we were also looking for any inappropriate lobbying pressure that may have attempted to influence a decision one way or another. In the end, we found that although the Schaghticoke Tribal Nation acknowledgment decision was highly controversial, OFA and the Principal Deputy Assistant Secretary for Indian Affairs conducted themselves in keeping with the requirements of the administrative process, their decision-making process was made transparent by the administrative record, and those parties aggrieved by the decision sought relief in the appropriate administrative forum — each, as it should be.

If I may, I would like to comment briefly on outside influences that impact the federal acknowledgment process and Indian gaming. As this Committee recently demonstrated, greater care must be exercised by gaming tribes when they are approached by unsavory Indian gaming lobbyists promising imperceptible services for astonishing fees. We know of no statutory or regulatory safeguard protections against such lobbying efforts or the often-questionable financial backing of the federal acknowledgment process. That being said, however, given the spate of recent media reports of alleged improper lobbying influences relating to Indian programs, the Office of Inspector General now includes in its scope of investigation an inquiry into any lobbying or other financial influences that might bear on the issue or program at hand, with a view toward targeting improper lobbying access and/or influence on the Department of the Interior.

The transparency that attaches itself to the federal acknowledgment process itself is often obscured when it comes to those who would use this process as an instant opportunity for opening a casino. Last year, in a prosecution stemming from one of our investigations, the U.S. Attorney's Office for the Northern District of New York secured a guilty plea by an individual who had submitted fraudulent documents in an effort to obtain federal acknowledgment for a group known as the Western Mohegan Tribe and Nation of New York. Throughout trial, the prosecution contended that the fraudulent application was made in the hope of initiating gaming and casino operations in upstate New York. We are hopeful that this conviction has sent a clear message to others who would attempt to corrupt the federal acknowledgment process, particularly when motivated by gaming interests.

This murky underbelly is fraught with potential for abuse, including inappropriate lobbying activities and unsavory characters gaining an illicit foothold in Indian gaming operations. We will continue to aggressively investigate allegations of fraud or impropriety in the federal acknowledgment process.

Notes and Questions

1.   Scrutinizing the BIA process. In recent years, the BIA's recognition process has come under fire for alleged secrecy, bias, and other improprieties. At the same time, competing gaming tribes, non-tribal governments, and outside investors have been accused of tainting the process. The 2001 events mentioned in Deputy Inspector General

Kendall's testimony refer to the controversial acknowledgment decisions of outgoing Assistant Secretary for Indian Affairs Kevin Gover (and then Michael Anderson, Gover's replacement at the end of the Clinton administration). Gover, now a law professor, issued preliminary approvals for the Eastern Pequot Tribe and Paucatuck Eastern Tribe, both in Connecticut, and the Little Shell Chippewa in Montana. Gover also issued a final determination to recognize the Chinook Nation of Washington on his last day in office. Shortly thereafter, Anderson preliminarily approved the Nipmuc Nation of Massachusetts and the Duwamish Tribe of Washington. In all six cases, Gover and Anderson went against the findings by professional staff in the Branch of Acknowledgment and Research. In his first term of office, President Bush named Neal McCaleb as Assistant Secretary for Indian Affairs, who promised to review the Gover and Anderson decisions. The controversy resulted in a 2001 federal General Accounting Office (GAO) investigation, which concluded that

> the end result [of such cases] could be that the resolution of tribal recognition cases will have less to do with the attributes and qualities of a group as an independent political entity deserving of a government-to-government relationship with the United States and more to do with the resources that petitioners and third parties can marshal to develop a successful political and legal strategy.

U.S. General Accounting Office, Indian Issues: Improvements Needed in Tribal Recognition Process, GAO-02-49 (November 2001), at 19. Following the GAO report, the BIA adopted a strategic plan to increase transparency and efficiency in the administrative process of tribal acknowledgment. One change under the plan was the restructuring of the Branch of Acknowledgment and Research, resulting in the Office of Federal Acknowledgment in 2003.

2.   *Long wait, long odds.* Some tribal representatives have pointed out that the BIA's administrative process takes years, and very few petitions for recognition have been granted. Since 1978, when Congress authorized the BIA to recognize tribes, it has approved about 15 applications and has denied roughly 20. Rand & Light, Indian Gaming Law and Policy, at 156. Over 200 applications are awaiting a decision (more than 50 of which originate in California alone), while a number of tribal applications have been in the queue for more than twenty years—that is, predating IGRA, as the next excerpt discusses. On the BIA's glacial pace in reviewing applications, see Miller, Forgotten Tribes.

Given a growing perception that federal recognition is the gateway to Indian gaming, the perceptions of the acknowledgment process, if not the process itself, have become increasingly politicized and arguably, more exacting for tribal groups. Fueling concerns and perhaps generating a backlash, some tribes have enlisted the assistance of outside investors and commercial backers to bankroll the expensive and time-consuming process of seeking recognition.

Renee Ann Cramer
Cash, Color, and Colonialism:
The Politics of Tribal Acknowledgment
95–103 (2005)

Although the relatively modest available sources of funding have proven invaluable to most of the tribes seeking acknowledgment, they are often inadequate to pay for the research demands of the BAR (BIA's Branch of Acknowledgment and Research), the lobbying and research demands of Congress, or the legal demands of the court system. The gaming industry, seeing a need in the community and a payoff in the form of potentially lucrative tribal casino contracts, has rushed to fill in the gaps left by other sources of funding.

As a result of investments made by casino developers and gaming tribes, some hopeful groups are able to finance massive work on their petitions, or hire lobbyists in aid of legislative recognition. This certainly helps to ensure that some deserving tribes will not be denied recognition simply because they could not afford to hire the research work necessary for their petition. It may also, however, create or exacerbate tribal splits over the idea of gaming, which could lead to economic and power disparities within the petitioning groups.

It is, in part, the availability of gaming financing and the publicly aired factionalization of some petitioning groups that have led to gross oversimplifications about acknowledgment, such as Connecticut television station that reported the following when the Golden Hill Paugussetts were denied by the BAR: "Golden Hill Paugussett Tribe denied a gambling permit by the Federal Bureau of Indian Affairs." The conflation of gaming with acknowledgment by the media and BAR staff alike is unfair for those groups who sought recognition long before the passage of the IGRA, and are merely taking advantage of new laws to achieve economic self-sufficiency.

Resentment against Indian tribes as they pursue land claims or economic development is nothing new. However, there has been a dramatic escalation of tensions between the towns, the tribes, and unrecognized groups in Connecticut since the advent of casino gaming. In the most pressing instances, Connecticut legislators have called for the dissolution of state recognition for the Golden Hill Paugussetts, and for a federal investigation into the acknowledgment of the Mashantucket Pequots. The tensions have also risen to a national level, with a number of anti-gaming bills being introduced since the IGRA.

Nationally and regionally, those who resent Indian casino success have voiced three primary concerns. These concerns focus on the supposed immorality and criminality of gaming, the perception that local towns and cities are not benefiting economically from Indian gaming, and the perception that the tribes are using their increasing political power to steamroll citizens concerned about uncontrolled development of tribal lands.

Though most of its premises are unfounded, the backlash against casino operations is quickly spilling over into a backlash against recognizing new tribes. And, while BAR staff maintains that its processes are above such backlash, congressional processes certainly are not.

It is hard to judge whether the BAR's outcomes and processes are affected by the casino issue; none of the tribes that have been recognized since 1978 were post-1988 petitioners. In other words, none of the fifteen newly recognized tribes are likely to have been motivated solely by high-stakes casino gaming when they filed their first correspondence with the BAR. Only one of the fifteen groups denied by the BAR was a post-1988 petitioner; this leaves no argument that the BAR staff's decisions against tribes came about due to concerns regarding the petitioners' gaming motivations.

One significant aspect of BAR processes and decisions, however, has been affected by casino gaming. The accelerating rate of litigation of BAR decisions, as states side with their non-Indian residents in suits fighting tribal acknowledgment, subjects the BAR to increasing scrutiny, costly research and litigation, and a sense of being embattled on all fronts. BAR proceedings are subject to backlash, like it or not. Certainly, the same is true for groups hoping to achieve acknowledgment.

Notes and Questions

1. *State recognized tribes.* As mentioned above, a number of tribes are state-recognized, but not federally recognized. Such tribes reside in several states, including Alabama, Connecticut, Louisiana, Massachusetts, Michigan, New Jersey, New York, North Carolina, Ohio, Oklahoma, and Virginia. For more on state and federal recognition, see Margo S. Brownell, *Who Is an Indian? Searching for an Answer to the Question at the Core of Federal Indian Law*, 34 U. Mich. J.L. Reform 275 (2000); Sharon O'Brien, *Tribes and Indians: With Whom Does the United States Maintain a Relationship?*, 66 Notre Dame L. Rev. 1461 (1991). Tribes whose governmental authority is recognized only by the state are not "Indian tribes" for purposes of IGRA. With the advent of Indian gaming, some states have opposed federal recognition of tribes that have been recognized by the state, often since colonial times. On state recognition and IGRA, see Alexa Koenig & Jonathan Stein, *Lost in the Shuffle: State-Recognized Tribes and the Tribal Gaming Industry*, 40 U.S.F. L. Rev. 327 (2006).

2. *The Mashantucket Pequots and Foxwoods.* Perhaps the most important reason why federal recognition is so controversial has nothing to do with the BIA's administrative recognition process; rather, it stems from Congress's legislative recognition of the Mashantucket Pequots, signed into law by President Reagan. For a detailed summary of the Pequots' story and its implications, see generally Light & Rand, Indian Gaming and Tribal Sovereignty, at 105–18. The unparalleled economic success of the Foxwoods Resort Casino in Connecticut — one of the world's largest and most lucrative casinos — has made the Mashantucket Pequots the most intensely scrutinized and highly criticized tribe in the U.S. The story of the Pequots and their resurrection by tribal president Richard "Skip" Hayward is oft-recounted, yet apparently never ceases to provoke amazement as well as anger. After a long battle featuring lawsuits over land claims and a settlement by the state of Connecticut, Congress recognized the Pequots through the Connecticut Indian Land Claims Settlement Act of 1983, 25 U.S.C. §§ 1751–1760. The tribe subsequently built a successful bingo hall in the mid-1980s. After Congress passed IGRA, the tribe pursued casino-style gaming in the face of state and local opposition. In 1990, a federal court ruled that because Connecticut allowed casino-style gaming for charitable purposes, the tribe could open a casino on its reservation. See *Mashantucket Pequot Tribe v. Connecticut*, 913 F.2d 1024 (2d Cir. 1990) (excerpted in Chapter 5). A compact featuring the first revenue-sharing agreement — a 25 percent cut of slot revenue for the state — and financing from a Malaysian construction magnate paved the way for Foxwoods and its annual billion-dollar grosses. For differing accounts of the Pequots' recognition and its implications, compare Paul Pasquaretta, Gambling and Survival in Native North America (2003) and The Pequots in Southern New England (Laurence M. Hauptman & James D. Wherry eds., 1990) with Kim Isaac Eisler, Revenge of the Pequots: How a Small Native American Tribe Created the World's Most Profitable Casino (2001) and Jeff Benedict, Without Reservation: The Making of America's Most Powerful Indian Tribe and Foxwoods, The World's Largest Casino (2000); see also Kathryn R.L. Rand, *There Are No Pequots on the Plains: Assessing the Success of Indian Gaming*, 5 Chapman L. Rev. 47 (2002) (critiquing and contextualizing several of these accounts).

3. *Additional recent controversies in Connecticut.* Professor Cramer also referenced the recent controversial recognition efforts of the Golden Hill Paugussett, a tribal group

based in Trumbull, Connecticut. Fanning the fire, shopping mall developer Tom Wilmot and Subway Restaurants founder Frederick A. DeLuca each backed the group's recognition attempt to the tune of about $10 million. The Paugussett were forthright in their intent to build a casino in Bridgeport upon federal acknowledgment. Connecticut state officials expressed outrage over the recognition attempts by the Paugussett as well as the (temporarily) successful efforts of the Eastern Pequots—at one time bankrolled by Donald Trump—and the Schaghticoke Tribal Nation. Connecticut attorney general Richard Blumenthal condemned the BIA's affirmative decision on the Schaghticokes as "arbitrary and lawless." On the Schaghticoke, see Light & Rand, Indian Gaming and Tribal Sovereignty, at 60–63, 191 n.59. The Interior Department subsequently reversed its position on the Eastern Pequots and the Schaghticokes. *See* U.S. Department of the Interior, The Department of the Interior Issued Reconsidered Final Determination to Decline Federal Acknowledgment of the Schaghticoke Tribal Nation, Press Release (Oct. 12, 2004).

4.   Second-class sovereignty? In May 2007, the U.S. House of Representatives passed a bill that would grant federal recognition to six tribes in Virginia, coinciding with the 400th anniversary of the Jamestown settlement. H.R. 1294, 110th Cong., 1st Sess. (2007). But federal acknowledgment would come at a price: the bill conditioned the tribes' recognition on their waiver of gaming rights. This is the latest manifestation of the view that federal recognition is a "license" to operate a casino, rather than a straightforward acknowledgement of a tribe's status as a sovereign government. By conditioning the Virginia tribes' recognition on waiver of gaming rights, House members may have believed they had hit upon a happy compromise: the tribes would receive federal recognition, and Virginia would get a guarantee that the tribes cannot open casinos. Beyond that, however, the bill may be a harbinger of a long-term trend. Suppose Congress—and perhaps tribal groups desperate for federal acknowledgement—displays a willingness to use the legislative recognition process conditioned upon the abrogation of gaming rights. Would this new form of federal acknowledgement effectively fiat a "second-class" tier of tribal sovereignty: federally recognized tribes without all of the inherent rights that historically have been acknowledged through recognition?

Critics of conditional legislative acknowledgment assert that tribal rights are not granted to tribes by Congress; instead, they stem from tribes' status as separate, sovereign governments. Moreover, in instances like this one, the Virginia tribes have long been recognized by the state, and before that, entered into treaties as sovereign governments with England. Would conditioning their recognition on the abrogation of gaming rights be a victory of politics over principle? Would it truly be a "voluntary" decision on the part of the tribes? Is it paternalistic to suggest otherwise?

Problem 10.3: Tribal Recognition

You are a key tribal official for a small, impoverished tribal group in a populous state. The tribal group has been waiting for nearly a decade for a final determination on its administrative petition for federal acknowledgment. A member of your state's congressional delegation is on the U.S. Senate's Indian Affairs Committee, and you believe she would be willing to sponsor a bill that would grant federal recognition of your tribe via federal statute, as long as it waives the right to game. Several members of the tribal group's governing body are interested in pursuing gaming as part of an economic development plan; others are critical of a possible gaming proposal, raising concerns about its impacts on traditional tribal culture as well as the prevalence of problem and pathological gambling. With so much more at stake than gaming—many tribal members believe strongly that acknowledgment carries with it a valuable recognition of tribal sovereignty, and others believe access to federal programs and services would help lift tribal members from poverty — you are charged with making a recommendation to the tribal council about what to do. Articulate the arguments for and against pursuing federal recognition accompanied by an abrogation of the right to game.

E. Tribal Casinos as Employers

Tribal gaming enterprises directly employ more than 325,000 people, most of whom are non-Indian. *See* MEISTER, INDIAN GAMING INDUSTRY REPORT, at 3. Not surprisingly, the rapid growth of the Indian gaming industry has given rise to a number of employment-related issues. As reflected in *Cabazon*'s analysis, state labor laws do not apply to tribal enterprises. Tribes have developed their own employment and labor laws and personnel policies, and some compacts specifically incorporate state and/or tribal employment-related laws.

Tribal casinos, as government-operated businesses, often are exempt from federal employment law. Title VII of the 1964 Civil Rights Act, for example, expressly excludes tribes from the employers covered by the statute. 42 U.S.C. § 2000e(1); *see also* 42 U.S.C. § 12111(b) (similar provision in Title I of the Americans with Disabilities Act). Federal laws of general applicability raise the issue of whether tribal governments, neither expressly exempted nor included, are subject to the law's requirements. In the context of Indian gaming, a significant issue has arisen regarding the applicability of the National Labor Relations Act to — and by extension, the authority of the National Labor Relations Board over — tribal casinos. In 2007, the D.C. Circuit weighed in on the issue of the NLRB's authority in Indian country.

San Manuel Indian Bingo & Casino v. NLRB
475 F.3d 1306 (D.C. Cir. 2007)

In this case, we consider whether the National Labor Relations Board (the "Board") may apply the National Labor Relations Act, 29 U.S.C. §§ 151 *et seq.* (the "NLRA"), to employment at a casino the San Manuel Band of Serrano Mission Indians ("San Manuel" or the "Tribe") operates on its reservation.

San Manuel owns and operates the San Manuel Indian Bingo and Casino (the "Casino") on its reservation in San Bernardino County, California. This proceeding arose out of a competition between the Communication Workers of America ("CWA") and the Hotel Employees & Restaurant Employees International Union ("HERE"), each seeking to organize the Casino's employees. According to HERE's evidence, the Casino is about an hour's drive from Los Angeles. It includes a 2300-seat bingo hall and over a thousand slot machines. It also offers live entertainment. HERE's evidence further suggests the Tribe actively directs its marketing efforts to non-Indians, and the Board found that "many, and perhaps the great majority, of the casino's patrons are nonmembers who come from outside the reservation." The Tribe does not contract with an independent management company to operate the Casino, and therefore many Tribe members hold key positions at the Casino. Nevertheless, given the Casino's size, the Tribe must employ a significant number of non-members to ensure effective operation.

According to San Manuel's evidence, its tribal government consists of a "General Council," which elects from among its members a "Business Committee." The General Council includes all tribal members twenty-one years of age or older. The record is not specific in regards to the size of the Tribe, but the Tribe's "Articles of Association" call for monthly meetings of the General Council, suggesting the Tribe is relatively small. The record also does not indicate the Casino's gross annual revenues, but HERE submitted a declaration indicating that, as of February 8, 2000, the Casino's website was advertising in regard to its bingo operation "Over 1 BILLION Dollars in Cash and Prizes awarded since July 24th, 1986." Revenues from the Casino are used to fund various tribal government programs and to provide for the general welfare of Tribe members.

In the Tribe's case, IGRA appears to have fulfilled its purpose, as the Casino has markedly improved the Tribe's economic condition. The Tribe's evidence indicates its one-square-mile reservation consists primarily of steep, mountainous, arid land, most of it unsuitable to economic development. For many years, the Tribe had no resources, and many of its members depended on public assistance. As a result of the Casino, however, the Tribe can now boast full employment, complete medical coverage for all members, government funding for scholarships, improved housing, and significant infrastructure improvements to the reservation. In addition, according to the Tribe's evidence, the tribal government is authorized to make direct per capita payments of Casino revenues to Tribe members, suggesting that improved government services are not the only way Tribe members might benefit from the Casino.

On January 18, 1999, HERE filed an unfair labor practice charge with the Board. The charge asserted the Casino "has interfered with, coerced and restrained employees in the exercise of their [collective bargaining] rights, and has dominated and discriminatorily supported the [CWA] by allowing CWA representatives access to Casino property . . . , while denying the same-or any-right of access to representatives of [HERE]." The Tribe appeared specially, seeking dismissal for lack of jurisdiction. The Tribe asserted the NLRA does not apply to the actions of tribal governments on their reservations.

The Board began by reviewing its past decisions regarding application of the NLRA to tribal governments. In *Fort Apache*, the Board had ruled the NLRA did not apply to a tribal government operating a timber mill on Indian land, finding the mill to be akin to a "political subdivision" of a state government and therefore exempt. *Fort Apache Timber Co.*, 226 N.L.R.B. 503 (1976). This ruling would arguably apply wherever the tribal government's enterprise was located, but in *Sac & Fox Industries, Ltd.*, 307 N.L.R.B. 241 (1992), the Board found the NLRA applicable to *off-reservation* tribal enterprises. Analyzing these precedents, the Board acknowledged reliance on two basic premises — that location is determinative and that the text of the NLRA supported this location-based rule — and found both flawed. First, the Board concluded that the NLRA applies to tribal governments by its terms and that the legislative history of the NLRA does not suggest a tribal exemption. Next, the Board held federal Indian policy does not preclude application of the NLRA to the commercial activities of tribal governments.

In regard to the latter point, the Board cited the Supreme Court's statement in *Federal Power Commission v. Tuscarora Indian Nation*, 362 U.S. 99 (1960), that "a general statute in terms applying to all persons includes Indians and their property interests." The Board noted several contexts in which courts had followed *Tuscarora* and applied federal laws to Indian tribes. In *Donovan v. Coeur d'Alene Tribal Farm*, 751 F.2d 1113 (9th Cir. 1985), for example, the Ninth Circuit found the Occupational Safety and Health Act applicable to a farm operated by a tribe and located on the tribe's reservation. The *Coeur d'Alene* court identified only three exceptions to *Tuscarora*'s statement that federal statutes apply to tribes. According to the Ninth Circuit, an exception to this general rule is appropriate when: "(1) the law touches 'exclusive rights of self-governance in purely intramural matters'; (2) the application of the law to the tribe would 'abrogate rights guaranteed by Indian treaties'; or (3) there is proof 'by legislative history or some other means that Congress intended [the law] not to apply to Indians on their reservations. . . .'" (quoting *United States v. Farris*, 624 F.2d 890, 893–94 (9th Cir. 1980)). The Board adopted the *Tuscarora-Coeur d'Alene* framework in this case, thus overruling the *Fort Apache* decision, and it concluded that none of the three *Coeur d'Alene* exceptions applied and that therefore what it characterized as *Tuscarora*'s general rule was controlling.

But the Board did not stop there. Having found the NLRA applicable according to its terms, and having concluded federal Indian law did not preclude application of the NLRA, the Board considered as a matter of discretion whether to exercise its jurisdiction in light of the need to "accommodate the unique status of Indians in our society and legal culture." Here, the Board went beyond the *Coeur d'Alene* exceptions, asking if the assertion of jurisdiction would "effectuate the purposes of the [NLRA]," and noting that when a tribe "is fulfilling traditionally tribal or governmental functions" that do not "involve non-Indians [or] substantially affect interstate commerce," "the Board's interest in effectuating the policies of the [NLRA] is likely to be lower." The Board considered the location of the tribal government's activity (that is, whether on or off the Tribe's reservation) relevant but not determinative. Because here "the casino is a typical commercial enterprise [that] employs non-Indians[ ] and ... caters to non-Indian customers," the Board found the exercise of jurisdiction appropriate. [Accordingly,] the Board issued a cease-and-desist order requiring the Tribe to give HERE access to the Casino and also to post notices in the Casino describing the rights of employees under the NLRA.

Several factors make resolution of this case particularly difficult. We have before us conflicting Supreme Court canons of interpretation that are articulated at a fairly high level of generality. In addition, the NLRA was enacted by a Congress that in all likelihood never contemplated the statute's potential application to tribal employers, and probably no member of that Congress imagined a small Indian tribe might operate like a closely held corporation, employing hundreds, or even thousands, of non-Indians to produce a product it profitably marketed to non-Indians. Further, the casino at issue here, though certainly exhibiting characteristics that are strongly commercial (non-Indian employees and non-Indian patrons), is also in some sense governmental (the casino is the primary source of revenue for the tribal government). Finally, out-of-circuit precedent is inconsistent as to the applicability of general federal laws to Indian tribes.

The gravitational center of San Manuel's case is tribal sovereignty, but even if we accept the paramount significance of this factor, our resolution of the case depends on how the Supreme Court and Congress have defined the contours and limits of tribal sovereignty. Our central inquiry is whether the relation between the Tribe's sovereign interests and the NLRA is such that the ambiguity in the NLRA should be resolved against the Board's exercise of jurisdiction. By focusing on the sovereignty question and addressing it first, we find the statutory interpretation question resolves itself fairly simply. Thus, we analyze this case in two parts: (1) Would application of the NLRA to San Manuel's casino violate federal Indian law by impinging upon protected tribal sovereignty? and (2) Assuming the preceding question is answered in the negative, does the term "employer" in the NLRA reasonably encompass Indian tribal governments operating commercial enterprises?

When we begin to examine tribal sovereignty, we find the relevant principles to be, superficially at least, in conflict. First, we have the Supreme Court's statement in *Tuscarora* that "a general statute in terms applying to all persons includes Indians and their property interests." This *Tuscarora* statement is, however, in tension with the longstanding principles that (1) ambiguities in a federal statute must be resolved in favor of Indians and (2) a clear expression of Congressional intent is necessary before a court may construe a federal statute so as to impair tribal sovereignty. Moreover, *Tuscarora*'s statement is of uncertain significance, and possibly *dictum*, given the particulars of that case. Unlike the NLRA, the Federal Power Act at issue in *Tuscarora* included a specific limitation on eminent domain on Indian reservations. This limitation supported the inference that Congress intended in other circumstances to include Indians within the Federal Power Act's eminent domain provision.

As discussed above, the Board steered its way between these various rules by following the Ninth Circuit's lead in *Coeur d'Alene*, which identified three exceptions to *Tuscarora*'s general statement. The Board concluded none of the exceptions applied, and therefore *Tuscarora*'s general statement controlled. Because the Board's expertise and delegated authority does not relate to federal Indian law, we need not defer to the Board's conclusion. Therefore, we decide *de novo* the implications of tribal sovereignty on the statutory construction question before us.

Each of the cases petitioners cite in support of the principle that statutory ambiguities must be construed in favor of Indians (as well as the cases we have found supporting the principle) involved construction of a statute or a provision of a statute Congress enacted specifically for the benefit of Indians or for the regulation of Indian affairs. We have found no case in which the Supreme Court applied this principle of pro-Indian construction when resolving an ambiguity in a statute of general application.

With regard to the alternative principle relied on by petitioners, that a clear statement of Congressional intent is necessary before a court can construe a statute to limit tribal sovereignty, we can reconcile this principle with *Tuscarora* by recognizing that, in some cases at least, a statute of general application can constrain the actions of a tribal government without at the same time impairing tribal sovereignty.

Tribal sovereignty is far from absolute, as the Supreme Court has explained:

> Indian tribes are distinct, independent political communities, retaining their original natural rights in matters of local self-government. Although no longer possessed of the full attributes of sovereignty, they remain a separate people, with the power of regulating their internal and social relations.... As the Court ... [has] recognized, however, Congress has plenary authority to limit, modify or eliminate the powers of local self-government which the tribes otherwise possess.

Santa Clara Pueblo v. Martinez, 436 U.S. 49 (1978). An examination of Supreme Court cases shows tribal sovereignty to be at its strongest when explicitly established by a treaty, or when a tribal government acts within the borders of its reservation, in a matter of concern only to members of the tribe. Conversely, when a tribal government goes beyond matters of internal self-governance and enters into off-reservation business transaction with non-Indians, its claim of sovereignty is at its weakest. In the latter situation, courts recognize the capacity of a duly established tribal government to act as an unincorporated legal person, engaging in privately negotiated contractual affairs with non-Indians, but the tribal government does so subject to generally applicable laws. The primary qualification to this rule is that the tribal government may be immune from suit.

Many activities of a tribal government fall somewhere between a purely intramural act of reservation governance and an off-reservation commercial enterprise. The determinative consideration appears to be the extent to which application of the general law will constrain the tribe with respect to its governmental functions. If such constraint will occur, then tribal sovereignty is at risk and a clear expression of Congressional intent is necessary. Conversely, if the general law relates only to the extra-governmental activities of the tribe, and in particular activities involving non-Indians, then application of the law might not impinge on tribal sovereignty. Of course, it can be argued any activity of a tribal government is by definition "governmental," and even more so an activity aimed at raising revenue that will fund governmental functions. Here, though, we use the term "governmental" in a restrictive sense to distinguish between the traditional acts governments perform and collateral activities that, though perhaps in some way related to the foregoing, lie outside their scope.

Cases involving the application of state law to Indian activities are also instructive. Generally speaking, state laws do not apply to the activities of tribal Indians on their reservations. Nevertheless, the location of the activity is not the only consideration the Supreme Court has applied in these cases, and though the application of state law raises very different issues and therefore these cases are not directly on point, we find significant that the Court has defined tribal sovereignty in these cases partly in terms of governmental functions. In sum, the Supreme Court's decisions [with regard to state regulation] reflect an earnest concern for maintaining tribal sovereignty, but they also recognize that tribal governments engage in a varied range of activities many of which are not activities we normally associate with governance. These activities include off-reservation fishing, investments in non-residential private property, and commercial enterprises that tend to blur any distinction between the tribal government and a private corporation. The Supreme Court's concern for tribal sovereignty distinguishes among the different activities tribal governments pursue, focusing on acts of governance as the measure of tribal sovereignty. The principle of tribal sovereignty in American law exists as a matter of respect for Indian communities. It recognizes the independence of these communities as regards internal affairs, thereby giving them latitude to maintain traditional customs and practices. But tribal sovereignty is not absolute autonomy, permitting a tribe to operate in a commercial capacity without legal constraint.

Of course, in establishing and operating the Casino, San Manuel has not acted solely in a commercial capacity. Certainly its enactment of a tribal labor ordinance to govern relations with its employees was a governmental act, as was its act of negotiating and executing a gaming compact with the State of California, as required by IGRA. Moreover, application of the NLRA to employment at the Casino will impinge, to some extent, on these governmental activities. Nevertheless, impairment of tribal sovereignty is negligible in this context, as the Tribe's activity was primarily commercial and its enactment of labor legislation and its execution of a gaming compact were ancillary to that commercial activity. The total impact on tribal sovereignty at issue here amounts to some unpredictable, but probably modest, effect on tribal revenue and the displacement of legislative and executive authority that is secondary to a commercial undertaking. We do not think this limited impact is sufficient to demand a restrictive construction of the NLRA.

Therefore, we need not choose between *Tuscarora*'s statement that laws of general applicability apply also to Indian tribes and *Santa Clara Pueblo*'s statement that courts may not construe laws in a way that impinges upon tribal sovereignty absent a clear indication of Congressional intent. Even applying the more restrictive rule of *Santa Clara Pueblo*, the NLRA does not impinge on the Tribe's sovereignty enough to indicate a need to construe the statute narrowly against application to employment at the Casino. First, operation of a casino is not a traditional attribute of self-government. Rather, the casino at issue here is virtually identical to scores of purely commercial casinos across the country. Second, the vast majority of the Casino's employees and customers are not members of the Tribe, and they live off the reservation. For these reasons, the Tribe is not simply engaged in internal governance of its territory and members, and its sovereignty over such matters is not called into question. Because applying the NLRA to San Manuel's Casino would not impair tribal sovereignty, federal Indian law does not prevent the Board from exercising jurisdiction.

The second question before us, whether the term "employer" in the NLRA encompasses Indian tribal governments operating commercial enterprises, requires a much briefer analysis. The Board concluded the NLRA's definition of employer extended to San Manuel's commercial activities. Neither the text of the NLRA, nor any other reliable indicator of Congressional intent, indicates whether or not Congress specifically intended to include the commercial enterprises of Indian tribes when it used the term "employer." Therefore, Congress has not "directly spoken to the precise question at issue," *Chevron U.S.A. Inc. v. Natural Resources Defense Council*, 467 U.S. 837 (1984), and the question is therefore one Congress has implicitly delegated to the Board for determination. Under these circumstances, the scope of our review is limited, the matter falling under step two of *Chevron*'s analytical diptych. Specifically, if the Board's interpretation is "a permissible construction of the statute," we must give that interpretation "controlling weight."

Section 2(2) of the NLRA defines "employer" in only very general terms, stating agents of employers are themselves employers and then listing certain specific entities that are *not* employers. The NLRA never actually states descriptively what an employer is, but by listing certain entities that are not employers, the NLRA arguably intends to include everything else that might qualify as an employer. *Black's Law Dictionary* defines employer as "[a] person who controls and directs a worker under an express or implied contract of hire and who pays the worker's salary or wages." Under this generic definition of the term employer, we have no doubt it was reasonable for the Board to conclude the Tribe is an employer of its Casino workers. The Tribe does not suggest that it lacks control over these workers, or that it has no contract of hire with these workers, or that these workers are unpaid. Certainly, then, the Tribe is an employer in the ordinary sense of that term; indeed, the Tribe calls its Casino workers "employees" in its briefs filed in this court. Thus, the Tribe does not seriously contend it is not an employer; rather it contends it falls within one of the NLRA's listed exceptions.

Section 2(2) states that "[t]he term 'employer'... shall not include the United States or any wholly owned Government corporation, or any Federal Reserve Bank, or any State or political subdivision thereof, or any person subject to the Railway Labor Act, as amended from time to time, or any labor organization." The Tribe asserts it falls within the exception for "any State or political subdivision thereof," calling this exception a "governmental exemption." The Tribe's argument is certainly plausible, but we cannot say the Board's more restrictive reading of the NLRA's government exception is not "a permissible construction of the statute." The exception is limited by its terms to *state* governments (and their political subdivisions), and we can hardly call it impermissible for an agency to limit a statutory phrase to its ordinary and plain meaning. In short, the Board could reasonably conclude that Congress's decision not to include an express exception for Indian tribes in the NLRA was because no such exception was intended or exists.

San Manuel argues, however, that nothing in the legislative history or text of the NLRA indicates a Congressional intent to apply the NLRA to tribal governments. This point is irrelevant in light of our conclusion above that the NLRA does not impinge on the Tribe's sovereignty enough to warrant construing the statute as inapplicable. In the absence of a presumption against application of the NLRA, the legislative history need not expressly anticipate every category of employer that might fall within the NLRA's broad definition.

San Manuel also argues Congress intended, by enacting IGRA, to give tribes and states a primary role in regulating tribal gaming activities, including labor relations, and that Congress therefore, by implication, foreclosed application of the NLRA to tribal gaming. Among other things, IGRA requires tribes that engage or intend to engage in "class III gaming" (the broad category of gaming at issue here) to negotiate, enter into, and comply with a compact between the tribe and the state in which the gaming will occur.

The compact San Manuel entered into with the State of California specifically addresses labor relations, requiring San Manuel to adopt "an agreement or other procedure acceptable to the State for addressing organizational and representational rights of Class III Gaming Employees." San Manuel satisfied this requirement by enacting a detailed labor relations ordinance, which differs substantively from the NLRA.

San Manuel argues that IGRA, by authorizing tribes and states to enter into compacts addressing labor-relations issues and by mandating a tribal ordinance or resolution regulating gaming activities, contemplates tribal and state control over gaming and therefore implicitly restricts the scope of the NLRA.

We think San Manuel reads too much into IGRA. IGRA certainly permits tribes and states to regulate gaming activities, but it is a considerable leap from that bare fact to the conclusion that Congress intended federal agencies to have no role in regulating employment issues that arise in the context of tribal gaming. This is not a case in which Congress enacted a comprehensive scheme governing labor relations at Indian casinos, and then the Board sought to expand its jurisdiction into that field. We find no indication that Congress intended to limit the scope of the NLRA when it enacted IGRA, and certainly nothing strong enough to render the Board's interpretation of the NLRA impermissible.

In sum, the Board has given the NLRA a natural interpretation that falls within the range of interpretations the NLRA permits, and regardless of whether we think the Board's decision wise, we are without authority to reject it.

Brian P. McClatchey
Tribally-Owned Businesses Are Not "Employers": Economic Effects, Tribal Sovereignty, and NLRB v. San Manuel Band of Mission Indians
43 IDAHO L. REV. 127 (2006)

Indian gaming presents a particularly salient example of the utility as well as the source of tribal sovereignty. Indian gaming arose from the desperate need to fund tribal operations from a "homegrown" source, rather than the erratic funding from the BIA. To put a slightly sharper point on it, for many tribes, without gaming revenues, the tribe will cease to exist as an entity — as a matter of history, the other shoe will drop.

In response to *Cabazon*, Congress enacted the Indian Gaming Regulatory Act ("IGRA"). One motivation for the statute was to resolve conflicts between the asserted power of the states to prohibit gaming and the asserted power of the tribes to be free from state inter-ference in operating gaming enterprises for the provision of governmental revenue. Bingo parlors and the later full-fledged casinos became the primary means for some tribes to fund tribal governmental operations. State regulation threatened to drown this source of tribal governmental revenues in the bathtub, so to speak, killing it before it could grow to maturity.

Armed with *Cabazon* and the IGRA, tribes expanded their operations. The rest, as they say, is history. With this source of funding, tribes can be and are more effective sov-ereigns now than before the advent of Indian gaming.

Tribal gaming has produced a very real, and apparently sustained, benefit for many Indian communities. Indian gaming, along with the corresponding outside investment in Indian Country in the last decade, has created great momentum in the economic de-velopment of Indian Country. *San Manuel* threatens to make the long road to economic parity the tribes must travel longer still.

The clearest and simplest reform to address the problem created by the NLRB's deci-sion in the *San Manuel* case would be for Congress to amend the NLRA by adding the phrase "and federally recognized Indian tribes" to the list of exempt entities. Simple in form, while dramatic in substance, such an amendment would recognize the governmental status of Indian tribes and their powers as sovereigns, and would ensure that non-Indians respect this governmental status. Tribes need the proceeds from tribal gaming operations and their other, non-gaming enterprises, to fund crucial governmental functions. Absent a tax base, on many reservations, tribes have no way other than their tribally-owned en-terprises to fund the day-to-day functioning of their governments. Tribal gaming is a di-rect analog to state lotteries—the proposed simple reform would recognize and codify that fact.

Labor unions are the obvious critics of this proposal, since they have now gained the blessing of the NLRB for unionization of Indian tribal enterprises. Unions would not want to allow any reduction in their power, or any reduction in their potential member-ship pool, given recent market conditions. Another part of this opposition is founded on the unwarranted assumption that tribes and tribally-owned organizations would not enter into agreements with unions. In fact, the reverse is true: some tribes have already done just that, even before San Manuel was decided. Under this reform, tribes would have the incentive to enter into labor agreements in order both to gain allies in organized labor and valuable public relations recognition regarding their progressive labor policies.

Aside from the dubious legal foundations of the *San Manuel* decision, another aspect of it must be addressed. Part of the basis for the decision was that tribal commercial ac-tivity simply does not fit the model of traditional tribal functions, a statement the NLRB has made time and time again. By doing so, the NLRB attempts to freeze tribes in time by romanticizing them as simple, unsophisticated, and thoroughly un-modern people. The notion that a tribe can have commercial dealings while retaining sovereignty appears for-eign to the NLRB, despite the fact that states engage in commercial dealings every day without losing an iota of their sovereignty. There should be real discussion as to why this proposition is not more widely challenged, but action by Congress to rule out this line of inquiry would force courts to look at other, more rational, factors.

One objection to the thesis of this article is that tribes, in the gaming context, are not acting purely for governmental purposes. Tribes, the argument runs, are operating in-credibly lucrative gaming operations, in essence, for profit. In fact, this was part of the basis for the decision in *San Manuel*. However, it is belied by *Cabazon*, in which the

Supreme Court effectively held that an inability to obtain gaming revenue is, in an important sense, an inability to obtain governmental revenue. Since tribes have historically had no tax base, they have had to gain creative means of financing their government operations. This case is no exception.

Even were it true that profit is first and foremost for some tribes, a wise application of policy requires that the tribes without lucrative operations be exempt from the NLRA, just as those more fortunate tribes. It should be noted that not all gaming operations are the incredible success often portrayed in the media. The National Indian Gaming Commission's recent figures show that around 15% of the Indian gaming operations are responsible for nearly 70% of the revenue derived from Indian gaming nationally. However, the NLRB's ruling falls on all tribal gaming operations, not just the wealthy ones.

There are other concerns. Who decides what is or is not "a traditional tribal function"? There is a strong argument that any economic development project (for example, anything that provides for the tribe's sustenance and self-sustaining nature) for a tribe is "a traditional tribal function." To throw the point into sharper relief, under the reasoning of *San Manuel*, state lotteries are a state function, but Indian casinos are not.

The emphasis on "traditional services" is also misplaced. The NLRB decision repeatedly relies on the notion that tribes, properly conceptualized, only engage in traditional activities, without elaborating upon the point:

> At times, the tribes continue to act in a manner consistent with that mantle of uniqueness. They do so primarily when they are fulfilling traditionally tribal or governmental functions that are unique to their status as Indian tribes.... Thus, when the Indian tribes are acting with regard to this particularized sphere of traditional tribal or governmental functions, the Board should take cognizance of its lessened interest in regulation and the tribe's increased interest in its autonomy.

Indians, according to this view, aren't really acting as Indians unless they reject the modern world and stay within their "particular sphere." To restrict tribal governmental and commercial ventures by removing gaming and other highly lucrative ventures on this basis reeks of the paternalism and ethnocentrism that has confounded federal Indian policy for generations. To the extent we reject this in other areas of law, we should do so even more strongly in cases like *San Manuel*.

The NLRB's conception of "Indian tribe" is sorely lacking. The Supreme Court's precedents state that tribes are "more than 'private, voluntary organizations,'" but it is not, in the current environment where tribes operate for-profit (albeit with significant restrictions on how they may dispose of that profit) enterprises as well as provide governmental services, always clear in which category tribes belong: are they (and their gaming enterprises) businesses, or are they governments? The most correct answer is "both" and "neither."

One aspect of modern Indian tribalism is the dual nature of tribes. Unlike the sharp distinction between governmental operations and commercial concerns, modern tribes blend both of these, and more, into one coherent whole. The notion that tribes provide for their people is no empty phrase; tribal governments are charged with providing housing, health care, education, law enforcement, courts, roads, jobs, and more, all while maintaining and fostering the unique culture that each tribe possesses. In doing so, tribes have had to be resourceful, to provide the funds to carry out their responsibilities. While it may be satisfying, on a simplistic level, to assume that tribes cease functioning as governments when they enter into the commercial world, that assumption simply doesn't work in practice.

We should also inquire as to the effects of labor regulation on tribes, just as we would inquire as to the effects of mandatory labor regulation of state and local governments. Requiring tribes to shoulder the burden of increased labor costs decreases the amount of revenue they can apply to legitimate tribal government needs, just as mandatory union-ization increases the costs of public services provided by state and local governments. States, it must be remembered, have the tax bases that tribes lack. Unless and until tribes are able to utilize a tax base for revenue, tribally-owned businesses fulfill the same func-tion for tribal governments that property taxes, sales taxes, excise taxes, and the like ful-fill for state and local governments. The survival of tribes depends, in large part, upon their ability to generate revenue without having to rely upon the whims of the federal government. It is no new statement that, for many tribes, subjecting them to labor reg-ulation under the NLRA threatens tribal survival.

What can be learned from this episode, where the NLRB has cast aside its precedents in the pursuit of a redefinition of Indian tribes without basis in law or reality? For one thing, it should be clear to any student of Indian affairs with more than a casual interest that it is indeed a topsy-turvy world: those disinclined to favor the strengthening of labor unions in general react with approval to a decision which does that very thing in the con-text of Indian tribal businesses. The rhetoric of rugged individualism, the entrepreneur-ial spirit, and the desire to free oneself from dependency on the federal government that animates many conservatives is missing in the debate over this kind of regulation of In-dian tribal governments. Also, the *San Manuel* decision will divert to labor unions some of the casino dollars that have done so much to help so many Indians since *Cabazon*. *San Manuel* highlights the resounding hypocrisy so often displayed by non-Indians regarding Indian affairs and Indian policy. Decisions like this reduce concepts of "self-determina-tion" and "government-to-government relationship" into empty rhetoric.

The reform proposal in this article is grounded in common sense: because tribes act as states (by employing people in their government-owned and operated enterprises), they should be treated as states. This means according tribes the same deference under federal labor law that states receive. However, the NLRB has persisted in the notion that bad law, outdated assumptions, and an incorrect assessment of the facts on the ground justify federal jurisdiction over tribally-owned businesses, despite repeated Supreme Court guidance to the contrary. As tribes continue their economic rise, tribal labor issues will remain. Congress should act to amend the NLRA to include tribes as governments within the Act, to ensure that tribal sovereignty is respected, and federal policy is uniform. This is a historic moment for the Indians of North America, and history will be kind to those who allow tribes to develop their economies and take their place in the economic main-stream of America.

Notes and Questions

1. "Commercial" operations vs. "traditional governmental functions." The court in *San Manuel* distinguished between "commercial" and "governmental" operations. The court stated that governmental activities are ones which governments "traditionally perform," not all of the actions of a government. Is this distinction logical? Legally ten-able? The court asserted that "tribal governments engage in a varied range of activities many of which are not activities we normally associate with governance. These activi-ties include off-reservation fishing, investments in non-residential private property, and commercial enterprises that tend to blur any distinction between the tribal government and a private corporation." Are tribal governments fundamentally distinct from other governments in this regard? Compare attorney McClatchey's arguments to the court's. The court found that "operation of a casino is not a traditional attribute of self-government. Rather, the casino at issue here is virtually identical to scores of purely commercial casinos across the country." Again, compare McClatchey's arguments. If the public policy goals underlying the operation of a tribal casino are different than those of a commercial casino, is the function different? Can a state-sanctioned gambling operation, i.e., a state lottery, ever be a "traditional government function"? What about a tribal casino? For additional critique of the NLRB opinion that gave rise to *San Manuel*, see Wenona Singel, *Labor Relations and Tribal Self-Governance*, 80 N.D. L. Rev. 691 (2004).

2.   *A* San Manuel *"fix."* In response to the NLRB's assertion of authority over tribal enterprises (but prior to the D.C. Circuit's decision in *San Manuel*), U.S. House Representative J.D. Hayworth (R-Ariz.) introduced legislation to overturn the agency decision. Hayworth said that tribal casinos, as government-operated businesses, should be exempt from the National Labor Relations Act. He asserted the bill had "nothing to do with unions and everything to do with tribal sovereignty." *See* Tony Batt, *Congressman: Tribes Should Be Exempted From Labor Act*, Las Vegas Gaming Wire, Jul. 21, 2006, available at http://www.casinocitytimes.com/news/article.cfm?contentID=159900. In that light, should Congress adopt the reform suggested by McClatchey? Why or why not?

3.   *Implications of* San Manuel. Does the D.C. Circuit's reasoning open the door for every federal law of general applicability to apply to tribal casinos? Are there arguments in tribes' favor regarding the impact on tribal sovereignty that could arise in the context of other federal statutes?

4.   *The business side of tribal casinos.* Consider this view of the degree to which tribal governments interact with private business:

> Indian tribes are not merely casino entrepreneurs or cigarette wholesalers. In conjunction with America's largest corporations, Indians are now engaged in real estate development, banking and finance, telecommunications, wholesale and retail trade, and tourism.... U.S. tribes have become economic, legal and political forces to be reckoned with.... Both the cause and effect of the dramatic rise in Indian economic development is the increased interaction of tribes and non-tribal parties who seek business, employment or recreation on Indian reservations. Consequently, Indian tribes and non-Indians are executing billions of dollars in commercial transactions and frequently litigating those deals....

> Corporate America is witnessing firsthand both the tremendous rise in Indian economic development and an array of business dealings and commercial litigation matters arising in Indian Country. With Fortune 500 companies increasingly doing business on reservations, Indian law has been transformed from a niche practice to a body of law intersecting every area of practice and engaging lawyers and clients of all types.

> Indian law, however, defies boilerplate contract language, standard business negotiations, and common understandings of civil procedure and jurisdiction in the commercial litigation arena. For these reasons, it is vital that today's business lawyers have some understanding of basic Indian law, particularly those whose clients are doing business and seek to do business in Indian Country.

Gabriel S. Galanda, *Getting Commercial in Indian Country*, Business Law Today, July/Aug. 2003. Should more attorneys be exposed to federal Indian law and tribal law? If so, how should that be accomplished?

5.   *Other employment issues.* Tribal casinos are not the only context in which employment issues arise. Like state and local governments, tribes employ people in government, law enforcement, housing authorities, schools and colleges, social services, health clinics, and so on. In gaming and other business enterprises, tribes employ hundreds of thousands of tribal members as well as non-Indians across the U.S. Accordingly, tribes have adopted or are in the process of adopting laws and policies governing the employment relationship. To ensure that jobs created by tribal governments benefit tribal members, many tribes have adopted an "Indian preference" in hiring. A practical factor affecting employment decisions and practices in many tribes is that tribal communities are relatively small, and members often share some degree of family ties. In such close communities, tribal government typically is highly accessible to its constituents. Consider Professor Matthew Fletcher's view of the unique role that tribes play as employers:

> Most Tribal Members employed by a Tribe are ingrained in the community. Many were born and raised in the community. They typically have several generations of relatives living in the area. The adult employees of a Tribe likely grew up with the members of the Tribal Council and may themselves be former or future Tribal Council Members. They know each other intimately: their strengths and weaknesses, their relations, and their "skeletons." In many ways, the situation is no different from a small town where the chief of city police is the wife of the vice-chairman of the city council and the first cousin of the town mayor.

> There are incredible advantages to such close-knit circumstances [in many tribal communities]. Tribal Members live and grow up together. They work together and they either stand or fall together. The Tribal Council and the front-line employees realize almost instantly the impact that their decisions have on the community.

> Contrast a Tribal government employer to a large corporate board of directors. A Tribal government employer must continually justify itself to its employees, many of whom will vote periodically in Tribal Council elections. A corporate board of directors may have to respond to thousands of shareholders, but few of these shareholders will be able to successfully pierce the corporate veil or force a board to be more accountable. Most often, members of a board of directors will not have to go home to the same neighborhood as their front-line employees, or even the same city or state if the corporation is large enough. Tribes exist to provide a conduit for direct governmental services to Members, services such as housing, health care, education, social services, and even employment. Meanwhile, corporations exist to make a profit. The United States Congress enacted the Fair Labor Standards Act, the Indian Civil Rights Act of 1968, the National Labor Relations Act, and other remedial pro-employee statues because corporations and other employers are not accountable to their employees and cannot be trusted, on the whole, to treat employees fairly. While some critics complain that Tribes do not have adequate labor laws or employment protection laws, there is a remedy in place. If Tribal Council Members victimize employees, they can expect to be removed from the political process.

> Indian Tribes also employ increasing numbers of non-Tribal Members. Many of these non-Tribal Members are Indians from other Indian Tribes who have married into the community or who have became part of the community in some other way. However, a significant number of these employees are non-Indians. As tribal governments grow, fueled by federal and state grants and fund-

ing and by improving tribal business enterprises, many tribes simply do not have enough Tribal Members to fill all of their employment slots. Tribal government jobs are usually better jobs than those that private employers offer. In the author's experience, Tribal employees maintain better relationships with co-workers and the employer.

Matthew L.M. Fletcher, *Tribal Employment Separation: Tribal Law Enigma, Tribal Governance Paradox, and Tribal Court Conundrum* 38 U. Mich. J.L. Reform 273, 285–87 (2005).

Problem 10.4: The *San Manuel* Case

Suppose that the U.S. Supreme Court has decided to review the D.C. Circuit's decision in *San Manuel Indian Bingo & Casino v. NLRB*. You are an attorney for the San Manuel Band. What persuasive arguments would you make to the Supreme Court? Marshaling what you have learned throughout this course, what principles or matters of law did the D.C. Circuit overlook or misconstrue?

Appendix

The Indian Gaming Regulatory Act of 1988

Public Law No. 100-497, 102 Stat. 2467
(October 17, 1998)
Codified at 25 U.S.C. §§ 2701–2721

§ 2101. Findings

The Congress finds that—

(1) numerous Indian tribes have become engaged in or have licensed gaming activities on Indian lands as a means of generating tribal governmental revenue;

(2) Federal courts have held that section 81 of this title requires Secretarial review of management contracts dealing with Indian gaming, but does not provide standards for approval of such contracts;

(3) existing Federal law does not provide clear standards or regulations for the conduct of gaming on Indian lands;

(4) a principal goal of Federal Indian policy is to promote tribal economic development, tribal self-sufficiency, and strong tribal government; and

(5) Indian tribes have the exclusive right to regulate gaming activity on Indian lands if the gaming activity is not specifically prohibited by Federal law and is conducted within a State which does not, as a matter of criminal law and public policy, prohibit such gaming activity.

§ 2702. Declaration of policy

The purpose of this chapter is—

(1) to provide a statutory basis for the operation of gaming by Indian tribes as a means of promoting tribal economic development, self-sufficiency, and strong tribal governments;

(2) to provide a statutory basis for the regulation of gaming by an Indian tribe adequate to shield it from organized crime and other corrupting influences, to ensure that the Indian tribe is the primary beneficiary of the gaming operation, and to assure that gaming is conducted fairly and honestly by both the operator and players; and

(3) to declare that the establishment of independent Federal regulatory authority for gaming on Indian lands, the establishment of Federal standards for gaming on Indian lands, and the establishment of a National Indian Gaming Commission are necessary to meet congressional concerns regarding gaming and to protect such gaming as a means of generating tribal revenue.

§ 2703. Definitions

For purposes of this chapter—

(1) The term "Attorney General" means the Attorney General of the United States.

(2) The term "Chairman" means the Chairman of the National Indian Gaming Commission.

(3) The term "Commission" means the National Indian Gaming Commission established pursuant to section 2704 of this title.

(4) The term "Indian lands" means—

(A) all lands within the limits of any Indian reservation; and

(B) any lands title to which is either held in trust by the United States for the benefit of any Indian tribe or individual or held by any Indian tribe or individual subject to restriction by the United States against alienation and over which an Indian tribe exercises governmental power.

(5) The term "Indian tribe" means any Indian tribe, band, nation, or other organized group or community of Indians which—

(A) is recognized as eligible by the Secretary for the special programs and services provided by the United States to Indians because of their status as Indians, and

(B) is recognized as possessing powers of self-government.

(6) The term "class I gaming" means social games solely for prizes of minimal value or traditional forms of Indian gaming engaged in by individuals as a part of, or in connection with, tribal ceremonies or celebrations.

(7) (A) The term "class II gaming" means—

(i) the game of chance commonly known as bingo (whether or not electronic, computer, or other technologic aids are used in connection therewith)—

(I) which is played for prizes, including monetary prizes, with cards bearing numbers or other designations,

(II) in which the holder of the card covers such numbers or designations when objects, similarly numbered or designated, are drawn or electronically determined, and

(III) in which the game is won by the first person covering a previously designated arrangement of numbers or designations on such cards, including (if played in the same location) pull-tabs, lotto, punch boards, tip jars, instant bingo, and other games similar to bingo, and

(ii) card games that—

(I) are explicitly authorized by the laws of the State, or

(II) are not explicitly prohibited by the laws of the State and are played at any location in the State, but only if such card games are played in conformity with those laws and regulations (if any) of the State regarding hours or periods of operation of such card games or limitations on wagers or pot sizes in such card games.

(B) The term "class II gaming" does not include—

(i) any banking card games, including baccarat, chemin de fer, or blackjack (21), or

(ii) electronic or electromechanical facsimiles of any game of chance or slot machines of any kind.

(C) Notwithstanding any other provision of this paragraph, the term "class II gaming" includes those card games played in the State of Michigan, the State of North Dakota, the State of South Dakota, or the State of Washington, that were actually operated in such State by an Indian tribe on or before May 1, 1988, but only to the extent of the nature and scope of the card games that were actually operated by an Indian tribe in such State on or before such date, as determined by the Chairman.

(D) Notwithstanding any other provision of this paragraph, the term "class II gaming" includes, during the 1-year period beginning on October 17, 1988, any gaming described in subparagraph (B)(ii) that was legally operated on Indian lands on or before May 1, 1988, if the Indian tribe having jurisdiction over the lands on which such gaming was operated requests the State, by no later than the date that is 30 days after October 17, 1988, to negotiate a Tribal-State compact under section 2710(d)(3) of this title.

(E) Notwithstanding any other provision of this paragraph, the term "class II gaming" includes, during the 1-year period beginning on December 17, 1991, any gaming described in subparagraph (B)(ii) that was legally operated on Indian lands in the State of Wisconsin on or before May 1, 1988, if the Indian tribe having jurisdiction over the lands on which such gaming was operated requested the State, by no later than November 16, 1988, to negotiate a Tribal-State compact under section 2710(d)(3) of this title.

(F) If, during the 1-year period described in subparagraph (E), there is a final judicial determination that the gaming described in subparagraph (E) is not legal as a matter of State law, then such gaming on such Indian land shall cease to operate on the date next following the date of such judicial decision.

(8) The term "class III gaming" means all forms of gaming that are not class I gaming or class II gaming.

(9) The term "net revenues" means gross revenues of an Indian gaming activity less amounts paid out as, or paid for, prizes and total operating expenses, excluding management fees.

(10) The term "Secretary" means the Secretary of the Interior.

§ 2704. National Indian Gaming Commission

(a) Establishment

There is established within the Department of the Interior a Commission to be known as the National Indian Gaming Commission.

(b) Composition; investigation; term of office; removal

(1) The Commission shall be composed of three full-time members who shall be appointed as follows:

(A) a Chairman, who shall be appointed by the President with the advice and consent of the Senate; and

(B) two associate members who shall be appointed by the Secretary of the Interior.

(2) (A) The Attorney General shall conduct a background investigation on any person considered for appointment to the Commission.

(B) The Secretary shall publish in the Federal Register the name and other information the Secretary deems pertinent regarding a nominee for membership on the Commission and shall allow a period of not less than thirty days for receipt of public comment.

(3) Not more than two members of the Commission shall be of the same political party. At least two members of the Commission shall be enrolled members of any Indian tribe.

(4) (A) Except as provided in subparagraph (B), the term of office of the members of the Commission shall be three years.

(B) Of the initial members of the Commission

(i) two members, including the Chairman, shall have a term of office of three years; and

(ii) one member shall have a term of office of one year.

(5) No individual shall be eligible for any appointment to, or to continue service on, the Commission, who—

(A) has been convicted of a felony or gaming offense;

(B) has any financial interest in, or management responsibility for, any gaming activity; or

(C) has a financial interest in, or management responsibility for, any management contract approved pursuant to section 2711 of this title.

(6) A Commissioner may only be removed from office before the expiration of the term of office of the member by the President (or, in the case of associate member,

by the Secretary) for neglect of duty, or malfeasance in office, or for other good cause shown.

(c) Vacancies

Vacancies occurring on the Commission shall be filled in the same manner as the original appointment. A member may serve after the expiration of his term of office until his successor has been appointed, unless the member has been removed for cause under subsection (b)(6) of this section.

(d) Quorum

Two members of the Commission, at least one of which is the Chairman or Vice Chairman, shall constitute a quorum.

(e) Vice Chairman

The Commission shall select, by majority vote, one of the members of the Commission to serve as Vice Chairman. The Vice Chairman shall serve as Chairman during meetings of the Commission in the absence of the Chairman.

(f) Meetings

The Commission shall meet at the call of the Chairman or a majority of its members, but shall meet at least once every 4 months.

(g) Compensation

(1) The Chairman of the Commission shall be paid at a rate equal to that of level IV of the Executive Schedule under section 5315 of title 5.

(2) The associate members of the Commission shall each be paid at a rate equal to that of level V of the Executive Schedule under section 5316 of title 5.

(3) All members of the Commission shall be reimbursed in accordance with title 5 for travel, subsistence, and other necessary expenses incurred by them in the performance of their duties.

§ 2705. Powers of Chairman

(a) The Chairman, on behalf of the Commission, shall have power, subject to an appeal to the Commission, to—

(1) issue orders of temporary closure of gaming activities as provided in section 2713 (b) of this title;

(2) levy and collect civil fines as provided in section 2713 (a) of this title;

(3) approve tribal ordinances or resolutions regulating class II gaming and class III gaming as provided in section 2710 of this title; and

(4) approve management contracts for class II gaming and class III gaming as provided in sections 2710 (d)(9) and 2711 of this title.

(b) The Chairman shall have such other powers as may be delegated by the Commission.

§ 2706. Powers of Commission

(a) Budget approval; civil fines; fees; subpoenas; permanent orders

The Commission shall have the power, not subject to delegation—

(1) upon the recommendation of the Chairman, to approve the annual budget of the Commission as provided in section 2717 of this title;

(2) to adopt regulations for the assessment and collection of civil fines as provided in section 2713 (a) of this title;

(3) by an affirmative vote of not less than 2 members, to establish the rate of fees as provided in section 2717 of this title;

(4) by an affirmative vote of not less than 2 members, to authorize the Chairman to issue subpoenas as provided in section 2715 of this title; and

(5) by an affirmative vote of not less than 2 members and after a full hearing, to make permanent a temporary order of the Chairman closing a gaming activity as provided in section 2713(b)(2) of this title.

(b) Monitoring; inspection of premises; investigations; access to records; mail; contracts; hearings; oaths; regulations

The Commission—

(1) shall monitor class II gaming conducted on Indian lands on a continuing basis;

(2) shall inspect and examine all premises located on Indian lands on which class II gaming is conducted;

(3) shall conduct or cause to be conducted such background investigations as may be necessary;

(4) may demand access to and inspect, examine, photocopy, and audit all papers, books, and records respecting gross revenues of class II gaming conducted on Indian lands and any other matters necessary to carry out the duties of the Commission under this chapter;

(5) may use the United States mail in the same manner and under the same conditions as any department or agency of the United States;

(6) may procure supplies, services, and property by contract in accordance with applicable Federal laws and regulations;

(7) may enter into contracts with Federal, State, tribal and private entities for activities necessary to the discharge of the duties of the Commission and, to the extent feasible, contract the enforcement of the Commission's regulations with the Indian tribes;

(8) may hold such hearings, sit and act at such times and places, take such testimony, and receive such evidence as the Commission deems appropriate;

(9) may administer oaths or affirmations to witnesses appearing before the Commission; and

(10) shall promulgate such regulations and guidelines as it deems appropriate to implement the provisions of this chapter.

(c) Report

The Commission shall submit a report with minority views, if any, to the Congress on December 31, 1989, and every two years thereafter. The report shall include information on—

(1) whether the associate commissioners should continue as full or part-time officials;

(2) funding, including income and expenses, of the Commission;

(3) recommendations for amendments to the chapter; and

(4) any other matter considered appropriate by the Commission.

§ 2707. Commission staffing

(a) General Counsel

The Chairman shall appoint a General Counsel to the Commission who shall be paid at the annual rate of basic pay payable for GS-18 of the General Schedule under section 5332 of title 5.

(b) Staff

The Chairman shall appoint and supervise other staff of the Commission without regard to the provisions of title 5 governing appointments in the competitive service. Such staff shall be paid without regard to the provisions of chapter 51 and subchapter III of chapter 53 of such title relating to classification and General Schedule pay rates, except that no individual so appointed may receive pay in excess of the annual rate of basic pay payable for GS-17 of the General Schedule under section 5332 of that title.

(c) Temporary services

The Chairman may procure temporary and intermittent services under section 3109 (b) of title 5, but at rates for individuals not to exceed the daily equivalent of the maximum annual rate of basic pay payable for GS-18 of the General Schedule.

(d) Federal agency personnel

Upon the request of the Chairman, the head of any Federal agency is authorized to detail any of the personnel of such agency to the Commission to assist the Commission in carrying out its duties under this chapter, unless otherwise prohibited by law.

(e) Administrative support services

The Secretary or Administrator of General Services shall provide to the Commission on a reimbursable basis such administrative support services as the Commission may request.

§ 2708. Commission — access to information

The Commission may secure from any department or agency of the United States information necessary to enable it to carry out this chapter. Upon the request of the Chairman, the head of such department or agency shall furnish such information to the Commission, unless otherwise prohibited by law.

§ 2709. Interim authority to regulate gaming

Notwithstanding any other provision of this chapter, the Secretary shall continue to exercise those authorities vested in the Secretary on the day before October 17, 1988, relating to supervision of Indian gaming until such time as the Commission is organized and prescribes regulations. The Secretary shall provide staff and support assistance to facilitate an orderly transition to regulation of Indian gaming by the Commission.

§ 2710. Tribal gaming ordinances

(a) Exclusive jurisdiction over class I and class II gaming activity

(1) Class I gaming on Indian lands is within the exclusive jurisdiction of the Indian tribes and shall not be subject to the provisions of this chapter.

(2) Any class II gaming on Indian lands shall continue to be within the jurisdiction of the Indian tribes, but shall be subject to the provisions of this chapter.

(b) Regulation of class II gaming activity; net revenue allocation; audits; contracts

(1) An Indian tribe may engage in, or license and regulate, class II gaming on Indian lands within such tribe's jurisdiction, if—

(A) such Indian gaming is located within a State that permits such gaming for any purpose by any person, organization or entity (and such gaming is not otherwise specifically prohibited on Indian lands by Federal law), and

(B) the governing body of the Indian tribe adopts an ordinance or resolution which is approved by the Chairman.

A separate license issued by the Indian tribe shall be required for each place, facility, or location on Indian lands at which class II gaming is conducted.

(2) The Chairman shall approve any tribal ordinance or resolution concerning the conduct, or regulation of class II gaming on the Indian lands within the tribe's jurisdiction if such ordinance or resolution provides that—

(A) except as provided in paragraph (4), the Indian tribe will have the sole proprietary interest and responsibility for the conduct of any gaming activity;

(B) net revenues from any tribal gaming are not to be used for purposes other than—

(i) to fund tribal government operations or programs;

(ii) to provide for the general welfare of the Indian tribe and its members;

(iii) to promote tribal economic development;

(iv) to donate to charitable organizations; or

(v) to help fund operations of local government agencies;

(C) annual outside audits of the gaming, which may be encompassed within existing independent tribal audit systems, will be provided by the Indian tribe to the Commission;

(D) all contracts for supplies, services, or concessions for a contract amount in excess of $25,000 annually (except contracts for professional legal or accounting services) relating to such gaming shall be subject to such independent audits;

(E) the construction and maintenance of the gaming facility, and the operation of that gaming is conducted in a manner which adequately protects the environment and the public health and safety; and

(F) there is an adequate system which—

(i) ensures that background investigations are conducted on the primary management officials and key employees of the gaming enterprise and that oversight of such officials and their management is conducted on an ongoing basis; and

(ii) includes—

(I) tribal licenses for primary management officials and key employees of the gaming enterprise with prompt notification to the Commission of the issuance of such licenses;

(II) a standard whereby any person whose prior activities, criminal record, if any, or reputation, habits and associations pose a threat to the public interest or to the effective regulation of gaming, or create or enhance the dangers of unsuitable, unfair, or illegal practices and methods and activities in the conduct of gaming shall not be eligible for employment; and

(III) notification by the Indian tribe to the Commission of the results of such background check before the issuance of any of such licenses.

(3) Net revenues from any class II gaming activities conducted or licensed by any Indian tribe may be used to make per capita payments to members of the Indian tribe only if—

(A) the Indian tribe has prepared a plan to allocate revenues to uses authorized by paragraph (2)(B);

(B) the plan is approved by the Secretary as adequate, particularly with respect to uses described in clause (i) or (iii) of paragraph (2)(B);

(C) the interests of minors and other legally incompetent persons who are entitled to receive any of the per capita payments are protected and preserved and the per capita payments are disbursed to the parents or legal guardian of such minors or legal incompetents in such amounts as may be necessary for the health, education, or welfare, of the minor or other legally incompetent person under a plan approved by the Secretary and the governing body of the Indian tribe; and

(D) the per capita payments are subject to Federal taxation and tribes notify members of such tax liability when payments are made.

(4) (A) A tribal ordinance or resolution may provide for the licensing or regulation of class II gaming activities owned by any person or entity other than the Indian tribe and conducted on Indian lands, only if the tribal licensing requirements include the requirements described in the subclauses of subparagraph (B)(i) and are at least as restrictive as those established by State law governing similar gaming within the jurisdiction of the State within which such Indian lands are located. No person or entity, other than the Indian tribe, shall be eligible to receive a tribal license to own a class II gaming activity conducted on Indian lands within the jurisdiction of the Indian tribe if such person or entity would not be eligible to receive a State license to conduct the same activity within the jurisdiction of the State.

(B) (i) The provisions of subparagraph (A) of this paragraph and the provisions of subparagraphs (A) and (B) of paragraph (2) shall not bar the continued operation of an individually owned class II gaming operation that was operating on September 1, 1986, if—

(I) such gaming operation is licensed and regulated by an Indian tribe pursuant to an ordinance reviewed and approved by the Commission in accordance with section 2712 of this title,

(II) income to the Indian tribe from such gaming is used only for the purposes described in paragraph (2)(B) of this subsection,

(III) not less than 60 percent of the net revenues is income to the Indian tribe, and

(IV) the owner of such gaming operation pays an appropriate assessment to the National Indian Gaming Commission under section 2717(a)(1) of this title for regulation of such gaming.

(ii) The exemption from the application of this subsection provided under this subparagraph may not be transferred to any person or entity and shall remain in effect only so long as the gaming activity remains within the same nature and scope as operated on October 17, 1988.

(iii) Within sixty days of October 17, 1988, the Secretary shall prepare a list of each individually owned gaming operation to which clause (i) applies and shall publish such list in the Federal Register.

(c) Issuance of gaming license; certificate of self-regulation

(1) The Commission may consult with appropriate law enforcement officials concerning gaming licenses issued by an Indian tribe and shall have thirty days to notify the Indian tribe of any objections to issuance of such license.

(2) If, after the issuance of a gaming license by an Indian tribe, reliable information is received from the Commission indicating that a primary management official or key employee does not meet the standard established under subsection (b)(2)(F)(ii)(II) of this section, the Indian tribe shall suspend such license and, after notice and hearing, may revoke such license.

(3) Any Indian tribe which operates a class II gaming activity and which—

(A) has continuously conducted such activity for a period of not less than three years, including at least one year after October 17, 1988; and

(B) has otherwise complied with the provisions of this section may petition the Commission for a certificate of self-regulation.

(4) The Commission shall issue a certificate of self-regulation if it determines from available information, and after a hearing if requested by the tribe, that the tribe has—

(A) conducted its gaming activity in a manner which—

(i) has resulted in an effective and honest accounting of all revenues;

(ii) has resulted in a reputation for safe, fair, and honest operation of the activity; and

(iii) has been generally free of evidence of criminal or dishonest activity;

(B) adopted and is implementing adequate systems for—

(i) accounting for all revenues from the activity;

(ii) investigation, licensing, and monitoring of all employees of the gaming activity; and

(iii) investigation, enforcement and prosecution of violations of its gaming ordinance and regulations; and

(C) conducted the operation on a fiscally and economically sound basis.

(5) During any year in which a tribe has a certificate for self-regulation—

(A) the tribe shall not be subject to the provisions of paragraphs (1), (2), (3), and (4) of section 2706 (b) of this title;

(B) the tribe shall continue to submit an annual independent audit as required by subsection (b)(2)(C) of this section and shall submit to the Commission a complete resume on all employees hired and licensed by the tribe subsequent to the issuance of a certificate of self-regulation; and

(C) the Commission may not assess a fee on such activity pursuant to section 2717 of this title in excess of one quarter of 1 per centum of the gross revenue.

(6) The Commission may, for just cause and after an opportunity for a hearing, remove a certificate of self-regulation by majority vote of its members.

(d) Class III gaming activities; authorization; revocation; Tribal-State compact

(1) Class III gaming activities shall be lawful on Indian lands only if such activities are—

(A) authorized by an ordinance or resolution that—

(i) is adopted by the governing body of the Indian tribe having jurisdiction over such lands,

(ii) meets the requirements of subsection (b) of this section, and

(iii) is approved by the Chairman,

(B) located in a State that permits such gaming for any purpose by any person, organization, or entity, and

(C) conducted in conformance with a Tribal-State compact entered into by the Indian tribe and the State under paragraph (3) that is in effect.

(2) (A) If any Indian tribe proposes to engage in, or to authorize any person or entity to engage in, a class III gaming activity on Indian lands of the Indian tribe, the governing body of the Indian tribe shall adopt and submit to the Chairman an ordinance or resolution that meets the requirements of subsection (b) of this section.

(B) The Chairman shall approve any ordinance or resolution described in subparagraph (A), unless the Chairman specifically determines that—

(i) the ordinance or resolution was not adopted in compliance with the governing documents of the Indian tribe, or

(ii) the tribal governing body was significantly and unduly influenced in the adoption of such ordinance or resolution by any person identified in section 2711 (e)(1)(D) of this title.

Upon the approval of such an ordinance or resolution, the Chairman shall publish in the Federal Register such ordinance or resolution and the order of approval.

(C) Effective with the publication under subparagraph (B) of an ordinance or resolution adopted by the governing body of an Indian tribe that has been approved by the Chairman under subparagraph (B), class III gaming activity on the Indian lands of the Indian tribe shall be fully subject to the terms and conditions of the Tribal-State compact entered into under paragraph (3) by the Indian tribe that is in effect.

(D) (i) The governing body of an Indian tribe, in its sole discretion and without the approval of the Chairman, may adopt an ordinance or resolution revoking any prior ordinance or resolution that authorized class III gaming on the Indian lands of the Indian tribe. Such revocation shall render class III gaming illegal on the Indian lands of such Indian tribe.

(ii) The Indian tribe shall submit any revocation ordinance or resolution described in clause (i) to the Chairman. The Chairman shall publish such ordinance or resolution in the Federal Register and the revocation provided by such ordinance or resolution shall take effect on the date of such publication.

(iii) Notwithstanding any other provision of this subsection—

(I) any person or entity operating a class III gaming activity pursuant to this paragraph on the date on which an ordinance or resolution described in clause (i) that revokes authorization for such class III gaming activity is published in the Federal Register may, during the 1-year period beginning on the date on which such revocation ordinance or resolution is published under clause (ii), continue to operate such activity in conformance with the Tribal-State compact entered into under paragraph (3) that is in effect, and

(II) any civil action that arises before, and any crime that is committed before, the close of such 1-year period shall not be affected by such revocation ordinance or resolution.

(3) (A) Any Indian tribe having jurisdiction over the Indian lands upon which a class III gaming activity is being conducted, or is to be conducted, shall request the State in which such lands are located to enter into negotiations for the purpose of entering into a Tribal-State compact governing the conduct of gaming activities. Upon receiving such a request, the State shall negotiate with the Indian tribe in good faith to enter into such a compact.

(B) Any State and any Indian tribe may enter into a Tribal-State compact governing gaming activities on the Indian lands of the Indian tribe, but such compact shall take effect only when notice of approval by the Secretary of such compact has been published by the Secretary in the Federal Register.

(C) Any Tribal-State compact negotiated under subparagraph (A) may include provisions relating to—

(i) the application of the criminal and civil laws and regulations of the Indian tribe or the State that are directly related to, and necessary for, the licensing and regulation of such activity;

(ii) the allocation of criminal and civil jurisdiction between the State and the Indian tribe necessary for the enforcement of such laws and regulations;

(iii) the assessment by the State of such activities in such amounts as are necessary to defray the costs of regulating such activity;

(iv) taxation by the Indian tribe of such activity in amounts comparable to amounts assessed by the State for comparable activities;

(v) remedies for breach of contract;

(vi) standards for the operation of such activity and maintenance of the gaming facility, including licensing; and

(vii) any other subjects that are directly related to the operation of gaming activities.

(4) Except for any assessments that may be agreed to under paragraph (3)(C)(iii) of this subsection, nothing in this section shall be interpreted as conferring upon a State or any of its political subdivisions authority to impose any tax, fee, charge, or other assessment upon an Indian tribe or upon any other person or entity authorized by an Indian tribe to engage in a class III activity. No State may refuse to enter into the negotiations described in paragraph (3)(A) based upon the lack of authority in such State, or its political subdivisions, to impose such a tax, fee, charge, or other assessment.

(5) Nothing in this subsection shall impair the right of an Indian tribe to regulate class III gaming on its Indian lands concurrently with the State, except to the extent that such regulation is inconsistent with, or less stringent than, the State laws and regulations made applicable by any Tribal-State compact entered into by the Indian tribe under paragraph (3) that is in effect.

(6) The provisions of section 1175 of title 15 shall not apply to any gaming conducted under a Tribal-State compact that—

  (A) is entered into under paragraph (3) by a State in which gambling devices are legal, and

  (B) is in effect.

(7) (A) The United States district courts shall have jurisdiction over—

    (i) any cause of action initiated by an Indian tribe arising from the failure of a State to enter into negotiations with the Indian tribe for the purpose of entering into a Tribal-State compact under paragraph (3) or to conduct such negotiations in good faith,

    (ii) any cause of action initiated by a State or Indian tribe to enjoin a class III gaming activity located on Indian lands and conducted in violation of any Tribal-State compact entered into under paragraph (3) that is in effect, and

    (iii) any cause of action initiated by the Secretary to enforce the procedures prescribed under subparagraph (B)(vii).

  (B) (i) An Indian tribe may initiate a cause of action described in subparagraph (A)(i) only after the close of the 180-day period beginning on the date on which the Indian tribe requested the State to enter into negotiations under paragraph (3)(A).

    (ii) In any action described in subparagraph (A)(i), upon the introduction of evidence by an Indian tribe that—

      (I) a Tribal-State compact has not been entered into under paragraph (3), and

      (II) the State did not respond to the request of the Indian tribe to negotiate such a compact or did not respond to such request in good faith,

    the burden of proof shall be upon the State to prove that the State has negotiated with the Indian tribe in good faith to conclude a Tribal-State compact governing the conduct of gaming activities.

    (iii) If, in any action described in subparagraph (A)(i), the court finds that the State has failed to negotiate in good faith with the Indian tribe to conclude a Tribal-State compact governing the conduct of gaming activities, the court shall order the State and the Indian Tribe to conclude such a compact within a 60-day period. In determining in such an action whether a State has negotiated in good faith, the court—

      (I) may take into account the public interest, public safety, criminality, financial integrity, and adverse economic impacts on existing gaming activities, and

      (II) shall consider any demand by the State for direct taxation of the Indian tribe or of any Indian lands as evidence that the State has not negotiated in good faith.

(iv) If a State and an Indian tribe fail to conclude a Tribal-State compact governing the conduct of gaming activities on the Indian lands subject to the jurisdiction of such Indian tribe within the 60-day period provided in the order of a court issued under clause (iii), the Indian tribe and the State shall each submit to a mediator appointed by the court a proposed compact that represents their last best offer for a compact. The mediator shall select from the two proposed compacts the one which best comports with the terms of this chapter and any other applicable Federal law and with the findings and order of the court.

(v) The mediator appointed by the court under clause (iv) shall submit to the State and the Indian tribe the compact selected by the mediator under clause (iv).

(vi) If a State consents to a proposed compact during the 60-day period beginning on the date on which the proposed compact is submitted by the mediator to the State under clause (v), the proposed compact shall be treated as a Tribal-State compact entered into under paragraph (3).

(vii) If the State does not consent during the 60-day period described in clause (vi) to a proposed compact submitted by a mediator under clause (v), the mediator shall notify the Secretary and the Secretary shall prescribe, in consultation with the Indian tribe, procedures—

(I) which are consistent with the proposed compact selected by the mediator under clause (iv), the provisions of this chapter, and the relevant provisions of the laws of the State, and

(II) under which class III gaming may be conducted on the Indian lands over which the Indian tribe has jurisdiction.

(8) (A) The Secretary is authorized to approve any Tribal-State compact entered into between an Indian tribe and a State governing gaming on Indian lands of such Indian tribe.

(B) The Secretary may disapprove a compact described in subparagraph (A) only if such compact violates—

(i) any provision of this chapter,

(ii) any other provision of Federal law that does not relate to jurisdiction over gaming on Indian lands, or

(iii) the trust obligations of the United States to Indians.

(C) If the Secretary does not approve or disapprove a compact described in subparagraph (A) before the date that is 45 days after the date on which the compact is submitted to the Secretary for approval, the compact shall be considered to have been approved by the Secretary, but only to the extent the compact is consistent with the provisions of this chapter.

(D) The Secretary shall publish in the Federal Register notice of any Tribal-State compact that is approved, or considered to have been approved, under this paragraph.

(9) An Indian tribe may enter into a management contract for the operation of a class III gaming activity if such contract has been submitted to, and approved by, the Chairman. The Chairman's review and approval of such contract shall be governed by the provisions of subsections (b), (c), (d), (f), (g), and (h) of section 2711 of this title.

(e) Approval of ordinances

For purposes of this section, by not later than the date that is 90 days after the date on which any tribal gaming ordinance or resolution is submitted to the Chairman, the Chairman shall approve such ordinance or resolution if it meets the requirements of this section. Any such ordinance or resolution not acted upon at the end of that 90-day period shall be considered to have been approved by the Chairman, but only to the extent such ordinance or resolution is consistent with the provisions of this chapter.

§ 2711. Management contracts

(a) Class II gaming activity; information on operators

(1) Subject to the approval of the Chairman, an Indian tribe may enter into a management contract for the operation and management of a class II gaming activity that the Indian tribe may engage in under section 2710(b)(1) of this title, but, before approving such contract, the Chairman shall require and obtain the following information:

(A) the name, address, and other additional pertinent background information on each person or entity (including individuals comprising such entity) having a direct financial interest in, or management responsibility for, such contract, and, in the case of a corporation, those individuals who serve on the board of directors of such corporation and each of its stockholders who hold (directly or indirectly) 10 percent or more of its issued and outstanding stock;

(B) a description of any previous experience that each person listed pursuant to subparagraph (A) has had with other gaming contracts with Indian tribes or with the gaming industry generally, including specifically the name and address of any licensing or regulatory agency with which such person has had a contract relating to gaming; and

(C) a complete financial statement of each person listed pursuant to subparagraph (A).

(2) Any person listed pursuant to paragraph (1)(A) shall be required to respond to such written or oral questions that the Chairman may propound in accordance with his responsibilities under this section.

(3) For purposes of this chapter, any reference to the management contract described in paragraph (1) shall be considered to include all collateral agreements to such contract that relate to the gaming activity.

(b) Approval

The Chairman may approve any management contract entered into pursuant to this section only if he determines that it provides at least—

(1) for adequate accounting procedures that are maintained, and for verifiable financial reports that are prepared, by or for the tribal governing body on a monthly basis;

(2) for access to the daily operations of the gaming to appropriate tribal officials who shall also have a right to verify the daily gross revenues and income made from any such tribal gaming activity;

(3) for a minimum guaranteed payment to the Indian tribe that has preference over the retirement of development and construction costs;

(4) for an agreed ceiling for the repayment of development and construction costs;

(5) for a contract term not to exceed five years, except that, upon the request of an Indian tribe, the Chairman may authorize a contract term that exceeds five years but does not exceed seven years if the Chairman is satisfied that the capital investment required, and the income projections, for the particular gaming activity require the additional time; and

(6) for grounds and mechanisms for terminating such contract, but actual contract termination shall not require the approval of the Commission.

(c) Fee based on percentage of net revenues

(1) The Chairman may approve a management contract providing for a fee based upon a percentage of the net revenues of a tribal gaming activity if the Chairman determines that such percentage fee is reasonable in light of surrounding circumstances. Except as otherwise provided in this subsection, such fee shall not exceed 30 percent of the net revenues.

(2) Upon the request of an Indian tribe, the Chairman may approve a management contract providing for a fee based upon a percentage of the net revenues of a tribal gaming activity that exceeds 30 percent but not 40 percent of the net revenues if the Chairman is satisfied that the capital investment required, and income projections, for such tribal gaming activity require the additional fee requested by the Indian tribe.

(d) Period for approval; extension

By no later than the date that is 180 days after the date on which a management contract is submitted to the Chairman for approval, the Chairman shall approve or disapprove such contract on its merits. The Chairman may extend the 180-day period by not more than 90 days if the Chairman notifies the Indian tribe in writing of the reason for the extension. The Indian tribe may bring an action in a United States district court to compel action by the Chairman if a contract has not been approved or disapproved within the period required by this subsection.

(e) Disapproval

The Chairman shall not approve any contract if the Chairman determines that—

(1) any person listed pursuant to subsection (a)(1)(A) of this section—

(A) is an elected member of the governing body of the Indian tribe which is the party to the management contract;

(B) has been or subsequently is convicted of any felony or gaming offense;

(C) has knowingly and willfully provided materially important false statements or information to the Commission or the Indian tribe pursuant to this chapter or has refused to respond to questions propounded pursuant to subsection (a)(2) of this section; or

(D) has been determined to be a person whose prior activities, criminal record if any, or reputation, habits, and associations pose a threat to the public interest or to the effective regulation and control of gaming, or create or enhance the dangers of unsuitable, unfair, or illegal practices, methods, and activities in the conduct of gaming or the carrying on of the business and financial arrangements incidental thereto;

(2) the management contractor has, or has attempted to, unduly interfere or influence for its gain or advantage any decision or process of tribal government relating to the gaming activity;

(3) the management contractor has deliberately or substantially failed to comply with the terms of the management contract or the tribal gaming ordinance or resolution adopted and approved pursuant to this chapter; or

(4) a trustee, exercising the skill and diligence that a trustee is commonly held to, would not approve the contract.

(f) Modification or voiding

The Chairman, after notice and hearing, shall have the authority to require appropriate contract modifications or may void any contract if he subsequently determines that any of the provisions of this section have been violated.

(g) Interest in land

No management contract for the operation and management of a gaming activity regulated by this chapter shall transfer or, in any other manner, convey any interest in land or other real property, unless specific statutory authority exists and unless clearly specified in writing in said contract.

(h) Authority

The authority of the Secretary under section 81 of this title, relating to management contracts regulated pursuant to this chapter, is hereby transferred to the Commission.

(i) Investigation fee

The Commission shall require a potential contractor to pay a fee to cover the cost of the investigation necessary to reach a determination required in subsection (e) of this section.

§ 2712. Review of existing ordinances and contracts

(a) Notification to submit

As soon as practicable after the organization of the Commission, the Chairman shall notify each Indian tribe or management contractor who, prior to October 17, 1988, adopted an ordinance or resolution authorizing class II gaming or class III gaming or entered into a management contract, that such ordinance, resolution, or contract, including all collateral agreements relating to the gaming activity, must be submitted for his review within 60 days of such notification. Any activity conducted under such ordinance, resolution, contract, or agreement shall be valid under this chapter, or any amendment made by this chapter, unless disapproved under this section.

(b) Approval or modification of ordinance or resolution

(1) By no later than the date that is 90 days after the date on which an ordinance or resolution authorizing class II gaming or class III gaming is submitted to the Chairman pursuant to subsection (a) of this section, the Chairman shall review such ordinance or resolution to determine if it conforms to the requirements of section 2710(b) of this title.

(2) If the Chairman determines that an ordinance or resolution submitted under subsection (a) of this section conforms to the requirements of section 2710(b) of this title, the Chairman shall approve it.

(3) If the Chairman determines that an ordinance or resolution submitted under subsection (a) of this section does not conform to the requirements of section 2710(b) of this title, the Chairman shall provide written notification of necessary modifications to the Indian tribe which shall have not more than 120 days to bring such ordinance or resolution into compliance.

(c) Approval or modification of management contract

(1) Within 180 days after the submission of a management contract, including all collateral agreements, pursuant to subsection (a) of this section, the Chairman shall subject such contract to the requirements and process of section 2711 of this title.

(2) If the Chairman determines that a management contract submitted under subsection (a) of this section, and the management contractor under such contract, meet the requirements of section 2711 of this title, the Chairman shall approve the management contract.

(3) If the Chairman determines that a contract submitted under subsection (a) of this section, or the management contractor under a contract submitted under subsection (a) of this section, does not meet the requirements of section 2711 of this title, the Chairman shall provide written notification to the parties to such contract of necessary modifications and the parties shall have not more than 120 days to come into compliance. If a management contract has been approved by the Secretary prior to October 17, 1988, the parties shall have not more than 180 days after notification of necessary modifications to come into compliance.

§ 2713. Civil penalties

(a) Authority; amount; appeal; written complaint

(1) Subject to such regulations as may be prescribed by the Commission, the Chairman shall have authority to levy and collect appropriate civil fines, not to exceed $25,000 per violation, against the tribal operator of an Indian game or a management contractor engaged in gaming for any violation of any provision of this chapter, any regulation prescribed by the Commission pursuant to this chapter, or tribal regulations, ordinances, or resolutions approved under section 2710 or 2712 of this title.

(2) The Commission shall, by regulation, provide an opportunity for an appeal and hearing before the Commission on fines levied and collected by the Chairman.

(3) Whenever the Commission has reason to believe that the tribal operator of an Indian game or a management contractor is engaged in activities regulated by this chapter, by regulations prescribed under this chapter, or by tribal regulations, ordinances, or resolutions, approved under section 2710 or 2712 of this title, that may result in the imposition of a fine under subsection (a)(1) of this section, the permanent closure of such game, or the modification or termination of any management contract, the Commission shall provide such tribal operator or management contractor with a written complaint stating the acts or omissions which form the basis for such belief and the action or choice of action being considered by the Commission. The allegation shall be set forth in common and concise language and must specify the statutory or regulatory provisions alleged to have been violated, but may not consist merely of allegations stated in statutory or regulatory language.

(b) Temporary closure; hearing

(1) The Chairman shall have power to order temporary closure of an Indian game for substantial violation of the provisions of this chapter, of regulations prescribed by the Commission pursuant to this chapter, or of tribal regulations, ordinances, or resolutions approved under section 2710 or 2712 of this title.

(2) Not later than thirty days after the issuance by the Chairman of an order of temporary closure, the Indian tribe or management contractor involved shall have a right to a hearing before the Commission to determine whether such order should be made permanent or dissolved. Not later than sixty days following such hearing, the Commission shall, by a vote of not less than two of its members, decide whether to order a permanent closure of the gaming operation.

(c) Appeal from final decision

A decision of the Commission to give final approval of a fine levied by the Chairman or to order a permanent closure pursuant to this section shall be appealable to the appropriate Federal district court pursuant to chapter 7 of title 5.

(d) Regulatory authority under tribal law

Nothing in this chapter precludes an Indian tribe from exercising regulatory authority provided under tribal law over a gaming establishment within the Indian tribe's jurisdiction if such regulation is not inconsistent with this chapter or with any rules or regulations adopted by the Commission.

§2714. Judicial review

Decisions made by the Commission pursuant to sections 2710, 2711, 2712, and 2713 of this title shall be final agency decisions for purposes of appeal to the appropriate Federal district court pursuant to chapter 7 of title 5.

§2715. Subpoena and deposition authority

(a) Attendance, testimony, production of papers, etc.

By a vote of not less than two members, the Commission shall have the power to require by subpoena the attendance and testimony of witnesses and the production of all books, papers, and documents relating to any matter under consideration or investigation. Witnesses so summoned shall be paid the same fees and mileage that are paid witnesses in the courts of the United States.

(b) Geographical location

The attendance of witnesses and the production of books, papers, and documents, may be required from any place in the United States at any designated place of hearing. The Commission may request the Secretary to request the Attorney General to bring an action to enforce any subpoena under this section.

(c) Refusal of subpoena; court order; contempt

Any court of the United States within the jurisdiction of which an inquiry is carried on may, in case of contumacy or refusal to obey a subpoena for any reason, issue an order requiring such person to appear before the Commission (and produce books, papers, or documents as so ordered) and give evidence concerning the matter in question and any failure to obey such order of the court may be punished by such court as a contempt thereof.

(d) Depositions; notice

A Commissioner may order testimony to be taken by deposition in any proceeding or investigation pending before the Commission at any stage of such proceeding or investigation. Such depositions may be taken before any person designated by the Commission and having power to administer oaths. Reasonable notice must first be given to the Commission in writing by the party or his attorney proposing to take such deposition, and, in cases in which a Commissioner proposes to take a deposition, reasonable notice must be given. The notice shall state the name of the witness and the time and place of the taking of his deposition. Any person may be compelled to appear and depose, and to produce books, papers, or documents, in the same manner as witnesses may be compelled to appear and testify and produce like documentary evidence before the Commission, as hereinbefore provided.

(e) Oath or affirmation required

Every person deposing as herein provided shall be cautioned and shall be required to swear (or affirm, if he so requests) to testify to the whole truth, and shall be carefully examined. His testimony shall be reduced to writing by the person taking the deposition, or under his direction, and shall, after it has been reduced to writing, be subscribed by the deponent. All depositions shall be promptly filed with the Commission.

(f) Witness fees

Witnesses whose depositions are taken as authorized in this section, and the persons taking the same, shall severally be entitled to the same fees as are paid for like services in the courts of the United States.

§ 2716. Investigative powers

(a) Confidential information

Except as provided in subsection (b) of this section, the Commission shall preserve any and all information received pursuant to this chapter as confidential pursuant to the provisions of paragraphs (4) and (7) of section 552(b) of title 5.

(b) Provision to law enforcement officials

The Commission shall, when such information indicates a violation of Federal, State, or tribal statutes, ordinances, or resolutions, provide such information to the appropriate law enforcement officials.

(c) Attorney General

The Attorney General shall investigate activities associated with gaming authorized by this chapter which may be a violation of Federal law.

§ 2717. Commission funding

(a) (1) The Commission shall establish a schedule of fees to be paid to the Commission annually by each gaming operation that conducts a class II or class III gaming activity that is regulated by this chapter.

(2) (A) The rate of the fees imposed under the schedule established under paragraph (1) shall be —

(i) no more than 2.5 percent of the first $1,500,000, and

(ii) no more than 5 percent of amounts in excess of the first $1,500,000, of the gross revenues from each activity regulated by this chapter.

(B) The total amount of all fees imposed during any fiscal year under the schedule established under paragraph (1) shall not exceed $8,000,000.

(3) The Commission, by a vote of not less than two of its members, shall annually adopt the rate of the fees authorized by this section which shall be payable to the Commission on a quarterly basis.

(4) Failure to pay the fees imposed under the schedule established under paragraph (1) shall, subject to the regulations of the Commission, be grounds for revocation of the approval of the Chairman of any license, ordinance, or resolution required under this chapter for the operation of gaming.

(5) To the extent that revenue derived from fees imposed under the schedule established under paragraph (1) are not expended or committed at the close of any fiscal year, such surplus funds shall be credited to each gaming activity on a pro rata basis against such fees imposed for the succeeding year.

(6) For purposes of this section, gross revenues shall constitute the annual total amount of money wagered, less any amounts paid out as prizes or paid for prizes awarded and less allowance for amortization of capital expenditures for structures.

(b) (1) The Commission, in coordination with the Secretary and in conjunction with the fiscal year of the United States, shall adopt an annual budget for the expenses and operation of the Commission.

(2) The budget of the Commission may include a request for appropriations, as authorized by section 2718 of this title, in an amount equal the amount of funds derived from assessments authorized by subsection (a) of this section for the fiscal year preceding the fiscal year for which the appropriation request is made.

(3) The request for appropriations pursuant to paragraph (2) shall be subject to the approval of the Secretary and shall be included as a part of the budget request of the Department of the Interior.

§ 2717a. Availability of class II gaming activity fees to carry out duties of the Commission

In fiscal year 1990 and thereafter, fees collected pursuant to and as limited by section 2717 of this title shall be available to carry out the duties of the Commission, to remain available until expended.

§ 2718. Authorization of appropriations

(a) Subject to section 2717 of this title, there are authorized to be appropriated, for fiscal year 1998, and for each fiscal year thereafter, an amount equal to the amount of funds derived from the assessments authorized by section 2717(a) of this title.

(b) Notwithstanding section 2717 of this title, there are authorized to be appropriated to fund the operation of the Commission, $2,000,000 for fiscal year 1998, and $2,000,000 for each fiscal year thereafter. The amounts authorized to be appropriated in the preceding sentence shall be in addition to the amounts authorized to be appropriated under subsection (a) of this section.

§ 2719. Gaming on lands acquired after October 17, 1988

(a) Prohibition on lands acquired in trust by Secretary

Except as provided in subsection (b) of this section, gaming regulated by this chapter shall not be conducted on lands acquired by the Secretary in trust for the benefit of an Indian tribe after October 17, 1988, unless—

(1) such lands are located within or contiguous to the boundaries of the reservation of the Indian tribe on October 17, 1988; or

(2) the Indian tribe has no reservation on October 17, 1988, and—

    (A) such lands are located in Oklahoma and—

        (i) are within the boundaries of the Indian tribe's former reservation, as defined by the Secretary, or

        (ii) are contiguous to other land held in trust or restricted status by the United States for the Indian tribe in Oklahoma; or

    (B) such lands are located in a State other than Oklahoma and are within the Indian tribe's last recognized reservation within the State or States within which such Indian tribe is presently located.

(b) Exceptions

    (1) Subsection (a) of this section will not apply when—

    (A) the Secretary, after consultation with the Indian tribe and appropriate State and local officials, including officials of other nearby Indian tribes, determines that a gaming establishment on newly acquired lands would be in the best interest of the Indian tribe and its members, and would not be detrimental to the surrounding community, but only if the Governor of the State in which the gaming activity is to be conducted concurs in the Secretary's determination; or

    (B) lands are taken into trust as part of—

        (i) a settlement of a land claim,

        (ii) the initial reservation of an Indian tribe acknowledged by the Secretary under the Federal acknowledgment process, or

        (iii) the restoration of lands for an Indian tribe that is restored to Federal recognition.

    (2) Subsection (a) of this section shall not apply to—

    (A) any lands involved in the trust petition of the St. Croix Chippewa Indians of Wisconsin that is the subject of the action filed in the United States District Court for the District of Columbia entitled St. Croix Chippewa Indians of Wisconsin v. United States, Civ. No. 86-2278, or

    (B) the interests of the Miccosukee Tribe of Indians of Florida in approximately 25 contiguous acres of land, more or less, in Dade County, Florida, located within one mile of the intersection of State Road Numbered 27 (also known as Krome Avenue) and the Tamiami Trail.

    (3) Upon request of the governing body of the Miccosukee Tribe of Indians of Florida, the Secretary shall, notwithstanding any other provision of law, accept the transfer by such Tribe to the Secretary of the interests of such Tribe in the lands described in paragraph (2)(B) and the Secretary shall declare that such interests are held in trust by the Secretary for the benefit of such Tribe and that such interests are part of the reservation of such Tribe under sections 465 and 467 of this title, subject to any encumbrances and rights that are held at the time of such transfer by any person or entity other than such Tribe. The Secretary shall publish in the Federal Register the legal description of any lands that are declared held in trust by the Secretary under this paragraph.

(c) Authority of Secretary not affected

Nothing in this section shall affect or diminish the authority and responsibility of the Secretary to take land into trust.

(d) Application of Internal Revenue Code of 1986

(1) The provisions of the Internal Revenue Code of 1986 (including sections 1441, 3402(q), 6041, and 6050I, and chapter 35 of such Code) concerning the reporting and withholding of taxes with respect to the winnings from gaming or wagering operations shall apply to Indian gaming operations conducted pursuant to this chapter, or under a Tribal-State compact entered into under section 2710(d)(3) of this title that is in effect, in the same manner as such provisions apply to State gaming and wagering operations.

(2) The provisions of this subsection shall apply notwithstanding any other provision of law enacted before, on, or after October 17, 1988, unless such other provision of law specifically cites this subsection.

§ 2720. Dissemination of information

Consistent with the requirements of this chapter, sections 1301, 1302, 1303 and 1304 of Title 18 shall not apply to any gaming conducted by an Indian tribe pursuant to this chapter.

§ 2721. Severability

In the event that any section or provision of this chapter, or amendment made by this chapter, is held invalid, it is the intent of Congress that the remaining sections or provisions of this chapter, and amendments made by this chapter, shall continue in full force and effect.

Index